MENTAL DISORDER AND THE CRIMINAL TRIAL PROCESS

Canadian Legal Textbook Series

CARROTHERS:	*Collective Bargaining Law in Canada*
WILLISTON AND ROLLS:	*The Law of Civil Procedure*
REID:	*Administrative Law and Practice*
SACK AND LEVINSON:	*Ontario Labour Relations Board Practice*
SOPINKA AND LEDERMAN:	*The Law of Evidence in Civil Cases*
FEENEY:	*The Canadian Law of Wills - Probate*
CASTEL:	*Canadian Conflict of Laws (2 volumes)*
RUBY:	*Sentencing*
WILLIAMS:	*The Law of Defamation*
JOHNSTON:	*Canadian Securities Regulation*
LINDEN:	*Canadian Tort Law*
SCHIFFER:	*Mental Disorder and The Criminal Trial Process*
PALMER:	*Labour Arbitration in Canada*

MENTAL DISORDER AND THE CRIMINAL TRIAL PROCESS

Marc E. Schiffer,
LL.B., LL.M., D.Jur.

BUTTERWORTHS

TORONTO

CANADA: BUTTERWORTH & CO. (CANADA) LTD.
                       TORONTO: 2265 MIDLAND AVENUE, SCARBOROUGH, M1P 4S1

UNITED KINGDOM: BUTTERWORTH & CO. (PUBLISHERS) LTD.
                       LONDON: 88 KINGSWAY, WC2 B 6AB

AUSTRALIA: BUTTERWORTH PTY. LTD.
                       SYDNEY: 586 PACIFIC HIGHWAY, CHATSWOOD, NSW 2067
                       MELBOURNE: 343 LITTLE COLLINS STREET, 3000
                       BRISBANE: 240 QUEEN STREET, 4000

NEW ZEALAND: BUTTERWORTHS OF NEW ZEALAND LTD.
                       T & W BUILDING
                       77-85 CUSTOMHOUSE QUAY
                       CPO BOX 472
                       WELLINGTON 1

SOUTH AFRICA: BUTTERWORTH & CO. (SOUTH AFRICA) (PTY.) LTD.
                       DURBAN: 152/154 GALE STREET

© by BUTTERWORTH & CO. (CANADA) LTD. 1978

Canadian Cataloguing in Publication Data

Schiffer, Marc E., 1951-
    Mental disorder and the criminal trial process

(Canadian legal text series)

Originally presented as the author's thesis,
University of Toronto Law School.

Includes index.
ISBN 0-409-865-605

1. Forensic psychiatry. 2. Insanity—
Jurisprudence—Canada. 3. Criminal procedure—
Canada. I. Title. II. Series.

KE8839.S34   345′.71′067   C77-001709-6

Printed and bound in Canada by John Deyell Company

To My Family

Preface

The greater part of this book was originally written as a doctoral thesis at the University of Toronto Law School. My aim in writing it was to explore as thoroughly as I could the relationship of psychiatry to criminal law in Canada. As popular as the subject has always been amongst members of the legal and psychiatric professions, I was surprised to find that there existed no comprehensive Canadian text on criminal law and psychiatry.

It is hoped that this work will be of use not only to lawyers and law students, but to forensic psychiatrists and students of criminology as well. Many of the issues examined herein are as much matters of psychiatry, ethics and social policy as they are questions of law.

While the raw material was derived mainly from case reports, articles and legal texts, it has been supplemented by a certain amount of field work. During the course of my research, I visited the forensic wards of several psychiatric hospitals and consulted with many forensic psychiatrists as well as with several judges.

I wish to express my sincere gratitude to Professor M.L. Friedland, Dean of the University of Toronto Law School, for the constant advice and encouragement he has given me throughout the preparation of this work. I am indebted as well to The Honourable Mr. Justice G.A. Martin, to Dr. Basil Orchard and to Professors A.W. Mewett, J.Ll.J. Edwards and S.M. Waddams for their helpful criticisms and suggestions. I wish also to thank the University of Toronto for its financial support in the form of a Doctoral Fellowship, the editors of the *Osgoode Hall Law Journal, University of Toronto Faculty of Law Review* and *Saskatchewan Law Review* for allowing me to use articles of mine which appeared in their publications, and Shirley Hinterauer and Jim Michaud of Butterworths for their tireless assistance in the final preparation of this book.

Marc E. Schiffer
November, 1977

Table of Contents

Preface vii

Table of Cases xiii

Introduction 1

PART I: THE PRE-TRIAL STAGE 5-79

CHAPTER 1: PRE-TRIAL DIVERSION OF THE
     MENTALLY DISORDERED 7
 I. Introduction 7
 II. Police Screening 9
 III. Prosecutorial Discretion 16
 IV. Diversion by Provincial Authorities 17
 V. Diversion by the Court 19
 VI. Conclusions 25

CHAPTER 2: PROBLEMS ARISING OUT OF PRE-TRIAL
      PSYCHIATRIC EXAMINATION 31
 I. The Question of Psychiatrist-Accused Privilege 31
  A. The Problem 31
  B. The Present Law 32
  C. The Case for Extending the Privilege 34
 II. The Question of "Self-Incrimination" 36
  A. The Problem 36
  B. The Present Law 36
  C. The Case Against Application of the Privilege
   Against Self-Incrimination 40
  D. The Case for a Privilege Against Compulsory
   Psychiatric Examination 42
 III. Conclusions 46

CHAPTER 3: FITNESS TO STAND TRIAL 51
 I. Introduction 51
 II. Remand and Examination 52
 III. When is the Issue Tried? 58
 IV. The Judge's Discretion to Try the Issue 62
 V. Trial of the Issue 65
  A. The Test of Fitness 65
  B. Onus of Proof 73
  C. Expert Evidence 76
 VI. Results of the Trial of the Issue 77

VII. Conclusions.. 78

PART II: THE TRIAL STAGE................................... 81-224

CHAPTER 4: AUTOMATISM 83
  I.   Introduction... 83
  II. Automatism Defined 83
  III. When is Automatism Not a Defence?..................... 89
      A.   When Caused by a Disease of the Mind.............. 89
           (i) Epilepsy 90
           (ii) Cerebral Arteriosclerosis............................ 93
           (iii) Brain Tumour 94
      B.   When Caused by Voluntary Consumption of
           Alcohol and/or Drugs 95
  IV. Causes of Non-Insane Automatism....................... 99
      A.   Head Injury.. 99
      B.   Hypoglycemia 100
      C.   "Psychological Blow".. 101
      D.   Sleep 107
      E.   Hypnosis? 111
  V.   Evidence... 112
  VI. Conclusions... 118

CHAPTER 5: INSANITY AS A DEFENCE...................... 121
  I.   Introduction... 121
  II. The Procedure 122
  III. Warrants of the Lieutenant-Governor................... 124
      A.   The Insane Defendant....................................... 124
      B.   The Mentally Ill Prisoner................................. 125
  IV. The Substantive Law 126
      A.   "Natural Imbecility"... 126
      B.   "Disease of the Mind"....................................... 127
      C.   "Appreciating the Nature and Quality of an Act or
           Omission" 130
      D.   "Knowing That an Act or Omission is Wrong" 132
      E.   Delusions 136
      F.   Irresistible Impulse 138
  V.   Evidence... 141
  VI. Conclusions... 144

CHAPTER 6: REDUCED RESPONSIBILITY.................... 153
  I.   Introduction... 153
  II. Incapacity to Form Specific Intent Due to Intoxication .. 153
      A.   "Specific Intent"... 154
      B.   Incapacity to Form Specific Intent 157
           (i)   Alcohol-Induced States.............................. 158
                (a) *Delirium Tremens*........................... 158
                (b) Korsakov's Psychosis 158
                (c) Alcoholic Paranoia 159
                (d) Pathological Intoxication.................. 159
                (e) Other Alcoholic Hallucinosis 160
                (f) Confusional States............................. 160
           (ii) Drug-Induced States.............................. 160
                (a) Amphetamines.................................. 160

(b) Barbiturates 161
(c) Cocaine 161
(d) Hallucinogens... 162
(e) Marijuana 162
(f) Minor Tranquilizers and Non-Barbiturate
    Sedative Hynotics.. 162
(g) Opiate Narcotics.. 162
(h) Volatile Substances (Inhalants)....................... 163
III. Lack of *Mens Rea* Due to Mental Disorder Other Than
    Intoxication.. 163
    A.   Lack of Specific Intent 163
    B.   Lack of Knowledge...................................... 165
    C.   Lack of Planning or Deliberation 166
    D.   Evidence 169
IV. Provocation.. 170
    A.   The Objective Test...................................... 171
    B.   The Subjective Test 176
V. Infanticide.. 178
    A.   "The Effects of Giving Birth".................... 180
       (i)   Manic Depressive Psychosis 181
       (ii) Schizophrenia..................................... 182
       (iii) Delirious Reactions 182
    B.   "The Effect of Lactation"........................... 182
VI. Diminished Responsibility in English Law...................... 183
VII. Conclusions.. 186

CHAPTER 7: PSYCHIATRIC EVIDENCE AT TRIAL 189
  I.   Introduction.. 189
  II.   Competence, Credibility and Character 190
      A.   Competence... 190
      B.   Credibility.. 191
      C.   Character 195
  III.   Qualifications of the Psychiatric Witness 196
  IV.   Basis of Opinion 201
  V.   Hypothetical Questions.. 202
  VI.   The Ultimate Issue Rule... 208
  VII. Weight... 211
  VIII. Why Do Psychiatrists Disagree? 215
  IX.   Can the Court Call Psychiatric Witnesses?...................... 216
  X.   Conclusions.. 221

PART III: THE POST-TRIAL STAGE.................... 225-332

CHAPTER 8: SENTENCING... 227
  I.   Introduction.. 227
  II.   Remand.. 228
  III   Psychiatric Reports 229
  IV.   Possible Sentences 235
      A.   Fine.. 237
      B.   Probation 239
       (i)   Following Imprisonment 239
       (ii) Following a Conditional Discharge or
           Suspended Sentence............................... 240
      C.   Imprisonment 244
       (i)   With No Special Interest in Treatment 244

(ii) With a Recommendation for Treatment............ 247
D.   Hospital Orders?.. 251
V.   Conclusions... 254

CHAPTER 9: DANGEROUS (SEXUAL) OFFENDERS................ 263
I.   Introduction... 263
II.   The Procedure... 265
III.   The Substantive Law... 268
    A.   "Failure to Control His Sexual Impulses"................. 270
    B.   "Likelihood of His Causing Injury, Pain or Other
        Evil Through Failure in the Future to Control His
        Sexual Impulses"... 272
IV.   Evidence... 278
V.   Preventive Detention... 281
VI.   Conclusions... 286

CHAPTER 10: PSYCHIATRIC TREATMENT............................ 289
I.   Introduction... 289
II.   The Right to Treatment... 290
    A.   Under Statute... 290
        (i)   The Insane Accused... 290
        (ii) The Federal Prisoner...................................... 291
        (iii) The Provincial Prisoner................................. 292
        (iv) The Hospitalized Offender............................ 293
    B.   Under the Canadian Bill of Rights............................ 294
        (i)   Cruel and Unusual Treatment or Punishment.. 294
        (ii) Due Process.. 295
            (a) The Diverted Defendant............................ 295
            (b) The Unfit Accused...................................... 298
            (c) The Dangerous Offender............................ 298
            (d) The Accused Acquitted Under S. 16................ 298
    C.   Under Tort Law... 299
III.   The Standard of Treatment.. 300
IV.   The Right Not to be Treated.. 304
    A.   The Doctrine of Voluntary Informed Consent......... 304
    B.   Cruel and Unusual Treatment or Punishment......... 311
V.   Remedies... 313
    A.   Tort Action... 314
    B.   *Habeas Corpus*.. 314
    C.   *Mandamus*.. 314
    D.   Injunction... 315
    E.   Ombudsman... 315
VI.   The Therapist's Dilemma.. 315
VII.   Conclusions... 320

CHAPTER 11: RELEASE... 323
I.   Introduction... 323
II.   Release From a Warrant of the Lieutenant-Governor...... 323
III.   The Civilly Committed Defendant..................................... 327
IV.   The Preventive Detainee... 329
V.   The Psychiatrist as Jailer... 331
VI.   Conclusions... 332

Table of Statutes... 333
Index.. 337

Table of Cases

A.B. v. C.D. (1851), 14 Dunlop 177 32
Advocate (H.M.) v. Braithwaite, [1945] S.C. (J.) 53 184
Advocate (H.M.) v. Brown, [1907] S.C. (J.) 67 67
Advocate (H.M.) v. Dingwall (1867), 5 Irv. 466 183
Advocate (H.M.) v. Fraser (1878), 4 Couper 70 108
Advocate (H.M.) v. McLean (1876), 3 Coup. 334 183
Advocate (H.M.) v. Ritchie, [1926] S.C. (J.) 45 99
Advocate (H.M.) v. Robertson (1891), 3 White 6 (Scot.) 72
Aiken v. Clary (1965), 396 S.W. 2d 668.. 306
Aitcheson v. Mann (1882), 9 P.R. 473 (C.A.) 28, 62
Application of D.D. (1971), 118 N.J. Super. 1 (App. Div.) 301
Armstrong v. Clarke, [1957] 2 Q.B. 391 .... 96, 100
Ashby v. State (1911), 124 Tenn. 684 198
A.-G. v. Hitchcock (1847), 1 Ex. 91, 154 E.R. 38 190
A.-G. v. Mulholland; A.-G. v. Foster, [1963] 1 All E.R. 767 32
A.-G. Ceylon v. Perera, [1953] A.C. 200 (P.C.) 170
A.-G. Northern Ireland v. Gallagher, [1961] 3 W.L.R. 619 (H.L.) 95
A.-G. Que. v. Begin, [1955] S.C.R. 593, 21 C.R. 217, 112 C.C.C. 209, [1955] 5
    D.L.R. 394 .... 36, 45
A.-G. South Australia v. Brown, [1960] A.C. 432 (P.C.) 140

B and M, Re (1975), 33 C.R.N.S. 362 (Ont. Prov. Ct.) 124
Bank of Upper Canada v. Baldwin, Re (1829), Draper 55 314
Beatty v. Gillbanks (1882), 9 Q.B.D. 308 9
Beatty and Mackie v. Kozak (1958), 120 C.C.C. 1, 13 D.L.R. (2d) 1, [1958] S.C.R.
    177 16
Bedder v. D.P.P., [1954] 2 All E.R. 801 (H.L.)............................. 171, 172
Bleta v. The Queen, [1964] S.C.R. 561, 44 C.R. 193, [1965] 1 C.C.C. 1, 48 D.L.R.
    (2d) 139 .... 100, 203, 204
Boase v. Paul, [1931] 1 D.L.R. 562, 66 O.L.R. 237; affd [1931] 4 D.L.R. 435,
    [1931] O.R. 625 (C.A.) 304
Boivin v. The Queen, [1970] S.C.R. 917, 14 C.R.N.S. 140, 14 D.L.R. (3d) 601, 1
    C.C.C. (2d) 403 169
Bowater v. Rowley Regis Corp., [1944] 1 K.B. 476 308
Bowyer, Re (1930), 66 O.L.R. 378, 54 C.C.C. 392 329
Brady v. State (1931), 116 Tex. Crim. 427.. 198
Branco, Ex p., [1971] 3 O.R. 575, 4 C.C.C. (2d) 183 .... 21, 23, 24, 53
Bratty v. A.-G. Northern Ireland, [1961] 2 W.L.R. 965, 46 Cr. App. R. 1
    (H.L.) 85, 87, 90, 94, 95, 99, 102, 105, 112, 114, 115, 117, 129, 141, 157, 184
Brodie v. The Queen; Dansky v. The Queen; Rubin v. The Queen, [1962] S.C.R.
    681, 37 C.R. 120, 32 D.L.R. (2d) 507, 132 C.C.C. 161 201
Broham v. State (1904), 143 Ala. 28 198
Brooks' Detention, Re (1961), 38 W.W.R. 51, 37 C.R. 348, 133 C.C.C. 204 *sub*
    nom. Brooks v. The Queen (Alta.) 326
Building Products Ltd. v. B.P. Canada Ltd. (1961), 36 C.P.R. 121, 21 Fox Pat. C.
    130 (Ex. Ct.)... 201

Burnham v. Department of Public Health (Georgia) (1972), 349 F. Supp. 1335
(N.D. Ga.) 302

Campbell and The Queen, Re (1974), 16 C.C.C. (2d) 573, [1974] 4 W.W.R. 765
sub nom. R. v. Campbell (B.C.); affd 22 C.C.C. (2d) 65, [1975] 3 W.W.R. 593
(C.A.)... 283
Carnochan, Re, [1941] S.C.R. 470, [1941] 3 D.L.R. 700, 76 C.C.C. 301 328
Champagne v. Plouffe and A.-G. Que. (1940), 77 C.C.C. 87 (Que.) 125
Chan Kau v. The Queen, [1955] A.C. 206 (P.C.) 112
Chartrand v. The Queen (1975), 26 C.C.C. (2d) 417, 64 D.L.R. (3d) 145
(S.C.C.)... 130
Citadel Brick Ltd. v. Garneau, [1937] 3 D.L.R. 169 (S.C.C.)................... 223
Clark v. The King (1921), 61 S.C.R. 608, 35 C.C.C. 261, 59 D.L.R. 121, [1921] 2
W.W.R. 446; revg 48 N.B.R. 342... 143
Clatterbuck v. Harris (1968), 295 F. Supp. 84 (D.D.C.) 301, 321
Constanineau and Jones, Re (1912), 5 D.L.R. 483, 26 O.L.R. 160............... 124
Cook v. Ciccone (1970), 312 F. Supp. 822 (W.D. Mo.) 303
Cooper v. McKenna, Ex p. Cooper, [1960] Qd. R. 406 (F.C.)............... 99, 100
Corbett v. The Queen (1973), 14 C.C.C. (2d) 385, 42 D.L.R. (3d) 142, 25 C.R.N.S.
296, [1974] 2 W.W.R. 524 (S.C.C.) 214
Crabbe v. S., [1925] 2 W.W.R. 701, [1925] 3 D.L.R. 1069 *sub nom.* Crabbe v.
Shields, 36 B.C.R. 89 (C.A.) 212
Crane v. D.P.P., [1921] 2 A.C. 299 (H.L.) 74
Curr v. The Queen, [1972] S.C.R. 889, 18 C.R.N.S. 281, 7 C.C.C. (2d) 181, 26
D.L.R. (3d) 603.. 36, 45, 297

Dack, Re (1914), 5 O.W.N. 774.. 328
Dagenais v. Corp. of the Town of Trenton (1893), 24 O.R. 343, 2 C. & S.
445 124
Davidson, Re (1915), 8 O.W.N. 481 329
Davy v. Morrison, [1932] O.R. 1, [1931] 4 D.L.R. 619 (C.A.) 210
Davy v. Sullivan (1973), 354 F. Supp. 1320 298
DeClerq v. The Queen, [1968] S.C.R. 902, 4 C.R.N.S. 205, [1969] 1 C.C.C. 197, 70
D.L.R. (2d) 530... 37
Delorme v. Sisters of Charity of Quebec (1924), 40 C.C.C. 218, 24 Que. P.R.
435 126
Dembie v. Dembie (1963), 21 R.F.L. 46 (Ont.) 33, 46
Dion v. The Queen, [1965] Que. Q.B. 238 (C.A.); appeal to S.C.C. dismissed [1965]
S.C.R. *v*.. 140
D.P.P. v. Beard, [1920] A.C. 479 (H.L.)........................ 154, 155, 157, 184
D.P.P. v. Majewski, [1976] 2 All E.R. 142 (H.L.) 155
Dominion News and Gifts (1962) Ltd. v. The Queen, [1964] S.C.R. 251, 42 C.R.
209, [1964] 3 C.C.C. 1 201
Donaldson v. O'Connor (1974), 493 F. 2d 507 .... 296, 302
Doyle v. The Queen (1976), 35 C.R.N.S. 1, 68 D.L.R. (3d) 270, [1977] 1 S.C.R.
597 .... 23, 52
Ducharme v. The Queen (1969), 8 C.R.N.S. 287 (Que. C.A.) 170
Duclos, Re (1907), 12 C.C.C. 278, 8 Que. P.R. 372 *sub nom.* Duclos v. Sisters of
Charity, 32 Que. S.C. 154 *sub nom.* Duclos v. L'Asile de St. Jean de Dieu . 298
Duncan v. Jones, [1936] 1 K.B. 218 9
Durham v. United States (1954), 214 F. 2d 862.............................. 146

Edwards v. The Queen, [1973] 1 All E.R. 152 (P.C.) 173

Fain v. The Commonwealth (1879), 78 Ky. 183 .... 110, 118
Fawcett v. A.-G. Ont., [1964] S.C.R. 625, 44 C.R. 201, [1965] 2 C.C.C. 262, 45
D.L.R. (2d) 579; affg [1964] 1 C.C.C. 164, 45 D.L.R. (2d) at p. 579, [1964] 2
O.R. 399 (C.A.); affg [1963] 3 C.C.C. 134, 40 D.L.R. (2d) 942, [1963] 2 O.R.
718 .... 24, 329
Fenwick v. Bell (1844), 1 Car. & Kir. 313 (N.P.) 210

Fisher v. The Queen *See* R. v. Fisher
Frensom v. New Westminster (1897), 2 C.C.C. 52 (B.C.) 28, 62

Galpin v. Page (1873), 85 U.S. 350 27
Gibson, Re (1907), 15 O.L.R. 245 (C.A.) 329
Glasbrook Brothers Ltd. v. Glamorgan County Council, [1925] A.C. 270 (H.L.) 9
Glover v. State (1907), 129 Ga. 717 198
Goldhar v. The Queen (1960), 126 C.C.C. 337, 25 D.L.R. (2d) 401, 33 C.R. 71, [1960]
   S.C.R. 431 ....:... 124, 314
Gootson v. The King, [1947] 4 D.L.R. 568, [1947] Ex. C.R. 514; affd [1948] 4 D.L.R. 33
   (S.C.C.)... 91
Green v. Gaskell (1833), 1 Myl. & K. 98... 36
Green v. Livermore; Green v. Brickenden, [1940] 4 D.L.R. 678, [1940] O.R. 381, 74
   C.C.C. 240 24
Greenwood, Re (1855), 24 L.J.Q.B. 148 329
Grock v. United States (1923), 289 F. 544 (D.C.) 146

Hales v. Petit (1562), 1 Plowd. 260... 15
Halls v. Mitchell, [1928] S.C.R. 125, [1928] 2 D.L.R. 97 32
Hamilton Dairies Ltd. and Town of Dundas, Re (1927), 33 O.W.N. 113 (C.A.) 315
Hardy v. Merrill (1875), 56 N.H. 227.. 146
Harris v. D.P.P., [1952] A.C. 694 (H.L.) 32
Haynes v. Harwood, [1935] 1 K.B. 146.. 9
Hill v. Baxter, [1958] 1 All E.R. 193 (Q.B.D.) 31, 74, 85, 99, 102, 112, 113, 115
Hill v. The Queen (No. 2) (1975), 25 C.C.C. (2d) 6, 62 D.L.R. (3d) 193, 7 N.R. 373
   (S.C.C.)... 248
Hoban's Glynde v. Firle Hotel (1973), 41 S.A.S.R. 503 201
Holloway v. United States (1945), 148 F. 2d 665 (D.C. Cir.) 146
Holmes v. D.P.P., [1946] 2 All E.R. 124 (H.L.) 170
Holt v. State (1947), 84 Okla. Crim. 283 198
Humphrey v. Cady (1974), 405 U.S. 504 295

Ibrahim v. The King, [1914] A.C. 599 (P.C.) 37, 309

Jackson v. Indiana (1972), U.S. 715 (U.S.S.C.) 296
Jackson v. The Queen (1962), 36 A.L.J.R. 198 (H.C.) 192
Johnson v. U.S. (1948), 366 U.S. 46 223
Julius v. Bishop of Oxford (1880), 5 App. Cas. 214 (H.L.) 28, 62

Kaimowitz et al. v. Department of Mental Health (Mich.) (unreported) 310
Kay v. Butterworth (1945), 61 T.L.R. 452 99
Kelliher v. Smith, [1931] S.C.R. 672, [1931] 4 D.L.R. 102; affg [1930] 2 W.W.R. 638,
   [1930] 4 D.L.R. 938, 25 Sask. L.R. 65 (C.A.); revg [1929] 3 W.W.R. 655, [1930] 1
   D.L.R. 878, 24 Sask. L.R. 198 .... 76, 197
Kennedy v. Tomlinson (1959), 126 C.C.C. 175, 20 D.L.R. (2d) 273 (Ont. C.A.); leave to
   appeal to S.C.C. refused [1959] S.C.R. ix 23, 54
Kenny v. Lockwood, [1932] 1 D.L.R. 507, [1932] O.R. 141 (C.A.) 304
King, Re, [1917] 1 W.W.R. 132, 30 D.L.R. 599 (Man.) 329
Kleinys' Habeas Corpus Application, Re (1965), 51 W.W.R. 597, 46 C.R. 141 *sub nom.* Re
   Kleinys 49 D.L.R. (2d) 225, [1965] 3 C.C.C. 102, *sub nom* Ex p. Kleineys
   (B.C.)... 125, 294, 295, 326
Klippert v. The Queen, [1967] S.C.R. 822, 2 C.R.N.S. 319, 61 W.W.R. 727, [1968] 2
   C.C.C. 129, 65 D.L.R. (2d) 698 .... 269, 270
Knecht v. Gillman (1973), 488 F. 2d 1136 (8th Cir.) 312, 313
Kolacz, [1950] V.L.R. 200 61
Kuruma, Son of Kaniu v. The Queen, [1955] A.C. 197 (P.C.) 32
Kwaka Mensah v. The King, [1946] 1 A.C. 83 170

Lacey v. Laird (1956), 166 Ohio St. 12 304
Latour v. The King, [1951] S.C.R. 19, 11 C.R. 1, 98 C.C.C. 258, [1951] 1 D.L.R 834 .. 170

Leary v. The Queen *See* R. v. Leary
Lee v. Erie County Ct. (1971), 267 N.E. 2d 452 .... 41, 42, 50
Lee v. Tahash (1965), 352 F. 2d 970 312
Lelance and Grosjean Mfg. Co. v. Haverman (1898), 87 Fed. 563 (C.C.S.D.N.Y.) 35
Lessard v. Schmidt (1972), 349 F. Supp. 1078 321
Ley's Case (1828), 1 Lewin 239 73
Lindala v. Canadian Copper Co. (1920), 51 D.L.R. 565, 47 O.L.R. 28 (C.A.) 214
Lingley v. Hickman, [1972] F.C. 171, 10 C.C.C. (2d) 362, 33 D.L.R. (3d) 593 326
Lingley v. N.B. Board of Review, [1973] F.C. 861, 13 C.C.C. (2d) 303, 41 D.L.R. (3d)
  259 326
Lowe v. State (1903), 118 Wis. 641 198
Lowery v. The Queen, [1974] A.C. 85 .... 193, 195, 196
Lowther v. The Queen (1957), 26 C.R. 150 (Que. C.A.) 142, 171, 219

MacDonald v. The Queen (1976), 29 C.C.C. (2d) 257, 68 D.L.R. (3d) 649 (S.C.C.); affg 22
  C.C.C. (2d) 129 (Ct. Mar. A.C.) 169
Mackey v. Procunier (1973), 477 F. 2d 877 (9th Cir.) 312
Maddox, Re (1957), 88 N.W. 2d 470 .... 303, 321
Male v. Hopmans, [1967] 2 O.R. 457, 64 D.L.R. (2d) 105 (C.A.) 304
Mancini v. D.P.P., [1942] A.C. 1 .... 170, 172
Mark, Re, [1964] 2 C.C.C. 398, 43 C.R. 39, 46 W.W.R. 381, *sub nom.* Re Mark's
  Application (B.C.) 267
Martarella v. Kelley (1972), 349 F. Supp. 575 (S.D.N.Y.) 294, 295
Matticks, Ex p. (1972), 10 C.C.C. (2d) 438 (Que. C.A.); affd 15 C.C.C. (2d) 213n
  (S.C.C.) 283
McElroy v. State (1922), 146 Ten. 442 198
McMartin v. The Queen, [1964] S.C.R. 484, 43 C.R. 403, 47 W.W.R. 603, 46 D.L.R. (2d)
  372; revg 41 C.R. 147, 43 W.W.R. 483, [1964] 1 C.C.C. 217 (B.C.C.A.) 168
Midland Railway Co. v. Robinson (1890), 15 App. Cas. 19 127
Millard v. Cameron (1966), 373 F. 2d 468 (D.C. Cir.) 301
Minehan, Re (1925), 28 O.W.N. 263 328
Miranda v. Arizona (1966), 384 U.S. 436 50
M'Naghten's Case (1843), 10 Cl. & Fin. 200, 8 E.R.
  718 .... 90, 112, 121, 131, 136, 145, 146, 152
Mohr v. Williams (1905), 95 Minn. 261 304
More v. The Queen, [1963] S.C.R. 522, 41 C.R. 98, [1963] 3 C.C.C. 289, 41 D.L.R. (2d)
  380; revg 43 W.W.R. 30 (Man. C.A.) 166, 168, 212
Morris, Re *See* R. v. Hume, Ex p. Morris

Nason v. Superintendent of Bridgewater State Hospital (1968), 233 N.E. 2d
  908 .... 296, 303, 314
Nelson v. Heyne (1972), 355 F. Supp. 451 (N.D. Ind.); affd 491 F. 2d 352 (U.S.C.A. 7th
  Cir.) 312, 313
Noor Mohamed v. The King, [1949] A.C. 182 (P.C.) 32
Nuttall v. Nuttall and Twyman (1964), 108 Sol. Jo. 605 32

Ochse, Re (1951), 238 P. 2d 561 (Cal. S.C.) 34
O'Donnell, Re (1915), 7 O.W.N. 605 328
Oliver v. State (1936), 232 Ala. 5 198
Orvis v. Brickman (1952), 196 F. 2d 762 (D.C. Cir.) 12

Palomba v. The Queen (1975), 32 C.R.N.S. 31, [1975] Que. C.A. 340, 24 C.C.C. (2d) 19
  sub nom. R. v. Palomba (No. 3) 197
Parkes v. The Queen (1956), 116 C.C.C. 86, 6 D.L.R. (2d) 449, [1956] S.C.R. 768, 24 C.R.
  279 267
Parnerkar v. The Queen, [1974] S.C.R. 449, 21 C.R.N.S. 129, [1973] 4 W.W.R. 298, 10
  C.C.C. (2d) 253, 33 D.L.R. (3d) 683; affg 16 C.R.N.S. 347, [1972] 1 W.W.R. 161, 5
  C.C.C. (2d) 11 (Sask. C.A.) 103, 104, 105, 122, 171, 175
Paulsen v. Gundersen (1935), 218 Wis. 578 308
Pearson v. Le Corre (unreported, October 13, 1973) 283
Peek v. Ciccone (1968), 288 F. Supp. 329 (W.D. Mo.) 312, 313

People v. Esposito (1942), 39 N.E. 2d 925 (N.Y.C.A.) 44
People v. Hilliker (1971), 185 N.W. 2d 831 (Mich. C.A.) 34
People v. Kearse (1967), 282 N.Y.S. 2d 136 (App. Div.) 301
People v. Leyra (1951), 98 N.E. 2d 553 43
People (A.-G.) v. Manning (1953), 89 I.L.T. 155 .... 31, 115
People v. Schmidt (1915), 216 N.Y. 324 132
People v. Wells (1949), 202 P. 2d 53, cert. denied 338 U.S. 836 49
People ex. rel. Apicella v. Superintendent of Kings County Hospital (1940), 18 N.Y.S. 2d
    523 (Sup. Ct. Kings Co.) 64
Perras v. The Queen (1973), 22 C.R.N.S. 160, [1973] 5 W.W.R. 275, [1974] S.C.R. 659, 35
    D.L.R. (3d) 596, 11 C.C.C. (2d) 449 .... 38, 39
Perrault v. The Queen, [1971] S.C.R. 196, 74 W.W.R. 607, [1970] 5 C.C.C. 217, 12 D.L.R.
    (3d) 480 .... 157, 171
Piché v. The Queen, [1971] S.C.R. 23, 11 D.L.R. (3d) 700, [1970] 4 C.C.C. 27, 74 W.W.R.
    674, 12 C.R.N.S. 222 37
Pilon v. The Queen, [1966] 2 C.C.C. 53, 46 C.R. 272 (Que. C.A.) 168
Police v. Beaumont, [1958] Crim. L.R. 620 99
Ponton v. The Queen (1959), 127 C.C.C. 325, 31 C.R. 347 (Que. C.A.) 266
Pope v. United States (1967), 372 F. 2d 710 (8th Cir.) 41
Powell v. Texas (1968), 392 U.S. 514 321
Pratt v. Davis (1906), 224 Ill. 300 304
Preeper and Doyle v. The Queen (1888), 15 S.C.R. 401 199
Prescott v. Jarvis (1849), 5 U.C.Q.B. 489 (C.A.) 190
Prinsep and East Indian Co. v. Dyce Sombre (1856), 10 Moo. P.C.C. 232, 14 E.R. 480   75
Provincial Board of Health for Ont. and City of Toronto, Re (1920), 46 O.L.R. 587, 51
    D.L.R. 444 (C.A.) 315

R. v. Aarons, [1964] Crim. L.R. 484 244
R. v. Abramovitch (1912), 7 Cr. App.R. 145 (C.C.A.) 143
R. v. Adamcik, [1977] 3 W.W.R. 29, 38 C.R.N.S. 101, 33 C.C.C. (2d) 11 (B.C. Co.
    Ct.) 136
R. v. Alexander (1913), 9 Cr. App.R. 139 (C.C.A.) 172
R. v. Allen (1954), 108 C.C.C. 239, 20 C.R. 301, 11 W.W.R. 454 (B.C.C.A.) .   242, 254, 260
R. v. Anderson (1914), 22 C.C.C. 455, 16 D.L.R. 203, 5 W.W.R. 1052, 7 Alta. L.R. 102
    (C.A.) 143
R. v. Ashcroft, [1965] Qd. R. 81 194
R. v. Aughet (1918), 13 Cr. App.R. 101 (C.C.A.) 139
R. v. Bailey (1800), Russ. & Ry. 1 149
R. v. Baker, [1970] 1 C.C.C. 203, 7 C.R.N.S. 298 (N.S. Co. Ct.) 100, 115
R. v. Bakun (1967), 50 C.R. 178, 58 W.W.R. 129, [1967] 2 C.C.C. 214 (B.C.C.A.) 170
R. v. Ballard (1897), 1 C.C.C. 96, 28 O.R. 489 315
R. v. Baltzer (1974), 10 N.S.R. (2d) 561, 27 C.C.C. (2d) 118 (C.A.) 130
R. v. Barbour (1938), 13 M.P.R. 203 (N.B.C.A.); affd [1938] S.C.R. 465, 71 C.C.C. 1,
    [1939] 1 D.L.R. 65 .... 143, 170
R. v. Barker, [1954] Crim. L.R. 423, 482 44
R. v. Barlow (1693), 2 Salk. 609, 91 E.R. 516 .... 28, 62
R. v. Barnett, [1956] Crim. L.R. 560 (C.C.A.) 220
R. v. Bastian, [1958] 1 W.L.R. 413 .... 141, 184
R. v. Beauvais, [1965] 3 C.C.C. 281 (B.C.) 197
R. v. Benson and Stevenson (1951), 100 C.C.C. 247, 13 C.R. 1, 3 W.W.R. 29
    (B.C.C.A.) 55, 234, 235
R. v. Bentley, [1960] Crim. L.R. 777 97
R. v. Berger (1975), 27 C.C.C. (2d) 357 (B.C.C.A.); leave to appeal to S.C.C. refused 27
    C.C.C. (2d) 357n (S.C.C.) 173, 177
R. v. Berry (1876), 1 Q.B.D. 447 .... 59, 60, 61, 65
R. v. Beynon, [1957] 2 W.L.R. 956 .... 60, 61
R. v. Binette, [1965] 3 C.C.C. 216 (B.C.C.A.) 276
R. v. Blackmore (1967), 1 C.R.N.S. 286, 53 M.P.R. 141 (N.S.C.A.) 163
R. v. Boisvert and Lupien (1967), 10 Crim. L.Q. 25 (B.C. Co. Ct.) 238, 254
R. v. Bolduc (1973), 16 C.C.C. (2d) 280 (Que. C.A.) 266, 279, 280
R. v. Boomhower (1974), 20 C.C.C. (2d) 89, 27 C.R.N.S. 188 (Ont. C.A.) ...   251, 252, 253

R. v. Borg, [1969] S.C.R. 551, [1969] 4 C.C.C. 262, 6 D.L.R. (3d) 1, 7 C.R.N.S. 85 .... 130, 140
R. v. Bouchard (1912), 20 C.C.C. 95, 4 D.L.R. 317 (Que. Ct. Sess.) 20
R. v. Bouchard (1973), 24 C.R.N.S. 31, 12 C.C.C. (2d) 554 (N.S. Co. Ct.) 207, 220
R. v. Boucher, [1963] 2 C.C.C. 241, 39 C.R. 242, 40 W.W.R. 663 (B.C.C.A.) 156
R. v. Bourque, [1969] 4 C.C.C. 358, 7 C.R.N.S. 189, 69 W.W.R. 145 (B.C.C.A.) 157
R. v. Boylen (1972), 18 C.R.N.S. 273 (N.S. Mag. Ct.) 67, 68
R. v. Bradbury (1973), 23 C.R.N.S. 293, 14 C.C.C. (2d) 139 (Ont. C.A.)   249, 250, 251, 254
R. v. Bray (1975), 24 C.C.C. (2d) 366 (Ont. Co. Ct.) 97
R. v. Brockenshire and Clarkson, [1932] 1 D.L.R. 156, [1931] O.R. 806, 56 C.C.C. 340 (C.A.).. 115, 143
R. v. Brown (1776), Leach 148 171
R. v. Bruzas, [1972] Crim. L.R. 357 170
R. v. Bryson, [1966] 3 C.C.C. 182 (B.C.C.A.) 267
R. v. Buckler, [1970] 2 C.C.C. 4, [1970] 2 O.R. 614 (Prov. Ct.)....................... 281
R. v. Budic (1977), 35 C.C.C. (2d) 272 (Alta. C.A.) 73
R. v. Burkart; R. v. Sawatsky, [1965] 3 C.C.C. 210, 45 C.R. 383, 50 W.W.R. 515 (Sask. C.A.) 194
R. v. Burles, [1970] 2 Q.B. 191 (C.A.) 59
R. v. Burns (1974), 58 Cr. App.R. 364.. 97, 156
R. v. Burnshine (1974), 15 C.C.C. (2d) 505, 44 D.L.R. (3d) 53, 25 C.R.N.S. 270, [1974] 4 W.W.R. 49, 2 N.R. 53 (S.C.C.) 284
R. v. Byrne, [1960] 3 All E.R. 1 (C.C.A.) 184, 185
R. v. Canning, [1966] 4 C.C.C. 379, 49 C.R. 13, 56 W.W.R. 466 (B.C.C.A.) 279
R. v. Cardinal (1953), 17 C.R. 373, 10 W.W.R. 403 (Alta. C.A.).................... 132, 143
R. v. Carter, [1959] V.R. 105 .... 100, 112
R. v. Casey (1947), 63 T.L.R. 487 (C.C.A.) 141
R. v. Cave, [1965] Crim. L.R. 448 243
R. v. Chan Ming Luk, [1962] H.K.L.R. 651 (S.C.) 141, 219, 220
R. v. Chapman (1838), 8 C. & P. 558 220
R. v. Chard (1971), 56 Cr. App.R. 268.. 189
R. v. Charlebois (unreported, 1973 Ont. C.A.) 163
R. v. Charlson, [1955] 1 All E.R. 859 (C.C.A.)................................. 85, 87, 94
R. v. Chupiuk, [1949] 2 W.W.R. 801, 8 C.R. 398, 95 C.C.C. 189 (Sask. C.A.) 143
R. v. Clark, [1975] 2 W.W.R. 385, 22 C.C.C. (2d) 1 (Alta. C.A.); affd [1976] 2 W.W.R. 570, 5 N.R. 599 (S.C.C.) 173, 177, 193
R. v. Clarke, [1972] 1 All E.R. 219, 56 Cr. App.R. 225 (C.A.) 165, 189
R. v. Clarke (1973), 16 C.C.C. (2d) 310 (N.S.) 115
R. v. Cleary (1964), 48 Cr. App.R. 116 39
R. v. Codere (1916), 12 Cr. App.R. 21 .... 130, 132, 133
R. v. Coelho (1914), 10 Cr. App.R. 210 139
R. v. Coleman (1927), 47 C.C.C. 148 (N.S.)...................................... 126, 291
R. v. Connolly (1965), 49 C.R. 142, [1966] 4 C.C.C. 101, 52 M.P.R. 11 (N.S.C.A.) 84, 85, 87, 165
R. v. Cottle, [1958] N.Z.L.R. 999...................................... 85, 87, 102, 114
R. v. Couture (1947), 4 C.R. 323 (Que. C.A.) 63
R. v. Cracknell, [1931] O.R. 634, 56 C.C.C. 190, [1931] 4 D.L.R. 657 (C.A.)........... 132
R. v. Craig. [1975] 2 W.W.R. 314, 22 C.C.C. (2d) 212 (Alta.); vard 28 C.C.C. (2d) 311 (C.A.).. 130
R. v. Creighton (1908), 14 C.C.C. 349 (Ont.) 139
R. v. Cullum (1973), 14 C.C.C. (2d) 294 (Ont. Co. Ct.)............ 32, 88, 98, 104, 106, 107
R. v. Cunningham, [1958] 3 All E.R. 711 170
R. v. Curtis (1972), 8 C.C.C. (2d) 240, 19 C.R.N.S. 11 (Ont. C.A.) 154
R. v. Cusack (1971), 3 C.C.C. (2d) 527, 1 N. & P.E.I.R. 496 (P.E.I.C.A.) 114
R. v. D. (1971), 5 C.C.C. (2d) 366, [1972] 1 O.R. 405, 16 C.R.N.S. 9 *sub nom.* R. v. Doran (C.A.).. 227, 241, 242
R. v. Dart (1878), 14 Cox C.C. 143 143
R. v. Dashwood, [1943] 1 K.B. 1 (C.C.A.) 61, 64
R. v. Davies (1853), 3 Car. & Kir. 328, 175 E.R. 575 .... 73, 74, 75
R. v. Davies (1913), 8 Cr. App.R. 211 87
R. v. Davies, [1962] 3 All E.R. 97 197

R. v. Davis (1881), 14 Cox C.C. 563 158
R. v. Dawe (1973), 10 C.C.C. (2d) 520 (Ont. C.A.) 154
R. v. Dawson, [1970] 3 C.C.C. 212, 8 C.R.N.S. 395, 71 W.W.R. 455 (B.C.C.A.) 278
R. v. DeCoste (1974), 10 N.S.R. (2d) 94 (C.A.) 240
R. v. Deforge (1971), 5 C.C.C. (2d) 255, [1972] 1 O.R. 515 (Dist. Ct.) 21, 55
R. v. DeSeve (unreported, June 9, 1966, B.C.) 254
R. v. Desjarlais and Ferguson (unreported, 1963, B.C. Mag. Ct.) 240, 254
R. v. Desmoulin (1976), 30 C.C.C. (2d) 517 (Ont. C.A.) 191
R. v. De Tonnancourt and Paquin (1956), 115 C.C.C. 154, 24 C.R. 19, 18 W.W.R. 337
   (Man. C.A.) 212, 222
R. v. Dhlamini, [1955 (1)] S.A. 120 (T.P.D.) 110
R. v. Dietrich, [1970] 3 O.R. 725, 11 C.R.N.S. 22, 1 C.C.C. (2d) 49 (C.A.) 192
R. v. Ditto (1962), 132 C.C.C. 198, 38 C.R. 32, 38 W.W.R. 480 (Alta. C.A.) 91, 130
R. v. Dixon, [1961] 3 All E.R. 460n 115, 143
R. v. Dobson (1975), 11 N.S.R. (2d) 81 (C.A.) 238
R. v. Donnelly (1968), 52 Cr. App.R. 731 245
R. v. Doran *See* R. v. D.
R. v. Doucet, [1971] 1 O.R. 705, 2 C.C.C. (2d) 433 (C.A.) 234, 247, 255
R. v. Dubois (1890), 17 Q.L.R. 203 201
R. v. Dubois (1976), 30 C.C.C. (2d) 412 (Ont. C.A.) 177
R. v. Duffy, [1949] 1 All E.R. 932 (C.C.A.) 177
R. v. Duke, [1963] 1 Q.B. 120 143
R. v. Dunbar, [1958] 1 Q.B. 1 184
R. v. Dunning; R. v. Simpson, [1965] Crim. L.R. (C.C.A.) 191
R. v. Dwyer, [1977] 2 W.W.R. 704 (Alta. C.A.) 273, 280
R. v. Dyson (1831), 7 C. & P. 305n 68, 70, 74
R. v. Eades, [1972] Crim. L.R. 99 194
R. v. Enright, [1961]V.R. 663 171
R. v. F. (1910), 74 J.P. 384 127
R. v. Fisher, [1961] O.W.N. 94, 34 C.R. 320 (C.A.); affd [1961] S.C.R. 535, 35 C.R. 107,
   130 C.C.C. 1 .... 76, 200, 202
R. v. Fisher (1973), 24 C.R.N.S. 129, [1973] 6 W.W.R. 1, 12 C.C.C. (2d) 513 (Alta.
   C.A.) 205
R. v. Fisher (1975), 23 C.C.C. (2d) 449, 17 Crim. L.Q. 246 (Ont. C.A.) .. 244, 245, 250, 255
R. v. Fitton, [1956] S.C.R. 958, 24 C.R. 371, 116 C.C.C. 1, 6 D.L.R. (2d) 529 37
R. v. Five Accused Persons (unreported, July 12, 1961, Man. Prov. Ct.) 238, 254
R. v. Flannery, [1969] V.R. 31 156
R. v. Frances (1849), 4 Cox C.C. 57 210
R. v. Frank (1971), 12 C.R.N.S. 339, [1971] 1 O.R. 693, 2 C.C.C. (2d) 287 .. 115, 142, 218
R. v. Fryer (1915), 24 Cox C.C. 403 138
R. v. Galbraith (1971), 5 C.C.C. (2d) 37, [1972] 1 W.W.R. 586 (B.C.C.A.); leave to appeal
   to S.C.C. refused 6 C.C.C. (2d) 188n, [1972] 2 W.W.R. 80 (S.C.C.) 267
R. v. Galgay, [1972] 2 O.R. 630, 6 C.C.C. (2d) 539 (C.A.) 171
R. v. George, [1960] S.C.R. 871, 34 C.R. 1 .... 156, 157
R. v. German (1947), 89 C.C.C. 90, 3 C.R. 516, [1947] O.R. 395, [1947] 4 D.L.R. 68
   (C.A.) 197
R. v. Giannotti (1956), 115 C.C.C. 203, 23 C.R. 259, [1956] O.R. 349 (C.A.) 157, 170
R. v. Gibbons (1946), 86 C.C.C. 20, [1946] O.R. 464, 1 C.R. 522 (C.A.) 62, 67, 71
R. v. Gillis (1973), 13 C.C.C. (2d) 362 (B.C. Co. Ct.) 91, 116, 117, 130, 141, 143, 185
R. v. Glynn, [1972] 1 O.R. 403, 15 C.R.N.S. 343, 5 C.C.C. (2d) 364 (C.A.) 195
R. v. Goode (1837), 7 Ad. & El. 536, 112 E.R. 572 76
R. v. Gottschalk (1974), 22 C.C.C. (2d) 415 (Ont. Prov. Ct.) 165
R. v. Governor of Stafford Prison, Ex p. Emery, [1909] 2 K.B. 81 .... 68, 70, 74
R. v. Grant, [1960] Crim. L.R. 424 184
R. v. Greedy, [1964] Crim. L.R. 669 243
R. v. Green, [1962] Crim. L.R. 823 (C.C.A.) 61
R. v. Green (1972), 5 N.S.R. (2d) 41, 20 C.R.N.S. 340, 9 C.C.C. (2d) 289 (C.A.) 171
R. v. Grobb (1906), 13 C.C.C. 92, 6 W.L.R. 727, 17 Man. R. 191 (C.A.) 197
R. v. Gross (1913), 23 Cox C.C. 455 170
R. v. Gunewardine, [1951] 2 All E.R. 290 (C.C.A.) 191
R. v. Gunnell (1956), 50 Cr. App.R. 242 247

R. v. H. (1965-66), 8 Crim. L.Q. 11 (Ont. Co. Ct.) 242, 260
R. v. Haig (1974), 26 C.R.N.S. 247 (Ont. C.A.) 249
R. v. Haight (1976), 30 C.C.C. (2d) 168 (Ont. C.A.).................................. 177
R. v. Hall (1928), 21 Cr. App.R. 48... 170
R. v. Hally, [1962] Qd. R. 214 (C.C.A.).. 200
R. v. Harms, [1936] 2 W.W.R. 114, 66 C.C.C. 134, [1936] 3 D.L.R. 497 (Sask C.A.)... 170
R. v. Harper (1913), 9 Cr. App. R. 41 136
R. v. Harris, [1927] All E.R. Rep. 473... 220
R. v. Harrison-Owen, [1951] 2 All E.R. 726 117
R. v. Harrop, [1940] 3 W.W.R. 77, 48 Man. R. 113, 74 C.C.C. 228, [1940] 4 D.L.R. 80
   (C.A.)... 122, 130, 132
R. v. Hartridge (1966), 57 D.L.R. (2d) 332, [1967] 1 C.C.C. 346, 48 C.R. 389, 56 W.W.R.
   385 (Sask. C.A.) 89, 95, 154, 157
R. v. Hatchwell, [1974] 1 W.W.R. 307, 14 C.C.C. (2d) 256 (B.C.C.A.); revd [1975] 4
   W.W.R. 68, 21 C.C.C. (2d) 201, 54 D.L.R. (3d) 419, 3 N.R. 351 (S.C.C.) .. 283, 284, 285
R. v. Hawke (1975), 29 C.R.N.S. 1, 7 O.R. (2d) 145, 22 C.C.C. (2d) 19 (C.A.) 190
R. v. Hay (1911), 22 Cox C.C. 268.. 138
R. v. Haymour (1974), 21 C.C.C. (2d) 30 (B.C. Prov. Ct.) 143
R. v. Head (1970), 1 C.C.C. (2d) 436 (Sask. C.A.)........................... 245, 254
R. v. Herrman and Singer (unreported, 1963, B.C. Mag. Ct.) 240, 254
R. v. Hill (1851), 2 Den. 254, 169 E.R. 495 190
R. v. Hill, [1963] Crim. L.R. 525 243
R. v. Hill (1974), 15 C.C.C. (2d) 145 (Ont. C.A.); affd 23 C.C.C. (2d) 321, 58 D.L.R. (3d)
   697, 6 N.R. 413 (S.C.C.) 248, 249
R. v. Hilton (unreported, May 5, 1977, Ont. C.A.) 154
R. v. Hodgson (1967), 52 Cr. App.R. 113 249
R. v. Holden (1838), 8 C. & P. 606 220
R. v. Holmes, [1960] W.A.R. 122 94
R. v. Holmes, [1953] 1 W.L.R. 686 .... 132, 208
R. v. Holt (1920), 15 Cr. App.R. 10 139
R. v. Holte and Landry (unreported 1963, B.C. Mag. Ct.)....................... 240, 254
R. v. Hopper, [1915] 2 K.B. 431.. 170
R. v. Hornbuckle, [1945] V.L.R. 31 156
R. v. Hough, [1965] Crim. L.R. 665 241
R. v. Hubach, [1966] 4 C.C.C. 114, 48 C.R. 252, 55 W.W.R. 536 (Alta. C.A.) ... 67, 71, 72
R. v. Hubbert (1975), 31 C.R.N.S. 27, 29 C.C.C. (2d) 279, 11 O.R. (2d) 464 (C.A.); affd 38
   C.R.N.S. 381, 33 C.C.C. (2d) 207n (S.C.C.) 199
R. v. Hume, Ex p. Morris, [1965] 3 C.C.C. 118, 49 W.W.R. 756 *sub nom.* Re Morris
   (B.C.); revd [1965] 3 C.C.C. 349, 50 W.W.R. 576, 46 C.R. 203, *sub nom.* R. v. Morris
   (C.A.)... 267
R. v. Ireland, [1910] 1 K.B. 654 142
R. v. J. (1957), 118 C.C.C. 30, 26 C.R. 57, 21 W.W.R. 248 (Alta. C.A.) 201
R. v. Jackson, [1941] 1 W.W.R. 418, 75 C.C.C. 306, [1941] 2 D.L.R. 119 (Sask.
   C.A.) 170, 171
R. v. James (1974), 30 C.R.N.S. 65 (Ont.) 101
R. v. Jeanotte, [1932] 2 W.W.R. 283 (Sask. C.A.) 132
R. v. Jefferson (1908), 24 T.L.R. 877 62
R. v. Jennion, [1962] 1 W.L.R. 317 212
R. v. Jessamine (1912), 21 O.W.R. 392 (C.A.) 132
R. v. Johnson, [1946] Que. S.C. 101 125
R. v. Johnston (1965), 51 W.W.R. 280, [1965] 3 C.C.C. 42 (Man. C.A.) 37, 48, 276
R. v. Jones (1956), 115 C.C.C. 273, 23 C.R 364, [1956] O.W.N. 396 (C.A.) 246
R. v. Jones (1971), 3 C.C.C. (2d) 153, [1971] 2 O.R. 549 (C.A.) 244, 255
R. v. K., [1971] 2 O.R. 401, 3 C.C.C. (2d) 84 .... 32, 87, 101, 102
R. v. Kanester, [1968] 1 C.C.C. 351 (B.C.C.A.) 280
R. v. Kasperek (1951), 101 C.C.C. 375, [1951] O.R. 776, 13 C.R. 206 (C.A.) 99
R. v. Kelly (1971), 16 C.R.N.S. 72, 6 C.C.C. (2d) 186n (Ont. C.A.)............... 213, 214
R. v. Kelman (1971), 4 C.C.C. (2d) 8 (B.C.) 271
R. v. Kemp, [1957] 1 Q.B. 399 .... 93, 115, 128, 141
R. v. Kierstead (1918), 42 D.L.R. 193, 30 C.C.C. 175, 45 N.B.R. 553 (C.A.) . 115, 143, 197
R. v. Kierstead (No. 2) (1918), 33 C.C.C. 288 (N.B.) 73, 198

R. v. King, [1962] S.C.R. 746, 38 C.R. 52, 133 C.C.C. 1, 35 D.L.R. (3d) 386 ... 87, 97, 154
R. v. Knight (1975), 27 C.C.C. (2d) 343 (Ont.) 280
R. v. Kopsch (1925), 19 Cr. App. R. 50 139
R. v. Krawchuk, [1941] 3 W.W.R. 540, 75 C.C.C. 16, 56 B.C.R. 7 (C.A.); affd 75 C.C.C.
219, [1941] 2 D.L.R. 353 (S.C.C.) 171
R. v. Kuzmack (1954), 110 C.C.C. 338, 20 C.R. 365, 14 W.W.R. 595 (Alta. C.A.); affd
[1955] S.C.R. 292, 111 C.C.C. 1, 20 C.R. 337 .... 76, 197, 199
R. v. Kyselka, [1962] O.W.N. 160, 37 C.R. 391, 133 C.C.C. 103 (C.A.) 194
R. v. Lachance, [1963] 2 C.C.C. 14, 36 C.R. 127 (Ont. C.A.) 166
R. v. LaChance and Bliss (unreported, 1963, B.C. Mag. Ct.) 240, 254
R. v. Lanfear, [1968] 1 All E.R. 683 213
R. v. Larkins (1911), 6 Cr. App R. 194 62
R. v. Laycock, [1952] O.R. 908, 104 C.C.C. 274, 15 C.R. 292 (C.A) 122, 132
R. v. Leary (1975), 31 C.R.N.S. 199, 26 C.C.C. (2d) 522 (B.C.C.A.); affd 37 C.R.N.S. 60,
33 C.C.C. (2d) 473, 74 D.L.R. (3d) 103 (S.C.C.) 156, 157, 186
R. v. Lee Kun, [1916] 1 K.B. 337 51
R. v. Leech (1973), 21 C.R.N.S. 1, [1973] 1 W.W.R. 744, 10 C.C.C. (2d) 149
(Alta.) 130, 131, 140, 242, 249
R. v. Leggo (1962), 133 C.C.C. 149, 38 C.R. 290, 39 W.W.R. 385 (B.C.C.A.) 37, 203
R. v. Lenchitsky, [1954] Crim. L.R. 216 163
R. v. Lesbini, [1914] 3 K.B. 1116 (C.C.A.) 172
R. v. Leshley (unreported, Ont.) 270
R. v. Letenock (1917), 12 Cr. App. R. 221 171
R. v. Levionnois (1956), 114 C.C.C. 266, [1956] O.R. 267, 23 C.R. 230 (C.A.) 75
R. v. Leys (1910), 17 C.C.C. 198, 1 O.W.N. 958 (C.A.) 63
R. v. Liddle (1928), 21 Cr. App. R. 3 220
R. v. Lipman, [1969] 3 All E.R. 410, [1970] 1 Q.B. 152 (C.A.) 96, 154
R. v. Lloyd (1927), 20 Cr. App. R. 139 .... 123, 143
R. v. Lloyd, [1966] 1 All E.R. 107 (C.C.A.) 185
R. v. Lobell, [1957] 1 Q.B. 547 112
R. v. Louison, [1975] 6 W.W.R. 289 (Sask. C.A.) 173
R. v. Loysen (1973), 13 C.C.C. (2d) 202 (B.C.) 276, 280
R. v. Luknowsky (1976), 19 Crim. L.Q. 18 (B.C.C.A.) 250
R. v. Lupien, [1970] S.C.R. 263, 9 C.R.N.S. 165, 71 W.W.R. 110, [1970] 2 C.C.C. 193, 9
D.L.R. (3d) 1; revg 4 C.R.N.S. 250, 64 W.W.R. 721, [1969] 1 C.C.C. 32
(B.C.C.A.) 77, 189, 195, 205, 206, 208, 238
R. v. MacCarthy (or McCarthy), [1966] 2 W.L.R. 555 64
R. v. MacDonald (1966), 9 Crim. L.Q. 239 (N.S.) 197
R. v. MacIsaac (1968), 11 Crim. L.Q. 234 (Ont. Dist. Ct.) 95, 96
R. v. Mack (1975), 27 C.R.N.S. 270, [1975] 4 W.W.R. 180, 22 C.C.C. (2d) 257 (Alta.
C.A.) 96
R. v. Mackie, [1933] 1 W.W.R. 273, 59 C.C.C. 254, [1933] 2 D.L.R. 685, 41 Man. R. 9
(C.A.) 211
R. v. Manchuk, [1938] S.C.R. 18 .... 170, 171
R. v. Marshall (unreported, May 4, 1966, B.C.) 254
R. v. McAmmond, [1970] 1 C.C.C. 175, 7 D.L.R. (3d) 346, 7 C.R.N.S. 210, 69 W.W.R. 277
(Man. C.A.) 48, 269, 272, 279
R. v. McCarthy, [1954] 2 Q.B. 105 172
R. v. McCoskey (1926), 47 C.C.C. 122, [1927] 2 D.L.R. 539, 60 O.L.R. 44 (C.A.) 122
R. v. McKay, [1967] N.Z.L.R. 139 (C.A.) 192
R. v. McKenzie, [1965] 3 C.C.C. 6, 46 C.R. 153, 51 W.W.R. 641 (Alta. C.A.) .. 37, 39, 270
R. v. McMahon (1933), 24 Cr. App. R. 97 220
R. v. McMillan (1975), 29 C.R.N.S. 191, 7 O.R. (2d) 750, 23 C.C.C. (2d) 160 (C.A.); affd
33 C.C.C. (2d) 360, 73 D.L.R. (3d) 759 (S.C.C.) 196
R. v. Marchello (1951), 12 C.R. 7, 100 C.C.C. 137, [1951] 4 D.L.R. 751, [1951] O.W.N.
316 .... 178, 179
R. v. Marks (1952), 103 C.C.C. 368, 15 C.R. 47, [1958] O.W.N. 608 (Co. Ct.) 197
R. v. Marple (1973), 6 N.S.R. (2d) 389 (C.A.) 238
R. v. Martin (1854), 2 N.S.R. 322 125
R. v. Mason (1911), 7 Cr. App. R. 67 210
R. v. Matheson, [1958] 2 All E.R. 87 .... 213, 214

R. v. Mathews (1953), 17 C.R. 241, 9 W.W.R. 649 (B.C.C.A.) 132
R. v. Meadus (unreported, Oct. 8, 1976, Ont.) 135, 136
R. v. Minor (1955), 112 C.C.C. 29, 21 C.R. 377, 15 W.W.R. 433 (Sask. C.A.) 89, 100
R. v. Mitchell, [1965] 1 C.C.C. 155, 46 D.L.R. (2d) 384, 43 C.R. 391, 47 W.W.R. 591,
    [1964] S.C.R. 471; affg [1964] 2 C.C.C. 1, 42 C.R. 12, 45 W.W.R. 199 (B.C.C.A.) ... 168
R. v. Moke, [1917] 3 W.W.R. 575, 12 Alta. L.R. 18, 28 C.C.C. 296, 38 D.L.R. 441
    (C.A.) 122, 213
R. v. Morris *See* R. v. Hume, Ex p. Morris
R. v. Morris, [1961] 2 Q.B. 237 236
R. v. Morrison (1957), 40 M.P.R. 58 (N.S.C.A.) 170
R. v. Mulligan (1974), 26 C.R.N.S. 179, 18 C.C.C. (2d) 270 (Ont. C.A.); affd 66 D.L.R.
    (3d) 627, 28 C.C.C. (2d) 266 (S.C.C.) 106, 163
R. v. Murphy (1972), 15 Crim. L. Q. 13 (Ont. C.A.) 247, 255
R. v. Neil [1957] S.C.R. 685, 26 C.R. 281, 119 C.C.C. 1, 11 D.L.R. (2d)
    545 .... 202, 203, 271, 273, 279
R. v. Nesbitt, [1965] 2 C.C.C. 360, 49 D.L.R. (2d) 22, 46 C.R. 260, 50 W.W.R. 453 (Sask.
    C.A.) 169, 171
R. v. Nott (1958), 43 C.R. App.R. 8 .... 143, 184
R. v. Nowell, [1948] 1 All E.R. 794 213
R. v. O. (1960-61), 3 Crim. L. Q. 151 .... 132, 136
R. v. O'Brien (1965), 56 D.L.R. (2d) 65, [1966] 3 C.C.C. 288 (N.B.C.A.) ... 89, 91, 94, 130
R. v. O'Donoghue (1927), 20 Cr. App. R. 132 179
R. v. Oldham (1970), 1 C.C.C. (2d) 141, 11 C.R.N.S. 204, 74 W.W.R. 151 (B.C.C.A.) .. 192
R. v. Ortt, [1969] 1 O.R. 461, [1970] 1 C.C.C. 223, 6 C.R.N.S. 233, 11 Crim. L. Q. 328
    (C.A.) 157
R. v. Oxford (1840), 9 C. & P. 525 138
R. v. P., [1968] 3 C.C.C. 129, 3 C.R.N.S. 302, 63 W.W.R. 222 (Man. C.A.) 201
R. v. Pascoe (1974), 17 Crim. L. Q. 142 (Ont. C.A.) 246
R. v. Payne [1963] 1 W.L.R. 637 (C.C.A) 32
R. v. Petrov, [1973] B.N. 57 (Ont.C.A.) 252
R. v. Phillion (1972), 21 C.R.N.S. 169, [1973] 2 O.R. 209, 10 C.C.C. (2d) 562, 34 D.L.R.
    (3d) 99; affd 37 C.R.N.S. 361 at p. 362, 5 O.R. (2d) 656, 20 C.C.C. (2d) 191, 53 D.L.R.
    (3d) 319 (C.A.); affd 37 C.R.N.S. 361, 33 C.C.C. (2d) 535, 74 D.L.R. (3d) 136
    (S.C.C.) 44, 192, 193
R. v. Phinney (No. 1) (1903), 6 C.C.C. 469, 36 N.S.R. 264 (C.A.) 122
R. v. Pickstone [1954] Crim. L. R. 565 60
R. v. Pitrie (1971), 3 C.C.C. (2d) 380, [1971] 5 W.W.R. 270, 16 C.R.N.S. 226, *sub nom.*
    Pitrie v. The Queen (B.C.C.A.) 97
R. v. Podola, [1959] 3 W.L.R. 718 .... 62, 68, 69, 75
R. v. Porter (1936), 55 C.L.R. 182 131
R. v. Potvin (1971), 16 C.R.N.S. 233 (Que. C.A.) 32
R. v. Prairie Schooner News Ltd. and Powers (1970), 1 C.C.C. (2d) 251, 12 Crim. L.Q.
    462, 75 W.W.R. 585 (Man. C.A.) 201
R. v. Price, [1963] 2 Q.B. 1 .... 143, 184
R. v. Prince (1972), 16 C.R.N.S. 73, [1972] 2 O.R. 252, 6 C.C.C. (2d) 183 (C.A.) 214
R. v. Pritchard (1836), 7 C. & P. 303, 173 E.R. 135 .... 65, 68, 70, 74
R. v. Quarmby (1921), 15 Cr. App. R. 163 139
R. v. Quick and Paddison (1973), 57 Cr. App. R. 722, [1973] Q.B. 910 .... 96, 97, 112
R. v. Rabey (unreported, March 17, 1977, Ont. C.A.) 107
R. v. Rasim Taka (unreported, September, 1969, Ont.) 163
R. v. Rivett (1950), 34 Cr. App. R. 87 .... 71, 76, 77, 210
R. v. Roberts, [1953] 2 All E.R. 340 .... 59, 60, 66, 67, 70
R. v. Roberts, [1963] 1 O.R. 280, [1963] 1 C.C.C. 27, 36 D.L.R. (2d) 696, 39 C.R. 1
    (C.A.) 227
R. v. Roberts (1975), 24 C.C.C. (2d) 539, [1975] 3 W.W.R. 742 (B.C.C.A.) 76
R. v. Robertson, [1968] 3 All E.R. 577 (C.C.A.) 71, 75
R. v. Robertson (1975), 29 C.R.N.S. 141, 21 C.C.C. (2d) 385 (Ont. C.A.); application for
    leave to appeal to S.C.C. dismissed 21 C.C.C. (2d) 385n 195
R. v. Robinson (1974), 19 C.C.C. (2d) 193 (Ont. C.A.) 231, 249, 253, 254

R. v. Roestad (1971), 19 C.R.N.S. 190, [1972] 1 O.R. 814, 5 C.C.C. (2d) 564 (Co. Ct.);
application for leave to appeal to C.A. dismissed 19 C.R.N.S. 235*n*
(C.A.).. 272, 280, 282, 285
R. v. Rogers, [1964] 1 C.C.C. 303, 40 C.R. 207, 42 W.W.R. 605, *sub nom.* Re Rogers
Prohibition Application (B.C.).. 267
R. v. Rogers (1965), 48 C.R. 90 (B.C.C.A.) 97
R. v. Rosik (1970), 2 C.C.C. (2d) 351, [1971] 2 O.R. 47, 13 C.R.N.S. 129, 13 Crim. L.Q.
224 (C.A.); affd 2 C.C.C. (2d) 393*n*, [1971] 2 O.R. 89*n*, 14 C.R.N.S. 400 (S.C.C.) 207
R. v. Ross Tucket (1844), 1 Cox C.C. 103 143
R. v. Rowton (1865), 10 Cox C.C. 25 195
R. v. Russell (1964), 48 Cr. App.R. 62 143
R. v. St. Pierre, [1973] 1 O.R. 718, 10 C.C.C. (2d) 164; revd 3 O.R. (2d) 642, 17 C.C.C.
(2d) 489 (C.A.).. 200
R. v. Sampson (1934), 8 M.P.R. 328, 63 C.C.C. 24, [1935] 2 D.L.R. 197 (N.S.C.A.); affd
[1935] S.C.R. 634, 63 C.C.C. 384, [1935] 3 D.L.R. 197 170
R. v. Sanders, [1966] 2 C.C.C. 345, 54 W.W.R. 529 (B.C.) 276
R. v. Sanders. [1968] 4 C.C.C. 156 (B.C.C.A.) 267
R. v. Santinon (1973), 21 C.R.N.S. 323, [1973] 3 W.W.R. 113, 11 C.C.C. (2d) 121
(B.C.C.A.).. 192
R. v. Saunders, [1965] Crim. L.R. 250.. 244
R. v. Saxon, [1975] 4 W.W.R. 346, 22 C.C.C. (2d) 370 (Alta. C.A.).................... 97
R. v. Sayle, [1974] 5 W.W.R. 766, 28 C.R.N.S. 21, 18 C.C.C. (2d) 56 *sub nom.* Ex p. Sayle
(B.C.).. 17, 25
R. v. Schmidt and Gole (1972), 9 C.C.C. (2d) 101 (Ont. C.A.) 156
R. v. Schonberger (1960), 126 C.C.C. 113, 33 C.R. 107, 31 W.W.R. 97 (Sask. C.A.).. 88, 98
R. v. Scroggic, [1974] 2 W.W.R. 641, 15 C.C.C. (2d) 309 *sub nom* Re R. and Scroggie
(B.C.).. 143
R. v. Searle (1831), 1 Mood. & R. 75 210
R. v. Sharp, [1957] 1 All E.R. 577... 74, 75
R. v. Sibbles, [1959] Crim. L.R. 660 .... 84, 98
R. v. Simcox, [1964] Crim. L.R. 402 (C.C.A.).. 185
R. v. Simpson (1977), 35 C.C.C. (2d) 337 (Ont. C.A.) 116, 117, 135, 142, 143
R. v. Sloane (1930), 1 M.P.R. 546, 53 C.C.C. 342, [1930] 4 D.L.R. 129 (N.S.C.A.)..... 122
R. v. Smith (1910), 6 Cr. App. R. 19 .... 112, 141
R. v. Smith (1912), 8 Cr. App. R. 72 143
R. v. Smith (1915), 31 T.L.R. 617 210
R. v. Smith, [1936] 1 D.L.R. 717, 65 C.C.C. 231, [1936] 1 W.W.R. 67
(Sask.C.A.) 53, 61, 63, 66
R. v. Smith (1967), 5 C.R.N.S. 162 (Ont.) 140
R. v. Smith (1970), 1 C.C.C. (2d) 457, 2 N.S.R. (2d) 375 (C.A.); remitted to trial court for
sentence on substantive offence 8 C.C.C. (2d) 279*n*, 3 N.S.R. (2d) 520 (S.C.C.) 267
R. v. Smith (1976), 32 C.C.C. (2d) 224 (Nfld. Dist. Ct.) 178
R. v. Smyth, [1963] V.R. 737 112
R. v. Soanes, [1948] 1 All E.R. 289 (C.C.A.) 178
R. v. Spriggs, [1958] 1 Q.B. 270 184
R. v. Sproule (1975), 30 C.R.N.S. 56 (Ont. C.A.); revg 19 C.R.N.S. 384 .... 96, 113
R. v. Stamford, [1972] 2 All E.R. 427 201
R. v. Starecki, [1960] V.L.R. 141 (Vict. S.C.) 192
R. v. Stewart (1972), 56 Cr. App. R. 272 192
R. v. Stones, [1956] S.R. (N.S.W.) 25 .... 112, 155
R. v. Swanson (1950), 10 C.R. 81, [1950] 1 W.W.R. 1001, 96 C.C.C. 227 (B.C.C.A.) ... 171
R. v. Sweeney (No. 2) (1977), 35 C.C.C. (2d) 245 (Ont. C.A.) 36
R. v. Szymusiak, [1972] 3 O.R. 602, 8 C.C.C. (2d) 407, 19 C.R.N.S. 373 (C.A.).... 95, 114
R. v. Taylor, [1915] 2 K.B. 709 142
R. v. Taylor, [1959] O.W.N. 1 (C.A.) 227
R. v. Thomas (1911), 7 Cr. App. R. 36 139
R. v. Tilley, [1953] O.R. 609, 106 C.C.C. 42, 17 C.R. 1 (C.A.), affg 104 C.C.C. 315 204
R. v. Times Square Cinema Ltd., [1971] 3 O.R. 688, 4 C.C.C. (2d) 229 (C.A.) 201
R. v. Tolson (1889), 23 Q.B.D. 168 .... 84, 87, 108
R. v. Tousignant, [1957] O.W.N. 573 (C.A.) 279
R. v. Trapnell (1910), 22 O.L.R. 219, 17 C.C.C. 346 (C.A.) 295

R. v. Tregear, [1967] 1 All E.R. 989 (C.C.A.) 220
R. v. Tripodi, [1955] S.C.R. 438, 21 C.R. 192, 112 C.C.C. 66, [1955] 4 D.L.R. 445 170
R. v. Turner (1969), 53 Cr. App. R. 590 .... 251, 260
R. v. Turner, [1975] 1 Q.B. 834 .... 177, 193
R. v. Turpin (unreported, May 4, 1966, B.C.) 254
R. v. Turton (1854), 6 Cox C.C. 385 73
R. v. Twine, [1967] Crim. L.R. 710 170
R. v. Vandervoot (1961), 130 C.C.C. 158, [1961] O.W.N. 141, 34 C.R. 380 (C.A.) 156
R. v. Vent (1935), 25 Cr. App. R. 55 63
R. v. Vlcko (1972), 10 C.C.C. (2d) 139 (Ont. C.A.) 154
R. v. Volk (1973), 12 C.C.C. (2d) 395, [1973] 6 W.W.R. 29 (Alta. C.A.) 270
R. v. Wakefield (1957), 75 W.N. (N.S.W.) 66 100
R. v. Wallace (1973), 11 C.C.C. (2d) 95 (Ont. C.A.) 248, 250
R. v. Wardrope, [1960] Crim. L.R. 770 .... 171, 172
R. v. Warren (1973), 14 C.C.C. (2d) 188, 6 N.S.R. (2d) 323, 24 C.R.N.S. 349 32
R. v. Webb, [1969] 2 Q.B. 278 (C.A.) 59
R. v. Welsh (1869), 11 Cox C.C. 336 .... 170, 171
R. v. White, 1941 S.R. 1 108
R. v. Williams (1929), 50 C.C.C. 230, [1929] 1 D.L.R. 343, 63 O.L.R. 191 (C.A.) 61
R. v. Windle, [1952] 2 Q.B. 826 132
R. v. Wolfson, [1965] 3 C.C.C. 304, 51 D.L.R. (2d) 428, 46 C.R. 8, 51 W.W.R. 321 (Alta.
    C.A.) 63, 139
R. v. Woltucky (1952), 103 C.C.C. 43, 15 C.R. 24, 6 W.W.R. 72 (Sask.
    C.A.) 65, 67, 71, 75, 77
R. v. Wray, [1971] S.C.R. 272, 11 C.R.N.S. 235, [1970] 4 C.C.C. 1, 11 D.L.R. (3d) 673 . 33
R. v. Wright (1967), 62 W.W.R. 449, 3 C.R.N.S. 136, [1968] 3 C.C.C. 168 (Sask. C.A.);
    affd 66 W.W.R. 631, [1969] 3 C.C.C. 258, 2 D.L.R. (3d) 529, [1969] S.C.R. 335.. 171, 177
R. and Lester, Re (1971), 6 C.C.C. (2d) 227, [1972] 2 O.R. 330 (C.A.) 122
R. ex rel. Taggart v. Forage (1968), 3 C.R.N.S. 117 (Ont.) 204, 205, 206
R. ex rel. Johannesson v. Rural Munic. of Cartier (1922), 68 D.L.R. 741 (Man.) 314
Ragsdale v. Overholser (1960), 281 F. 2d 943 (U.S. App. D.C.) 299
Reference re R. v. Gorecki (No. 1) (1976), 32 C.C.C. (2d) 129, 14 O.R. (2d) 212 (C.A.) . 61
Reid, Re (1953), 10 W.W.R. (N.S.) 383 (B.C.) 328
Rogers Prohibition Application, Re *See* R. v. Rogers
Rolater v. Strain (1914), 39 Okla. 572 304
Rose v. The Queen, [1961] A.C. 496 184
Rouse v. Cameron (1966), 373 F. 2d 451 (D.C. Cir.) 301, 302, 303, 321
Russell v. H.M. Advocate, [1946] S.C. (J.) 37 .... 67, 68, 73

Salamon v. The Queen, [1959] S.C.R. 404, 30 C.R. 1, 123 C.C.C. 1, 17 D.L.R. (2d)
    685 173
San Francisco (City and County of) v. Superior Court (1951) 231 P. 2d 26 (Cal. S.C.) . 34
Sarault, Re (1905), 9 C.C.C. 448 (Que. K.B.) 20
Sas v. Maryland (1964), 334 F. 2d 506 (4th Cir.); cert. dismissed *sub nom.* Murel v.
    Baltimore City Crim. Ct. (1972), 407 U.S. 355 298
Sayle, Ex p. *See* R. v. Sayle
Schmerber v. California (1964), 384 U.S. 757 40
Schwartz v. The Queen (1976), 34 C.R.N.S. 138, 29 C.C.C. (2d) 1, 67 D.L.R. (3d)
    716 .... 132, 134, 135
Sevanson v. Hood (1918), 99 Wash. 506 198
Shumiatcher, Re, [1962] S.C.R. 38, 31 D.L.R. (2d) 2 .... 124, 314
Shuttleworth, Re (1846), 9 Q.B.D. 329
Sinclair v. The Queen (1946), 73 C.L.R. 316 (Aust. H.C.) 192
Smith v. Mason (1901), 1 O.L.R. 594 197
Smith v. United States (1929), 36 F. 2d 548 (D.C. Cir.) 146
Smythe v. The King, [1941] S.C.R. 17, 74 C.C.C. 273, [1941] 1 D.L.R. 497 143
Smythe v. The Queen (1971), 13 C.R.N.S. 7, [1971] 2 O.R. 209 at p. 211, 17 D.L.R. (3d)
    389 at p. 391, 3 C.C.C. (2d) 97 at p. 98, 70 D.T.C. 6382; affd 13 C.R.N.S. 33, [1971] 2
    O.R. 209, 17 D.L.R. (3d) 389, 3 C.C.C. (2d) 97, 71 D.T.C. 5090 (C.A.); affd 16 C.R.N.S.
    147, [1971] S.C.R. 680, 19 D.L.R. (3d) 480, 3 C.C.C. (2d) 366, 71 D.T.C. 5252 284
Sommer, Re (1958), 27 C.R. 243 (Que.) 20

Soquet v. State (1888), 72 Wis. 659 198
Sportun v. Murphy and Smith, [1955] 2 D.L.R. 248 (Ont. C.A.) 99
Stapleton v. The Queen (1952), 86 C.L.R. 358 (Aust. H.C.) 132, 133
State v. Anderson (1973), 509 P. 2d 80 50
State v. Boyce (1901), 24 Wash. 514 198
State v. Cerar (1922), 207 P. 597 (Utah S.C.) 41
State v. Corbin (1973), 516 P. 2d 1314 50
State v. Esser (1962), 115 N.W. 2d 505 145
State v. Jones (1871), 50 N.H. 369 .... 109, 146
State v. Lange (1929), 168 La. 958 222
State v. Liolios (1920), 285 Mo. 1 198
State v. McClendon (1966), 419 P. 2d 60 (Ariz.) 67
State v. Pike (1870), 49 N.H. 399 146
State v. Rose (1917), 271 Mo. 17 198
State v. Shaw (1970), 471 P. 2d 715, cert. denied (1971), 40 U.S. 1009 49
State v. White (1962), 374 P. 2d 942, cert. denied 375 U.S. 883 145
State v. Whitlow (1965), 210 A. 2d 763 40
State ex rel. LaFollette v. Raskin (1967), 150 N.W. 2d 318 49
State ex rel. Berger v. Superior Court (1970), 476 P. 2d 666 49
Steinberg v. The King, [1931] 4 D.L.R. 8, [1931] S.C.R. 421, 56 C.C.C. 9 190
Sun Ins. Office v. Roy, [1927] S.C.R. 8, [1927] 1 D.L.R. 17 210

Tabor v. Scobel (1952), 254 S.W. 2d 474 (Ky. C.A.) 304
Taylor v. Gray, [1937] 4 D.L.R. 123, 11 M.P.R. 588 (N.B.C.A.) 76, 197
Taylor v. The Queen (1947), 3 C.R. 475, [1947] S.C.R. 462, 89 C.C.C. 209 .... 170, 171
Taylor v. United States (1955), 222 F. 2d 398 (D.C. Cir.) 35
Tendrup v. State (1927), 193 Wis. 482 198
Thomas v. The Queen, [1972] N.Z.L.R. 34 192
Thomas v. Sawkins, [1935] 2 K.B. 249 9
Thompson v. The King, [1918] A.C. 221 195
Thornton v. Corcoran (1969), 407 F. 2d 695 (D.C. Cir.) 41
Toohey v. Metropolitan Police Comm'rs, [1965] 1 All E.R. 506 (H.L.) 191, 194
Travers v. United States (1895), 6 App. D.C. 450 146
Trenholm, Re, [1939] O.W.N. 224, [1939] 3 D.L.R. 627, 72 C.C.C. 71; affd by C.A.
    unreported; revd *sub nom.* Trenholm v. A.-G. Ont., [1940] S.C.R. 301, [1940] 1 D.L.R.
    497, 73 C.C.C. 129 126
Trepanier, Re (1885), 12 S.C.R. 111 .... 124, 314
Trial of Elizabeth, Duchess of Kingston (1776), 20 Howell's State Tr. 573 32

United States v. Albright (1968), 388 F. 2d 719 (4th Cir.) 41
United States v. Baird (1959), 414 F. 2d 700 (2nd Cir.) 40, 41
United States v. Bennett (1970), 460 F. 2d 822 (D.C. Cir.) 49
United States v. Bohle (1971), 445 F. 2d 54 (7th Cir.) 41
United States v. Brawner (1972), 471 F. 2d 969 (D.C. Cir.) 146, 147, 187, 188
United States v. Currens (1961), 290 F. 2d 751 (3rd Cir.) 145, 146, 148, 149
United States v. Malcolm (1973), 475 F. 2d 420 (9th Cir.) 41
United States v. Weiser (1969), F. 2d 932 (2nd Cir.) 40

Vaillancourt v. The Queen (No. 2) (1975), 31 C.R.N.S. 81, 21 C.C.C. (2d) 65, 54 D.L.R.
    (3d) 512 (S.C.C.); affg 31 C.R.N.S. 81 at p. 82, 16 C.C.C. (2d) 137 (Ont. C.A.) ... 36, 44

Walker v. The King, [1939] S.C.R. 214, 71 C.C.C. 305, [1939] 2 D.L.R. 353 ...... 37, 309
Warner v. The State (1948), 297 N.Y. 395 10
Watmore v. Jenkins, [1962] 2 All E.R. 868 .... 84, 101
Watson v. State (1915), 133 Ten. 198 198
Watts v. Indiana (1949), 338 U.S. 40 42
Westcott et al. and Corp. of the County of Peterborough, Re (1873), 33 U.C.Q.B. 280 315
Wheeler v. Le Marchant (1881), 17 L.R. Ch. D. 675 32
Whitree v. State (1968), 290 N.Y.S. 2d 486 (Ct. Cl.) 299, 305, 306
Wilband v. The Queen, [1967] S.C.R. 14, 2 C.R.N.S. 29, 60 W.W.R. 292, [1967] 2 C.C.C.
    6 .... 37, 39, 202, 230, 279, 280, 283

William v. Field (1969), 416 F. 2d 483 (9th Cir.) 312
Wilson v. Buttery, [1926] S.A.S.R. 150 113
Wilson v. Lehman (1964), 379 S.W. 2d 478 .... 305, 306
Wilson v. United States (1968), 391 F. 2d 460 (D.C. Cir.) 67
Winn v. State (1939), 136 Tex. Crim. 513 198
Winters v. Miller (1969), 306 F. Supp. 1158 (E.D.N.Y.) 317
Wise v. Dunning, [1902] 1 K.B. 167 9
Woods v. Brumlop (1962), 71 N.M. 221 308
Woolmington v. D.P.P., [1935] A.C. 462 (H.L.) 74, 75, 112, 169, 170
Wright v. The Queen *See* R. v. Wright
Wyatt v. Aderholt (1974), 503 F. 2d 1305 321
Wyatt v. Stickney (1971), 325 F. Supp. 781 (M.D. Ala.) 296, 303
Wyatt v. Stickney (No. 2) (1971), 334 F. Supp. 1341 (M.D. Ala.) 303
Wyatt v. Stickey (1972), 344 F. Supp. 373 300

Younts v. St. Francis Hospital and School of Nursing Inc. (1970), 205 Kan. 292 304

Zoldoske v. State (1892), 82 Wis. 580 198

Introduction

The relationship of mental abnormality to crime has long been a favourite topic of discussion amongst lawyers, judges, psychiatrists and members of the general public. Traditionally, the involvement of psychiatry in the criminal law has centred on the problem of separating those accused who are mentally blameworthy from those who are not. With the so-called "psychiatrization" of contemporary criminal law, however, psychiatry has succeeded in extending its influence into virtually every phase of the trial process. Experts in the field may now be called upon to assist in the determination of such issues as fitness to stand trial, credibility of witnesses, competence to give testimony, insanity, automatism, drunkenness, provocation, dangerousness, curability, deterability, and more. As to the value of the opinions offered and of the contribution which psychiatry has to make, there has been rather widespread disagreement. Though the profession's growth and advance have assuaged much of the scepticism which it encountered in its early days, there are still those who subscribe to the view that psychiatry has no place in the legal process. Sociologist Michael Hakeem has written:

> ". . . psychiatrists have not attained the level of competence and scientific reliability and validity necessary to make their testimony eligible for serious consideration by the courts. Neither should it be looked upon as an objective and sound basis for coercive decisions, judicial or correctional. The courts should not allow psychiatric testimony to be heard, irrespective of whether the psychiatrists are partisan or court-appointed, attached to a court clinic or to a hospital . . . . It is astounding that judges and correctional officials continue to view psychiatrists as experts on human behaviour when there is considerable experimental and other research which shows laymen to be superior to psychiatrists and associated personnel in the judgment of people's motives, emotions, abilities, personality traits, and action tendencies."[1]

---

[1] Hakeem, "A Critique of the Psychiatric Approach to Crime and Correction" (1958), 23 Law and Contemporary Problems 650 at pp. 681-2.

1

The fact remains that psychiatrists have become key participants in the trial of mentally disordered defendants. Their services are sought by defence counsel, by counsel for the prosecution, and by the courts themselves. Unfortunately, however, the use of psychiatric expertise involves some rather complex legal problems. Owing to the adversarial role in which forensic psychiatrists have been cast, a defendant's mental abnormality may either assist in his defence or place him at a distinct disadvantage. Besides mitigating responsibility or punishment, an accused's mental disorder may result in either a partial deprivation of those rights and privileges which mentally sound defendants are accorded, or a more severe form of punishment than would normally be imposed.

This book will concern itself with several problems and procedures peculiar to the trial of mentally disordered defendants in Canada. The first part will deal with pre-trial diversion, fitness to stand trial, and some evidentiary difficulties arising out of pre-trial psychiatric examination. Owing to the present procedure regarding fitness to stand trial and to the practice of pre-trial diversion, the disordered defendant stands a good chance of being incarcerated for long periods of time without having been convicted of any offence. With characteristic cynicism, Thomas Szasz has partially accounted for the law's affinity for psychiatry in these rather disrespectful terms:

"For the prosecution, establishing the defendant's insanity, instead of his guilt, may become an easy method of securing 'conviction' and 'imprisonment'. The defendant will be incarcerated in a psychiatric institution for an indefinite period. This is a sentence at least as severe and probably more so than would result from conviction and sentencing to a penitentiary. To the judge, too, establishing the defendant's incapacity to stand trial may be tempting. It will save him the effort of conducting a trial that might be filled with distressing emotional and moral problems. If the defendant can be shown to be crazy, both he and the jury will be spared a taxing experience." [2]

Even if allowed to assert his mental abnormality as a defence at trial, the accused's chances of success may be seriously impaired by the current law surrounding the use of information obtained through psychiatric examination. Should communications which pass between an accused and the psychiatrist who examines him be privileged? Should they be subject to a "privilege against self-incrimination" or to the voluntariness rule regarding confessions?

The second part of the book focuses on what may loosely be called the "psychiatric defences". This section will involve a detailed discussion of the various ways in which mental disorder or abnormality may be asserted at trial to negative or reduce criminal responsibility. Included are such defences as automatism, insanity, intoxication, lack of *mens rea* produced by mental disorder, provocation, and infanticide. Also in this section is a chapter dealing with the use of psychiatric evidence at trial.

[2] Szasz, *Law, Liberty and Psychiatry* (New York, Collier, 1963) at p. 161.

The third part of the book focuses upon the ultimate consequences which may flow from a determination that the accused is mentally abnormal. Once a defendant has been labelled "insane", "mentally ill" or simply "dangerous", then what? Of what legal and practical effect are such classifications? Specifically, the discussion will deal with the issues of sentencing, treatment and release of disordered offenders. Historically, the chief function of psychiatry has been that of classifying and isolating mentally abnormal individuals. The "alienist" of the nineteenth century was more an agent of social control than a healer.[3] To what extent has this situation changed in modern times? It is submitted that so far as the specialty of forensic psychiatry is concerned, the answer is: very little. Although law and criminology tend to speak increasingly of such things as "rehabilitation" and "correction", there is little evidence of these concepts being effectively applied to the case of mentally disturbed offenders. Once identified as such, the disordered accused may well be dealt with in a different manner from other offenders, although the likelihood of his being rehabilitated by psychiatry is small indeed.

The major piece of legislation which is discussed in this book is, of course, the Criminal Code.[4] In many instances, however, reference is made to various provisions in provincial mental health statutes which are germane to the thesis. While it would be impractical to embark upon a detailed analysis of each provincial statute which may affect the mentally disordered defendant, Ontario's Mental Health Act[5] has occasionally been singled out for close examination.

---

[3] Halleck, *Psychiatry and the Dilemmas of Crime: A Study of Causes, Punishment and Treatment* (Berkeley, University of California Press, 1971) at p. 205. See also Freedman, "Forensic Psychiatry", in Freedman and Kaplan eds., *Comprehensive Textbook of Psychiatry* (Baltimore, Williams and Wilkins Co., 1967) at p. 1588: "Both psychiatry and law are concerned with the social deviant, the person who has violated the 'rules' of society and whose behaviour represents a problem, not only because his deviance diminishes his ability to function effectively, but because it affects the functioning of the community adversely."

[4] R.S.C. 1970, c. C-34, as amended.

[5] R.S.O. 1970, c. 269.

Part I

The Pre-Trial Stage

Chapter 1

Pre-Trial Diversion Of The Mentally Disordered

"The mental problems of most people begin before they come into contact with the criminal process; they bring their mental disorder with them. It is important therefore, that the mentally disordered be identified as early as possible in the process to assure that they will be treated in legally and medically appropriate ways. One way of dealing with the mentally disordered before trial is to divert them from the criminal law altogether."[1]

I. Introduction

In the United States, it has been estimated that less than 10 per cent of all persons charged with criminal offences ever undergo a full-scale trial.[2] This statistic has led at least one commentator to conclude that: "The pre-trial stage is far more important than the trial stage in the administration of criminal justice."[3] Although the same may be true in Canada, it is surprising how little attention has focused upon such pre-trial procedures as plea bargaining and the phenomenon which has come to be known as "diversion". Avoidance of the criminal process, especially where disordered persons are concerned, may involve legal and ethical consequences of no small significance.

Diversion in the context of mentally disordered persons usually refers to the invocation of civil commitment proceedings in preference to criminal trial. Although the underlying philosophy is seldom expressly articulated, it would seem that the choice of one process over the other results

---

[1] Law Reform Commission of Canada, *Report: The Criminal Process and Mental Disorder (Working Paper 14)* (Ottawa, Information Canada, 1975) at p. 23.
[2] Slovenko, "The Psychiatric Patient, Liberty and The Law" (1964-65), 13 U. Kansas L. Rev. 59 at p. 69, footnote 39.
[3] *Ibid.*

from a subjective assessment as to which is more "appropriate" in the circumstances;[4] it is not necessarily premised upon any consideration of an individual's fitness to stand trial in the strictly legal sense. As one psychiatrist has put it:

> "There are many offenders, who are legally fit to stand trial and who are legally sane under Section 16, who are considered by our society more in need of treatment than of punishment. These include the sexual offender, many arsonists and the psychopathic personality. Should they be treated within the prison system or should they be a responsibility of the Department of Health? At present, many such offenders are considered, quite properly, certifiable as mentally ill and sent to Oak Ridge for incarceration and treatment rather than sent to court, although they are technically fit to stand trial."[5]

As the wording here perhaps demonstrates, the disordered accused may not always benefit from the presumption of innocence. Inasmuch as his guilt may be taken for granted, the decision to divert is essentially both adjudicative and dispositional in nature. Removal from the criminal process is seen as a means of sparing him from the full force of that "very blunt and powerful instrument called criminal law,"[6] while at the same time imposing what amounts to a type of therapeutic sentence designed to cure the "offender" of his presumed tendency toward misbehaviour.

Unlike the criminal process, the diversionary process is not necessarily presided over by a judge. Consistent with the comparatively high attrition rate amongst the mentally disordered,[7] a great many potential defendants will have been channelled out of the system long in advance of the trial stage. In fact, it is only when the police, the prosecutor and perhaps certain provincial officials have failed to exercise their diversionary discretion that the decision will rest with the judge. Even then, as will be seen, the ultimate authority to divert (*i.e.*, to commit civilly) remains in the hands of the examining psychiatrist, who must screen and make the final judgment on those candidates presented to him.

This chapter will deal with the various methods by which mentally disordered persons may be channelled away from the criminal justice system and into the waiting arms of institutional psychiatrists. In par-

---

[4] See Brakel and South, "Diversion from the Criminal Process in the Rural Community" (1968-69), 7 Am. Crim. L.Q. 122 at p. 124 where it is noted: "[Diversionary] practices, widespread already in many urban areas, are largely a response to the 'inappropriate' characterization as 'criminal' of behaviour that is perhaps 'sick', perhaps 'deviant', perhaps offensive or a nuisance, perhaps contrary to prevalent social morality . . . . Diversion thus is an elastic term. Prosecution of 'full criminal disposition' is thought to be 'inappropriate' for some citizens who are then 'diverted' from the criminal process to the presumably more hospitable climes of the mental hospitals . . .".

[5] Boyd, "Our Jails and the Psychiatric Examination and Treatment of the Disturbed Offender" (1964), 6 Can. J. Crim. and Corr. 477 at pp. 478-9.

[6] *Working Paper 14*, at p. 23.

[7] With characteristic cynicism, Thomas Szasz has explained this fact by comparing the criminal trial process to a type of morality play; because the mentally disordered make poor actors, they are seldom cast in the role of defendant. See Szasz, *Psychiatric Justice* (New York, Collier, 1965) at p. 25.

ticular, it will examine the various provisions contained in Canada's Criminal Code and provincial mental health legislation which allow for a circumvention of the trial process and the possibility of civil commitment. Rather than attempt a detailed examination of the procedure within each province, the discussion will focus on pre-trial diversion as it is practiced in Ontario. Besides canvassing the relevant statutory provisions and explaining their operation it will in addition touch upon the various ethical and philosophical issues which their use involves. Finally, in light of the serious consequences which diversion may produce, suggestions will be made for safeguarding more adequately the liberty of mentally ill defendants. As will be seen, the law leaves something to be desired in this regard.

II. Police Screening

"When people feel threatened or annoyed by the bizarre or irrational conduct of another, they usually call the police. So the mentally ill's first official contact with the criminal process is often in the person of a police officer. The traditional police response, where the evidence is sufficient, is to dispose of the incident through charging. This should not always be the case; in appropriate circumstances the police should divert the mentally ill away from the criminal process."[8]

When a peace officer chooses to divert someone whom he feels to be mentally ill away from the trial process, he may do one of two things: (a) he may simply ignore the offending behaviour and exercise his discretion not to charge the individual;[9] or (b) he may exercise the authority conferred on him both by common law and by provincial mental health statutes for dealing with such persons. This latter authority is derived principally from two sources. First, there is the general constabulary duty to prevent the commission of crimes,[10] protect life and property,[11] and otherwise preserve the Queen's peace.[12] In Ontario, these common law functions have been set out in s-s. 46(1) of the Police Act.[13] Secondly, there is the more specific power (exercisable by anyone) which existed at common law to detain the dangerously mentally ill.[14] In *Warner v. The*

---

[8] *Working Paper 14* at p. 24. See also *Mental Illness and Law Enforcement*, Burger ed. (St. Louis, Law Enforcement Study Centre, Washington University, 1970).

[9] Goldstein, *The Insanity Defense* (New Haven, Yale University Press, 1967) at p. 173 has noted: "Statutes in a great many states require the police to prosecute *all* crimes coming to their notice. But nowhere are such statutes taken seriously. The police are regarded in such states, and elsewhere, as having a broad discretion to arrest or not."

[10] Halsbury, *Laws of England*, 3rd ed., Vol. 30, p. 129.

[11] *Haynes v. Harwood*, [1935] 1 K.B. 146.

[12] *Glasbrook Brothers Ltd. v. Glamorgan County Council*, [1925] A.C. 270 (H.L.); *Duncan v. Jones*, [1936] 1 K.B. 218; *Beatty v. Gillbanks* (1882), 9 Q.B.D. 308; *Wise v. Dunning*, [1902] 1 K.B. 167; *Thomas v. Sawkins*, [1935] 2 K.B. 249.

[13] R.S.O. 1970, c. 351.

[14] See Blackstone, *Commentaries on the Laws of England*, Book IV, 1st ed. (Oxford, Clarendon Press, 1769) at p. 25; Fox and Erickson, *Apparently Suffering from Mental Disor-*

State,[15] a leading American authority, the New York Court of Appeals explained and clarified this power as follows:

> "The common law recognized the power to restrain, summarily and without court process, an insane person who was dangerous at the moment. The power was to be exercised, however, only when 'necessary to prevent the party from doing some immediate injury to himself or to others' and 'only when the urgency of the case demands immediate intervention.' On the other hand, insane persons who were not dangerous were 'not liable to be thus arrested and restrained.' And upon one who did the restraining rested the burden of showing, in order to justify it, the urgency and necessity for the immediate restraint."

Today in Canada this latter power is embodied in provincial police and mental health statutes. Clause 46(1)(c) of Ontario's Police Act [16] states:

> "46 (1) It is the duty of the members of the Ontario Provincial Police Force. . .
>
> . . .
>
> (c) to perform all duties that may be lawfully performed by constables in relation to the escort and conveyance of convicts and other prisoners and mentally incompetent persons to and from any courts, places of punishment or confinement, hospitals or other places ..."

Section 10 of Ontario's Mental Health Act [17] provides:

> "10. Where a constable or other peace officer observes a person,
> (a) apparently suffering from mental disorder; and
> (b) acting in a manner that in a normal person would be disorderly,
> the officer may, if he is satisfied that,
> (c) the person should be examined in the interests of his own safety or the safety of others; and
> (d) the circumstances are such that to proceed under section 9[18] would be dangerous,

---

der: An Examination of the Exercise of Police Power under s. 10 of the Mental Health Act of Ontario (Toronto Centre of Criminology, University of Toronto, 1972) at p. 3; and Matthews, *Mental Disability and the Criminal Law* (Chicago, American Bar Foundation, 1970) at pp. 171-2.

[15] (1948), 297 N.Y. 395, *per* Fuld J. at p. 401.

[16] R.S.O. 1970, c. 351.

[17] R.S.O. 1970, c. 269.

[18] With only slight variation, the mental health legislation of every province in Canada authorizes a second method of apprehending and detaining mentally "ill", "disordered" or "defective" persons: procedure by warrant. Once again, Ontario's provision may be referred to as typical. Section 9 of the province's Mental Health Act reads as follows:
> "9(1) Where information upon oath is brought before a justice of the peace that a person, within the limits of his jurisdiction,
> (a) is believed to be suffering from mental disorder; and

take the person to an appropriate place where he may be detained for medical examination."

Section 11 of the Act defines the time and place of examination and detention in these terms:

"11. An examination referred to in section 9 or 10 should be conducted forthwith and, wherever practicable, the place of examination shall be a psychiatric or other health facility."

When it is not "practicable" to take the individual to a mental hospital, the police may simply escort him to the psychiatric unit of the local jail. The Mental Health Act prefers, however, that the individual be taken to a "psychiatric facility" which is defined by cl. 1(k) as follows:

"1. In this Act,

. . .

(k) 'psychiatric facility' means a facility for the observation, care and treatment of persons suffering from mental disorder, and designated as such by the regulations".

Those hospitals which have been designated as psychiatric facilities in Ontario are set out in s. 1 of Regulation 576.[19] Although the length of time for which any diverted individual may be detained in a psychiatric facility is not specified in s. 10, he clearly runs the risk of being civilly committed for an indefinite period.[20]

(b) should be examined in the interest of his own safety or the safety of others, the justice may, if he is satisfied that,
    (c) such examination is necessary; and
    (d) such examination can be arranged in no other way,
issue his order for examination in the prescribed form.
"(2) In every order under this section it shall be stated and shown clearly that the justice issuing the order made due inquiry into all of the facts necessary for him to form a satisfactory opinion.
"(3) An order under this section may be directed to all or any constables or other peace officers of the locality within which the justice has jurisdiction and shall name or otherwise describe the person with respect to whom the order has been made.
"(4) An order under this section shall direct, and is sufficient authority for, any constable or other peace officer to whom it is addressed to take the person named or described therein to an appropriate place where he may be detained for medical examination."
[19] R.R.O. 1970, as amended.
[20] According to s. 8 of Ontario's Mental Health Act:
"8(1) Any person who,
    (a) suffers from mental disorder of a nature or degree so as to require hospitalization in the interest of his own safety or the safety of others; and
    (b) is not suitable for admission as an informal patient,
may be admitted as an involuntary patient to a psychiatric facility upon application therefor in the prescribed form signed by a physician.
"(2) It shall be stated and shown clearly that the physician signing the application personally examined the person who is the subject of the application and made due inquiry into all of the facts necessary for him to form a satisfactory opinion.
"(3) The physician signing the application shall also in the application state the

Besides Ontario, there are six other provinces whose mental health legislation allows police to apprehend mentally disordered persons without a warrant.[21] While the mental health statutes in some provinces require the prior issuance of a warrant, Fox and Erickson have astutely pointed out that lack of official countenance by no means precludes police from exercising their common law authority to apprehend informally.[22]

The philosophy which underlies police diversion is one which should be seriously questioned where mentally abnormal persons are concerned. One criminologist has rationalized the procedure in these terms: "By implication the police officer observes behaviour amounting to disorderly conduct but decides the person is not guilty by reason of insan-

---

facts upon which he has formed his opinion of the mental disorder, distinguishing the facts observed by him from the facts communicated to him by others, and shall note the date upon which the examination was made.

"(4) Every such application shall be completed no later than seven days after the examination referred to therein, and no person shall be admitted to a psychiatric facility upon an application except within fourteen days of the date on which the application was completed.

"(5) Such an application is sufficient authority,

(a) to any person to convey the person who is the subject of the application to a psychiatric facility; and

(b) to the authorities thereof to admit and detain him therein for a period of not more than one month."

Under s. 13, the period of detention for involuntary patients may be renewed periodically *ad infinitum*:

"13(1) The period of detention of an involuntary patient may be extended upon the completion of a certificate of renewal in the prescribed form by the attending physician after personal examination.

"(2) The attending physician shall not complete a certificate of renewal unless the patient,

(a) suffers from mental disorder of a nature or degree so as to require further hospitalization in the interest of his own safety or the safety of others; and

(b) is not suitable to be continued as an informal patient.

"(3) A certificate of renewal is authority to detain the patient as follows:

1. First certificate — not more than two additional months.
2. Second certificate — not more than three additional months.
3. Third certificate — not more than six additional months.
4. Fourth certificate — not more than twelve additional months.
5. Each subsequent certificate — not more than twelve additional months.

"(4) An involuntary patient whose authorized period of detention has expired shall be deemed to be an informal patient.

"(5) An involuntary patient whose authorized period of detention has not expired may be continued as an informal patient upon completion of the prescribed form by the attending physician."

[21] British Columbia: Mental Health Act, 1964 (B.C.), c. 29, s. 27 as am. by 1968, c. 27, s. 10; 1970, c. 24, s.1; 1973, c. 84, s. 12; Alberta: Mental Health Act, 1972 (Alta.), c. 118, s. 34; Saskatchewan: Mental Health Act, R.S.S. 1965, c. 345, s. 20; Newfoundland: Health and Public Welfare Act, R.S.N. 1970, c. 151, s. 108; New Brunswick: Mental Health Act, R.S.N.B. 1973, c. M-10, s.10; Prince Edward Island: Mental Health Act, R.S.P.E.I. 1974, c. M-9, s. 12.

[22] Fox and Erickson, *op. cit.* footnote 14, at p. 5. See also Matthews, *op. cit.* footnote 14 at p. 172 where the author, citing *Orvis v. Brickman* (1952), 196 F. 2d 762 (D.C.Cir.), states that "even where a statute authorizes emergency detention, there is authority for the proposition that the common law power of emergency detention survives; in some jurisdictions it may be broader than the statutory power."

ity and then takes him to the hospital."[23] Unfortunately, this justification is premised upon three rather weak assumptions. First, it is
assumed that the individual's behaviour is *prima facie* criminal. Fox and
Erickson have pointed out, however, that there exists "no authority
indicating the 'disorderly' conduct which must be observed ... under s.10
need be narrowly limited to conduct of a type which would constitute an
offence . . .".[24] Secondly, it is assumed that the individual, if charged,
would raise the defence of insanity at trial. This possibility, it is submitted, is rather unlikely; the cumbersome defence of insanity is generally
reserved for crimes of a more serious nature. Thirdly, it is assumed that
the individual, were he to raise insanity, would in fact be successful with
that defence. This proposition, once again, is by no means self-evident.
Apart from the fact that statistically the defence of insanity stands little
chance of succeeding, one must consider that the concept of mental disorder under s. 10 of the Mental Health Act is considerably looser than
that of insanity under s. 16 of the Criminal Code.

The use of "disorderly conduct" as a justification for police apprehension of the mentally abnormal seems to be an extension of the former
practice of arresting and detaining such persons on the slim pretext of
vagrancy. This practice was one both rooted in tradition and judicially
accepted. In his *Commentaries on the Laws of England*, Blackstone
wrote:

"It was the doctrine of our ancient law, that persons deprived of
their reason might be confined till they recovered their senses, without waiting for the forms of a commission or other special authority
from the Crown: and now, by the vagrant acts, a method is chalked
out for imprisoning, chaining and sending them to their proper
homes."[25]

The rationale given for this procedure were twofold. First, "in the case of
absolute madmen, as they are not answerable for their actions, they
should not be permitted the liberty of acting ...".[26] Unfortunately, this
reasoning holds water only if criminal insanity is the criterion for detention. However, nowhere in Canada must an individual be judged criminally insane in order to be committed by civil process. Blackstone's
second justification was apparently that of dangerousness. Mentally disordered persons, in his words, "ought not to be suffered to go loose, to
the terror of the King's subjects."[27] With respect, this is the sounder of
the two reasons put forward. Nor is it surprising that the criterion of
dangerousness is currently embodied in cls. 10(c) and (d) of Ontario's
Mental Health Act. The problem which remains, however, is one of defi-

---

[23] Matthews, "Observations on Police Policy and Procedures for Emergency Detention of
the Mentally Ill" (1970), 61 J. Crim. Law, Crimin. and Police Sci. 283 at p. 286.
[24] *Supra,* footnote 14, at p. 11. As the authors have noted (at p. 10), disorderly conduct, in
order to constitute an offence, must fall within types of behaviour described in ss. 169-
175 of the Criminal Code.
[25] *Supra,* footnote 14, at p. 25.
[26] *Ibid.*
[27] *Ibid.*

nition. What is dangerousness? Blackstone seems to have believed that all disordered people were dangerous because they terrified the King's subjects. Although the Mental Health Act defines the concept in terms of the individual's own safety and the safety of others, it contains what must be regarded as the same fundamental error. By relying on the policeman's purely subjective assessment, it fails to draw any distinction between perceived danger and actual danger. In order to apprehend a disordered and disorderly individual, the police officer need only be "satisfied" in his own mind that such person is dangerous. In 1968 the McRuer Civil Rights Commission[28] criticized this use of subjective standards as failing to sufficiently safeguard individual rights. Noting that the subjective approach conferred on police officers a much wider power than the usual power of arrest, the Commission recommended the adoption of more objective criteria. Exercise of police power under s. 10, it said, should be premised upon a *reasonable* belief that the conditions of cls. (c) and (d) have been satisfied.

But even if one assumes the implementation of objective standards with regard to the assessment of dangerousness, there remain several philosophical arguments against interfering with a citizen's liberty "in the interest of his own safety or the safety of others." The first is that put forward by John Stuart Mill, who maintained that "The only purpose for which power can be rightfully exercised over any member of a civilized community, against his will, is to prevent harm to others. His own good, either physical, or moral, is not sufficient warrant."[29] While acceptance of this view has never been unanimous, Szasz has pointed out that in most instances the principle is adhered to. "Some types of dangerous behaviour", he has noted, "are even rewarded. Race-car drivers, trapeze artists, and astronauts receive admiration and applause."[30] Why, then, are the mentally disordered restrained from behaving in a manner dangerous to themselves? Presumably it is because they are incapable of exercising a rational choice as to whether or not they should behave dangerously. The problem with this reasoning, however, is that it assumes that an unnecessary gamble with one's life can in some instances be the product of rational motivation. Do the goals of fame and fortune make risk-taking any more rational than that of escaping life's miseries? True, there may be other ways than suicide to alleviate unhappiness (such as psychotherapy). But then there are other ways to become rich and famous besides fighting Muhammad Ali. Why do we impose alternatives on the potential suicide but not on the professional daredevil?

Rather than restrict the right of all persons, mentally disordered or otherwise, to do with their lives as they wish, Szasz has argued for the repeal of all laws which effectively prohibit the mentally disordered from behaving in a manner dangerous to themselves. "In a free society" he has stated, "a person must have the right to kill or injure himself. I

---

[28] McRuer, *Royal Commission Inquiry into Civil Rights* (Report No. 1, Vol. 3) (Toronto, Queen's Printer, 1963) at p. 1233.
[29] Mill, *On Liberty* (Chicago, Henry Regnery, 1955) at p. 13.
[30] Szasz, *Law, Liberty and Psychiatry* (New York, Collier, 1963) at p. 46.

think Mill was right when he asserted that there is no moral justification for depriving a person of his liberty in order to treat him."[31] In saying this, however, Szasz seems to have distorted Mill's words somewhat. Mill, after all, did not say that no justification existed for depriving a person of his liberty. Rather, he expressly stated that the prevention of harm to others constituted sufficient justification. Szasz has apparently ignored the grievous emotional (and often financial) harm which suicides inflict upon their friends and families. Indeed, it was this harm to others — and not sheer "therapeutic paternalism"[32] — upon which the one-time illegality of suicide was originally founded.[33] Thus while Szasz has eloquently demonstrated the illogic of singling out the mentally disordered as unwilling beneficiaries of the *parens patriae* doctrine, he has failed to undermine the ethical basis for psychiatric intervention where the well-being of persons other than the suicide himself is indirectly threatened.

There is in fact a case to be made against s. 10 intervention even in cases where the safety of others is *directly* threatened. Such interference with individual liberty may be criticized on the simple ground that it derives from the preventive theory of criminal justice, as opposed to the more traditional reactive theory. Although police action under the Mental Health Act may be technically described as "civil" in nature, reliance on this fact would be taking the easy way out. In Kittrie's words: "To date, we have warded off the most searching . . . questions . . . by resorting to a semantic double-talk which differentiates between 'criminal' and 'non-criminal' proceedings and sanctions . . .". Such distinction, he has argued, is one which is "not carefully drawn, not easily defensible, and liable to accelerated legal attack in the future."[34] It may be argued with some force that s. 10 of the Mental Health Act in reality amounts to a statement of arrest procedure for persons "charged" with being mentally ill.[35]

A final and purely practical criticism which may be levelled against police apprehension of the mentally ill is that the police are inherently ill-suited for the task. As they themselves "disavow all competence in matters pertaining to psychopathology",[36] the risk of unnecessary apprehension would at first glance appear to be great. Moreover, it has been argued (usually by police officers) that the conveyance of mentally ill

---

[31] *Ibid.*, at p. 229.

[32] Szasz's term.

[33] In *Hales v. Petit* (1562), 1 Plowd. 260 at p. 261 Brown J. described suicide as "an offence against nature: because to destroy oneself is contrary to nature, and a thing most horrible. Also against God, because breach of the commandment; and against the king, in that thereby he has lost one of his mystical members." Similarly, Blackstone in his *Commentaries* (Book IV at p. 189) wrote: "The suicide is guilty of a double offence: one spiritual, in evading the prerogative of the Almighty, and rushing into his immediate presence uncalled for: the other temporal, against the king, who hath an interest in the preservation of all his subjects."

[34] Kittrie, *The Right to be Different* (Baltimore, Penguin, 1973) at p. 8.

[35] See Szasz, at p. 47.

[36] Bittner, "Police Discretion in Emergency Apprehension of Mentally Ill Persons", *The Making of a Mental Patient*, Price and Dennereds, eds (New York, Holt, Rinehart and Winston, 1973) 46 at pp. 48-9.

persons to psychiatric facilities is a cumbersome and time-consuming procedure "incompatible with the officially propounded conception of the policeman's principal vocation."[37] Paradoxically, though, it is precisely these arguments which speak loudest in favour of police involvement. While the creation of a special psychiatric emergency team has been frequently advocated as an alternative,[38] it is submitted that such a step could be disastrous from a civil libertarian point of view. For it is the policeman's very uncertainty in psychological matters and his distaste for the tedious procedure which the use of s. 10 involves that induce him to resort to emergency apprehension with caution and only in the most compelling circumstances — hopefully, only where an offence has been committed. One wonders whether a professional "goon squad" whose very livelihood depended upon the recruitment of mental patients would exercise the same restraint.

III. Prosecutorial Discretion

As a general rule, police officers seem quite reluctant to exercise their diversionary powers with respect to the mentally disordered.[39] Rather than route an individual toward civil commitment, they tend to lay charges — especially where offences of a more serious nature are concerned.[40] Once an information or complaint has been sworn before a justice of the peace and process issued, the discretion to divert a mentally disordered accused passes from the police to the prosecutor.[41]

Essentially, the alternatives to prosecution are twofold: (1) withdrawal of the charges on the condition that the accused seek psychiatric assistance;[42] and (2) withdrawal of the charges in exchange for the accused's voluntary civil commitment.[43] From the Crown's point of view, the decision to pursue these options may arise from considerations other than that of sheer benevolence. It may, for instance, be motivated by a desire to exercise control over the defendant in excess of that which would result from conviction. As Bittner has put it:

---

[37] *Ibid.*, at p. 51.

[38] See Fox and Erickson, *op. cit.* footnote 14, at p. 144.

[39] Bittner, at p. 48. No doubt, such reluctance is enhanced by the decision of the Supreme Court of Canada in *Beatty and Mackie v. Kozak* (1958), 120 C.C.C. 1, a case in which two policemen were successfully sued for false imprisonment. See Macdonald, "The Police and the Mentally Ill" (1958-9), Crim. L.Q. 400 at p. 400.

[40] Goldstein, *op. cit.* footnote 9, at p. 174.

[41] Grosman, in his book, *The Prosecutor: An Inquiry into the Exercise of Discretion* (Toronto, University of Toronto Press, 1969) at p. 20 has pointed out that technically "although empowered to initiate criminal proceedings by complaint or information, in practice the prosecutor rarely participates in the charging stage and does not assume responsibility for prosecution until after the charge has been laid."

[42] *Working Paper 14*, at p. 26.

[43] *Ibid.*

"In some cases, persons who appear to suffer from a psychological deficit would, if prosecuted successfully, receive a short sentence or probation. But if the deficit is interpreted as an omen of greater mischief, then prosecutors may wish to avert this by hospitalizing the person in a mental institution."[44]

Where the defendant is perceived as dangerously sick but the chances of obtaining a conviction are poor, the tactic of diversion may become especially attractive.[45]

In light of the serious consequences which a withdrawal of charges may entail for the accused and the possibility that the Crown may be bargaining from weakness, participation by defence counsel would seem essential to pre-trial negotiations of this sort. Unfortunately, however, it has been observed that despite the "right to retain and instruct counsel without delay" which the Bill of Rights[46] guarantees, many accused remain unrepresented at arraignment.[47] In practice, of course, the danger of non-representation may not be as great as it seems; prosecutors seldom have time to consider a case before the preliminary hearing or trial stage anyway.[48]

IV. Diversion By Provincial Authorities

Once an individual has been charged with a criminal offence and detained in prison, the prosecutor is not the only person with authority to remove him from the criminal process. By virtue of certain provisions contained in the mental health statutes of several provinces, the option of pre-trial diversion rests also in the hands of designated provincial officials. One such provision is s. 28 of British Columbia's Mental Health Act.[49] It states:

"28. The Lieutenant-Governor in Council, upon receiving two medical certificates completed in accordance with section 23 in respect of the mental condition of any person imprisoned or detained in any gaol or lock-up in the Province or in any child care resource

---

[44] Bittner, "The Concept of Mental Abnormality in the Administration of Justice Outside the Courtroom", in de Reuck and Porter, eds., *The Mentally Abnormal Offender* (London, Churchill, 1968) 201 at p. 207.

[45] *Ibid.*

[46] R.S.C. 1970, App. III, subpara. 2(c)(ii).

[47] Schlatter, "An Empirical Study of Pre-Trial Detention and Psychiatric Illness in the Montreal Area — Legal, Psychiatric and Administrative Aspects" (1969), 15 McGill L.J. 326 at p. 327.

[48] Grosman, at p. 20.

[49] 1964 (B.C.), c. 29, as amended by 1973 (2nd Sess.), c. 127, s. 17. See also the Mental Health Act of Saskatchewan R.S.S. 1965, c. 345, s-s. 16(1). For a case in which non-compliance with the strict provisions of the British Columbia statute resulted in the granting of an application for *habeas corpus*, see *R. v. Sayle*, [1974] 5 W.W.R. 766 (B.C.).

as defined in the *Protection of Children Act* established under any
Act of the Legislature, may order the removal of the person to a
Provincial mental health facility, whereupon

(a) the Warden or other person in charge of the gaol, lock-up,
or child care resource as defined in the *Protection of Children Act* shall, in accordance with the order, cause the person to be conveyed to the Provincial mental health facility
named in the order and send to the Superintendent of the
Provincial mental health facility an application for admission in the form prescribed by the Lieutenant-Governor in
Council by regulation, together with copies of the medical
certificates; and

(b) the person shall be detained in that Provincial mental
health facility or in such other Provincial mental health facility as the Lieutenant-Governor in Council may from
time to time order until his complete or partial recovery or
until other circumstances justifying his discharge from the
Provincial mental health facility are certified to the satisfaction of the Lieutenant-Governor in Council, who may
then order him back to imprisonment or detention if then
liable thereto or otherwise to be discharged."[50]

---

[50] In a like fashion, s. 24 of Quebec's Mental Patients Institutions Act, R.S.Q. 1964, c. 166
conferred a similar power upon the Minister of Health of that province. The section provided:

"24. When the sheriff of a district has reason to believe that a person detained in a
gaol or other place of correction is suffering from mental illness, he shall have him
examined by the superintendent of a hospital or by another physician designated by
the Minister of Health; if the examination establishes that the prisoner is mentally
deranged, the examining physician shall forward forthwith a report to that effect to
the Minister of Health.

"The latter shall then issue an order for the conveyance of the prisoner to a hospital and such order shall justify the superintendent in keeping the patient there for
close treatment; but the latter cannot be admitted to any home contemplated in section 28."

Section 25 of that Act further provides:

"25. When a patient from a gaol or other place of correction is cured or when his
health is so improved that he may be returned, the superintendent shall so notify the
Minister of Health and the latter shall issue an order to that effect."

The Mental Patients Institutions Act was replaced by the Mental Patients Protection
Act, 1972 (Que.), c. 44. Although there is no anologous provision in the current statute, s.
64 provides, *inter alia*, that "Every person under close treatment in a hospital within the
meaning of the Mental Patients Institutions Act ... at the time of the coming into force
of this act shall remain under such treatment as if he had been admitted thereto under
this act."

V. Diversion By The Court

Assuming that the charges facing the accused have not been withdrawn and that provincial authorities have not diverted him, the ultimate discretion to divert then rests in the hands of the court. Although there exist no statutory provisions which openly empower a court to permanently remove disordered accused persons from the trial process, those provisions which allow a justice, court, judge or magistrate to remand for psychiatric examination may be used toward the same end. In Ontario, the combined effect of federal and provincial legislation (the Criminal Code and Mental Health Act respectively) is to provide a total of at least four[51] (possibly six)[52] such provisions. Of these, the first which should be examined is contained in s. 465 of the Code, which enumerates the powers of a justice conducting a preliminary inquiry. Subsection 465(1) reads:

"465(1) A justice acting under this Part may

. . .

(c) by order in writing,
(i) direct an accused to attend, at a place or before a person specified in the order and within a time specified therein, for observation, or
(ii) remand an accused to such custody as the justice directs for observation for a period not exceeding thirty days,

where, in his opinion, supported by the evidence, or where the prosecutor and the accused consent, by the report in writing, of at least one duly qualified medical practitioner, there is reason to believe that
(iii) the accused may be mentally ill, or
(iv) the balance of the mind of the accused may be disturbed, where the accused is a female person charged with an offence arising out of the death of her newly-born child ..."

Subsection (2) of s. 465 further provides:

"(2) Notwithstanding paragraph 1(c), a justice acting under this Part may remand an accused in accordance with that paragraph
(a) for a period not exceeding thirty days without having heard the evidence or considered the report of a duly qualified medical practitioner where compelling circumstances exist for so doing and where a medical practitioner is not

---

[51] Criminal Code, ss. 543(2) and (2.1), 544, 738(5) and (6); Ontario, Mental Health Act, s-s. 15(1).
[52] Subsections 14(1) and (3) of Ontario's Mental Health Act are perhaps not strictly remand provisions insofar as the word "remand" is not used.

readily available to examine the accused and give evidence
or submit a report; and

(b) for a period of more than thirty days but not exceeding
sixty days where he is satisfied that observation for such a
period is required in all the circumstances of the case and
his opinion is supported by the evidence or, where the
prosecutor and the accused consent, by the report in writing, of at least one duly qualified medical practitioner."

Although s-s. 465(1) does not spell it out, it is essential that the
accused be brought before the remanding justice before the provisions
contained therein may be resorted to. This fact was made clear by the
decision of the Quebec Court of King's Bench in *Re Sarault*.[53] In that
case a magistrate had remanded the accused for observation upon being
advised by the arresting police officers that he showed signs of insanity,
but without having had the accused brought before him. Discharging
the accused on a writ of *habeas corpus*, Hall J. remarked:

"I cannot think it possible that this procedure can validly take
place, out of the view and hearing of the accused person, as one can
easily imagine, if such a method were adopted, that a flagrant abuse
of personal liberty might be effected under the colour of legal
proceedings."[54]

Also not referred to in the remand provision itself, though worth keeping in mind, is the accused's right to cross-examine the medical witness.
As was decided in *Re Sommer*[55] a denial by the remanding justice of this
right runs "contrary to common law, to the provisions of s. [468(1)(a)] of
The Criminal Code, and to the tenets of natural justice"[56] and renders
the remand illegal. Presumably, this holds true whenever an accused is
remanded for observation under the Criminal Code, since the right to
cross-examine exists at all stages of the trial.[57]

The Code's other psychiatric remand provisions are virtually identical
to that in s. 465. They provide ample opportunity for diversion at any
stage of the trial process. Subsections 543(2) and (2.1) apply "at any
time before verdict or sentence" and are used primarily as a means for
gathering psychiatric information relevant to the issue of fitness to
stand trial.

Perhaps the most interesting remand provisions are those contained
in s. 544 and s-ss. 738(5) and (6). The former allows for the application of
s. 543's remand provision in circumstances "Where an accused who is
charged with an indictable offence is brought before a court, judge or

---

[53] (1905), 9 C.C.C. 448.
[54] *Ibid.*, at p. 449. This is not to say, however, that the accused must be brought before the
court for the purpose of extending the period of remand under para. 465(2)(b). See *R. v.
Bouchard* (1912), 20 C.C.C. 95 (Que. Ct. of Sessions of the Peace) which distinguished *Re
Sarault* on this ground.
[55] (1958), 27 C.R. 243 (Que.).
[56] *Ibid.*, at p. 247.
[57] See Criminal Code, s. 575, s-s. 610(2) and s. 737.

magistrate *to be discharged for want of prosecution* and the accused appears to be insane."[58] The latter permits a summary conviction court to remand for psychiatric observation "at any time before convicting a defendant or making an order against him *or dismissing the information*, as the case may be."[59] Clearly these provisions go a step beyond diversion; rather than spare an accused from the criminal law consequences of his actions, they may be used as a method of exposing him to civil consequences (*i.e.*, commitment) where no criminal liability has in fact been established.

Turning to the Mental Health Act, s-s. 15(1) should first be examined. It states:

> "15(1) Where a judge has reason to believe that a person in custody who appears before him charged with an offence suffers from mental disorder, the judge may, by order, remand that person for admission as a patient to a psychiatric facility for a period of not more than two months."

From the relatively recent decision of the Ontario High Court of Justice in *Ex parte Branco*[60] it might appear that the words "in custody" here are superfluous. In that case Addy J. held:

> "For the purposes of s-s.(1) of s. 15 of the *Mental Health Act, 1967*, when considering the jurisdiction of a Judge over any person in custody, an accused, who is before the Court presided over by that Judge for the purpose of his trial on a criminal charge, is within the custody of that Court and it is immaterial whether, immediately previous to his appearance before that Court, he had been free on bail or free on his own recognizance or held in actual custody ..."[61]

Note, however, that a court, in order to have custody of an accused appearing before it charged with an offence, must be the same court which is trying him on the indictment or information. Thus where counsel for the accused applied to have him remanded by a court different from the one which was trying his case it was held in *R. v. Deforge*[62] that the court lacked jurisdiction under the Mental Health Act. It may be wondered whether the Criminal Code could have been used in this case or whether the words "at any time before the verdict or sentence" in s-s. 543(2) imply that custody, in the sense that it is used in the Mental Health Act, is necessary here too.

Section 14 of the Mental Health Act contains no limitation whatsoever concerning custody. By far the broadest provision of its type, s-s. (1) reads:

---

[58] Emphasis added.
[59] Emphasis added.
[60] [1971] 3 O.R. 575.
[61] *Ibid.*, at p. 578.
[62] (1971), 5 C.C.C. (2d) 255 (Ont. Dist. Ct.).

"14(1) Where a judge has reason to believe that a person who appears before him charged with or convicted of an offence suffers from mental disorder, the judge may order the person to attend a psychiatric facility for examination."

Not only does this provision dispense with a limitation upon the length of time for which the accused may be detained, but it endows the court with a power not available through the use of other sections referred to. Rather than depend upon the examining physician to admit the accused as an involuntary patient under s-s. 8(1), the judge may himself compel the accused's submission to treatment. Subsections (2) and (3) of s. 14 state:

"(2) Where an examination is made under this section, the senior physician shall report in writing to the judge as to the mental condition of the person.
"(3) If the senior physician reports that the person examined needs treatment, the judge may order the person to attend a psychiatric facility for treatment."[63]

The legality of using provincial legislation as a method of diverting persons charged under the Criminal Code may be seriously questioned. The first issue which bears examination is whether or not someone charged with a Criminal Code offence may be remanded for examination under s-ss. 14(1) and 15(1) of the Mental Health Act. In considering this issue, the following provisions of the British North America Act, 1867[64] should be kept in mind:

"91. It shall be lawful for the Queen, by and with the Advice and Consent of the Senate and House of Commons, to make Laws for the Peace, Order and good Government of *Canada*, in relation to all Matters not coming within the Classes of Subjects by this Act assigned exclusively to the Legislatures of the Provinces; and for greater Certainty, but not so as to restrict the Generality of the foregoing Terms of this Section, it is hereby declared that (notwithstanding anything in this Act) the exclusive Legislative Authority of the Parliament of *Canada* extends to all Matters coming within the Classes of Subjects next hereinafter enumerated; that is to say, —
...
27. The Criminal Law, except the Constitution of Courts of Criminal Jurisdiction, but including the Procedure in Criminal Matters.
...
"92. In each Province the Legislature may exclusively make Laws

---

[63] The writer has been informed, from personal communication with forensic psychiatrists, that this subsection is in practice used as a method of compelling the accused to receive psychiatric treatment as an *out-patient*. There is nothing in this section which precludes certification, however.
[64] 1867 (U.K.), c. 3.

in relation to Matters coming within the Classes of Subjects next hereinafter enumerated; that is to say, —

> ...
>
> 7. The Establishment, Maintenance, and Management of Hospitals, Asylums, Charities, and Eleemosynary Institutions in and for the Province, other than Marine Hospitals
>
> ...
>
> 13. Property and Civil Rights in the Province."

Because the enactment of provisions which purport to govern criminal procedure would be clearly *ultra vires* the provincial legislatures, it may be argued that the word "offence" which appears in both s-ss. 14(1) and 15(1) pertains solely to offences under provincial statute. Unfortunately, the only direct authority on this point comes by way of *obiter* from the Ontario Court of Appeal decision in *Kennedy v. Tomlinson*.[65] In that case an accused who was remanded under an analogous section of the 1950 Ontario Mental Hospitals Act[66] (s. 35) brought an action against the magistrate for false imprisonment. Because the Court felt that various provisions in the Mental Hospitals Act and Public Authorities Protection Act[67] protected the magistrate from liability in any event, it was not necessary to decide the constitutionality of the section in question.[68] Nevertheless, Schroeder J.A. did express the opinion that because the provision referred to persons charged with "any offence", it was "not by its terms limited to offences against provincial enactments."[69]

If this reasoning holds true with regard to s-ss. 14(1) and 15(1) of the Mental Health Act, what is their constitutional position? Once again the only opinion on this question appears in the form of *obiter dicta*. In the case of *Ex parte Branco*,[70] Addy J. of the Ontario High Court of Justice had this to say:

> "A remand for mental examination of a person in custody pursuant to s. 15(1) is neither a criminal trial nor a criminal proceeding. It is, on the contrary, a procedure under a provincial statute, which the Legislature of Ontario has enacted under its property and civil rights jurisdiction pursuant to s. 92 of the *B.N.A. Act, 1867,* by which a criminal proceeding may be interrupted, if the Judge has reason to believe that the accused should be examined mentally. It is not a proceeding against an accused but, on the contrary, it is a proceeding conceived and enacted for the protection and benefit of the accused."[71]

---

[65] (1959), 126 C.C.C. 175 (Ont. C.A.).
[66] R.S.O. 1950, c. 229.
[67] R.S.O. 1950, c. 303.
[68] At p. 215 of the judgment, Schroeder J.A. expressly stated: "Clearly, therefore, the constitutional issue does not fall to be decided in this case, and we do not find it necessary to express nor do we express any opinion upon it."
[69] *Supra*, footnote 65 at p. 214.
[70] [1971] 3 O.R. 579.
[71] At p. 579. *Cf. Doyle v. The Queen* (1976), 35 C.R.N.S. 1 (S.C.C.) *per* Ritchie J. at p. 6 and the doctrine of paramountcy.

But while *Ex parte Branco* did involve the use of provincial remand provisions for an accused charged under the Code, Addy J.'s statement must once again be taken as *obiter*, since the court had not been called upon to decide the constitutional issue.

The next question which should be considered is whether or not a judge may use s-s. 14(3) of the Mental Health Act to order an accused charged under the Code to attend for treatment. If one accepts the *dicta* in *Green v. Livermore*,[72] the answer would seem to be "yes". In that case the constitutionality of s. 35 of the 1937 Mental Hospitals Act was disputed. The section, which is perhaps similar to both ss. 14 and 15, read in part:

> "35(1) Any person may be admitted to an institution upon the order of a judge or magistrate where such person has been apprehended either with or without warrant and charged with any offence..."

With regard to this procedure, Greene J. of the Ontario Supreme Court had this to say:

> "The action of the Magistrate in sending the plaintiff to the hospital does not arise from any crime of the plaintiff. It is a step in the control of persons who have always been dealt with by the Province in legislation of the nature of the *Mental Hospitals Act.*"[73]

But because that particular case involved the remand of an accused charged under provincial legislation (Ontario's Liquor Control Act[74]), this statement cannot be taken as decisive on the matter of *ultra vires*.[75]

In the famous (infamous?) case of *Fawcett v. A.-G. Ont.*[76] the Supreme Court of Canada stated unequivocally that s. 38 of the 1960 Mental Hospitals Act (which was virtually identical to s. 35 of the 1937 Act) was *intra vires* the Ontario Legislature. Although this ruling would appear to have settled the matter with regard to ss. 14 and 15 of the Mental Health Act as well, there is one problem. Because that case involved the admission and subsequent certification of a prisoner remanded for psychiatric observation under the provisions of the Criminal Code, the courts were only called upon to decide the constitutional status of those provisions under which the *hospital authorities* had acted. At best, therefore, the case decided that the provision of s. 38 requiring the hospital authorities to *admit* was *intra vires* the Ontario Legislature. Any suggestion that the section was also *intra vires* with respect to its regulation of judicial remand procedure was *obiter*.

One question which the *Fawcett* case does seem to have settled per-

---

[72] [1940] 4 D.L.R. 678 (Ont.).
[73] *Ibid.*, at p. 681.
[74] R.S.O. 1937, c. 294, now R.S.O. 1970, c. 249, as amended.
[75] Poole, "Committing the Mentally Ill in Ontario" (1963-64), 6 Crim. L.Q. 92 at pp. 93-4.
[76] [1964] S.C.R. 625; affg 45 D.L.R. (2d) at p. 579 (Ont. C.A.); affg 40 D.L.R. (2d) 942 (H.C.).

tains to the effect of civil commitment upon the criminal process. Under Ontario's mental health legislation there is nothing inherently unlawful about a hospital's committing an accused person who has been remanded for observation. Provided that the court or Crown do not seek his return for trial[77] and, assuming that the statutory admission procedures have been complied with, such person may remain confined in hospital indefinitely.

VI. Conclusions

What social policies underlie the practice of pre-trial diversion? The most obvious rationale is the humanitarian one. By channelling a disordered accused away from the criminal justice system we spare him the stigma of criminalization. And as Professor Goldstein has suggested, "the increasing concern about 'labeling' a man as a criminal — with the attending stigma and the influence it may have on fixing him in that role — presses toward making the choice [to divert] as early as possible."[78] There are, however, several problems with this reasoning. To begin with there is Goldstein's own criticism:

> "It is not at all clear, however, that it is possible at so early a stage to make a sensible choice between a criminal process and a civil one. For one thing, the facts are not yet in and cannot possibly be. For another, the policeman is hardly cast ideally to make the decision on medical grounds, or moral grounds, or even on grounds of deterrence or retribution."[79]

Despite the policeman's subjective belief in an individual's guilt,[80] one must remember that conviction (and thus stigmatization) is by no means a certainty.

Another problem which the humanitarian argument does not take into consideration is the stigma which being labelled "mentally ill" itself imposes. Commitment as an involuntary patient under s-s. 8(1) of the Mental Health Act can in fact have grave social consequences of its own.

---

[77] Usually in such cases the charges are withdrawn. Where the charges are not withdrawn, it has been suggested in the case of *R. v. Sayle*, [1974] 5 W.W.R. 766 (B.C.), *per* Munroe J. in *obiter*, that the accused has a right to be returned to have his fitness to stand trial determined.

[78] *The Insanity Defense,* at pp. 173-4.

[79] *Ibid.,* at p. 174.

[80] As Grosman has pointed out in his book *The Prosecutor: An Enquiry into the Exercise of Discretion* (Toronto, University of Toronto Press, 1969) at p. 44: "The decision to arrest is, in most situations, made only when the police officer has decided that the accused is guilty of the offence for which he is being arrested . . . . If he, as a professional law enforcement agent, had not believed the accused guilty he would not have arrested him." See also Boydell, "The Administration of Criminal Justice: Continuity Versus Conflict" (1974), 16 Can. J. Crim. and Corr. 14 at p. 25.

Thomas Szasz has stated the mental patient's plight in these rather dramatic terms:

> "... once a person is cast into the role of mental patient, there is a permanent record of his deviance. Like the inquisitor, the psychiatrist can 'sentence' a person to mental illness, but cannot wipe out the stigma he himself has imposed. In psychiatry, moreover, there is no pope to grant absolute pardon from a publicly affirmed diagnosis of mental illness."[81]

The practical consequences of civil commitment may, from the patient's point of view, be far more severe than those which might have resulted from his subjection to the criminal process. Because diversion most commonly occurs in cases where the offence involved is relatively minor, a person directed to a psychiatric hospital may quite conceivably spend more time behind bars than he would have as a convicted offender. Moreover, it has been pointed out that an individual's very status as a mental patient paradoxically impedes his chances of release. As Professor Waddams has succinctly put it:

> "... an inmate applying to a review board is not in as good a position to argue his case as is a man at liberty. His access to legal and medical advice may be restricted, he has no automatic right to an inquiry by the review board unless he applies for it, indeed he has no absolute right to a hearing at all, and there is the danger of a presumption against one who is already hospitalized."[82]

Perhaps the best argument in favour of diversion is the economic one. As Grosman has noted, "the . . . avoidance of time, expense, and the uncertainty of trial are regarded by police, prosecutors, defence lawyers, and even judges as important factors in the efficient functioning of the criminal courts."[83] Our criminal justice system is simply not equipped with sufficient resources to prosecute all alleged infringements of the law. While another method of alleviating the courts' burden might be to reduce the volume of "victimless" crimes which the criminal law prohibits,[84] this would by no means constitute a complete solution. There are, after all, a great many problems which cannot merely be defined out of existence[85] yet, for which criminal prosecution serves no useful purpose.

But have economics taken precedence over individual liberty? In 1873

---

[81] Szasz, *The Manufacture of Madness* (New York, Dell, 1970) at pp. 55-6. See also pp. 207-37.

[82] Waddams, "Are the Mentally Ill Deprived of Rights?" (1972), 20 Chitty's L.J. 301 at p. 302.

[83] *Supra*, footnote 80, at p. 34.

[84] Fox and Erickson, *op. cit.* footnote 14, at p. 3. See also the Law Reform Commission of Canada, *Report: Diversion (Working Paper 7)* (Ottawa, Information Canada, 1975) at p. 1.

[85] The Law Reform Commission of Canada, *op.cit.* footnote 84 at p. 1 has commented that "Even when offences are eliminated, problematic behaviour often remains, has to be dealt with, and may lead to the use of other charges."

an American Supreme Court Justice proclaimed it to be "a rule as old as the law . . . that no one shall be personally bound until he has had his day in court. . .".[86] Today in Canada, however, the tactic of pre-trial diversion may be seen as a convenient method for depriving the mentally ill of their freedom without benefit of the traditional (but inexpedient) day in court. By removing a "mental case" from the criminal process, we simultaneously divest the object of our benevolence of those rights and safeguards which have been built into the criminal justice system. Specifically, we deny him the right to a fair hearing,[87] the right to make full answer and defence,[88] and the right to cross-examine witnesses.[89] While these rights are available to anyone standing trial in a Canadian criminal court, they remain entirely alien to the present process of civil commitment.

It is submitted that diversion of the mentally disordered is an option which must remain open to courts, prosecutors and law enforcement officers in appropriate circumstances. As the Law Reform Commission has recently put it, "some of the people who find their way into the criminal process shouldn't have been let in or shouldn't be required to go further."[90] But it is also submitted that our good intentions are not enough. "Hell", said Samuel Johnson, "is paved with good intentions."[91] Because, in our zeal to treat certain individuals (rather than prosecute them) we have tended to ignore the possibility of providing them with rights, perhaps we should now direct our efforts to the alleviation of this unfortunate side-effect. Kittrie has stated the challenge in these terms:

> ". . . if we are to preserve the opportunity for social experimentation in the crime and delinquency prevention area, we must seriously and expeditiously consider the question: What should the role and applicability of the traditional. . .guarantees, designed and developed in conjunction with criminal law, be in the 'civil' borderlands of criminal justice?"[92]

Although provincial civil commitment procedures have effectively escaped the purview of the Canadian Bill of Rights,[93] this constitutional fact cannot justify the laxity with which the liberty of mentally disordered persons has been safeguarded. As the President's Commission on Law Enforcement and Administration of Justice expressed it:

> "Alternative ways of disposing of criminal cases that involve close supervision or institutional commitment without conviction, call for protections from their abuse, protections that should be roughly comparable to those of the criminal law. Experience with civil pro-

---

[86] Field J. in *Galpin v. Page* (1873), 85 U.S. 350 at p. 368.
[87] Canadian Bill of Rights, R.S.C. 1970, App. III, para. 2(e).
[88] Criminal Code, s-ss. 577(3), 737(1).
[89] Criminal Code, para. 468(1)(a), s. 575, s-ss. 610(2), 737(2).
[90] *Working Paper 14*, at p. 23.
[91] Quoted by Szasz, *The Manufacture of Madness* (New York, Dell, 1970) at p. xviii.
[92] *Supra,* footnote 34, at p. 8.
[93] Subparagraph 2(c)(ii).

cedures for the commitment of the mentally ill, for so-called sexual psychopaths, and for similar groups demonstrates that there are dangers of such programs developing in ways potentially more oppressive than those foreclosed by the careful traditional protections of the criminal law."[94]

To avoid the development of oppressive practices with regard to pre-trial diversion, it is submitted that several key changes must be made in both the Ontario Mental Health Act and the Criminal Code. To begin with, the exercise of police powers under s. 10 of the Mental Health Act should be premised upon more objective criteria; the words "if he is satisfied" should be replaced by the words "if he has reasonable grounds to believe".[95] With regard to prosecutorial diversion, it is suggested that a form of "double jeopardy" should apply; because it would run contrary to public policy for a diverted individual to be tried upon his release from a psychiatric hospital, the withdrawal of charges in such circumstances ought to constitute a bar to further prosecution.[96] As far as the diversionary powers of certain provincial officials are concerned, it is submitted that these should be removed altogether. The broad and virtually unreviewable discretion conferred by provincial legislation is inconsistent with the proper administration of justice where unconvicted accused persons are concerned.

Except in emergency situations, the decision to commit civilly should be made by a tribunal required to hold a hearing for that purpose.[97] Any person facing loss of liberty for an indefinite period ought at least to be afforded those safeguards contained in Ontario's Statutory Powers Procedure Act, 1971.[98] Moreover, review of a patient's detention by way of hearing should be made mandatory. Subsection 29(1) of the Mental Health Act, which provides that the review board *may* hold a hearing, is insufficient. While there is authority for the proposition that the word "may" must be treated as imperative wherever the purposes of the provision in which it appears is the furtherance of justice or the enforcement of a legal right,[99] the word "may" in s-s. 27(1) is *prima facie* permissible[100] and should be replaced by the word "shall".

On the philosophical (as opposed to legislative) plain it is recommended that diversionary practices be tempered with an element of restraint. Because diversion may amount to a method of sentencing without trial, the instances where a short-circuiting of the criminal pro-

---

[94] President's Commission on Law Enforcement and Administration of Justice, *Report: The Challenge of Crime in a Free Society* (Washington, D.C., U.S. Gov't. Printing Office, 1967) at p. 134.
[95] McRuer Civil Rights Commission, Report No. 1, at p. 1233.
[96] *Working Paper 7*, at pp. 19-20.
[97] Waddams, *op. cit.* footnote 82, at p. 301.
[98] 1971 (Ont.), Vol 2, c. 47.
[99] See Crankshaw, *Criminal Code of Canada,* 6th ed. (1935) at p. 17; *Frensom v. New Westminster* (1879), 2 C.C.C. 52 (B.C.); *R. v. Barlow* (1693), 2 Salk 609, 91 E.R. 516; *Aitcheson v. Mann* (1882), 9 P.R. 473 (C.A.); *Julius v. Bishop of Oxford* (1880), 5 App. Cas. 214 (H.L.).
[100] Ontario Interpretation Act, R.S.O. 1970, c. 225, s. 30, cl. 16.

cess will serve the accused's best interests may be rare indeed. While no right to be tried exists in Canada, it has been suggested that "a system which presumes innocence requires that preconviction sanctions be kept at a minimum consistent with assuring an opportunity for the process to run its course."[101]

---

[101] Goldstein, "Police Discretion Not to Invoke the Criminal Process: Low-Visibility Decisions in the Administration of Justice" (1960), 69 Yale L.J. 543 at pp. 549-50.

Chapter 2

Problems Arising Out Of Pre-Trial Psychiatric Examination

I. The Question Of Psychiatrist-Accused Privilege

A. THE PROBLEM

Though perhaps a luxury at one time, the psychiatric expert has become a tactical (if not legal) necessity in many criminal cases. Where counsel wishes to raise his client's mental abnormality as a defence, his chances of success will be seriously impaired unless he can enlist the support of at least one or two psychiatrists. Indeed, referring to the defence of automatism raised in *Hill v. Baxter*,[1] Devlin J. (as he then was) remarked that he did not see how the layman could differentiate between real and feigned automatism without expert assistance. Similarly, in *People (A.-G.) v. Manning*[2] it was held that a trial judge was entitled to state in his charge to the jury that he had never seen a case where the defence of insanity was successfully established without expert evidence having been called.

This being the case, it is not surprising that lawyers who suspect mental disorder in their clients should have them psychiatrically examined at some point before their trial. In addition to assisting counsel in his determination of what defence he will put forward, the doctor's findings may well aid in pre-trial strategy and the process of plea-bargaining.

Because defence counsel is usually not an expert in such matters himself, it stands to reason that his suspicions concerning his client's state of mind may not always be borne out by the psychiatrist he has retained. Moreover, where several psychiatrists have been consulted, the possibility of disagreement becomes distinct. In such cases, it is only

---

[1] [1958] 1 All E.R. 193 at p. 197 (Q.B.D.).
[2] (1953), 89 I.L.T. 155.

natural for counsel to select as expert witnesses the doctors whose opinions are most favourable to the defence. If, for example, two out of three
examining psychiatrists feel that the accused was in a state of
"psychological blow" automatism[3] at the time of the alleged crime, yet
the third believes the accused merely to have been provoked, defence
counsel will obviously elect not to call the third psychiatrist as a witness
for the defence. Or should all three psychiatrists agree that the defendant was insane at the time of the offence, counsel may prefer not to call
any of them as witnesses if a less drastic defence presents itself.

Where does this leave the examining psychiatrist? Having been told
that his services as a witness will not be required by the defence, does he
become a free agent? Armed with the highly sensitive and potentially
damaging information which the accused has himself provided, may the
doctor testify to all he knows for the prosecution? This section deals
with the doctrine of testimonial privilege and its relevance to the above-
stated questions. Should communications between an accused and his
psychiatrist be subject to such privilege, the possibility of a defence-retained expert turning "double agent" would become remote.

B. THE PRESENT LAW

It has been amply demonstrated that the common law attaches no testimonial privilege either to the relationship between psychiatrist and
patient,[4] or to that between doctor and patient generally.[5] As a matter of
fact, the only relationship protected by professional privilege is that
which exists between a solicitor and his client.[6] While it is true that a
doctor's betrayal of professional confidences *outside* the courtroom may
be generally reprehensible and perhaps even actionable by civil suit,[7] the
law is settled that "to give that information in a court of justice, which
by the law of the land he is bound to do, will never be imputed to him as
any indiscretion whatever".[8]

Despite the technical absence of medical or psychiatric privilege, it
would appear from such cases as *Noor Mohamed v. The King*[9] and
Kuruma, Son of Kaniu v. The Queen[10] that the courts retain a discretion

---

[3] For cases involving this type of automatism, see *R. v. K.*, [1971] 2 O.R. 401 and *R. v.
Cullum* (1973), 14 C.C.C. (2d) 294 (Ont. Co. Ct.), discussed *post* in Chapter 4.

[4] *R. v. Potvin* (1971), 16 C.R.N.S. 233 (Que.C.A.); *R. v. Warren* (1973), 14 C.C.C. (2d) 188
(N.S.); *Nuttall v. Nuttall and Twyman* (1964), 108 Sol. Jo. 605.

[5] See *Wheeler v. Le Marchant* (1881), 17 L.R. Ch.D. 675, and *A.-G. v. Mulholland; A.-G.
v. Foster,* [1963] 1 All E.R. 767. Note, however, the statutory exceptions under the Civil
Code, 1965, Vol. 2, s. 308 and Medical Act, 1973 (Que.), c. 46, s. 40.

[6] See Freedman, "Medical Privilege" (1954), 32 Can. Bar Rev. 1 at p. 2.

[7] See *The Trial of Elizabeth, Duchess of Kingston* (1776), 20 Howell's State Tr. 573 at p.
574; *A.B. v. C.D.* (1851), 14 Dunlop 177; and *Halls v. Mitchell,* [1928] S.C.R. 125, *per*
Duff J. at pp. 136, 138; and see Freedman, at p. 13.

[8] *The Trial of Elizabeth, Duchess of Kingston, supra,* footnote 7 at p. 574.

[9] [1949] A.C. 182 (P.C.), *per* Lord Du Parq at pp. 191-2.

[10] [1955] A.C. 197 (P.C.), *per* Lord Goddard at pp. 203-4 . See also *Harris v. D.P.P.,* [1952]
A.C. 694 (H.L.), *per* Viscount Simon at p. 707 and *R. v. Payne,* [1963] 1 W.L.R. 637
(C.C.A.), *per* Lord Parker C.J. at p. 638.

to exclude relevant and admissible evidence when it would be contrary to the interest of justice to admit it.[11] This discretion has apparently been utilized on occasion to exclude confidential communications made to psychiatric witnesses. In the well-known Ontario High Court case of *Dembie v. Dembie* [12] Stewart J. exercised his prerogative in these words:

"When the laws involving privilege were first developed and promulgated there was no such thing as a psychiatrist, and, indeed, the surgeon was basically a barber and the physician little more than a herbalist, and it was perfectly suitable — and for other reasons — that there should be an absence of privilege which exists between solicitor and client, but today the situation is quite otherwise, and it is recognized in general that the psychiatrist is as important as the physician or surgeon, in therapy in general, and, indeed, there is no other form of therapy which can be dealt with as by a psychiatrist. That is, it is a new form of medicine and must be recognized as such. . . . I think it is inimical to a fair trial to force a psychiatrist to disclose the things he has heard from a patient, and, in addition to that, I think it rather shocking that one profession should attempt to dictate the ethics of another, which the courts are doing when they see fit to state what a doctor will say and what he will not. They are forcing a breach of oath, and the legal concept that the doctor is not breaching it, that he shall not disclose anything a patient shall tell him unless mete to do so, the idea that it is mete when he gets in the witness box is nonsense, and I have no intention of forcing Doctor Kyne to repeat what his patient told him."[13]

In light of the Supreme Court of Canada's decision in *R. v. Wray*,[14] however, it may be seriously questioned whether Stewart J.'s ruling was supportable by the law. In *Wray* a majority of the Supreme Court[15] held that the trial judge's discretion to exclude relevant and admissible evidence was confined to situations where such evidence was of "trifling" probative value and of great prejudicial effect.

It is an interesting question in Canada whether the *solicitor-client* privilege might not be invoked to protect the confidentiality of communication between an accused and his psychiatrist. The solicitor-client privilege, it is true, embraces only those communications which pass

---

[11] See Kennedy, "Exclusion of Relevant and Admissible Evidence — Doctors and Priests" (1964), 13 Chitty's L.J. 41 at p. 42.

[12] (1963), 21 R.F.L. 46.

[13] Quotation taken from Tollefson, "Privileged Communications in Canada" (1966), 4 Col. I. Dr. Comp. 32 at pp. 44-5. At p. 45, the author comments: "With respect [Stewart J.'s], suggestion that one profession should not dictate the ethics of another seems to be altogether too sweeping. What is a profession? If the legal profession cannot dictate the ethics of another profession it would seem logical that neither can the legal profession determine what other vocations in society constitute professions. Stretching the argument to the limit, it would appear necessary for the court to recognize and respect 'honour among thieves' if they were professional thieves."

[14] [1971] S.C.R. 272.

[15] Fauteux, Abbott, Martland, Ritchie and Pigeon JJ.; Cartwright C.J.C., Hall and Spence JJ. dissented.

between a client and his attorney. If, however, the two choose to communicate through their agents, any information passed to a "transmission agent" may be subject to the privilege as well. The key question therefore becomes whether or not a psychiatric expert retained by one's lawyer is a transmission agent for the purposes of privilege. In several American cases, the courts have decided that he is. In cases such as *City and County of San Francisco v. Superior Court;*[16] *In re Ochse,*[17] and *People v. Hilliker,*[18] for instance, it was reasoned that a psychiatrist who examines an individual at the request of his attorney is analogous to an interpreter, since his function is merely that of communicating and interpreting the client's mental condition to the attorney. It is submitted, however, that such reasoning is pure legal fiction since, as one critic has pointed out, "the client is not aware of the facts which the expert is hired to ascertain and interpret for the lawyer".[19] Moreover, by the time the communication reaches the lawyer, it has been transformed into something quite different from what the client intended to communicate.[20] For these reasons, and owing to the absence of definitive case law on point, the question of whether or not a psychiatrist may be a transmission agent remains unanswered in Canada.

C. THE CASE FOR EXTENDING THE PRIVILEGE

What rationale underlies the recognition of a testimonial privilege? According to Wigmore,[21] such privilege is justifiable only where the following four conditions are met:

(1)   Communications must originate in a *confidence* they will not be disclosed;

(2)   Confidentiality must be *essential* to the full and satisfactory maintenance of the relationship;

(3)   The *relation* must be one which, in the opinion of the community, ought to be fostered sedulously; and,

(4)   The *injury* that might inure to the relation by the communications' disclosure must be greater than the benefit thereby gained for the correct disposal of litigation.

As regards the question of medical privilege generally, Wigmore felt that communications between patient and physician should not be privileged, since they satisfied only the third of his four conditions.[22] But because the learned professor did not specifically consider the psychiatrist-patient relationship in formulating his test,[23] it is submitted that a special evaluation under Wigmore's four points is in order.

---

[16] (1951), 231 P. 2d 26 (Cal. S.C.).

[17] (1951), 238 P. 2d 561 (Cal. S.C.).

[18] (1971), 185 N.W. 2d 831 (Mich. C.A.).

[19] Gardner, "Agency Problems in the Law of Attorney-Client Privilege: The Expert Witness" (1964-65), 42 U. Det. L.J. 473 at pp. 478-9, footnote 22.

[20] *Ibid.*, at p. 476, footnote 13.

[21] *Wigmore on Evidence*, 3rd ed. (Boston, Little Brown, 1940) s. 2285, at p. 527.

[22] *Ibid.*, s. 2285 at p. 528.

[23] Kennedy, "The Psychotherapist's Privilege" (1972-73), 12 Washburn L.J. 297 at p. 302;

Do communications by accused persons to defence-retained psychiatrists originate in a confidence that they will not be disclosed? At least one commentator has suggested that they do not. Referring to the situation of retained experts generally, it has been asserted that "it is expected from the time he enters the case that at the proper time the expert will take the witness stand and testify to all that he knows about the case".[24] It is submitted, however, that such a point of view cannot realistically be supported in the present context. In the first place, a candidate for mental examination is unlikely to appreciate the full ramifications of the psychiatric interview. He may well view the doctor whom his lawyer has retained as a confidant who is 100 per cent on his side. It seems reasonable, in fact, for him to see the psychiatrist as an integral element of the "defence team", working in conjunction with his lawyer. As one American court has put it: "a party substantially retains an expert to conduct the case almost as associate counsel with the solicitor. In such case it would seem fair to apply the same rule to the expert as to the counsel".[25]

Is confidentiality essential to the relationship? Yes. Pre-trial psychiatric examination is of little value unless the accused co-operates fully with the examining expert. If the accused does not feel he can trust the doctor, his responses may be evasive or disingenuous, thus jeopardizing the accuracy of the diagnosis. In Freud's words, "the whole undertaking becomes lost labour if a single concession is made to secrecy".[26]

Should the relationship be fostered by the community? Once again the answer must be yes. While certain critics have argued that psychiatry has no place in the trial process,[27] one can easily imagine the difficulty a mentally disordered accused would have defending himself in the absence of psychiatric assistance. Indeed the classic rationale for solicitor-client privilege could be well applied in support of a psychiatrist-accused privilege. More than a century ago, Lord Brougham stated the basis of the former privilege in these terms:

> "The foundation of this rule is not difficult to discover . . . . It is out of regard to the interests of justice which cannot be upholden, and to the administration of justice, which cannot go on without the aid of men skilled in jurisprudence, in the practice of the courts, and in those matters affecting rights and obligations which form the subject of all judicial proceedings. If the privilege did not exist at all, every one would be thrown upon his own legal resources; deprived of all professional assistance, a man would not venture to consult any skilful person, or would only dare to tell his counsellor half his

---

Louisell, "The Psychologist in Today's Legal World: Part II" (1957), 41 Minn. L. Rev. 731 at pp. 745-6.

[24] Gardner, at pp. 478-9.

[25] *Lelance and Grosjean Mfg. Co. v. Haverman* (1898), 87 Fed. 563 at p. 564 (C.C.S.D.N.Y.).

[26] Freud, *Collected Papers* (London, Hogarth Press, 1956), vol. II at p. 356, footnote 1. See also *Taylor v. United States* (1955) 222 F. 2d 398 at p. 401, (D.C.Cir.).

[27] See, for example, Hakeem, "A Critique of the Psychiatric Approach to Crime and Correction" (1958), 23 Law and Contemporary Problems 650 at pp. 681-2.

case. . . ."[28]

Would the injury to the relationship caused by courtroom disclosure of communications be greater than the social benefit gained therefrom? As we have seen, the injury which non-confidentiality may cause to the relationship between defendant and psychiatrist is considerable. It is submitted, moreover, that the benefits to be gained by full disclosure in the courtroom are negligible. Certainly a recognition of psychiatrist-accused privilege would impose minimal hardship upon the administration of justice; it would not unduly frustrate the Crown to exclude the evidence of a witness who possesses no independent knowledge of the case (apart from what he has learned by assisting defence counsel).[29]

II. The Question of "Self-Incrimination"

A. THE PROBLEM

As mentioned in Chapter 1, the Criminal Code and mental health statutes of most provinces contain numerous provisions which allow for the compulsory psychiatric examination of potentially disordered accused persons.[30] In addition, it is clear that as a matter of practice Crown counsel may occasionally choose to have a defendant examined in the absence of any court order and without the consent of either the defendant or his counsel.[31] Should the accused reveal to the psychiatrist information which may be damaging to his defence, a rather serious evidentiary and ethical problem arises. Will and should statements obtained under such circumstances be admissible as evidence against the accused at trial?

B. THE PRESENT LAW

In Canada, it would appear that the concept of self-incrimination has no application whatsoever to pre-trial statements made to persons in authority.[32] This being the case, there would seem to be only one possi-

---

[28] *Green v. Gaskell* (1833), 1 Myl. & K. 98 at p. 103.

[29] Gardner, at p. 498.

[30] Though the courts may not have jurisdiction to order a remanded accused to submit to examination, evidence of his refusal may be relevant and admissible where he raises insanity at trial. See *R. v. Sweeney (No. 2)* (1977), 35 C.C.C. (2d) 245 (Ont. C.A.).

[31] See *Vaillancourt v. The Queen (No. 2)* (1975), 31 C.R.N.S. 81 (S.C.C.).

[32] Ratushny, "Is There a Right Against Self-Incrimination in Canada?" (1973), 19 McGill L.J. 1 at p. 9, citing *A.-G. Que. v. Begin,* [1955] S.C.R. 593. See also *Curr v. The Queen* (1972), 7 C.C.C. (2d) 181 (S.C.C.) at pp. 199-200, where it was held that s. 2(d) of the Bill of Rights, R.S.C. 1970, App. III, pertained solely to "the giving of evidence at the behest of a Court or like tribunal."

ble ground upon which admissions elicited through compulsory pre-trial psychiatric examination could be impugned: lack of voluntariness. Must such statements be proved to have been made voluntarily in order to be admissible?

The answer, of course, turns on whether or not the examining psychiatrist can be said in such circumstances to have taken on the character of a "person in authority" for the purposes of the voluntariness rule.[33] In *R. v. Leggo*[34] this was, in fact, held to be the case. There a majority of the British Columbia Court of Appeal felt that Crown-appointed psychiatrists who examined a prisoner prior to a dangerous sexual offender hearing were "performing a function in connection with the administration of justice."[35] Sheppard J.A. dissented, however, saying that a dangerous sexual offender hearing was distinguishable from a hearing involving the charge of a crime. Although not referred to, Sheppard J.A.'s reasoning was later adopted by the Manitoba Court of Appeal in *R. v. Johnston*,[36] where it was held that the law relating to the voluntariness of admissions and confessions had no application to statements made to psychiatrists prior to a dangerous sexual offender hearing, even if the accused had not been advised of the purpose of the examination. The same thing was held by the majority of the Alberta Supreme Court, Appellate Division in *R. v. McKenzie*,[37] although in *obiter* it was suggested that a psychiatrist might well become a person in authority by holding himself out to be one. McDonald J.A. dissented in this case, basically for the reasons set down by the majority in *Leggo*, saying[38] also that the psychiatrist's appointment by the Attorney-General certainly made him a person in authority.

In *Wilband v. The Queen*[39] the question came before the Supreme Court of Canada. After referring to *Leggo, Johnston* and *McKenzie*, Fauteux J. rejected the former case and upheld the latter two decisions for the following reasons:

> [1] "The issue, in these proceedings which can only be resorted to if the accused has been convicted of a sexual offence, is not whether he should be convicted of another offence, but solely whether he is afflicted by a state or condition that makes him a dangerous sexual offender within the meaning of s. 659 (*b*) of the *Criminal Code*. To be so afflicted is not an offence. . . .

---

[33] *Per* Lord Summer in *Ibrahim v. The King,* [1914] A.C. 599 at pp. 609-10:

"It has long been established as a positive rule of English criminal law, that no statement by an accused is admissible in evidence against him unless it is shown by the prosecution to have been a voluntary statement, in the sense that it has not been obtained from him either by fear of prejudice or hope of advantage exercised or held out by a person in authority."

See also *Walker v. The King,* [1939] S.C.R. 214; *R. v. Fitton,* [1956] S.C.R. 958; *De Clerq v. The Queen,* [1968] S.C.R. 902; *Piche v. The Queen,* [1971] S.C.R. 23.

[34] (1962), 133 C.C.C. 149.

[35] *Ibid.,* at p. 171.

[36] (1965), 51 W.W.R. 280.

[37] [1965] 3 C.C.C. 6.

[38] *Ibid.,* at p. 27.

[39] [1967] S.C.R. 14.

[2] "The confession rule, which excludes incriminatory statements not affirmatively proved to have been made voluntarily, is a rule which has been designed for proceedings where, broadly speaking, the guilt or innocence of a person charged with an offence is the matter in issue. The rule has not been established for proceedings related to the determination of a sentence. ...

[3] "Another reason why the confession rule does not obtain to exclude statements made by a sexual offender to psychiatrists examining him pursuant to subs. 2 of s. 661 of the Code, is that the latter are not, as it has been decided particularly by the Court of Appeal for Alberta in *Regina v. McKenzie, supra,* persons in authority. Indeed, the nature of their position, in relation to the proceedings under s. 661 of the Code, does not enable them to control or influence the course of such proceedings in the sense and the manner in which the course of proceedings may be controlled or influenced by persons who have a concern with the apprehension, prosecution or examination of prisoners conducted to collect evidence leading to conviction of an offence. On the contrary, and as the purpose to be inferred from subs. 2 of s. 661 of the Code indicates, the position of the psychiatrists, in relation to the proceedings under s. 661, is that of free and independent medical experts, specialists in mental health, whose only part and concern in the proceedings is to give the Court the assistance, which the latter is required by subs. 2 to seek from them, for the assessment of the mental state or condition of a sexual offender and the determination of the application made under the section. Except in rare cases, where indications to the contrary might possibly appear, — and none have been shown in this case — psychiatrists called to assist the Court in these proceedings cannot be considered as being persons in authority. In this respect, their position, in relation to proceedings under s. 661 of the Code, does not differ from their position in relation to proceedings where insanity is raised as an issue, and never, as far as I know, was it suggested that, in the latter case, they have the status of persons in authority."[40]

The matter was taken out of the context of dangerous sexual offender hearings in *Perras v. The Queen.*[41] There the accused had been charged with murder and examined by a psychiatrist while in custody at the request of the police. The psychiatrist was Director of the Psychiatric Services Branch of the Department of Public Health for the Province of Saskatchewan. Conceding that the doctor was a person in authority, the Crown nevertheless proposed to call him as a witness. It was further contended that no *voir dire* needed to be held to determine the voluntary quality of statements made by the accused to the doctor, since the prose-

---

[40] *Ibid.*, at pp. 19-21.
[41] (1973), 22 C.R.N.S. 160 (S.C.C.).

cution did not intend to have such statements introduced into evidence. The issues which reached the Supreme Court of Canada were: (1) whether the trial judge was correct in holding a *voir dire*, and (2) whether the psychiatrist could give evidence at all where the defence could not safely cross-examine him without the statements made by the accused becoming evidence. Judson J. speaking for the majority (Fauteux C.J.C., Abbott and Martland JJ.) relied heavily on *Wilband* in answering the first question in the negative and the second question in the affirmative. Ritchie, Spence and Laskin JJ. dissented. Regarding the applicability of *McKenzie* and *Wilband* to the case at hand, Spence J. (with whom Laskin J. concurred) had this to say:

> "In those cases, there was no question of guilt or innocence. The accused person had already been convicted and what was left to determine was whether he should be adjudged to have the status of a dangerous sexual offender. Therefore, the problem of admissions, against interest by the accused simply did not come up for decision and, in my view, the statement of the present Chief Justice of this Court in *Wilband v. The Queen*, supra, at pp. 20-1 is applicable only to the situation dealt with in that case. In the present case, the circumstances are very different indeed.
>
> "The accused was being held, either charged with or suspected of murder, in the offices of the R.C.M.P. in Regina and had, in fact, been confined to a cell for about 12 hours. At the request of the police, he was examined by Dr. Demay and the purpose of the examination could only have been to meet a plea of lack of intent due to intoxication. It was quite evident in the cross-examination of Dr. Coburn that when this defence was advanced by counsel for the accused, it was the intention of the Crown to adduce the evidence of Dr. Demay to meet that defence. In short, the examination by Dr. Demay and the attempt to produce his evidence was part of the prosecution of the accused person, and Dr. Demay might well be described as part of the prosecution team just as much as the said staff sergeant, the officer who arrested the appellant, or any of the others. Under such circumstances, and applying the subjective test that we should apply, I have no reason to doubt that Dr. Demay was a person in authority."[42]

What then is the state of the present law in Canada? Despite the majority decisions of the Supreme Court in *Wilband* and *Perras*, two commentators have concluded: "It seems clear enough that in each individual case the facts must be looked at and the subjective test applied to determine whether or not a psychiatrist is in law a person in

---

[42] *Ibid.,* at p. 171. For support of this reasoning (although perhaps by way of a slightly strained analogy), consider the interesting decision of the English Court of Appeal in *R. v. Cleary* (1964), 48 Cr. App. R. 116, where it was held that the jury should have been left to consider whether the accused's father, by his presence at the time the accused made his statement while in police custody, had not in effect taken on the character of a legal "person in authority".

authority."[43] Though the courts have not entirely extinguished the possibility that a psychiatrist might, in some circumstances, amount to a person in authority, the criteria for making such characterization remain a mystery at this time.

C. THE CASE AGAINST APPLICATION OF THE PRIVILEGE AGAINST SELF-INCRIMINATION

Should the concept of self-incrimination be extended to apply to examination by Crown-appointed psychiatrists? In the United States, several arguments have been advanced in opposition to such suggestion. There the courts have, for the most part, resisted extension of the privilege by resorting to two legal fictions in particular: (1) the "real evidence" fiction; and (2) the doctrine of "constructive waiver".

Both American and Canadian jurisprudence indicate that the privilege against self-incrimination has never been more than a *testimonial* privilege. While the American privilege (unlike the Canadian privilege) has been held to apply to statements made by an accused *prior* to his trial, it has never prohibited the compelled production of so-called "real evidence". The accused may, therefore, be required to supply blood or breath samples, try on clothing, appear in a police line-up and so on. By the use of a somewhat strained analogy, compulsory mental examination has been justified as an attempt to acquire real evidence and nothing more. Psychiatric examination is comparable to physical exhibition of the accused's body, the argument goes, since, "the aim of the examination is merely to show forth an obscure part of the body — *viz.*, the brain or mind."[44]

Although the real evidence theory has been accepted by the courts in several American cases,[45] there remains one fundamental problem. As Brennan J. observed in the case of *Schmerber v. California*,[46] there are many instances in which the distinction between "real" and "testimonial" response from an accused cannot readily be drawn:[47]

> "Some tests seemingly directed to obtain 'physical evidence' ... may actually be directed to eliciting responses which are essentially testimonial. To compel a person to submit to testing in which an effort will be made to determine his guilt or innocence on the basis of physiological responses, whether willed or not, is to evoke the spirit and history of the Fifth Amendment."[48]

---

[43] Manning and Mewett, "Psychiatric Evidence" (1975-76), 18 Crim. L.Q. 325 at p. 349.

[44] Berry, "Self-Incrimination and the Compulsory Mental Examination: A Proposal" (1973), 15 Ariz. L. Rev. 919 at p. 940.

[45] See *e.g., United States v. Weiser* (1969), F. 2d 932 (2nd Cir.); *United States v. Baird* (1959), 414 F. 2d 700 (2nd Cir.); and *State v. Whitlow* (1965), 210 A. 2d 763.

[46] (1966), 384 U.S. 757.

[47] *Ibid.*, at p. 764.

[48] *Ibid.*

While Brennan J. seems to have considered the method of examination less relevant to the distinction between real and testimonial evidence than the nature of the information elicited and the uses to which it might be put, several courts have held that the method used to obtain evidence may automatically render such evidence testimonial. In *Thornton v. Corcoran,*[49] for example, it was felt that evidence arising from a psychiatric interview would always be testimonial, since "the words of the accused are critically important in determining his mental condition" and, ultimately, his guilt or innocence. Similarly, in *Lee v. Erie County Ct.,*[50] the real evidence theory was rejected, the court stating that "Inasmuch as [the responses to questions asked in a psychiatric interview] are relevant on a material element of the crime, *mens rea,* we are unable to analogize them to the mere exhibition of one's body."

Owing perhaps to the deficiencies inherent in the "real evidence" approach, some American courts have invoked the doctrine of constructive waiver as a means of blocking the extension of the privilege. Stated simply, the principle does in fact recognize a right to remain silent, yet deems such right to have been voluntarily forfeited by any accused who places his mental condition in issue. It rests on the common sense reasoning that "It certainly would be strange doctrine to permit one charged with a public offense to put in issue his want of mental capacity to commit the offense, and in order to make his plea of want of capacity invulnerable prevent all inquiry into his mental state or condition."[51] Such reasoning has been used in numerous American decisions as a basis for compelling accused persons to submit to pre-trial examination.[52] The problem with this approach, however, is that it assumes that the accused's state of mind may be divorced from the issue of guilt.[53] As one commentator has succinctly put it: "since unlawful intent is an essential element of the crime, the import of the court's logic is that one cannot simultaneously assert that he is 'not guilty' of the crime charged and that he is entitled to the privilege against self-incrimination."[54]

Another rationale for compulsory psychiatric examinations concerns the burden of proof which rests on the prosecution. In the United States it has been argued that "To allow the defendant to choose the only psychiatrist who may testify on the basis of an in-depth interview ... would weigh the scales at trial in favour of the defendant in those jurisdictions requiring the prosecution to prove legal sanity beyond a reasonable doubt."[55] While it may be sporting to give the accused a slight edge, the

---

[49] (1969), 407 F. 2d 695 at p. 700 (D.C.Cir.).

[50] (1971), 267 N.E. 2d 452 at p. 456.

[51] *State v. Cerar* (1922), 207 P. 597 at p. 602. (Utah S.C.).

[52] See *e.g., United States v. Bohle* (1971), 445 F. 2d 54 (7th Cir.); *United States v. Baird* (1969), 414 F. 2d 700 (2nd Cir.); *United States v. Malcolm* (1973), 475 F. 2d 420 (9th Cir.); *United States v. Albright* (1968), 388 F. 2d 719 (4th Cir.); *Pope v. United States* (1967), 372 F. 2d 710 (8th Cir.).

[53] Meister, "*Miranda* on the Couch: An Approach to Problems of Self-Incrimination, Right to Counsel, and *Miranda* Warnings in Pre-Trial Psychiatric Examinations of Criminal Defendants" (1975), 11 Columbia J. Law and Social Problems 403 at p. 433.

[54] Comment, "Psychiatry v. Law in the Pre-Trial Mental Examination: The Bifurcated Trial and Other Alternatives" (1971-72), 40 Fordham L.Rev. 827 at p. 837.

[55] *Ibid.,* at p. 836.

burden which this type of advantage places on the prosecution has been described as "insurmountable".[56] But because in Canada the burden of proving insanity (on a balance of probabilities) rests upon the accused in all cases, it is submitted that the "insurmountable burden" rationale would be invalid in our law.

D. THE CASE FOR A PRIVILEGE AGAINST COMPULSORY PSYCHIATRIC EXAMINATION

Several policy arguments may be advanced in opposition to compulsory pre-trial psychiatric examination. To begin with, it may be argued that the procedure relieves the Crown of its burden of producing independent evidence of a defendant's guilt and thus "run[s] contrary to the policy of the accusatorial system."[57] As Frankfurter J. remarked in the case of *Watts v. Indiana*:[58]

> "Ours is the accusatorial as opposed to the inquisitorial system. Such has been the characteristic of Anglo-American criminal justice since it freed itself from practices borrowed by the Star Chamber from the Continent whereby an accused was interrogated in secret for hours on end . . . . Under our system society carries the burden of proving its charge against the accused not out of his own mouth. It must establish its case, not by interrogation of the accused even under judicial safeguards, but by evidence independently secured through skillful investigation."

The difficulty with the independent evidence rationale, however, is that it ignores the fact that the Crown is entitled to rely upon the voluntary and unsolicited statements made by an accused.[59]

Perhaps the most compelling argument in favour of a privilege against compulsory psychiatric examination arises from the insidious nature of the investigatory techniques which may be employed.[60] Because those provisions of the Criminal Code and provincial mental health legislation which authorize psychiatric remands are silent on the method of examination to be used, the psychiatrist would appear to have a *carte blanche*

---

[56] *Lee v. Erie County Ct., supra,* footnote 52 at p. 456.

[57] Meister, at p. 424.

[58] (1949), 338 U.S. 40 at pp. 54-5.

[59] See Aronson, "Should the Privilege Against Self-Incrimination Apply to Compelled Psychiatric Examinations?" (1973), 26 Stan. L.Rev. at pp. 87-8.

[60] See Diamond and Louisell, "The Psychiatrist as an Expert Witness: Some Ruminations and Speculations" (1965), 63 Mich. L.Rev. 1335 at p. 1349, where the authors have asserted that "Psychiatry, with its special investigatory devices of persuasion, insinuation, into a subject's confidence, 'lie detection', hypnosis, 'truth serums', projective tests, and other procedures, can flagrantly violate basic constitutional and other personal rights." And see Meister, at p. 419, where it is noted: "Because the psychiatric examination is so comprehensive, the type of information sought so personal and self-revealing, and the psychiatric techniques employed so effective at eliciting information about the defendant, the likelihood that ultimately the defendant will be compelled or induced to incriminate himself is substantial."

in this regard. Presumably, he may resort to any technique which he deems proper or efficacious.[61]

Although the procedures used for mental examination of a criminal defendant may vary from psychiatrist to psychiatrist or from institution to institution, a thorough psychiatric examination is generally comprised of three elements: physical testing, mental testing, and the personal interview. The following is a brief description of each.

The Interview

Typically the first encounter between psychiatrist and accused takes the form of a simple interview. Because it is necessary that a medical history be taken, the opening questions are routinely aimed at discovering whether the patient/accused has been hospitalized, incarcerated or psychiatrically treated elsewhere; if such has been the case, any medical, prison or probation records available may be sent for as corroborative material to aid the examiner in his diagnosis. The doctor may also ask if a statement has been made to the police, so that it might be obtained as an additional source of information. Oftentimes the patient is asked to give a detailed day-by-day account of the period (perhaps weeks) leading up to the day in question. In this context, the patient may literally be asked what he ate for breakfast that morning, as his answer may prove significant should a low blood sugar later be diagnosed. Both the accused's recollection of the events leading up to the alleged crime and those immediately following it are of particular importance. Subsequent amnesia, depression, elation or confusion may all be relevant clues in pinpointing mental disorder. It is important to note that throughout the course of the interview, communication is transpiring on two levels, the "subjective" component being what the patient says and the "objective" element being what the psychiatrist observes independently.

Where the accused is uncooperative and refuses to answer the doctor's interrogatories, several methods are available for weakening his resistance. One technique which has come under harsh criticism from commentators as well as judges is the use of deception and false promises:[62]

> ". . . the psychiatrist, calling himself defendant's doctor, playing upon the latter's natural fears and hopes, pressing his hands upon defendant's head with accompanying commands, and suggesting details to an unwilling mind by persistent and unceasing questioning; informing defendant that he was not morally responsible; making deceptive offers of friendship and numerous promises, express and implied; giving assurances in a pseudo-confidential atmosphere of physician and patient ...".[63]

Another technique available is the use of so-called "truth drugs" such as scopolamine, sodium amytal, or metrazol. While supporters of narcoanalysis have asserted that "a drug induced interview may be a valuable

---

[61] Meister, at p. 414.
[62] Meister, at p. 417.
[63] *People v. Leyra* (1951), 98 N.E. 2d at p. 558.

adjunct to an otherwise thorough psychiatric examination",[64] they have also noted its limitations. As one group of medico-legal commentators have pointed out, "some [subjects] are able to withhold information and some, especially character neurotics, are able to lie."[65] More importantly, "Others are so suggestible they will describe, in response to suggestive questioning, behaviour which never in fact occurred."[66] Despite these difficulties, there is nothing in Canadian case law which suggests that a psychiatric opinion formed partially on the basis of a drug-induced confession would be ruled inadmissible in evidence.[67] Nor would the present law prevent the confession itself and the circumstances which surrounded it from being disclosed to the jury, unless, perhaps, the psychiatrist could be shown to be a "person in authority" for the purposes of the voluntariness rule. As indicated by the decision of the Ontario Court of Appeal in *Vaillancourt v. The Queen (No. 2)*,[68] however, the question as to whether or not a psychiatrist is such a person becomes "irrelevant" in cases "where the testimony being proffered ... by Crown psychiatrists is limited solely to their opinion as to the mental capacity of the accused in relation to the offence charged . . .".[69] It would seem, therefore, that statements made under the influence of "truth drugs", though they might not be admissible as proof of the truth of their contents,[70] could nevertheless be used by the prosecution as evidence tending to establish guilt. In the American case of *People v. Esposito,*[71] for example, information obtained through narco-analysis was held to be admissible for the purpose of rebutting the defence of insanity. The court, however, hastened to add:

"... we do not pass upon the question whether testimony of the examining and observing psychiatrists was admissible to establish a confession of guilt or admissions evidencing guilt while the defendants were subject to the influence of the drugs which had been administered to them. We are not now prepared in view of the record presented here and of present medical knowledge and experimentation disclosed therein, to hold that such testimony is competent."[72]

---

[64] Dession, Freedman, Donnelly and Redlich, "Drug-Induced Revelation and Criminal Investigation" (1953), 62 Yale L.J. 315 at p. 319.

[65] *Ibid.*

[66] *Ibid.* See also Macdonald, "Truth Serum" (1955), 46 J. Crim. L. and Crimin. 259 at p. 263 where the author has stated that "Criminal suspects, while under the influence of drugs, may deliberately withhold information, persist in giving untruthful answers, or falsely confess to crimes they have not committed." And see generally Gall, "The Case Against Narcointerrogation" (1962), 7 J.For.Sci. 29.

[67] Although there are no cases directly on point, there is the case of *R. v. Phillion* (1972), 21 C.R.N.S. 169, in which the Ontario Supreme Court admitted evidence of a defence psychiatrist which was based on the results of psychological, sodium amytal and polygraph tests conducted on the accused; affd 37 C.R.N.S. 361 at p. 362 (C.A.); appeal was heard by the Supreme Court of Canada on another issue 37 C.R.N.S. 361.

[68] (1974), 31 C.R.N.S. 81 at p. 82.

[69] *Ibid., per* Gale C.J.O. at p. 89, and affd by the Supreme Court of Canada 31 C.R.N.S. 81.

[70] *Ibid.,* and see *R. v. Barker,* [1954] Crim. L.R. 423 and 482.

[71] (1942), 39 N.E. 2d 925 (N.Y.C.A.).

[72] *Ibid.,* at p. 929.

Although in Canada the trial judge would be required to instruct the jury not to interpret a drug-induced confession as proof that its contents are true, it is unrealistic to suppose that a jury would take such evidence merely as the basis of the psychiatrist's opinion and totally ignore its more damaging aspects.[73]

Physical Testing
The next phase of the examination is usually organic testing. The tests include routine blood and urine analyses for detecting possible diabetes, hypoglycemia, lead or alcohol poisoning, anemia, and so on. Besides a routine chest X-ray, skull X-rays may also be taken as well as pneumoencephalographs, spinal tap and electroencephalogram, where organic brain disorders such as meningitis or tumours are suspected. Although the electroencephalogram is a standard part of the examination, it is rarely helpful since (a) organic brain disorders are a comparatively rare cause of criminal behaviour, and (b) the EEG is not foolproof. What is referred to as a "sleep EEG", however, may be particularly useful as a means of corroborating a claim by the patient that he suffers from somnambulism.

Although the purpose of subjecting a defendant to organic testing is to "discover information about his mental processes relevant to the issue of his guilt",[74] it is doubtful that such procedure could ever be successfully attacked as a denial of substantive due process under the Canadian Bill of Rights.[75] The compulsory donation of blood and breath samples have, after all, been ruled to be consistent with due process of law in Canada.[76] The physical tests which may be employed in the psychiatric setting, though perhaps somewhat more drastic, seem unlikely to produce the "revulsion and shock of conscience" which Laskin J. (as he then was) intimated in *Curr v. The Queen*[77] might be necessary for a substantive due process argument to succeed.

Mental Testing
Once the physical tests have been completed, the patient is asked to participate in a series of psychological tests which are normally conducted by a psychologist. Although there are a veritable battery of possible tests which may be used, the essentials are: (1) an intelligence test of some sort, commonly the Stanford-Binet or Wechsler scales; (2) a physi-

---

[73] See Manning and Mewett, *op. cit.* footnote 43, at pp. 352-3, where the authors have made the same point with regard to hearsay evidence which forms the basis of psychiatrist's opinion. And see Comment, *supra,* footnote 56 at p. 835, where the author has noted: "While the appropriate instruction to the jury might protect the defendant's privilege against self-incrimination in a theoretical sense, practically speaking the result is a severe infringement of the privilege because of the likelihood that the jury will be unable to avoid the implications of the psychiatrist's testimony on the issue of whether the defendant committed the actus reus."

[74] Meister, at p. 415.

[75] R.S.C. 1970, App. III.

[76] See *A.-G. Que. v. Begin,* [1955] S.C.R. 593 and *Curr v. The Queen,* [1972] S.C.R. 889 respectively.

[77] [1972] S.C.R. 889 at p. 898.

cal disability test such as the self-administered Cornell Health Index (not strictly a psychological test at all, though it is convenient to give such test at this point); (3) a self-report inventory such as the Minnesota Multiphasic Personality Inventory (which has a built-in "lie score" for detecting malingerers); (4) a sexual behaviour questionnaire; and (5) optional specific projective tests such as the Rorschach (ink blot) or Thematic Apperception (suggestive picture) tests. Once the scores on these tests have been calculated (usually by a computer), they are analysed and a detailed report is sent to the psychiatrist in charge.

Although, like the organic tests, psychological tests do not compel an accused to reveal any information which pertains specifically to the offence with which he is charged, they do require him to supply information of a potentially incriminating nature.[78] The results of such testing may, for example, reveal in the defendant a peculiar propensity for behaviour of the type involved in the crime. Moreover, the defendant may be quite unaware of the significance of what he is disclosing at the time he is being tested.

III. Conclusions

Despite the frequent arguments which have been made in favour of recognizing a general physician-patient privilege, none has succeeded in altering Canada's law thus far.[79] In 1968, the McRuer Civil Rights Commission expressed the opinion that "Apart from the psychiatric cases, no convincing evidence has been forthcoming to establish that the public interest is not being well served by the law as it now is ...".[80] Despite the convincing evidence which psychiatric cases apparently presented, the Commission went on to criticize the ruling in *Dembie v. Dembie*[81] for giving the Hippocratic Oath precedence over the rule of law. "The law", it said, "cannot recognize any power in professional bodies to impose on their members declarations of secrecy (if they do) which would override the right of the individual to a disclosure of the truth before a court of justice. This would be an invasion of civil rights which ought not to be tolerated".[82] On the matter of psychiatric privilege, the Commission concluded as follows:

> "Where a psychiatrist has been called to give opinion evidence, it is essential that he should give the foundation for his opinion. State-

---

[78] Meister, at p. 416.

[79] See Kennedy, "Exclusion of Relevant and Admissible Evidence — Doctors and Priests" (1964), 13 Chitty's L.J. 41 at pp. 43-5, where a bill to amend the Canada Evidence Act is reproduced. This bill was defeated in Parliament.

[80] McRuer, *Report of the Royal Commission Inquiry Into Civil Rights*, Vol. 2 (Ottawa, Queen's Printer, 1968) at p. 822.

[81] (1963), 21 R.F.L. 46 (Ont.). See also the discussion, *supra*, footnote 13.

[82] *Supra*, footnote 80 at p. 823.

ments made by the patient very frequently form at least a part of the foundation . . . . To exclude them by law would require very persuasive evidence of public necessity, which evidence has not been put before this Commission."[83]

It is submitted that in the context of pre-trial psychiatric examination of someone who has been accused of a criminal offence, persuasive evidence of public necessity does in fact exist. In fighting to preserve his liberty, the criminal defendant requires special safeguards to offset the vast investigatory powers of the state.[84] Should defence counsel believe his client to have been insane or in a state of automatism when the offence was allegedly committed, he should be free to explore the possibility without fear of having his own expert called as a witness against his client.[85] Permitting the Crown to call such a witness would, in a sense, make things too easy for the prosecution; it might allow a mistake in defence strategy to make up for any weakness of the Crown's case.[86] Perhaps for these reasons, the federal Law Reform Commission has recently proposed that the doctrine of testimonial privilege be modified in certain ways.[87] In the model Evidence Code which it has drafted, the Commission has included sections dealing with "general professional privilege" as well as with privilege regarding work done "in contemplation of litigation".[88] Psychiatrist-accused privilege could fall within either category. The former provision reads as follows:

"41. A person who has consulted a person exercising a profession for the purpose of obtaining professional services, or who has been rendered such services by a professional person, has a privilege against disclosure of any confidential communication reasonably made in the course of the relationship if, in the circumstances, the public interest in the privacy of the relationship outweighs the public interest in the administration of justice."

The latter provision states:

"42(2) A person has a privilege against disclosure of information obtained or work produced in contemplation of litigation by him or his lawyer or a person employed to assist the lawyer, unless, in the case of information, it is not reasonably available from another source and its probative value substantially outweighs the disadvantages that would be caused by its disclosure."

The maxim *nemo tenetur siepsum accusare* is a grand aphorism which, unhappily, has had precious little impact upon the trial of men-

---

[83] *Ibid.*
[84] Gardner, op. cit. footnote 19, at p. 498.
[85] *Ibid.*, at p. 499.
[86] *Ibid.*
[87] Law Reform Commission of Canada, *Report: Evidence* (Ottawa, Information Canada, 1975).
[88] *Ibid.*, at pp. 30-1.

tally disordered defendants. What can be done to remedy the present situation regarding compelled pre-trial mental examination? The most obvious alternative to the current procedure would be a total elimination of all non-consensual psychiatric probing. While certain *dicta* emanating from the Manitoba Court of Appeal suggest a willingness to uphold an accused's objection to examination,[89] it is submitted that at present there exists no legal basis for compelling a court to do so. A second alternative would be to allow compulsory pre-trial examination, but make all statements made by the defendant during such examination inadmissible at any proceeding to determine his guilt or innocence. Unfortunately, however, the concealment of facts which form the basis of an expert's opinion may well effect the defendant in an adverse manner. It has been noted that "The absolute barring of the defendant's statements would result in an increased transfer of the jury function to the expert, who alone would evaluate the medical and moral facts then 'report' his decision to the court and jury."[90] Unaware of the facts upon which the prosecution's expert has based his opinion, the jury may well accord such opinion either more or less weight than it deserves.

A third alternative would be to render any statements made by the accused during the course of his compulsory examination admissible only at his option. In Arizona such solution has in fact been implemented by statute. Rule 11.7 of that State's Rules of Criminal Procedure provides:

"RULE 11.7 PRIVILEGE

a. GENERAL RESTRICTION. No evidence of any kind obtained under these provisions shall be admissible at any proceedings to determine guilt or innocence unless the defendant presents evidence intended to rebut the presumption of sanity.

b. PRIVILEGED STATEMENTS OF DEFENDANT
(1) No statement of the defendant obtained under these provisions, or evidence resulting therefrom, concerning the events which form the basis of the charges against him shall be admissible at the trial of guilt or innocence, or at any subsequent proceeding to determine guilt or innocence, without his consent.
(2) No statement of the defendant or evidence resulting therefrom obtained under these provisions, concerning any other events or transactions, shall be admissible at any proceeding to determine his guilt or innocence of criminal charges based on such events or transactions."

A fourth and more complex alternative would be the bifurcated trial. Several American courts and legislatures have opted for this solution.[91]

---

[89] See *R. v. Johnston* (1965), 51 W.W.R. 280 (Man. C.A.) *per* Miller C.J.M. at pp. 284, 287; *R. v. McAmmond,* [1970] 1 C.C.C. 175 (Man. C.A.) *per* Dickson J.A. (as he then was) at p. 178.
[90] Berry, *op. cit.* footnote 44, at p. 945.
[91] See *Cal. Penal Code,* s. 1026 (West, 1970); *Tex. Code Crim. Pro. Ann.*, art. 46.02, s.1

The "traditional" bifurcated trial involves a splitting of the trial process into two separate stages: the first proceeding is directed at a determination of the defendant's "guilt", excluding the issue of his possible insanity; and the second proceeding (which becomes necessary only if the accused is found "guilty" at the first) involves the issue of insanity.

Because experience has shown that psychiatric testimony unrelated to insanity may still creep into the first stage of a bifurcated trial,[92] several modifications of the basic scheme have been proposed. First, it has been suggested that the trial could be split by issues into two parts: psychiatric and non-psychiatric. "The first trial would involve such issues as commission of the acts by the defendant . . . and the existence of any other circumstances that might be essential to liability. In addition, this first phase would include a determination of state of mind *if* this would not require the use of evidence of mental illness."[93] The second trial, should it become necessary, would deal with any psychiatric defences which might be put forward by the defendant.

A more complicated proposal would divide the trial into at least three phases, establishing a "sequential order of proof":

> "The first stage would be on the issue of defendant's commission of the overt act. All evidence not relevant to the commission of the overt act would be excluded at this point. . . .In the second stage the prosecution would have to prove beyond a reasonable doubt that the defendant had the required mens rea apart from any defence of mental disorder. Evidence of mental disorder would again be excluded. . . .The third stage would consider the issues involving psychiatric testimony. Depending on the jurisdiction's holdings with regard to the consideration of mental disorder to reduce the grade of the crime, the issue at this stage would be either the grade of the crime, the criminal incapacity of the defendant, or both."[94]

But the obvious problem with all bifurcated trial procedures described is that "there is still a sacrifice of the self-incrimination privilege since defendant's admissions to the psychiatrist may be used to help convince the jury that he is not legally insane . . .".[95] The only advantage to be gained lies in the fact that the jury will not be prejudiced in the first trial by any incriminating statements he may have made as to overt acts.

It is submitted that the fairest and most sensible solution would be to

---

(supp. 1972-73); *State ex rel. Berger v. Superior Court* (1970), 476 P. 2d 666; *United States v. Bennett* (1970), 460 F. 2d 822 (D.C.Cir.); *State ex rel. La Follette v. Raskin* (1967), 150 N.W. 2d 318.

[92] See *People v. Wells* (1949), 202 P. 2d 53, cert. denied, 338 U.S. 836 and *State v. Shaw* (1970), 471 P. 2d 715, cert. denied (1971), 40 U.S. 1009.

[93] Dix, "Mental Illness, Criminal Intent, and the Bifurcated Trial" (1970), Law and the Social Order 559 at p. 575, quoted in Comment, "Psychiatry v. Law in the Pre-Trial Mental Examination: The Bifurcated Trial and Other Alternatives" (1971-72), 40 Fordham L. Rev. 827 at p. 855.

[94] Comment, at p. 858.

[95] *Ibid.*, at p. 849.

do away with compelled pre-trial psychiatric investigation altogether. Psychiatric examination should be premised upon the accused's voluntary informed consent[96] and should entail such fundamental safeguards as a *Miranda*[97] type warning and the right to have counsel present. Although our law does not require the *Miranda* caution in other circumstances, it has been pointed out that:

> "Psychiatric examination is unlike examination or being questioned by police officers in that the accused is psychologically trusting of the psychiatrist. He or she will feel that the psychiatrist is there to assist the accused rather than to hurt the accused . . . There are many accused who are surprised to find the psychiatrist, to whom they have freely spoken, standing in the witness box and testifying against them."[98]

Owing to the fact that court-appointed and Crown-appointed psychiatrists are potential adversaries of the accused, and that his mental examination may be a critical stage of the proceedings, the presence of counsel (at least during the interview stage of the examination) seems only fair and reasonable.[99]

---

[96] See Manning and Mewett, "Psychiatric Evidence" (1975-76), 18 Crim. L.Q. 325 at p. 350.
[97] *Miranda v. Arizona* (1966), 384 U.S. 346.
[98] Manning and Mewett, at p. 350.
[99] For American cases in which the courts have adopted this reasoning, see *Lee v. Erie County Ct.* (1971), 267 N.E. 2d 452; *State v. Corbin* (1973), 516 P. 2d 1314; *State v. Anderson* (1973), 509 P. 2d 80.

Chapter 3

Fitness To Stand Trial

I. Introduction

The idea that persons of unsound mind should not be made to stand trial is one rooted in age-old concepts of fair play and fundamental justice. Originally, jurists may have viewed a defendant's affliction with mental illness as a sign of demoniacal possession[1] or as evidence of direct intervention by the Almighty;[2] in either case, it was thought unwise to proceed.

Besides being a measure to appease the supernatural forces, the fitness requirement is both the product of the traditional right of an accused to make full answer and defence[3] (which dates back to biblical teachings[4]) and a logical extension of the rule which evolved at common law prohibiting trials *in absentia*.[5] But despite its noble heritage, the fitness requirement, as it exists within our modern criminal justice system, is an imperfect contraption. It involves some rather complex statutory machinery which, unfortunately, is capable of being misused, half-used, or altogether ignored.

This chapter focuses on the procedure used for determining fitness to stand trial in Canada, with a special emphasis on the Ontario practice.

---

[1] Szasz, "Psychiatry, Ethics and the Criminal Law" (1958), 58 Columbia L. Rev. 183 at p. 184.

[2] Maxwell, "Competency for Trial in North Dakota" (1973), 49 North Dakota L. Rev. 799 at p. 799.

[3] Embodied in s-s. 577(3) of the Criminal Code.

[4] "Doth our law judge any man, before it hear him, and know what he doeth?" (John 7:51).

[5] In *R. v. Lee Kun,* [1916] 1 K.B. 337, Lord Reading stated (at p. 341) that the accused's presence in the courtroom must be mental as well as physical. See also Tremeear, *Criminal Code,* 6th ed. (1964) at p. 934; Ryan, "Insanity at the Time of Trial Under the Criminal Code of Canada" (1967), 3 U.B.C. L. Rev. 36 at p. 37; Foote, "A Comment on Pre-Trial Commitment of Criminal Defendants" (1960), 108 U.Pa.L. Rev. 832 at p. 834. The accused's right to be physically present during his trial is set forth in s-s. 577(1) of

II. Remand And Examination

Although the law does not require it,[6] a remand of the accused for psychiatric examination is usually ordered by the court before the issue of fitness is tried.[7] The trial judge who wishes to have a defendant psychiatrically examined must choose either to proceed under the Criminal Code or under the provincial mental health statute.[8] Although it seems that the Code is more frequently selected in Ontario,[9] this is rather difficult to understand since the Ontario Mental Health Act would appear from a practical standpoint to be far less awkward. While an order under s-s. 543(2) of the Code generally requires the "evidence or ... report in writing of one duly qualified medical practitioner" to be given in support of the remand, no such requirement exists in either s-ss. 14(1) or 15(1) of the Mental Health Act. Furthermore, the Code is unclear on the procedure involved in obtaining the necessary medical evidence in the first place. In actual practice, however, no difficulty really arises. Usually where mental illness is suspected the defence has had its doctor examine the accused long before the trial stage.[10] Where it is the prosecution which anticipates raising the issue, the Crown may have the accused examined during the three-day remand provided for at the time of a "show cause" hearing under ss. 457 and 457.1.[11] In addition, s-s. (2.1) of s. 543 dispenses with the necessity for medical evidence where the circumstances are compelling and a physician is not readily available.

At first blush, there does not appear to be a great deal of difference

---

the Criminal Code. Note that this right is subject to certain exceptions however, one of which being that a court may cause an accused to be removed from the courtroom during the trial of the fitness issue. This seems somewhat paradoxical.

[6] Note the use of the permissive word "may" in s-s. 543(2) of the Code.

[7] From personal communication with Provincial Court Judges. See also the Law Reform Commission of Canada, Study Paper, "Fitness to Stand Trial", May 1973 (Ottawa: Project on the General Principles of the Criminal Law) at p. 3. It has been recommended that such procedure be made mandatory. The Study Group proposes substitution of the word "shall" for "may" in s-s. 4(1) of its Draft Legislation would have this effect.

[8] It should be noted that this choice arises from the appearance of the word "may" in the pertinent sections of both statutes. It has been recommended by the recent Study Group's report (*supra,* footnote 7) that the word "shall" be substituted in s. 543 of the Code, thus eliminating the option of using provincial legislation. For reasons which will become apparent, the Study Group feels that provincial remand provisions are potentially more dangerous than s. 543 of the Code.

[9] In 1973 the Clarke Institute of Psychiatry in Toronto admitted 50 patients remanded under the Criminal Code as compared to 35 remanded under the Mental Health Act. Judges seem to prefer using the Code whenever the accused has been charged under the Code. See *Doyle v. The Queen* (1976), 35 C.R.N.S. 1 (S.C.C.) *per* Ritchie J. at p. 6.

[10] If not, *i.e.,* in cases where the accused has been assigned counsel under s-s. 543(3), the examination may take place in the lock-up during a brief adjournment.

[11] Should the accused refuse to voluntarily submit to an examination, the justice will ask the Crown attorney if he wishes to show cause why the accused should be detained in custody. In order that the Crown may use the "secondary ground" (para. 457(7)(b)) a three-day remand will be ordered. If the accused persists in his refusal to be examined, the doctor may either infer mental abnormality from this behaviour or else the Crown may repeatedly request remands until he does submit, despite the fact that s. 457.1 stip-

between the tests which must be satisfied under both pieces of legislation in order for a judge to remand. The Code requires the court to be of the opinion that there is reason to believe that:

> "(2) (a) an accused is *mentally ill,* or
>   (b) *the balance of the mind of an accused is disturbed,* where the accused is a female person charged with an offence arising out of the death of her newly-born child." [Emphasis added.]

It is worth noting that s. 544 will only operate if the accused "appears to be insane". What then is the practical distinction between these various tests? Perhaps "mental illness" connotes something less severe than "insanity"; likewise, a disturbance of the mind's balance may be less severe even than "mental illness", as it implies a more temporary state. The significance of para. (b) of s-s. (2) has been explained this way:

> "That portion of the amendment pertaining to the female accused appears to be a legislative recognition . . . [that] 'post-partum depression' cases ... might not otherwise be classed under the generic term of 'mental illness', and thus would not have been subject to medical observation after the issue of fitness to stand trial was raised."[12]

The Mental Health Act, in comparison, may be used wherever the judge "has reason to believe"[13] that the accused "suffers from a mental disorder".[14] It is possible that the term "mental disorder" encompasses all of the terms which the Code uses and more. One writer has pointed out[15] that although the congenital mental defective would likely rank among those considered unfit to stand trial,[16] it may be that he is not subject to remand under the wording of s-s. 543(2). Because medical examination is probably the best way of gathering the information necessary to a determination of fitness[17] it is fortunate that the Mental Health Act fills the apparent gap left by the Criminal Code; it may more easily be said that a mental defective suffers from a "mental disorder" than from a "mental illness".

Once the defendant has been remanded, where does he go? For how long? Under para. 543(2)(d) of the Code, he may be placed in "such custody as the court, judge or magistrate directs for observation ...". Theo-

---

ulates that "no such adjournment shall be for more than three clear days except with the consent of the accused."

[12] Ryan, *op. cit.* footnote 5, at p. 40.

[13] In *Ex parte Branco,* [1971] 3 O.R. 575, it was held that although a superior court could decide whether there were reasonable grounds on which this discretion could be exercised, the Provincial Court Judge's exercise of the discretion could not itself be reviewed.

[14] Section 1(f) of the Act defines "mental disorder" as "any disease or disability of the mind".

[15] Ryan, at p. 40.

[16] See *R. v. Smith,* [1936] 1 D.L.R. 717 (Sask. C.A.).

[17] Ryan, at p. 40.

retically, this could mean simple incarceration in the lock-up for 30 days. In contrast, s-ss. 14(1) and 15(1) of the Mental Health Act are more precise in their wording, providing that the accused must be sent to a "psychiatric facility". In addition, s. 16 offers the following insurance:

> "16. A judge shall not make an order under section 14 or 15 until he ascertains from the senior physician of a psychiatric facility that the services of the psychiatric facility are available to the person to be named in the order."[18]

A potential source of difficulty with the Act, however, is that the maximum period of remand is longer here than in the Code. The prescribed period under s-s. 15(1) is two months. Under para. (b) of s. 543(2.1) of the Code, a remand for more than 30 days (with a maximum of 60 days) can only be ordered when supported by the evidence or report of at least one doctor. By s-s. 14(3) of the Mental Health Act such evidence is sufficient to commit the accused for an indefinite period of treatment.

The fact that s. 14 is susceptible to abuse cannot be doubted. In a relatively recent empirical study made in Nova Scotia[19] an examination of hospital records revealed that although only eight out of 76 cases detained in hospital as a result of remand under equivalent provincial mental health legislation were summary conviction offences, the defendants in three of these cases had been charged with vagrancy. They ended up remaining in the hospital for five, 22 and 33 years. The maximum sentence for a vagrancy conviction under the Code was six months.[20]

Until recently, s. 14 of the Mental Health Act was the only provision which allowed for mental examination to take place on an out-patient basis. With the passage of Bill C-71,[21] however, this situation has been changed. By para. 543(2)(c) of the Criminal Code, the court is empowered to "direct the accused to attend, at a place or before a person specified in the order and within a time specified therein, for observation . . .". The utility of such procedure may be readily seen when one considers the fact that actual examination time normally comprises only a fraction of the remand period.[22] Out-patient examination would seem

---

[18] Note that technically this provision relates solely to availability of psychiatric services; it does not really guarantee an accused any right to examination or treatment.

[19] Jobson, "Commitment and Release of the Mentally Ill Under Criminal Law" (1969), 11 Crim. L.Q. 186 at p.197.

[20] The author has concluded (at p. 197): "It is quite probable that there were good medical reasons for these three persons being confined for such long periods of time, but it is inappropriate that the criminal law should be forced to appear as an instrument of oppression, sweeping the helpless from the streets into the hospitals." For a reported case in which the accused was committed under provincial mental health legislation pursuant to his arrest on a vagrancy charge see *Kennedy v. Tomlinson et al.* (1959), 126 C.C.C. 175 (Ont.C.A.); leave to appeal to S.C.C. refused [1959] S.C.R. ix.

[21] Criminal Law Amendment Act, 1975, 1974-75-76 (Can.), c. 93, assented to 30 March 1976, proclaimed in force 26 April 1976 with exceptions.

[22] Jobson, at p. 197. It should be kept in mind, however, that nothing prevents the court from ordering a remand for *less* than 30 days or from having the accused returned from the psychiatric hospital before the period of remand has expired if the remainder of the time is not required.

particularly appropriate for a defendant who is not in actual custody at the time the order is made. The fact is, however, that this alternative is rarely used in Ontario,[23] although an equivalent measure which is sometimes employed is the making of judicial interim release conditional upon the signing of an undertaking to submit to out-patient psychiatric examination.[24]

One apparent flaw in s-s. 543(2) of the Code is that it does not require the examining psychiatrist to submit a report of what he has discovered about the defendant's fitness during the period of "observation". Because observation is in itself useless without such report, common practice is for the doctor to submit one anyway.[25] When remand has been ordered under the Mental Health Act, however, both s-ss. 14(2) and 15(2) require that "the senior physician shall report in writing to the judge as to the mental condition of the person."[26] While these words would seem to fill a gap which s. 543 leaves open, this point might be debated by counsel who would prefer that a potentially prejudicial report not fall into the hands of a judge who is trying the case alone.[27] It has been pointed out that a written report of this nature may not be received as evidence at the fitness hearing because it is hearsay and not subject to cross-examination[28] (which is why, in practice, the psychiatrist's opinion on the fitness issue is given *viva voce*); however, the case of *R. v. Deforge*[29] makes clear the fact that a judge may receive reports submitted subsequent to remand regardless of the evidentiary rules which may apply at trial. In the words of Vannini D.C.J. of the Algoma District Court:

> "Many a Provincial Judge who sits alone upon the trial of an accused has such reports before him received pursuant to an order made under . . . the *Criminal Code* or under ss. 14 or 15 of the *Mental Health Act, 1967*, and the trial proceeds notwithstanding.
>
> "I am satisfied that a Judge sitting alone to try an accused will not in any way be prejudiced by any information which may be

---

[23] From personal communication with Provincial Court Judges and forensic psychiatrists.

[24] *Ibid.*

[25] *Ibid.*

[26] Beyond this, the Study Group has recommended in s. 5 of its Draft Legislation, *supra*, footnote 7 at p. 39, that the Code set out a specific list of details which must be contained in each report. This provision is a statutory embodiment of what is already common practice.

[27] For this reason, counsel for the defence in *R. v. Deforge* (1971), 5 C.C.C. (2d) 255 (Ont. Dist. Ct.) attempted (unsuccessfully) to have his client remanded under the Mental Health Act by a judge different from the one who was trying the accused on the indictment.

[28] Poole, "Committing the Mentally Ill in Ontario" (1963-64), 6 Crim. L.Q. 92 at p. 94. The author makes this point with regard to s-s. 38(2) of the Mental Hospitals Act, R.S.O. 1960, c. 236 which contained, at that time, virtually the same remand provision which exists now under s-ss. 14(2) and 15(2) of the Mental Health Act. See also *R. v. Benson and Stevenson* (1951), 100 C.C.C. 247 (B.C.C.A.). Swadron, "Remands for Psychiatric Examination in Ontario" (1963-64), 6 Crim. L.Q. 102 points out (at p. 110) that if Poole is correct, then the same evidentiary problem exists with reports provided as a result of remand under the Code.

[29] (1971), 5 C.C.C. (2d) 255 (Ont. Dist. Ct.).

placed before him under s. 15 of the *Mental Health Act, 1967* ..."[30]

Because law and psychiatry agree that most people are fit, it is the philosophy of most psychiatrists that the criteria used should be such that most people will be found fit. In his examination of the accused, therefore (which may take as little as ten minutes), the psychiatrist will typically ask the following questions:

1. Does the accused know what he is charged with?
2. Does he know the consequences of a conviction on the charge(s)?
3. Does he know what an oath is?
4. Does he know the penalty for lying under oath?
5. Does he know the purpose of the trial?
6. Does he know who the people in the courtroom are?
7. Does he know what pleas are open to him?
8. Does he know the consequences of the pleas?

In addition, the accused's ability to concentrate and participate will be assessed, as will his ability to instruct (or perhaps more accurately, receive instructions from) counsel.

Although it is usually only necessary in the more difficult cases,[31] some psychiatrists may run the patient/accused through a whole series of organic and psychological tests as a part of standard procedure. The advantage of doing this is to enable the doctor to make a diagnosis which may assist defence counsel in deciding whether or not to raise the defence of insanity and perhaps later substantiate that defence. Normally where this defence is contemplated, however, counsel will have had the accused thoroughly examined well in advance of the arraignment. One further advantage is to provide the basis for a pre-sentence report by the psychiatrist in the event that the accused is convicted.

Besides an assessment of the accused's fitness to be tried, a psychiatrist will typically include in his report an opinion as to whether the accused requires immediate treatment (in cases where he is suicidal, for example), whether he is certifiable, and whether it is necessary for his mental health that the trial take place without unnecessary delay. Where the accused is charged with a relatively minor offence, the psychiatrist may express an opinion that although technically fit, the accused ought to be hospitalized rather than tried.

It is fair to say that the substantial majority of those persons remanded for psychiatric examination are ultimately found fit by the courts to stand their trial.[32] In a relatively recent statistical study[33] con-

---

[30] *Ibid.*, at p. 258.

[31] Two of the more troublesome disorders with which an examining psychiatrist may be confronted are the paranoid and manic depressive psychoses. In the case of the former, the patient may be extremely secretive and uncooperative with the doctor. In the case of the latter, the patient may be perceptive and keenly alert, yet susceptible to abnormally imprudent judgment. See Coon, " Psychiatry for the Lawyer: The Principal Psychoses" (1946), 31 Cornell L.Q. 327 at p. 331 and Cooper, "Fitness to Proceed: A brief look at some aspects of the medico-legal problem under the New York criminal procedure law" (1972), 52 Nebraska L. Rev. 44 at p. 51.

[32] See Law Reform Commission of Canada, Study Paper, "Fitness to Stand Trial", at p. 24.

[33] Jobson, *op. cit.* footnote 19, at p. 196.

ducted in Nova Scotia over a period of two years, the figure was found to be 78 per cent.[34] Although the frequency of remanding defendants for examination varies depending on the judge, prosecutor or defence counsel,[35] it is legitimate to ask whether in light of the apparent rarity of unfitness the remand procedure is being unnecessarily employed. One Provincial Court Judge with whom the writer consulted said that although he has had the issue of fitness tried before him many times and has therefore frequently utilized s-s. 543(2), he has not yet in his career found an accused unfit. Perhaps the most satisfactory explanation for this problem lies in the disparity between the statutory tests used for determining "remandability" and those used for determining fitness. A judge may well be proven correct in his belief that the accused is "mentally ill" or "mentally disturbed" or that the "balance of the mind of an accused is disturbed", without the accused being necessarily legally "insane". In fact, the judge's suspicion seems most often to be confirmed by the examining doctors. In a study made in 1966 in England[36] it was discovered that only 29 per cent[37] of those persons remanded were considered by the examining doctors to be mentally normal. Yet psychiatrists are reluctant to equate abnormality with unfitness; though abnormality among remand cases may be common, unfitness is rare.[38]

Another point which must be considered is that a prisoner who is unfit at the time he is remanded not uncommonly regains sufficient stability during the 30 or 60-day period to be considered fit to be tried by the end of that time. As Wily and Stallworthy have noted: "Some patients may be very temporarily unfit to plead, as a result of acute manic, depressive or schizophrenic episodes, but with modern treatment a very few weeks in a psychiatric ward will usually make them well enough to stand their trial ... ".[39] In the case of mentally defective or retarded patients, the examination period may, in fact, be used to "coach" the patient on what his trial is all about, in order that he will have sufficient understanding to be found fit.[40] On the other hand, some defendants who are either guilty or are certain they will be found guilty if tried, make very poor patients for the simple reason that they have no incentive to become fit;

---

[34] This percentage represented 72 out of the 97 accused persons remanded for 30-day observation periods.

[35] Schlatter, "An Empirical Study of Pre-Trial Detention and Psychiatric Illness in the Montreal Area — Legal, Psychiatric and Administrative Aspects" (1969), 15 McGill L.J. 326 at p. 334. "Some judges", says the author, "send as many as 50 per cent of their cases for assessment. In the experience of a Crown Prosecutor, of approximately 500 cases prosecuted, only 5-6 were sent for pre-trial assessment. In the experience of a Defense Attorney, over a period of 15 years, he came across only 10 cases dealing with insanity and unfitness to stand trial in Montreal."

[36] Sparks, "The Decision to Remand for Mental Examination" (1966), 6 Brit. J. Criminology 6. See table II at p. 10.

[37] This percentage represents 143 out of a sample of 494 accused persons remanded for examination.

[38] Wily and Stallworthy, in their book *Mental Abnormality and the Law* (New Zealand, N. M. Peryer Ltd., 1962), stress (p. 362) that "from a psychiatric point of view, it is rare that a prisoner is unfit to plead ...".

[39] *Ibid.*

[40] From communication with forensic psychiatrists.

their anxiety at the approach of the end of the remand period often produces a relapse.[41]

In summation, both the Criminal Code and Mental Health Act have their problems. Although in theory the primary purpose of the remand for mental examination is to obtain evidence which will aid in a determination of the accused's capacity to undergo a trial, what happens very often is that it is used as a speedy method of commitment. Perhaps one explanation for the frequency of remands and relative scarcity of unfit defendants is that judges use the remand procedure as a means for diverting from the criminal trial process persons whom they feel are mentally ill. And, of course, it is arguable in the case where a very minor charge (such as vagrancy) has been laid that the accused never really belonged in the criminal process to begin with.

The role of the examining psychiatrist is an odd one. Along with the unusually influential position come many serious ethical questions which the psychiatrist is left alone to decide. Personal judgment will determine whether a mentally defective defendant should be coached into a borderline state of fitness, whether institutionalization should be recommended for a mentally ill but technically fit person, or whether a remand case should be admitted as an involuntary patient.

III. When Is The Issue Tried?

There are no provisions in provincial statutes for a formal trial of the fitness issue. Subsection 543(1) of the Criminal Code is the only one which may be used. It provides that the issue may be raised "at any time before verdict". Once the issue of fitness to stand trial arises, the trial judge retains a discretionary power to delay trying the issue. As para. (4) (a) and s-s. (7) of s. 543 state:

> "(4) (a) where the issue arises before the close of the case of the prosecution, the court, judge or magistrate may postpone directing the trial of the issue until any time up to the opening of the case for the defence;
>
>   ...
>
> "(7) where the court, judge or magistrate has postponed directing the trial of the issue pursuant to paragraph (4) (a) and the accused is acquitted at the close of the case for the prosecution, the issue shall not be tried."

The practical effect of these subsections is to allow the court, if it chooses, to test the validity of the charges in order to see whether or not the trial itself need continue. There may, for instance, be a lack of jurisdiction; or the indictment may be defective or totally unsupported by

---

[41] *Ibid.*

evidence.[42] In such case, a quashed indictment, directed verdict or non-suit would render the question of fitness to proceed academic. Because the criteria upon which the court must exercise its discretion are not set out in the Code, the question arises whether a decision not to postpone trial of the fitness issue is reviewable. In England, where the equivalent of para. 543(4)(a) provides that the court must have regard to "the nature of the supposed disability", expediency, and "the interests of the accused",[43] it has been held that either a failure to exercise discretion or an incorrect exercise of that discretion may quash a subsequent finding of unfitness.[44] It may be questioned whether similar criteria are not impliedly applicable in Canada.

Paragraph 543(4)(a) and s-s. (7) are the result of an amendment to s-s. 524(2) of the 1967 Code under s. 47 of the Criminal Law Amendment Act[45] and are modelled after s-s. 4(2) of England's Criminal Procedure (Insanity) Act 1964.[46] Although these provisions have no doubt affected trial practice in both countries, it may be questioned whether prior to their enactment the courts were precluded by procedural law from reserving the fitness issue. In the 1953 English case of *R. v. Roberts*,[47] Devlin J. (as he then was) held:

> "I can find no authority in the cases cited which would prevent counsel for the defence, who wishes to test the prosecution's case on the general issue, from having the right to do so, at the same time preserving all those rights which flow to the defence from the fact that the defendant is a person, if it be so established, who is incapable of being communicated with or from instructing counsel for his defence. Were it otherwise, I think the gravest mischief and injustice might follow. The defence might wish to tender a witness who, if he was believed, could prove that the defendant was ten miles away at the time of the alleged crime. It cannot, I think, be our law that, by some formality of procedure, counsel for the defendant should be prevented from laying matters of that sort before the jury, and so achieving for his client, if he can, a verdict of Not Guilty."[48]

Here Devlin J. implied that the state of the law at that time was such that the entire case for both sides could be presented before determination of the fitness issue. He relied on *R. v. Berry*,[49] where the issue of fitness was left with the jury to decide at the same time as the general issue of guilt or innocence,[50] producing in that case a verdict of "guilty

---

[42] These examples were suggested in the Report of the Study Group, "Fitness to Stand Trial", at p. 4.

[43] Subsection 4 (2) of the Criminal Procedure (Insanity) Act, 1964 (U.K.), c. 84.

[44] See *R. v. Webb*, [1969] 2 Q.B. 278 (C.A.) and *R. v. Burles*, [1970] 2 Q.B. 191 (C.A.). These cases outline fully the English criteria upon which the discretion should be exercised.

[45] 1968-69 (Can.), c. 38.

[46] *Supra*, footnote 43.

[47] [1953] 2 All E.R. 340.

[48] *Ibid.*, at p. 344.

[49] (1876), 1 Q.B.D. 447.

[50] Hereinafter referred to as "the general issue".

but unfit". If the decisions in these cases accurately reflected the law in Canada as well as England, it would seem that the postponement provisions enacted by the Criminal Procedure Insanity Act 1964 in England and the Criminal Law Amendment Act 1968-69 in Canada constitute a restriction of procedural freedom since they demand a trial of the fitness issue before the opening of the case for the defence. Although *Berry* and *Roberts* were followed in the case of *R. v. Pickstone*,[51] when the matter arose four years later in *R. v. Beynon*,[52] the court said: "I know of no case which says that [trying the fitness issue as soon as it arises] is not the proper course to take, apart from *Roberts* case."[53] Rather than apply *Roberts,* the court chose to rely upon a well-known extract from Hale's *Pleas of the Crown* to the following effect:

> "If a man in his sound memory commits a capital offence and before his arraignment becomes absolutely mad, he ought not by law to be arraigned during such his phrensy, but be remitted to prison until that incapacity be removed; the reason is because he cannot advisedly plead to the indictment ... "[54]

It has been pointed out,[55] however, that the decision in *Beynon* should be given little weight in light of the fact that this quotation (which was supplied by the prosecution) was lifted out of context. Lord Hale had qualified his remarks by saying:

> "... in case any doubt appear upon the evidence touching the guilt of the fact ... and if there be no colour of evidence to prove him guilty ... then upon the same favour of life and liberty it is fit it should be proceeded in the trial, in order to his acquittal and enlargement."[56]

Regardless of what the former state of the law was, it is now clear that under para. (4)(a) of s. 543 the issue of unfitness must be tried before an allegedly unfit defendant is allowed to present his defence. By s-s. (6) a verdict of unfitness means suspension of the trial and indefinite detention of the accused in custody. Apart from the fact that this procedure may result in the long-term imprisonment of an innocent person, it has often been pointed out[57] that the passage of time may seriously jeopardize the defence's case when and if it is ultimately presented. For this reason, it has been recommended by the Law Reform Commission of Canada that the fitness issue be postponable until after a complete trial

---

[51] [1954] Crim. L.R. 565.
[52] [1957] 2 W.L.R. 956.
[53] *Ibid.*, at p. 959.
[54] Hale, *Pleas of the Crown* (London, Professional Books Ltd., 1911), vol. 1, at p. 34.
[55] Swayze, "Fitness to Plead under Section 524 of the Criminal Code" (1966), 2 U.B.C. L. Rev. 514 at p. 519. See also Ryan, *op. cit.* footnote 5, at p. 48.
[56] Hale, at pp. 35-6.
[57] See Note (1961), 59 Michigan L. Rev. 1028 at p. 1094; Halyk, "Prosecution Only of the Criminally Responsible" (1969), 17 Chitty's L.J. 298 at p. 301; Law Reform Commission of Canada, Study Paper, "Fitness to Stand Trial", at p. 5.

of the general issue.[58] This approach is, in effect, a return to the practice advocated in the *Berry* case;[59] the fitness issue need only be tried should the accused be found "guilty", in which case a finding of unfit would quash that verdict.

It is clear that the issue of fitness may be raised by the prosecution[60] or by the presiding judge acting on his own motion,[61] despite the objections of the defence.[62] It is, however, most often the case that the defence brings the matter to the court's attention.[63] Because he owes a duty not only to his client but to the court as well, the defence counsel who has doubts concerning the accused's mental condition is in a difficult spot. It may be that the accused, having no desire to spend an indeterminate amount of time in prison or in a mental hospital (with no guarantee he will ever come to trial) should he be found unfit, would object strenuously to any suggestion that the issue be raised. Whether counsel should respect such objection, however, in turn depends on whether his client is competent to instruct him.[64] On the other hand, counsel may have what he feels is an excellent defence which does not depend on his client's participation. Even assuming the defence were to fail, *R. v. Williams*[65] has held that a failure by defence counsel to raise the fitness issue will not deprive his client of his right under s. 543.

As the *Williams* case demonstrates, the issue of fitness may actually be raised after the verdict, *i.e.*, on appeal. This is true even where the appellant is appealing on grounds relating solely to the trial of the general issue and despite his wishes. In *R. v. Green*[66] evidence of unfitness arose several days after an application for leave to appeal a murder conviction was filed. It was held that although no statutory provision existed for such procedure in England, the issue of fitness had to be tried before the appeal would be heard.

---

[58] Law Reform Commission of Canada, *Mental Disorder in the Criminal Trial Process* (Ottawa, Information Canada, 1976) at pp. 16-7.

[59] (1876), 1 Q.B.D. 447.

[60] See British Royal Commission on Capital Punishment, 1949/53, *Report,* Cmnd. 8932 (London, H.M.S.O., 1953) at p. 77.

[61] *R. v. Beynon, supra,* footnote 52 *per* Byrne J. at p. 958; see also Williams, *Criminal Law: the General Part,* 2nd ed. (London, Stevens and Sons, 1961) at p. 434. Furthermore, in *R. v. Dashwood,* [1943] 1 K.B. 1 Humphreys J. stated (at p. 4): "It does not matter whether the information comes to the court from the defendant himself or his advisors or the prosecution, or an independent person, such as, for instance, the medical officer of the prison where the defendant has been confined." And see the Committee on Legislation and Psychiatric Disorder, *The Law and Mental Disorder Three: Criminal Process,* C.M.H.A., 1973, at p. 130.

[62] Law Reform Commission of Canada, Study Paper, "Fitness to Stand Trial", at p. 2.

[63] Whitlock, *Criminal Responsibility and Mental Illness* (London, Butterworths, 1963) at p. 127.

[64] Counsel is thus faced with an ethical problem for which logic provides no solution. He will be forced to resolve the question on the basis of what he feels to be his client's state of mind. See Swadron, *Detention of the Mentally Disordered* (Toronto, Butterworths, 1964) at pp. 284-5; and *The Law and Mental Disorder Three, supra,* footnote 61 at p. 130.

[65] (1929), 50 C.C.C. 230 (Ont. C.A.). See also *R. v. Smith,* [1936] 1 D.L.R. 717 (Sask. C.A.) and *Kolacz,* [1950] V.L.R. 200; *Reference re R. v. Gorecki (No. 1)* (1976), 32 C.C.C. (2d) 129 (Ont. C.A.).

[66] [1962] Crim. L.R. 823 (C.C.A.).

Although by virtue of the 1968-69 amendment to the Criminal Code[67] there now exists in Canada the right to appeal against a verdict of unfitness,[68] there does not appear to be any appeal from a finding of fitness to stand trial. Rather, a finding that the accused is fit is *reviewable* only upon an appeal against conviction; an incorrect finding of fitness will overturn the conviction.[69]

IV. The Judge's Discretion To Try The Issue

Subsection (1) of s. 543 provides that a trial of the issue of fitness *"may ... where it appears that there is sufficient reason"*[70] be directed by the court. The wording here suggests two things: first, that the test is subjective in that there needn't actually *be* sufficient reason to doubt the accused's fitness; secondly, as the word "may"[71] implies, even where a judge has decided there is sufficient reason to doubt the accused's fitness, he may still choose *not* to have the issue tried. The cases, however, do not support such interpretation.[72]

To begin with, the issue of whether or not there is sufficient reason to doubt the accused's fitness has been held to be a question of law, not fact. This makes a judge's "discretion" under s-s. 543(1) reviewable by

---

[67] Paragraph 603(2)(a) as enacted by s. 55 of the Criminal Law Amendment Act, 1968-69 (Can.), c. 38.

[68] Paragraph 603(2)(a) provides:

"(2) A person who
    (a) is found unfit, on account of insanity, to stand his trial may appeal to the court of appeal against that verdict. . . ."

In England, this right was established for the first time by s. 2 of the Criminal Procedure (Insanity) Act, 1964. The first appeal under this section was *R. v. Clarke,* [1966] Crim. L.R. 447. Formerly, it was held that as a finding of insanity at the time of trial was not a conviction, there could be no appeal therefrom. See *R. v. Larkins* (1911), 6 Cr. App. R. 194.

[69] *R. v. Gibbons* (1946), 86 C.C.C. 20 (Ont. C.A.), *per* Hope J.A. at pp. 32-3. It may be questioned whether this state of affairs corresponds with the English law. While *R. v. Jefferson* (1908), 24 T.L.R. 877 has been interpreted as standing for the general principal that no appeal lies against a finding of fit to plead (see Wily and Stallworthy, *op. cit.* footnote 38, at p. 365), it should be noted (1) that the appeal in that case was filed *after* conviction (thus rendering the principle *obiter* when applied to appeals immediately pursuant to the finding of fitness) and (2) that according to the more recent decision of *R. v. Podola,* [1959] 3 W.L.R. 718, the English Court of Criminal Appeal has jurisdiction to hear an appeal against a finding of fitness which is brought after conviction on the main issue. *Quaere* whether this is not really an appeal against the conviction itself.

[70] Emphasis added.

[71] "May" according to s. 28 of the Interpretation Act, R.S.C. 1970, c. I-23, is a permissive term, as opposed to the imperative "shall" which appears in s-s. 543(3).

[72] The authorities indicate that the word "may" must be treated as *imperative* wherever the purpose of the provision in which it appears is the furtherance of justice or the enforcement of a legal right. See Crankshaw, *Criminal Code of Canada,* 6th ed. (1935) at p. 17; *Frensom v. New Westminster* (1897), 2 C.C.C. 52 (B.C.); *R. v. Barlow* (1693), 2 Salk. 609, 91 E.R. 516; *Aitcheson v. Mann* (1882), 9 P.R. 473 (C.A.); *Julius v. Bishop of Oxford* (1880), 5 App. Cas. 214 (H.L.).

the appeal courts. In *R. v. Couture,*[73] the Quebec Court of King's Bench said:

"By the terms of s. 967 [now 543(1)] of The Criminal Code, the judge may exercise his discretion only when it appears to him that there is some good reason for doubting that the accused is then, because of insanity, in condition to conduct his defence. If he has not some good reason for doubt, the matter is closed. That is a question of law reserved for the judge, foreign to the jury, which is called upon to adjudicate only upon the evidence that may be adduced before it on the question of the mental sanity of the accused."[74]

The appeal courts have made it their policy to second-guess the trial judge, ascertaining for themselves whether grounds for doubt in fact (in law?) existed. In the old Ontario Court of Appeal case of *R. v. Leys*[75] for instance, a magistrate's failure to direct a preliminary trial on the question of the defendant's sanity when there was sufficient reason to doubt fitness resulted in an order for the accused's discharge. There the convicting magistrate was aware of pending proceedings to commit the accused. Similarly, in *R. v. Smith*[76] the Saskatchewan Court of Appeal found that psychiatric evidence adduced during the course of the trial that the appellant was a "congenital mental defective with a mental age of an average normal child of about eight and a half years"[77] should have made it apparent to the court that there was sufficient reason to doubt the accused's fitness.

The question which must now be raised is: what constitutes sufficient reason to doubt a defendant's fitness to stand trial ? In *R. v. Wolfson*[78] it was held that the mere insistence by counsel for the defence was not, without the production of evidence in support of the application, sufficient to raise doubt in the trial judge's mind. "To hold otherwise", said Smith C.J.A., "would amount to the conclusion that [the trial judge] was bound to submit this issue to the jury even though he had no sufficient reason to doubt that the accused was fit to conduct his defence."[79] It may be questioned, however, whether Canadian courts would be justified in adopting the procedure followed in the English case of *R. v. Vent.*[80] That was also a case of the trial judge's refusing to have the issue tried upon the unsupported application of defence counsel, although there the judge consulted with the prison medical officer before reaching that decision. If counsel's application was not in itself sufficient to raise doubt in the judge's mind, why speak with the medical officer? The Court of Criminal Appeal held that in light of the opinion that the medical officer had given, there had been no sufficient reason to empanel

[73] (1947), 4 C.R. 323.
[74] *Ibid.,* at p. 325.
[75] (1910), 17 C.C.C. 198.
[76] [1936] 1 D.L.R. 717.
[77] *Ibid.*
[78] [1965] 3 C.C.C. 304 (Alta. C.A.).
[79] *Ibid.,* at p. 316.
[80] (1935), 25 Cr. App. R. 55.

a jury, ignoring the possibility that the judge may have resolved his doubts by, in effect, trying the issue of fitness himself and calling his own witnesses.[81] It should be noted that since the enactment of the Criminal Procedure (Insanity) Act 1964 in England it has been held that the fact that the trial judge doubted the accused's fitness and on the strength of that doubt adjourned the case in order to read medical reports and question the prison doctor, was insufficient to require a trial of any preliminary issue of fitness.[82]

The type of evidence that will give rise to doubt as to an accused's fitness is discussed by implication in the case of *R. v. Dashwood*.[83] There the English Court of King's Bench, in holding that the trial court had properly exercised its discretion in not directing a preliminary trial of the fitness issue, said:

> "We ask ourselves: Where is the evidence that that was his state of mind at the time of the trial? No medical report or statement of any sort or description has been furnished to us which would afford any ground for such a holding by us. When we look at the nature of the crime ... and the circumstances of the crime ... and the long, careful, well-expressed statement which was made by the appellant ... we can find no justification for assuming that the appellant was so insane at the time of the trial that he was unable to appreciate his own action in refusing to raise a defence ...".[84]

When there is nothing else to go on, judges will sometimes direct a trial of the accused's fitness solely on the basis of the nature of the offence with which the accused is charged.[85] According to some judges, however, this is clearly incorrect. As one American Superior Court Judge has put it: "... it must appear that there is reasonable ground and the Court must exercise discretion. . . .It cannot be done arbitrarily, or merely because of the nature of the charge."[86]

One final point. In all of the reported cases referred to, the issue on appeal has been whether the trial judge was justified in *not* directing a trial of the issue fitness. It is interesting that although cases can be found appealing a finding of unfitness, there is a dearth of situations in which the trial judge's decision to try the issue of fitness has itself been challenged as being an incorrect exercise of discretion. The decisions

---

[81] On the other hand, there seems to be little difference between the procedure followed here and the possibility provided by the Code of the judge's remanding the accused for observation and later deciding on the basis of the psychiatric report not to have the issue tried.

[82] See *R. v. MacCarthy or (McCarthy)*, [1966] 2 W.L.R. 555. This case highlights the distinction between English and Canadian legislation. In England, under s-s. 4(1) of the Criminal Procedure (Insanity) Act, 1964 the issue must "arise" before it will be tried; mere doubt in the mind of the trial judge does not, apparently, raise the issue.

[83] [1943] 1 K.B. 1.

[84] *Ibid.*, at pp. 3-4.

[85] From communication with Provincial Court Judges.

[86] *People ex rel. Apicella v. Superintendent of Kings County Hospital* (1940), 18 N.Y.S. 2d 523 at p. 524 (Sup. Ct. King's County).

referred to, in justifying a judge's refusal to try the issue for lack of sufficient reason, only serve to emphasize the difficulty in establishing the proper circumstances in which a direction should be made. Is this because the judge's discretion, though reviewable when no trial is ordered is non-reviewable when a trial is ordered needlessly? If this is so, then in such circumstances the test of "sufficient reason" is indeed subjective as the wording of s-s. 543(1) originally indicated.

V. Trial Of The Issue

A. THE TEST OF FITNESS

The issue which must be determined, according to s-s. 543(1) is "whether the accused is then, on account of insanity, unfit to stand his trial". Because the wording of the subsection seems to equate fitness to stand trial with capacity to conduct one's defence, the implication is that "insanity" by itself will not amount to unfitness; it must be a type which renders the accused incapable of conducting his own defence. Conversely, it appears that incapacity to conduct one's defence is not sufficient to call for a finding of unfitness; the incapacity must be due to insanity.[87]

What is involved in the capacity to conduct one's defence? To begin with, it has often been said that an ability to "understand the proceedings",[88] or to "understand the *nature* of the proceedings", [89] or to "[follow] the evidence with understanding"[90] is required. Because it has been held that a certain amount of intellect is necessary for this task,[91] the problem which has arisen is one of degree: how much intellect is necessary?

In *R. v. Pritchard*[92] the trial judge stressed that "it is not enough that [the accused] may have a general capacity of communicating on ordinary matters."[93] In that case the jurors were told that the accused must

---

[87] Perhaps this is putting too fine a point on the matter. Ryan, at p. 45, has suggested that what appears at first to be a double-barrelled test is in fact illusory; "the definitions of legal insanity all include, by necessary implication", he says , "the fact of fitness to stand trial". The author concludes that "There is, in reality, only one test — that of fitness to stand trial — and the use of the word 'insanity' in the section serves only as moral justification for the subsequent incarceration of the person found to be unfit". But note the contrasting viewpoint of Lewin, "Incompetency to Stand Trial: Legal and Ethical Aspects of an Abused Doctrine" (1969), Law and Social Order 233 at p. 239, to the effect that the question of fitness is, in practice, frequently submerged in "the rhetoric of psychiatric diagnosis".

[88] *R. v. Woltucky* (1952), 103 C.C.C. 43 at p. 47 (Sask. C.A.).

[89] *R. v. Berry* (1876), 1 Q.B.D. 447 at p. 451.

[90] Wily and Stallworthy, *op. cit.* footnote 38, at p. 360.

[91] *R. v. Berry, supra,* footnote 89.

[92] (1836), 7 C. & P. 303, 173 E.R. 135.

[93] *Ibid.,* at p. 135 E.R.

understand the *details* of the trial. The practical difficulty which this test produces for the examining psychiatrist has been expressed in this way:

> "To be able to detail his reasons why the defendant lacks capacity to understand the proceeding against him ... involves the psychiatrist in a process fraught with professional peril. He must himself 'understand' the proceeding to be able to gauge the lack of understanding of the defendant. The fact that many psychotics are manifestly incapable of understanding matters of far less complexity does not logically qualify the psychiatrist to undertake the task. Many who are referred for his examination will not be psychotics; it is equally true that many may fail to understand the proceedings on grounds quite irrelevant to the state of their mental health."[94]

On the other hand, it is unlikely that in order to be fairly tried an accused person must be a graduate from Harvard Law School. It is most probable that the accused, to be fit, need only have a general comprehension of the proceedings and the evidence. As one Crown attorney has put it:

> "You cannot expect a person to be able to understand in the finer terms because even our learned gentlemen of the Bench at times have difficulty doing that. His understanding need only be in those terms in which the ordinary person would understand what was going on."[95]

As a matter of fact, it may well be that a defendant whose intellectual capacity is less than that of a normal person will be found fit. Because there are gradations of mental defectiveness and retardation, persons of subnormal intelligence have been held to be unfit in some instances[96] and fit in others.[97] Perhaps the most carefully formulated[98] expression of the "understanding" test, then, appears in words of Devlin J. (as he then was) in the *Roberts* case:

---

[94] Cooper, "Fitness to Proceed: A brief look at some aspects of the medico-legal problem under the New York criminal procedure law" (1972), 52 Nebraska L. Rev. 44 at p. 51. See also Figari, "Competency to Stand Trial in Texas" (1971), 25 S.W.L.J. 279 at p. 284 where the author states: "The need for the psychiatrist to be fully aware of the nature of the proceedings facing the accused cannot be over-emphasized. No opinion on the competency of an accused can be complete without consideration of the severity of the charges, the complexity of the case, and the demands which may be made upon the accused during the course of trial. Obviously, standing trial on a charge of murder or tax evasion involves the need for considerably greater ability to assist counsel than does standing trial for theft or driving while intoxicated. If the psychiatrist underestimates the level of mental competency required, he may send an incompetent accused to face proceedings he does not understand. On the other hand, if he overestimates the demands that will be placed upon the accused, he will unfairly deprive a competent accused of his right to a speedy trial."
[95] Bull, "Fitness to Stand Trial" (1965-66), 8 Crim. L.Q. 290 at p. 294.
[96] See *R. v. Smith*, [1936] 1 D.L.R. 717 (Sask.C.A.) for example.
[97] See the *Garbella* case noted by Bull, at pp. 291-2 and 294 for example.
[98] For the reason outlined in footnote 94.

"... if there are no certain means of communication with the defendant so that there are no certain means of making sure that he will *follow as much as it is necessary that he should follow of the proceedings at his trial,* he should then be found unfit to plead."[99]

Another familiar element of the capacity to conduct one's defence is the ability to "instruct counsel".[100] It has been suggested that this term is a misnomer; in reality, it has been said, a defendant only supplies counsel with whatever information he may have concerning the case to enable counsel to in turn advise him and handle his defence.[101] If one accepts that the ability either to instruct or to inform counsel is a necessary prerequisite to making a proper defence, it is difficult to see why retrograde amnesia has not in itself been held to render an accused person unfit to stand his trial in Canada.[102] How can someone who does not remember the incident out of which the charge arose, adequately inform his counsel of what took place? Indeed, the "sound memory" rationale for the fitness rule propounded by Lord Hale suggests that such person should not be tried.[103] In *H. M. Advocate v. Brown,*[104] a case in which the accused was found unfit by reason of insanity unrelated to amnesia, Lord Dunedin of the Scottish Court of Justiciary said in *obiter*:

"There is something which is not generally asked about, and that is that the person who is giving these instructions should not only intelligently, but without obliteration of memory as to what has happened in his life, give a true history of the circumstances of his life at the time the supposed crime was committed." [105]

In the 1946 case of *Russell v. H. M. Advocate,*[106] however, where the accused who was indicted for fraud claimed to be suffering from hysterical amnesia, the *dicta* in *Brown* was expressly not followed. It having been found as a fact that the prisoner suffered from a genuine loss of memory, Lord Sorn held that she was nevertheless capable of instructing counsel, being of otherwise sound mind. Lord Cooper said:

"I do not consider that [the *dicta* in *Brown's* case] were intended to be understood, or are capable of being understood, literally as ap-

---

[99] *R. v. Roberts,* [1953] 2 All E.R. 340 at p. 341 (emphasis added).
[100] See Thompson, "Proof in a Criminal Case" (1955), Law Society of Upper Canada Special Lectures (Evidence) 71 at p. 81; Wily and Stallworthy, *op. cit.* footnote 38, at p. 360; *R. v. Hubach,* [1966] 4 C.C.C. 114 (Alta.C.A.); *R. v. Woltucky* (1952), 103 C.C.C. 43 (Sask.C.A.); *R. v. Gibbons* (1946), 86 C.C.C. 20 (Ont.C.A.).
[101] Bull, at pp. 294-5.
[102] See *R. v. Boylen* (1972), 18 C.R.N.S. 273 (N.S. Mag. Ct.) discussed *infra.* For American cases where amnesia has successfully formed the basis for a finding of incompetency see *Wilson v. United States* (1968), 391 F. 2d 460 (D.C. Cir.); *State v. McClendon* (1966), 419 P. 2d 60 (Ariz.).
[103] Hale, *Pleas of the Crown* (London, Professional Books Ltd., 1911), Vol 1, at pp. 34-5.
[104] [1907] S.C. (J.) 67.
[105] *Ibid.,* at p. 77.
[106] [1946] S.C. (J.) 37.

plying to the case of a sane prisoner ... "[107]

Lord Cooper did concede, however, that loss of memory might be evidence of insanity.[108] What is perhaps noteworthy about this case is that the court seems to have taken the strict approach that in order to be found unfit the accused must first be proven insane.[109] While this implies that insanity has a legal or medical meaning independent of the fitness test, the English approach (as will be more fully discussed below)[110] has been to answer the question of capacity to conduct a defence first; if the accused is found incapable he is automatically stamped with the label "insane". The *Russell* case was approved in the *dicta* of Lord Parker C.J. in the classic *Podola* case.[111] There it was said that had the amnesia been genuine (it was feigned in that case) it would not in itself have amounted to unfitness in the case of an otherwise sane accused. Furthermore, Lord Hale's use of the word "memory" (which was relied on by the defence in this case) was interpreted not as relating to recollection but to a state of mind.[112]

It must be remembered that in both the *Russell* and *Podola* cases, the amnesia being claimed was hysterical. Though both cases imply that where amnesia is symptomatic of an organic or functional psychosis the accused would probably be unfit to stand trial, they are not necessarily authoritative on the subject of organic amnesia.[113] If perhaps an undisclosed reason behind rejecting hysterical amnesia as a ground for unfitness is that it is difficult to differentiate from malingering,[114] it would seem that a claim of organic amnesia would have a better change of succeeding, provided there is medical evidence to support it.

In *R. v. Boylen*[115] a Nova Scotia Magistrate's Court had to consider on a preliminary motion made at the opening of a preliminary inquiry whether amnesia which resulted from a concussion would deprive the accused of his right under s-s. 577(3) of the Criminal Code to make full answer and defence, and of his right to a fair hearing under para. 2(e) of the Canadian Bill of Rights.[116] In coming to its conclusion on the second issue[117] that amnesia, though it might be a disadvantage to the accused, would not render his trial unfair, the Court had this to say:

---

[107] *Ibid.*, at p. 47.

[108] *Ibid.*, at p. 48.

[109] Under s. 2 of the Criminal Lunatics Act 1800 insanity was in fact the only test.

[110] See *R. v. Dyson* (1831), 7 C. & P. 305n; *R. v. Pritchard* (1836), 7 C. & P. 303, 173 E.R. 135; and *R. v. Governor of Stafford Prison, Ex p. Emery* , [1909] 2 K.B. 81, discussed *infra*.

[111] [1959] 3 W.L.R. 718.

[112] *Ibid.*, at p. 731.

[113] This may be caused by cerebral trauma, alcohol, drugs, epilepsy, etc.

[114] See Hays, Note (1961), 29 Medico-Legal J. 27.

[115] (1972), 18 C.R.N.S. 273.

[116] R.S.C. 1970, App. III.

[117] With regard to the first, it was held that s-s. 577(3) was purely procedural and could not be asserted where the accused had yet to be tried since it could not at that time be said that the accused had been denied its protection.

"The fact that *he is not able to instruct counsel* as to the events is part of his defence to the charge ... that fact, of itself, cannot excuse an accused from trial and *does not render him unfit to stand trial.* The point is made by Edmund Davies J. in *Podola* at p. 424:

'Such a plea is easy to advance, and it may be extremely difficult to refute. It affords an obvious and convenient refuge to a person finding himself or herself in a position of grave difficulty and danger — and, the graver the danger the greater the motive for making an assertion of this kind'.

"The inability of an accused, who is otherwise normal, to recall events and not to be able to instruct counsel as is normally done, in my opinion, does not deny him the right to a fair hearing." [118]

What is interesting is that the Court, though it said it accepted as a fact that the accused suffered from a genuine organic amnesia, nevertheless relied on the reasoning which was used in *Podola* for holding a malingerer to be fit. The implication here is that the Court was fearful that the accused was in fact faking. Furthermore, the Court seems to have conceded that the accused was unable to instruct counsel (at least on some important points) yet expressed the opinion that he was still fit to stand trial.

Also involved in the capacity to conduct one's defence are the abilities to challenge jurors,[119] examine and cross-examine witnesses,[120] distinguish and choose between the various pleas available,[121] and testify on one's own behalf.[122] Although it is difficult to conceive of a situation where the accused would possess all of the requisite abilities except the last,[123] it is an interesting question whether in such circumstances the accused would have been found unfit. Perhaps the trial of such person would deprive him of the right to make full answer and defence guaranteed under s-s. 577(3) of the Code. But on the other hand, there are many trials in which the accused never takes the witness stand. What if the accused and his counsel have worked out an excellent defence which does not require the accused's testimony?

The next obvious question which must be answered is what constitutes "insanity" for the purposes of the fitness test. Unhappily, the only definition of the word which appears in the Code[124] pertains to the *defence* of insanity and is of doubtful application to s. 543. In spite of (or perhaps because of) the fact that insanity is a strictly legal concept formulated without regard to medical characterization,[125] it is doubtful

---

[118] *Supra*, footnote 115 at p. 278 (emphasis added).

[119] Wily and Stallworthy, *Mental Abnormality and the Law*, at p. 360.

[120] *Ibid.*

[121] *Ibid.* And see Thompson, *op. cit.* footnote 100, at p. 81.

[122] Bull, *op. cit.* footnote 95, at p. 295.

[123] One psychiatrist with whom the writer consulted recalled a patient/accused who was distracted from his testimony by imaginary electric shocks which were being administered to his testicles by the prosecutor. The intensity of the shocks increased with the intensity of the cross-examination, to the point that the fellow was incapable of answering the questions put to him.

[124] Subsection 16(2).

[125] See Karpman, "Criminality, Insanity and the Law" (1949), 39 J. Crim. L. & C. 584 at p.

whether the word is clearly definable by law. As one author has force-fully stated the problem:

> "'Insanity' as used in the section under consideration is merely the traditionally improper usage of a bundle of vague legal concepts, and its unfortunate choice by Parliament only serves to give an air of certainty to the law where in reality there is none. It adds nothing to the test of whether the accused is capable of conducting his defence, except perhaps to direct the mind of the trier of fact to the mental capabilities of the accused, and it has the obvious defect of either not meaning what it says or being a word so larded over with secondary meanings, conflicting legal and medical definitions and preconceptions, as to be of no value in the Criminal Code."[126]

While "insanity" is generally understood by the psychiatric profession as meaning *psychosis,* the case law demonstrates that there is much truth to the understatement that "law and medicine do not always speak the same language".[127] The law has traditionally stamped with the label "insanity" a variety of disorders falling outside the medical classification of psychosis.[128] As was pointed out by Devlin J. (as he then was) in *R. v. Roberts:*[129] "It is clear from the authorities that it is not merely defects of the mind which may bring about [the result of unfitness]. Defects of the senses, whether or not combined with some defect of the mind, may do so ...".[130] In actual practice, a finding of incapacity to conduct a defence seems inevitably to carry with it a finding of insanity, which suggests that for the law's purposes insanity and incapacity may be the same thing.[131] In *R. v. Dyson,*[132] for instance, the jurors were instructed that "if they were satisfied that the prisoner had not then, from a defect of her faculties, intelligence enough to understand the nature of the proceedings against her, they ought to find her *not sane*".[133] In *R. v. Pritchard*[134] the jurors were told that if they found that there was no certain method of communicating the details of the trial to the accused, they should find him *insane*. And similarly in *R. v. Governor of Stafford Prison, Ex p. Emery*[135] it was held that a finding that the accused was unable to communicate or be communicated with by others amounted to a finding of *insanity* within the meaning of the Criminal

---

585: "It must be first clearly understood that insanity is entirely a legal term comprising behaviour that is grossly and obviously abnormal ...".
[126] Ryan, *op. cit.* footnote 5, at p. 43.
[127] Cooper, *op. cit.* footnote 94, at pp. 54-5.
[128] *E.g.,* deafness, muteness and, at one time, lack of familiarity with the English language.
[129] [1953] 2 All E.R. 340.
[130] *Ibid.,* at p. 341. See also Bull, *op. cit.* footnote 95, at p. 293.
[131] Thus the Code's stipulation that the accused's incapacity must result from insanity in order for a verdict of unfitness to be supported would seem, in practice, to be a red herring.
[132] (1831), 7 C. & P. 305n (emphasis added).
[133] *Ibid.*
[134] (1836), 7 C. & P. 303, 173 E.R. 135
[135] [1909] 2 K.B. 81.

Lunatics Act 1800.[136]

It is an interesting question whether, conversely, medical insanity (*i.e.,* psychosis) must as a rule result in a finding of unfitness. The trend in England appears to be that such is definitely not the case. In *R. v. Rivett*,[137] for example, uncontradicted evidence that the accused was schizophrenic and, in the opinion of the medical witnesses, insane, failed to amount to unfitness in the eyes of an English jury. Although the 1953 British Royal Commission on Capital Punishment[138] suggested that perhaps fitness to plead and medical sanity had become synonymous as far as murder cases were concerned,[139] *R. v. Robertson*[140] would suggest otherwise. There it was held by the Court of Criminal Appeal that if the accused had a complete understanding of the legal proceedings he could be found fit to plead and to conduct his defence notwithstanding the fact that he was a delusional paranoic incapable of acting in his own best interests.

By way of contrast, Canadian courts have tended to equate psychosis with unfitness. In *R. v. Gibbons*,[141] for example, it was the opinion of the Ontario Court of Appeal that a delusional psychosis would in itself render the accused incapable of conducting his defence because it would necessarily impair his ability to instruct counsel. In the case of a paranoid psychotic who suffered from delusions of being persecuted by the police, Martin C.J.S. of the Saskatchewan Court of Appeal said:

> "I cannot think that the accused, while suffering from the delusion as to the machine in the hands of the police, which interfered with his thinking and affected his bodily sensations would be able to follow and understand the proceedings, and to instruct his counsel."[142]

More recent, and perhaps more interesting, is the decision in *R. v. Hubach*.[143] This case involved a depressive psychotic who was disputedly suffering from paranoid delusions. Relying on the *Gibbons* case, Smith C.J.A. of the Alberta Supreme Court Appellate Division ruled: (1) that regardless of the accused's high intelligence, psychosis would deprive him of sufficient *intellect* to instruct his counsel; and (2) that delusions in themselves gave rise to an inference of unfitness. Dissenting on the second point was Johnson J.A. (with whom McDermid J.A. concurred) who said:

> "It would appear to me that many delusions, even those which would justify a person being confined to an institution for the protection of himself and the public, would not necessarily render him

---

[136] 1800 (U.K.), c. 94.
[137] (1950), 34 Cr. App. R. 87.
[138] *Report,* Cmnd. 8932 (London, H.M.S.O., 1953) at p. 77.
[139] *Ibid.,* at para. 220.
[140] [1968] 3 All E.R. 557.
[141] (1946), 86 C.C.C. 20, *per* Robertson C.J.O. at pp. 22, 24.
[142] *R. v. Woltucky* (1952), 103 C.C.C. 43 at pp. 50-1.
[143] [1966] 4 C.C.C. 114 (Alta.C.A.).

unfit to stand trial."[144]

The reasoning behind this statement is perhaps the same as that of the modern text writer who has written:

> "When a Court determines the fitness to stand trial issue, it must take into account the specific crime with which the accused is charged and the particular facts which surround it. An accused person may appear normal in most respects, yet a mental disorder is noticed when reference is made to certain subjects about which he has delusions. If this is true, it would appear possible that a person who is charged with several crimes may be fit to stand trial in respect of some charges, but not in respect of others."[145]

This view is apparently based upon an analogy to the "specific delusions" subsection of s. 16's insanity defence.[146] It is submitted, however, that even if one assumes a relationship between s. 16's definition of insanity and the type of insanity required by s. 543, the delusion rationale should be viewed with a healthy scepticism. Can a man be sane in all other respects excepting the fact that he thinks he's a duck? The assumption that a person might suffer from specific delusions and yet remain otherwise unaffected mentally seems to be based upon the now-discredited theories of phrenology and monomania. Monomania was believed to be a state of mind characterized by the predominance of one insane idea while the rest of the mind remained normal. Phrenology envisioned the brain as being composed of some 27 separate organs each capable of producing a separate trait in an individual.[147] Today it is widely accepted among psychiatrists that delusions are symptomatic of a psychosis, and that so-called focal delusions are always evidence of a wider spread psychopathology.[148]

Although not referred to in the dissenting judgment of Johnson J.A. in *Hubach,* the old Scottish case of *H. M. Advocate v. Robertson*[149] evidences similar reasoning. In holding that the accused was in that case *unfit* to stand trial, the court said :

---

[144] *Ibid.,* at p. 131.

[145] Swadron, *op. cit.* footnote 64, at p. 282.

[146] Subsection 16(3) provides:

> "(3) A person who has specific delusions, but is in other respects sane, shall not be acquitted on the ground of insanity unless the delusions caused him to believe in the existence of a state of things that, if it existed, would have justified or excused his act or omission."

[147] Weihofen, *Mental Disease as a Criminal Defense* (Buffalo, Dennis, 1954) at p. 110.

[148] In 1956 the Royal Commission on the Law of Insanity recommended in its Report (Ottawa 1956) that s-s. (3) be dropped from s. 16. Chapter 10 of the Report stated: "The preponderance of medical evidence condemned the wording of this subsection on the ground that it describes a person who could not exist. The opinion of these witnesses was that no one who has 'specific delusions' could be in other respects sane. We think that from a medical point of view the arguments put forward in support of this opinion are conclusive."

[149] (1891), 3 White 6 (Scot.).

"The peculiarity of the case is that the insanity from which the prisoner suffers is *monomania* referring to particular matters, and that he is not insane upon other points — upon other points he might be entirely intelligent. It is a case of monomania, *but the monomania relates to the very subject matter of the charge.* . . ."[150]

The court went on to apply the *M'Naghten* test of insanity, in effect, saying:

". . . after the evidence of the doctors who examined the prisoner, it is clear that he is *unable, from his mental state, to distinguish between right and wrong,* and cannot give any reasonable instructions for the conduct of his defence."[151]

B. ONUS OF PROOF

In the old English case of *R. v. Davies,*[152] the court considered the matter of fitness a "preliminary inquiry for the information of the Court"[153] as opposed to "an issue joined" and ruled that the onus was, therefore, on the prosecution to prove fitness. Despite the fact that the prosecutor thereupon called several medical witnesses, the jury found the prisoner to be insane. The next year, however, *Davies* was rejected in the case of *R. v. Turton.*[154] There Cresswell J. said:

"Why is a man to be presumed *insane* when called upon to plead? The presumption is that he is sane. I do not see any sufficient reason for deviating from the old practice. If you suggest that the prisoner is not in such a state of mind as to be able to plead to the indictment, you must give evidence of the fact."[155]

Similarly, in the 1918 New Brunswick case of *R. v. Kierstead (No. 2),*[156] the King's Bench of the Supreme Court ruled that the onus of proving unfitness rested on the defence. Relying on *M'Naghten's Case*[157] it was also held that the insanity must be proved to the satisfaction of the jury but not beyond a reasonable doubt. And in 1946 the Scottish Court of Justiciary said in *Russell v. H. M. Advocate*[158] that "The onus is always on the accused to justify a plea in bar of trial . . . to the satisfaction of the

---

[150] *Ibid.,* at pp. 16-7 (emphasis added).
[151] *Ibid.,* at p. 17 (emphasis added).
[152] (1853), 3 Car. & Kir. 328, 175 E.R. 575
[153] *Ibid.,* at p. 575. See also *Ley's Case* (1828), 1 Lewin 239. See *R. v. Budic* (1977), 35 C.C.C. (2d) 272 at p. 278 (Alta. C.A.) where the court expressed the opinion, in *obiter,* that no burden of proof rested on anyone!
[154] (1854), 6 Cox C.C. 385.
[155] *Ibid.,* at p. 385.
[156] (1918), 33 C.C.C. 288.
[157] (1843), 10 Cl. & Fin. 200, 8 E.R. 718.
[158] [1946] S.C. (J.) 37.

court."[159]

Just looking at these four cases it would be easy to conclude that the correct law is that which was stated in the latter three cases, and that the decision in the first should be discounted as an erroneous quirk. As a matter of fact, however, the matter is far from clear cut. In *Halsbury's Laws of England*[160] it is stated that the burden of proving fitness falls upon the prosecutor once the issue is raised. One writer has further stated that this view corresponds with the weight of judicial thinking on the subject.[161] In *R. v. Sharp*[162] Salmon J. held that where the prisoner stood mute, the onus was on the Crown to prove *beyond a reasonable doubt* that he was "mute of malice" as opposed to "mute by the visitation of God".[163] This decision appears to have rested on the reasoning that the Crown's scepticism amounted to an allegation of fraud. The jury having found the accused's muteness to be genuine, the court ruled that although the prisoner was originally presumed to have been fit, the burden of proving fitness shifted to the Crown once doubt arose.

The legitimacy of the view expressed in *Davies* and *Sharp* may be supported by two separate lines of reasoning. First, it has been suggested[164] that because unfitness seems in English law to have arisen otherwise than from insanity (*e.g.*, from muteness), even assuming that the law placed the onus of proving insanity of the defendant in all cases, it would not necessarily follow that the burden of proving unfitness lay on him as well. The problem with this argument, however, is that whenever the English courts have found unfit persons who were not mentally disordered, they have nevertheless insisted on bringing them within the word "insane" as demanded by s. 2 of the Criminal Lunatics Act, 1800.[165] Even if this difficulty were overcome with regard to the English situation, it is submitted that Canadian case law and the wording of s. 543 of our Criminal Code, which requires that the unfitness be the product of insanity, would most certainly preclude the application of this theory in Canada.

The second argument which has been advanced[166] is that the general rule in *Woolmington v. D.P.P.*[167] should apply; that it is the prosecution's duty to establish all the elements of its case beyond a reasonable doubt. Applying *Crane v. D.P.P.*,[168] it may be contended that because the question of whether a person should have been "given in charge to the jury"[169] is one of the "facts necessary to establish guilt",[170]

---

[159] *Ibid.*, at p. 44.

[160] 3rd ed., Vol. 10 at p. 403.

[161] Prevezer, "Fitness to Plead and the Criminal Lunatics Act, 1800", [1958] Crim. L.R. 144 at p. 150.

[162] [1957] 1 All E.R. 577.

[163] This test was propounded by Alderson B. in *R. v. Pritchard* (1836), 7 C. & P. 303, 173 E.R. 135.

[164] Note, "Fitness to Plead and Onus of Proof" (1959), 103 Sol. J. 781.

[165] See *Dyson, Pritchard* and *Ex parte Emery, supra,* at p. 70.

[166] Dean, "Fitness to Plead", [1960] Crim. L.R. 79 at pp. 82-3.

[167] [1935] A.C. 462 (H.L.).

[168] [1921] 2 A.C. 299 (H.L.).

[169] *Ibid.*, at p. 319.

[170] *Hill v. Baxter,* [1958] 1 All E.R. 193.

the prosecution cannot be said to have met its responsibility under *Woolmington* until that question is answered by the Crown with affirmative proof.

In *R. v. Podola*[171] the *M'Naghten* exception to the *Woolmington* general rule was, in effect, applied and the cases of *Davies* and *Sharp* overruled. [172] The rules concerning onus of proof were stated as follows:

"1. In all cases in which a preliminary issue as to the accused person's sanity is raised, whether that issue is contested or not, the jury should be directed to consider the whole of the evidence and to answer the question 'Are you satisfied upon that evidence that the accused person is insane so that he cannot be tried upon the indictment?' If authority were needed for the principle, it is to be found in the very words of the section itself.

"2. If the contention that the accused is insane is put forward by the defence and contested by the prosecution, there is, in our judgment, a burden upon the defence of satisfying the jury of the accused's insanity. In such a case, as in other criminal cases in which the onus of proof rests upon the defence, the onus is discharged if the jury are satisfied on the balance of probabilities that the accused's insanity has been made out.

"3. Conversely, if the prosecution alleges and the defence disputes insanity, there is a burden upon the prosectuion of establishing it."[173]

With regard to this last point, it was held in *R. v. Robertson*[174] that unfitness, if alleged by the prosecution, must be proved beyond a reasonable doubt.[175]

What effect does a prior finding of unfitness have upon the onus of proof in the case of an accused who, after detention in custody, is returned for trial? Where this issue arose in the case of *R. v. Woltucky*,[176] the Saskatchewan Court of Appeal held, applying *Prinsep and East Indian Co. v. Dyce Sombre*,[177] that in these circumstances it becomes the Crown's task to establish the prisoner's sanity. Yet four years later *R. v. Levionnois*[178] raised the possibility that *Woltucky* was decided incorrectly and that s-s. 16(4) of the Criminal Code placed the burden on the accused in all cases. The problem was not solved here because the judge considered it unnecessary to decide the question, there having been no injustice to the appellant-accused on this account as the burden had in fact been placed upon the Crown by the trial judge. Relying on *Wigmore On Evidence*[179] the Court held that any presumption of insani-

---

[171] [1959] 3 W.L.R. 718 (C.C.A.).

[172] *Ley's Case* (1891), 3 White 6 (Scot.) was also overruled.

[173] *Supra,* footnote 171 at p. 729.

[174] [1968] 3 All E.R. 577 (C.C.A.).

[175] What if the issue is raised by the court? In this situation, might the onus of proving sanity fall on the prosecutor? If so, what would be the quantum of proof required?

[176] (1952), 103 C.C.C. 43.

[177] (1856), 10 Moo. P.C.C. 232, 14 E.R. 480.

[178] (1956), 114 C.C.C. 266 (Ont.C.A.).

[179] 3rd ed. (Boston, Little Brown, 1940), vol. IX, s. 2491 , at p. 289-90.

ty, if it existed, disappeared upon the crown's adducing *some* evidence to the contrary. In *R. v. Roberts*,[180] however the standard of proof borne by the Crown was "to the reasonable satisfaction of the jury".

C. EXPERT EVIDENCE

In the old English case of *R. v. Goode*[181] it was held that a jury might, solely from their own observation of his demeanour and without medical evidence being adduced, find the defendant unfit to plead. This case, if it is still good law, calls into question both the strength of the presumption of fitness and the value of psychiatric evidence. With regard to the first problem, one commentator has concluded that the presumption exists only to the extent that neither the prosecution nor defence need prove fitness, and that it can be rebutted simply by raising a reasonable doubt![182]

With regard to the second problem, *R. v. Rivett*[183] is another case worth noting. There it was held by the English Court of Criminal Appeal that a jury was entitled to entirely overrule the unchallenged evidence of three eminent medical witnesses that the accused was insane and unfit to stand his trial. The Court said:

> "... it is for the jury and not for medical men of whatever eminence to determine the issue. Unless and until Parliament ordains that this question is to be determined by a panel of medical men, it is to the jury, after a proper direction by a Judge, that by the law of this country the decision is to be entrusted. This Court has said over and over again that it will not usurp the functions of the jury..."[184]

What is interesting about this case is the fact that the medical witnesses were allowed to express their opinions on the issue of fitness in the first place. As a general rule of evidence, expert testimony will not be *admissible* unless the subject-matter of the trial or inquiry involves issues beyond the competence of a lay jury to determine if unaided by such experts.[185] According to *Goode*, unfitness would seem to be an issue entirely within the jury's competence to decide by themselves. Certainly it is not one which the medical witness has been specifically trained to determine. As one writer has pointed out:

> "It should be noted that the concept of incompetency as it exists in the law does not exist in medicine. No physician within the frame-

---

180 (1975), 24 C.C.C. (2d) 539 at p. 549 (B.C.C.A.).

181 (1837), 7 Ad. & El. 536, 112 E.R. 572.

182 Note, "Fitness to Plead and Onus of Proof" (1954), 103 Sol. J. 781.

183 (1950), 34 Cr. App. R. 87.

184 At p. 94.

185 *Kelliher v. Smith*, [1931] S.C.R. 672; affg [1930] 2 W.W.R. 638 (Sask.C.A.) which reversed [1929] 3 W.W.R. 655; *Taylor v. Gray*, [1937] 4 D.L.R. 123 (N.B.C.A.); *R. v. Kuzmack* (1954), 110 C.C.C. 338 (Alta.C.A.) affd without reference to this point, [1958] S.C.R. 292; *R. v. Fisher,* [1961] O.W.N. 94 (C.A.).

work of his science or his experience alone can sensibly state that a given individual is incompetent. Incompetency is a legal definition, not amenable to precise medical standards of mental health."[186]

Furthermore, the admission of psychiatric opinion on the issue of fitness would seem to be an obvious violation of the ultimate issue rule.[187] It is doubtful whether this means much, however, in light of the impotence to which that rule has been reduced in recent years. It is noted in *Halsbury's Laws of England*, for instance, that the rule does not apply to cases where insanity is raised as a defence to accusations of crime.[188] The judgment of Hall J. in *R. v. Lupien*[189] suggests that it may be on the way out in all cases where psychiatric opinion is expressed on the issue of intent. In practice, psychiatric witnesses are commonly required to express an opinion not only as to their diagnosis of the accused but as to his fitness to be tried.[190] And despite the result produced in *Rivett,* where the issue is tried by a judge alone (as is most often the case in Canada) it is extremely rare in practice that the opinion which the psychiatrist expresses will be rejected.

VI. Results Of The Trial Of The Issue

If the accused is found fit to stand his trial, the trial of the general issue will proceed without further delay.[191] Should the accused be found unfit, s-s. 543 (6) has this to say:

> "(6) Where the verdict is that the accused is unfit on account of insanity to stand his trial, the court, judge or magistrate shall order that the accused be *kept in custody until the pleasure of the lieutenant governor of the province is known,* and any plea that has been pleaded shall be set aside and the jury shall be discharged."[192]

Although one would expect the normal procedure to be the speedy removal of the accused to a psychiatric facility, the Code is hardly explicit on this point. It seems quite possible under s. 545 for an accused person to remain *jailed* indefinitely without ever being sent to a mental hospital.[193] Furthermore, although para.(1)(b) of that section empowers

---

[186] Comment, "Criminal Law — Insane Persons — Competency to Stand Trial" (1961), 59 Mich. L. Rev. 1078 at p. 1100.
[187] *Halsbury's Laws of England,* 3rd ed., vol. 15, at p. 323 expresses the rule this way: "An expert cannot usually be asked to express an opinion upon any of the issues, whether of law or fact, which the court or jury have to determine ...".
[188] Vol. 15 at p. 323.
[189] [1970] 2 C.C.C. 193 at p. 205 (S.C.C.).
[190] See *R. v. Woltucky* (1952), 103 C.C.C. 43 (Sask.C.A.).
[191] Subsection 543(5).
[192] Emphasis added.
[193] See Chapter 8, *post.*

the lieutenant-governor to discharge the accused, this must be read in the light of s-s. 543(8):

> "(8) No proceeding pursuant to this section shall prevent the accused from being tried subsequently on the indictment unless the trial of the issue was postponed pursuant to paragraph (4)(a) and the accused was acquitted at the close of the case for the prosecution."[194]

Another interesting point about s. 545 is that it allows the lieutenant-governor to make an order once the accused has been found to be "insane". The test is *not* whether the accused is incapable of conducting his defence by reason of insanity (which was the issue determined by the trial). So it would seem possible for an order to be made concerning an accused person who has been found insane, yet perfectly capable of conducting his defence, if such person exists.

VII. Conclusions

The requirement that an accused person be mentally fit to stand his trial, though it sounds simple enough, is an extremely difficult one to implement. When Parliament enacted s. 543 it knew that it just was not cricket to try a mentally incapacitated person, for the simple reason that the poor fellow would not have a sporting chance. That would be like hunting moose with a bazooka. Yet civil libertarians would contend that it is equally unsportsmanlike to deprive a presumably innocent individual of his freedom for a long period of time. In response to this argument, it is submitted that Parliament should adopt the recent proposal of the federal Law Reform Commission for dealing with the issue of fitness. Such proposal would make the issue postponable either until the Crown has established a *prima facie* case *or* until the end of the trial itself.[195] In the Law Reform Commission's words:

> "After presentation of the case for the prosecution, the trial judge has three possibilities: he may, on motion by the defence, acquit the accused; he may, on motion by the defence, postpone the issue to the end of the trial; or he may order a hearing on the accused's fitness to stand trial. He would only postpone the determination of the issue to the end of the trial where defence counsel has demon-

---

[194] In practice it is relatively rare, unless the charge is an extremely serious one, for the accused to be returned for trial upon his recovery. See Whitlock, *op. cit.* footnote 63, at p. 128. Apart from the fact that the passage of time could seriously harm the accused's defence, a subsequent trial might work grave injustice in the event of conviction if no reduction in sentence were received for the amount of time spent in detention.

[195] See Law Reform Commission of Canada, *Mental Disorder in the Criminal Trial Process*, pp. 16-7.

strated that he has a case to present and that it would be in the interests of justice to proceed on the merits of the charge."[196]

It is further submitted that the lieutenant-governor's warrant is an inappropriate means for disposing of those persons who are ultimately found to be unfit to stand trial. For this reason the Law Reform Commission has recommended that a variety of orders be available to the courts. Where the accused is chronically unfit but of no apparent danger to himself or others, he should be released subject to the possibility of reindictment and trial if his condition improves sufficiently.[197] Where the accused is not dangerous and can be effectively treated as an out-patient, an order to attend a psychiatric facility for treatment would seem preferable to institutionalization.[198] Lastly, where the accused is considered to be in need of intensive treatment and supervision, he should be made the subject of an "order for mandatory hospitalization". Such order would differ from a warrant of the lieutenant-governor in that it would avoid the possibility of indefinite incarceration in jail:

"An order for mandatory hospitalization [runs] until the accused regains fitness or until six months have elapsed . . . . If at the end of the six month maximum the accused has not regained fitness, the disposition must be reviewed by the court. It can be then renewed for subsequent periods of up to one year, but in cases where the charge is not one for which imprisonment is an appropriate sanction, or where the length of time the accused has been detained as unfit approximately equals the sentence of imprisonment to which, in the opinion of the judge, the accused would have been sentenced if his trial had proceeded and he had been found guilty, the order should not be renewed. If, at that time, the accused is so mentally deranged as to warrant further hospitalization, he could be detained under the appropriate provincial legislation."[199]

---

[196] *Ibid.*, at p. 16.
[197] *Ibid.*, at pp. 18-9.
[198] *Ibid.*, at p. 19.
[199] *Ibid.*

Part II

The Trial Stage

Chapter 4

Automatism

I. Introduction

The defence of automatism is one which the courts have traditionally received with a great deal of scepticism — and for good reason. It is a defence in which the accused, in effect, says: "I did it, but I didn't do it". Frequently asserting that mental impairment was responsible for his actions (or omissions), the accused nevertheless defends his sanity and demands to be allowed to leave the courtroom a free man at the end of the day.

The law pertaining to automatism is complex and fraught with inconsistencies. During the course of this chapter an attempt will be made to discern judicial trends and reconcile policies. Primarily the discussion will endeavour to define automatism in the context of its relationship to other defences, as well as survey the circumstances which may give rise to the defence and explain their medical and/or psychiatric bases. In addition, some evidentiary problems will be examined and, in the end, suggestions offered for reforming the law of automatism.

II. Automatism Defined

Automatism, though it may vitiate the mental element in crime, does not necessarily derive its status as a defence from a negation of *mens rea*. More fundamentally, it is a denial of criminal liability's other essential ingredient — *actus reus*.[1] In order to explain the reasoning behind

---

[1] For a differing opinion, see Smith and Hogan, *Criminal Law,* 3rd ed. (London, Butterworths, 1973) at pp. 34-5.

this proposition it is necessary to resort to basic principles and terminology.

An act, for legal purposes, has been defined by Holmes[2] as a muscular contraction produced by an operation of the *will.* The dictionary in turn defines will as: (1) "the power of *conscious* and deliberate action or choice"; or (2) "the process of *volition*".[3] From this it would seem that in the absence of either consciousness or volition no exercise of the will and, therefore, no act is possible.

Before defining consciousness, let us examine the concept of volition. As one would expect, the dictionary calls it simply "the act of willing; exercise of the will".[4] Can volition exist without consciousness? Judging from this somewhat circular definition plus the fact that will depends on consciousness (whatever that is) the answer would seem to be no.[5] Consciousness, on the other hand, is not a function of volition. It is clear, however, that consciousness alone is an insufficient basis for criminal liability. If there is consciousness but no volition there can be no exercise of the will, therefor no act, and hence no crime. It is upon this premise that the defence of physical compulsion,[6] for example, rests.

Given this background, how exactly does automatism fit into the picture? Is the essence of the defence simply the lack of volition; or must this lack of volition stem from unconsciousness? Differences in the way this question has been answered indicate the unwholesome ambiguity which the term automatism has traditionally had in law. In *Watmore v. Jenkins,*[7] for example, Winn J. of the English Queen's Bench remarked that the word automatism was "no more than a modern catchphrase which the courts have not accepted as connoting any wider or looser concept than *involuntary* movement of the body or limbs of a person."[8] Similarly in *R. v. Sibbles*[9] it was said that the defence would cover any unexpected circumstances which deprived the defendant of all control — such as a swarm of bees attacking the driver of a car.

Other cases, however, suggest that unconsciousness is the essence of the defence. Indeed, the weight of authority seems to point toward this view. As early as 1889, for instance, Stephen J. stated the defence of automatism in this way:

"... can anyone doubt that a man who, though he might be perfectly sane, committed what would otherwise be a crime in a state of somnambulism, would be entitled to be acquitted? And why is this? Simply because he would not *know* what he was doing."[10]

---

[2] *The Common Law* (Boston, Little Brown, 1963) at pp. 45-6.
[3] *Webster's New Twentieth Century Dictionary,* 2nd ed. (New York, World, 1971) (emphasis added).
[4] *Ibid.*
[5] But this would seem to depend upon the way in which the word "consciousness" is used. See *R. v. Connolly* (1965), 49 C.R. 142 (N.S.C.A.) discussed *infra.*
[6] *E.g.,* where A seizes B's hand and by superior force compels him to strike C.
[7] [1962] 2 All E.R. 868.
[8] *Ibid.,* at p. 874 (emphasis added).
[9] [1959] Crim. L.R. 660 *per* Paull J. at p. 661.
[10] *R. v. Tolson* (1889), 23 Q.B.D. 168 at p. 187 *in obiter* (emphasis added).

Likewise in *R. v. Charlson*[11] the question to be answered, according to Barry J., was whether the accused "knew what he was doing" when he struck his son with a mallet. If he did not, then he could not be held responsible.

In the famous *Bratty*[12] decision, the Court of Criminal Appeal in Northern Ireland defined automatism as "unconscious involuntary action" and said it was a defence "because the mind does not go with what [is] being done." Similarly, the New Zealand Court of Appeal said in *R. v. Cottle*[13] that automatism was simply "action without knowledge of acting, or action with no consciousness of doing what was being done." And in *Hill v. Baxter*,[14] Lord Goddard suggested that automatism was the mere performance of acts in a state of unconsciousness.

If automatism is essentially unconscious behaviour the next question which must logically be asked is whether *all* unconscious behaviour is necessarily automatism in law. Psychiatrically the term seems to have been confined to "*complex* activity of the *voluntary musculature* occurring in a person who is in a state of defective consciousness."[15] The behaviour, in other words, must be something more than the random movements of sleep or epileptic seizure. Though the legal definitions do not appear to have adopted this distinction[16] one might well wonder why not. Must reflex and convulsive movements of the type mentioned be labelled automatism in order to escape being classified as acts in the strict legal sense? Textwriters have traditionally categorized them as non-acts without the slightest mention of the term.[17] Surely the lumping of basic autonomic reflex behaviour together with the intricate and seemingly purposeful actions of a sleepwalker under the broad umbrella of "automatism" only serves to detract precision from the word.

In at least one Canadian decision the court refrained from categorizing what it found to be "unconscious" behaviour as automatism. The case of *R. v. Connolly*[18] was an unusual instance where unconsciousness provided an entirely different defence. There the accused had been convicted of unlawfully assaulting a peace officer engaged in the execution of his duty. According to the evidence, the officer had been struck while attempting to assist the accused who was bleeding profusely as the result of a head injury suffered in a fight. Medical evidence indicated

---

[11] [1955] 1 All E.R. 859 at p. 864.
[12] *Bratty v. A.-G. Northern Ireland,* [1961] 3 W.L.R. 965 at p. 972 (H.L.).
[13] [1958] N.Z.L.R. 999 at p. 1020.
[14] [1958] 1 All E.R. 193 at p. 195.
[15] McCaldon, "Automatism" (1964), 91 Can. Med. Assoc. J. 914 at p. 914 (emphasis added). "This definition", the writer points out, "excludes complex movements under autonomic control, for example, intestinal peristalsis, and simple movements of the limbs such as those made during sleep or anesthesia."
[16] In *Bratty v. A.-G. Northern Ireland, supra,* footnote 12 at p. 978, Lord Denning said that automatism included "an act which is done by the muscles without any control by the mind such as a spasm, a reflex action or a convulsion; or an act done by a person who is not conscious of what he is doing such as an act done whilst suffering from concussion or whilst sleep-walking."
[17] See Hall, *Principles of the Criminal Law* (Indianapolis, Bobbs-Merrill, 1947) at p. 388; Holmes, at pp. 45-6.
[18] (1965), 49 C.R. 142 (N.S.C.A.).

that by the time the accused had reached the hospital he had lost so much blood that he was in danger of going into shock. The doctor who administered the treatment said "it was definitely possible that Connolly at an earlier time could have had no control over or knowledge of his motions; that the nature of the injury could cause a loss of consciousness so that he would not know what he was doing."[19] On this basis a finding of guilty was overturned by the Nova Scotia Supreme Court in Banco. The reasons for this decision, however, are surprising. Rather than conclude that the defendant was suffering from automatism at the time of the alleged assault,[20] the Court preferred to rule that the Crown had not established *mens rea* with regard to the essential elements of the crime. Specifically, the majority held, it was not shown that the accused in his injured state knew that the person he was hitting was a police officer. In the words of Currie J. (MacQuarrie, Bissett, and Coffin JJ. concurring):

> "It is my opinion that due to the severity of the injuries to his forehead and to the vortex of the skull, the accused was not able to form a rational intent to unlawfully assault a peace officer in the execution of his duty. . . .
> "The evidence here does not establish that there was a criminal intent to commit the unlawful act charged in the information. No doubt the condition of his mind was blameworthy, but it was rendered so by the beating he received at the restaurant and not by any motive of an assault upon the policeman. In other words, so far as the act of violence against the policeman is concerned, it was an unconscious act *qua* the policeman."[21]

And later:

> "I am satisfied upon the evidence and under all the circumstances of the case that the accused did not have the specific knowledge at the time of the assault that the man he assaulted was a police officer in the execution of his duty...
> "If there is any doubt as to the accused's mental condition at the time of the assault, that doubt should be resolved in favour of the accused. The accused had no recollection of having assaulted a policeman. His evidence should not lightly be regarded. At the same time *I do not think that there should be applied to his condition the term automatism.*"[22]

Although the Court referred to the accused's attack on the police officer as an "unconscious act",[23] it is clear that the meaning it attached

---

[19] *Ibid.*, at p. 146.
[20] The author of the practice note which is appended to this case as reported has concluded that in fact lack of *actus reus* (in the form of automatism) was the underlying basis for the acquittal here.
[21] *Supra,* footnote 18 at p. 148.
[22] At p. 149 (emphasis added).
[23] *Ibid.,* at pp. 148-9.

to the term "unconscious" was different from that associated with automatism. In quoting *R. v. Davies*[24] it is apparent that the Court placed *mistake* in the category of unconscious acts. In *Davies,* Channell J. had said:

> "It may be that the criticism of counsel for appellant is correct and the judge was misled into drawing the wrong deduction from the maxim that the law presumes a man to intend the natural consequences of his acts, which can only mean his conscious acts, not his mistakes."[25]

The *Connolly* case, therefore, dramatizes the ambiguity of the term "unconscious". Because automatism would seem to depend on unconsciousness, the significance of assigning a meaning to the word must be apparent. The law assumes that one is either conscious or one is not.[26] Medicine, on the other hand, prefers to speak of various levels of consciousness. McCaldon,[27] for instance, has listed five. They are:
1. full awareness;
2. clouded consciousness;
3. delirium;
4. stupor;
5. coma.

Coma, he has pointed out, is no consciousness at all. In the legal sense, therefore, the movements (if any) of a person in a comatose condition can truly be said to be unconscious. And yet such movements are not what is meant medically by automatism. Rather, says McCaldon, it is in the states of clouded consciousness, delirium or stupor that automatism may occur.

Although McCaldon offers five degrees of consciousness, it is submitted that these are as arbitrary as the law's brutal conscious/unconscious distinction. To speak of two or five or three or sixteen levels of consciousness is pointless; who is to say how many there are? Surely between any two designated states there are infinite shadings of consciousness. The point to be made is that consciousness and unconsciousness are not absolute terms in medicine. The difficulties, therefore, in proving unconsciousness by means of expert evidence are considerable.

What do the courts mean when they say that an automaton must not "know" what he is doing?[28] How does one prove that an accused person did not know what he was doing at a certain time in the past? Is it sufficient proof that someone did not know what he was doing if he can-

---

[24] (1913), 8 Cr. App. R. 211.

[25] *Ibid.,* at p. 213.

[26] The practice note to *R. v. King* (1962), 38 C.R. 52 (S.C.C.) (states flatly at p. 53) "There are (1) conscious acts; and (2) unconscious acts." But see *R. v. K.,* [1971] 2 O.R. 401 at p. 404 where Lacourciere J. spoke of the accused (who was acquitted) as having been in a state of "*diminished* consciousness" (emphasis added).

[27] "Automatism" (1964), 91 Can. Med. Assoc. J. 914 at p. 914.

[28] See *R. v. Tolson* (1889), 23 Q.B.D. 168; *R. v. Charlson,* [1955] 1 All E.R. 859; *Bratty v. A.-G. Northern Ireland,* [1961] 3 W.L.R. 965 (H.L.) and *R. v. Cottle,* [1958] N.Z.L.R. 999.

not remember it afterwards? In *R. v. Schonberger* [29] Culliton J.A. (as he then was) of the Saskatchewan Court of Appeal expressed the view that "amnesia itself would not be a defence to the charge of murder", and that "It is only evidence of a state of mind that might be a defence to the charge."[30]

Amnesia, though it is nearly always present after an automatic episode, is not in itself medical proof of automatism either. Usually, however, memory is irretrievable in true cases of automatism.[31] This fact can be explained by reference to the well-recognized theory in psychiatry that memory involves three consecutive processes: *registration, retention* and *recall*.[32] Suffice it to say that registration is something analogous to the formation of an image on a photographic plate. Basically it is the simple result of one's paying attention.[33] Psychiatrists have found that mental disorder may impair attentiveness.[34] Retention means exactly what it says: the permanent fixing of a memory in the mind once it has registered. Lastly, recall is the ability to "remember" a memory which has been registered, retained and, in effect, filed away. Psychogenic automatism (*i.e.,* automatism resulting from inorganic causes[35]) and so-called "normal" automatism (*e.g.,* somnambulism) are said to impair registration, thus making recall impossible. This seems logical since, by definition, an automaton is unconscious and registration depends on attentiveness. Organic automatism (*i.e.,* caused by cerebral trauma, drugs, alcohol, temporal lobe epilepsy, etc.) will perhaps impair retention as well as registration. Grossly defective recall, on the other hand, may simply be feigned amnesia or may be symptomatic of a genuine *hysterical* amnesia.[36] Hysterical amnesia which represents a failure of recall alone[37] is *not* indicative of automatism, being merely an exaggeration of the natural human tendency to repress unpleasant memories.[38] Furthermore, the fact that this form of amnesia is potentially recoverable — either through hypnosis, the use of abreactive drugs, or quite often spontaneously — is proof of prior registration and retention.[39] In short, the presence of this form of amnesia points to conscious behaviour rather than to automatism. Some writers have gone so far as to argue that repression is indicative of guilt and that amnesia due

---

[29] (1960), 126 C.C.C. 113.

[30] *Ibid.,* at p. 123.

[31] McCaldon, *op. cit.* footnote 27, at p. 914; Whitlock, *Criminal Responsibility and Mental Illness* (Butterworths, London, 1963) at p. 119; Wily and Stallworthy, *Mental Abnormality and the Law* (Christchurch, N.Z., Peryer, 1962) at p. 398.

[32] McCaldon, at p. 915; O'Connell, "The Defence of Amnesia" (1958), 26 Medico-Legal J. 25 at p. 25.

[33] O'Connell, at p. 25.

[34] *Ibid.*

[35] See *R. v. Cullum* (1973), 14 C.C.C. (2d) 294 (Ont. Co. Ct.).

[36] For a discussion of the difference between feigned amnesia and hysterical amnesia see Hays, "Hysterical Amnesia in the Podola Trial" (1961), 29 Medico-Legal J. 27.

[37] Hysterical amnesia can also represent a dissociative reaction. See McCaldon, at p. 918; *R. v. Parnerkar, infra; R. v. Cullum, infra,* pp. 104-6.

[38] O'Connell at pp. 25-6.

[39] *Ibid.,* at p. 25.

[40] *Ibid.,* at p. 26.

to failure of recall should weigh against the accused rather than in his favour.[40]

III. When Is Automatism Not A Defence?

Hopefully the uncertainties surrounding the meaning of the word automatism have been adequately demonstrated. It is perhaps safe to say that whatever else automatism may be it is *generally* a complete defence to all criminal charges, including those which involve strict liability. In *R. v. Minor*,[41] Martin C.J.S. stated that "when a person is unconscious *from any cause* ... he has a good defence to a criminal act performed by him when in that condition." However, since the cause of automatism in that case was brain damage resulting from a blow to the eye, the remarks of Martin C.J.S. must be taken as *obiter* insofar as they seek to encompass unconscious behaviour resulting from other causes.[42] In fact there are two instances in which automatism will *not* in itself amount to a defence. They are: (1) when it is caused by "disease of the mind";[43] and (2) when it is caused by the voluntary consumption of alcohol and/or drugs.

A. WHEN CAUSED BY A DISEASE OF THE MIND

An unconscious accused, by definition, cannot know what he is doing at the time of an alleged offence. Couched in these terms, the defence of automatism is strongly reminiscent of s. 16's definition of insanity:

> "(2) For the purposes of this section a person is insane when he is in a state of natural imbecility or has disease of the mind to an extent that renders him incapable of appreciating the nature and quality of an act or omission or of knowing that an act or omission is wrong."

Because s. 16 has been held not to exclude from its provisions any person behaving automatically while rendered unconscious by disease of the mind,[44] any automatism caused by such disease will be labelled "insane automatism". In these circumstances the result is that the defence of

---

[40] *Ibid.*, at p. 26.
[41] (1955), 112 C.C.C. 29 at p. 34 (Sask. C.A.) (emphasis added.).
[42] *R. v. Hartridge* (1966), 57 D.L.R. (2d) 332 at p. 348 (Sask. C.A.).
[43] Technically, one might say that automatism caused by disease of the mind is not automatism at all, but rather insanity. While some writers speak of "insane automatism" and "sane (or non-insane) automatism", Morris and Howard, *Studies in Criminal Law* (Oxford, Clarendon, 1964) at p. 62 have confined the term automatism to "involuntary action performed in a state of unconsciousness not amounting to insanity".
[44] *R. v. O'Brien* (1965), 56 D.L.R. (2d) 65 (N.B.C.A.) *per* Ritchie J.A. at p. 80.

insanity *alone* is left open to the accused.[45]

Below are some examples of what the law has recognized as being diseases of the mind.

(i) Epilepsy

Medically, epilepsy has been defined as a chronic functional disease characterized by seizures.[46] These seizures are the product of what are called "neuronal discharges" in the brain and may take different forms, depending upon the part of the brain in which the discharges originate. Where the discharge originates in the upper brain stem or diencephalon, a *grand mal* or *petit mal* attack may ensue.[47] While a *grand mal* seizure involves unconsciousness and extreme convulsions, the *petit mal* variety involves unconsciousness only.[48] Following either form of seizure, an individual may pass into a state of altered consciousness ("fugue state") in which he may behave in an automatic fashion.[49] Where the discharge originates in the cortex of the cerebrum's temporal or frontal lobes, *psychomotor* epilepsy may result.[50] Here the epileptic may suffer a major motor seizure, sometime followed by a fugue, or pass directly into the fugue state.[51]

Epilepsy may result from a variety of causes such as tumours, chemical and metabolic disorders, brain injury, or infections of the nervous system such as meningitis.[52] The organic origin of the disease and the fact that many epileptics do not show signs of their abnormality except while suffering attacks has led many neurologists and psychiatrists to describe epilepsy as a disease of the brain — not the mind. In *Bratty v. A.-G. Northern Ireland,*[53] however, the House of Lords held the accused's psychomotor epilepsy to be a disease of the mind for the purposes of the *M'Naghten* rules. In doing so, they raised the question of whether all forms of epilepsy necessarily constituted diseases of the mind in all circumstances. Both Viscount Kilmuir L.C. and Lord Morris of Borth-Y-Gest, relying on the medical testimony adduced at trial, accepted without question that psychomotor epilepsy was in all cases such a disease. It is to be remembered, however, that Lord Denning justified his classification of the disease on these grounds:

"The major mental diseases, which the doctors call psychoses, such as schizophrenia, are clearly diseases of the mind. But in *Charlson's*

---

[45] *Bratty v. A.-G. Northern Ireland,* [1961] 3 W.L.R. 965 (H.L.).

[46] Dorland, *The American Illustrated Medical Dictionary* (1951), cited in Smith, "Medico-Legal Facets of Epilepsy" (1953), 31 Texas L. Rev. 765 at p. 766 and in Mitchell, "Legal Problems of Epilepsy" (1956), 29 Temple L.Q. 364 at p. 364.

[47] Knox, "Epileptic Automatism and Violence" (1968), 8 Med. Sci. and The Law 96 at p. 96.

[48] Mitchell, at p. 373-4.

[49] Knox, at p. 96.

[50] *Ibid.*

[51] *Ibid.*

[52] Fabing and Barrow, "Medical Discovery as a Legal Catalyst: Modernization of Epilepsy Laws to Reflect Medical Progress" (1955), 59 Nw. U.L. Rev. 42.

[53] *Supra,* footnote 45.

case, Barry J. seems to have assumed that other diseases such as epilepsy or cerebral tumour are not diseases of the mind, even when they are such as to manifest themselves in violence. I do not agree with this. It seems to me that *any mental disorder which has manifested itself in violence and is prone to recur is a disease of the mind.* At any rate it is the sort of disease for which a person should be detained in hospital rather than be given an unqualified acquittal."[54]

Under this test the legal status of epilepsy which has resulted in non-violent behaviour remained in doubt. In *R. v. Ditto,*[55] however, the fact that psychomotor epilepsy had been held to provide an insanity defence to a charge of theft passed without exception in the Alberta Supreme Court (Appellate Division). In *R. v. O'Brien*[56] the New Brunswick Court of Appeal decided that psychomotor epilepsy was a disease of the mind in all circumstances,[57] despite the fact that the specific charge in that case was attempted murder. Ritchie J.A. reasoned:

> "Applying a fair, large and liberal construction to s. 16 and, notwithstanding the difference in the medical opinion testimony, having regard to the *Bratty* case, *supra,* and also to the *Ditto* case, *supra,* I am clearly of the opinion that the expression 'disease of the mind', as used therein, must be interpreted to include a disease of the brain which has affected the mind, even though such effect is of only temporary duration."[58]

Important here is the fact that diseases of the brain which *may* affect the mind have not been included; the learned judge referred only to those which *have.* What then is the position of the epileptic who has become unconscious at the wheel of his car as the result of a *grand mal* or *petit mal* seizure? Assuming he was unaware of his disease until that point, could he not raise the defence of non-insane automatism on the ground that the attack was confined to his brain and did not produce a fugue state? In Canada there is a dearth of authority on this point, the reported cases being confined to complex automatic behaviour resulting from psychomotor seizures. In *Gootson v. The King* [59] (a civil damages case) it was held that an epileptic driver who caused an accident as the result of an attack could not be found guilty of negligence in the absence of evidence that he knew of his condition. But what if the accused had been charged with dangerous driving? From a policy standpoint it would seem grossly unfair to commit such a person to a hospital for the insane. The justification for detention of violent epileptics, according to Lord Denning, is that of dangerousness. Because our hypothetical epileptic

---

[54] *Ibid.*, at p. 981 (emphasis added).
[55] (1962), 132 C.C.C. 198 (Alta. C.A.).
[56] *Supra,* footnote 44.
[57] See also *R. v. Gillis* (1973), 13 C.C.C. (2d) 362 (B.C. Co. Ct.).
[58] *Supra,* footnote 44 at p. 81.
[59] [1947] 4 D.L.R. 568 (Ex. Ct.); affd [1948] 4 D.L.R. 33 (S.C.C.).

driver is dangerous only when operating a dangerous piece of machinery such as a car, a prohibition from engaging in such activity in the future would seem sufficient.

It is open to debate whether the indefinite detention of violent or larcenous epileptics is a sound policy. Since it has been estimated that over 50 per cent of those subject to convulsive seizures can gain complete control through the use of drugs[60] and that many epileptics whose seizures result from brain injury may respond to surgery,[61] some writers have argued that alternative procedures such as probation with compulsory treatment should be provided by the Criminal Code.[62] On the other hand, there remain those epileptics for whom a reduction in seizures is the most that can be affected through the use of traditional medical techniques. Can it be said that such persons, many of whom behave quite normally for the most part, belong in a facility for the criminally insane? For those who subscribe to Freudian psychology, justification may well exist. Podolsky has suggested that despite the organic origins of the disease, "the seemingly unmotivated, impulsive outburst of dangerous aggression is, in actuality, not without purpose, but is always in some definite, meaningful relation to unconscious conflicts."[63] Furthermore, he has pointed out, *grand mal* convulsions are generally accepted in psychoanalytic circles as being psychosomatic in the sense that they represent a physical expression of pent up destructiveness and rage; nor does the consideration of epilepsy as a purely physiological (as opposed to a psychogenic) condition conflict with this premise.[64] Where no convulsions occur, as in psychomotor seizures, a popular theory is that acts of violence represent the prevail of an unconscious unrestrained by *ego*[65] over the substituted somatization (*i.e.,* convulsions).[66] This theory may be supported by empirical studies which indicate that a high proportion of murderers suffer from epilepsy. In a sample taken by Hill and Pond[67] in 1952, for example, the incidence of epilepsy among murderers tested at random was found to be 32 times that of the general population. What is significant is that none of the murderers showed any indication of having committed their crimes while in a state of epileptic automatism. This finding is consistent with the established view of forensic

---

[60] *President's Committee on the Employment of the Physically Handicapped, Performance 9* (1954), cited in Mitchell, *op. cit.* footnote 46, at p. 365.

[61] Penfield and Jasper, "Epilepsy and the Functional Anatomy of the Human Brain", cited in Fabing and Barrow.

[62] See Beck, "Voluntary Conduct: Automatism, Insanity and Drunkenness" (1966-67), 9 Crim. L.Q. 315 at p. 319; and Edwards, "Automatism and Social Defence" (1965-66), 8 Crim. L.Q. 258 at p. 288.

[63] Podolsky, "The Epileptic Murderer" (1962), 30 Medico-Legal J. 176 at p. 179.

[64] *Ibid.* Stekel, Freud and Fenischel are cited as authority.

[65] *Ibid.* And see Mitchell, *op. cit.* footnote 46, at p. 374.

[66] Podolsky, at p. 179 says: "Extensive individual analysis of Rorschach projections of eighteen murderers by Ernest Schneider suggests that murder could be substituted for an epileptic seizure, whereby the accumulated aggressive impulses are directed against another person instead of against the subject himself."

[67] Cited in Walton, "Some Observations on the Value of Electroencephalography in Medico-Legal Practice" (1963), 31 Medico-Legal J. 15 at p. 21. See also Gunn, "The Prevalence of Epilepsy Among Prisoners" (1969), 62 Proc. Roy. Soc. Med. 60.

experts that murders are very rarely committed as the result of epileptic seizures.[68] As a matter of fact, statistical studies indicate that: (1) violent behaviour of any sort is unusual in epileptic automatisms;[69] (2) the vast majority of epileptics have never experienced fugue state automatism;[70] and (3) amongst those who do experience fugue state automatism it is a relatively rare occurrence for most of them.[71]

(ii) Cerebral Arteriosclerosis

Arteriosclerosis, in plain terms, is a hardening and thickening of arterial walls which reduces blood flow to various organs of the body.[72] In the case of cerebral arteriosclerosis it is the arteries to the brain which are affected.[73] Since this condition is a degenerative process associated with ageing, old or elderly persons are those most commonly afflicted.[74]

Because consciousness is dependant upon the concentration of oxygen in cerebral vessels,[75] it is easy to see how a reduction of blood flow might result in a state of automatism. Although cerebral arteriosclerosis may also lead to a permanent organic psychosis (*i.e.,* medical "insanity"[76]) in the form of *senile dementia,* it is significant that the law has not considered the presence of organic psychosis necessary in order to label arteriosclerotic automatism insanity. In *R. v. Kemp,*[77] for example, the accused was charged with causing grievous bodily harm to his wife when he struck her with a hammer during a lapse of consciousness. The English Court of Queen's Bench found the accused's arteriosclerosis to be a disease of the mind which rendered him temporarily insane within the meaning of the *M'Naghten* rules — despite the following finding of fact:

"There is no general medical opinion upon what category of diseases ought properly to be called diseases of the mind, but it was agreed that arteriosclerosis can in time produce a degeneration of the brain cells by interfering with their blood supply. In the case of the accused, however, the disease had not progressed so far and it

---

[68] Walton, at p. 21.

[69] In the study made by Knox, *op. cit.* footnote 47, none of the 43 epileptics studied had ever exhibited violent behaviour.

[70] In a sample taken by Knox, only 64 out of 434 epileptic patients had ever experienced fugue state automatism.

[71] Knox, at p. 98 has reported that: (1) in 60 per cent of the patients studied it occurred in a minority of attacks; (2) in only 30 per cent did it occur in the majority of attacks; and (3) in only seven per cent was a fit invariably associated with automatic behaviour.

[72] Wily and Stallworthy, *Mental Abnormality and the Law,* at p. 69.

[73] *Ibid.*

[74] *Ibid.,* at p. 20. The authors point out, however, that arteriosclerosis may cause gross physical or mental impairment in persons in their forties or fifties, particularly where high blood pressure is present as well.

[75] Lovett-Doust, Note (1951), 44 Proc. Soc. Med. 347.

[76] Whitlock in his book *Criminal Responsibility and Mental Illness,* at p. 27 has stated: "There is no generally accepted definition of disease of the mind but usually it is assumed to mean one of the major functional or organic psychoses."

[77] [1957] 1 Q.B. 399.

was merely a transient upset of the blood to the brain that caused the temporary state of unconsciousness in which the attack was made."[78]

Similarly, in *R. v. Holmes*[79] Jackson S.P.J. of the Supreme Court of Western Australia instructed the jury that arteriosclerosis, though it was a physical disease, was capable of being considered a disease of the mind insofar as it could affect the mind by temporarily restricting the brain's blood supply.

Should someone who has misbehaved as the result of a transient arteriosclerotic episode be committed to a mental hospital? If an injustice exists, perhaps it is not so great as in the case of epileptic automatons, since arteriosclerosis is an irreversible degenerative process which often leads to a permanent *senile dementia*.[80] The disease generally affects aged people who have a comparatively short time to live and require care and attention anyway.

(iii) Brain Tumour

It is difficult to say whether a cerebral tumour is legally classified as disease of the mind or not. In *R. v. Charlson*[81] Barry J. was clearly of the opinion that it is not. In view of the test laid down by Lord Denning in *Bratty,* however, it may be doubted whether *Charlson* is a good law today. Lord Denning made a point of disagreeing[82] with the assumption of Barry J. that organic brain diseases such as epilepsy and brain tumours would not be diseases of the mind even when they manifested themselves in violent behaviour. It is to be remembered, however, that the remarks of both judges were *obiter* insofar as they pertained to the legal status of diseases upon which they were not required to rule. Nevertheless, the decision in *O'Brien* indicates that Lord Denning's rationale will be followed with regard to all diseases of the brain which affect the mind. And so the problems cited with regard to epilepsy will also exist with regard to brain tumours and most other organic diseases of the mind. Should someone who has misbehaved *non-violently* as the result of a brain tumour be detained indefinitely in a hospital for the criminally insane? Is this the appropriate disposition for an accused who suffers from a brain tumour which can be removed by surgery?

---

[78] *Ibid.,* at p. 400.
[79] [1960] W.A.R. 122.
[80] As Wily and Stallworthy, *op. cit.* footnote 31, at p. 70 have written: "A diffuse and generalized narrowing of all the arteries to the brain may gradually but progressively so reduce the blood flow that many small areas of the brain die from lack of oxygen; although there is no obvious stroke, the patient becomes increasingly irritable, forgetful, unable to concentrate, uninhibited and childish until, perhaps, he arrives at a grossly demented, virtually mindless state."
[81] [1955] 1 All E.R. 859.
[82] [1961] 3 W.L.R. 905 at p. 981.

B. WHEN CAUSED BY VOLUNTARY CONSUMPTION OF ALCOHOL AND/OR DRUGS

The basic rule regarding alcoholic automatism was succinctly stated by Lord Denning in *Bratty*. According to His Lordship: "When the only cause that is assigned for an involuntary act is drunkenness, then it is only necessary to leave drunkenness to the jury, with the consequential directions, and not to leave automatism at all."[83] Although this was the precise situation in *R. v. Hartridge*,[84] Culliton C.J.S. decided in the course of his judgment to expand somewhat on Lord Denning's statement,[85] producing a formula which, in light of the facts, must be taken as partly *obiter*. ". . . where the possibility of an unconscious act depends on, and only on, drunkenness", he stated, "then, depending upon the evidence the defence is either insanity or drunkenness, and not automatism."[86] In other words, if drunkenness causes non-insane automatism, the only defence is drunkenness. But if drunkenness causes insane automatism the defence is insanity.

Hartridge was recently followed by the Ontario Court of Appeal in *R. v. Szymusiak*[87] and seems to be good law in Canada. Whether or not it is fair law is another matter. Professor Beck has criticized the decision[88] on the basis that it resulted from a moral judgment of the act of drinking: "If acute intoxication so affects the brain that an actor is rendered unconscious by his behaviour," he has argued, "he ought not to be held responsible for his acts."[89] Contending, however, that neither an outright acquittal nor a verdict of insanity would be appropriate in such circumstances, Beck has proposed the creation of a separate offence of being drunk and dangerous.[90]

The law regarding drug-induced automatism has in essence developed by way of analogy to alcoholic automatism. The cases suggest, however, that in some circumstances different considerations might apply.

In *R. v. MacIsaac*[91] the accused pleaded not guilty to charges of attempted robbery, robbery, breaking and entering, and theft, saying in his defence that he had been under the influence of LSD. The court found that this had not in fact been the case, adding in *obiter* that the accused's having taken LSD would not have provided him with the

---

[83] *Ibid.,* at p. 982.

[84] (1966), 57 D.L.R. (2d) 332 (Sask. C.A.).

[85] The learned judge seems to have combined this statement with the following remarks made by Lord Denning in *A.-G. Northern Ireland v. Gallagher,* [1961] 3 W.L.R. 619 at p. 640: "If a man by drinking brings on a distinct disease of the mind such as delirium tremens, so that he is temporarily insane within the M'Naghten Rules, that is to say, he does not at the time know what he is doing or that it is wrong, then he has a defence on the ground of insanity: see *Reg.* v. *Davis* and *Beard's* case ...".

[86] *Supra,* footnote 84 at p. 354.

[87] [1972] 3 O.R. 602.

[88] "Voluntary Conduct: Automatism, Insanity and Drunkenness" (1966-67), 9 Crim. L.Q. 315 at p. 315.

[89] *Ibid.,* at p. 322.

[90] See Chapter 6 *post* at pp. 186-7.

[91] (1968), 11 Crim. L.Q. 234 (Ont. Dist. Ct.).

defences of insanity or automatism anyway. In the words of McAndrew
D.C.J.:

> "... the defence advanced is on the same footing as that of drunken-
> ness in that both result from the voluntary consumption of mind-
> changing agents. It may be noted that s. 223 of the Code dealing
> with impaired driving uses the words 'by alcohol or a drug.' "[92]

This view has been accepted in England, as shown by the case of *R. v.
Lipman.*[93] There Widgery L.J. said:

> "For the purposes of criminal responsibility we see no reason to
> distinguish between the effect of drugs voluntarily taken and
> drunkenness voluntarily induced."[94]

As in *MacIsaac,* LSD was the drug involved here. For this reason, it is
submitted that the rulings in both of the above cases are *obiter* insofar
as they seek to encompass drugs other than LSD. Because, as Professor
Beck has pointed out, the law regarding alcoholic automatism has
sprung from a moral judgment of the act of drinking, there may indeed
be reason to distinguish between drunkenness and the effect of drugs
taken for purposes other than intoxication.

What if the accused in *Lipman* or *MacIsaac* had taken insulin instead
of LSD? In *Armstrong v. Clarke*[95] the accused, who was a diabetic, had
gone into hypoglycemic coma while driving, due to an overreaction to an
insulin injection taken previously. He was denied the defence of automatism and convicted of driving "while under the influence of drink or
drug" contrary to England's Road Traffic Act, 1930.[96] It does not follow
from this decision, however, that McAndrew D.C.J.'s reference in
MacIsaac to Canada's impaired driving provisions was a helpful one.
Liability for the offence of impaired driving is founded on considerations
somewhat different from those which underlie the crime of robbery
(which, among other things, is what MacIsaac was charged with). The
ratio decidendi in *Armstrong v. Clarke* was simply that "if people happen to be in a condition of health that renders them subject to comas or
take remedies which may send them into a coma, they must not drive
because they are a danger to the rest of Her Majesty's subjects."[97] Had
Clarke been charged with committing a robbery just prior to the onset of
coma, it is submitted that hypoglycemic automatism would have been
open to him as a viable defence. In *R. v. Quick and Paddison*[98] the
English Court of Appeal held that it was for the *jury* to decide whether
automatism which is self-induced through insulin should provide a complete defence.[99] Indeed juries have acquitted sufferers of self-induced

---

[92] *Ibid.,* at p. 237.
[93] [1969] 3 All E.R. 410 (C.A.).
[94] *Ibid.,* at p. 412. See also *R. v. Mack* (1975), 29 C.R.N.S. 270 (Alta. C.A.).
[95] [1957] 2 Q.B. 391.
[96] 1930 (U.K.), c. 43.
[97] *Supra,* footnote 95 at p. 395
[98] (1973), 57 Cr. App. R. 722.
[99] In *R. v. Sproule* (1975), 30 C.R.N.S. 56 (Ont. C.A.) at p. 64, Kelly J.A. remarked in *obiter,*

hypoglycemia on several occasions.[100]

The voluntary consumption of drugs for medical purposes is distinguishable from the ingestion of alcohol on one very fundamental ground: while in the case of alcohol the physical effects are generally foreseeable, in the case of drugs they may not be. Though it has been held[101] that a condition of impairment, from whatever cause, carries with it a rebuttable presumption that the condition has been voluntarily induced, this presumption will be more easily displaced in the case of drugs. Thus in *R. v. King*,[102] where an accused whose dentist had injected him with sodium pentothal was involved in a car accident on his way home, he was able to state that he knew nothing of the drug's after-effects and avoid conviction for impaired driving.[103]

Interestingly, the presumption of voluntary impairment may be more difficult to rebut when alcohol is consumed after drugs have been taken. *R. v. Pitrie*[104] was another impaired driving case. There the accused had taken a Valium tablet at breakfast, had had several drinks at lunch, and at dinner time was found slumped over the wheel of his car in a ditch on the wrong side of the road. The accused's physician testified that he had prescribed the drug and had not warned Pitrie of the danger of drinking shortly afterward. Despite this evidence, a conviction was entered and was later affirmed on appeal to the British Columbia Court of Appeal. This decision rests, it is submitted, upon the assumption expressed most recently in *R. v. Saxon*[105] that reasonable men are capable of foreseeing the impairing effects of tranquilizers and alcohol when mixed.[106]

---

however, that self-induced hypoglycemia is incapable of being a defence which would entitle a jury to bring a verdict of acquittal.

[100] See *Horton* and *R.*, referred to *infra* at p. 101. Admittedly, these cases involved neither diabetes nor the injection of insulin, and it could be argued that an overdosed diabetic would have the defences of insanity alone open to him. *Quick* expressly held, however, that the temporary effects of an overdose of a drug could not be called "disease of the mind" and that the defence of insanity, therefore, was *not* the only defence open to an overdosed diabetic. (See also the commentary on *R. v. Bentley,* [1960] Crim. L.R. 777). Furthermore, the courts have refrained from calling diabetes itself a disease of the mind. In *R. v. Rogers* (1965), 48 C.R. 90 the British Columbia Court of Appeal avoided the issue by ascertaining that the accused in any event appreciated the nature and quality of his actions and knew that they were wrong.

[101] *R. v. King* (1962), 38 C.R. 52 (S.C.C.).

[102] *Ibid.*

[103] See also *R. v. Bray* (1975), 24 C.C.C. (2d) 366 (Ont. Co. Ct.), where an accused who had consumed a large amount of alcohol after taking a medication which his psychiatrist had prescribed was acquitted on a charge of impaired driving. The court accepted that the accused was in a state of automatism *before* he drank the alcohol as a result of the unforeseen effects of the medication.

[104] (1971), 3 C.C.C. (2d) 380 (B.C.C.A.).

[105] [1975] 4 W.W.R. 346 (Alta. C.A.).

[106] But see *R. v. Burns* (1974), 58 Cr. App. R. 364. In that case the trial judge had failed to direct the jury on the defence of automatism where such condition was allegedly caused by a combination of brain damage, alcohol and drugs. The Court of Appeal concluded (at p. 375) that "there was some evidence of other factors operating upon a disease of the appellant's mind, and of the possibility that he did not appreciate the effect which they might have" and "There was therefore misdirection or nondirection on the issue of automatism ...". The appeal was dismissed, however, on the ground that no miscarriage of justice had occurred, since the jury had obviously disbelieved the accused's story that he was unaware of his actions at the time of the offence.

As shown dramatically by the case of *R. v. Cullum,*[107] the mere fact that alcohol or drugs have combined with other factors to produce a state of automatism does not limit the accused to the defences of drunkenness and insanity. Once drinking or drug-taking enter into the picture, however, there is a tendency for the courts to treat other contributing causes as secondary. *R. v. Sibbles*[108] is a case in point. There the accused was charged with dangerous driving causing death. Sibbles, who had had high blood pressure for several years and had suffered from dizzy spells at one time in his life, went into a state of automatism at the wheel of his car one day after having "about five bottles" of beer. Just prior to the accident he had been arrested on a drunk driving charge but let go again by the police. The defence argued that the emotional disturbance Sibbles had suffered on being arrested had affected his blood pressure, causing a dizzy spell. The dizzy spell had then caused Sibbles to keel over, hitting his head on the windshield. It was this bump, the defence contended, which had ultimately produced the state of automatism. The court rejected this scenario and convicted the accused, saying that either high blood pressure alone or a combination of alcohol and high blood pressure had caused the so-called automatism. In charging the jury the court said: (1) that a man who was subject to dizzy spells ought not to drive, and that such dizzy spells could therefore be no defence; and (2) that a man who drinks knowing he has high blood pressure ought not to drive, and that any resulting automatism is no defence since the defence of automatism was intended to cover totally unexpected circumstances only.

If the offence is one involving specific intent, the inclusion by the defence of factors other than alcohol as an alleged cause of automatism may prove significant even where the defence is not sufficiently made out to be left to a jury. In *R. v. Schonberger*[109] the accused raised organic amnesia as a defence to a charge of murder. In effect, this amounted to a defence of automatism since the amnesia was supposed to have "deprived him of the ability of conscious reason."[110] The defence, however, only seems to have argued lack of specific intent. In any event, it was asserted that this organic amnesia had been induced either by drugs, alcohol, head injury, or a combination thereof. The trial judge left the defence of drunkenness to the jury. On appeal it was held that a new trial should be ordered. In giving his reasons, Culliton J.A. (as he then was) of the Saskatchewan Court of Appeal said:

> "A careful study and review of the full charge made by the learned trial judge satisfies me that he put to the jury only the defence of drunkenness; or it may be more fairly said that he so emphasized the question of alcohol as to leave the jury with the impression that once it had disposed of the question of drunkenness, there was no other defence. ...
>
> "It was for the jury to say on all of the evidence whether the ac-

---

[107] (1973), 14 C.C.C. (2d) 204 (Ont. Co. Ct.), discussed *infra* at pp. 104-6.
[108] [1959] Crim. L.R. 660.
[109] (1960), 126 C.C.C. 113 (Sask. C.A.).
[110] *Ibid.,* at p. 115.

cused had the necessary intent, or whether, not on the question of drunkenness alone, but because of injury, drugs and alcohol, or a combination of these, there was a reasonable doubt as to the capacity of the accused to have such an intent."[111]

IV. Causes Of Non-Insane Automatism

In order for the defence of automatism to be raised successfully some cause for the unconscious behaviour must be offered; a bald statement by the accused that he "blacked out" is in itself insufficient.[112] The category of possible causes is extremely wide, however, with few limitations in theory. With the exceptions of alcohol, drugs and diseases of the mind, any illness[113] or external force[114] which may produce unexpected unconsciousness[115] is a potential basis for the defence of non-insane automatism. While it is not proposed at this point to enumerate each and every circumstance which may give rise to the defence, some of the more interesting ones which have received judicial recognition are set out below.

A. HEAD INJURY

Cerebral trauma is perhaps the classic cause of non-insane automatism. Although *contusion* (bruising) or *laceration* (tearing) of the brain will produce unconsciousness, complex automatic behaviour is more likely to occur in someone who has suffered a less severe injury such as a *concussion*. Concussion may be defined as a temporary paralysis of nervous function and dazed unconsciousness resulting from a violent movement of the brain inside the skull.[116]

---

[111] *Ibid.*, at p. 126.
[112] *Cooper v. McKenna, Ex p. Cooper*, [1960] Qd. R. 406 (F.C.) *per* Stable J. at p. 419; *Bratty v. A.-G. Northern Ireland*, [1961] 3 W.L.R. 965 *per* Lord Denning at p. 982; *Hill v. Baxter*, [1958] 1 All E.R. 193 *per* Lord Goddard at p. 195; *R. v. Kasperek* (1951), 101 C.C.C. 375 (Ont. C.A.) *per* Bowlby J.A. at p. 384.
[113] *Kay v. Butterworth* (1945), 61 T.L.R. 452 *per* Humphreys J. at p. 453. See *Police v. Beaumont*, [1958] Crim. L.R. 620 where a woman who collapsed unconscious at the wheel of her car from pneumonia was acquitted of dangerous driving.
[114] See *H. M. Advocate v. Ritchie*, [1926] S.C. (J.) 4 (Scot.) where carbon monoxide poisoning was raised as a defence to a charge of causing death by reckless driving.
[115] In *Hill v. Baxter*, [1958] 1 All E.R. 193 at p. 195 it was said that "it would be impossible as well as disastrous to hold that falling asleep at the wheel was any defence to a charge of dangerous driving. If a driver finds that he is getting sleepy he must stop." See also *Kay v. Butterworth, supra,* footnote 113. In *Beaumont, supra,* footnote 113 the accused admitted feeling very tired, but in view of the medical evidence that she may not have noticed any pronounced symptoms of pneumonia, the court apparently felt this was not enough to inculpate her. Note that sudden illness which does not result in unconsciousness at the material time may not give rise to the defence. See *Sportun v. Murphy and Smith*, [1955] 2 D.L.R. 248 (Ont. C.A.).
[116] Wily and Stallworthy, *Mental Abnormality and the Law,* at p. 75.

Any blow to the face or head of sufficient force carries with it the possibility of concussion, and, therefore, automatism. Thus in *R. v. Minor,*[117] where medical evidence was given that the accused had suffered injury to his brain resulting from a punch in the eye, the Saskatchewan Court of Appeal ordered a new trial because the trial judge had instructed the jury that insanity was the only defence to the charge of motor manslaughter which the accused faced. Similarly in *R. v. Carter*[118] and *Cooper v. McKenna*[119] the courts of Victoria and Queensland respectively held that post-traumatic automatism could be raised as a defence to a charge of dangerous driving. In *Bleta v. The Queen*[120] the Supreme Court of Canada recognized post-traumatic automatism as a defence to non-capital murder. An interesting feature of that case was the fact that the accused had supposedly suffered his concussion during the course of the fatal fight with the victim! The acquittal not only demonstrates the odds which may be surmounted by the defence of automatism, but suggests also that it may more easily be asserted when head injury is the alleged cause.[121]

B. HYPOGLYCEMIA

Hypoglycemia is an abnormally depleted level of sugar in the blood. Because sugar and oxygen react chemically in the brain much the same as gasoline and oxygen react within an internal combustion engine, a deficiency of sugar, like a deficiency of oxygen, may be expected to impair mental functioning.[122] Retrocession of consciousness will necessarily vary proportionately with the severity of sugar or oxygen lack; extreme depletion may result in coma or even death.[123]

Any number of causes may produce a hypoglycemic state, though most commonly it is the result of an over-production of insulin by the pancreas or an over-injection of insulin by diabetic patients.[124] If an alleged crime is committed by someone acting in a state of hypoglycemic automatism, liability will probably depend on the nature of the offence and the cause of the hypoglycemia. As demonstrated by the case of *Armstrong v. Clarke,*[125] noted earlier, hypoglycemic automatism which results from an insulin injection will not constitute a defence to an impaired driving charge. It may, however, be a defence to a charge of

---

[117] (1955), 112 C.C.C. 29. See also *R. v. Wakefield* (1957), 75 W.N. (N.S.W.) 66.

[118] [1959] V.R. 105 (S.C.).

[119] [1960] Qd. R. 406 (F.C.).

[120] [1964] S.C.R. 561.

[121] As the headnote to *R. v. Baker,* [1970] 1 C.C.C. 203 (N.S. Co. Ct.) at pp. 203-4 says:
   "The possibility of a concussion resulting in an organic amnesia and a state of automatism is a proposition which does not need medical evidence to support it."

[122] Wily and Stallworthy, at p. 183.

[123] *Ibid.*

[124] *Ibid.*

[125] [1957] 2 Q.B. 391.

robbery or murder.[126] In *R. v. Horton*[127] hypoglycemic automatism which was self-induced by prolonged dieting provided a defence to a charge of theft. In *R. v. R.*[128] the same causes provided a defence to a charge of murder.

Watmore v. Jenkins[129] was a rather odd decision in which England's Court of Queen's Bench refused to accept that a hypoglycemic episode so severe as to result in coma was a case of automatism at all. It is submitted that this ruling was incorrect as it was based on an unduly narrow conception of what automatism is. Confining the definition to involuntary muscular movements in the nature of reflexes, the Court convicted the accused of dangerous driving on the grounds that a genuine automaton could not have driven five miles of curved road at all!

C. "PSYCHOLOGICAL BLOW"

Emotional stress may, in the absence of other physical factors such as illness or external force, produce what psychiatry terms a *psychogenic* form of automatism. Whether or not such condition will be labelled "insanity" within the meaning of the law seems largely dependent on the duration of the emotional derangement involved. As indicated by the Ontario Supreme Court in *R. v. James*,[130] a chronic pathological condition which develops from constant emotional stress and results in involuntary unconscious action will be categorized as mental disease for the purposes of s. 16. However, in cases where the psychological stress has taken the form of a sudden jolt or blow to the accused, the court may be more willing to treat a short-lived bout of automatism as sane. Because the automatism, in order to be a defence in itself, must be an "on the sudden" reaction to psychological stress, the defence of "psychological blow automatism" may be seen as somewhat analogous to the defence of provocation.

An excellent example of psychological blow automatism appeared in the case of *R. v. K.*[131] There the accused, who had apparently been undergoing psychiatric treatment for a severe obsessive-compulsive neurosis, killed his wife after hearing from a neighbour that she planned to leave him. Psychiatric evidence was given to the effect that:

> "[The accused suffered] a severe psychological shock arising from the telephone call, when he was told that his wife was leaving him, and he believed it. This, in the doctor's opinion, was the blow, or the psychological blow or stress, which produced in the accused, in his opinion, a state of automatism, where the mind registered little, and from then on the accused did not know what was happening, his

[126] See the discussion *supra*, at pp. 96-7.
[127] *Manchester Guardian,* 20 July 1951.
[128] (1965), 33 Medico-Legal J. 72.
[129] [1962] 2 All E.R. 868.
[130] (1974), 30 C.R.N.S. 65.
[131] [1971] 2 O.R. 401.

mind no longer being in control of his actions."[132]

On the basis of this testimony the accused was acquitted.

The facts in *R. v. K.* were particularly interesting in that they differed only slightly from a situation in which the defence of provocation might have been raised. Before killing his wife, the accused had apparently confronted her and begged her not to leave him.[133] There is no evidence as to what her response was. The accused testified that at that point the rest of what happened became dreamlike.[134] Presumably an accused using the defence of provocation would be limited to that defence by the fact of his consciousness at the time of the homicide; automatism is supposedly the defence of the unconscious. If we examine the testimony of the defence psychiatrist under cross-examination, however, we see that:

> "... he states that the mind of the accused had not stopped functioning completely, that he was able to recognize his wife, his concern about her leaving him, that he had a *diminished awareness*. In other words, that the accused knew that he put his arms around her — the accused admits that — that he saw her on the ground, called for help, but that he had a *decreased or diminished awareness, consciousness, of what was going on....*".[135]

On this evidence K's mental state would appear to have been a far cry from the state of total unconsciousness demanded in the earlier formulations of the defence of automatism,[136] though it is in line with medical interpretation of the term.[137] "Diminished consciousness" reminds one of the term "diminished responsibility", which is not, of course, a defence in Canadian law.[138]

Now imagine the following hypothetical set of facts. Bozo, upon hearing that his wife is deserting him, confronts her with the rumour and begs her not to leave. She replies with a "wrongful act or insult". This deprives him of his self-control and he proceeds to squeeze Mrs. Bozo to death. Bozo is subsequently charged with murder and must choose a defence. If he opts for provocation he will be convicted of manslaughter instead of murder — provided he succeeds. In order to do so, he must show that the wrongful act or insult uttered by his wife not only deprived *him* of his self-control, but that it would have deprived an ordinary person of the power of self-control.[139] This troubles Bozo, who suspects that the phrase "your mother wears army boots" might not enrage

---

[132] *Ibid.,* at p. 404.
[133] *Ibid.,* at p. 403.
[134] *Ibid.*
[135] At p. 404 (emphasis added).
[136] See *Bratty v. A.-G Northern Ireland,* [1961] 3 W.L.R. 965 (H.L.); *Hill v. Baxter,* [1958] 1 All E.R. 193 (Q.B.D.) and especially *R. v. Cottle,* [1958] N.Z.L.R. 999.
[137] McCaldon, *op. cit.* footnote 15, at p. 914 defines automatism as "complex activity of the voluntary musculature occurring in a person who is in a state of *defective* consciousness" (emphasis added).
[138] See Chapter 6 *post* at pp. 183-5.
[139] Criminal Code, s-s. 215 (2).

others as it had enraged him that fateful night. If, on the other hand, he
opts for "psychological blow automatism" he need only show that he
was out of control owing to the fact that he was not fully conscious. And
if he succeeds, he will be acquitted. It now seems to Bozo that he was in
a dreamlike state when he squeezed poor Mrs. Bozo to death and that
his consciousness was "diminished".

In *Parnerkar v. The Queen*[140] the accused was charged with the murder of his girl friend. The evidence was that he had stabbed her to death
when she told him she would not marry a black man and then tore up
certain letters she had written him. The psychiatric testimony given at
trial has been summed up as follows:

> "... the most important part of the doctor's evidence appears to me
> to be the expression of his opinion that the appellant was in a disso-
> ciated state at the time when Anna was killed and that this state
> commenced when she tore up the letter and lasted until he pulled
> the knife from Anna's stomach and realized that he had a knife in
> his hand. The doctor also expressed his opinion that there was a
> possibility of the appellant having suffered an 'hysterical amnesia'
> following the psychological blow occasioned by the tearing up of the
> letter. In describing this dissociated state, the doctor said that while
> it lasted the appellant would be incapable of forming any intent; in-
> capable of appreciating the nature and quality of the act he com-
> mitted, or that such act was wrong; that he could not appreciate the
> probable and natural consequences of his act. He further stated that
> during the period of dissociation, Parnerkar's acts would be auto-
> matic or, in other words, he would be in a state of automatism and
> would have no recollection or control over the events which occur-
> red during that period."[141]

On the basis of this evidence, the trial judge left the defences of
psychological blow automatism, insanity and provocation to the jury.
What is interesting is that the jury rejected both insanity and automatism, returning instead a verdict of manslaughter based on the defence
of provocation! One might well conclude that in doing so, the jury suspected the real situation to be something along the lines of the hypothetical posed earlier. On appeal by the Crown a new trial was ordered for
Parnerkar, one of the grounds being that the defence of provocation
should not have been left to the jury.[142] A further appeal by the accused
was dismissed by the Supreme Court of Canada, the majority[143] being of
the opinion that there was no evidence of an act or insult sufficient to
constitute provocation.[144] It was also held by the Saskatchewan Court of

---

[140] (1973), 10 C.C.C. (2d) 253 (S.C.C.).
[141] *Ibid.,* at pp. 259-60.
[142] (1971), 5 C.C.C. (2d) 11 (Sask. C.A.).
[143] Fauteux, C.J.C., Abbott, Martland, Judson and Pigeon JJ.
[144] Ritchie J. (Spence J. concurring) held that the question of law for the trial judge was
   whether there was any evidence of an act or insult *simpliciter,* but agreed that because
   there was no such evidence the defence of provocation had been erroneously left to the
   jury.

Appeal, and affirmed by the Supreme Court, that the defence of non-in-sane automatism should not have been left to the jury. The reasons for this decision were stated by Culliton C.J.S. as follows:

> "In my opinion, if the evidence of Dr. Benjamin is accepted, that Parnerkar was in a dissociated state at the time he killed Anna, he was, at that time, suffering from a disease of the mind within the McNaghten rules as defined by this Court. If the acts committed by Parnerkar were unconscious acts, they depended upon a defect of reason from disease of the mind, and consequently the defence, if any, was one of insanity, and not of automatism. Therefore, in my respectful view, the learned trial Judge erred in law in putting the defence of automatism to the jury. I would also point out that Dr. Benjamin stated, if Parnerkar was in a dissociated state, then during that time he was temporarily insane."[145]

In light of the decision in *R. v. Cullum*,[146] a case which came before an Ontario County Court only seven months after the *Parnerkar* decision, one might conclude that the defence of psychological blow automatism failed for *Parnerkar* as the result of unskilled psychiatric testimony. In *Cullum*, the defence psychiatrist was careful to state that the dissociated state from which the accused, in his opinion, suffered did *not* constitute a disease of the mind, with the result that Cullum was acquitted.

The facts in *Cullum* were as follows. The accused was charged with criminal negligence causing death (under s. 203 of the Criminal Code) when his car, which was travelling eastbound and at excessive speed in Highway 401's westbound lane, struck another car head-on. The evidence given at trial showed that some time before the collision the accused had been drinking beer with some friends in a tavern. During that time he observed one of his friends "making out with the chicks", as he put it, and began behaving in the following manner:

> "...the accused directed some smart remarks to a couple of girls at the next table. Both were somewhat surprised and considered this to be completely out of character for the accused. . . . The accused grabbed a girl by the leg. The manager came over and cautioned the accused about his conduct. . . . The accused started pinching girls again and he was ejected ..."[147]

Once outside the tavern with his friends, the accused apparently decided to attack single-handedly a group of five men. This manoeuvre resulted in his being punched, knocked down and kicked in the head by the men.

Approximately three hours later, the accused's car was spotted by an O.P.P. officer. Cullum was travelling eastward at 112 m.p.h. while strad-dling the westbound lanes of Highway 401. His car's headlights were on high beam. He seemed oblivious when the police officer drove beside him

---

[145] *Supra,* footnote 140 at p. 260, quoting from 5 C.C.C. (2d) 11 at p. 24.
[146] (1973), 14 C.C.C. (2d) 294 (Ont. Co. Ct.).
[147] *Ibid.,* at pp. 299-300.

although the siren and flasher were on. Shortly afterwards the collision occurred. The accused, who was remarkably uninjured, appeared to the police officer to be intoxicated when he got out of his car. He refused a breathalyzer test, however, demanding to be taken to a hospital instead. In the course of his examination there, the accused shoved an orderly and knocked down a police officer. During interrogation, the accused said he did not understand why he had been arrested. When told of the collision his only comment was to ask how his car was.

In essence, the psychiatric testimony boiled down to this. Cullum, a man of 30 who had very little social contact and had never had sexual intercourse, was given to repressing his sexual and aggressive impulses. Upon seeing his friend's apparent success with the women in the bar, he went into a "dissociative state" which existed at the time of the collision, lasted until 8:00 a.m. the following morning and produced amnesia[148] for that period of time. This dissociative state, in the opinion of the doctors, did not result from the kick in the head which Cullum had received but was "most likely triggered by alcohol and the girls."[149]

In finding the accused not guilty by reason of automatism, Zalev Co.Ct.J. ruled out the possibility of temporary insanity. Referring to *Parnerkar,* the learned Judge had this to say:

> "In some cases, dissociative state has been equated with insanity. In the case of *R. v. Parnerkar* ... the defence psychiatrist testified that at the time of the offence the accused was in a dissociative state, a disease of the mind and was accordingly momentarily insane.
>
> ...
>
> "However, I must decide this case on the evidence before me. It may be that there are different types or degrees of dissociative state. Dr. Cassidy said that the dissociative state in this case did not constitute a disease of the mind. He described the state as a functional disorder or personality problem. The evidence before me does not, therefore, justify any finding of insanity."[150]

Interesting here is the reliance placed by the Court on the opinion of the defence psychiatrist as to whether or not the dissociative state amounted to disease of the mind. One should recall that in *R. v. Kemp*[151] Devlin J. (as he then was) pointed out that medical opinions as to what constitute diseases of the mind within the meaning of the *M'Naghten* rules were not binding upon the court.[152] In the *Bratty* case,[153] Lord Denning said:

---

[148] The amnesia here was total with two exceptions. The accused recalled (1) being in his car with the lights of the traffic coming towards him, and (2) being in the back seat of the O.P.P. cruiser with the officer saying (p. 299) "If you make one more move, I'll smash you in the mouth". Even under sodium amytal the accused could remember no more than this.

[149] *Supra,* footnote 146 at p. 302.

[150] *Ibid.,* at p. 303.

[151] [1957] 1 Q.B. 399.

[152] *Ibid.,* at p. 406.

[153] [1961] 3 W.L.R. 965.

"Upon the other point discussed by Devlin J., namely what is a 'disease of the mind' within the M'Naughten Rules, I would agree with him that this is a question for the judge."

He emphasized that:

"... any mental disorder which has manifested itself in violence and is prone to recur is a disease of the mind. At any rate it is the sort of disease for which a person should be detained in hospital rather than be given an unqualified acquittal."[154]

Cullum's dissociative state clearly manifested itself in violence if not vis-à-vis the collision in a literal sense, then vis-à-vis the fight outside the tavern and the scuffle in the hospital. What is more, the defence psychiatrist admitted that recurrence was a possibility. But "although recurrence was possible", the Court noted, "he did not think that he would require the accused to submit to psychiatric treatment."[155]

So it would appear that a "dissociated" or "dissociative" state brought on by a "psychological blow" or by "emotional stress", as it was called in *Cullum*,[156] may produce insane or non-insane automatism, depending upon the psychiatric witness called to testify. In fact, authority can be found for the proposition that a dissociated state, unless it is the product of psychosis, constitutes *neither* sane automatism nor insanity. In describing the behaviour of hysterical neurotics in a dissociated state, Weihofen has written:

"Their actions are *almost* automatic. . . . Their crimes may be impulsive or premeditated. After they have once started carrying them out, they develop a state of dissociation that lasts out the crime, so that *they go through the various steps understandingly,* but in a state of emotional numbness. Recollection of the crime is often incomplete, with a spotty amnesia that may only partially clear up under sodium pentothal or other abreactive drug. Since *these individuals cannot be said to have been completely incapable of knowing*[157] *the nature and quality of their acts and their wrongfulness,* they are generally held to be responsible and punishable."[158]

A more recent case in which a dissociated state was raised as a defence is that of *R. v. Mulligan*.[159] In that case the accused was charged with

---

[154] *Ibid.,* at p. 981.
[155] *Supra,* footnote 146 at p. 302.
[156] *Ibid.,* at p. 301.
[157] Section 16 of the Criminal Code substitutes the word "appreciating" here. *Quaere* whether this fact would have affected the author's opinion vis-à-vis insanity in Canada.
[158] Weihofen, *Mental Disorder as a Criminal Defense* (Buffalo, Dennis, 1954) at p. 19 (emphasis added).
[159] (1974), 26 C.R.N.S. 179 (Ont. C.A.); affd 66 D.L.R. (3d) 627 (S.C.C.). For a discussion of the accused's appeal to the Supreme Court of Canada on another point, see Chapter 6 *post* at pp. 163-4.

murdering his wife. The evidence was that Mulligan, who had drunk a "substantial amount",[160] stabbed Mrs. Mulligan to death when, according to the accused's testimony, she attempted to induce a miscarriage with a wire coathanger. It was later revealed by autopsy that Mrs. Mulligan had not in fact been pregnant. Psychiatric evidence was led by the defence to the effect that the accused had suffered an acute dissociative reaction brought about by the combination of psychological stress and alcohol. In this respect, the defence was the same as that in *Cullum*. Unfortunately for the accused, however, the defence psychiatrist was of the opinion that the dissociative state was a disease of the mind which rendered him incapable of appreciating the nature and quality of the act. Furthermore, when asked whether the accused had been intoxicated, the doctor answered yes, although not to the extent that leaving aside the dissociated state he would have been incapable of forming the intent to kill.

On the basis of this evidence, the jury convicted the accused of murder, despite the fact that the defences of insanity, provocation and intoxication had been left to them. As pointed out by the Ontario Court of Appeal:

> "[It was not] open to the jury to return a verdict of acquittal based on non-insane automatism, since on the evidence the only causes which could have produced a condition of automatism were 'a disease of the mind' or 'intoxication'. . . . Indeed, the psychiatric evidence did not indicate that the accused's conduct was involuntary in the sense that he was not conscious of it."[161]

In the more recent case of *R. v. Rabey*,[161a] the Ontario Court of Appeal classified the accused's dissociative state as a "disease of the mind". Here the Court has attempted, by way of *obiter*, to confine the category of non-insane psychological blow automatism to automatisms "produced by some specific external factor".

D. SLEEP

Although somnambulism is sometimes treated as being a separate phenomenon distinguishable (medically) from automatism,[162] McCaldon has described somnambulism as a "normal" form of automatism and defined it as "a state of dissociation in which, with the usual personality asleep, some fragment of the personality directs the person into the performance of some complicated act."[163] A similar definition is provided by Podolsky:

---

[160] *Ibid.,* at p. 181.
[161] *Ibid.,* at p. 186.
[161a] 17 March 1977 (not yet reported).
[162] Podolsky, "Somnambulistic Homicide" (1960-61), 1 Med. Sci. and The Law 260 at p. 264 appears to have based this distinction solely upon the fact that somnambulism originates from a prior state of unconsciousness (sleep), while in other forms of automatism the subject begins from a conscious situation.
[163] "Automatism" (1964), 91 Can. Med. Assoc. J. 914 at p. 915.

"Somnambulism (sleep-walking) is a form of sleep in which a person is able to function without any awareness of his motivations and actions. In somnambulism a greater or smaller part of the personality takes command and dictates the general behaviour, the rest of the normal personality becoming apparently incapable of consciousness for the time being and having no influence on conduct. . . . Somnambulism, like dreaming, is a dissociative reaction, which H.P. Laughlin . . . describes as 'co-ordinated physical activity which has been split off or dissociated from the normal stream of consciously directed and purposeful activity'."[164]

When it is said that somnambulistic automatism is "normal" it should be remembered that normal is usually accepted by psychiatrists as meaning mildly neurotic. Glueck,[165] however, seems to have attributed somnambulism solely to those occasional borderline neurotics who inhabit the twilight zone between neurosis and psychosis. McCaldon has acknowledged,[166] as has Williams,[167] that somnambulism may be symptomatic of ego-fragmentation and regression (*i.e.*, psychosis). The cumulative effect of these opinions leads one to the conclusion that an isolated somnambulistic episode may occur in anyone — normal neurotic, borderline neurotic, psychotic or psychopath — and is really in itself symptomatic of nothing. It is submitted, however, that individual quirks of personality and character and the presence or absence of psychopathology may well determine the quality of somnambulism experienced and the type of automatic behaviour exhibited therein. While sleepwalking is a fairly common phenomenon, the commission by sleepwalkers of brutally violent acts is not. For this reason one may question the wisdom of acquitting without qualification a somnambulistic killer who, though not legally insane, could benefit from psychiatric counselling. Except in the case of insanity, however, Canada's Criminal Code does not provide for qualified acquittals, and because s. 662.1 premises conditional discharge upon a finding of guilt, the alternative suggested nearly one hundred years ago in *H.M. Advocate v. Fraser*[168] is precluded. *Fraser* was a case in which a Scottish jury found a man not to have been responsible for killing his child by reason of somnambulism. The accused was discharged, however, only once he had given an undertaking never to sleep in a room with others.

The principle laid down by Stephen J. in *R. v. Tolson*[169] is that somnambulism is a condition demanding absolute acquittal of an otherwise sane accused. Despite the relative rarity of somnambulistic violence, the legal literature is not without examples of this principle in operation.[170]

---

[164] *Supra*, footnote 162 at pp. 260-1.
[165] *Mental Disorder and the Criminal Law* (Boston, Little Brown, 1925) at p. 29.
[166] McCaldon, *op. cit.* footnote 15, at p. 915.
[167] *Criminal Law: The General Part*, 2nd ed. (London, Stevens and Sons, 1961) at p. 12.
[168] (1878), 4 Couper 70.
[169] (1889), 23 Q.B.D. 168.
[170] For examples other than those set out herein, see *R. v. Gnypiuk, London Times* 20 December 1960 (C.C.A.); *R. v. White* 1941 S.R. 1; and Podolsky, *op. cit.* footnote 162.

In *R. v. Paltridge,*[171] a defendant who axed his wife while sleepwalking was acquitted of attempted murder. In the case of *Boshears*[172] an American Air Force Sergeant was acquitted of murdering a girl whom he had strangled in his sleep. *R. v. Cogdon*[173] was a case in which a mother who dreamt that her daughter was being seduced by a soldier axed the girl to death; apparently she thought she was killing the imagined soldier. Despite the fact that she killed the wrong person, the accused knew in her dream she was killing a human being in circumstances which, even if true, would not establish a defence. Yet the mother was found not guilty of murder because, as Glanville Williams has put it, "dream 'knowledge' is not knowledge for legal purposes."[174]

The facts in *Cogdon* bring to mind another defence distinct from automatism. Included in the Criminal Code's insanity provisions is what may be called the "delusion defence". It goes as follows:

"16 (3)A person who has specific delusions, but is in other respects sane, shall not be acquitted on the ground of insanity unless the delusions caused him to believe in the existence of a state of things that, if it existed, would have justified or excused his act or ommission."

The implications of s-s. 16(3) and its relation to the distinct but similar defence of somnambulism may be demonstrated by four simple propositions:
(1) Bozo is perfectly sane in other respects but thinks (literally) that his wife is a giant salami. If, acting on this belief, he one day slices her up in little pieces with a meat cleaver, he is not guilty of murder by reason of insanity.
(2) Bozo is sane in other respects but has the specific paranoid delusion that Mrs. Bozo has been cheating him at pinochle. If he makes hamburger out of her to teach her a lesson he has no defence.
(3) *But* if Bozo *dreams* that Mrs. Bozo has been cheating him at pinochle and (using the meat cleaver he keeps tucked under his pillow) performs free-lance open heart surgery on her while sleepwalking, he will be acquitted by the defence of automatism.
(4) *And* if Bozo, *dreaming* that his wife is a giant salami, makes a sandwich out of her in his sleep, he will not be limited to the defence of insanity but will be acquitted by reason of automatism instead.

It is submitted that the disparity in result between situations (2) and (3) is unfair and ridiculous. Under the delusion defence the law holds a man whom it recognizes to be under the influence of an insane delusion to the same standard of responsibility as a sane man; he is expected to behave rationally and ethically within the framework of his delusion.[175]

---

171 *Daily Telegraph,* 18 February 1961.
172 *London Times,* 18 February 1961.
173 *Daily Telegraph,* 20 December 1950.
174 *Criminal Law: The General Part,* at p. 483.
175 In *State v. Jones* (1871), 50 N.H. 369 at pp. 387-8, Ladd J. called the reasoning behind the delusion defence "exquisite inhumanity" in that "it practically holds a man con-

Under the defence of somnambulism the law assumes the defendant to be sane yet permits him to behave irrationally and unethically with impunity.

In situation (4) it is doubtful that the Crown would be able to successfully rebut the defence of automatism with s-s. 16(3) insanity. If this tactic were permitted the somnambulist who has behaved rationally within the framework of his dream would be in a worse position than the one who has not. Two examples of somnambulistic homicide occurring as a "rational" reaction to dream facts are seen in the cases of *R. v. Dhlamini*[176] and *Fain v. The Commonwealth.*[177] In *Dhlamini* a native of the Transvaal was found not guilty in the stabbing death of a chum with whom he shared sleeping quarters. Apparently the accused had dreamt that he was being attacked and that he was defending himself; he was described by the court as having just "half-awakened out of a nightmare"[178] when he stabbed the deceased, who made a move toward him. In *Fain* the accused, who had fallen asleep in a hotel bar, gunned down a porter who tried to awaken him at closing time. In acquitting the accused of murder, the Kentucky Appeal Court drew a distinction between the responsibility of someone who is asleep and someone who is "half-awake":

> "If, as claimed, the appellant was unconscious when he fired the first shot, it cannot be imputed to him as a crime. Nor is he guilty if partially conscious, if, upon being partially awakened, and finding the deceased had hold of him and was shaking him, he imagined he was being attacked, and believed himself in danger of losing his life or of sustaining great bodily injury at the hands of his assailant, he shot in good faith, believing it necessary to preserve his life or his person from great harm."[179]

The Court further distinguished between the responsibility of someone "half-awake" and someone fully conscious, saying:

> "In such circumstances, it does not matter whether he had reasonable grounds for his belief or not. He had been asleep, and could know nothing of the surrounding circumstances."[180]

It is doubtful whether these distinctions would be made in Canada. As mentioned earlier, our law recognizes no middle ground between consciousness and unconsciousness. Consequently, the "half-awake" defendant would most likely be treated as a somnambulist.

---

fessed to be insane, accountable for the exercise of the same reason, judgment and controlling mental power that is required of a man of perfect mental health. It is, in effect, saying to the jury, the prisoner was mad when he committed the act, but he did not use sufficient reason in his madness".

[176] [1955 (1)] S.A. 120 (T.P.D.).
[177] (1879), 78 Ky. 183.
[178] *Supra,* footnote 176 at p. 122.
[179] *Supra,* footnote 177 at p. 189.
[180] *Ibid.*

E. HYPNOSIS?

Hypnosis has been classified along with somnambulism as a "normal" form of automatism in that it is said to be a state of hysterical dissociation which can be induced in normal people.[181] The commission of alleged crimes while in the hypnotic state is not a common situation by any means, however, and it is perhaps for this reason that the legal effect of hypnosis is a matter of interesting debate.

Paragraph 2(a) of s. 2.01 of the American Law Institute's Model Penal Code lists conduct during hypnosis or resulting from hypnotic suggestion as an involuntary act for which an accused person should not be held liable. One wonders, however, whether such blanket immunity is supportable by law. Should inquiry not be made as to whether the accused submitted voluntarily to the hypnosis?[182] It will be remembered that a person who voluntarily consumes alcohol or mind-altering drugs may be restricted to the defences of drunkenness and insanity should automatism result.[183]

Glanville Williams has taken the position that conduct under hypnosis is really not automatic behaviour at all:

"Hypnosis is not a state of unconsciousness. . . . It is, therefore, doubtful whether a relevant distinction can be made between hypnotic suggestion and insane impulse, the law being that the latter does not exclude the possibility of an 'act'."[184]

Williams, in speaking of "insane impulse" probably meant "irresistible impulse". Morris and Howard have stated[185] that automatism and irresistible impulse are distinguishable in that while the former is not conscious the latter is. According to Williams, "Where there is consciousness, a party is capable of 'acting' even though he is subject to an uncontrollable impulse."[186] If one assumes that the hypnotic state is a form of irresistible impulse, one is left with an anomaly. Perhaps the only impulses which can be called irresistible with any degree of medical certainty are those which exist in a state of automatism. But because the law prefers to separate unconscious involuntary conduct from what it calls "irresistible impulse", the term is rendered ambiguous to the point of being virtually indefinable. If a person genuinely cannot control himself, how can he be held responsible for his actions? Even in cases where it is established that an accused was quite understandably "deprived of the power of self-control"[187] (*i.e., provoked* in the legal sense), the most the law will do is to reduce a charge of murder to manslaughter.

---

[181] McCaldon, *op. cit.* footnote 15, at p. 915. In a similar fashion, O'Driscoll, Practice Note (1966-67), 49 C.R. 142 lists as one cause of automatism "automatism caused by a 'normal' state — *e.g.,* by sleepwalking or hypnosis."

[182] Allen, "Hypnotism and its Legal Import" (1934), 12 Can. Bar Rev. 14 has refined the issue, saying (at p. 87) that the fact that the subject "did not enter this state for the purpose of receiving a criminal suggestion" need only be proved.

[183] See discussion on pp. 95-9, *supra.*

[184] Williams, *op. cit.* footnote 167, at pp. 768-9.

[185] Morris and Howard, *Studies in Criminal Law* (Oxford, Clarendon, 1964) at p. 62.

[186] At p. 13.

[187] Criminal Code, s-s. 215(2).

As Williams has pointed out, there is in fact no English authority on whether conduct under the influence of hypnosis amounts to non-insane automatism.[188] Nor, it seems, are there any Canadian cases on the matter. French and German law, however, treat hypnosis as relevant to the question of *mens rea*.[189] It has been suggested that this is the state of law in Britain[190] (and in Canada?). Williams has posited, however, that because, under one theory, the hypnotized subject cannot (presumably) be forced to do things repugnant to his nature, *mens rea* will necessarily have existed for any crime which the subject is induced to commit; the hypnotist can at best remove inhibitions.[191] But this argument may be refuted by the fact that unconscious motivation is not recognized by law.[192] As one author has put it: "The fact that the *inner mind* of the accused was prepared to accept the criminal suggestion would not in my opinion affect the position since the law only recognizes the normal consciousness as the seat of criminal responsibility."[193]

V. Evidence

As a general rule in criminal cases the "legal" or "persuasive" burden of establishing every element of an offence (including its voluntariness) beyond a reasonable doubt rests upon the Crown at the outset and does not shift in the course of the trial.[194] Exceptions to this rule may be found in some statutes[195] which contain special rules governing the question of onus, or in the case of insanity[196] where the legal burden rests on the accused to establish the defence on a balance of probabilities. So far as non-insane automatism[197] is concerned, however, there is a lighter "evidential" burden which must be discharged by an accused who seeks to raise the defence.[198] The evidential burden is said to be one of produc-

---

[188] At p. 768. See *R. v. Quick and Paddison* (1973), 57 Cr. App. R. 722 at p. 734, however, where Lawton L.J., in *obiter*, grouped hypnosis in with possible causes of non-insane automatism.

[189] De Vabes, *Droit Criminal,* at p. 203; Ebermacher, Lobe and Rosenberg, St. G.B. 4th ed., at p. 280, cited by Williams, at p. 768.

[190] Cuddon, "Hypnotism and the Law" (1954), 22 Medico-Legal J. 107 at p. 112.

[191] Williams, *op. cit.* footnote 167, at p. 12.

[192] This fact is recognized by Williams himself, at p. 12.

[193] Cuddon, at p. 112.

[194] *Woolmington v. D.P.P.,* [1935] A.C. 462 (H.L.).

[195] See *Cross on Evidence* (London, Butterworths, 1967) at p. 72.

[196] *M'Naghten's Case* (1843), 10 Cl. & Fin. 200, 8 E.R. 718; *R. v. Smith* (1910), 6 Cr. App. R. 19. For criticism see Williams, at p. 516.

[197] Along with other defences such as self-defence (*R. v. Lobell,* [1957] 1 Q.B. 547); provocation (*Chan Kau v. The Queen,* [1955] A.C. 206 (P.C.)); drunkenness (*R. v. Stones,* [1956] S.R. 25 (N.S.W.)); and duress (*R. v. Smyth,* [1963] V.R. 737).

[198] *R. v. Carter,* [1959] V.R. 105 at p. 111; *Bratty v. A.-G. Northern Ireland,* [1961] 3 W.L.R. 965 at p. 983. This fact was not always clear, as evidenced by the remarks of Lord Goddard C.J. in *Hill v. Baxter,* [1958] 1 All E.R. 193. The learned Chief Justice

ing evidence sufficient to require the judge to leave the issue to the jury, or, if there is no jury, to compel the court to consider the evidence when determining whether the legal burden has been discharged.[199]

As Cross has pointed out,[200] no precise formulae exist regarding the quantum of proof necessary to discharge an evidential burden. The reason given for this is that the evidential burden is not something upon which the jury need ever be instructed. As a consequence, the amount of evidence which must be adduced for the defence of automatism to "pass the judge", as Wigmore has put it,[201] will vary from case to case. In *Hill v. Baxter*,[202] Devlin J. (as he then was) was of the opinion that in order for the defence to be considered at all, *prima facie* evidence must at least be produced. When *prima facie* evidence is required of an accused in criminal cases, the term must generally be taken to mean sufficient evidence as would leave a reasonable tribunal in reasonable doubt on the point if uncontradicted.[203] By way of contrast, a *prima facie* case can be made by the Crown in a criminal case or by either party in a civil case only by establishing a *balance of probability* in favour of the inference which is sought to be drawn.[204] Recently in *R. v. Sproule*[205] the Ontario Supreme Court seems to have demanded this latter form of *prima facie* case from an accused. In that case evidence indicating a 30 per cent possibility of psychological blow automatism was ruled insufficient to allow the defence to be put before a jury. Referring to the testimony of the defence psychiatrist, Lerner J. said:

> "...the telling part, as I say, in his evidence was where he said, 'In my opinion, there is a possibility ...' the emphasis being in my view on the word 'possibility', that he was at that time in a state of automatism resulting from that particular psychological blow.
>
> *"Now, we cannot deal in possibilities. We have to deal in probabilities.* And had it been left alone, I might have had some trouble; but then he went on to say that that possibility goes to the extent of 30 per cent. That does not put it in the realm of consideration, in my view, in this type of case, or in any case for that matter."[206]

---

was of the opinion that, as in cases of insanity, the legal burden rested upon the accused to establish the defence of automatism. He said at p. 195 "... undoubtedly the onus of proving that he was in a state of automatism must be on [the accused]. This is not only akin to a defence of insanity but it is a rule of the law of evidence that the onus of proving a fact which must be exclusively within the knowledge of a party lies on him who asserts it. This no doubt is subject to the qualification that where an onus is on the defendant in a criminal case the burden is not as high as it is on a prosecutor."

[199] Cross, at pp. 68-9.
[200] *Ibid.*, at p. 99.
[201] *Wigmore, On Evidence,* 3rd ed. (Boston, Little Brown, 1940), Vol. IX, s. 2494, at p. 293.
[202] [1958] 1 All E.R. 193 at p. 196.
[203] Cross, at p. 99.
[204] *Wilson v. Buttery,* [1926] S.A.S.R. 150, *per* Napier C.J. at p. 154.
[205] (1972), 19 C.R.N.S. 384.
[206] *Ibid.,* at p. 389 (emphasis added).

Lerner J.'s ruling resulted in a new trial being ordered by the Ontario Court of Appeal,[207] though not on the ground that the wrong quantum of proof had been required of the defence in discharging its evidential burden. Cited instead was the fact that the trial judge had made his ruling at the close of a *voir dire* and had not permitted the defence to lead any evidence of automatism in the trial proper. This, said Kelly J.A., was an infringement of the accused's right to make full answer and defence as provided for by s-s. 577(3) of the Criminal Code. Noting that the evidence in question was not inadmissible by reason of any of the exclusionary rules or by virtue of the "probative value versus prejudicial effect", test, Kelly J.A. held:

> "The rejection of the evidence otherwise legally admissible sought to be placed before the jury for the purpose of establishing a defence in this case really brought about the rejection of the defence itself, and it goes so directly to the very root of the principle of trial by jury as to constitute a fundamental error ..."[208]

It is submitted, however, that the mere fact that the evidence had been rejected in a *voir dire* did not in itself constitute a "substantial wrong or miscarriage of justice"[209] sufficient to warrant a new trial. Indeed, there may have been merit in Lerner J.'s reason for holding a trial within a trial: if the defence did not in fact have evidence of automatism suitable for a jury's consideration, he would have to make that ruling eventually; snuffing out the issue in a *voir dire* would be a more effective means of withdrawing the defence from the jury's consideration than the traditionally confusing instruction to disregard. What made the trial judge's ruling a miscarriage of justice, it is contended, was the application of an unduly onerous standard of proof, the demand for evidence which made automatism probable.

In order for the accused to discharge his evidential burden it has been held necessary to lay a "proper foundation" for the defence of automatism.[210] In practice this has generally meant adduction of positive evidence, although in *R. v. Szymusiak*[211] it was suggested that the mere cross-examination of prosecution witnesses might be sufficient.[212] In *Bratty,* Lord Denning remarked that a bare statement by the accused would not in itself constitute a proper foundation,[213] although in *Szymusiak* the court considered it essential for the accused to testify.[214]

---

[207] (1975), 30 C.R.N.S. 56.

[208] *Ibid.,* at p. 63.

[209] Criminal Code, subpara. 613(1) (b) (iii).

[210] *R. v. Cottle,* [1958] N.Z.L.R. 999. See also *R. v. Cusack* (1971), 3 C.C.C. (2d) 527 (P.E.I. C.A.).

[211] [1972] 3 O.R. 602 (Ont. C.A.).

[212] *Per* Schroeder J.A. at p. 607.

[213] [1961] 3 W.L.R. 965 at p. 982.

[214] *Supra,* footnote 211 at p. 613: "It is difficult to conceive of such a defence prevailing in a case in which the accused failed to testify, and counsel for the accused admitted to the Court that he had been unable to find any case in which the defence of automatism was entertained in which there was a failure on the part of the accused man to give evidence

In addition, most courts view the production of medical witnesses as mandatory. The reason for this was expressed by Devlin J. (as he then was) in *Hill v. Baxter* when he said:

> "I do not doubt that there are genuine cases of automatism and the like, but I do not see how the layman can safely attempt without the help of some medical or scientific evidence to distinguish the genuine from the fraudulent."[215]

Convincing as this reasoning may be, it is not conclusive on the matter of medical proof. Indeed if it expressed an evidentiary rule it would be difficult to reconcile with the fact that psychiatric evidence has been held to be unnecessary in order to justify a jury's finding of *insanity,* on the basis that an accused's mental state may be inferred from his acts.[216] The best view would seem to be that medical evidence is a practical necessity, though not a technical one, in the cases of both insanity and automatism. In *People (A.-G.) v. Manning*[217] it was held on appeal from a conviction for murder that the trial judge was entitled to remark in his charge to the jury that he had never seen a case where the defence of insanity was successfully established without expert evidence having been called. Similarly, in the *Bratty* case Lord Denning stated that the accused's evidence of automatism "will *rarely* be sufficient"[218] to displace the presumption of mental capacity unless supported by medical evidence. The Halifax County Court case of *R. v. Baker*[219] is an example of such rare occurrence. There it was held that the possibility of a concussion resulting in a state of automatism raised a reasonable doubt despite the fact that there was no medical proof offered in support.

The practice of allowing the Crown to adduce medical evidence of the accused's insanity once the accused's state of mind has been put in issue by the defence is exemplified in the case of *R. v. Kemp.*[220] There it was held that medical evidence of insanity could be called by the prosecution in rebuttal of the defence's claim that the accused was acting in a state of automatism at the time of the alleged crime. The decision in *Kemp* was approved in *Bratty,* where Lord Denning went a step farther by asserting that in such circumstances a positive duty rested upon the Crown to call medical evidence:

---

in support of his defence." But see *R. v. Clarke* (1973), 16 C.C.C. (2d) 310, where the Nova Scotia Supreme Court held it to be unnecessary for the accused to give evidence himself in order for the defence of automatism to be put to the jury.

[215] [1958] 1 All E.R. 193 at p. 197.

[216] *R. v. Kierstead* (1918), 42 D.L.R. 193 (N.B.C.A.). See also *R. v. Brockenshire and Clarkson,* [1932] 1 D.L.R. 156 (Ont. C.A.).

[217] (1953), 89 I.L.T. 155.

[218] [1961] 3 W.L.R. 965 at p. 983 (emphasis added).

[219] [1970] 1 C.C.C. 203.

[220] [1957] 1 Q.B. 399. Although *R. v. Dixon,* [1961] 3 All E.R. 460n, stated expressly that psychiatric evidence of insanity could not be placed before the jury during the prosecution's case in-chief, in the relatively recent case of *R. v. Frank* (1971), 12 C.R.N.S. 339 the Supreme Court of Ontario ruled that it was open to the Crown to introduce reply evidence of insanity even where the accused had *not* put his mental state in issue.

"My Lords, I think that Devlin J. was quite right in *Kemp's* case in putting the question of insanity to the jury, even though it had not been raised by the defence. When it is asserted that the accused did an involuntary act in a state of automatism, the defence necessarily puts in issue the state of mind of the accused man: and thereupon it is open to the prosecution to show what his true state of mind was. The old notion that only the defence can raise the defence of insanity is now gone. The prosecution are entitled to raise it and it is their *duty* to do so rather than allow a dangerous person to be at large."[221]

In practice, the easiest way for the prosecution to raise the defence of insanity in rebuttal of non-insane automatism is to concede that the accused acted unconsciously but allege that the automatism was caused by disease of the mind. In cases where the Crown knows, for example, that the accused is an epileptic, this tactic would stand an excellent chance of suceeding. For this reason it is difficult to understand the criticism which has been made by some writers with respect to the unequal burdens of proof borne by sane and insane automatism. The complaint is that "Someone who alleges that he acted in a state of automatism due to psychomotor epilepsy must prove his case on the balance of probabilities, while someone who alleges that he was suffering from concussion due to a blow on the head need only raise a reasonable doubt in the mind of the jury".[222] While this criticism may be valid in theory, it is questionable whether it has a pragmatic basis. In practice the epileptic accused need only raise the defence of non-insane automatism and leave the rest up to the Crown. If anything, it is the *likelihood* of a finding of insane automatism which should trouble the accused in such circumstances. Because in the case of indictable offences a verdict of insanity will result in detention "until the pleasure of the lieutenant governor of the province is known",[223] insane automatism will probably only be raised when there is no other defence available.

What is the burden of proof resting upon the prosecution when it has raised the defence of insanity to rebut automatism? Need the Crown only prove insanity on the balance of probabilities as is the case when it is raised by the defence? Or must it prove insanity beyond a reasonable doubt? In the relatively recent case of *R. v. Gillis*[224] these very questions were asked. McClellan Co. Ct. J., relying on the opinion of Lord Denning in the *Bratty* case, decided that a balance of probabilities was sufficient. The same conclusion was reached by the Ontario Court of Appeal in *R. v. Simpson*.[225] It is submitted, however, that the effect of these decisions is to alter the entire evidential burden of proof resting on the accused, and to deprive him of the right to be acquitted if he raises a reasonable doubt. In effect, it places on the accused the burden of prov-

---

[221] *Supra,* footnote 218 at p. 980 (emphasis added).
[222] Cross, "Reflections on Bratty's Case" (1962), 78 L.Q.R. 236 at p. 241.
[223] Criminal Code, s-s. 542 (2).
[224] (1973), 13 C.C.C. (2d) 363 (B.C. Co. Ct.).
[225] (1977), 35 C.C.C. (2d) 337 (Ont. C.A.).

ing non-insane automatism on a balance of probabilities! A reasonable possibility that the accused was suffering from non-insane automatism would no longer be sufficient; the mere fact that the automatism is more likely the insane variety would, according to *Gillis* and *Simpson*, be sufficient to produce a verdict of insanity.

It is an interesting question to what extent, if any, similar fact evidence can be used by the Crown to rebut a defence of automatism. The only case on point would seem to be *R. v. Harrison-Owen*,[226] a decision of the English Court of Criminal Appeal. There the accused, who had been found in someone's house at 1:00 a.m., answered a burglary charge by stating that he had entered the house while in a "black-out". In order to negative this defence the trial judge directed counsel for the prosecution to question the accused about previous convictions for similar offences. The conviction which resulted was quashed on appeal on the grounds that the defence of automatism, if proved, denied *actus reus;* similar fact evidence was appropriate only as a means of rebutting a defence based on lack of *mens rea*. Inasmuch as the decision here suggests that similar fact evidence is *never* permissible to rebut a defence of automatism, it has been widely criticized.[227] Glanville Williams has argued[228] that the decision is wrong (1) because of the very technical nature of the distinction between lack of *mens rea* and absence of the mental element in an act; and (2) because "previous convictions are of great probative force in displacing a defence of automatism, and the defence may be difficult to rebut in any other way."[229] Williams' contention, in effect, seems to be that similar fact evidence should *invariably* be admissible to rebut automatism.[230] Cross, on the other hand, has argued that similar fact evidence should be admissible only when a nexus exists between the accused's conduct on the occasion under investigation and that on other occasions. This nexus would have to be something in the nature of a strikingly similar *modus operandi*. In opposition to Williams', second argument, Cross has suggested that proof of previous convictions without more evidence as to details shows only that the accused is the type of person who would commit the offence in question. Even where the accused's supposedly unconscious conduct is *identical* to the conscious conduct which led to conviction for offences in the past, it is submitted that the probative value of such past conduct remains questionable. Of those writers who have criticized the decision in *Harrison-Owen*, none

---

[226] [1951] 2 All E.R. 726.

[227] In the *Bratty case,* [1961] 3 W.L.R. 965 at p. 980, Lord Denning remarked: "I should have thought that, in order to rebut this defence, he could have been cross-examined about his previous burglaries: but the Court of Criminal Appeal ruled otherwise. I venture to doubt that decision". See also Cross, *op. cit.* footnote 122, at pp. 243-4; Williams, *op. cit.* footnote 167, at pp. 14-5; Walton, "The Defence of Automatism" (1959), 109 L.J. 454 at p. 454; Prevezer, "Automatism and Involuntary Conduct," [1958] Crim. L.R. 361 at pp. 444-5.

[228] *Criminal Law: The General Part,* at p. 14.

[229] *Ibid.,* at p. 15.

[230] "To prevent abuse of this defence", says Williams at p. 15, "it is necessary to allow the prosecution to put in evidence every fact tending to show that the alleged automatism is a fake".

has offered psychiatric evidence tending to show that an automaton would not do things unconsciously in much the same way as he has done them consciously. One would have thought such proof fundamental to a discussion of the probative value of similar facts evidence.

VI. Conclusions

The law surrounding the defence of automatism is unsatisfactory in a number of areas. As is the case with any defence which lends itself to the introduction of psychiatric opinion evidence, a defendant who raises automatism gambles on the outcome of the inevitable "battle of the experts" which must ensue. The odds on coming out a winner are decidedly stacked against him. He may hit the jackpot and be acquitted outright, although he is more likely to be found insane, drunk or 100 per cent responsible.

As a means of making the defence a less risky proposition, some more acceptable alternative dispositions ought to be provided. Rather than forcing the courts to label insane those defendants they wish to keep an eye on, the Criminal Code could be amended to provide, in effect, for a special verdict of "not guilty by reason of automatism" which would involve the possibility of probation and compulsory treatment following acquittal.[231] It is, in fact, arguable that all automatons who have committed serious acts of violence should be compelled to receive psychiatric treatment, if only on an out-patient basis. Furthermore, a separate offence of being drunk and dangerous could be created to deal with the accused whose automatism resulted from acute intoxication;[232] such offence would carry with it the possibility of a short prison term. Were liability to be based on negligence,[233] the Code's present provisions for conditional discharge (which requires a determination of guilt) and probation could be used as a means of treating and supervising persons whose automatic misbehaviour was foreseeable and resulted from drunkenness, careless drug overdoses, failure to take medication, etc. Traditionally, however, the courts have not inquired into whether automatism was preceded by negligence except where charges such as dangerous driving are involved.[234] Why not involve the concept of negligence to deal with diabetics, epileptics, or even somnambulists who, knowing their propensity for violent behaviour, have failed to take precautionary measures?[235]

---

[231] See Beck, "Voluntary Conduct: Automatism, Insanity and Drunkenness" (1966-67), 9 Crim. L.Q. 315 at p. 319. For a more detailed discussion of this proposal, see Chapter 6 *post*, under the heading "Conclusions".

[232] Beck, at p. 322.

[233] *I.e.*, by laying charges under ss. 203 or 204 of the Code.

[234] Prevezer, at p. 448.

[235] In *Fain v. Commonwealth* (1879), 78 Ky. 183 at pp. 192-3, the court said: "If the pris-

Perhaps the defence of automatism should be codified if for no other purpose than to supply a clear definition of the term itself. Simple reflex and convulsive movements should be excluded from the definition (being non-acts in themselves) in an effort to give the word more precision in law. Also included in the codification should be a provision concerning burden of proof. When the Crown seeks to rebut the defence of non-insane automatism, it should be required to do so beyond a reasonable doubt.

oner is and has been afflicted in the manner claimed, and knew, as he no doubt did, his prospensity to do acts of violence when aroused from sleep, he was guilty of a grave breach of social duty in going to sleep in the public room of a hotel with a deadly weapon on his person, and merits, for that reckless disregard of the safety of others, some degree of punishment, but we know of no law under which he can be punished."

Chapter 5

Insanity As A Defence

I. Introduction

In 1843, following the controversial acquittal of Daniel M'Naghten on a charge of murder,[1] England's House of Lords addressed to the judges of that country a series of questions regarding the law of insanity as a defence in criminal cases. It is upon the rules laid down by those judges which Canada's law relating to the defence of insanity presently rests. In what amounts to a synopsis of the original opinion of the judges, s. 16 of our Criminal Code sets out the law as follows:

> "16(1) No person shall be convicted of an offence in respect of an act or omission on his part while he was insane.
>
> "(2) For the purposes of this section a person is insane when he is in a state of natural imbecility or has disease of the mind to an extent that renders him incapable of appreciating the nature and quality of an act or omission or of knowing that an act or omission is wrong.
>
> "(3) A person who has specific delusions, but is in other respects sane, shall not be acquitted on the ground of insanity unless the delusions caused him to believe in the existence of a state of things that, if it existed, would have justified or excused his act or omission.
>
> "(4) Every one shall, until the contrary is proved, be presumed to be and to have been sane."

This chapter will deal with substantive, procedural and evidential aspects of our insanity defence, as well as with the ideological conflicts which protracted adherence to the *M'Naghten* rules has created. In view of the severe criticisms which both psychiatrists and legal scholars have heaped upon the rules, alternative suggestions will also be examined.

---

[1] (1843), 10 Cl. & Fin. 200, 8 E.R. 718.

II. The Procedure

Subsection 16(1) of the Criminal Code provides that: "No person shall be convicted of an offence in respect of an act or omission on his part while he was insane." Regardless of whether or not defence counsel has raised the defence of insanity at trial,[2] it has been held that the question of whether sufficient evidence exists to go to the jury (where there is one) is a question of law for the judge to decide.[3] Where the evidence does disclose insanity, the effect of s-s. 16(1) is to place a duty upon the trial judge to instruct the jury on that defence even where counsel has not chosen to rely upon it.[4]

It is incumbent upon the trial judge to instruct the jury carefully in the law. If the defence has presented evidence both as to specific delusions and general insanity, it would no doubt be an error for the judge to leave only the question of delusional insanity to the jury.[5] Moreover, in instructing the jury on general insanity, a failure to refer to both branches of the test set out in s-s. 16(2) might render the charge defective and necessitate a new trial.[6] Because the judge's charge must ensure a "due appreciation of the value of the evidence" at trial, reference must be made to any medical evidence which bears directly on the issue of insanity; a mere reference to the statements made by the accused himself is insufficient.[7]

Insanity is a question of fact to be decided on the evidence presented at the trial.[8] As regards the verdict, s-s. 542(1) of the Code provides:

> "542(1) Where, upon the trial of an accused who is charged with an indictable offence,[9] evidence is given that the accused was insane at the time the offence was committed and the accused is acquitted,
> (a) the jury, or
> (b) the judge or magistrate, where there is no jury,
> shall find whether the accused was insane at the time the offence was committed and shall declare whether he is acquitted on account of insanity."

Alternatively, of course, it is open for the court to convict the accused. However, where there is evidence of insanity a jury should not be

---

[2] Insanity is raised by a plea of "not guilty", rather than by a "special plea": *R. v. McCoskey* (1926), 47 C.C.C. 122 (Ont. C.A.); *R. v. Sloane* (1930), 1 M.P.R. 546 (N.S.C.A.); *Re R. and Lester* (1971), 6 C.C.C. (2d) 227 (Ont. C.A.).

[3] *R. v. Phinney (No. 1)* (1903), 6 C.C.C. 469 (N.S.C.A.).

[4] *R. v. Parnerkar* (1971), 5 C.C.C. (2d) 11 (Sask. C.A.); affd 10 C.C.C. (2d) 253 (S.C.C.).

[5] *R. v. Moke*, [1917] 3 W.W.R. 575 (Alta. C.A.).

[6] *R. v. Harrop*, [1940] 3 W.W.R. 77 (Man. C.A.).

[7] *R. v. Laycock*, [1952] O.R. 908 (C.A.) *per* Pickup C.J.O. at p. 921.

[8] *R. v. McCoskey* (1926), 47 C.C.C. 122 (Ont. C.A.).

[9] This section should not be interpreted as restricting application of the defence of insanity to indictable offences only. Any such restriction would run contrary to s-s. 737(1) of the Criminal Code, which provides all persons charged with summary offences the right to make full answer and defence.

encouraged to find the accused guilty and simply add a recommendation for mercy.[10]

An accused found not guilty by reason of insanity may, according to para. 603(2)(b) of the Code, appeal to the court of appeal on the same grounds set out for persons appealing against conviction.[11] As regards the powers of the court of appeal, these are set out in s. 613;[12] para. (1)(d) and subpara. (4)(b)(ii) are worthy of special note. The former empowers the court of appeal to set aside a conviction and substitute therefor a verdict of not guilty by reason of insanity; the latter allows a special verdict of insanity to be replaced by conviction, except in cases where the original verdict resulted from trial by jury.

Section 620 of the Code deals with appeals to the Supreme Court of Canada. It provides:

"620(1) A person who has been found not guilty on account of insanity and
  (a) whose acquittal is affirmed on that ground by the court of appeal, or
  (b) against whom a verdict of guilty is entered by the court of appeal under subparagraph 613(4)(b)[ii],
may appeal to the Supreme Court of Canada."[13]

---

[10] *R. v. Lloyd* (1927), 20 Cr. App. R. 139.

[11] According to para. 603(1)(a) of the Code:
  "603(1) A person who is convicted by a trial court in proceedings by indictment may appeal to the court of appeal
    (a) against his conviction
      (i) on any ground of appeal that involves a question of law alone,
      (ii) on any ground of appeal that involves a question of fact or a question of mixed law and fact, with leave of the court of appeal or a judge thereof or upon the certificate of the trial judge that the case is a proper case for appeal, or
      (iii) on any ground of appeal not mentioned in subparagraph (i) or (ii) that appears to the court of appeal to be a sufficient ground of appeal, with leave of the court of appeal."
  As s-s. 771(2) indicates, this section is applicable in the case of summary conviction offences as well.

[12] That section reads in part as follows:
  "613(1) On the hearing of an appeal against a conviction or against a verdict that the appellant is unfit, on account of insanity, to stand his trial, or against a special verdict of not guilty on account of insanity, the court of appeal
    (a) may allow the appeal where it is of the opinion that
      (i) the verdict should be set aside on the ground that it is unreasonable or cannot be supported by the evidence,
      (ii) the judgment of the trial court should be set aside on the ground of a wrong decision on a question of law, or
      (iii) on any ground there was a miscarriage of justice;
    (b) may dismiss the appeal where
      (i) the court is of the opinion that the appellant, although he was not properly convicted on a count or part of the indictment, was properly convicted on another count or part of the indictment..."
  According to s-s. 771(2), this section applies to summary conviction offences as well.

[13] Paragraph 620(1)(b) of the Code as it presently stands refers to subpara. 613(4)(b)(i), not subpara (ii). This is an obvious error.

This procedure differs somewhat from the normal situation, in that persons whose acquittals have been set aside are generally entitled to appeal to the Supreme Court on questions of law only.[14]

In cases where the accused has been tried for a summary conviction offence, the result of a finding of insanity is unqualified acquittal. As the Ontario Provincial Court pointed out in *Re B. and M.*,[15] "the provisions of s. 542 of the Criminal Code are only available 'upon the trial of an accused who is charged with an indictable offence'." Where an accused has been tried for an indictable offence, the result of a special verdict of not guilty by reason of insanity is detention in custody at the pleasure of the provincial lieutenant-governor. According to s-s. 542(2) of the Code:

> "(2) Where the accused is found to have been insane at the time the offence was committed, the court, judge or magistrate before whom the trial is held shall order that he be kept in strict custody in the place and in the manner that the court, judge or magistrate directs, until the pleasure of the lieutenant governor of the province is known."

III. Warrants Of The Lieutenant-Governor

A. THE INSANE DEFENDANT

Once an accused has been found either unfit to stand trial or not guilty by reason of insanity, the law provides for his mandatory detention in custody "until the pleasure of the lieutenant governor of the province is known".[16] Until the lieutenant-governor makes known his pleasure, it is doubtful that a valid detention order issued by a court of competent jurisdiction may be reviewed by way of *habeas corpus*.[17] If however, the lieutenant-governor fails to exercise his discretionary powers within a reasonable length of time, there would seem to be no reason why *mandamus* should not issue to compel him to act.[18]

As to the options which are open to the lieutenant-governor, these are set out in s-s. 545(1) of the Code, which provides:

---

[14] Paragraph 618(2)(a) provides:
    "(2) A person
        (a) who is acquitted of an indictable offence other than by reason of the special verdict of not guilty on account of insanity and whose acquittal is set aside by the court of appeal ...
    may appeal to the Supreme Court of Canada on a question of law."
[16] Criminal Code, s-ss. 542(2) and 543(6).
[17] See *Re Shumiatcher*, [1962] S.C.R. 38; *Re Trepanier* (1885), 12 S.C.R. 111; *Goldhar v. The Queen* (1960), 126 C.C.C. 337 (S.C.C.).
[18] See *Re Constanineau and Jones* (1912), 5 D.L.R. 483 (Ont.); *Dagenais v. The Corp. of the Town of Trenton* (1893), 24 O.R. 343.

"545(1) Where an accused is, pursuant to this Part, found to be insane, the lieutenant governor of the province in which he is detained may make an order

(a) for the safe custody of the accused in a place and manner directed by him, or

(b) if in his opinion it would be in the best interest of the accused and not contrary to the interest of the public, for the discharge of the accused either absolutely or subject to such conditions as he prescribes."

B. THE MENTALLY ILL PRISONER

With regard to persons who have been convicted of an offence and sentenced to terms in provincial prison, s. 546 of the Code makes the following provision:

"546(1) The lieutenant governor of a province may, upon evidence satisfactory to him that a person who is insane, mentally ill, mentally deficient or feeble-minded is serving a sentence in a prison in that province, order that the person be removed to a place of safe-keeping to be named in the order.

"(2) A person who is removed to a place of safe-keeping under an order made pursuant to subsection (1) shall, subject to subsections (3) and (4), be kept in that place or in any other place of safe-keeping in which, from time to time, he may be ordered by the lieutenant governor to be kept."

The power which ss. 545 and 546 have conferred upon provincial lieutenant-governors was derived originally from common law. By virtue of its inherent prerogative as *parens patriae* the Crown was entitled to the custody of all insane persons.[19] Although attacked as *ultra vires*,[20] the transfer of this power has been held to be a valid exercise by the Dominion Parliament of its right, when acting in matters within its own sphere of jurisdiction,[21] to impose duties on officials of provincial governments.[22]

Under ss. 545 and 546 the lieutenant-governor's authority is extremely broad. As regards the initial decision to remove a prisoner[23] to a "place of safe-keeping" under the latter provision, it has been held that once an order is issued the lieutenant-governor has "exclusive judicial control"[24]

---

[19] See *R. v. Martin* (1854), 2 N.S.R. 322 *per* Haliburton C.J. at p. 324.

[20] See *Re Kleinys' Habeas Corpus Application* (1965), 51 W.W.R. 597 at p. 600 (B.C.).

[21] In the *Kleinys* case, it was argued that s. 527 (now s. 546) purported to legislate either on matters of civil rights or the "establishment, maintenance and management of asylums", both of which lie within the sphere of provincial jurisdiction. Section 527 was held to pertain solely to the incarceration of criminals, however, and thus fell squarely within the purview of the Federal Government's criminal jurisdiction.

[22] *Kleinys, supra,* footnote 20.

[23] Such person must be in legal custody. See *R. v. Johnson*, [1946] Que. S.C. 101.

[24] *Champagne v. Plouffe and A.-G. Que.* (1940), 77 C.C.C. 87 at p. 89 (Que.).

over the prisoner and "exercises an executive power which is not subject to control on the part of the Courts".[25] It is only the lieutenant-governor who need be satisfied as to an individual's insanity, mental illness, mental deficiency or feeble-mindedness. As the cases of *Re Trenholm*[26] and *Delorme v. Sisters of Charity of Quebec*[27] indicate, an order is not itself reviewable by the courts. In the former case the accused had been transferred from prison to a psychiatric hospital. Rejecting his argument that "in all matters where the liberty of the subject is involved, the acts of the Crown, its Ministers and the Executive, are subject to revision and control by the Courts. . ."[28] the Ontario High Court dismissed the prisoner's application for *habeas corpus*. In the latter case a prisoner transferred under a lieutenant-governor's order to an asylum petitioned for *habeas corpus* on the ground that he was and always had been of sound mind.[29] There it was held that a judge of the Quebec Court of King's Bench lacked jurisdiction to issue a writ of *habeas corpus* to declare that the prisoner was illegally detained. The proper procedure was to apply to the lieutenant-governor himself under s-s. 546(3).

With regard to the place and manner of confinement which may be ordered, the Nova Scotia Supreme Court pronounced simply in *R. v. Coleman*[30] that a lieutenant-governor possessed "the widest discretion".[31] Such confinement may therefore range from simple incarceration in jail (as was the case in *Coleman*) to a bed in a minimum security psychiatric hospital.

IV. The Substantive Law

A. "NATURAL IMBECILITY"

Because mental deficiency might not in all cases be properly categorized as a "disease of the mind", the inclusion of the phrase "natural imbecility" in s. 16 of the Criminal Code is not entirely superfluous. It is doubtful, however, that the term, as used here, refers to anything more than mental subnormality in general.[32] Any attempt to discover a more precise interpretation results in something of an absurdity.

Although the definition of the expression "feeble-minded person" in s.

---

[25] *Ibid.*
[26] [1939] O.W.N. 224; affd by C.A. unreported; revd on other grounds *sub. nom. Trenholm v. A.-G. Ont.*, [1940] S.C.R. 301.
[27] (1924), 40 C.C.C. 218 (Que.).
[28] *Supra*, footnote 26 at p. 228.
[29] The petitioner in fact filed a declaration by the asylum's superintendent which stated (at p. 219) that the petitioner "has shown no evident sign of imbecility, insanity or madness from the first days of his confinement down to the present time...".
[30] (1927), 47 C.C.C. 148.
[31] *Ibid.*, at p. 148.
[32] See Williams *Criminal Law: The General Part*, 2nd ed. (London, Stevens and Sons, 1961) at p. 147.

2 suggests that imbecility is a form of mental defectiveness more severe than feeble-mindedness,[33] no further reference to the phrase "natural imbecility" is to be found within the Criminal Code. This being the case, it has been suggested that "rules of statute interpretation require reference to the dictionary and *to no other source* to ascertain the meaning of the word[s]."[34] Referring to *Webster's New Twentieth Century Dictionary*[35] we see that an imbecile is:

"a mentally deficient person with an intelligence quotient ranging from 25 to 50; a person mentally equal to a child between three and eight years old; *imbecile* is the second lowest classification of mental deficiency, above *idiot* and below *moron*."

Since it would be rather arbitrary practice to allow only those mental defectives with I.Q.'s ranging between 25 and 50 the benefit of the insanity defence, the utility of the above definition as an aid to statutory interpretation remains questionable. Though case law interpretations might be resorted to in the absence of satisfactory dictionary definition,[36] it is submitted that the type of definition to be found in England's jurisprudence sheds little light, if any, upon the problem. In the 1910 case of *R. v. F.*,[37] for instance, an imbecile was defined as someone "who has once had a mind of some kind, but owing to decay or other mental or physical courses, ceases to have a mind".

Williams has asserted that when *M'Naghten's Case* was decided the word "imbecility" was generally accepted as meaning mental deficiency.[38] The term natural imbecility, presumably, was used in contradistinction to a state of mental subnormality which had been produced by a disease of the mind. Owing to the more specific and contradictory meanings which the term has taken on since 1843, it is a wonder why Parliament has not seen fit to replace it with more up-to-date terminology.

B. "DISEASE OF THE MIND"

It has been forcefully argued that when the *M'Naghten* judges used the term "disease of the mind" they could not possibly have been referring to anything other than a medical condition.[39] This conclusion would

---

[33] The definition in s. 2 of the Code reads as follows:
" 'feeble-minded person' means a person in whom there exists and has existed from birth or from an early age, mental defectiveness not amounting to imbecility, but so pronounced that he requires care, supervision and control for his protection or for the protection of others".

[34] Applegath, "Sexual Intercourse With a Feeble-Minded Female Person: Problems of Proof" (1964-65), 7 Crim. L. Q. 480 at p. 483.

[35] 2nd ed.(New York, World, 1970).

[36] See *Midland Railway Co. v. Robinson* (1890), 15 App. Cas. 19 at pp. 34-5.

[37] (1910), 74 J.P. 384.

[38] At p. 147.

[39] Mueller, "*M'Naghten* Remains Irreplaceable: Recent Events in the Law of Incapacity" (1961), 50 Georgetown L.J. 105 at p. 110.

seem inevitably to flow from the fact that no legal concept of mental disease existed prior to the formulation of the *M'Naghten* rules. Today, however, it must be equally apparent that the question of whether or not specific psychiatric diagnoses amount to mental disease for the purposes of the insanity defence is a legal question and not a medical one.[40] As Devlin J. (as he then was) stated in the case of *R. v. Kemp*:[41]

> "... there is ... no general medical opinion upon what category of diseases are properly to be called diseases of the mind ... Doctors' personal views, of course, are not binding upon me. I have to interpret the rules according to the ordinary principles of interpretation ..."

The learned Justice pointed out, however, that he derived assistance from medical opinions "inasmuch as they illustrate the nature of the disease and the matters which from the medical point of view have to be considered in determining whether or not it is a disease of the mind."[42]

Although there exists no one definition of mental disease which is generally accepted by the medical profession,[43] Whitlock has observed that the term "disease of the mind" is "usually ... assumed to mean one of the major functional or organic psychoses".[44] Psychosis is a psychiatric term encompassing a variety of disorders characterized by varying degrees of personality disintegration and the failure to test and evaluate correctly external reality.[45] The current Canadian *Manual for the Classification of Psychiatric Diagnoses*[46] states:

> "Patients are described as psychotic when their mental functioning is sufficiently impaired to interfere grossly with their capacity to meet the ordinary demands of life. The impairment may result from a serious distortion in their capacity to recognize reality. Hallucinations and delusions, for example, may distort their perceptions. Alterations of mood may be so profound that the patient's capacity to respond appropriately is grossly impaired. Deficits in perception,

---

[40] Smith and Hogan, *Criminal Law*, 2nd ed. (London, Butterworths, 1973) at p. 134.
[41] [1957] 1 Q.B. 399 at p. 406.
[42] *Ibid.*
[43] See Fingarette, *The Meaning of Criminal Insanity* (Berkeley, University of California Press, 1972) at pp. 26-28, where the author, citing the psychiatric literature, has pointed out: "When the problem of defining mental disease is raised explicitly, it is in fact resolved by some personal decision, or at times a hospital decision, and in any of the following different ways: (1) There is no such medical entity as mental disease, or we would do well not to use the phrase. (2) Mental disease is psychosis but not neurosis. (3) Mental disease is any significant and substantial mental disturbance, or is any condition at all that is authoritatively dealt with by the psychiatrist or physician treating mental conditions. (4) Mental disease means substantial social maladaptation, or incompetence, or both as judged by legal criteria. (5) Mental disease is the failure to realize one's nature, capacities, or true self."
[44] Whitlock, *Criminal Responsibility and Mental Illness* (London, Butterworths, 1963) at p. 27.
[45] *American Psychiatric Association Standard Nomenclature*, Washington D.C. (1952).
[46] Information Canada, Ottawa, 1974 at p. 13.

language and memory may be so severe that the patient's cap.
for mental grasp of his situation is effectively lost."

A psychosis, as previously mentioned, may be organic in origin or it may
be functional, *i.e.*, emotional in origin. Generally speaking, in a psychosis
the *ego* is incapable of coping with instinctual life. The result of this failure may be (1) impulsive acts of an aggressive or sexual nature or both;
(2) hallucinations; or (3) delusions. The psychotic may commit acts of
violence or thievery as the result of paranoid thinking — *i.e.*, acting on
ideas of persecution, revenge, grandiose omnipotence, depressive delusions or on fear of imaginary dangers.

Neuroses, on the other hand, are conditions in which the patient is
disturbed by psychic or physical symptoms which represent his emotional reaction to his problems or difficulties.[47] All so-called normal people are thought to be neurotic to some degree; it is only when one's neurosis becomes incapacitating or results in antisocial behaviour that it is
considered abnormal. While sexual or aggressive acts may be committed
by a neurotic, they are differentiated from those of the psychotic in the
sense that they are in this case the product of a mind with an *ego* capable of reality testing. Where the psychotic may have hallucinations or
delusions, the neurotic experiences fantasies and illusions of various
kinds. The neurotic may have paranoid-like ideas, grandiose feelings,
depressive illusions; he may wish to seek revenge against real or imagined wrongs — but these wishes are normally buffered by an *ego* that
knows the law, morality, ethics and demands of the community in which
he lives. A neurotic, in short, is able to differentiate his subjective feelings from object reality and is not *generally* regarded by psychiatrists as
suffering from a disease of the mind within the meaning of s. 16.[48]

Possibly the major "criminal type" (if such thing in fact exists) is the
psychopath. Although there has been widespread disagreement upon
the meaning of this term, the psychopath is generally characterized by
his hairtrigger emotions, impulsive and explosive behaviour, narcissism,
callousness, total lack of conscience or remorse, defective judgment, and
inability to profit from experience.[49] While psychopathy is not often
accompanied by any other form of mental disorder, psychiatric diagnosis
is not always easy, since there may be a deep psychosis or neurosis hidden behind the outward facade. Canadian psychiatrists have tended to
classify psychopathy as a "personality state" rather than as a "disease of
the mind".[50]

Though most psychiatrists would probably interpret the phrase
"disease of mind" as being roughly equivalent to the psychiatric term
psychosis (thus excluding neurosis and psychopathy), the courts have

---

[47] Wily and Stallworthy, *Mental Abnormality and the Law* (Christchurch, N.Z., Peryer 1962) at p. 125.
[48] Ryan, "Mental Abnormalities and the Criminal Law" (1967), 17 U.N.B. L.J. 1 at p. 6, citing *8th Annual Report, Forensic Clinic, Toronto Psychiatric Hospital* (1965), Appxs. viii and ix.
[49] Weihofen, *Mental Disease as a Criminal Defense* (Buffalo, Dennis, 1954) at p. 23.
[50] Ryan, at p. 6.

insisted upon giving the phrase a scope which far exceeds the boundaries of current medical opinion. Perhaps the broadest interpretation to date is that given by Lord Denning in *Bratty v. A.-G. Northern Ireland.*[51] Having acknowledged that "the major mental diseases, which the doctors call psychoses ... are clearly diseases of the mind",[52] the learned Justice went on to assert that "any mental disorder which has manifested itself in violence and is prone to recur is a disease of the mind."[53]

In *Bratty*, psychomotor epilepsy was ruled a disease of the mind.[54] In *R. v. Borg*,[55] the Supreme Court of Canada seems to have accepted psychopathy as being a disease of the mind.[56] As pointed out in the previous chapter on automatism,[57] the phrase has also been held to include such disorders as brain tumour and cerebral arteriosclerosis.

C. "APPRECIATING THE NATURE AND QUALITY OF AN ACT OR OMISSION"

The phrase "nature and quality of an act" has been held to refer solely to the physical aspect of the act in question, as opposed to its legal or moral character.[58] But what precisely is meant by the physical nature and quality of an act? Williams has asserted that the phrase pertains to the *actus reus* of the crime. *Actus reus*, he has argued, "includes not only the physical act, the muscular movement, but also its consequences".[59] If, for example, Bozo slices off his mother-in-law's head thinking he is removing a giant wart, he cannot be said to appreciate the nature and quality of his actions even though he knows he is using a Black and Decker chain saw. Conversely, if Bozo blasts the old lady to kingdom-come with what he believes to be a .44 magnum, Bozo is guilty of murder even though unaware that he was in fact using a .357 magnum. As Williams has noted: ". . . the *actus reus* in murder is killing a human being, and if the accused knew that he was doing that there is no mis-

---

[51] [1961] 3 W.L.R. 965 (H.L.).

[52] *Ibid.*, at p. 981.

[53] *Ibid.*

[54] See also the cases of *R. v. Ditto* (1962), 132 C.C.C. 198 (Alta. C.A.); *R. v. O'Brien* (1965), 56 D.L.R. (2d) 65 (N.B.C.A.) and *R. v. Gillis* (1973), 13 C.C.C. (2d) 362 (B.C. Co. Ct.) discussed in Chapter 4.

[55] [1969] S.C.R. 551. But see the more recent decision of *R. v. Leech* (1973), 21 C.R.N.S. 1 in which the Alberta Supreme Court refused to call psychopathy a disease of the mind, saying (at p. 12): "...without deciding whether psychopathy is to be classed as a 'disease of the mind' from the medical point of view, it is clear that he did and does suffer from a disorder of the mind ...".

[56] See also *Chartrand v. The Queen* (1975), 26 C.C.C. (2d) 417 (S.C.C.); *R. v. Craig*, [1975] 2 W.W.R. 314 at p. 317 (Alta.), sentence vard 28 C.C.C. (2d) 311 (C.A.).

[57] See Chapter 4.

[58] *R. v. Codere* (1916), 12 Cr. App. R. 21 at p. 27; *R. v. Harrop*, [1940] 3 W.W.R. 77 (Man.C.A.). But see *R. v. Baltzer* (1974), 10 N.S.R. (2d) 561 (C.A.) at p. 582, where Mac-Donald J.A. remarked: "The capacity to *appreciate* the nature and quality of the act committed clearly imports the requirement of capacity to understand the moral significance of the act."

[59] Williams, *op. cit.* footnote 32, at p. 480.

take as to the nature and quality of his act . . . . For what is relevant is the killing, not the mode of killing."[60]

But what if Bozo were to open fire on his mother-in-law with a 12-gauge shotgun, mistaking the weapon for his secret "death ray"? According to Williams, the first branch of the *M'Naghten* rules would not exculpate him; despite his confusion, Bozo would still have had sufficient *mens rea* to be convicted. It should be pointed out, however, that the *M'Naghten* rules speak of a person who suffers from a disease of the mind being exculpated from criminal liability if the disease rendered him "incapable of *knowing* the nature and quality of the act".[61] By way of contrast, our Criminal Code provision substitutes the word "appreciating" for "knowing". Under this test, it is submitted that Bozo would be found insane. For as the Royal Commission on the Law of Insanity as a Defence in Criminal Cases pointed out, "the word 'appreciating', not being a word that is synonymous with 'knowing', requires far reaching legal and medical consideration when discussing Canadian law".[62] The major effect of this substitution is to require of the defendant an understanding of his actions which goes beyond *mens rea*. Although the Alberta Supreme Court held in the case of *R. v. Leech*[63] that ". . . it is not necessary [in order that the defence fail] that the accused appreciate or be sensible beyond the fact that his action will result in the actus reus", it is submitted that forsight of the *actus reus* is not synonymous with a full appreciation of the physical nature and quality of the act. Appreciation necessarily requires a capacity to perceive object reality in a more or less accurate manner. To appreciate, says the New Oxford Dictionary, is "To estimate aright, to perceive the full force of. B. Esp. to be sensitive to, or sensible of, any delicate impression or distinction".[64] While an accused who fires his "death ray" at someone may indeed intend the *actus reus* of killing, he would certainly not appreciate the physical reality of his actions if he was so disordered as not to realize that his weapon was in fact a shotgun.

From a psychiatric standpoint, it is possible that the use of the word "appreciating" in s. 16 brings the criminal law definition of insanity closer to the concept of psychosis. In the United States, where the *M'Naghten* rules have been adopted with the word "knowing" included, the complaint has arisen that "there are some instances of psychosis in which under all legal formulae of responsibility the defendant might well be found responsible."[65] It is doubtful, however, that psychosis (which, by definition, involves a failure to evaluate correctly external reality) would permit an appreciation of one's actions sufficient to meet the test of criminal responsibility in Canada. Taken in its broadest sense, it may in fact be argued that the word "appreciate" connotes a

---

[60] *Ibid.*, at p. 479.
[61] *M'Naghten's Case* (1843), 10 Cl. & Fin. 200 at p. 210, 8 E.R. 173 (emphasis added).
[62] *Report*, Ottawa, 1956, c. 5.
[63] (1973), 21 C.R.N.S. 1 at p. 11.
[64] Cited in *R. v. Leech* at p. 11.
[65] Guttmacher, "What Can the Psychiatrist Contribute to the Issue of Criminal Responsibility?" (1963), J. Nerv. and Ment. Disease 103 at p. 105.

metaphysical understanding of which even the sanest of men are incapable.[66]

D. "KNOWING THAT AN ACT OR OMISSION IS WRONG"

Regardless of whether he was capable of appreciating the nature and quality of an act, an accused may be found insane within the meaning of s. 16 if natural imbecility or a disease of the mind prevented him from knowing that the act was wrong.[67] But does "wrong" mean *morally* wrong or merely illegal? Since the decision of *R. v. Codere*,[68] the word's interpretation has been the subject of considerable controversy. In that case the English Court of Criminal Appeal ambiguously held that the test was "whether according to the ordinary standard adopted by reasonable men the act was right or wrong".[69] While Canadian decisions like *R. v. Cracknell*;[70] *R. v. Harrop*;[71] *R. v. Jeanotte*[72] and *R. v. O.*[73] have placed a moral connotation on the word "wrong",[74] others such as *R. v. Cardinal*;[75] *R. v. Wolfson*;[76] *R. v. Jessamine*[77] and *R. v. Mathews*[78] have been supportive of the view expressed in the English case of *R. v. Windle*,[79] namely, that "wrong" means legally wrong and nothing more.[80]

Recently the matter came before the Supreme Court of Canada. In

---

[66] See Fingarette, *op. cit.* footnote 43, at p. 150 and Williams, *op. cit.* footnote 32, pp. 491-2. See also the case of *R. v. Porter* (1936), 55 C.L.R. 182 at p. 188 (Aust. H.C.), where Dixon J. (as he then was) stated in his address to the jury: "In a case where a man intentionally destroys life he may have so little capacity for understanding the nature of life and the destruction of life, that to him it is no more than breaking a twig or destroying an inanimate object. In such a case he would not know the physical nature of what he was doing. He would not know the implications and what it really amounted to." Here it seems that Dixon J. was using the word "know" in the broader sense of "appreciate". Commenting on this passage, Williams has written (*op. cit.* footnote 32, at p. 491): "If this refers to a case where the accused does not realise that he is killing (as it probably does), the opinion accords with generally accepted principles. If it refers to a case where the accused knows he is killing, but, because of his insanity, sets no value on life, it goes beyond them". *Quaere* whether Dixon J.'s statement, if given the latter interpretation, would be an appropriate direction to give a Canadian jury.

[67] *R. v. Cardinal* (1953), 17 C.R. 373 (Alta. C.A.), applying *R. v. Holmes* [1953] 1 W.L.R. 686.

[68] (1916), 12 Cr. App. R. 21.

[69] *Ibid.*, at pp. 27-8.

[70] [1931] O.R. 634 (C.A.).

[71] [1940] 3 W.W.R. 77 (Man. C.A.).

[72] [1932] 2 W.W.R. 283 (Sask. C.A.).

[73] (1960-61), 3 Crim. L.Q. 151.

[74] See also *R. v. Laycock*, [1952] O.R. 908 (C.A.); *Stapleton v. The Queen* (1952), 86 C.L.R. 358 (Aust. H.C.); *People v. Schmidt* (1915), 216 N.Y. 324.

[75] (1953), 17 C.R. 373 (Alta. C.A.).

[76] [1965] 3 C.C.C. 304 (Alta. C.A.)

[77] (1912), 21 O.W.R. 392 (C.A.).

[78] (1953), 17 C.R. 241 (B.C.C.A.).

[79] [1952] 2 Q.B. 826

[80] See also *R. v. Holmes*, [1953] 1 W.L.R. 686.

Schwartz v. The Queen[81] a majority of the nine-man bench (Martland, Judson, Ritchie, Pigeon and de Grandpré JJ.) opted for the latter interpretation. Martland J., speaking for the majority, stated:

> "In brief, it is my opinion that the effect of s. 16(2) is to provide protection to a person suffering from disease of the mind who has committed a crime if, in committing the crime, he did not appreciate what he was doing or, if he did have that appreciation, he did not know that he was committing a crime."[82]

Commenting on the test propounded in *Stapleton v. The Queen*[83] (which was similar to that stated in *Codere*) Martland J. continued:

> "The test as to knowledge of 'wrong' which is stated by Dixon C.J. in the *Stapleton* case is as to whether the accused knew that his act was wrong according to the ordinary principles of reasonable men. I find it difficult to see how this test really differs from the test as to whether he knew he was committing a crime. Surely, according to the ordinary principles of reasonable men, it is wrong to commit a crime. This must be so in relation to the crime of murder. If there is a difference between these tests, and it could be contended that the commission of a particular crime, though known to be illegal, was considered to be morally justifiable in the opinion of ordinary men, I do not see why a person who committed a crime in such circumstances should be protected from conviction if suffering from disease of the mind and not protected if he committed the crime when sane."[84]

The minority of the Court (Laskin C.J.C., Spence, Dickson and Beetz JJ.) relied on rules of statutory construction to support its view that the word "wrong" in s. 16 had acquired a moral connotation. In the words of Dickson J.:

> "Accepted legal authorities respecting statutory construction confirm the validity of construing one part of a statute by reference to another part of the same statute. If Parliament had intended 'wrong' to mean 'contrary to law', one might expect use of the word 'unlawful', which is used in sections of the Code dealing with assembly (s. 64), riots (s. 65), drilling (s. 71) and solemnization of marriage (s. 258) or possibly the word 'illegal', which is used in s. 215(4) of the Code dealing with arrests."[85]

Having surveyed the case law, as well as the historical origins of the right-wrong test, Dickson J. concluded: "The question for the jury is

---

[81] (1976), 34 C.R.N.S. 138.
[82] *Ibid.*, at p. 149.
[83] (1952), 86 C.L.R. 358 (Aust. H.C.).
[84] *Supra*, footnote 81 at pp. 149-50.
[85] *Ibid.*, at p. 153.

whether mental illness so obstructed the thought processes of the accused as to make him incapable of knowing that his acts were morally wrong."[86] He added that " 'Moral wrong' is not to be judged by the personal standards of the offender but by his awareness that society regards the act as wrong."[87]

Presumably, the reasoning behind wishing to make the test whether or not the accused knew that an act was morally wrong by his own personal standards would be to benefit the victim of mental disease who may not know the difference between right and wrong even though he knows his act is illegal. In his *A History of the Criminal Law of England*,[88] Stephen has provided the following example to illustrate the operation of this rationale:

> "A kills B knowing that he is killing B, and knowing that it is illegal to kill B, but under an insane delusion that the salvation of the human race will be obtained by his execution for the murder of B, and that God has commanded him (A) to produce that result by those means. A's act is a crime if the word 'wrong' means illegal. It is not a crime if the word 'wrong' means morally wrong."

It has been suggested, however, that to interpret wrongfulness according to the accused's personal moral standards would "undermine the foundations of criminal law";[89] no offender should be allowed to escape criminal responsibility simply because he or she has a clear conscience. If, on the other hand, we were to judge wrongfulness by the moral standards of society (as the minority in *Schwartz* suggested), it is submitted that the right-wrong test would become virtually meaningless. In the case of certain crimes (*e.g.* abortion), even the most lucid individual would have trouble appraising society's views without conducting an opinion poll. In the case of other crimes (*e.g.* rape) the most severe psychotic might know that they are morally condemned by society.[90] Unfortunately, this latter difficulty inheres as well in the Supreme Court's equation of wrongfulness with simple illegality.[91]

Though he rejects the right-wrong test altogether, Fingarette, in his *The Meaning of Criminal Insanity*, has suggested that the best way to interpret wrongfulness is according to the personal moral standards of the defendant. Although, he has argued, "we cannot generally allow a person to be exculpated of criminal responsibility simply because in his own mind, for whatever reasons, he believed his act not to be wrong",[92] he has pointed out that there is a "crucial difference . . . if the person's own moral view of his act comes from mental disease."[93] Fingarette has expanded on the argument as follows:

---

[86] *Ibid.*, at p. 161.
[87] *Ibid.*, at p. 151.
[88] (New York, Burt Franklin, 1883), vol. II at p. 149.
[89] Fingarette, *op. cit.* footnote 43, at p. 154.
[90] *Ibid.*, at pp. 153-4.
[91] *Ibid.*, at p. 153.
[92] *Ibid.*, at p. 154.
[93] *Ibid.*

"... we normally do not allow a person's moral convictions to serve as a defense to criminal charges because we normally and tacitly assume that a person is not acting out of mental disease. No doubt a good many criminals believe even in their own minds that they did wrong in violating the law as they did; but other criminals — whether because of social, economic, political, religious, or other reasons — judge their conduct to have been morally right even though illegal. Nevertheless, regardless of his personal moral views, the average citizen must expect to have to 'take his medicine,' to suffer the consequences if he violates the law and is apprehended. For the law generally presumes men to be sane, and it is this tacit presumption that makes it seem right to us to hold him responsible for his law violations. We do not say his moral views cancel the law but that they call for him, in his opinion, to do what violates the law; and the moral person stands, and should be ready to stand, responsible for what he does. But if the moral views on which the person acts are due to mental disease, should we not then consider him insane and refrain from blame and condemnation? Is not the question of normality or disease somehow always in the back of our mind?"[94]

The precise effect of the *Schwartz* decision is difficult to assess. In the recent case of *R. v. Meadus*,[95] Wright J. of the Ontario Supreme Court remarked (in the jury's absence): "The opinions in the *Schwartz* case were not necessary for the decision of the appeal by the majority and are not strictly binding on anyone."[96] The learned Justice pointed out that the majority had offered its interpretation "only because the matter was fully argued before us, and it would be desirable that an expression of opinion on this point by this Court should now be made."[97] Wright J. then went on to charge the jury in part as follows:

" 'Wrong' can mean two things. It can mean wrong as contrary to the law or as a crime or it can mean wrong in the moral sense, that is wrong in that it is contrary to what you consider would be the view of reasonable men in our society as to good or evil. I have put it to you that if *either* of these conditions are so, he is entitled to a verdict of not guilty by reason of insanity. That is to say, if you find on a preponderance of evidence that owing to the disease of his mind he was unable to know that the act was contrary to the Criminal law or is a crime, he is entitled to the verdict of not guilty by reason of insanity, or if you find that because of his disease of the mind he was incapable of knowing that his act was morally wrong, that is, was contrary to the generally accepted moral standard of good and evil held by reasonable people in our society, if either of those conditions existed in your opinion, then my instructions to you are that

---

[94] *Ibid.*, at pp. 154-5.
[95] Unreported, 8 October 1976.
[96] At p. 8 of the original judgment.
[97] *Schwartz, supra*, footnote 81 at p. 144.

he is entitled to a verdict of not guilty by reason of insanity."[98]

The jury found the accused not guilty by reason of insanity.

In the more recent case of *R. v. Simpson*,[99] however, the Ontario Court
of Appeal adopted the Supreme Court of Canada's interpretation without discussion. Commenting on the broad direction given by McRuer
C.J.H.C. in *R. v. O.*[100] (which was similar to that in *Meadus*), Martin J.A.
stated simply:

> "The above direction with respect to the meaning of the word
> 'wrong' in the second branch of the test of insanity under s. 16(2)
> must now be taken to be incorrect. In *Schwartz v. The Queen* ... the
> Supreme Court of Canada held that knowledge that the act is
> 'wrong' means knowledge on the part of the accused that he was
> committing a criminal act."[101]

E. DELUSIONS

Evidence that an accused suffers from delusions is not in itself proof of
criminal insanity.[102] Subsection 16(3) of our Criminal Code provides,
however, that a person who suffers from specific delusions yet is otherwise sane may raise the defence of insanity if those delusions caused him
to believe in the existence of a state of things which, if it existed, would
have provided justification or excuse for his behaviour. The trouble with
this provision is that it provides a defence for someone who, from a medical standpoint, could not exist. It exculpates the man who is sane in all
other respects save for his specific delusion that his wife is a salami. In
1956 the Royal Commission on the Law of Insanity recommended in its
report that s-s. (3) be dropped from the Criminal Code. The Report
stated:[103]

> "The preponderance of medical evidence condemned the wording of
> this subsection on the ground that it describes a person who could
> not exist. The opinion of these witnesses was that no one who has
> 'specific delusions' could be 'in other respects sane'. We think that
> from a medical point of view the arguments put forward in support
> of this opinion are conclusive."

However, the Commission did not elaborate on what these arguments
were. The idea that an individual might suffer from specific delusions
and yet remain otherwise unaffected mentally seems to be premised

---

[98] *Meadus, supra*, footnote 95 at pp. 4-5 of the original judgment.
[99] (1977), 35 C.C.C. (2d) 337.
[100] (1960-61), 3 Crim. L.Q. 151.
[101] *Supra*, footnote 99 at p. 353.
[102] *R. v. Harper* (1913), 9 Cr. App. R. 41.
[103] McRuer, *Report of the Royal Commission on The Law of Insanity as a Defence in Criminal Cases* (Hull, Queen's Printer, 1956) at p. 36. Note that a deluded accused could still
assert lack of appreciation. See *R. v. Adamcik*, [1977] 3 W.W.R. 29 (B.C. Co. Ct.).

upon the apparent belief of the judges in *M'Naghten's Case* in the now-discredited theories of phrenology and monomania.[104]

The major legal complaint with respect to the delusion defence is that a person acting under a delusion is judged by the same standard as a sane person. Assuming that the delusion is reality to the person experiencing it, the law requires that he act rationally within the framework of that delusion. In the words of Isaac Ray:

> "This is virtually saying to a man, 'You are allowed to be insane; ... but have a care how you manifest your insanity; there must be method in your madness. Having once adopted your delusion, all the subsequent steps connected with it must be conformed to the strictest requirements of reason .... In short, having become fairly enveloped in the clouds of mental disorder, the law expects you will move as discreetly and circumspectly as if the undimmed light of reason were shining upon your path'."[105]

It may be that a person who was in all other respects sane would be capable of exercising reason within the context of his delusions but, as stated earlier, such person is unknown to medical science.

It has been pointed out[106] that persons who commit criminal acts while operating under delusions would be found insane without having to resort specifically to the "delusion defence" embodied in s-s. 16(3). Suppose, for example, that Bozo harpoons his wife in the bathtub while under the insane delusion that Mrs. Bozo is the great white whale. In such circumstances, Bozo might rely upon the first limb of s-s. 16(2), *i.e.* lack of appreciation of the nature and quality of his actions. The only reason to invoke s-s. (3) specifically might be to dispense with the necessity of proving natural imbecility or disease of the mind.

Even if we assume that specific delusions need not be symptomatic of a "disease of the mind", the delusion defence is not without its difficulties. Let us suppose that Bozo is sane in all respects save for the specific delusion that Parliament has given him an unqualified licence to kill. Were he to liquidate his cousin Maury for cracking his knuckles too loudly, Bozo would presumably be found insane. If, however, Bozo were sane except for the delusion that God had ordered him to "slay thy cousin Maury", things would be different. If Bozo knew that such an act was illegal, he would not be able to premise an insanity defence upon s-s. 16(3).[107] As Stephen once remarked, "if a special Divine order were given to a man to commit murder, I should certainly hang him for it, unless I got a special Divine order not to hang him."[108] Interestingly, a delusion that he was the Angel of Death would have exculpated Bozo since the

---

[104] See Chapter 3 *ante* at p. 72.

[105] Isaac Ray, *Medical Jurisprudence*, 4th ed., at pp. 46-7, as quoted by Williams, *op. cit.* footnote 32, at p. 505.

[106] Smith and Hogan, *op. cit.* footnote 40, at p. 138; Williams, at pp. 500-1.

[107] *I.e.*, if an act is illegal even within the delusional framework, there can be no justification or excuse for it, even assuming the delusional fact situation to have been true. See Williams at p. 503.

[108] Stephen, *op. cit.* footnote 88, at p. 160, footnote 1.

criminal law of Canada binds men, not angels.[109]

It is submitted that the disparate results which the above hypothetical situations produce illustrate graphically the fatal flaw of the delusion rationale. While all three situations involve an accused who suffers from grandiose delusions of similar proportion, the law does not in fact consider them on an equal footing. Distinguishing delusions on the basis of minute details (details which, from a psychological standpoint, are probably quite inconsequential) the law fails to consider one feature common to them all, namely, that each is the product of severe mental disorder. Examining the first and second hypothetical situations, it is indeed curious to note that the law excuses an act of aggression where the defendant's only delusion was that he would escape conviction (so where is the delusion?), yet condemns the same act if motivated by a genuine but deluded belief in its morality.

A further consequence of the preoccupation with details inherent in the delusion defence has been pointed out by Glanville Williams. Where the delusion involves a complicated fact situation, the court might end up having to try a make-believe case based on delusional "facts" in order to ascertain whether the imagined situation, if real, would have afforded justification or excuse for the accused's act or omission. In Williams' words:

"Suppose that a lunatic shoots a person whom he believes to be Guy Fawkes, about to blow up the Houses of Parliament. According to the delusional facts, the act is justifiable, provided that there was no other means of preventing the supposed culprit from executing his nefarious purpose. We therefore have to inquire into the imagination of the accused in order to determine what stage the supposed Guy Fawkes was supposed to have reached in his plot, what help the lunatic supposed was available to arrest the conspirators, at what part of Guy Fawkes' body he supposed he was shooting, and so on. Only an exceptionally clear-headed lunatic would be able to furnish all these details of his delusion. Yet without them the case cannot be decided, except indeed with the aid of an artificial rule relating to burden of proof."[110]

F. IRRESISTIBLE IMPULSE

Medically, perhaps the only impulses which can be called irresistible with certainty are those produced by a state of automatism. Automatism is a situation, however, where the subject is deprived of conscious will and the law calls the conduct of such person involuntary. Because the law seems to separate involuntary conduct from what it calls "irresistible impulse",[111] the meaning of the term is not altogether clear.

From the few English cases in which irresistible impulse has afforded

---

[109] See Williams, at p. 502.
[110] *Ibid.*
[111] See Morris and Howard, *Studies in Criminal Law* (Oxford, Clarendon, 1964) at p. 62.

the defence of insanity,[112] it would seem that the expression is applicable in situations where the accused appreciates the nature and quality of his act and knows that it is wrong, but, through mental disease, is unable to control his actions. Because such situations fall outside the scope of the *M'Naghten* rules, however, the prevailing view is that the separate defence of irresistible impulse is unknown in English law.[113] It is for this reason, moreover, that the *M'Naghten* rules have received their most severe criticism. As Hart has pointed out:[114]

> "From the start English critics denounced these rules because their effect is to excuse from criminal responsibility only those whose mental abnormality resulted in a lack of knowledge: in the eyes of these critics this amounted to a dogmatic refusal to acknowledge the fact that a man might know what he was doing and that it was wrong or illegal and yet because of his abnormal mental state might lack the capacity to control his action. This lack of capacity, the critics urged, must be the fundamental point in any intelligible doctrine of responsibility. The point just is that in a civilized system only those who *could have* kept the law should be punished. Why else should we bother about a man's knowledge or intention or other mental element except as throwing light on this?"

According to Smith and Hogan, the recognition of irresistible impulse has been opposed "on the ground of the difficulty — or impossibility — of distinguishing between an impulse which proves irresistible because of insanity and one which is irresistible because of ordinary motives of greed, jealousy or revenge."[115] Sceptical as to whether or not any impulses are truly irresistible, the courts have preferred to make examples of those defendants who have succumbed rather than allow them a defence. As Riddell J. remarked in *R. v. Creighton*:[116] "If you cannot resist an impulse in any other way, we will hang a rope in front of your eyes, and perhaps that will help."

It would appear that the notion of irresistible impulse has failed as well to gain unanimous support amongst psychiatrists. While some have asserted that "Every tenet of modern psychiatry points toward the acceptance of the 'irresistible impulse' plea as a proper defense in criminal law",[117] others have maintained that the concept is not psychiat-

---

[112] See *R. v. Oxford* (1840), 9 C. & P. 525; *R. v. Hay* (1911), 22 Cox C.C. 268; *R. v. Gill*, 2 Hamilton and Godkin's Leg. Med. 248; *R. v. Fryer* (1915), 24 Cox C.C. 403.
[113] See *R. v. Aughet* (1918), 13 Cr. App. R. 101; *R. v. Holt* (1920), 15 Cr. App. R. 10; *R. v. Kopsch* (1925), 19 Cr. App. R. 50; *R. v. Coelho* (1914), 10 Cr. App. R. 210; *R. v. Quarmby* (1921), 15 Cr. App. R. 163; *R. v. Thomas* (1911), 7 Cr. App. R. 36. In England, an individual suffering from irresistible impulses may, however, escape conviction for murder by asserting the defence of diminished responsibility. See Chapter 6 *post* at pp. 183-5.
[114] Hart, *Punishment and Responsibility* (Oxford, Clarendon, 1968) at p. 189.
[115] Smith and Hogan, *op. cit.* footnote 40, at p. 139.
[116] (1908), 14 C.C.C. 349 at p. 350 (Ont.).
[117] Hoedemaker, " 'Irresistible Impulse' as a Defense in Criminal Law" (1948), 23 Washington L. Rev. 1 at p. 7. See also the authorities cited by Keedy, "Irresistible Impulse in Criminal Law" (1952), 100 U. Pa. L. Rev. 956 at p. 989, footnote 201.

rically sound.[118]

Although Canadian courts have refused to recognize irresistible impulse as a form of insanity *per se*,[119] it was held by the Judicial Committee for the Privy Council in *A.-G. South Australia v. Brown*[120] that while there was no presumption that irresistible impulse is a disease of the mind, medical evidence might be given to show (a) that the accused's irresistible impulses were symptoms of a disease of the mind, and (b) that such irresistible impulses might prevent him from appreciating the nature and quality of an act or from knowing that it was wrong. This ruling was approved of by Hall J. (with whom Spence J. concurred) in the Supreme Court of Canada decision in *R. v. Borg*.[121] It seems, however, that where the term "irresistible impulse" has been applied to the motivations of persons tried in Canada, the accused has generally been diagnosed as a psychopathic personality. And although juries have been free to find psychopathy a disease of the mind which may have prevented the defendant from appreciating the nature and quality of an act or from knowing that it was wrong, they have been reluctant indeed to do so.[122] The word "irresistible" would seem to be an adjective ill-suited for the impulses of a psychopath, since the psychopath with his defective *ego* makes no real attempt to resist them. Perhaps more compelling as an excuse is the impulsive behaviour of some neurotics, although here, too, irresistible impulse has yet to entitle the neurotic to the insanity defence in Canada. In the United States, however, what is termed an "impulse neurosis" may well afford such defence in those jurisdictions which recognize irresistible impulse as a separate branch of insanity.[123] Persons suffering from this affliction may occasionally perform unusual or bizarre acts in the hope of achieving pleasure.[124] Typical impulsive neurotics are kleptomaniacs, pyromaniacs, voyeurs and exhibitionists. While it cannot be said that the compulsive neurotic does not feel that his acts are wrong, his impulses are to him quite overpowering even though he has tried hard to resist them. It may be questioned, also, whether the hysterical neurotic acting in what is called a "dissociated state" is not suffering from what approaches being an irre-

---

[118] See Davidson, "Irresistible Impulse and Criminal Responsibility" (1956), J. For. Sci. 1 at p. 6. And see the authorities cited by Keedy, at p. 989, footnote 202.

[119] *R. v. Wolfson*, [1965] 3 C.C.C. 304 (Alta. C.A.); *R. v. Creighton* (1908), 14 C.C.C. 349 (Ont.); *R. v. Borg*, [1969] S.C.R. 551; *Dion v. The Queen*, [1965] Que. Q.B. 238 (C.A.), appeal to the Supreme Court dismissed [1965] S.C.R.; *R. v. Leech* (1973), 21 C.R.N.S. 1 (Alta.). Canadian courts have, however, recognized irresistible impulse as a factor which may negative the requirement of planning and deliberation in first degree murder cases. See Chapter 6 *post* at pp. 166-9.

[120] [1960] A.C. 432.

[121] [1969] S.C.R. 551.

[122] Note, however, the jury's finding in *R. v. Smith* (1967), 5 C.R.N.S. 162 (Ont.) that the accused, who was diagnosed as a "pathological personality" (a vague term meaning nothing more than "sick"), was insane. It is unclear from the report whether or not the accused was in fact a psychopath, although counsel for the defence seems to have used the term "pathological personality" and "psychopath" interchangeably in his address to the jury.

[123] Weihofen, *Mental Disease as a Criminal Defense* (Buffalo, Dennis, 1954) at p. 21.

[124] *Ibid.*

sistible impulse produced by a disease of the mind. Such severe neurotics are responsible for their share of murders.[125] Although they may appear normal in their day-to-day life and conform quietly to the laws of the land on a regular basis, they may become overpowered by some combination of circumstances and "explode", committing violent crimes in a state of confused consciousness.[126] If produced by a psychosis, a dissociated state may well support the defence of insanity. Where it is the product of hysterical neurosis, however, it may be argued that a verdict of insanity would be unfounded because the individual would have sufficient appreciation of the nature and quality of his actions and knowledge of their wrongfulness.[127] As demonstrated in a previous chapter,[128] however, dissociated states have provided accused persons with the defence of non-insane automatism.

V. Evidence

For a long time, it appears to have been the practice in England to allow only the defence to bring forth evidence of an accused's insanity at the time of the alleged offence.[129] The decisions in cases like *R. v. Smith*[130] and *R. v. Casey*[131] would seem to lend support to the contention that this was the law, although it has since been suggested that such was never the case — that although it was common practice it was never a procedural rule.[132] The practice of allowing the Crown to adduce medical evidence of an accused's insanity once the accused's state of mind has been put in issue by the defence is exemplified by the case of *R. v. Kemp*.[133] There it was held that medical evidence of insanity could be called by the prosecution in rebuttal of the defence's claim that the accused was acting in a state of non-insane automatism at the time of the alleged crime. The decision in *Kemp* was approved of in the well-known case of *Bratty v. A.-G. Northern Ireland*,[134] where Lord Denning went a step further by asserting that in such circumstances a positive duty rested

---

[125] *Ibid.*, at p. 18.

[126] *Ibid.*, at p. 19.

[127] *Ibid.* But see the *Manual for the Classification of Psychiatric Diagnoses* (Ottawa, Information Canada, 1974) at p. 33, where it is stated: "The neuroses, as contrasted to the psychoses, manifest neither gross distortion or misinterpretation of external reality nor gross personality disorganization. A possible exception to this is hysterical neurosis, which some believe may occasionally be accompanied by hallucinations and other symptoms encountered in psychoses."

[128] See Chapter 4 *ante* at pp. 101-2, 104-6.

[129] See Royal Commission on Capital Punishment, 1949/53; *Report*, Cmnd. 8932 (London, H.M.S.O., 1953).

[130] (1910), 6 Cr. App. R. 19.

[131] (1947), 63 T.L.R. 487 (C.C.A.).

[132] See *R. v. Chan Ming Luk*, [1962] H.K.L.R. 651 at pp. 656-7.

[133] [1957] 1 Q.B. 399. See also *R. v. Bastian*, [1958] 1 W.L.R. 413.

[134] [1961] 3 W.L.R. 965.

upon the Crown to call medical evidence of insanity rather than allow a dangerous individual to be at large.[135] Both *Kemp* and *Bratty* have been followed in Canada.[136]

It would appear from some relatively recent Canadian decisions that the prosecution is entitled to lead evidence of an accused's insanity even in cases where the accused has not raised mental disorder as a defence. According to Martin J.A. in *R. v. Simpson*,[137] the rule is that a trial judge may "exclude evidence of insanity when tendered by the prosecution unless he is satisfied that the evidence of insanity proposed to be tendered is sufficiently substantial that the interest of justice requires that it be adduced." His Lordship elaborated as follows:

> "In no case would the interest of justice require the prosecution to adduce such evidence until evidence had been previously adduced which would warrant a jury being satisfied beyond a reasonable doubt that the accused committed the act charged with the requisite criminal intent, apart from a condition of insanity.
>
> "Where the prosecution seeks to adduce evidence that the accused was insane at the time of the act, the proper test, in my view, is not whether, if advanced by the accused, the evidence would be sufficient to require the defence of insanity to be submitted to the jury by the trial Judge, but whether it is sufficiently substantial and creates such a grave question whether the accused had the capacity to commit the offence that the interest of justice requires it to be adduced."[138]

Moreover:

> "In any case where the prosecution adduces evidence of insanity and the accused denies the commission of the act, it is incumbent upon the trial Judge to direct the jury that they are not to consider the evidence of insanity unless and until they are satisfied beyond a reasonable doubt that the accused committed the act charged with the requisite criminal intent."[139]

In *R. v. Frank*[140] it was held that the Crown could introduce reply evidence of insanity though the accused did not wish his mental condition to become an issue and had expressly disclaimed insanity.[141] While psy-

---

[135] *Ibid.*, at p. 980.

[136] See *R. v. Gillis* (1973), 13 C.C.C. (2d) 362 (B.C. Co. Ct.).

[137] (1977), 35 C.C.C. (2d) 337 (Ont. C.A.).

[138] *Ibid.*, at p. 362.

[139] *Ibid.*, at p. 363.

[140] (1971), 12 C.R.N.S. 339 (Ont.).

[141] Here the court placed great reliance on *Lowther v. The Queen* (1957), 26 C.R. 150, where it was held by the Quebec Court of Queen's Bench (at p. 158) that it was the duty of the presiding judge to direct the jury's attention to any evidence which disclosed possible insanity "despite the protestations to the contrary of counsel for the defence". May it be assumed from the reasoning in the *Frank* case that the power of the prosecution to adduce evidence of the accused's mental condition extends to non-insane auto-

chiatric evidence of insanity cannot normally be placed before the jury during the prosecution's case in-chief,[142] there is an important exception to this rule. Where the accused wishes to enter a plea of guilty, it would appear from the recent decisions in *R. v. Scroggie*[143] and *R. v. Haymour*[144] that the court may (or indeed must) refuse to accept such plea in order that the Crown be permitted to show that the person is not guilty by reason of insanity.

It seems clear from cases like *R. v. Dart*[145] and *R. v. Lloyd*[146] that medical or scientific evidence need not be produced in order to justify a finding of insanity, since a jury is entitled to infer insanity from the accused's actions. Moreover, inferences may be drawn from the defendant's conduct before, during and after the alleged offence.[147] While legal insanity may not be inferred from the existence of mental disorder in the accused's family or ancestors, it was held in the case of *R. v. Barbour*[148] that such evidence might well be corroborative of independent evidence that the accused was suffering from mental disorder at the time of the alleged crime.

As regards the burden of proof, s-s. 16(4) of the Criminal Code provides that until the contrary is proved everyone is presumed to be and to have been sane. In order to displace this presumption, it seems that the party raising insanity (be it the defence or prosecution)[149] must prove the facts necessary to constitute that defence on a balance of probabilities basis.[150] It is not necessary to prove insanity beyond a reasonable doubt.[151] Moreover, it would appear from such cases as *R. v. Chupiuk*[152]

---

matism as well as insanity? It is doubtful that in practice the situation would arise. While a verdict of insanity means detention of the accused in a mental institution at the pleasure of the provincial lieutenant-governor, a finding of non-insane automatism results in acquittal. The general duty resting upon the Crown to make evidence available which tends to substantiate a defence probably does not extend to the actual calling of witnesses. Although they were not referred to in the judgment, the English cases of *R. v. Ireland*, [1910] 1 K.B. 654 and *R. v. Taylor*, [1915] 2 K.B. 709 would seem to lend support to the decision of Moorehouse J.

[142] *R. v. Dixon*, [1961] 3 All E.R. 460n. Nor can psychiatric evidence of the accused's sanity: *R. v. Smith* (1912), 8 Cr. App. R. 72. But see *R. v. Abramovitch* (1912), 7 Cr. App. R. 145. The normal case is for the prosecution to call psychiatric evidence to *rebut* the defence of insanity once it has been raised. See *R. v. Nott* (1958), 43 Cr. App. R. 8 for instance. There the prosecution called evidence of diminished responsibility. Six years later the tactic of leading evidence of diminished responsibility to rebut insanity, and *vice versa* (*R. v. Russell* (1964), 48 Cr. App. R. 62), was to become regulated, at least in murder trials, by s. 6 of England's Criminal Procedure (Insanity) Act, 1964, c. 84. This Act overruled *R. v. Price*, [1963] 2 Q.B. 1, putting an end to the "conflict of practice" referred to by Lord Parker C.J. In *R. v. Duke*, [1963] 1 Q.B. 120 at p. 124.

[143] [1974] 2 W.W.R. 641 (B.C.).

[144] (1974), 21 C.C.C. (2d) 30 (B.C. Prov. Ct.).

[145] (1878), 14 Cox C.C. 143.

[146] (1927), 20 Cr. App. R. 139.

[147] *R. v. Brockenshire and Clarkson*, [1932] 1 D.L.R. 156 (Ont. C.A.).

[148] (1938), 13 M.P.R. 203 (N.B.C.A.); affd [1938] S.C.R. 465. See also *R. v. Ross Tucket* (1844), 1 Cox C.C. 103.

[149] *R. v. Gillis* (1973), 13 C.C.C. (2d) 362 at pp. 367-8 (B.C. Co. Ct.); *R. v. Haymour* (1974), 21 C.C.C. (2d) 30 at p. 42 (B.C. Prov. Ct.); *R. v. Simpson* (1977), 35 C.C.C. (2d) 337 (Ont. C.A.).

[150] *Smythe v. The King*, [1941] S.C.R. 17.

[151] *R. v. Anderson* (1914), 22 C.C.C. 455 (Alta. C.A.); *Clark v. The King* (1921), 61 S.C.R. 608, overruling *R. v. Kierstead* (1918), 42 D.L.R. 193 (N.B.C.A.).

[152] [1949] 2 W.W.R. 801 (Sask. C.A.).

and *R. v. Cardinal*[153] that it is a misdirection for the trial judge to instruct the jury that to establish the defence it must be "clearly proved" that the accused has fulfilled the requirements of s. 16.

It has been pointed out[154] that requiring an accused to establish the defence of insanity by producing a preponderance of evidence may conflict with the general rule requiring the Crown to prove *mens rea* beyond reasonable doubt. Where the accused is relying on the first limb of the insanity defence, he must prove that because of "natural imbecility" or "disease of the mind" he was "incapable of appreciating the nature and quality of an act or omission". But this seems contradictory to the general rule regarding *mens rea* which, in effect, requires the prosecution to prove that the defendant *did* appreciate the nature and quality of his act.[155] Williams has reconciled the difficulty by asserting that "The confusion arises through failing to distinguish between the burden of introducing evidence and the burden of proof or persuasive burden".[156] He has argued that "It is only in the first sense that the burden in respect of the defence of insanity lies on the accused."[157] As Smith and Hogan have noted,[158] this inconsistency does not arise where the accused relies on the second limb of the insanity defence and asserts that natural imbecility or mental disease rendered him incapable of knowing that an act or omission was wrong. Such knowledge need not be proved by the prosecution in order to establish *mens rea*.

VI. Conclusions

Hopefully the foregoing discussion has served to clarify the procedural, substantive and evidential law surrounding the defence of insanity. A more fundamental problem which remains to be considered is whether or not the present law deals adequately with the mentally disordered defendant as regards the question of criminal responsibility. Should Canadian law continue to base its formulation of the insanity defence upon the *M'Naghten* rules of 1843?

Defenders of the *M'Naghten* rules have advanced several arguments in their support. It has been asserted, first, that their simplistic nature, rather than being a drawback, is the principle justification for their continued use.[159] As one commentator has stated, "they provide tests that

---

[153] (1953), 17 C.R. 373 (Alta. C.A.).
[154] Smith and Hogan, *op. cit.* footnote 40, at p. 141.
[155] *Ibid.*
[156] Williams, *Criminal Law: The General Part*, at p. 518.
[157] *Ibid.*
[158] *Criminal Law* at p. 141.
[159] Kuh, "The Insanity Defense — An Effort to Combine Law and Reason" (1962), 110 U. Pa. L. Rev. 771 at p. 784; Slovenko, "Psychiatry, Criminal Law, and the Role of the Psychiatrist" (1963), Duke L.J. 395 at p. 403.

are so elementary that trial jurors can readily understand and follow them . . .".[160] Moreover, the relative simplicity of the *M'Naghten* rules (as compared with a rule incorporating sophisticated psychiatric concepts)[161] reduces the dependency of jurors upon expert testimony. "Although there may have been testimony involving reports of psychiatric examinations", it has been argued, "this merely provides background, possibly helpful, but not vital to the jury's determination. *McNaughton* jurors are free to disregard this kind of information or to minimize its importance."[162] The narrow scope of the *M'Naghten* rules has received approval for promoting general deterrence of crime. Presumably by excluding the possibility of irresistible impulse being raised as a defence, the present insanity test has the virtue of "subjecting to punishment all who are capable of being deterred".[163]

The *M'Naghten* rules have been severely criticized on psychological grounds. Concerned primarily with defects in cognition, they have been denounced for placing an inordinate value on the intellectual factor[164] while at the same time ignoring the possibility of emotional or volitional impairment.[165] Moreover, the rules have been said to ignore the role of the unconscious, the *M'Naghten* judgment having come 50 years before the explorations of Sigmund Freud.[166] It has been this type of criticism which has prompted the American courts to formulate alternative insanity defences.

One response to the evils of *M'Naghten* has been the test propounded in *United States v. Currens*.[167] In that case the Court of Appeals for the Third Circuit stated that an accused should be acquitted on the ground of insanity if "as a result of mental disease or defect", which existed at the time of the alleged offence, he "lacked substantial capacity to con-

---

[160] Kuh, at p. 784. The author has further stated that "Although the words 'nature and quality of the act' and knowledge that 'he was doing what was wrong' may at first blush, seem cloudy, our law allows them to be communicated by concrete examples which have unmistakable meaning for lay jurors".

[161] See Glueck, *Mental Disorder and the Criminal Law* (New York, Kraus, 1966) at p. 265.

[162] Kuh, at p. 785. The author has further maintained: "Although the standards in theory require that the inability to know the nature and quality of one's acts or to distinguish right from wrong stem from 'a defect of reason, from disease of the mind', a finding of such disease or defect follows almost automatically when it is found that a defendant was in such a state that he did not know the nature, quality, or wrongfulness of his actions. Hence, under McNaughton, no emphasis need be placed on the medical question of illness".

[163] Kennalley, "Modern Insanity Tests — Alternatives" (1976), 15 Washburn L.J. 88 at p. 100, citing *State v. White* (1962), 374 P. 2d 942, cert. denied (1963), 375 U.S. 883; *State v. Esser* (1962), 115 N.W. 2d 505.

[164] Aschaffenburg, "Psychiatry and Criminal Law" (1941), 32 J. Crim. Law and Criminology 3 at p. 5; Glueck, at pp. 226-7.

[165] Goldstein, *The Insanity Defense* (New Haven, Yale University Press, 1967) at p. 46; Weihofen, *op. cit.* footnote 49, at p. 66; Davidson, "Criminal Responsibility: The Quest for a Formula", in Hoch and Zubin, eds., *Psychiatry and the Law*, 1955 at p. 68.

[166] Weihofen, at p. 66. The author has pointed out (at p. 3) that in 1843 an accepted psychological theory was that of *phrenology*. That doctrine, invented by the Viennese physician Francis Gall, taught that each function of the mind was localized in its own corner of the brain, so that the phrenologist could calibrate a man's "ambition", "docility" or "amativeness" by measuring the corresponding bumps on his cranium.

[167] (1961), 190 F. 2d 751 (3rd Cir.).

form his conduct to the requirements of the law which he is alleged to have violated."[168] While this rule takes into account the accused's capacity to control his behaviour it is submitted that its chief drawback lies in its complete rejection of the criteria which *M'Naghten* focused upon, namely, the accused's capacity to understand the significance of his actions.

An alternative suggested by Jerome Hall would exculpate by reason of insanity "anyone who, because of a mental disease, is unable to understand what he is doing and to control his conduct at the time he commits a harm forbidden by criminal law".[169] This test focuses on both cognitive and volitional incapacities, thus combining the philosophies of *M'Naghten* and *Currens*, but ends up being narrower than either of the two previous tests. In order to raise a successful defence of insanity an accused must establish *both* volitional and cognitive impairment. Furthermore, such impairment must be total, as contrasted with the *substantial* impairment which the *Currens* test requires.

In 1954 the District of Columbia Circuit Court of Appeals abandoned the *M'Naghten* rules and adopted instead the so-called New Hampshire Rule[170] of 1870. In its landmark decision in *Durham v. United States*,[171] the court held that "an accused is not criminally responsible if his unlawful act was the product of mental disease or mental defect". This test was broader than *M'Naghten*, *Currens* or Hall's proposal, allowing defects in either volition or cognition to constitute a defence. It went a step beyond the mere appending of an irresistible impulse clause to the *M'Naghten* rules,[172] taking into account both impulsive loss of control and loss of control which may be preceded by long periods of brooding and reflection.

Although the court in *Durham* shied away from the use of medical or psychiatric terminology in an apparent effort to avoid domination of experts in the courtroom,[173] *Durham* seems nevertheless to have died in the stranglehold of forensic psychiatrists. As Bazelon C.J. stated in the case of *United States v. Brawner*:[174] "The term 'mental disease or mental defect' was saddled with an unintended and astringent medical meaning. And the 'productivity' requirement was perversely viewed as a locked door which could only be opened by an expert's key". In *Brawner*

---

[168] *Ibid.*, at p. 774.
[169] Hall *General Principles of Criminal Law*, 2nd ed. (Indianapolis, Bobbs-Merrill, 1960) at p. 521.
[170] See *State v. Jones* (1870), 50 N.H. 369; *State v. Pike* (1870), 49 N.H. 399, overruled on other grounds; *Hardy v. Merrill* (1875), 56 N.H. 227.
[171] (1954), 214 F. 2d 862 at pp. 874-5.
[172] The District of Columbia used a combination of *M'Naghten* and the irresistible impulse test for several years: *Holloway v. United States* (1945), 148 F. 2d 665 (D.C. Cir.); *Smith v. United States* (1929), 36 F. 2d 548 (D.C. Cir.). Previously *M'Naghten* alone had been used: *Grock v. United States* (1923), 289 F. 544 (D.C.); *Travers v. United States* (1895), 6 App. D.C. 450.
[173] See also Brady, "Abolish the Insanity Defense? — No!" (1971), 8 Houston L. Rev. 629 at p. 646 where it has been pointed out that "an approach which identifies the symptoms of mental disease or defect which excuse tends, as the history of *M'Naghten* shows, to perpetuate outmoded psychology."
[174] (1972), 471 F. 2d 969 at p. 1011 (D.C. Cir.).

the United States Court of Appeals for the District of Columbia scrapped the *Durham* rule and substituted therefor the rule stated in s-s. 4.01(1) of the American Law Institute's Model Penal Code.[175] That section provides:

"(1) A person is not responsible for criminal conduct if at the time of such conduct as a result of mental disease or defect he lacks substantial capacity either to appreciate the criminality [wrongfulness] of his conduct or to conform his conduct to the requirements of the law."

In adopting this formula, the majority of the Court expressly rejected a sweeping proposal made by the British Royal Commission on Capital Punishment in 1953.[176] Under that proposal a jury would be required to determine, without the aid of more specific guidelines, whether "at the time of the act the accused was suffering from disease of the mind (or mental deficiency) to such a degree that he ought not to be held responsible."[177] The major difficulty with the test, the Court felt, was that an instruction couched in terms of justice would allow juries to acquit or convict without reference to any legal standard. In the Court's words:

"It is one thing ... to tolerate and even welcome the jury's sense of equity as a force that affects its application of instructions which state the legal rules that crystallize the requirements of justice as determined by the lawmakers of the community. It is quite another to set the jury at large, without such crystallization, to evolve its own legal rules and standards of justice."[178]

In his dissenting judgment, Bazelon C.J. argued that the ALI test itself failed to offer any "legal rules that crystallize the requirements of justice" and that the test "merely reshuffles and obfuscates the *Durham* components,[179] [doing] nothing to sort out for the jury the difference between its function and the function of the expert witnesses".[180] Prefer-

---

[175] (Philadelphia, 1961). The ALI formulation was, in effect, recommended in s. 1-3C2 of c. 3C of U.S. Senate Bill 1 (93d Cong. 2nd Sess.) for inclusion in the proposed American Federal Criminal Code. According to that proposal:
"It is a defense that when a defendant engages in conduct which otherwise constitutes an offense, as a result of mental illness or defect he lacks substantial capacity to appreciate the character of his conduct or to control his conduct. 'Mental illness or defect' does not include any abnormality manifested by repeated criminal or otherwise anti-social conduct."
[176] Royal Commission on Capital Punishment, 1949/53; *Report* Cmd. 8932 (London, H.M.S.O., 1953).
[177] *Ibid.*, at p. 116.
[178] *Brawner, supra*, footnote 174 at p. 989.
[179] The learned Chief Justice further remarked (at p. 1031): "If the ALI test is indeed an improvement, it is not because it focuses attention on the *right* question, but only because it makes the *wrong* question so obscure that jurors may abandon the effort to answer it literally".
[180] *Supra*, footnote 174 at p. 1034.

ring the type of approach taken by the British Royal Commission, the learned Justice stated:

> "Our instruction to the jury should provide that a defendant is not responsible *if at the time of his unlawful conduct his mental or emotional processes or behaviour controls were impaired to such an extent that he cannot justly be held responsible for his act.* This test would ask the psychiatrist a single question: what is the nature of the impairment of the defendant's mental and emotional processes and behaviour controls? It would leave for the jury the question whether that impairment is sufficient to relieve the defendant of responsibility for the particular act charged."[181]

An alternative more drastic than that proposed by either Bazelon C.J. or by the British Royal Commission is the simple abolition of the insanity defence, leaving evidence of mental abnormality a factor which might cast doubt upon a material element of the crime (*i.e., mens rea* or *actus reus*).[182] Professors Goldstein and Katz have argued[183] that because any mental disorder which is severe enough to fall within the *M'Naghten* test would necessarily vitiate the element of *mens rea*,[184] there is in fact no need for a separate insanity defence.[185] It should be noted, however, that this line of reasoning is premised upon the authors' own assumptions concerning the nature of mental abnormality, and not upon a theoretical comparison between the doctrine of *mens rea* and the insanity defence. In theory, at least, the *M'Naghten* rules provide a defence for persons who would not necessarily lack *mens rea*. Besides excusing the accused who (because of delusions, "natural imbecility" or mental disease) did not appreciate the nature and quality of his actions, they permit lack of knowledge that an act is illegal to exculpate a defendant (provided such ignorance was produced by delusions, "natural imbecility" or mental disease). Under normal circumstances, knowledge of an act's illegality is not necessary for *mens rea*.[186]

Goldstein and Katz have supported their contention by reference to

---

[181] *Ibid.*, at p. 1032.

[182] See Goldstein and Katz, "Abolish the 'Insanity Defense' — Why Not?" (1963), 72 Yale L.J. 853 at p. 863.

[183] *Ibid.*, at pp. 862-3.

[184] Glanville Williams, *op. cit.* footnote 32, at p. 490 has stated that mental impairment severe enough to constitute insanity under the *M'Naghten* rules would in fact negative the mental element in *actus reus* as well (*i.e.,* volition).

[185] This would appear to have been the reasoning behind s. 502 of c. 5 of U.S. Senate Bill 1400 (93rd Cong. 2nd Sess.), dealing with the proposed American Federal Criminal Code. Under that proposal, the following formulation was suggested:

> "It is a defense to a prosecution under any federal statute that the defendant, as a result of mental disease or defect, lacked the state of mind required as an element of the offense charged. Mental disease or defect does not otherwise constitute a defense."

For criticism of this formulation, see Pollock, "The Insanity Defense as Defined by the Proposed Federal Criminal Code" (1976), 4 Bull. Am. Academy of Psychiatry and the Law II.

[186] See Smith and Hogan, *op. cit.* footnote 40, at p. 54.

the *Currens* decision.[187] In that case both the *M'Naghten* and *Durham* rules were criticized for the following reason:

> "They do not take account of the fact that an 'insane' defendant commits the crime not because his mental illness causes him to do a certain prohibited act but because the totality of his personality is such, because of mental illness, that he has lost the capacity to control his acts in the way that the normal individual can and does control them. If this effect has taken place he must be found not to possess the guilty mind, the *mens rea*, necessary to constitute his prohibited act a crime."[188]

"Without the essential element of *mens rea*", the authors have concluded, "there is no crime from which to relieve the defendant of liability and consequently, since no crime has been committed, there is no need for formulating an insanity defence."[189]

Although the defence of insanity is theoretically wider than the concept of *mens rea*, the logical foundations of this fact may be seriously questioned. Why should ignorance of the law be an excuse if produced by mental disease yet not if produced by other factors? One might assume that the distinction is attributable to the notion that when mental disease causes ignorance of the law, the accused *cannot help* his ignorance. But are there not other circumstances, apart from mental disorder, in which an accused might quite unavoidably be ignorant of the law?[190] Even if this had been the reasoning of the *M'Naghten* judges, one wonders why they did not simply express the defence of insanity in terms of an inability to conform to the law as the result of mental impairment (*i.e.*, adopt the *Currens* rule).

Goldstein and Katz have asserted that the real reason for the existence of a separate insanity defence is not in fact to exculpate "mentally ill" defendants who would otherwise be convicted of criminal offences. The defence's real function, "is to authorize the state to hold those 'who must be found not to possess the guilty mind *mens rea*', even though the criminal law demands that no person be held criminally responsible if doubt is cast upon any material element of the offense charged."[191]

A proposal even more radical than that of simply abolishing the insanity defence is that advanced by Lady Wootton in 1963. In her short treatise on *Crime and the Criminal Law*,[192] she recommended that all inquiry into *mens rea* be abandoned prior to conviction. Arguing that

---

[187] (1961), 290 F. 2d 751 (3rd Cir.).

[188] *Ibid.*, at p. 774 quoted by Goldstein and Katz, at p. 862.

[189] At p. 863.

[190] See, for example, *R. v. Bailey* (1800), Russ. & Ry. 1, where the accused was convicted of an offence created by a statute which was passed while he was at sea. The offence was committed while he was aboard a ship and before he could possibly have known of the statute.

[191] At p. 864. As the authors have further pointed out, "This, in some jurisdictions, is found directly reflected in evidentiary rules making inadmissible testimony on mental health to disprove a state of mind necessary to constitute the crime charged".

[192] London, Stevens and Sons, 1963.

the aim of criminal law is prevention rather than retribution, she has maintained that an "offender's" state of mind is only relevant at the dispositional stage. The only question that should be decided at the time of the trial is whether or not the accused did in fact perform the act or acts which a particular crime involves. Unfortunately, this theory has the distinct disadvantage of subjecting to possible treatment individuals who though neither blameworthy nor mentally abnormal are considered to be dangerous.[193] "To show that you have struck or wounded another unintentionally or without negligence", Hart has observed, "would not save you from conviction and liability to such treatment, penal[194] or therapeutic, as the court might deem advisable on evidence of your mental state and character."[195]

Having noted what he considers to be the major flaw in Lady Wootton's proposal, Hart has put forward a "modified" version of her approach. Under his theory the doctrine of *mens rea* would be only partially eliminated. In this less extreme approach, evidence of mental abnormality could not be presented to cast doubt upon *mens rea*. In Hart's words "The innovation would be that no form of insanity or abnormality would bar a conviction, and this would no longer be investigated before conviction."[196] But if one adheres to Williams' view that mental abnormality severe enough to constitute insanity would necessarily negative the mental component of *actus reus* (*i.e.,* volition), or to the proposition that non-insane automatism is a form of mental abnormality which might bar conviction, Hart's statement would appear to advocate much more than a partial elimination of the doctrine of *mens rea*. It would seem to suggest the exclusion of any evidence of mental abnormality which might negative *actus reus* as well. From other statements, however, one gathers that Hart disputes the very notion that *actus reus* necessarily requires a volitional element in the first place,[197] and therefore disagrees with Williams' proposition that insanity can negative *actus reus*. Moreover, though he has not made this entirely clear, it would appear that Hart does not in fact consider non-insane automatism to be a form of mental abnormality. Thus he envisions non-insane automatons continuing to be acquitted without qualification under his system unless further provision is made.[198] It is submitted that this state of affairs makes Hart's theory rather difficult to implement. Given the fact that the question of whether a particular defendant's automatism was sane or insane is a matter for the court to determine,

---

[193] Such procedure would be a step beyond civil commitment insofar as it would require no finding of mental disorder *per se*.

[194] Under a modified form of Lady Wootton's proposal presented by Kennalley, *op. cit.* footnote 163, at pp. 114-8, punishment (as opposed to treatment) would require proof of criminal intent. But *quaere* how one distinguishes between punishment and treatment? See Chapter 10 *post* at pp. 303, 311-3.

[195] Hart, *Punishment and Responsibility*, at p. 195.

[196] *Ibid.,* at p. 195.

[197] *Ibid.,* at p. 90.

[198] *Ibid.,* at p. 202: "The courts could be given powers in the case of such physically harmful offences to order, notwithstanding an acquittal, any kind of medical treatment or supervision that seemed appropriate".

how does one prevent the defence from leading, as part of its case for non-insane automatism, extensive evidence concerning the accused's state of mind at the time of the alleged offence?

Another serious difficulty with Hart's scheme lies in its apparent failure to deal with the so-called doctrine of "partial responsibility". Partial responsibility is the theory which in some circumstances allows an accused who is charged with a particular offence to be convicted of a lesser included offence[199] where specific intent is not proved. Operation of this doctrine may necessitate the reception of evidence of mental abnormality which, though it may not amount to insanity, may be "relevant to negate a defining element"[200] of the offence charged. Under Hart's proposal, no evidence of mental abnormality could be presented prior to conviction, and thus the doctrine of partial responsibility would be seriously limited. This being the case, one commentator has asked:

> "Acknowledging ... that each element of an offense must be proved and that evidence disproving any element should be admissible, of what crime should we 'convict' the person if we exclude such evidence? If a killing occurs, and no evidence of mental abnormality is allowed to be presented to negate specific intent, do we convict for murder, manslaughter, or any other degree of homicide that the particular jurisdiction recognizes?"[201]

Of the abolitionist proposals, it is submitted that the solution offered by Goldstein and Katz is the most workable. The question which remains to be answered is whether abolition of a separate insanity defence is preferable to adoption of a modified test such as that endorsed by the majority in *Brawner* or that proposed by Bazelon C.J. in his dissenting judgment.

Kadish has argued[202] that the insanity defence is necessary to prevent mentally abnormal "offenders" from having a complete defence. Were it not for the insanity defence, such persons would assert their lack of *mens rea* and go completely free on acquittal. It is submitted, however, that the detention of potentially dangerous "offenders" might be accomplished by much simpler means (*i.e.*, by civil commitment).[203]

---

[199] Paragraph 589(1)(a) of the Criminal Code provides:
"589(1) A count in an indictment is divisible and where the commission of the offence charged, as described in the enactment creating it or as charged in the count, includes the commission of another offence, whether punishable by indictment or on summary conviction, the accused may be convicted
    (a) of an offence so included that is proved, notwithstanding that the whole offence that is charged is not proved..."

[200] Brady, *op. cit.* footnote 173, at p. 634.

[201] *Ibid.*

[202] Kadish, "The Decline of Innocence" (1968), 26 Camb. L.J. 273.

[203] See Law Reform Commission of Canada, *Report: Mental Disorder in the Criminal Process* (Ottawa, Information Canada, 1976) at p. 22 where it is in fact suggested that "[a verdict of] 'not guilty by reason of insanity' could be made a real acquittal, subject only to a post-acquittal hearing to determine whether the individual should be civilly detained on the basis of his psychiatric dangerousness." See also recommendation 25 at p. 46 of the Report, which states: "Section 542 of the Code dealing with the disposition

As a social justification for the continued existence of the insanity defence, Joseph Goldstein has pointed to the "vitally important distinction between illness and evil".[204] In his well-known text, *The Insanity Defense*, he has argued that the identification of a category of persons (the "insane") who are not responsible for their acts serves to reinforce in so-called normal individuals a "sense of obligation and responsibility."[205] The defence, in other words, tends to promote deterrence from crime. But even if one assumes that Professor Goldstein is correct in his evaluation of the communal conscience,[206] it is difficult to see how his argument can be asserted in opposition to all abolitionist proposals. While his argument might be used to counter schemes such as those put forward by Wootton and Hart, it is doubtful that the public's sense of personal responsibility would be weakened by a system which does away with the insanity defence yet leaves the doctrine of *mens rea* intact.

If Goldstein and Katz were correct in their assertion that *mens rea* would necessarily be negatived by any disorder severe enough to provide a defence under *M'Naghten*,[207] it follows that a separate insanity defence would be advantageous only if it were broader than both *M'Naghten* and the concept of *mens rea* itself. It is submitted that both the ALI rule and the test proposed by Bazelon C.J. would fill the bill in this regard. Couched in terms of "substantial" incapacity and "impaired" mental processes or behaviour controls respectively, the tests avoid the facile intent/lack of intent dichotomy upon which the doctrine of *mens rea* is partially founded. Under either formulation, therefore, it seems quite possible that a mentally abnormal defendant might be found not guilty by reason of insanity even though he satisfies the requirements of *mens rea*.

---

of the accused found not guilty by reason of insanity should be amended to provide only for a mandatory post-acquittal hearing to determine whether there are grounds to detain the accused under the provisions of the relevant provincial mental health legislation."

[204] Goldstein, *The Insanity Defense*, at p. 223.

[205] *Ibid.*, at p. 224.

[206] At least one commentator has disputed this, arguing that "The insanity defence ... affects the citizen's perception of responsibility in an unknown direction, if it affects that perception at all". See Monahan, "Abolish the Insanity Defense? — Not Yet" (1973), 26 Rutgers L. Rev. 719 at p. 725.

[207] See *supra* at p. 148.

Chapter 6

Reduced Responsibility

I. Introduction

Mental abnormality which does not necessarily amount to either automatism or insanity may still be asserted in mitigation of criminal responsibility. In addition to the complete defences previously discussed, there remain several other partial "defences" which might, in the appropriate circumstances, be particularly applicable to the case of mentally disordered defendants. Where, for example, the offence charged is one involving specific intent, knowledge of certain circumstances, or "planning and deliberation" as its *mens rea*, evidence of mental abnormality might be led to show that the accused lacked the mental state necessary to be found guilty of the full offence. Furthermore, even though it might not show a lack of *mens rea* on the part of the accused, psychiatric evidence may nevertheless be of great value in cases where the accused has been charged with murder. Where such evidence tends to show (a) that the accused was provoked, or (b) in cases where the accused is a female person charged with causing the death of her newly born child, that the accused was suffering from the effects of childbirth or lactation, the accused may be convicted of manslaughter, or infanticide respectively.

II. Incapacity To Form Specific Intent Due To Intoxication

Voluntary consumption of alcohol or drugs may help mitigate criminal liability in a number of ways. In extreme cases, where insanity has resulted therefrom, the accused may rely on s. 16 of the Criminal Code which provides a complete defence to criminal charges.[1] Where the effects of alcohol or drugs have been less profound, their consumption may still be considered by a jury in determining such questions as whether the accused planned and deliberated murder[2] or whether he was actually provoked into committing homicide.[3] It should be noted as well that *involuntary* intoxication is a complete defence to all charges.[4]

Apart from the above situations, there remains in our law a separate "defence"[5] of voluntary intoxication (or drunkenness)[6] which applies to reduce a defendant's criminal responsibility under certain rather narrowly circumscribed conditions. This "defence", as outlined by the House of Lords in *D.P.P. v. Beard*[7] is simply "That evidence of drunkenness which renders the accused *incapable of forming the specific intent* essential to constitute the crime should be taken into consideration with the other facts proved in order to determine whether or not he had this intent."

A.   "SPECIFIC INTENT"

The major limitation of the drunkenness defence propounded in *Beard* is that it is only applicable to so-called crimes of specific intent. In other words, it cannot be relied upon as a defence to crimes of general intent or in cases where the mental states of recklessness or knowledge (rather than intent) are sufficient to constitute the *mens rea* of the offence.[8] Just why this is so is not entirely clear, although the current state of the law seems more the result of policy considerations than of airtight logic. From a logical standpoint, there would seem to be no good reason why evidence of intoxication should not be relevant to the issues of knowledge or recklessness.[9] On occasion, the courts have in fact supported this view.[10] As a matter of policy, however, the courts have generally chosen

---

[1] *D.P.P. v. Beard,* [1920] A.C. 479 (H.L.); *R. v. Hartridge* (1966), 57 D.L.R. (2d) 332 at pp. 354-5 (Sask. C.A.); *R. v. Hilton* (Ont. C.A.) 5 May 1977 (not yet reported).

[2] See *infra* at pp. 166-9.

[3] See *infra* at pp. 176-7.

[4] *R. v. King,* [1962] S.C.R. 746; *R. v. Hartridge, supra,* footnote 1, at p. 354.

[5] Smith and Hogan, *Criminal Law,* 3rd ed. (London, Butterworths, 1973) have noted (at p. 151): "Drunkenness has never been a defence as such. When D relies on his drunkenness, he does so in order to show that he did not have the necessary *mens rea.* . . . As in the case of mistake, he is denying that the prosecution has proved its case."

[6] Insofar as the "drunkenness defence" formulated by the House of Lords in *D.P.P. v. Beard* applies where intoxicants other than alcohol have been used by the accused (*R. v. Lipman,* [1970] 1 Q.B. 152; *R. v. Curtis* (1972), 8 C.C.C. (2d) 240 (Ont. C.A.); *R. v. Dawe* (1973), 10 C.C.C. (2d) 520 (Ont. C.A.)) it is perhaps more appropriately referred to as the defence of intoxication.

[7] *Supra,* footnote 1 at pp. 501-2 (emphasis added).

[8] Gold, "An Untrimmed 'Beard': The Law of Intoxication as a Defence to a Criminal Charge" (1976), 19 Crim. L.Q. 34 at pp. 36-7.

[9] *Ibid.,* at p. 54.

[10] See, *e.g., R. v. Vlcko* (1972), 10 C.C.C. (2d) 139 (Ont. C.A.) where it was held that self-induced intoxication (with LSD) might constitute a defence to the charge of assaulting a police officer, as it might prevent the accused from knowing that the person whom he

to limit the ambit of the drunkenness defence to "those crimes for which there may be an alternative verdict leading to conviction of a lesser offence".[11] In doing so the courts have endeavoured to ensure that persons who cause injury or damage while drunk do not escape criminal liability altogether.[12] The underlying purpose of this approach would seem to be that of social defence. As Lord Simon stated in the case of *D.P.P. v. Majewski:*[13]

> "One of the prime purposes of the criminal law, with its penal sanctions, is the protection from certain proscribed conduct of persons who are pursuing their lawful lives. Unprovoked violence has, from time immemorial, been a significant part of such proscribed conduct. To accede to the argument on behalf of the appellant [regarding the illogic of *Beard*] would leave the citizen legally unprotected from unprovoked violence, where such violence was the consequence of drink or drugs having obliterated the capacity of the perpetrator to know what he was doing or what were its consequences."

Thus the goal of public protection has taken precedence over the strict application of general criminal law principles. Having recognized that the defendant's actual state of mind at the time he committed the harm in issue required total exculpation,[14] the House of Lords in *Majewski* nevertheless considered "the establishment and maintenance of order"[15] to be of paramount importance. In effect, therefore, Lord Birkenhead's suggestion in *Beard* that "the cause of the punishment is the drunkenness which has led to the crime, rather than the crime itself,"[16] was not far off the mark.

Setting aside the aforementioned difficulties for the moment, there

---

was alleged to have assaulted was a peace officer. And see *R. v. Stones,* [1956] S.R. (N.S.W.) 25 at p. 33, where it was held that "drunkenness can negative recklessness as an ingredient in the malicious homicide of murder ... ".

[11] Ashworth, "Reason, Logic and Criminal Liability" (1975), 91 L.Q.R. 102 at p. 113.

[12] *Ibid.*

[13] [1976] 2 All E.R. 142 at p. 152 (H.L.).

[14] *Per* Lord Edmund-Davies at p. 168.

[15] *Ibid.*

[16] *Supra,* footnote 1 at p. 500. See also Hogan, "The Killing Ground: 1964-73", [1974] Crim. L.R. 387 at p. 393. *Cf.* Stroud, *Mens Rea,* [1914] at p. 115 quoted in *Majewski, supra,* footnote 13 at p. 169 by Lord Edmund-Davies, where it is stated: " 'It has been suggested by various writers, in the explanation of the doctrine respecting voluntary drunkenness as an excuse for crime, that the effect is 'to make drunkenness itself an offence, which is punishable with a degree of punishment varying as the consequences of the act done' [Clark, *Analysis of Criminal Liability* (1880), p. 30]. This is not exactly correct, although it is not far from the true explanation of the rule. The true explanation is, that drunkenness is not incompatible with *mens rea,* in the sense of ordinary culpable intentionality, because mere recklessness is sufficient to satisfy the definition of *mens rea,* and drunkenness is itself an act of recklessness. The law therefore establishes a conclusive presumption against the admission of proof of intoxication for the purpose of disproving *mens rea* in ordinary crimes. Where this presumption applies, it does not make 'drunkenness itself' a crime, but the drunkenness is itself an integral part of the crime, as forming, together with the other unlawful conduct charged against the defendant, a complex act of criminal recklessness.' "

remains the additional problem of ascertaining what is actually meant by the phrase "specific intent". At least one critic has described it as "a meaningless expression"[17] and asserted that the distinction between crimes which require specific intent and those which do not "has no proper place in the law".[18] Certainly the ambiguity of the term has caused considerable confusion in law; in the case of certain offences it has created a real dilemma with regard to classification.[19]

In Canada, the leading authority on the subject of specific versus general intent is the decision of the Supreme Court of Canada in *R. v. George*.[20] In that case Fauteux J. (as he then was) expressed the view that:

> "In considering the question of *mens rea*, a distinction is to be made between (i) intention as applied to acts considered in relation to their purposes and (ii) intention as applied to acts considered apart from their purposes. A general intent attending the commission of an act is, in some cases, the only intent required to constitute the crime while, in others, there must be, in addition to that general intent, a specific intent attending the purpose for the commission of the act." [21]

Similarly, Ritchie J. was of the opinion that:

> "In considering the question of *mens rea*, a distinction is to be drawn between 'intention' as applied to acts done to achieve an immediate end on the one hand and acts done with the specific and ulterior motive and intention of furthering or achieving an illegal object on the other hand. Illegal acts of the former kind are done 'intentionally' in the sense that they are not done by accident or through honest mistake, but acts of the latter kind are the product of preconception and are deliberate steps taken towards an illegal goal. The former acts may be the purely physical products of momentary passion, whereas the latter involve the mental process of formulating a specific intent."[22]

---

[17] Commentary to *R. v. Burns,* [1975] Crim. L.R. 155 at p. 157.
[18] *Ibid.,* at p. 158.
[19] Rape, for example, has been classified as a crime of specific intent by some courts: *R. v. Schmidt and Gole* (1972), 9 C.C.C. (2d) 101 (Ont. C.A.); *R. v. Vandervoort* (1961), 130 C.C.C. 158 (Ont. C.A.); *R. v. Hornbuckle,* [1945] V.L.R. 31; *R. v. Flannery,* [1969] V.R. 31, but not by others: *R. v. Leary* (1975), 31 C.R.N.S. 199 (B.C.C.A.); *R. v. Boucher,* [1963] 2 C.C.C. 241 (B.C.C.A.). It is only recently that this conflict has been resolved; see *Leary v. The Queen* (1977), 37 C.R.N.S. 60 (S.C.C.).
[20] [1960] S.C.R. 871.
[21] *Ibid.,* at p. 877.
[22] *Ibid.,* at p. 890.

B. INCAPACITY TO FORM SPECIFIC INTENT

In his formulation of the defence of drunkenness in *Beard,* Lord Birken-head deemed fit for consideration "evidence of drunkenness which ren-ders the accused *incapable* of forming the specific intent". At first blush, this seems somewhat curious. Since the issue to be decided is whether or not the accused *in fact* formed the specific intent, one would have thought that any evidence of drunkenness would be appropriate for con-sideration on this issue, even though it might not have made formation of specific intent impossible. This, however, is not the case. Where drunkenness is the defence under consideration, juries are entitled to equate capacity to form specific intent with the actual formation of that intent. Why this should be so seems somewhat difficult to understand. Although Lord Birkenhead himself appears to have invoked the "presumption that a man intends the natural consequences of his acts"[23] to fill the logical gap left between capacity and actual formation, a series of more recent cases has cast considerable doubt upon the strength and indeed the very existence of that presumption.[24] Regardless of this fact, our courts continue to adhere to the rules in *Beard* as the correct articu-lation of the drunkenness defence in Canada.

How then might intoxication affect the capacity to form a specific intent? It is submitted that the only psychiatric diagnoses which *ipso facto* carry with them an automatic finding that the patient was incapa-ble of forming specific intent in law are those which describe a state of unconsciousness.[25] If, for example, the accused was in a state of alcoholic or drug-induced automatism at the time of the alleged crime, he cannot be found to have formed a specific intent,[26] even though his actions might unconsciously have been actuated by "the specific and ulterior motive and intention of furthering or achieving [the] illegal object [in

---

[23] [1920] A.C. 479 at p. 502: " ... evidence of drunkenness falling short of a proved incapac-ity in the accused to form the intent necessary to constitute the crime, and merely estab-lishing that his mind was affected by drink so that he more readily gave way to some violent passion, does not rebut the presumption that a man intends the natural conse-quence of his acts."

[24] See *R. v. Giannotti* (1956), 115 C.C.C. 203 (Ont. C.A.); *R. v. Ortt,* [1969] 1 O.R. 461 (C.A.); *R. v. Bourque,* [1969] 4 C.C.C. 358 (B.C.C.A.); *Perrault v. The Queen,* [1970] 5 C.C.C. 217 (S.C.C.), *per* Laskin J. (as he then was) at p. 224; *Leary v. The Queen* (1977), 37 C.R.N.S. 60 (S.C.C.) *per* Dickson J. at p. 80: " ... since *Hosegood v. Hosegood* (1950), 66 T.L.R. (Pt. 1) 735, the presumption that a man intends the natural consequences of his acts is now regarded as a proposition of good sense rather than a proposition of law."

[25] As pointed out earlier in Chapter 4, *ante,* at p. 87, psychiatry recognizes that there are varying degrees of consciousness, whereas the law seems to make an arbitrary distinc-tion between conscious acts and unconscious acts for the purpose of determining crimi-nal liability. The term "unconsciousness", as used here, refers to the legal concept.

[26] Note the opinion expressed by the British Columbia Court of Appeal in *R. v. Leary* (1975), 31 C.R.N.S. 199 *per* Bull J.A. *obiter* at p. 204 that drunkenness which amounts to automatism would be a defence to crimes of general intent as well, since such condition would rebut the presumption that a man intends the natural consequences of his acts. This statement contradicts the law set out in *Bratty v. A.-G. Northern Ireland,* [1961] 3 W.L.R. 965 at p. 982 (H.L.), and *R. v. Hartridge* (1966), 57 D.L.R. (2d) 332 at p. 354 (Sask. C.A.).

question]."[27] It will be recalled that the law places no significance whatever on the unconscious motivation of an accused.[28] In cases where the accused's sensorium has not been impaired to the extent that his condition fits within the law's conception of unconsciousness,[29] it is submitted that the mere affixing of a psychiatric label to his disorder will not in itself decide the question of capacity to form specific intent; in such circumstances the accused's capacity must be a matter for individual assessment.

(i) Alcohol-Induced States

Below are set out a number of psychiatric conditions which may result from alcoholic intoxication, and which *could* render impossible the formation of the specific intent required for any given crime. It should be noted that most of these conditions fall into the category of psychoses (*i.e.,* medical "insanity") and, therefore, stand a good chance of being considered "diseases of the mind" within the framework of the *M'Naghten* rules.

(a) Delirium Tremens
This temporary toxic state[30] is a form of acute brain syndrome[31] which occurs in chronic alcoholics.[32] Usually preceded by a period of restlessness, shakiness, insomnia and nightmares,[33] an attack of *delirium tremens* is characterized by delirium, tremors, and terrifying hallucinations, generally of the visual type.[34] The disorder has been judicially recognized as being a disease of the mind within the meaning of the *M'Naghten* rules.[35]

(b) Korsakov's Psychosis
In contrast with *delirium tremens,* Korsakov's Psychosis is a type of *chronic* brain syndrome,[36] which generally results in severe and irreversible intellectual damage.[37] Loss of memory, disorientation, childishness and general personality deterioration are among the typical symptoms.[38] Persons who suffer from this disorder also have a notable tendency to "confabulate" as a means of covering up gaps in memory.[39]

---

[27] *R. v. George,* [1960] S.C.R. 871 at p. 890.

[28] See Chapter 4, *ante,* at p. 112.

[29] See Chapter 4, *ante,* at pp. 85-7.

[30] Weihofen, *Mental Disorder as a Criminal Defense* (Buffalo, Dennis, 1954) at p. 127.

[31] *Manual for the Classification of Psychiatric Diagnoses* (Ottawa, Information Canada, 1974) at p. 14. Hereinafter cited as the *Diagnostic Manual.*

[32] Rozhnov, "Alcoholism and Other Drug Addictions", in Morozov and Kalashnik eds., *Forensic Psychiatry* (White Plains, N.Y., International Arts and Sciences Press, Inc., 1970) 343 at p. 361.

[33] Wily and Stallworthy, *Mental Abnormality and the Law* (Christchurch, N.Z., N.M. Peryer, 1962) at pp. 197-8; Rozhnov, at p. 361.

[34] *Diagnostic Manual* at pp. 14-5.

[35] *R. v. Davis* (1881), 14 Cox C.C. 563.

[36] *Diagnostic Manual* at p. 15.

[37] Wily and Stallworthy, at p. 198.

[38] *Ibid.*

[39] *Ibid.; Diagnostic Manual* at p. 15.

(c) Alcoholic Paranoia

Alcoholic paranoia is the term given to acute or prolonged paranoia which is the result of chronic alcoholism.[40] This disorder is typically characterized by unreasonable jealousy and delusions that one's spouse is being unfaithful.[41] Persons suffering from such delusions not uncommonly react with irrational aggression.[42]

(d) Pathological Intoxication

Excitement and aggressive behaviour are also characteristic of this form of alcoholic psychosis.[43] Also referred to as *mania à potu,*[44] pathological intoxication is the term applied to the temporary psychotic state which even small amounts of alcohol can produce in certain highly susceptible individuals. Fatigue, infectious disease, undernourishment or emotional agitation are all factors which may render an otherwise normal individual prone to this condition.[45] While repeated attacks in the same individual are theoretically possible, it is doubtful that a predictable pattern of pathological intoxication will be exhibited by individuals other than those suffering from craniocerebral trauma or epilepsy.[46] Although the symptoms of pathological intoxication may repeatedly occur in psychopathic personalities as the result of severe intoxication, the pre-existence of this form of mental disorder would seem to preclude the diagnosis of a genuine pathological intoxication. According to the definition provided by the Diagnostic and Statistical Manual of the American Psychiatric Association:

> "When without apparent preexisting mental disorder, there is a marked behavioural or psychotic reaction with an acute brain syndrome after minimal alcoholic intake, the case will be classified here. When a pre-existing psychotic, psychoneurotic, or personality disorder is made more manifest after minimal alcoholic intake, the case will be classified under the diagnosis of the underlying condition."[47]

The outward characteristics of pathological intoxication are distinguishable from those of simple drunkenness in a number of ways. Unlike the simple drunk, the pathological inebriate generally loses contact with the persons around him and speaks little, if at all.[48] Frequently he experiences delusions and hallucinations of a frightening nature.[49] Unlike the severe drunk, he retains equilibrium and motor co-ordination and, unless suffering from the epileptoid variety of the disorder, tends to

---

[40] *Ibid.*, at p. 16.
[41] *Ibid.*
[42] Rozhnov, at p. 368.
[43] Wily and Stallworthy, at p. 197.
[44] *Ibid.*
[45] Rozhnov, at p. 347.
[46] *Ibid.*, at pp. 347-8.
[47] Quoted by Macdonald, *Psychiatry and the Criminal* (Springfield, Ill., Charles C. Thomas, 1969) at p. 177.
[48] Rozhnov, at p. 349.
[49] *Ibid.*

retain at least a patchy recollection of his experiences.[50]

(e) Other Alcoholic Hallucinosis
This category is comprised simply of those alcoholic hallucinoses which cannot properly be classified under any other diagnosis. The condition is usually characterized by threatening or accusatory auditory hallucinations in a more or less clear state of consciousness.[51]

(f) Confusional States
Without resulting in a psychosis, severe acute intoxication may nevertheless produce significant disturbances of consciousness. One such disturbance, confusion, has been described as involving "impairment of the sensorium . . ., difficulty of grasp . . ., bewilderment, perplexity, disorientation, disturbance of association junctions and poverty of ideas."[52] According to psychiatrist Seymour Halleck, confusion may also entail "overwhelming anxiety, perceptual distortions and marked incoherence" as well as "difficulty in interpreting the source and meaning of signals from [one's] environment."[53] Whether or not an alcohol-induced confusional state will *ipso facto* obliterate the capacity to form a specific intent however, is another matter. Halleck has asserted that even without the presence of this condition, "The intoxicated individual's judgment is impaired and he often is unable to plan his behaviour in a rational way or to perceive its consequences."[54]

(ii) Drug-Induced States

The intoxicating effect of certain drugs may be vastly more complex and less predicitable than that of alcohol. This is especially true when drugs are mixed with alcohol or with each other. In general terms, however, the following is a brief description of the effects which the more common groups of intoxicating drugs might be expected to have when administered individually.

(a) Amphetamines
Taken in moderate amounts, amphetamines generally promote alertness, clarity of thought, elevation of mood, and increased initiative and activity.[55] In some circumstances, however, even small doses may produce a variety of unpleasant physical symptoms such as nausea, headache, blurred vision, dizziness, tremor, chest pains, chilliness, heart palpitation, and so on.[56] Possible adverse psychological reactions include

---

[50] *Ibid.*, at pp. 349-50.
[51] *Diagnostic Manual* at p. 15.
[52] Noyes, *Modern Clinical Psychiatry,* 6th ed. (Philadelphia, Saunders, 1963) quoted by Halleck, *Psychiatry and the Dilemmas of Crime: A Study of Causes, Punishment and Treatment* (Berkeley, University of California Press, 1971) at p. 159.
[53] *Diagnostic Manual* at p. 159.
[54] *Ibid.*, at p. 148.
[55] LeDain, *Report of the Commission of Inquiry into the Non-Medical Use of Drugs* (Ottawa, Information Canada, 1973) at p. 339.
[56] *Ibid.*

irritation, inability to concentrate, confusion and depersonalization.[57] Among the possible psychological effects are fear, panic, aggression, delirium and hallucinations.[58] The symptoms of an amphetamine overdose may closely resemble those of an acute paranoid schizophrenic reaction.[59]

(b) Barbiturates

Moderate doses of this type of hypnotic drug will normally induce a general depression of the central nervous system and reduce muscular activity.[60] The primary psychological symptoms which result are similar to those produced by alcohol.[61] An individual may either become drowsy and apathetic, or energetic and highly active.[62] He may become euphoric and behave in a jovial and affectionate manner, or become violent and aggressive.[63] Occasionally, excessive use of barbiturates may produce a psychotic state.[64] Medical authorities[65] have further attributed "deterioration of moral, volitional and intellectual powers" to the chronic misuse of hypnotic drugs.

(c) Cocaine

Cocaine is a stimulant drug pharmacologically similar to the amphetamines.[66] While the physiological and psychological effects of the two types of drug are similar, those of cocaine are somewhat more short-lived.[67] Once again a moderate dosage may result in increased capacity to concentrate, elevated mood and general improvement in mental function.[68] In a similar fashion, chronic use of cocaine in large amounts may create the type of toxic psychosis described earlier.[69] Although uncommon, a full-blown psychotic reaction may occur as the result of a single injection.[70]

---

[57] *Ibid.*

[58] *Ibid.*

[59] Group for the Advancement of Psychiatry (GAP), *Drug Misuse: A Psychiatric View of a Modern Dilemma* (New York, Scribner's, 1971) at p. 31, citing Oswald and Thacore "Amphetamine Phenmetrazine Addiction: Physiologic Abnormalities in the Abstinence Syndrome" (1963), 2 Brit. Med. J. 427.

[60] Le Dain, at p. 420.

[61] *Ibid.*, at p. 417.

[62] *Ibid.*

[63] *Ibid.*

[64] Rozhnov, at p. 374.

[65] *Ibid.*

[66] Le Dain, at p. 349.

[67] *Ibid.*, at p. 351.

[68] *Ibid.*

[69] *Ibid.*

[70] *Ibid.*, at p. 352. See also MacDonald, *Psychiatry and the Criminal* at p. 184, where the author has noted that "Cocaine by intravenous injection may lead to clouding of consciousness or frank delirium with disorientation, illusions, auditory and visual hallucinations as well as paranoid ideas or delusions."

(d) Hallucinogens
The terms psychotomimetic, psychedelic, hallucinogen and psychedelic-hallucinogen refer generally to LSD (d-lysergic acid diethylamide-25) and LSD-like drugs.[71] Included in this category are such substances as MDA (methylenedioxyamphetamine), DOM (dimethoxymethylamphetamine, also known as STP),[72] PCP (phencyclidine), mescaline and psilocybin. While the psychological effects of hallucinogenic drugs are to a large extent unpredictable and depend upon such factors as dosage, individual personality and the setting in which the drug is taken,[73] it is safe to say that the distortion or misrepresentation of object reality is a feature common to most psychedelic experiences.[74] Moreover, adverse psychotic reactions involving paranoid delusions, hallucinations, terror and a loss of emotional control are not uncommon.[75]

(e) Marijuana
While the effects of this substance are as yet poorly understood, some of the more recent clinical data suggests that in large doses marijuana may induce confusion, depersonalization, delusions and hallucinations.[76]

(f) Minor Tranquilizers and Non-Barbiturate Sedative Hypnotics
As with most drugs, the drugs in this category have varying effects, depending upon factors like dosage, personality of the user, setting, etc.[77] In general, however, their effect is not unlike that of alcohol.[78] Small doses usually depress nervous and muscular activity, inducing relaxation and a feeling of well-being.[79] Taken in large quantities, tranquilizers and sedatives may cause drowsiness, confusion, disorientation, rage, or a trance-like state.[80]

(g) Opiate Narcotics
Although the use of opiate narcotics may have a stimulating or invigorating effect on some individuals, the more common short-term effects of these drugs include euphoria, dizziness, drowsiness, apathy and inability to concentrate.[81] Higher doses may produce a dream-like state of clouded

---

[71] Le Dain, at p. 335.
[72] Drugs such as MMDA, TMA and DOET are related compounds of DOM. See Le Dain, at p. 356.
[73] Le Dain, at p. 364.
[74] See Pahnke and Richards, "Implications of LSD and Experimental Mysticism" (1966), 5 J. Religion and Health 175, cited by Le Dain, at pp. 364-6; GAP, at p. 32.
[75] Le Dain, at p. 365.
[76] GAP, at pp. 29-30, citing McGlothlin and West, "The Marijuana Problem: An Overview" (1968), 125 Am. J. Psychiat. 126; Keeler, "Adverse Reactions to Marijuana" (1967), 124 Am. J. Psychiat.; Keeler, "Marijuana-Induced Hallucinations" (1968), 29 Diseases of the Nervous System 314; Bromberg, "Marijuana Intoxication" (1934), 91 Am. J. Psychiat.; Dally, "Undesirable Effects of Marijuana " (1967), 3 Brit. Med. J. 367; Tylden "A Case for Cannabis" (1967), 3 Brit. Med. J. 556; Persyko, "Marijuana Psychosis" (1970), 212 J. Am. Med. Assoc. 1527.
[77] Le Dain, at p. 434.
[78] *Ibid.*
[79] *Ibid.*
[80] *Ibid.*
[81] *Ibid.*, at p. 309.

consciousness.[82]

(h) Volatile Substances (Inhalants)
The inhaling of volatile substances such as ether, glue, solvents, etc. may produce physiological and psychological effects similar to those of alcohol or barbiturates.[83] Large doses may result in dizziness, perceptual distortions, confusion, lack of behavioural control, delusions, hallucinations (usually visual), and perhaps unconsciousness. [84]

III. Lack of Mens Rea Due To Mental Disorder Other Than Intoxication

A. LACK OF SPECIFIC INTENT

Even where the accused's defence is not that of intoxication, psychiatric evidence may be used for the general purpose of rebutting *mens rea*. That mental disorder short of insanity might negative specific intent and thus constitute a partial defence in Anglo-Canadian law seems first to have been suggested in *R. v. Lenchitsky*.[85] In that case the English Court of Criminal Appeal upheld as correct a trial judge's direction that "feeble-mindedness" might render an accused incapable of forming the intention required for murder, *i.e.*, the intention to kill or cause bodily harm he knew was likely to cause death. Although it was not referred to specifically, the *Lenchitsky* rationale seems to have been taken a step further by the Nova Scotia Supreme Court (Appeal Division) in *R. v. Blackmore*.[86] In that case a conviction for non-capital murder was overturned on the grounds, *inter alia,* that the trial judge had neglected to instruct the jury to consider whether the appellant, suffering from a "reactive depression",[87] had formed the requisite intent. The result here is in sharp contrast with that in *R. v. Mulligan*,[88] however, where an

---

[82] *Ibid.*
[83] *Ibid.*, at p. 442.
[84] *Ibid.*, at p. 443; GAP, at p. 31.
[85] [1954] Crim. L.R. 216.
[86] (1967), 1 C.R.N.S. 286.
[87] Reactive depression is a psychiatric diagnosis not entirely alien to Canadian murder trials. *The Diagnostic Manual* (p. 35) defines it as a "disorder ... manifested by an excessive reaction of depression due to an internal conflict or to an indentifiable event such as the loss of a love object or cherished possession". *R. v. Rasim Taka* (Ontario, September, 1969), and *R. v. Charlebois* (Ontario, April and May, 1973) are two unreported cases in which reactive depression coupled with a severe "psychological blow" apparently produced a state of dissociation sufficient for the jury to consider when deciding whether the accused had formed the specific intent to kill. See Bayne, "Automatism and Provocation in Canadian Case Law" (1975), 31 C.R.N.S. 257 at pp. 268-70. Owing to the disparate results in *Blackmore* and *Mulligan,* however, it is an interesting question whether a failure of the trial judge to relate the evidence of the accused's mental condition to the issue of intent would have been grounds for appeal.
[88] (1974), 26 C.R.N.S. 179 at p. 186.

acute "dissociative reaction" was held by the Ontario Court of Appeal not to amount to the type of mental disorder which might be relevant to the issue of intent. The trial judge's failure to relate the psychiatric evidence of the accused's mental state separately to the issue of intent was therefore ruled insufficient as grounds for quashing the conviction. The accused brought further appeal to the Supreme Court of Canada[89] on the slightly different issue of whether or not the Court of Appeal erred "in failing to hold that the trial Judge erred in law in failing to put to the jury *on the issue of drunkenness* the medical evidence as to the accused's dissociative state of mind as having a bearing on the issue of intent *arising out of the defence of drunkenness.*"[90] The appeal was dismissed. Speaking for the majority, Martland J.[91] stated:

> "He [the trial judge] thus made it clear that it was only if the jury decided that the appellant had not proved the defence of insanity that they would need to go on to consider the defence of drunkenness. In substance this means that, if Dr. Butler's thesis of dissociative reaction was rejected, the defence of drunkenness would then require to be considered, because it is clear that, if that evidence were accepted by the jury, the defence of insanity would have been established. *The jury, by its verdict, has made it clear* that that evidence was not accepted.
>
> "In these circumstances, in my opinion, the learned trial Judge was under no obligation to instruct the jury specifically to consider again, when dealing with the defence of drunkenness, Dr. Butler's evidence concerning dissociative reaction.
>
> "I would dismiss the appeal."[92]

It is submitted, with respect, that the jury's verdict by no means "made it clear" that the medical evidence was rejected *in toto*. For this reason it is further submitted that the decision of the majority was incorrect. The jury might well have accepted the psychiatrist's diagnosis of a dissociative state even though it rejected his opinion on the ultimate issue of whether such state placed the accused within s. 16 of the Criminal Code. Apparently being of this opinion, Dickson J. felt that the evidence of the accused's dissociative state should have been specifically related to the issue of *mens rea*. In his dissenting judgment His Lordship stated:

> "When deciding whether an accused can rely on the defence of drunkenness to negative capacity to form the intent to kill, one must consider the effect of the alcohol alleged to have been consumed, upon the particular accused, at the particular time, and in his then mental state. Mental condition is a relevant, indeed essential, consideration to a determination of *mens rea* if, in conjunction

---

[89] (1976), 66 D.L.R. (3d) 627.
[90] *Ibid.*, at p. 628 (emphasis added).
[91] Judson, Ritchie, Pigeon, Beetz and de Grandpré JJ. concurring.
[92] *Supra*, footnote 89, p. 632 (emphasis added).

with alcohol, it affects capacity to form an intention. Mental condition as well as the effect of alcohol are relevant to the critical question, not placed before the jury in this case, of whether the accused *had* the necessary intent.

"The predominant question is intent. A rigid categorization of defences, keeping medical evidence of insanity entirely separate from evidence of drunkenness is not only unrealistic but a departure from all that is embraced in the phrase *mens rea*. The concern is with the particular accused and with his capacity to form the intent to kill when as here, for example, the defence contends the accused was in a dissociative state of mind, drunk and provoked. It was necessary for the jury to weigh and assess each of these elements separately; it was imperative also, in my view, to relate the evidence of drunkenness to the evidence of the mental state of the accused. These are not easy matters to explain to a jury. Obviously, the jury was confused here, as evidenced by the request for a recharge on provocation, insanity, and intent. The attempt must, however, be made. *If intent and capacity are to be anything more than catchwords, then all factors bearing upon capacity and intent, such as dissociative state, stress and drunkenness, must be considered jointly and severally as part of an over-all picture and their respective influences, each upon the other, assessed.*

"I would allow the appeal and direct a new trial."[93]

Judicial decisions as to what type of mental disorder might or might not be relevant to the issue of intent seem totally irreconcilable. Surely any form of mental disorder which causes confusion or a disturbance of consciousness is relevant to the issue of intent. In the case of *R. v. Gottschalk*[94] Ehgoetz Prov. Ct. J. decided that a state of "confusion, disorientation and depersonalization" which resulted from "chronic anxiety" was sufficient to raise a reasonable doubt as to whether the accused possessed the specific intent to steal.[95]

B. LACK OF KNOWLEDGE

As demonstrated by the case of *R. v. Connolly*,[96] mental abnormality may also vitiate *mens rea* without necessarily negativing specific intent. In *Connolly*, mental confusion caused by a bump on the head raised a reasonable doubt as to the accused's knowledge that the person whom he assaulted was a police officer.

---

[93] *Supra*, footnote 89, pp. 638-9 (emphasis added).
[94] (1975), 22 C.C.C. (2d) 415 (Ont. Prov. Ct.).
[95] See also *R. v. Clarke*, [1972] 1 All E.R. 219 (C.A.).
[96] (1965), 49 C.R. 142 (N.S.C.A.) discussed, *ante*, Chapter 4.

C. LACK OF PLANNING OR DELIBERATION

Subsection 214(2) of the Criminal Code defines first degree murder in part as murder which is "planned and deliberate". That mental disorder not amounting to legal insanity might provide a partial defence to this charge was first suggested in the 1962 case of *R. v. Lachance.*[97] There the Ontario Court of Appeal allowed an accused's appeal against conviction on the grounds *inter alia* that:

> " . . . the learned trial Judge should have charged the jury that it was their duty to decide whether or not the appellant was so affected by drink or mental stress not amounting to legal insanity, or both, as to be incapable not only of forming the intent to kill but of bestowing such forethought upon a prospective course of homicidal conduct as to bring it within the description of 'planned and deliberate' in s. 202A, subject always to the right of the accused to be afforded the benefit of a reasonable doubt upon this as upon other issues."[98]

Although the Court did not elaborate upon the degree of forethought which was required of an accused in order for his actions to be planned and deliberate, the Supreme Court of Canada addressed itself to this issue the very next year in the case of *More v. The Queen.*[99] That was a case in which the accused, who had been experiencing financial difficulties, shot his wife to death while she was sleeping and then attempted to commit suicide. The evidence showed that he had purchased the murder weapon, a hunting rifle, two days before the shooting. At trial the defence specifically disclaimed insanity but called two psychiatric witnesses who testified that the accused had suffered from a depressive psychosis at the time of the shooting which resulted in an "impairment of ability to decide even inconsequential things" and an "inability to make a decision in a normal kind of way."[100] Such evidence was, however, minimized by the trial judge in his charge to the jury and it was upon this ground that the accused appealed his conviction. Although a majority of the Manitoba Court of Appeal felt that the trial judge had misdirected the jury, it was also their opinion that such misdirection created no substantial wrong or miscarriage of justice. The majority of the Supreme Court of Canada did not agree. While it was felt that "The evidence that the murder was planned was very strong",[101] a crucial distinction was drawn between planning and deliberation. Deliberation, according to Cartwright J. (with whom Abbott, Judson, Ritchie and Hall JJ. concurred), required something more than either simple planning or a specific intent to commit homicide. It required that the act be considered and not impulsive or hasty. This being the case, Cartwright J. further stated:

---

[97] [1963] 2 C.C.C. 14.
[98] *Ibid.*, at p. 17.
[99] [1963] S.C.R. 522; revg 43 W.W.R. 30 (Man. C.A.).
[100] *Ibid.*, at p. 534.
[101] *Ibid.*, at p. 533, *per* Cartwright J.

" ... it was open to the jury to take the view that the act of the appellant in pulling the trigger was impulsive rather than considered and therefore was not deliberate. The evidence of the two doctors ... would have a direct bearing on the question whether the appellant's act was deliberate in the sense defined above; its weight was a matter for the jury."[102]

Fauteux J. (with whom Taschereau C.J.C. concurred) rejected the subtle distinction which the majority of the Court had drawn between the words planned and deliberate. In his dissenting judgment he expressed the view that the material feature common to the definitions of both words was a time element.[103] All that Parliament had intended in making planning and deliberation a constituent element of first degree murder was to exclude from that category of offence a murder committed on the spur of the moment.[104] Because the evidence as to planning (and, therefore, deliberation) was "uncontrovertible",[105] the learned Justice failed to see how psychiatric evidence which fell short of proving insanity could possibly affect the verdict in this case. Moreover, he asserted:

"Acceptance of appellant's submission that mental defect or disease not sufficient to render an accused legally irresponsible under s. 16 of the Code may nevertheless operate to reduce the degree of the crime charged is tantamount to introducing in the Canadian law a new and secondary test of legal irresponsibility as was done in England prior to the enactment of the provisions of s. 202A(2)(a) by the *Homicide Act 1957* ...

...

"Undoubtedly aware of these provisions, the Canadian Parliament deliberately refused to adopt them. If the appellant's submission is accepted, it follows that the Canadian Parliament has adopted rather obliquely a policy more generous than that of the English law. Contrary to what is the case in England, the prosecution in Canada would further have the burden of proving, as a constitutive element of the offence of capital murder, not only that the accused is mentally sane within the meaning of s. 16, but also that his mental responsibility is not affected to a lesser degree for which no legal standard is given. Again on appellant's submission there are two different tests of legal irresponsibility with respect to the offence of capital murder. The first being with respect to intent is defined in s. 16; the other being with respect to planning and deliberation is left to the arbitrament of the jury to define in each case. I am unable to read the section as implying such substantial innovations and changes in our Criminal Law."[106]

---

[102] *Ibid.*, at p. 534.
[103] *Ibid.*, at p. 530.
[104] *Ibid.*
[105] *Ibid.*, at p. 529.
[106] *Ibid.*, at pp. 531-2.

One year after the decision in *More,* the Supreme Court was again called upon to consider the importance of psychiatric evidence on the issue of planning and deliberation. In *McMartin v. The Queen*[107] the question arose as to whether the defence should have been allowed on appeal from a capital murder conviction to adduce fresh evidence directed towards proving that the appellant, though not legally insane, had long been suffering from a mental disorder characterized by impulsive, unpredictable and dangerous behaviour. The Supreme Court allowed the appeal. Having found that the appellant's counsel had exercised reasonable diligence in obtaining the psychiatric evidence before the trial, the Court went on to hold:

> "Under all the circumstances, it appears to me that the evidence of Dr. Tyhurst, like that of the doctors in *More v. R., supra,* might have caused the jury 'to regard it as more probable that the accused's final act was prompted by sudden impulse rather than by consideration'.
>
> ...
>
> "In my opinion, without the evidence of the appellant's mental history and condition, it cannot be said that all the circumstances bearing on the question of whether the murder was planned and deliberate have been passed upon by a jury, and I would accordingly allow this appeal, quash the conviction and direct that there be a new trial."[108]

The next year, in *R. v. Mitchell,*[109] the Supreme Court elaborated somewhat on *More* and *McMartin.* There it was held that on capital murder charges where the defences of provocation and drunkenness are raised it is incumbent upon the trial judge to relate those defences not only to the issue of whether murder should be reduced to manslaughter, but further to the question of whether the killing was planned and deliberate. In the words of Spence J. (with whom Fauteux, Martland, Ritchie and Hall JJ. concurred):

> "I believe some such procedure is necessary to illustrate to the jury the absolute necessity of considering the evidence first upon the issue of intent and the ameliorating provision as to provocation and then again, only if they find against the accused on the first issue, upon the issue of planning and deliberation. I adopt upon this latter issue the statement of Tysoe, J.A., in his reasons [p. 12]:
>
>> 'Our concern is with quite a different matter, namely, the effect of the drinking of the appellant and of the deceased's provocative conduct on the mind and mental processes of appellant in

---

[107] [1964] S.C.R. 484; revg 41 C.R. 147 (B.C.C.A.).

[108] *Ibid.,* at p. 495, *per* Ritchie J.

[109] [1965] 1 C.C.C. 155; affg [1964] 2 C.C.C. 1 (B.C.C.A.). See also *Pilon v. The Queen,* [1966] 2 C.C.C. 53 (Que. C.A.).

his then condition in relation to the issue of planning and deliberation on his part.' "[110]

Spence J. went on to add that:

"It might be preferable, in discussing insults and the accused's state
of mind as they affected deliberation, to avoid the use of the word
'provocation' as that word would, in the mind of the jury be associated with the exact technical sense in which the word is utilized in s.
203 [now 215]. Such circumstances have a broader and less exact
scope in the determination of whether the murder was
deliberate."[111]

D. EVIDENCE

Although the onus of proving each element of the offence charged generally rests upon the Crown in criminal cases,[112] the defendant who relies
upon mental disorder as negativing *mens rea* should in practice be prepared to lead psychiatric evidence to support this defence. It would
appear, moreover, from such cases as *R. v. Nesbitt* [113] and *MacDonald v.
The Queen*[114] that this type of evidence will be admitted regardless of
whether it offends the ultimate issue rule.[115] Note, however, that the
support of psychiatric experts may not always be enough. In *Boivin v.
The Queen*[116] a majority of the Supreme Court of Canada held that a
finding of planning and deliberation was both reasonable and supportable by the evidence where psychiatric witnesses were in disagreement.
There the jury had accepted a Crown psychiatrist's opinion that the
accused's action "could be more or less deliberate"[117] in preference to the
defence psychiatrist's opinion that the accused was incapable of premed-
itation and had acted impulsively.[118] In the *MacDonald* case, the
Supreme Court of Canada upheld a conviction for robbery where the
trial judge had refused to accept the *uncontradicted* testimony of a
defence psychiatrist that "the accused at the time of the alleged offense
was not so far free from mental defect, disease, derangement or any
other mental impairment as to be able, concerning the particular acts
charged to form or entertain the specific intent or other mental state
required."[119]

---

[110] [1965] 1 C.C.C. 155 at p. 163.
[111] *Ibid.*
[112] *Woolmington v. D.P.P.*, [1935] A.C. 462 (H.L.).
[113] (1965), 50 W.W.R. 453 (Sask. C.A.).
[114] (1976) , 29 C.C.C. (2d) 257 (S.C.C.); affg 22 C.C.C. (2d) 129 (Ct.Mar. A.C.).
[115] In *Nesbitt* a defence psychiatrist testified that the action of the accused was "not deliberate but impulsive", *supra*, footnote 113 at p. 461. In *MacDonald* a defence psychiatrist testified that the accused had no specific intent.
[116] [1970] S.C.R. 917.
[117] *Ibid.*, at p. 921.
[118] *Ibid.*
[119] *Supra,* footnote 114 at p. 261.

IV. Provocation

Provocation is a defence which operates independently of the doctrine of *mens rea*.[120] Unlike either drunkenness or simple lack of specific intent, it may only be raised in cases where the charge is that of murder.[121] According to s-s. 215(1) of the Code:

> "215(1) Culpable homicide that otherwise would be murder may be reduced to manslaughter if the person who committed it did so in the heat of passion caused by sudden provocation."

For the purposes of s. 215, provocation is defined in s-s. (2) as being a "wrongful act or insult" which satisfies two requirements. First, it must be "of such a nature as to be sufficient to deprive an ordinary person of the power of self-control ... ".[122] Secondly, the accused must have acted upon it "on the sudden and before there was time for his passion to cool."[123] Note also that the provocation itself must be sudden in order for it to give rise to the partial defence set out in s. 215. In *R. v. Tripodi*[124] the Supreme Court of Canada interpreted the expression "sudden provocation" as meaning "that the wrongful act or insult must strike upon a mind unprepared for it, that it must make an unexpected impact that takes the understanding by surprise and sets the passions aflame."

In cases where the accused wishes to rely upon the defence of provocation, the tactical burden of adducing some evidence in support thereof will rest on him. This is not to say, however, that the defendant is required to prove provocation beyond a reasonable doubt or even upon a preponderance of evidence.[125] All that is necessary is that a reasonable doubt be raised[126] as to whether the accused was provoked by the deceased or, in certain circumstances, by a third party[127] or through a

---

[120] *A.-G. Ceylon v. Perera*, [1953] A.C. 200 at pp. 205-6 (P.C.); *Taylor v. The Queen* (1947), 3 C.R. 475 at p. 490 (S.C.C.); *Woolmington v. D.P.P.*, [1935] A.C. 462 at p. 482; *R. v. Barbour* (1938), 71 C.C.C. 1 (S.C.C.); *R. v. Giannotti* (1956), 115 C.C.C. 203 (Ont. C.A.); *R. v. Hall* (1928), 21 Cr. App. R. 48 at p. 54; *R. v. Hopper*, [1915] 2 K.B. 431; *Kwaka Mensah v. The King*, [1946] 1 A.C. 83; *Mancini v. D.P.P.*, [1942] A.C. 1. But see *contra, Holmes v. D.P.P.*, [1946] 2 All E.R. 124 at p. 127 (H.L.); *R. v. Cunningham,* [1958] 3 All E.R 711 (C.C.A.); *R. v. Welsh* (1869), 11 Cox C.C. 336 at pp. 337-8.

[121] Criminal Code, s. 215; *R. v. Bakun* (1967), 50 C.R. 178 (B.C.C.A.). But see the interesting case of *R. v. Bruzas,* [1972] Crim. L.R. 367 and the comment which follows, suggesting that provocation might be a defence to a charge of attempted murder as well. See also English, "Provocation and Attempted Murder", [1973] Crim. L.R. 727.

[122] Subsection 215(2); *Taylor v. The Queen* (1947), 3 C.R. 475 (S.C.C.); *R. v. Harms*, [1936] 2 W.W.R. 114 (Sask. C.A.); *R. v. Sampson* (1934), 8 M.P.R. 328, (N.S.C.A.); affd [1935] S.C.R. 634; *R. v. Manchuk*, [1938] S.C.R. 18; *R. v. Morrison* (1957), 40 M.P.R. 58 (N.S.C.A.); *Ducharme v. The Queen* (1969), 8 C.R.N.S. 287 (Que. C.A.).

[123] *Ibid.*

[124] [1955] S.C.R. 438, *per* Rand J. at p. 443.

[125] *Latour v. The King*, [1951] S.C.R. 19.

[126] *Ibid.; Manchuk v. The King*, [1938] S.C.R. 18.

[127] *R. v. Jackson*, [1941] 1 W.W.R. 418 (Sask. C.A.); *R. v. Manchuk, supra,* footnote 126; *R. v. Twine*, [1967] Crim. L.R. 710; *R. v. Gross* (1913) , 23 Cox C.C. 455.

mistake of fact.[128]

A. THE OBJECTIVE TEST

While the question as to whether there is evidence of a wrongful act or insult for the jury to consider remains a matter of law for the court to decide,[129] the issue of whether or not a particular misdeed would be enough to cause an ordinary person to lose his control is a question of fact for the jury to determine.[130] In deciding this question, the jury are asked to use the familiar "reasonable man" test.[131] Although such standard would appear at first glance to be straightforward, it is submitted that the test's implementation may in fact involve some rather perplexing logical and practical dilemmas.

To begin with, there is a practical problem concerning the characteristics one ought to attribute to the ordinary or reasonable person. Various English cases would seem to indicate that the reasonable man is both physically and mentally "normal". In *Bedder v. D.P.P.*,[132] for instance, the House of Lords held that an accused's sexual impotence (which was found to be physical in nature) was not a factor which the jury could consider when deciding whether or not his victim's taunts fulfilled the objective criterion of provocation. Smith and Hogan have criticized the result in this case, however, calling it "utterly absurd" and asking: "Does it make sense to ask a jury to consider the effect of taunts of impotence on a man who is not impotent? or of taunts of being a hunchback and a dwarf on a man of six feet with a fine, military bearing? or of being a 'black ...!' on a man with a fair skin?"[133] Their point is well taken. In concluding, the authors have forcefully argued:

---

[128] *R. v. Jackson, supra,* footnote 127; *R. v. Manchuk, supra,* footnote 126; *R. v. Brown* (1776), Leach 148; *R. v. Letenock* (1917), 12 Cr. App. R. 221 (C.C.A.) (mistake arising from drunkenness); *R. v. Wardrope,* [1960] Crim. L.R. 770 (mistake arising from drunkenness). Note that the imagined provocation must still meet the objective standard, *i.e.,* it must be such as would deprive an ordinary man of the power of self-control.

[129] *R. v. Swanson* (1950), 10 C.R. 81 (B.C.C.A.); *R. v. Krawchuk,* [1941] 3 W.W.R. 540 (B.C.C.A.); affd 75 C.C.C. 219 (S.C.C.); *Taylor v. The Queen* (1947), 3 C.R. 475 (S.C.C.); *Parnerkar v. The Queen,* [1974] S.C.R. 449; *R. v. Nesbitt,* [1965] 2 C.C.C. 360 (Sask. C.A.); *R. v. Wright* (1968), 62 W.W.R. 449 (Sask. C.A.); affd 66 W.W.R. 631 (S.C.C.); *R. v. Green* (1972), 5 N.S.R. (2d) 41 (C.A.); *Perrault v. The Queen,* [1971] S.C.R. 196; *R. v. Galgay,* [1972] 2 O.R. 630 (C.A.).

[130] *Taylor v. The Queen* (1947), 3 C.R. 475 (S.C.C.); *Lowther v. The Queen* (1957), 26 C.R. 150 (Que. C.A.); *R. v. Nesbitt,* [1965] 2 C.C.C. 360 (Sask. C.A.).

[131] The reasonable man test was first applied to the defence of provocation in the case of *R. v. Welsh* (1869), 11 Cox C.C. 336. There Keating J. instructed the jury (at pp. 338-9) that it was for them to decide whether the provocation relied upon by the defence "was such that they can attribute the act to the violence of passion naturally arising therefrom, and likely to be aroused thereby in the breast of a reasonable man", and whether it was "something which might naturally cause an ordinary and reasonably minded man to lose his self-control and commit such an act". Although the terms "ordinary person" and "reasonable man" may be thought of as synonymous, and therefore used interchangeably, the Supreme Court of Victoria in *R. v. Enright,* [1961] V.R. 663 at p. 669 has suggested that a subtle distinction exists between the two on the ground that "ordinary person" is more consistent with a loss of self-control.

[132] [1954] 2 All E.R. 801 (H.L.).

[133] Smith and Hogan, *Criminal Law,* 3rd ed. (London, Butterworths, 1973) at p. 241.

"Surely there is only one characteristic of the reasonable man which is important for the present purpose and that is that he should show a reasonable degree of restraint in the actual circumstances, including his physical characteristics, whatever they be. In applying the test of the reasonable man at all we ask the jury, in effect, to put themselves into the situation in which D found himself, and to consider whether they, being presumably, a reasonable cross-section of the community, would have lost control of themselves. As the situation will probably be one which the jury have never before experienced anyway, this will be a most difficult task; will it be rendered so much more difficult by their attempting to visualise themselves as having also the physical characteristics of the accused?"[134]

While it is doubtful that *Bedder* is good law in Canada today, it is clear that a jury would not be entitled to visualize themselves as having the accused's mental or emotional characteristics when considering the first branch of the provocation test. Regardless of his physical quirks or disabilities, the reasonable man must be psychologically normal. In *R. v. Wardrope*[135] Edmund-Davies J. (as he then was) remarked that the reasonable man, by definition, could not be violent-tempered,[136] nor drunk.[137] In *R. v. Alexander,*[138] the English Court of Criminal Appeal refused to consider what would be sufficient provocation for a mentally deficient defendant. In *R. v. Lesbini*[139] the accused was precluded from relying upon "defective control" and "want of mental balance",[140] the court obviously feeling that such characteristics were hardly the attributes of a reasonable man.

It seems a curious inconsistency to allow an accused's physical characteristics to be considered by the jury when pondering the first limb of the provocation test and yet to exclude consideration of his psychological make-up. As Lord Simonds L.C. stated in the *Bedder* case:

"It would be plainly illogical not to recognise an unusually excitable or pugnacious temperament in the accused as a matter to be taken into account but yet to recognise for that purpose some unusual physical characteristic, be it impotence or another. Moreover, the proposed distinction appears to be to ignore the fundamental fact that the temper of a man which leads him to react in such and such a way to provocation, is, or may be, itself conditioned by some physical defect. It is too subtle a refinement for my mind or, I think, for that of a jury, to grasp that the temper may be ignored but the physical defect taken into account."[141]

---

[134] *Ibid.*
[135] [1960] Crim. L.R. 770.
[136] See also *Mancini v. D.P.P.,* [1942] A.C. 1 (H.L.).
[137] See also *R. v. McCarthy,* [1954] 2 Q.B. 105.
[138] (1913), 9 Cr. App. R. 139.
[139] [1914] 3 K.B. 1116 (C.C.A.).
[140] *Ibid.,* at p. 1117.
[141] *Supra,* footnote 132 at pp. 803-4.

Lord Simonds' remarks would seem particularly relevant to the case of an accused who suffers from a physical ailment known to affect the mind in a specific way. Diabetes[142] and intoxication are two such conditions. If a diabetic or intoxicated accused is wronged or insulted (*i.e.*, if his condition is ridiculed), should the jury be instructed to consider the physical component of his affliction but ignore the mental component?

If, as Smith and Hogan have contended, the reasonable man test requires the jury to ignore the defendant's mental or emotional peculiarities and yet "to put themselves into the situation in which D found himself . . . ",[143] we are faced with another difficult problem. What if the situation itself is inherently unreasonable? Does it make sense to ask how a reasonable man would behave in circumstances in which he would never find himself?[144] Paradoxical though it might seem, the courts appear to be doing just that with alarming frequency. Consider, for example, the case of *R. v. Berger*.[145] There, the trial judge instructed the jury to decide whether the average citizen who allows himself to be picked up by a homosexual and have his penis fondled would be provoked to violence if his new acquaintance remarked: "Come on, touch me a little bit. Come on Come on Come on — why not, you only like to fuck your damned girlfriend?"[146]

It is an interesting question whether psychiatric evidence may be heard on the issue of whether or not a particular wrongful act or insult would be sufficient to deprive an ordinary person of his powers of self-control. In *R. v. Clark*[147] it was argued on appeal that the admission of

---

[142] The acute irritability of diabetic patients at the onset of a hypoglycemic state has been well documented in medical literature. See Lawrence, *The Diabetic Life,* 17th ed. (London, J. & A. Churchill Ltd., 1965) at p. 119; Sussman, "Acute Problems: Hypoglycemia" *Diabetes Mellitus: Diagnosis and Treatment,* Danowski ed., vol. 1 (New York, American Diabetes Assoc., Inc., 1964) at p. 131; Lister, *The Clinical Syndrome of Diabetes Mellitus* (London, H.K. Lewis & Co. Ltd., 1959) at p. 93; Schmidt, *Diabetes for Diabetics: A Practical Guide* (Miami, Diabetes Press of America, Inc., 1965) at p. 210; Marble, "Hypoglycemia Due to Insulin", in Joslin, Root, White and Marble, *The Treatment of Diabetes* (Philadelphia, Lea & Febinger, 1959) at pp. 314-8.

[143] *Criminal Law* at p. 241.

[144] Where the act alleged to have been the provocation has resulted from the accused's own criminal behaviour, it may well be that the defence of provocation will not be open to the accused as a matter of law. According to s-s. (3) of s. 215:

"... no one shall be deemed to have given provocation to another by doing anything that he had a legal right to do, or by doing anything that the accused incited him to do in order to provide the accused with an excuse for causing death or bodily harm to any human being."

For a recent case in which this section was applied, see *R. v. Louison,* [1975] 6 W.W.R. 289 (Sask. C.A.). The decision of the Privy Council in *Edwards v. The Queen,* [1973] 1 All E.R. 152 would seem to indicate, however, that the inducement of provocation by means of criminal behaviour need not necessarily deprive an accused of that defence. But note that even where the act alleged to have been provocation resulted from the accused's *non-criminal* inducement, such unreasonable conduct on the part of the accused may nevertheless deprive him of the defence of provocation if it vitiates the element of suddenness. See *Salamon v. The Queen,* [1959] S.C.R. 404.

[145] (1975), 27 C.C.C. (2d) 357 (B.C.C.A.); leave to appeal to S.C.C. refused 27 C.C.C. (2d) 357n (S.C.C.).

[146] *Ibid.*, at p. 367.

[147] [1975] 2 W.W.R. 385 (Alta. C.A.); affd [1976] 2 W.W.R. 570 (S.C.C.).

such evidence at trial was an error in law. There a psychiatric witness for the defence had expressed the opinion (a) that the accused's mental and emotional condition made him "more susceptible to provocation"[148] than the ordinary person and (b) that a "normal person" without the accused's particular background would not have been provoked by the actions of the deceased. The latter opinion was elicited in response to cross-examination by Crown counsel. Although the appeal against conviction was dismissed, the Alberta Supreme Court (Appellate Division) was divided in its opinion regarding the admissibility of the psychiatric evidence. McDermid J.A. did not find it necessary to deal with the issue, holding that "Even if such evidence was inadmissible it was an error of law and this would be a case for the application of s. 613(1) (*b*) (iii) ...".[149] Smith C.J.A. (with whom Prowse J.A. concurred) considered the evidence to be inadmissible. Apparently feeling that the ultimate issue rule had been offended,[150] the learned Chief Justice relied on a passage from *Phipson on Evidence*,[151] to the effect that "neither experts nor ordinary witnesses may give their opinions upon *matters of legal or moral obligation, or general human nature, or the manner in which other persons would probably act or be influenced.*" Moreover, Smith C.J.A. was of the opinion that the admission of the psychiatric testimony had produced a substantial wrong or miscarriage of justice inasmuch as the trial judge (who was sitting alone) had relied upon the psychiatrist's evidence either in deciding that there was in law no evidence or provocation[152] or in determining "as a matter of fact that the evidence did not meet the requirements of the first objective test ... ".[153]

Clement J.A. (with whom Sinclair J.A. concurred) took a somewhat different approach. In his opinion the psychiatric evidence elicited in direct examination related solely to the subjective branch of the inquiry (*i.e.*, whether the accused had actually acted in the heat of passion) and was clearly admissible. While the evidence elicited in cross-examination related primarily to the objective branch of the inquiry (*i.e.*, whether a normal person would have lost his self-control), the learned Justice further felt that such evidence was at worst superfluous and that its admission was not incorrect. In his words:

> "The opinions expressed by Dr. Earp in his direct testimony open him to cross-examination not only to test the relevancy or credibility of his opinion, but also on the whole of the Crown's case: Phipson on Evidence, 11th ed., para. 1544; *Regina v. Parnerkar* (No. 2), [1974] 5 W.W.R. 101, 17 C.C.C. (2d) 113 (Sask. C.A.). Those opinions inherently involved a comparison of Clark's emotional condition with that of some standard he had in mind. In my opinion

---

[148] *Ibid.*, at p. 400.
[149] *Ibid.*, at p. 398.
[150] *Ibid.*, at p. 387.
[151] 10th ed. (London, Sweet & Maxwell, 1963), para. 1296, quoted at p. 387 of the judgment (emphasis included).
[152] *Supra*, footnote 147, p. 390.
[153] *Ibid.*

the Crown was entitled to cross-examine him on his standard of comparison to ascertain whether it was compatible with the standard prescribed by s. 215 — an ordinary person — upon which the issue in the first branch of the inquiry hinged in part. This was part of the Crown's burden. In some cases, if cross-examination were pursued it might disclose other criteria which could affect the credibility of the witnesses' opinions. Beyond this, the impugned answers were superfluous, since what is involved is the intuitive perception of human nature which judges, and I include appellate judges, are by common law deemed to be capable without the assistance of opinion evidence. It is the human nature and reactions of the ordinary person that provide the background in law against which the issue of fact under the second branch of the inquiry is to be tried, if it arises at all. The limits of cross-examination were not exceeded, and the matter would have to go farther than it has in the present case to prevent this Court from treating the evidence as superfluous and disregarding it in the first branch of the inquiry: *Carter v. Boehm* (1766), 3 Burr. 1905, 97 E.R. 1162 at 1168."[154]

It is submitted, however, that the decision of Clement J.A. is weakened somewhat by a flaw in his earlier reasoning. The notion that the psychiatrist's evidence was superfluous and capable of being disregarded seems to have been based on his assumption that "The inquiry under the first branch, the objective test, is a matter of *law* for the judge ...".[155] According to Clement J.A., "Evidence is not required for this purpose." since "It is the function *in law* of the judge, drawing upon his intuition, to postulate the reaction of an ordinary person in the given circumstances in order to determine whether or not such a person might have acted as the evidence discloses that the accused did."[156] This view of the law, however, seems to be a somewhat distorted version of the Supreme Court of Canada's interpretation of s-s. 215(3) of the Code. That subsection provides:

> "(3) For the purposes of this section the questions
>   (a) whether a particular wrongful act or insult amounted to provocation, and
>   (b) whether the accused was deprived of the power of self-control by the provocation that he alleges he received,
> *are questions of fact* ... "[157]

In *Parnerkar v. The Queen*[158] a majority of the Supreme Court[159] ruled that the section did not modify "the principle according to which the sufficiency of evidence, which is an issue only where there is some evi-

---

[154] *Ibid.*, at p. 402.
[155] *Ibid.*, at p. 401.
[156] *Ibid.* (emphasis added).
[157] Emphasis added.
[158] [1974] S.C.R. 449.
[159] Fauteux C.J.C. and Abbott, Martland, Judson and Pigeon JJ.

dence, is a question of fact for the jury and the absence of evidence is a question of law for the trial judge."[160] Accordingly, it was held that the trial judge could determine whether or not there was any evidence potentially enabling a reasonable jury acting judicially to find a wrongful act or insult which would satisfy the objective and subjective conditions set forth in s-s. 215(1).[161] This is something quite different from saying that the objective test is a matter of law for the trial judge.

B. THE SUBJECTIVE TEST

In order for a wrongful act or insult to amount to provocation, the subjective condition requires that "the accused acted upon it on the sudden and before there was time for his passion to cool."[162] From a scientific standpoint, this wording has been subject to severe criticism, chiefly on the grounds that it fails to accurately describe the phenomenon of provocation. In an article entitled "The Physiology of Provocation",[163] Peter Brett has in fact asserted that the criminal law's description of the phenomenon obscures physiological reality in some circumstances. To make his point, Brett has summarized the clinical reaction to provocation as follows:

> "Briefly, when anger is aroused, the pulse rate, blood pressure, peripheral circulation of the blood, and level of blood glucose all increase. Breathing becomes faster; the muscles of the limbs and trunk become more tensely contracted and less liable to fatigue. Blood is diverted from the internal organs; digestion and intestinal movements cease, and there is a lessening of sensory perception. All these changes serve the purpose of making the person more ready to fight or flee. They are initiated by a small area at the base of the brain called the hypothalamus, which functions as an integrated unit, with the central nervous and endocrine systems, to release hormones into the bloodstream. Apparently the circulating hormones quickly reach the brain and affect the hypothalamus, so that a circular reaction of the type known as positive feedback takes place. The brain initiates a reaction which in its turn stimulates the brain to produce a further reaction.
> "In this way the body, under stress, prepares for strenuous physical action. If such action occurs, as it often does, the process comes to an end fairly soon after the action has taken place; but in the absence of immediate physical action, the changes just described per-

---

[160] *Supra,* footnote 158 at p. 454.

[161] *Ibid.* Hall and Laskin JJ. dissented. According to Laskin J. (as he then was) at p. 470, "the function of the trial judge as arbiter on the law is to determine only whether there is any evidence of a wrongful act or insult, and ... the further question whether it was of such a nature as to deprive an ordinary person of the power of self-control was a question of fact for the jury ... ".

[162] Subsection 215(2).

[163] [1970] Crim. L.R. 634.

sist for some time, during which the anger that produced them continues."[164]

Having said this, the author has concluded that up to a point, the passage of time will enable an individual's anger to *increase* rather than diminish.[165] By requiring that an accused's actions be "on the sudden", however, our law tends to overlook this fact. "What matters," said Devlin J. (as he then was) in his "classic" direction to the jury in *R. v. Duffy*,[166] "is whether [the accused] had the time to say: 'Whatever I have suffered, whatever I have endured, I know that Thou shalt not kill'."

It is only when considering whether or not the accused acted in the heat of passion and was himself deprived of the power of self-control that the jury may take the possibility of mental disorder into account.[167] Where mental disorder is not asserted, it seems clear from the case of *R. v. Turner*[168] that psychiatric evidence may not be led as to the likelihood of the accused's having been provoked. In that case the English Court of Appeal said simply that "Jurors do not need psychiatrists to tell them how ordinary folk who are not suffering from any mental illness are likely to react to the stresses and strains of life."[169] So long as the psychiatric witness regards the accused as having been mentally abnormal at the time of the alleged murder, therefore, he will be permitted to testify directly on the issue of whether or not the accused acted in the heat of passion. Among the more common mental disorders which might render an individual abnormally susceptible to provocation are such conditions as brain damage, depression, psychopathy, intoxication, morbid jealousy (which may result from almost any mental disorder) and addiction.[170] In *R. v. Clark*,[171] several of these were relied upon by the defence's expert witness. The psychiatric testimony heard by the trial court in that case was summarized as follows:

> " 'Dr. Earp stated that at the time of this incident the accused had a personality problem, namely a morbid jealousy. This was compounded by depression or possible organic degeneration in the nervous system; and, therefore, the accused was more vulnerable to provocation than a person would ordinarily be.' "

---

[164] *Ibid.*, at p. 637.
[165] *Ibid.*, at p. 639.
[166] [1949] 1 All E.R. 932 at p. 932 (C.C.A.).
[167] *Wright v. The Queen,* [1969] S.C.R. 335 at p. 340; *R. v. Berger* (1975), 27 C.C.C. (2d) 357 at pp. 376-8 (B.C.C.A.); leave to appeal to S.C.C. refused 27 C.C.C. (2d) 357n (S.C.C.). It would seem, moreover, that a failure on the part of the trial judge to instruct the jury that they should take the accused's mental peculiarities into account when considering the second branch of the provocation defence is a non-direction providing grounds for appeal. See *R. v. Haight* (1976), 30 C.C.C. (2d) 168 (Ont. C.A.).
[168] [1975] 1 Q.B. 834.
[169] At p. 841. See also *R. v. Dubois* (1976), 30 C.C.C. (2d) 412 at p. 414 (Ont. C.A.).
[170] Gunn, *Violence* (New York, Praeger, 1973) at pp. 12-22.
[171] [1975] 2 W.W.R. 385 at p. 386 (Alta. C.A.); affd [1976] 2 W.W.R. 570 (S.C.C.).

V. Infanticide

In 1948 Parliament boradened the category of culpable homicide[172] by adding thereto the offence of infanticide. According to s. 216 of the current Criminal Code:

> "216. A female person commits infanticide when by a wilful act or omission she causes the death of her newly-born child, if at the time of the act or omission she is not fully recovered from the effects of giving birth to the child and by reason thereof or of the effect of lactation consequent on the birth of the child her mind is then disturbed."

The advent of this new offence has meant the stimultaneous creation of a new defence to charges of murder. As suggested by s-s. 589(3) of the Code,[173] a defendant charged with murder may in appropriate circumstances ask the jury to return a verdict of guilty of infanticide.[174] By s. 220 such verdict carries with it a maximum punishment of five years' imprisonment,[175] and is obviously preferable to conviction for either murder or manslaughter.

Although, strictly speaking, the onus of proof remains with the prosecution in any criminal case, the defendant who raises the defence of infanticide to a charge of murder bears an evidential burden.[176] In order for the offence of infanticide to be established, several things must be shown. According to McRuer C.J.H.C. in the case of *R. v. Marchello*,[177] it must be established (a) that the accused was a woman, (b) that she caused the death of her child, (c) that the child was newly born, (d) that the child was that of the accused, (e) that the child's death was caused by the accused's wilful act or omission, (f) that the accused was not fully recovered from the effects of giving birth to the child at the time of the

---

[172] See s-s. 205(4) of the current Criminal Code which states "Culpable homicide is murder or manslaughter or infanticide."

[173] That subsection provides:
> "(3) Subject to subsection (4), where a count charges murder and the evidence proves manslaughter or infanticide but does not prove murder, the jury may find the accused not guilty of murder but guilty of manslaughter or infanticide, but shall not on that count find the accused guilty of any other offence."

[174] Section 220 states:
> "220. Every female person who commits infanticide is guilty of an indictable offence and is liable to imprisonment for five years."

[175] Note that the jury is entitled to return such verdict even where the court has insisted that the accused be tried for murder despite the Crown's willingness to accept a guilty plea to the lesser offence of infanticide. See *R. v. Soanes,* [1948] 1 All E.R. 289 (C.C.A.) where the jury, on a charge of murder, found the accused guilty of infanticide despite the trial judge's earlier ruling that "nothing appears on the depositions which can be said to reduce the crime from the more serious offence charged to some lesser offence for which, under statute, a verdict may be returned ... " (p. 290).

[176] Smith and Hogan, *op. cit.* footnote 133, at p. 272.

[177] (1951), 12 C.R. 7 at p. 11 (Ont.). See also *R. v. Smith* (1976), 32 C.C.C. (2d) 224 (Nfld. Dist. Ct.).

offence, and (g) that the balance of the accused's mind was disturbed by the effects of childbirth or lactation. Where the accused has been charged with murder, the prosecution will have sought to establish several of the above elements. It will not be necessary, therefore, for the defence to lead evidence either that the accused caused the infant's death or that the act was wilfull. Moreover, it should not be difficult to establish that the accused is a woman and that the deceased infant was her child. It may, however, be somewhat more difficult to establish that the infant was a "newly-born" child within the meaning of s. 216. As indicated by the cases of *R. v. O'Donoghue*[178] and *R. v. Marchello,*[179] "newly-born" is an expression which has been neither judicially interpreted nor statutorily defined in Canada. In *O'Donoghue* and *Marchello* infants aged 35 days and four and one-half months respectively were held to fall outside the scope of the term.

Section 216 was modelled after s-s. 1(1) of England's Infanticide Act, 1938.[180] Commenting on the effect of that provision, Glanville Williams has noted[181] that the infanticide defence helps fill the gap between total responsibility and insanity. Owing to the limited scope of the *M'Naghten* rules (in particular, their failure to recognize "irrestible impulse" as a defence), it is doubtful that a mother suffering from postpartum hormonal imbalance or depressive psychosis would have the defence of insanity available to her.[182] Even if such defence were to succeed, the result would be indefinite detention of a defendant who might be neither dangerous nor acutely disturbed by that point.[183] Where, on the other hand, an accused is convicted of infanticide, she may benefit from judicial leniency at the time of sentencing. Statistics indicate that the maximum term of imprisonment is rarely imposed.[184] This situation may reflect the opinion of many judges that infanticide is a non-deterable crime.[185]

By way of criticism, Williams asserted that the infanticide defence constitutes "an illogical compromise between the law of murder and humane feeling".[186] While the defence spares a disordered defendant from the consequences of a murder conviction, it nevertheless allows an

---

[178] (1927), 20 Cr. App. R. 132.

[179] *Supra,* footnote 177.

[180] 1938 (U.K.), c. 36.

[181] Williams, *The Sanctity of Life and the Criminal Law* (New York, Knopf, 1957) at p. 26.

[182] *Ibid.*

[183] But see the remarks of Dr. W. C. Hood speaking before the British Royal Commission on Capital Punishment cited by Walker and McCabe, *Crime and Insanity in England,* vol. 2 (Edinburgh, Edinburgh University Press, 1973) at p. 5. It was Dr. Hood's opinion that infanticidal women should be detained until they were too old to bear children.

[184] See Williams, *Sanctity of Life and Criminal Law,* at p. 27, where he has stated: "In 1955, for example, thirteen women were charged in England with statutory infanticide and all were convicted, but most were discharged without punishment or merely put on probation; only two were sent to prison, one for a year and the other for three years."

[185] An interesting case has been reported in the Toronto *Globe and Mail,* January 7, 1977, where the Ontario Court of Appeal overturned a 1 year sentence and substituted therefor a conditional discharge. In doing so, the Court reasoned that a prison term would have no deterrent effect whatsoever.

[186] Williams, *op. cit.* footnote 181, at p. 37.

accused suffering from what Williams has suggested is "a real temporary insanity"[187] to be convicted of culpable homicide. Williams has noted also the peculiarity of limiting the infanticide defence to mothers who, as the result of post-partum disorder, kill their newly-born infants.[188] What about the woman who kills another child (or commits some other act of violence) while under the influence of a post-partum derangement? Should not her responsibility for the act be similarly reduced?

A. "THE EFFECTS OF GIVING BIRTH"

It is obvious that the trauma of childbirth has both physical and psychological components. On the physical side a woman must contend with severe metabolic and endocrinologic changes during pregnancy (not to mention alterations in the functions of the liver, kidneys, blood vessels and genital organs),[189] and with blood loss, tissue trauma, exhaustion, decrease in progesterone production, and the administration of anaesthetics, narcotics and hypnotics during and immediately after delivery.[190] From the psychological standpoint, childbirth may produce a variety of emotional responses, depending upon the individual involved. The trauma of biological separation may produce a disappointed and "empty" feeling in some women.[191] This, along with the sudden responsibilities of parenthood may induce depression or confusion which will vary in degree depending upon the woman's background, psychological makeup and her relationship with the child's father. Most women, of course, are able to cope adequately with the stress of childbirth and do not become psychiatric casualties. Usually, it is only when the mother's disturbances reach psychotic proportions that the life of her child is directly threatened.

In 1847 a physician named James Macdonald applied the term "puerperal insanity" to cases in which mental disorder accompanied childbirth.[192] Today, however, such expressions as "puerperal insanity" and "post-partum psychosis" have fallen out of use as diagnostic terms.[193] It is generally agreed that no such clinical entity exists and that the psychoses associated with childbirth occur in women whose psychological makeup predisposes them to such disorder.[194] While almost any

---

[187] *Ibid.*

[188] *Ibid.*, at p. 39.

[189] Brew and Seidenberg, "Psychotic Reactions Associated With Pregnancy and Childbirth" (1950), 111 J. Nerv. Ment. Dis. 408 at p. 408.

[190] *Ibid.*

[191] Benedek, "Sexual Functions in Women and Their Disturbances" *The Foundations of Psychiatry*, 2nd ed., Arieti ed., vol. 1 (New York, Basic Books, 1974) 569 at p. 583.

[192] (1847), 4 Am. J. Insan. 113.

[193] Bucove, "A Case of Prepartum Psychosis and Infanticide" (1968), 42 Psychiat. Q. 263 at p. 263; Brew and Seidenberg, at p. 408.

[194] Brew and Seidenberg, p. 408. But see Hemphill, "Incidence and Nature of Puerperal Psychiatric Illness" (1952), 11 Brit. Med. J. 1232 and Douglas, "Puerperal Depression and Excessive Compliance With the Mother" (1963), 36 Brit. J. Psychol. 271 at p. 271.

form of psychosis may occur during the post-partum period,[195] a brief description of the more common varieties is set out below.

(i) Manic Depressive Psychosis

Manic depressive psychoses are the most common of the mental disorders associated with childbirth.[196] According to Canada's current *Manual for the Classification of Psychiatric Diagnoses,*[197] these disorders may take one of three forms: manic, depressive or circular. Manic reactions, whether psychotic or otherwise, are characterized by excessive elation and excitement, grandiose ideas, rapid flow of thought, talkativeness and accelerated motor activity.[198] A relative rarity during gestation, manic reactions occur most commonly in the second or third week after childbirth.[199] Depressive reactions occur anywhere from several days to several weeks after delivery.[200] The clinical picture is generally one of physical and mental lethargy, motor retardation, profound sadness and a sense of worthlessness.[201] Feelings of apprehension, agitation and perplexity may also be experienced.[202] Owing to the sense of futility and hopelessness commonly experienced, psychotically depressed mothers pose a serious risk to their own safety and to that of their children.[203] Moreover, psychiatric studies indicate that rejection of the newly-born infant is a key feature of depressive post-partum reactions.[204] Finally, there is the circular type manic depressive psychosis. As its name suggests, this disorder is characterized by one or more dramatic mood changes during which the patient experiences alternating periods of mania and depression.[205]

Although they may be precipitated by any combination of biochemical, endochrinologic or psychological factors,[206] Boyd has suggested that manic depressive psychoses are most likely to occur in mothers who are predisposed by what is called a "syntonic temperament". In his words:

"Individuals of this type direct their energies and interests into the outside world rather than inwardly into their own mental life. Usually they are warm, tender, and sympathetic, responding emotionally in harmony with others and their environment. These individuals are often lively, energetic and socially active although some, because of shyness and lack of aggressiveness, give the impression of timidity and withdrawal. The whole group oscillate between the

---

[195] *Diagnostic Manual,* at p. 24.
[196] Boyd, "Mental Disorders Associated with Childbearing" (1942), 43 Am. J. Obstet. Gynec. 148 at p. 153.
[197] At pp. 29-30
[198] Boyd at p. 155; *Diagnostic Manual* at p. 29.
[199] Boyd at p. 155.
[200] *Ibid.,* at p. 157.
[201] *Ibid.; Diagnostic Manual* at p. 29.
[202] *Diagnostic Manual* at p. 29.
[203] Boyd at p. 156.
[204] Brew and Seidenberg at p. 414; Bucove, at p. 263.
[205] *Diagnostic Manual* at p. 30.
[206] Boyd at pp. 154-5.

poles of warm, infectious gayety and unobtrusive, taciturn somberness. Under the stress and pressure of psychologic conflicts or physiologic changes, it is possible that the underlying cyclic emotional swing may be so widened in amplitude that it constitutes obvious mental disorder. In the cases under consideration, pregnancy with its associated problems supplies the extra strain."[207]

(ii) Schizophrenia

Schizophrenia is another form of psychosis which may occur in predisposed[208] mothers during the post-partum period. Like the manic depressive psychosis, it may pose a grave threat to the safety of the newly-born child, psychiatric studies indicating that actual or symbolic rejection or destruction of the infant is not uncommon amongst schizophrenic mothers.[209] Schizophrenia is a broad category of psychosis marked by "alterations of concept formation which may lead to misinterpretation of reality ... ".[210] An individual suffering from this disorder may exhibit bizarre, regressive, withdrawn or inappropriate behaviour, and may experience hallucinations, delusions, and a general loss of empathy with others.[211] This form of disorder comprises perhaps 20 per cent of the so-called post-partum psychoses.[212]

(iii) Delirious Reactions

According to Boyd, delirious reactions comprise nearly 30 per cent of the puerperal psychoses.[213] These conditions generally occur in patients who have a basically unstable personality or have been under severe emotional strain during pregnancy.[214] The delirium is usually precipitated by infection, excessive hemorrhage, toxemias or severe exhaustion and is thought to constitute a "release of underlying conflicts in a symbolic form."[215] The principal characteristics of a delirious state are clouding of consciousness, confusion, hallucinations and/or delusions.

B. "THE EFFECT OF LACTATION"

Very little information exists in the medical literature concerning the psychological effect of lactation. Originally it was believed that diversion of milk from the mother's breast to her brain was responsible for a special form of post-partum psychosis known as "lactational insanity".[216]

---

207 *Ibid.*, at p. 155.
208 *Ibid.*, at p. 158.
209 Brew and Seidenberg at, p. 414.
210 *Diagnostic Manual*, at p. 25.
211 *Ibid.*, at p. 25; Boyd, at p. 159.
212 Boyd at p. 158.
213 *Ibid.*, at p. 161.
214 *Ibid.*
215 *Ibid.*
216 Boyd, at p. 148, citing Hippocrates, *Epidemics* I, III, (New York, Wm. Wood & Co.) and Esquirol, *Maladies Mentales* (Paris, 1838).

This theory was, however, disproved.[217] Although lactation is stimulated and maintained by the production of prolactin in the anterior lobe of the pituitary gland,[218] hormonal changes seem less likely to precipitate a severe behaviour disorder than do the exhaustion and depletion which sometimes result from prolonged nursing.[219]

VI. Diminished Responsibility In English Law

Section 2 of England's Homicide Act, 1957[220] introduced into the law of that country a special defence to murder known as "diminished responsibility". The defence, which originated in Scots law more than 100 years ago,[221] seems first to have been articulated by Lord Deas in *H.M. Advocate v. Dingwall.*[222] There, in the course of his charge to the jury, His Lordship stated that the accused could be convicted of manslaughter (rather than murder) if the jury found mental abnormality which fell short of either drunkenness or insanity. Referring to these instructions in the case of *H.M. Advocate v. McLean*[223] Lord Deas later explained:

> ". . . the state of mind of the prisoner might be an extenuating circumstance although not such as to warrant an acquittal on the ground of insanity; and he therefore could not exclude it from the consideration of the jury here, along with the whole other circumstances in making up their minds whether, if responsible to the law at all, the prisoner was to be held guilty of murder or culpable homicide."

Although the English doctrine of diminished responsibility operates to reduce the offence of murder to manslaughter, it is important to note that the defence, as currently formulated, in no way depends upon a lack of specific intent on the part of the accused. Section 2 of the Homicide Act states simply:

> "(1) Where a person kills or is a party to the killing of another, he shall not be convicted of murder if he was suffering from such abnormality of mind (whether arising from a condition of arrested or retarded development of mind or any inherent causes or induced by disease or injury) as substantially impaired his mental responsibility for his acts and omissions in doing or being party to the killing.

---

[217] *Ibid.*, citing Macdonald (1847), 4 Am. J. Insan. 113.

[218] Benedek, *op. cit.* footnote 191, at p. 583.

[219] See Boyd, at p. 148.

[220] 1957 (U.K.), c. 11.

[221] Topp, "A Concept of Diminished Responsibility for Canadian Criminal Law" (1975), 33 U. T. Fac. L. Rev. 205 at p. 205.

[222] (1867), 5 Irv. 466.

[223] (1867), 3 Coup. 334.

...

> "(3) A person who but for this section would be liable, whether as principal or as accessory, to be convicted of murder shall be liable instead to be convicted of manslaughter."

It is apparent that diminished responsibility is much broader than the Anglo-Canadian concept of legal insanity. As Lord Parker C.J. stated in the case of *R. v. Byrne*:[224]

> " 'Abnormality of mind'. . . means a state of mind so different from that of ordinary human beings that the reasonable man would term it abnormal. It appears to us to be wide enough to cover the mind's activities in all its aspects, not only the perception of physical acts and matters and the ability to form a rational judgment whether an act is right or wrong, but also the ability to exercise will-power to control physical acts in accordance with that rational judgment."

His Lordship further interpreted the phrase "such abnormality as substantially impairs his mental condition" as involving "a mental state which in popular language[225] (not that of the M'Naghten Rules) a jury would regard as amounting to partial insanity or being on the borderline of insanity."[226]

By s-s. 2(2) of the Homicide Act, the burden of proving diminished responsibility rests upon the defendant. As in the case of insanity, a balance of probabilities is all that need be established;[227] proof beyond reasonable doubt is not required. Once the accused has raised the defence, it is clear from s. 6 of the Criminal Procedure (Insanity) Act[228] that the Crown is entitled to lead evidence of the accused's insanity in rebuttal.[229] Conversely, it appears that the Crown may choose to assert diminished responsibility in cases where the accused has raised insanity.[230] Where this situation occurs, it has been held that the burden which the Crown must bear is that of proving the accused's insanity beyond a reasonable doubt.[231] While it is submitted that this view is the correct one, it seems to be in conflict with the law applicable to cases where the Crown seeks to prove insanity in rebuttal of the defence of automatism.[232] In *Bratty v. A.-G. Northern Ireland*[233] Lord Denning expressed the opinion that regardless of who raises the defence, the issue of insanity should be

---

[224] [1960] 3 All E.R. 1 at p. 4 (C.C.A.).

[225] See also *Rose v. The Queen*, [1961] A.C. 496.

[226] *Supra*, footnote 224 at p. 5. See also *H.M. Advocate v. Braithwaite*, [1945] S.C. (J.) 55, *per* Lord Cooper and *R. v. Spriggs*, [1958] 1 Q.B. 270 at p. 276, *per* Lord Goddard C.J.

[227] *R. v. Dunbar*, [1958] 1 Q.B. 1.

[228] 1964 (U.K.) c. 84.

[229] See also *R. v. Bastian*, [1958] 1 W.L.R. 413 where it was held that a positive *duty* rested on the Crown to do so. But *cf. R. v. Price*, [1963] 2 Q.B. 1 at p. 7, where Lawton J. remarked that "Prosecutors prosecute. They do not ask juries to return a verdict of acquittal". Section 6 of the Criminal Procedure (Insanity) Act has resolved this conflict.

[230] Section 6. See also *R. v. Nott* (1958), 43 Cr. App. R. 8.

[231] *R. v. Grant*, [1960] Crim. L.R. 424, *per* Paull J.

[232] See Chapter 4 *ante* at pp. 116-7.

[233] (1961), 46 Cr. App. R. 1 at p. 19.

decided on the balance of probabilities "inasmuch as the verdict is one of acquittal."[234]

Introduction of the doctrine of diminished responsibility into Canadian jurisprudence would fill a number of gaps which exist in our current law relating to crime and mental abnormality. To begin with, it would provide a partial defence to a murder charge for the accused whose particular disorder (*e.g.*, diabetes, intoxication) makes him unusually susceptible to provocation. Presently, such person has no defence unless the wrongful act or insult which he acted upon would have been sufficient to deprive the *ordinary* person of the power of self-control.[235] Under the doctrine of diminished responsibility, a partial defence would also exist for those persons who commit homicide while under the influence of so-called "irresistible impulse ". This fact was made clear by the decision of the English Court of Criminal Appeal in *Byrne*. There it was held that a sexual psychopath who had allegedly strangled and mutilated his victim on impulse was entitled to have the defence of diminished responsibility left to the jury. According to Lord Parker C.J.:

> "Inability to exercise will-power to control physical acts, provided that it is due to abnormality of mind from one of the causes specified in the parenthesis in the subsection, is, in our view, sufficient to entitle the accused to the benefit of the section; difficulty in controlling his physical acts, depending on the degree of difficulty, may be. It is for the jury to decide on the whole of the evidence whether such inability or difficulty has, not as a matter of scientific certainty but on the balance of probabilities, been established and, in the case of difficulty, whether the difficulty is so great as to amount in their view to a substantial impairment of the accused's mental responsibility for his acts." [236]

The major difficulties with the defence of diminished responsibility are twofold. First, the defence is partial, not total. In certain circumstances, it is submitted, this fact creates something of an absurdity. If, for example, an accused acts under the influence of truly irresistible impulses, it is submitted that he should be afforded a complete defence, since there is no question of moral blameworthiness. This reasoning applies as well to the individual who, though abnormally sensitive to provocation, has committed a violent act upon suffering a genuine loss of self-control. Only in cases where the accused has succumbed to *practically* irresistible impulses should he be held partially responsible in law. The second problem is that the defence of diminished responsibility, as set out in English Law, applies only where the offence charged is that of murder. Should not mental impairment of the type described in s-s. 2(1) of England's Homicide Act reduce criminal responsibility for other offences as well?

---

[234] This view was followed by a British Columbia County Court in its ruling in *R. v. Gillis* (1973), 13 C.C.C. (2d) 362 at p. 368.

[235] See the discussion *supra* at pp. 171-6.

[236] *Supra,* footnote 224 at p. 5. See also *R. v. Lloyd,* [1966] 1 All E.R. 107 (C.C.A.) and *R. v. Simcox,* [1964] Crim. L.R. 402 (C.C.A.).

VII. Conclusions

As they now stand, the "partial defences" which exist in our criminal
law are somewhat unsatisfactory. It is submitted, first of all, that the
rule in *Beard* ought to be abandoned. Preferable would be the approach
taken by Dickson J. in *Leary v. The Queen*.[237] In his dissenting judgment His Lordship remarked:

> "I would answer the question of law posed in this appeal in this
> manner — drunkenness, as such, is not a defence to a charge of rape
> but evidence of drunkenness may be considered by the jury, to-
> gether with all other relevant evidence, in determining whether the
> prosecution has proved beyond a reasonable doubt the mens rea re-
> quired to constitute the crime.
>
> . . .
>
> "From the acts and statements of the accused and all of the other
> evidence adduced, the jury should be entitled to draw inferences as
> to the mental state of the accused. The concern is with the mental
> state of the accused, in fact, and not merely with his capacity to
> have the necessary mental state. Intoxication is one factor which,
> with all of the other attendant circumstances, should be taken into
> account in determining the presence or absence of the requisite
> mental element. If that element is absent, the fact that it was ab-
> sent due to intoxication is no more relevant than the fact of intoxi-
> cation giving rise to a state of insanity."

Temporary mental disorder whether caused by self-induced intoxication
or otherwise, should be a defence to criminal liability wherever it raises a
reasonable doubt as to the accused's actual formation of the *mens rea*
requisite to the offence charged. This should be so regardless of whether
the crime is one involving planning and deliberation, specific intent, general intent, knowledge of certain circumstances, or recklessness. Should
Parliament wish to protect society from persons who commit violent
acts while intoxicated, it is always open to them to enact such legislation
as was recently proposed by England's Butler Committee on Mentally
Abnormal Offenders.[238] In the opinion of that Committee, "it should be

---

[237] (1977), 37 C.R.N.S. 60 at pp. 75, 87.

[238] Butler, *Report of the Committee on Mentally Abnormal Offenders,* Cmnd. 6244 (London, H.M.S.O., 1975). See also Beck and Parker "The Intoxicated Offender—A Problem
of Responsibility" (1966), 44 Can. Bar Rev. 536 at p. 609; Williams, *Criminal Law: The
General Part,* 2nd ed. (London, Stevens & Sons, 1961) at p. 573; Ashworth , "Reason,
Logic and Criminal Liability"(1975), 91 L.Q.R. 102 at pp. 112-9. In *Leary, supra,* footnote 237 at p. 86, Dickson J. approved of this proposal, remarking: "If sanctions against
drinking to excess be thought necessary then, in my view, they ought to be introduced
by legislation—as in a crime of being drunk and dangerous — and not by the adoption
of a legal fiction which cuts across fundamental criminal law precepts and has the effect
of making the law both uncertain and inconstant. If the point is deterrence from drink
then such deterrence ought to be specific and   se,   the form of a legislative
command."

an offence for a person while voluntarily intoxicated to do an act (or make an omission) that would amount to a dangerous offence if it were done or made with the requisite state of mind for such offence."[239] The maximum sentence recommended for the offence of "being drunk and dangerous" was one year imprisonment for a first offence and three years' imprisonment for any subsequent offence.[240]

It is further submitted that the defence of provocation needs to be reformulated. Parliament could begin by eschewing the "ordinary person" test from s. 215. If a person commits a violent act through genuine loss of self-control, he should be entitled to a complete defence,[241] regardless of whether his reaction to a particular wrongful act or insult corresponds to what might be expected from an ordinary person.[242] The fact that an ordinary person might or might not have lost control under similar circumstances should merely be treated as evidence bearing on the question of whether the accused in fact lost control.[243] Partial reduction of criminal responsibility would seem logical only in cases where the accused was partially deprived of his self-control.

In cases where the accused has suffered a total loss of self-control, there is no good reason why the defence of provocation should not operate as a complete defence *to any charge*. Where the loss of self-control is only partial, the defence of provocation should reduce responsibility for any violent crimes which contain lesser included offences; if the offence charged contains no lesser included offence partial loss of self-control should mitigate sentence.

Were Parliament to amend s. 16 of the Criminal Code and adopt the test suggested by Bazelon C.J. in *United States v. Brawner*,[244] it is submitted that an individual who is totally or even substantially deprived of self-control would have the defence of insanity open to him. This would leave s. 215 free to deal with those persons who are only partially

---

[239] Butler Report, at p. 236, para. 18.54. A less satisfactory alternative to this suggestion might be the adoption of a "special defence" of intoxication. An accused who successfully raised this defence would receive a special verdict of not guilty by reason of intoxication and, as in the case of insanity, be subject to indefinite detention for the purposes of treatment and public protection. See Berner, "The Defense of Drunkenness — A Reconsideration" (1971), 6 U.B.C. L. Rev. 309 at pp. 349-51.

[240] Although these sentences seem rather light, it should be noted that the enactment of such a provision would not preclude an accused from being convicted of either criminal negligence causing bodily harm (punishable by a maximum of ten years' imprisonment) or criminal negligence causing death (punishable by a maximum of life imprisonment) in cases where the accused knows before getting intoxicated that his doing so is likely to endanger the lives or safety of other persons. See Criminal Code, ss. 202-204.

[241] See Berger, "Provocation and the Involuntary Act" (1966-67), 12 McGill L.J. 202.

[242] In the case of automatism, the accused is certainly not held to the ordinary person standard, though he is provided with a complete defence. It is indeed odd that under the present formulation of the provocation defence, an individual whose behaviour is found to conform with that of the ordinary person may still be convicted of manslaughter.

[243] See Gordon, "Subjective and Objective Mens Rea" (1974-75), 17 Crim. L.Q. 355 at p. 368.

[244] (1972), 471 F. 2d 969 at p. 1032 (D.C. Cir.): "... a defendant is not responsible *if at the time of his unlawful conduct his mental or emotional processes or behaviour controls were impaired to such an extent that he cannot justly be held responsible for his act*" Emphasis added. See Chapter 5, *ante* at pp. 147-8.

deprived of self-control. Alternatively, if Parliament were to adopt the ALI test,[245] as did the majority in *Brawner*,[246] only mentally ill or defective individuals who are substantially deprived of self-control by provocation would have the insanity defence open to them. This would leave s. 215 to deal with (a) those persons who, though neither mentally ill nor defective, are totally deprived of self-control as the result of provocation, and (b) those mentally ill or defective persons who are only partially deprived of self-control as the result of provocation.

Replacement of the *M'Naghten* rules with the ALI test would also make the introduction of the "diminished responsibility" defence unnecessary in Canada. Moreover, any widening of the insanity defence would place considerable doubt upon the continued necessity for a separate infanticide provision in the Criminal Code.[247]

---

[245] Section 4.01(1) of the American Law Institute's Model Penal Code (Philadelphia, 1961) provides:

    "(1) A person is not responsible for criminal conduct if at the time of such conduct as a result of mental disease or defect he lacks substantial capacity either to appreciate the criminality [wrongfulness] of his conduct or to conform to the requirements of law."

[246] See Chapter 5, *ante* at p. 147.

[247] England's Butler Committee has recommended in its recent report both that the insanity defence be broadened and that the separate offence of infanticide be eliminated. See Butler, *op. cit.* footnote 238, pp. 223-30 and 248-51 respectively.

Chapter 7

Psychiatric Evidence At Trial

I. Introduction

As the previous chapters have indicated, psychiatric evidence is of great relevance where an accused's defence turns on the issue of his mental condition at the time of the alleged offence.[1] In addition, it is relevant to certain collateral questions which may arise at trial. These include the issues of competence to testify, credibility (of either a witness or the accused himself), and character (of a witness, the accused, or a third party). This chapter will discuss the admissibility of psychiatric evidence on these issues. It will also deal with some related considerations involved in the use of expert opinion, namely, basis of opinion, qualifications of the witness, the use of hypothetical questions, and the applicability of the ultimate issue rule. As will be seen, such considerations may have direct bearing upon the admissibility of psychiatric testimony, or upon the weight which such evidence is or should be accorded.

Another problem which this chapter will address itself to concerns the role of forensic psychiatry in the adversary system. Some writers have suggested that the present system, whereby each side retains one or more psychiatrists to "battle it out" in the courtroom, serves only to confuse courts and juries and to detract from the experts' credibility. In addition to discussing the problem of disagreement amongst psychiatrists, it is proposed to examine the admissibility of a statutory scheme for the judicial appointment of experts as well as the extent to which psychiatrists may already be called as witnesses by the court.

---

[1] Note, however, that where an accused's mental disorder at the time of the crime is not asserted, psychiatric evidence pertaining to the issue of intent may not be called: *R. v. Chard* (1971), 56 Cr. App. R. 268. This situation is to be distinguished, however, from that where some mild disorder or psychological peculiarity of the accused is raised to rebut the presumption of intent. See *R. v. Clarke* (1971), 56 Cr. App. R. 225; and *R. v. Lupien*, [1970] S.C.R. 263, discussed *infra* at pp. 205-6.

II. Competence, Credibility and Character

A. COMPETENCE

Competence to testify (that is, the ability to give sworn or affirmed evidence in court) involves the "capacity to observe, recollect and . . . communicate . . .".[2] Because such capacity may be affected by mental disorder, psychiatric evidence may be presented as an aid to the court in its determination of a witness' competence once the issue has arisen.

The competence of adult witnesses to give evidence is presumed unless an objection is raised.[3] Once made, the objection must be substantiated on a balance of probabilities basis[4] at a *voir dire*.[5] As indicated by the decision in *R. v. Hill*,[6] the mere fact that a witness is insane will not in itself render such person incompetent to testify. In that case the English Court of Crown Cases Reserved decided that a hallucinating mental patient was capable of giving evidence. This finding strikes one as rather odd, however, and seems to have been based on the belief that specific delusions might not affect the trustworthiness of a witness' testimony on unrelated subjects. According to Wigmore, "the mere fact of derangement or defect does not *in itself* exclude the witness" because "the various forms of monomania are no longer treated as equivalent to complete lunacy".[7] Furthermore, "the inquiry is always as to the relation of the derangement or defect to the *subject to be testified* about. If on this subject no aberration appears, the person is acceptable, however untrustworthy on other subjects".[8] As was pointed out in a previous chapter,[9] however, the theories of monomania and focal delusion have been largely abandoned by modern psychiatry. It is therefore extremely unlikely that a delusional psychotic would be ruled competent to give evidence in Canada today. Certainly where it is established that the delusions of a proposed witness relate to the very subject of his or her testimony, the evidence of such witness would have to be excluded as a matter of law. In the recent case of *R. v. Hawke*[10] it was held that the reception of such evidence was grounds for a mistrial.

---

[2] Manning and Mewett, "Psychiatric Evidence" (1975-76), 18 Crim. L.Q. 325 at p. 327.

[3] *Prescott v. Jarvis* (1849), 5 U.C.Q.B. 489 (C.A.); *Wigmore on Evidence,* 3rd ed. (Boston, Little Brown, 1940), vol. 2, s. 497, at pp. 588-9.

[4] Manning and Mewett, at p. 330.

[5] *A.-G. v. Hitchcock* (1847), 1 Ex. 91, 154 E.R. 38; *Steinberg v. The King,* [1931] 4 D.L.R. 8 (S.C.C.).

[6] (1851), 2 Den. 254, 169 E.R. 495.

[7] *Wigmore,* at p. 586.

[8] *Ibid.*

[9] See Chapter 3 *ante,* at p. 72.

[10] (1975), 29 C.R.N.S. 1 (Ont. C.A.).

B. CREDIBILITY

Though a witness may be either presumed or adjudged competent to give sworn evidence, the question of his or her credibility may still be open to dispute. Where the credibility of a particular witness relates to the possibility that such person is mentally disordered,[11] psychiatric evidence may be called.[12] What is not entirely clear, however, is the extent to which the rights of the prosecution and defence are similar with respect to the affirmation or impeachment of a witness' veracity by means of psychiatric evidence. Let us look first at the rights of the defence.

In the case of *R. v. Gunewardine*[13] the defence sought to elicit testimony from a doctor (it is unclear from the report whether he was a psychiatrist) to the effect that the Crown witness who had just been called was unbelievable because of his mental condition. Although, it was ruled, an opinion regarding the credibility of any witness might be given by a witness from the opposite party, the basis of that opinion could not be disclosed during the examination-in-chief. Since in the case of a medical man the basis of the opinion would have been obvious, the English Court of Criminal Appeal felt bound to exclude such evidence altogether.

In *Toohey v. Metropolitan Police Commissioners,*[14] the House of Lords overruled *Gunewardine* and admitted the evidence of a police surgeon pertaining to the veracity of the complainant. In his judgment, Lord Pearce held:

> "Medical evidence is admissible to show that a witness suffers from some defect or abnormality of mind that affects the reliability of his evidence. Such evidence is not confined to a general opinion of the unreliability of the witness, but may give all the matters necessary to show not only the foundation of and reasons for the diagnosis but also the extent to which the credibility of the witness is affected."[15]

In addition to impugning the veracity of a Crown witness, it would appear that the defence is entitled to lead psychiatric evidence attacking the credibility of the accused himself. Although s. 9 of the Canada Evidence Act[16] generally forbids a party who produces a witness from impeaching his credit by evidence of bad character, there certainly is

---

[11] For a discussion of the ways in which various mental disorders may affect a witness' credibility see Saxe, "Psychiatry, Psychoanalyis, and the Credibility of Witnesses" (1970), 45 Notre Dame Lawyer 238.

[12] Note, however, that where no evidence exists that a witness' mental abnormality effects his or her credibility, there is no foundation for the reception of medical evidence relating to that witness' credibility: *R. v. Desmoulin* (1976), 30 C.C.C. (2d) 517 at pp. 522-3 (Ont.C.A.).

[13] [1951] 2 All E.R. 290 (C.C.A.).

[14] [1965] 1 All E.R. 506 (H.L.). See also *R. v. Dunning; R. v. Simpson,* [1965] Crim. L.R. (C.C.A.).

[15] [1965] 1 All E.R. 506 at p. 512.

[16] R.S.C. 1970, c. E-10.

nothing to prevent the defence from discrediting prior statements made by the accused out of court, if such statements tend to reflect adversely on the accused. This tactic is indeed invited by the relatively recent decision of the British Columbia Court of Appeal in *R. v. Santinon:*[17]

> "An insane person is not normally incapacitated, because of insanity per se, from giving sworn evidence as a witness, and I can see no reason why his voluntary statements should be rendered inadmissible because of the same condition. Whether they should be believed is another matter entirely."

Consistent with this reasoning, though 11 years prior in chronology, was the decision of the Australian High Court in *Jackson v. The Queen.*[18] There it was held that a defence psychiatrist's opinion of the accused's mental state when he confessed to a charge of rape was relevant to the weight to be given to the confession and was, therefore, admissible. More recently, the Ontario Court of Appeal held in *R. v. Dietrich*[19] that psychiatric testimony could be given for the defence to show that the accused was untruthful and had lied in his confessions to a charge of murder. It was further held that the basis upon which the doctor's opinion had been formed was admissible as well. A more dramatic result was reached in the English case of *R. v. Stewart.*[20] There a "trial within a trial" was conducted to determine the admissibility of a series of confessions made by an accused who was mentally retarded. After hearing the evidence of two psychiatrists, the judge, exercising his discretion, *excluded* the confessions.[21] This case is apparently a step beyond *Santinon.*

At this point in time, it is not altogether clear in what circumstances the defence will be permitted to elicit psychiatric testimony to support the credibility of a witness. In the case of *R. v. McKay*[22] the New Zealand Court of Appeal held such evidence to be inadmissible, based as it was on exculpatory statements made by the accused to two psychiatrists while he was under the influence of methydrine, sodium pentothal and sodium amytal ("truth drugs"). An opinion that the accused was being truthful in his denial of guilt would, the Court ruled, offend the ultimate issue rule. In the more recent case of *R. v. Phillion,*[23] however, the Ontario Supreme Court allowed the defence to call psychiatric evidence

---

[17] (1973), 21 C.R.N.S. 323 at p. 326. See also *Sinclair v. The Queen* (1946), 73 C.L.R. 316 (Aust. H.C.); *R. v. Starecki,* [1960] V.L.R. 141 (Vict. S.C.).

[18] (1962), 36 A.L.J.R. 198 (H.C.).

[19] [1970] 3 O.R. 725.

[20] (1972), 56 Cr. App. R. 272.

[21] The "probative value vs. prejudicial effect" test was applied here. On this point, the British Columbia Court of Appeal decision in *R. v. Oldham* (1970), 1 C.C.C. (2d) 141 at p. 145 is worth noting. There, although the effect of drunkenness on an accused's confession was held only to be a matter of weight, and was consequently admitted, McFarlane J.A. expressed approval of the prejudicial effect rule's application in extreme cases.

[22] [1967] N.Z.L.R. 139 (C.A.). See also *Thomas v. The Queen,* [1972] N.Z.L.R. 34.

[23] (1972), 21 C.R.N.S. 169; appeal dismissed on another point, 37 C.R.N.S. 361 at p. 362 (C.A.); affd 37 C.R.N.S. 361 (S.C.C.).

that the accused was truthful, holding also that the basis of the psychiatrist's opinion — psychological, sodium amytal and polygraph tests — could be disclosed to the jury.

Since the decision of the trial court in *Phillion,* two rather interesting English decisions have been reported. The first is that in *Lowery v. The Queen,*[24] a case which dealt with the admissibility of expert opinion regarding the defendant's disposition to commit the type of offence involved. There the evidence of a psychologist was admitted to show that the appellant was more likely to have committed the crime in question (murder) than was his co-accused. Such evidence was not adduced by the Crown, however; it was adduced by the co-accused as part of his defence, and only after Lowery had placed his character at issue. Although the evidence related strictly to the relative characters of Lowery and his co-accused, it did in a sense pertain to the issue of the co-accused's veracity, insofar as it supported his claim of innocence and refuted Lowery's claim that he was lying. While the Privy Council felt that it would have been improper for the Crown to have lead such evidence in the circumstances,[25] it agreed with the following opinion of the Court of Criminal Appeal:

> "It is, we think, one thing to say that such evidence is excluded when tendered by the Crown in proof of guilt, but quite another to say that it is excluded when tendered by the accused in disproof of his own guilt. We see no reason of policy or fairness which justifies or requires the exclusion of evidence relevant to prove the innocence of an accused person."[26]

In *R. v. Turner*[27] the *Lowery* case was distinguished on its facts. This was a case in which the defence sought to adduce psychiatric evidence that the accused was not mentally disordered and was probably telling the truth when he testified that his act of homicide had been provoked.[28] The trial court refused to admit such evidence, however. Noting that the psychiatric testimony was not directed at rebutting any suggestion that the accused was an untruthful person, the English Court of Appeal upheld this ruling saying:

> "We adjudge *Lowery v. The Queen* . . . to have been decided on its special facts. We do not consider that it is an authority for the proposition that in all cases psychologists and psychiatrists can be called to prove the probability of the accused's veracity. If any such rule was applied in our courts, trial by psychiatrists would be likely to take the place of trial by jury and magistrates. We do not find that prospect attractive and the law does not at present provide for it."[29]

---

[24] [1974] A.C. 85.
[25] *Ibid.,* at p. 102.
[26] *Ibid.*
[27] [1975] 1 Q.B. 834 (C.A.).
[28] See also *R. v. Clark,* [1975] 2 W.W.R. 385 (Alta. C.A.); affd [1976] 2 W.W.R. 570 (S.C.C.).
[29] *Supra,* footnote 27 at p. 842.

Where the Crown has sought to bolster the credibility of its own witness, it has not been allowed to do so. In *R. v. Kyselka*[30] psychiatric evidence introduced for the sole purpose of establishing that the complainant was a truthful person was ruled by the Ontario Court of Appeal to be inadmissible. Similarly, in *R. v. Burkart; R. v. Sawatsky*[31] the Saskatchewan Court of Appeal (following *Kyselka*) refused to admit the testimony of a general practitioner called by the prosecution for the purpose of affirming that the complainant was likely to be truthful because of her low mentality. Because in both cases the Crown was attempting to call such evidence in-chief, the question is left open whether it would have been admissible in rebuttal, had the defence attempted to impeach the credit of a Crown witness.

It seems evident from the case of *R. v. Eades*[32] that the principle enunciated in *Toohey* applies to the accused as well as to witnesses for the prosecution. Once the accused takes the witness stand, his credibility may be attacked by psychiatric evidence in the same manner as any other witness. If the accused does not testify, however, it seems equally clear that the Crown may not call psychiatric evidence in-chief which impugns the veracity of a self-serving statement which has been tendered in evidence.[33]

It should be remembered that in both *Toohey* and *Eades,* psychiatric evidence was admitted for the sole purpose of establishing that some *mental disorder* destroyed or detracted from a witness' credibility. As demonstrated by the decision of the Queensland Court of Criminal Appeal in *R. v. Ashcroft,*[34] a psychiatrist's opinion that a witness is lying out of shrewdness or simple deceit is inadmissible. Such opinion is unprofessional and requires no special expertise in the field of psychiatry.[35]

---

[30] [1962] O.W.N. 160.

[31] [1965] 3 C.C.C. 210.

[32] [1972] Crim. L.R. 99.

[33] *Ibid.* For criticism of this ruling, see O'Reagan, "Impugning the Credit of the Accused by Psychiatric Evidence", [1975] Crim. L.R. 563 at pp. 566-7:

"... the Crown would be placed at a considerable disadvantage. At the end of the case the jury would have before it the accused's self-serving statement put in by the Crown but no psychiatric evidence to call its creditworthiness into question. The balance between prosecution and defence would be restored if the following procedure were adopted. If when the Crown closes its case the accused intimates that he does not propose to give evidence or make a statement from the dock then the Crown should be permitted to re-open its case and call psychiatric evidence impugning the veracity of the accused as a maker of the self-serving statement already tendered. A jury may be sceptical of any exculpatory statement which the accused is not prepared to verify at the trial. However adoption of the above procedure would make it clear that the accused is to be denied the benefit of the exculpatory statement unless he assumes the burden of vouching for its truth."

[34] [1964] Qd. R. 81.

[35] As Gibbs J. remarked at p. 85: "...the matter on which Dr. Parker gave evidence was not one upon which the competence to express an opinion could only be acquired by a course of study in psychiatry. If it were otherwise it would be necessary to substitute trial by psychiatrist for trial by jury in every criminal case."

C. CHARACTER

Character evidence has been described as pertaining to "the issue of whether, because of some disposition of the nature of a person, the person is more or less likely to have committed the relevant act or to have had the relevant *mens rea*".[36] In general, evidence of an accused's general character may be introduced in the form of evidence as to reputation only.[37] Once an accused has put his general character in issue, therefore, the Crown is not entitled to lead psychiatric evidence regarding the accused's disposition.[38] However, where an offence has distinctive characteristics which constitute "the hallmark of a specialized and extraordinary class", evidence is admissible for the purpose of showing that the accused does[39] or does not[40] fall within this class of persons. As the Ontario Court of Appeal explained in the case of *R. v. Glynn:*[41]

> "...where it was proved death could have been caused only by a left-handed person, evidence that the accused had the characteristic of being left-handed would clearly be admissible on the question of identity, so in this case where the death may well have been caused by a homosexual with certain characteristics it was proper to show that the accused was a homosexual with those characteristics."

If the features of a particular abnormal class fall within the area of expertise of a psychiatrist, it follows that psychiatric evidence will be admissible on the issue of disposition.[42] It should be noted, however, that "A *mere* disposition for violence ... is not so uncommon as to constitute a feature characteristic of an abnormal group falling within the special field of study of the psychiatrist...".[43] For this reason the Ontario Court of Appeal in *R. v. Robertson*[44] refused to allow psychiatric evidence to be given which showed that the accused lacked a disposition for violence. At first glance, this ruling would appear to be in conflict with the decision in *Lowery v. The Queen,*[45] noted earlier. That case involved the brutal and sadistic murder of a young girl. Psychological evidence led by a co-accused was admitted for the purpose of showing that Lowery was a psychopathic personality. In *Robertson*, Martin J.A. distinguished the two cases saying:

> "...the killing under consideration in the Lowery case was one with unusual features tending to identify the perpetrator as a member of a special and extra-ordinary class. ...

> ...

---

[36] Manning and Mewett, *op cit.* footnote 2 at p. 328; Wigmore, vol. 1, s. 55, at p. 450.
[37] *R. v. Rowton* (1865), 10 Cox C.C. 25, *per* Cockburn C.J. at p. 29.
[38] *Lowery v. The Queen,* [1974] A.C. 85 at p. 102.
[39] *Thompson v. The King,* [1918] A.C. 221.
[40] *R. v. Robertson* (1975), 29 C.R.N.S. 141 (Ont. C.A.).
[41] [1972] 1 O.R. 403 at p. 405.
[42] *R. v. Lupien,* [1970] S.C.R. 263, *per* Ritchie J. at pp. 275-6.
[43] *R. v. Robertson, supra,* footnote 40 at p. 189.
[44] *Supra,* footnote 40.
[45] [1974] A.C. 85.

> "In this case the evidence shows no more than that the young deceased was killed by an act of great brutality. It cannot be said that such an act would only be committed by a person with recognizable personality characteristics or traits."[46]

Interestingly, the Privy Council does not seem to have shared Martin J.A.'s view on the question of whether or not the offence in that case bore the hallmark of a distinctive class (*i.e.* psychopathy). Lord Morris of Borth-y-Gest expressed the view that it would have been improper for the Crown to have lead such evidence, apparently feeling that the case fell outside the "hallmark rule". He quoted with approval the Court of Criminal Appeal's statement to this effect:

> "It is ... established by the highest authorities that in criminal cases the Crown is precluded from leading evidence that does no more than show that the accused has a disposition or propensity or is the sort of person likely to commit the crime charged. ..."[47]

In the more recent case of *R. v. McMillan,*[48] Martin J.A. appears to have conceded that the real ground for admitting the psychologist's evidence in *Lowery* had nothing whatever to do with the hallmark theory. There he used the case as authority for the proposition that "Psychiatric evidence with respect to the personality traits or disposition of the accused, or another, ... is also admissible ... as bearing on the *probability* of the accused, or another, having committed the offence."[49] In the result, psychiatric evidence was admitted for the purpose of establishing that the accused's wife, a psychopath, was the more likely of the two to have murdered their two and a half week-old daughter. *McMillan* went a step beyond *Lowery*, however, holding in addition that by leading such evidence, the accused lost his protection against having his own disposition revealed to the jury by means of psychiatric evidence led by the Crown.[50] This ruling was upheld by the Supreme Court of Canada.[51]

III. Qualifications of the Psychiatric Witness

Although s. 7 of the Canada Evidence Act[52] provides for the use of "professional or other experts" as witnesses at a trial, nowhere is it stated in the Act exactly who such persons are. The general rule regarding qualifications of experts is that expert testimony will not be admissi-

---

[46] *Supra,* footnote 40 at pp. 189-90.
[47] *Supra,* footnote 45 at p. 102.
[48] (1975), 29 C.R.N.S. 191 (Ont. C.A.).
[49] *Ibid.,* at p. 206.
[50] *Ibid.,* at p. 210.
[51] (1977), 33 C.C.C. (2d) 360.
[52] R.S.C. 1970, c. E-10.

ble unless: (1) the subject-matter of the trial or inquiry involves issues beyond the competence of a lay jury to determine if unaided by such experts; and (2) the witness' expertise was gained though a course of study or habitual practical experience.[53]

It has been shown[54] that there are certain areas in which it is permissible for non-expert witnesses to state their opinions. It is submitted, however, that these areas are limited to situations where the lay person has fulfilled the requirement of practical experience, and the issue involved is not one which demands specialized assistance. The issue of an accused person's state of mind (and *a fortiori* insanity) would appear, then, to exclude lay opinion testimony,[55] although where the witness is a medical practitioner things become more interesting. Can an ordinary M.D. express an opinion on psychiatric issues?

In *R. v. Grobb*[56] the Manitoba Court of Appeal held that where a physician called by the Crown testified that he had no special experience in insanity cases and that he had not even examined the accused, his evidence on the issue of insanity could not be admitted since no proper foundation had been laid. A similar result was reached in the New Brunswick Supreme Court (Appeal Division) case of *R. v. Kierstead.*[57] There a doctor called by the defence stated several times that he was not an expert on the subject of insanity. With regard to the admissibility of the doctor's evidence, White J. stated:

> "... before a witness can be asked his opinion as to whether certain acts, conduct or expressions of the prisoner in his opinion indicate insanity, it must be shown that he is an expert, and as Dr. Kennedy does not appear to have been an expert, I think that Dr. Kennedy's opinion in evidence upon the question of the prisoner's insanity was

---

[53] *Kelliher v. Smith,* [1931] S.C.R. 672; affg [1930] 2 W.W.R. 638 (Sask. C.A.), which reversed [1929] 3 W.W.R. 655; *Taylor v. Gray,* [1937] 4 D.L.R. 123 (N.B.C.A.); *R. v. Kuzmack* (1954), 110 C.C.C. 338 (Alta. C.A.), affd without reference to this point, [1955] S.C.R. 292; *Smith v. Mason* (1901), 1 O.L.R. 594 at p. 598. *Quaere* how the first limb of this test when combined with the rule in *R. v. Kierstead* (1918), 42 D.L.R. 193 (N.B.C.A.) can be reconciled with the calling of expert evidence of insanity. In *Kierstead* it was held that insanity could be inferred by a lay jury from the accused's acts.

[54] See, for example *R. v. German* (1947), 89 C.C.C. 90 where the Ontario Court of Appeal held that a lay witness could give his opinion as to the accused's drunkenness. There, Robertson C.J.O. said (at p. 98): "No doubt, the general rule is that it is only persons who are qualified by some special skill, training or experience can be asked their opinion upon a matter in issue. The rule is not, however, an absolute one. There are a number of matters in respect of which a person of ordinary intelligence may be permitted to give evidence of his opinion upon a matter of which he has personal knowledge." See also *R. v. Marks* (1952), 103 C.C.C. 368 (Ont. Co. Ct.); *R. v. Beauvais,* [1965] 3 C.C.C. 281 (B.C.); *R. v. MacDonald* (1966), 9 Crim. L.Q. 239 (N.S.). But note *R. v. Davies,* [1962] 3 All E.R. 97 where it was held that though a non-expert opinion that the accused had been drinking was admissible, an opinion that he was unfit to drive due to intoxication was not.

[55] See the recent decision of the Quebec Court of Appeal in *Palomba v. The Queen* (1975), 32 C.R.N.S. 31, where it was held that a member of the clergy was not entitled to express an opinion on the accused's mental state because he was not a qualified psychiatrist.

[56] (1906), 13 C.C.C. 92.

[57] (1918), 42 D.L.R. 193.

improperly admitted."[58]

On a new trial[59] of the case, however (ordered for reasons unrelated to this ruling) it was held, *per* Chandler J.,[60] that any objection to the evidence given on insanity by the doctor went to weight and not to admissibility. Although this last finding strikes one as rather odd, it could well be the law in Canada. In the United States the general practitioner is *prima facie* held to qualify as an expert on insanity[61] regardless of the fact that he disclaims any such expertise, since his competence is a matter for the court's sole consideration.[62] At the very least, the Canadian cases referred to invite the inference that a physician — or, indeed, a non-M.D. — need not be stamped with the label "psychiatrist" in order to qualify as an expert on matters of the mind. Beyond that, it is unclear exactly *how qualified* an "expert" must be before he will be permitted to testify on very specific psychiatric issues. What about the doctor who has done extensive research on psychiatric topics but has had no practical experience in treating mental disorder?[63] Or what about the lay analyst (psychoanalyst with no M.D.) who has had vast practical experience treating emotionally disturbed patients but has done no forensic work? Doubtless, the admissibility of opinion from such experts will in each case be a question for the discretion of the judge, governed, as he is, by no apparent guidelines.[64]

Once a psychiatric expert has taken the stand to testify on issues beyond the competence of laymen, it is a tricky question where he oversteps the bounds of his competence by expressing an opinion on an area not outside the ken of the lay person; to do so would, in effect, render him no more expert than the members of the jury. In theory at least, non-professional opinions which venture beyond the witness' special knowledge should be ruled inadmissible. But in practice this does not always seem to be the case. In cases where the expert witness appears to have confined himself to expressing opinions on matters outside the jury's realm of knowledge, but has in the process apparently over-

---

[58] *Ibid.*, at p. 205.

[59] (1918), 33 C.C.C. 288.

[60] *Ibid.*, at p. 292.

[61] See Wigmore, s. 560 and the following American cases: *Holt v. State* (1947), 84 Okla. Crim. 283; *Oliver v. State* (1936), 232 Ala. 5; *Gast v. State* (1936), 232 Ala. 307; *Brady v. State* (1931), 116 Tex. Crim. 427; *Tendrup v. State* (1927), 193 Wis. 482; *Glover v. State* (1907), 129 Ga. 717.

[62] *Winn v. State* (1939), 136 Tex. Crim. 513; *Braunie v. State* (1920), 105 Neb. 355; *State v. Liolios* (1920), 285 Mo. 1; *State v. Rose* (1917), 271 Mo. 17; *Glover v. State* (1907), 129 Ga. 717; *Broham v. State* (1904), 143 Ala. 28; *State v. Boyce* (1901), 24 Wash. 514.

[63] In the States of Tennesee and Wisconsin, personal experience has been held to be essential. See, for example, *McElroy v. State* (1922), 146 Ten. 442; *Watson v. State* (1915), 133 Tenn. 198; *Ashby v. State* (1911), 124 Tenn. 684; *Lowe v. State* (1903), 118 Wis. 641; *Zoldoske v. State* (1892), 82 Wis. 580; *Soquet v. State* (1888), 72 Wis. 659. But see *contra Tendrup v. State* (1927), 193 Wis. 482; *Winn v. State* (1939), 136 Tex. Crim. 513 and *Sevanson v. Hood* (1918), 99 Wash. 506.

[64] See Wigmore, s. 561 at p. 641: "... the trial Court must be left to determine, absolutely and without review, the fact of possession of the required qualification by a particular witness."

reached his own expertise, contradictory decisions have arisen. In the case of *Preeper and Doyle v. The Queen,*[65] for example, a doctor who had examined the body of the victim of a gunshot wound was asked to estimate the distance from which the fatal shot was fired. Despite the fact that the doctor admitted to a lack of experience with firearms, the majority of the Supreme Court of Canada ruled his answer admissible. On the other hand, in *R. v. Kuzmack*[66] the admission into evidence of a doctor's non-professional guess at how certain stab wounds on the murder victim's fingers had been caused was held by the Alberta Supreme Court (Appellate Division) to be grounds for a new trial. The reasoning here was that since the doctor's opinion was no better than that which any member of the jury might have given (and neither opinion would have possessed the value of a *bona fide* expert in such matters) it was prejudicial to have expert weight attached to it. More recently in *R. v. Hubbert,*[67] the Ontario Court of Appeal ruled inadmissible a psychiatrist's opinion as to whether or not knowledge of the accused's incarceration in a mental institution would bias prospective jurors. The impact of such information upon members of the public was held to fall outside the scope of the psychiatrist's expertise.

Although the phrases "usurping the function of the jury" or "invading the province of the jury" are bandied about widely today in the context of expert opinion, it may be doubted whether they accurately describe the situations to which they are commonly applied. When such label is affixed to the expression by an expert witness of an opinion on an "ultimate issue" which the jury are to decide, it is submitted that the description is inaccurate.[68] If the expert is qualified in his field, the implication is that the opinion he is expressing is one which the triers of fact could not themselves have formulated; otherwise the expert would not be there in the first place. So when a psychiatrist expresses his opinion that an accused was insane at the time he committed an act, he is lending his special knowledge to the jury to aid them in performing their function. As Professor Wigmore has pointed out,[69] he in no sense replaces them. Neither does an expert "usurp" the jury's function when, as in the *Kuzmack* case, he expresses an opinion (whether on the ultimate issue or not) which neither he nor the jury are sufficiently knowledgeable to legitimately hold. Once again, if a lay jury possesses no special expertise in a certain area, their function has not been usurped, because forming an opinion outside their realm of competence was never their function to begin with. But where the term "usurping the function of the jury" may, it is submitted, more accurately be applied is in the situation where the expert, purporting to possess a unique wisdom, "point(s) out to the jury matters which it is within the ordinary capacity

---

[65] (1888), 15 S.C.R. 401.
[66] (1954), 110 C.C.C. 338 (Alta. C.A.), affd without reference to this point, [1955] S.C.R. 292.
[67] (1975), 31 C.R.N.S. 27, appeal to S.C.C. dismissed without written reasons 38 C.R.N.S. 381 (S.C.C.).
[68] See Wigmore, s. 1921.
[69] *Ibid.*

of jurors to decide for themselves".[70] Here the "expert" takes upon himself, with no better skill than the layman, the role of a thirteenth juror. While in a strictly procedural sense, as Wigmore has observed,[71] the witness has no power to prevent the jury from coming to their own decision, the court may produce a perilously similar result by cloaking such a witness in the mantel of expert.

In the Ontario Court of Appeal case of *R. v. Fisher*[72] Aylesworth J.A. stated:

> "It is trite to say that a witness may not give his opinion upon matters calling for special skill or knowledge unless he is an expert in such matters nor will an expert witness be allowed to give his opinion upon matters not within his particular field. Finally, *opinion evidence may not be given upon a subject-matter within what may be described as the common stock of knowledge.* Subject to these rules, the basic reasoning which runs through the authorities here and in England, seems to be that expert opinion evidence will be admitted where it will be helpful to the jury in their deliberations and it will be excluded only where the jury can easily draw the necessary inferences without it."[73]

In that case an accused, charged with murder by stabbing his victim some 15 times, raised the defence of drunkenness. A dispute arose as to the admissibility of a psychiatrist's opinion that any one capable of doing what the accused was alleged to have done would possess the capacity to form the intent to commit murder. Although the opinion seemed dangerously close to being non-professional, the Court rejected this contention, holding that the doctor was better qualified than the lay person to express such an opinion. On appeal, the Supreme Court of Canada upheld this decision,[74] adopting the reasons expressed by Aylesworth J.A.

A more recent case worth looking at is that of *R. v. St. Pierre.*[75] There, on a charge of gross indecency,[76] the defence sought to introduce in evidence a psychiatrist's opinion that the sexual acts which the accused was alleged to have committed were in fact normal within the Canadian community. Haines J. in the Ontario High Court refused to admit such testimony, on the ground that it would usurp the jury's function. In the words of Haines J., "the members of the jury have been selected, in theory, as a cross-section of Canadian mentality and it is they who are to decide what the standards of decency applicable in this case are to be."[77] However, the Ontario Court of Appeal reversed this ruling. Speaking for the Court, Dubin J.A. stated:

---

[70] *R. v. Hally,* [1962] Qd. R. 214 at pp. 228-9 (C.C.A.).
[71] Section 1921.
[72] [1961] O.W.N. 94.
[73] *Ibid.,* at pp. 94-5 (emphasis added).
[74] [1961] S.C.R. 535.
[75] [1973] 1 O.R. 718.
[76] The accused was also charged with rape.
[77] *Supra,* footnote 75 at p. 728.

"Attitudes relating to sexual behaviour are constantly changing. In determining whether the conduct of the accused was a very marked departure from decent conduct, it would have been of great assistance to the jury to have been appraised by an admittedly qualified expert as to sexual practices being carried on in this country, which are not regarded by many as abnormal or perverted. *In the absence of such evidence the jury would be left to make the determination dependent solely on their own private views and their own experience.*"[78]

In reaching its decision, the Court seems to have placed great reliance on the witness' qualifications as that of "a psychiatrist who has made a study of sexual behaviour".[79] Even if the witness had not possessed such qualifications, however, the words of Dubin J.A. imply that the jury's function could not have been usurped, since the issue in this case was beyond the competence of an unassisted lay jury to decide in the first place.

IV. Basis of Opinion

The calibre of psychiatric opinion, as with any other opinion, is naturally dependent on the basis upon which it is founded. Personal examination of the accused is doubtless the best source of diagnostic material. However, the law recognizes as acceptable other means of gathering information; some of these are good, some not so good. In the old Quebec case of *R. v. Dubois*[80] it was held that in cases where the defence of insanity has been raised, a medical expert who has heard all the evi-

---

[78] (1974), 3 O.R. (2d) 642 at pp. 649-50 (emphasis added). The decision here was consistent with the rulings in *R. v. J.* (1957), 118 C.C.C. 30 (Alta. C.A.) and *R. v. P.*, [1968] 3 C.C.C. 129 (Man. C.A.).

[79] At p. 649. Regarding the related topic of survey information as a basis of expert opinion, the case of *R. v. Times Square Cinema Ltd.*, [1971] 3 O.R. 688 (C.A.) is worth noting. That case involved the admissibility of expert opinion on the collective opinions of the lay public regarding obscenity. It was held that while both expert opinion on the community standard of tolerance and the opinion poll upon which the expert's view is based might be admissible in some cases, such evidence could not be admitted in the instant case. Because the sampling of people was so poor, the jury would have been in just as good a position to guess at community standards as the expert. See also *Building Products Ltd. v. B.P. Canada Ltd.* (1961), 36 C.P.R. 121 (Ex. Ct.) and *R. v. Prairie Schooner News Ltd. and Powers* (1970), 1 C.C.C. (2d) 251 (Man. C.A.) on the matter of survey evidence. Concerning the test for obscenity, see *Brodie v. The Queen; Dansky v. The Queen; Rubin v. The Queen*, [1962] S.C.R. 681 and *Dominion News and Gifts (1962) Ltd. v. The Queen*, [1964] S.C.R. 251. See also *Hoban's Glynde v. Firle Hotel* (1973), 41 S.A.S.R. 503 (S.C. of Aust. in Banco), where opinion poll evidence was rejected as being totally inadmissible "double hearsay", though without reference to it forming the factual basis of expert testimony. And note *R. v. Stamford*, [1972] 2 All E.R. 427, where the English Court of Appeal in an obscenity trial ruled expert opinion inadmissible as being in violation of the ultimate issue rule.

[80] (1890), 17 Q.L.R. 203.

dence presented in the courtroom could give his opinion, premised upon the truth of the facts stated, as to whether or not the accused was capable of distinguishing right from wrong. If the doctor had not even been present in court, it was further held that an opinion could be elicited which was founded solely upon the truth of depositions and a hypothetical account of the facts. In *Fisher v. The Queen,*[81] the Supreme Court of Canada seems to have used this rather undemanding standard to allow a psychiatrist to express his opinion as to the accused's capacity to form the intent requisite to murder, solely on the strength of having read the accused's statement.[82]

Many psychiatrists have expressed grave doubts *outside* the courtroom as to the ethics and utility of testifying "on the basis of wholly inadequate clinical information".[83] Yet counsel for either party do not seem to have much difficulty in finding psychiatrists who will testify without having conducted their own examination of the accused.

V. Hypothetical Questions

The status of the hypothetical question as a means for eliciting psychiatric opinion may be the subject of some confusion in Canadian criminal evidence. For the purpose of illustrating its usefulness, the Supreme Court of Canada case of *R. v. Neil*[84] is a good case to start with. There, the prosecution seems to have bungled its case rather badly in a sexual psychopath hearing through the improper use of a psychiatric witness. In its examination of the psychiatrist nominated by the Attorney-General, Crown counsel made it apparent that the witness (who had not examined the accused) had based his opinion entirely on the contradictory evidence which was adduced at the hearing. There was, therefore, no way of telling what facts about the accused the doctor had assumed to be true. He may have accepted all, some or none of the evidence against the accused. Cartwright J. said:

> "The objections to such a method of examination are obvious. The witness is being asked to weigh conflicting evidence ... The witness could not be expected to know the rules as to weighing the evidence of an accomplice or to appreciate the significance of the re-

---

[81] [1961] S.C.R. 535.
[82] *Quaere* what would happen if the statement were ruled inadmissible at trial. Could the doctor introduce it as the basis of his opinion? Would it make any difference if the doctor were a defence or Crown witness? What would happen if the defendant admitted to the psychiatrist that the involuntary confession is true? Perhaps the answer lies in the fact that the theoretical purpose of the doctor referring to the confession is not related to proof of the truth of the contents of the confession. (See *Wilband v. The Queen,* [1967] S.C.R. 14 at p. 21, discussed *post* in Chapter 9 at pp. 279-80.)
[83] Diamond, "The Psychiatrist as Advocate" (1973), 1 Psychiatry and Law 5 at p. 6.
[84] [1957] S.C.R. 685.

spondent not having been cross-examined."[85]

In *R. v. Leggo*[86] the opinions of psychiatrists at a sexual psychopath hearing were rendered useless partially because they had been based in part on an inadmissible unsworn statement of the circumstances of the offences made by the Crown prosecutor. Perhaps in both *Leggo* and *Neil* the use of hypothetical questions to elicit testimony would have avoided the problems created by Crown counsel. Had the witnesses been asked "assuming the following facts to be true, what would your opinion of the accused's mental state be doctor?" or something to that effect, their testimony might have been admitted. As to the necessity of using this particular format, *Bleta v. The Queen*[87] is in point. There automatism was raised in defence to a charge of murder. The psychiatrist who was called for the defence obtained his information only from his examination of the accused and from the evidence he heard at the trial. Ritchie J. said:

> "Provided that the questions are so phrased as to make clear what the evidence is on which an expert is being asked to found his conclusion, the failure of counsel to put such questions in hypothetical form does not of itself make the answers inadmissible. It is within the competence of the trial judge in any case to insist upon the foundation for the expert opinion being laid by way of hypothetical question if he feels this to be the best way in which he can be assured of the matter being fully understood by the jury, but this does not, in my opinion, mean that the judge is necessarily precluded in the exercise of his discretion in the conduct of the trial from permitting the expert's answer to go before the jury if the nature and foundation of his opinion has been clearly indicated by other means.
>
> "In the present case there does not appear to me to be any difficulty in concluding that in giving his opinion Dr. Stokes was proceeding on the hypothesis that the appellant's blow on the head and his conduct after receiving it were as described by the uncontradicted evidence of Crown witnesses, and that his condition as to amnesia, headaches and other symptoms was the condition which he himself described.
>
> "As he was required to do, the learned trial judge made it clear to the jury that they were not bound to accept the evidence upon which the doctor based his opinion or the opinion itself when he said: 'You may accept or reject the evidence of any witness in whole or in part and that applies to the experts — in this case the doctor — as it does to all other evidence'."[88]

---

[85] *Ibid.*, at p. 701.
[86] (1962), 133 C.C.C. 149 (B.C.C.A.).
[87] [1964] S.C.R. 561.
[88] *Ibid.*, at pp. 566-7.

In *R. ex rel Taggart v. Forage,*[89] where the accused was charged with contributing to juvenile delinquency by sexually assaulting a male student, psychiatric evidence rebutting peculiar propensity was allowed without a hypothetical base. Hartt J. stated:

> "Under normal circumstances, the admissibility of this type of opinion evidence could be open to serious question. However, in the light of evidence adduced by the Crown of the four boys other than the complainant, which evidence was realistically relevant only, in my opinion, to disposition, the psychiatric evidence, upon behalf of the defence and directed also to disposition, is admissible."[90]

This statement seems to have been construed by authors Maloney and Tomlinson[91] as the emergence of an *exception* to the hypothetical question "rule" in cases where the evidence is used to rebut similar fact evidence. A fact perhaps overlooked here is that the psychiatrist and psychologist had based their opinions on extensive examination and testing of the accused — not upon evidence they had listened to at trial. Was it ever the law that psychiatric testimony, in order to be admitted, had to have a hypothetical base? The only cases where this has been held have had one thing in common: the doctors had not examined the accused but based their opinions on conflicting evidence heard at the trial. Indeed in *R. v. Tilley*[92] Roach J.A. said:

> "The facts as to the indecent assault on Elizabeth White had been proved in evidence beyond a reasonable doubt because the jury found the accused guilty of that offence. It was allowable for the psychiatrists to base their evidence in whole or in part, as they might choose, on that evidence. It was also allowable for Dr. Tennant to base his evidence in part on his examination of the accused. It was improper to ask the psychiatrists to base any opinion on other *alleged* facts as to which evidence was given on the issue."[93]

And in *Bleta v. The Queen*[94] the Supreme Court of Canada said:

> "The case of *R. v. Holmes,* is illustrative of the fact that the opinion of experts on the very question at issue can be elicited without the aid of a hypothetical question if the basis for the opinion is made apparent to the jury. In that case the expert who had examined the accused before the trial was questioned as to his opinion based on his behaviour after the alleged murder had been committed."[95]

---

[89] (1968), 3 C.R.N.S. 117 (Ont.).
[90] *Ibid.,* at p. 119.
[91] "Opinion Evidence", *Studies in Canadian Criminal Evidence,* Salhany and Carter, eds. (Toronto, Butterworths, 1972), 219 at p. 239.
[92] [1953] O.R. 609 (C.A.); affg 104 C.C.C. 315.
[93] *Ibid.,* at p. 622 (emphasis added).
[94] *Supra,* footnote 87.
[95] *Per* Ritchie J. at pp. 565-6. Note also the statement of Smith C.J.A. in the Alberta

Maloney and Tomlinson[96] see the case of *R. v. Lupien*[97] as an expansion of the *Forage* "exception" — the admissibility of psychiatric testimony without a hypothetical basis even though its purpose is not to rebut similar facts evidence. But in *Lupien,* too, it is important to note that the opinion was based on examination. There the accused, who was charged with attempting to commit an act of gross indecency with another male, raised the defence that he had believed his companion to be a woman. In support of this defence, the accused sought to call psychiatric evidence that his strong aversion to homosexuality would have made him incapable of forming the intent requisite to the offence. The trial judge refused to allow such evidence and Lupien was convicted. On appeal, the British Columbia Court of Appeal set aside the conviction. To the Crown's contention that the psychiatrist's testimony "could only be based upon hypotheses founded upon Lupien's evidence about the facts, because the doctors had not seen him at the time",[98] counsel for the appellant argued that:

"... he was entitled to have had the psychiatric opinion elucidated to the jury on the broader base, as an opinion given solely on the facts of the incident in response to the truncated question could not possibly be a true evaluation of a state of mind, being without any consideration of the subject's mental processes and blocks, behaviour pattern, psychoses, inhibitions, urges, beliefs, and all the other indicia upon the analysis of which a true psychiatric evaluation could, and of necessity must, be made."[99]

Supreme Court (Appellate Division) case of *R. v. Fisher* (1973), 24 C.R.N.S. 129 at p. 137 to this effect:

> "I should state that on the argument of the appeal no objection was made to the manner in which many of the opinions of the experts were elicited, mostly without the aid of hypothetical questions, and in view of the decision of the Supreme Court of Canada in *Bleta v. The Queen,* [1964] S.C.R. 561, 44 C.R. 193, [1965] 1 C.C.C. 1, 48 D.L.R. (2d) 139, and *Regina v. Holmes,* [1953] 1 W.L.R. 686, 37 Cr. App. 61, [1953] 2 All E.R. 324, a decision of the Court of Criminal Appeal, I cannot see how there could have been a well-founded objection to this procedure."

[96] *Supra,* footnote 91, at p. 244.

[97] [1970] S.C.R. 263.

[98] (1968), 4 C.R.N.S. 250 at p. 252. It is interesting that the Crown suggests that the hypothetical basis for the psychiatrist's testimony be the truth of Lupien's account of the facts constituting the alleged offence. One would have thought the Crown would demand that the opinion be elicited on the assumption that Lupien's emotional responses to the psychiatrist were sincere. The psychiatrist himself seems to have disclosed a lack of faith in his objective powers of personality assessment in the following statement [1970] S.C.R. 263 at p. 267:

> "This is where I would have to assume the truthfulness of what he said referable to his background, his attitudes, his feelings, his beliefs, those things that would allow me to gain some idea and some opinion as to the sort of person that this man is, basically. As far as an answer to the question as to the state of this man's mind at the time or what happened at that time or what his thinking was at that time, no, it was not necessary to rely upon the truthfulness of what he had to say."

[99] *Supra,* footnote 98, at pp. 256-7. Note the incorrect use of the word "psychoses" here. Psychosis is a psychiatric term, defined by the American Psychiatric Assoc. Standard Nomenclature (Washington, D.C., 1952) as encompassing "a variety of disorders characterized by varying degrees of personality disintegration and the failure to test and evaluate correctly external reality."

Agreeing with this submission, Bull J.A. (speaking for the majority) rendered the following judgment respecting the admissibility of the psychiatrist's testimony:

> "Functional or organic disorders, disturbances, abnormalities and conditions of the mind, and its motivations, are clearly matters of scientific appraisal and evaluation, and where, as here, the issue is knowledge upon the presence of which intention to commit or repel acts of homosexual nature could properly be inferred, I conclude that properly extracted expert opinion evidence as to the heterosexual and homosexual psychoses of the appellant, with the resulting reaction or behaviourism whether conscious or otherwise, to establish that he had or had not any conscious awareness of any homosexual involvement with the person, had a great materiality and relevance."[100]

The Crown appealed to the Supreme Court of Canada and the conviction was restored. This was done in spite of the fact that a majority (Ritchie, Spence and Hall JJ.) were of the opinion that the psychiatrist's evidence should have been ruled admissible at trial, since an overwhelming abundance of evidence against the accused indicated no substantial wrong or miscarriage of justice had occurred. It is interesting that the two Justices who felt such evidence was inadmissible (Martland and Judson JJ.) based their decisions on the ground that the hearsay and ultimate issues rules would have been offended; the matter of hypothetical questions was not mentioned.

The result of the *Lupien* case, it is submitted, rather than being an exception to the rule that all psychiatric opinions must be elicited by means of hypothetical questions, is an affirmation that opinions based on examination of the accused never required a hypothetical basis in the first place. The *Lupien* case is significant only in the *type* of psychiatric evidence that was introduced. If it were true that prior to *Lupien* or *Forage* a hypothetical basis had to be laid before a psychiatrist voiced his opinion, what hypothetical question would be necessary to elicit the opinion of a psychiatrist that on the basis of extensive examination, he considered that the accused was a pathological liar, or had an organic psychosis?[101]

---

[100] *Supra*, footnote 98, at pp. 258-9. Once again the word "psychoses" is used in a meaningless context. This reveals an alarming degree of ignorance and lack of familarity with even the most basic psychiatric concepts and terminology.

[101] See Wigmore, s. 675, at p. 796 where it is expressly pointed out that hypothetical presentation of expert testimony becomes unnecessary where there has been personal observation: "... does it follow that, when the opinion comes from *the same witness* who has received the basis of it by actual observation, those premises must be stated beforehand, hypothetically or otherwise, by him or to him? .... In academic nicety, yes; practically, no; and for the simple reason that either on direct examination or on cross-examination each and every detail of the appearance he observed will be brought out and thus associated with his general conclusion as the grounds for it, and the tribunal will understand that the rejection of these data will destroy the validity of his opinion. Through failure to perceive this limitation, Courts have sometimes sanctioned the

Ideally, the psychiatrist who has examined a defendant will base his opinion of the individual's mental condition on fairly objective criteria (psychological and organic test results, observation and the like) rather than relying solely upon the truth of the facts which the accused has related to him. A distinction should be drawn, however, between the situation where the accused being interviewed still suffers from mental disorder and that where the disorder was temporary and has entirely cleared up by the time the psychiatrist sees him. In the latter case, the doctor may indeed be forced to depend upon what the accused tells him. Yet even in such case, the admissibility of psychiatric opinion need not be premised upon the use of hypothetical questions, so long as the basis of the doctor's opinion is made clear. As the case of *R. v. Rosik*[102] indicates, it is always open to the trial judge in such circumstances to instruct the jury that an accused's untruthfulness to the examining psychiatrist would destroy the foundation of the expert's evidence.

When conflicting evidence at the trial makes it necessary to demonstrate the basis upon which the opinion of the psychiatric witness was formed, the advisability of using hypothetical questions as a means of accomplishing this purpose might yet be open to criticism. As an advocacy tool, the hypothetical question may be wielded to achieve an unfair result; because it is counsel who selects the hypotheses, the opinion of the expert may be manipulated. The hypotheses chosen by either side run the risk of differing from the evidence adduced, producing an opinion which is not the opinion of the psychiatrist on the case at hand; yet the jury may be misled into believing that it is. This difficulty may, it is submitted, be alleviated by allowing experts to express their opinions directly and to provide the basis for them either beforehand or afterward on direct examination or cross-examination.[103] The former approach has been advocated by the Law Reform Commission of Canada in its recent report on evidence.[104] Section 68 of its draft Evidence Code provides:

> "68. The judge may require that a witness be examined with respect to the facts upon which he is relying before giving evidence in the form of an opinion for inference."

Interestingly, however, the Law Reform Commission has not suggested the elimination of the use of hypothetical questions as a means of eliciting opinion evidence. Section 71 of the draft Code states:

> "71. An expert witness may base an opinion or inference on ...
> (c) facts admitted or to be admitted in evidence in the pro-

---

requirement of an advance hypothetical statement even where the expert witness speaks from personal observation...".

[102] (1970), 2 C.C.C. (2d) 351 (Ont. C.A.); affd by the Supreme Court of Canada at p. 393*n*.

[103] Weihofen, in his *Mental Disorder as a Criminal Defense* (Buffalo, Dennis, 1954) at p. 284 has observed that this solution has been adopted in the United States. Note also that in *R. v. Bouchard* (1973), 24 C.R.N.S. 31 (N.S. Co. Ct.), discussed *infra* at pp. 220-1, the point is expressly made that an expert may offer an opinion first, leaving the factual underpinnings to be proved later.

[104] Law Reform Commission of Canada, *Report: Evidence* (Ottawa, Information Canada, 1975).

ceedings and assumed by the expert to be true for the purpose of giving the opinion or making the inference."

VI. The Ultimate Issue Rule

It is a general rule of evidence that "An expert cannot usually be asked
to express an opinion upon any of the issues, whether of law or fact,
which the jury have to determine. . .".[105] *Halsbury's Laws of England*
notes, however that "this rule is not applicable to ... all cases of insanity
as a defence to accusations of crime".[106] A rather backhanded application
of this exception may be seen in the case of *R. v. Holmes,*[107] where an
accused who was diagnosed by both Crown and defence psychiatrists as
a paranoid schizophrenic pleaded insanity to a charge of murder. Under
cross-examination, the defence's psychiatric witness testified that in his
opinion the accused knew (a) the nature of the act he was committing
and (b) that the act was contrary to law.[108] The defence appealed on the
grounds that this testimony had been elicited by the Crown in violation
of the ultimate issue rule, and should not have been admitted. The
Court of Criminal Appeal dismissed the appeal, however, holding that
"if the objection prevailed, it would put an insuperable difficulty in the
way of the *defence* whenever they were trying to establish insanity."[109]

In *Lupien,*[110] the central issue before the Supreme Court of Canada
was the admissibility of psychiatric opinion that the accused would not
knowingly have engaged in the homosexual practices with which he was
charged. Addressing himself to this issue, Martland J. (with whom Judson J. concurred) said:

> "The evidence which counsel for the respondent sought to lead was
> not to show that he was mentally incapable of forming the intent to
> commit the crime with which he was charged. Its purpose was to es-
> tablish (partly on the basis of what the respondent had told the wit-
> ness) that because the respondent normally reacted violently to ho-
> mosexual practices he must have been telling the truth when, in the
> proved situation in which he was discovered, he said he thought his
> companion was a woman. In other words, the psychiatrist is being
> asked for an opinion, not as to whether the respondent was men-
> tally capable of formulating an intent, but as to whether he did, on
> the facts of this case, formulate such intent. We have not been refer-
> red to any Canadian or English authority which establishes that the

---

[105] *Halsbury's Laws of England,* 3rd. ed., vol. 15 at p. 323.
[106] *Ibid.*
[107] [1953] 1 W.L.R. 686.
[108] Both limbs of the insanity defence in England differ from the current test in Canada.
Here, it is "appreciating" the nature and quality of an act, and knowing it is wrong.
[109] *Supra,* footnote 107, *per* Lord Goddard C.J. at p. 688.
[110] [1970] S.C.R. 263.

evidence of a psychiatrist can be introduced for a purpose such as this."[111]

And later:

"It is sought to adduce such opinion evidence on the very issue which the jury is bound to determine on the facts proved before it."[112]

Ritchie J. (with whom Spence J. concurred) had this to say, however:

". . .if the evidence had been tendered for the purpose of showing that Lupien was a normal man, the conclusion as to how he would have acted under the circumstances would have been a question for the jury; but, with all respect, as I understand the record, the evidence was not tendered for this purpose at all but rather for the purpose of proving the doctor's opinion that this particular man had a certain type of defence mechanism that made him react violently against homosexual behaviour."[113]

And later:

"In any event, it appears to me that the question of whether or not a man is homosexually inclined or otherwise sexually perverted is one upon which an experienced psychiatrist is qualified to express an opinion and that if such opinion is relevant it should be admitted at a trial such as this even if it involves the psychiatrist in expressing his conclusion that the accused does not have the capacity to commit the crime with which he is charged."[114]

But regardless of counsel's intention in eliciting the psychiatrist's opinion in this case, it is difficult to understand the distinction Ritchie J. drew between expressing an opinion upon the accused's capacity to form an intent, and expressing an opinion as to whether or not he acutally *did* form the intent. Surely in this case the two amounted to the same thing; an opinion that the accused was incapable of forming an intent would be an opinion that he did not in fact form that intent. This, in effect, is what was held by Martland J. (with whom Judson J. concurred), and it is interesting that for that reason Martland J. felt bound to rule the psychiatrist's opinion inadmissible. Conversely, it seems that Ritchie J. (with whom Spence J. concurred) felt that in order to rule the evidence admissible it was necessary to hold that it did not offend the ultimate issue rule. This, it is submitted, overlooks the exception laid down in the *Holmes* case. If an opinion on the ultimate issue can be expressed where the defence is insanity, why not in this case? In both situations the opin-

---

[111] *Ibid.*, at p. 268.
[112] *Ibid.*, at p. 270.
[113] *Ibid.*, at p. 275.
[114] *Ibid.*, at p. 278.

ion concerns capacity to form the intent requisite to the offence charged. The most lucid judgment, and the one which tipped the scales in favour of the psychiatrist's evidence being admitted, was put forth by Hall J.:

> "It is true, as Davey C.J.B.C. points out in his dissent, that the answer which the psychiatrist was expected to give 'comes too close to the very thing the jury had to find on the whole of the evidence'. I do not think that this is a valid reason for rejecting the evidence. Actually it cannot be considered an innovation in regard to medical evidence. Psychiatrists are permitted to testify that from their examination and study, sometimes long after the event, of an accused, including conversations with him and from facts proven in evidence, that the accused was incapable of forming the intent necessary to constitute the crime with which he is charged. That type of evidence is very close, *if not identical,* to the conclusion the jury must come to in such a case if it is to find that the accused was not guilty because he did not have intent necessary to support conviction."[115]

It would seem, then, that the ultimate issue rule is an artificial and functionless rule of semantics. While the rule has apparently been abandoned where the issue is insanity, and the judgment of Hall J. suggests that it may be on the way out in all cases where psychiatric opinion is expressed on the issue of intent, some judges prefer to continue performing semantic gymnastics. Although the rationale for the rule seems to be honourable enough — the prevention of an encroachment on the jury's function — Wigmore has described it as "one of those impracticable and misconceived utterances which lack any justification in principle."[116] The federal Law Reform Commission's report on evidence[117] has suggested that opinion on an ultimate issue should be dealt with in terms of weight instead of admissibility. In its draft of proposed legislation, the following provision is set out:

> "69. Testimony in the form of an opinion or inference otherwise admissible may be received in evidence notwithstanding that it embraces an ultimate issue to be decided by the trier of fact."

---

[115] *Ibid.,* at p. 279-80 (emphasis added).
[116] *Wigmore On Evidence,* vol. 3, s. 1921 at p. 19. In practice, there are numerous examples of the reception of opinion evidence on a variety of "ultimate issues". See, for example *R. v. Rivett* (1950), 34 Cr. App. R. 87; *R. v. Smith* (1915), 31 T.L.R. 617; *R. v. Mason* (1911), 7 Cr. App. R. 67; *R. v. Frances* (1849), 4 Cox C.C. 57; *R. v. Searle* (1831), 1 Mood. & R. 75 (N.P.). Note also the following civil cases: *Davy v. Morrison,* [1932] O.R. 1 (C.A.); *Sun Ins. Off. v. Roy,* [1927] S.C.R. 8; *Yorke* v. *Yorks Ins. Co.,* [1918] 1 K.B. 662; *Fenwick* v. *Bell* (1844), 1 Car. & Kir. 313 (N.P.).
[117] *Supra,* footnote 104.

VII. Weight

Assuming that psychiatric evidence has been admitted by a trial judge, the great problem for the jury then becomes the amount of weight they should attach to it in reaching their verdict. It is doubtful that any precise rule can be formulated, and it may be fair to say that the jury will ultimately have to rely on intuition in this regard. The legal literature abounds with a myriad of perplexing and contradictory guidelines, each having its own merits and its own inevitable prejudices. On the matter of expert evidence generally, *Phipson's Law of Evidence* offers this rather cynical direction:

> "The testimony of experts is often considered to be of slight value, since they are proverbially, though perhaps unwittingly, biased in favour of the side which calls them, as well as over-ready to regard harmless facts as confirmation of preconceived theories; moreover, support or opposition to given hypotheses can generally be multiplied at will. . . ."[118]

Such viewpoint is not atypical of the legal scholars; in *Taylor on Evidence* the idea is even more forcefully stated:

> "Perhaps the testimony which least deserves credit with a jury is that of *skilled witnesses.* These witnesses are usually required to speak, not to facts, but to *opinions,* and when this is the case, it is often quite surprising to see with what facility, and to what an extent their views can be made to correspond with the wishes or the interests of the parties who call them. They do not, indeed, wilfully misrepresent what they think, but their judgments become so warped by regarding the subject in one point of view, that, even when conscientiously disposed, they are incapable of forming an independent opinion. Being zealous partisans, their Belief becomes synonymous with Faith as defined by the Apostle . . . and it too often is but 'the substance of things *hoped for,* the evidence of things *not* seen.' To adopt the language of Lord Campbell, 'skilled witnesses come with such a bias on their minds to support the cause in which they are embarked that hardly any weight should be given to their evidence'."[119]

In apparent recognition that expert witnesses are not totally devoid of usefulness, the Canadian courts have refrained from such harsh scepticism and have adopted a somewhat more benevolent view of their testimony. In *R. v. Mackie,*[120] where the defence to a murder charge was insanity, the Manitoba Court of Appeal held that it was a misdirection for the trial judge to have read the passage from *Phipson* in his charge to

---

[118] 9th ed. (London, Sweet and Maxwell, 1952) at p. 403.
[119] 12th ed. (London, Sweet and Maxwell, 1931), vol. 1, at p. 59, para. 58.
[120] [1933] 1 W.W.R. 273.

the jury. Because the quotation unduly minimized the knowledge and skill of the psychiatrists who gave evidence, and prevented the jury from according their testimony proper weight, a new trial was ordered. More recently, in the capital murder case of *More v. The Queen*[121] both the passages from *Phipson* and from *Taylor* were quoted by the trial judge in the course of charging the jury as to how they should regard the evidence of two psychiatrists who had given evidence of the accused's mental condition. The Supreme Court of Canada held the quotations to be a misdirection amounting to a substantial miscarriage of justice. Cartwright and Judson JJ. (Abbott, Ritchie and Hall JJ. concurring) ruled:

> ". . . as generalizations, these statements are bad. They could, moreover, have no possible application to the evidence given in this case. All the judges in the Court of Appeal were of the opinion that the medical evidence was relevant and admissible and that there was error in the judge's instruction. In the context in which this instruction was given, the only possible reference is to the evidence of Dr. Adamson and Dr. Thompson and the probable result of this unwarranted disparagement of their evidence was its withdrawal from the jury's serious consideration. On a charge of capital murder, based on an allegation that the killing was planned and deliberate, it was virtually a withdrawal of the whole defence."[122]

It is doubtful, however, that the *More* case has had the effect of banning such expressions from Canadian judicial thinking altogether. Significant is the fact that in *R. v. De Tonnancourt and Paquin*[123] Adamson C.J.M. of the Manitoba Court of Appeal quoted from *Phipson* and *Taylor* in his judgment, and did so with apparent impunity. In light of this, probably the most that can be said is that while such views may be legitimately utilized by an appeal court judge in reaching his decision, it is improper that they be foisted upon a jury.

Despite (or perhaps because of) the frequent accusations of bias hurled at courtroom psychiatrists, the more prevalent tendency of judges today is to place an extremely high value on the opinions of *concurring* psychiatric experts. In *R. v. Jennion*,[124] for example, the English Court of Criminal Appeal decided that where there was a conflict of medical opinion on the issue of diminished responsibility, the decision rested with the jury.[125] Is it to be inferred from this statement that in the absence of any conflict of opinion the jury is bound to accept the doctors' evidence? Wigmore has stated emphatically that a jury is not bound to accept the opinion of any expert.[126] Of interest, however, is

---

[121] [1963] S.C.R. 522.

[122] *Ibid.*, at p. 538.

[123] (1956), 115 C.C.C. 155 at pp. 168-9.

[124] [1962] 1 W.L.R. 317.

[125] Note also the case of *Crabbe v. S.* [1925] 2 W.W.R. 701 (B.C.C.A.) which involved the issue of testamentary capacity. There it was held that the court did not need to accept expert medical opinion when it conflicted with the testimony of lay persons who came in contact with the party concerned.

[126] Section 1921.

the rather misleading statement appearing in the English appeal case of
R. v. Nowell[127] to this effect:

> "Our view is that the evidence of a doctor, whether he be a police
> surgeon or anyone else, should be accepted, unless the doctor him-
> self shows that it ought not to be, as the evidence of a professional
> man giving independent expert evidence with no other desire than
> to assist the court."

A slightly garbled form of this statement became the object of an appeal
in the case of *R. v. Lanfear,*[128] where the jury had been charged regarding their treatment of medical evidence as follows:

> "... his evidence is to be accepted as the evidence of a professional
> man giving independent expert evidence with the sole desire of
> helping the court. This, then, puts him into a position in which, in
> the absence of reasons for rejecting his evidence, his evidence ought
> to be accepted."[129]

Diplock L.J. (as he then was) ruled that such a direction was an
improper one and the result of a misapprehension of the meaning
intended in *Nowell*. What the passage really meant in the context of
that case was that "the evidence should be treated, as regards
admissibility and other matters of that kind, like that of any other independent witness; but taken out of its context, the use of the word
'accepted' may well ... give to the jury a false impression of the weight
to be given to that evidence."[130] In *R. v. Moke,*[131] where psychiatric evidence of insanity had been called as a defence to a charge of murder, it
was held on appeal that where the doctor had not been cross-examined
and his evidence remained uncontradicted, the trial judge need not
direct the jury that they were bound to accept such evidence as conclusive.

Even though it seems that Wigmore was technically correct in his
assertion that the jury need not accept the uncontradicted evidence of
experts, the practical consequences of rejecting it may be reversal on
appeal. In *R. v. Matheson,*[132] where the jury rejected uncontradicted
psychiatric evidence of diminished responsibility and convicted the
appellant on a charge of capital murder, the English Court of Criminal
Appeal reversed the verdict, holding it to have been "unsupported by
the evidence". In Canada, sub-para 613(1)(a)(i) of the Criminal Code
provides that a verdict may be reversed if it is "unreasonable or cannot
be supported by the evidence".[133] In *R. v. Kelly* the Ontario Court of

[127] [1948] 1 All E.R. 794 at p. 795.
[128] [1968] 1 All E.R. 683.
[129] *Ibid.,* at pp. 684-5.
[130] *Ibid.,* at p. 685 (emphasis added).
[131] [1917] 3 W.W.R. 575 (Alta. C.A.)
[132] [1958] 2 All E.R. 87. See also *R. v. Bailey,* [1961] Crim. L.R. 828.
[133] This section provides:

Appeal[134] substituted a finding of not guilty by reason of insanity because conviction contradicted the evidence of two defence psychiatrists whose evidence had not been "seriously challenged". But *quaere* the propriety of s. 613 being used to overturn a verdict of guilty which rejects non-conflicting psychiatric evidence of insanity. There being a presumption as to sanity residing in s-s. 16(4) of the Code,[135] might not the jury simply find the credibility of the experts insufficient to discharge the onus, which rests on the accused, of rebutting that presumption? Can it ever be said in reverse onus situations that the jury must *support* their verdict with evidence, and are precluded from relying on the presumption?[136] It may be that the ground of unreasonableness[137] would be sufficient to allow reversal, but surely the fact that the jury has refused to believe defence witnesses does not amount to unreasonableness *per se*. The jury may have had their own compelling reasons for disbelieving the psychiatric evidence adduced — reasons which might never become apparent to an appeal court from a reading of the transcript.[138]

In *R. v. Prince*[139] the Ontario Court of Appeal refused to substitute a verdict of not guilty by reason of insanity because (1) unlike *Kelly,* the psychiatric evidence here had been challenged in cross-examination, and (2) the Court felt that neither *Kelly* nor s. 613 should be applied without giving due weight to the presumption of sanity.

It has been suggested by some authors[140] that there are, in fact, many instances where a lay jury might properly reject the evidence of experts who are themselves in total accord. But such cases, it is said, are only those in which the issues inhabit that twilight zone between common and special knowledge. Once an issue strays beyond the layman's ken and enters the province of the specialist, the court and jury must rely upon expert evidence.[141] If this view is the correct one, it may be argued

---

"613(1) On the hearing of an appeal against a conviction or against a verdict that the appellant is unfit, on account of insanity, to stand his trial, or against a special verdict of not guilty on account of insanity the court of appeal
    (a) may allow the appeal where it is of the opinion that
        (i)   the verdict should be set aside on the ground that it is unreasonable or cannot be supported by the evidence."

[134] (1971), 16 C.R.N.S. 72.

[135] "(4) Every one shall, until the contrary is proved, be presumed to be and to have been sane."

[136] Note that in *Matheson* the defence of diminished responsibility carried with it a reverse onus.

[137] For a recent interpretation of the meaning of the word "unreasonable" by the Supreme Court of Canada, see *Corbett v. The Queen* (1973), 14 C.C.C. (2d) 385.

[138] For instance, there may have been only one "uncontradicted" psychiatrist called to testify. The psychiatrist may have appeared dishonest, incompetent, beligerent or uncertain to the jury. Perhaps he had not even examined the accused but testified solely on the basis of hypothetical questions.

[139] (1972), 16 C.R.N.S. 73.

[140] 11 C.E.D. (Ont. 3rd), *Evidence*, § 375, pp. 57-262-57-263.

[141] See also the Ontario Court of Appeal decision in *Lindala v. Canadian Copper Co.* (1920), 51 D.L.R. 565 at pp. 567-8 where Hodgins J.A., in *obiter* quoted the "rule" laid down by Lord Justice Bowen in *Fleet v. Managers of the Metropolitan Asylums District*, "The Times", 3 March 1886:

that the jury's function is genuinely usurped whenever experts agree on a matter which the jury does not understand. The vexing question now becomes: which issues fall within the exclusive jurisdiction of the psychiatrists (providing they concur), and which ones hang in limbo?

VIII. Why Do Psychiatrists Disagree?

The cynic will say that the reason psychiatric witnesses so often disagree is that they are paid to do so. A more charitable but equally facile answer is that there are good psychiatrists and there are bad ones. But while neither of these possibilities can be entirely disregarded, it just might not be that easy. For if one ascribes to the psychiatric profession a reasonable level of integrity — as the law obviously does — it is difficult to be satisfied with superficial, glib half-truths.

Oddly enough, one of the few subjects on which psychiatrists seem to be in substantial accord, is the reason for their lack of concurrence. Psychiatrists with whom the writer has consulted have inevitably stressed that their field, like any other branch of medicine, is not an exact science; individual judgment is always a factor. Although one would assume that disagreement could, to a large degree, be chalked up to the diversity of psychiatric "schools of thought", the writer has been assured, first, there is substantial uniformity in this regard in Canada, and, secondly, such diversity of theoretical orientation would not produce radical differences in testimony anyway.[142] One psychiatrist[143] has asserted that since today's psychiatric theories are all *genetic* in concept, the differences between Freudian and Jungian backgrounds are really inconsequential. He has also suggested, as have many of his colleaques, that differences in diagnoses are usually only quantitative; doctors observe the same things, but some see more than others. To put a finer point on this observation, it is perhaps worth noting the findings of what seems to be a relevant (although certainly not exhaustive) statistical control study.[144] Finding that the four participating psychiatrists were

---

"'If we are to act in the present instance, we must fall back upon the opinions of experts, and I wish emphatically to state my view, that in a matter like the present, so far from thinking the opinions of experts unsatisfactory, it is to the opinion of experts that I myself should turn with the utmost confidence and faith. Courts of Law and Courts of Justice are not fit places for the exercise of the inductive logic of science. . . . The result of the admission of this evidence, assuming it, as I do, to be admissible, has been, in my judgment, to shew that the endeavour to utilise such evidence launches us upon an inquiry fit only for the leisure of learned and scientific men, but for which the jury system and the judicial system are probably inadequate.'"

[142] From personal communication with forensic psychiatrists at Toronto's Clarke Institute of Psychiatry.

[143] Watson, "Untying the Knots: The Cross-Examination of the Psychiatric Expert Witness", in Sugarman, *Examining the Medical Expert* (Ann Arbor, Mich., Institute of Continuing Legal Education, 1969) 13 at p. 16.

[144] Beck, "Reliability of Psychiatric Diagnosis: 2. A Study of Consistency of Clinical Judgments and Ratings" (1962), 119 Am. J. Psychiat. 351.

unanimous in their diagnoses only slightly over half of the time,[145] the researcher concluded that although evaluation of information was consistent, individual interviewing techniques were responsible for the differences in the amount of information elicited. In other words, the capacities for observation were relatively equal, but the abilities to *extract* material differed. Unhappily, this disparity becomes magnified once psychiatrists, having been placed on the witness stand, are forced to translate their diagnoses into an assessment of the accused's behaviour at a specific point of time in the past.

Another point of view which has attracted a good deal of support is that "when there is disagreement between experts it is usually not on the technical medical issues but on the special questions that the law puts to them."[146] This, as far as legal argument is concerned, must surely be the nub of the matter. If the law is ever to exert its influence in achieving a higher degree of uniformity in expert testimony, then it is this last criticism to which it must address itself. The complaint of many psychiatrists is that they are constantly being seduced into expressing opinions on issues quite beyond their field of expertise. A psychiatrist may know that the accused is psychotic and is suffering from "a degree of personality disintegration and a failure to test and evaluate correctly external reality",[147] but should he be required to determine whether or not the accused "appreciated the nature and quality of an act or omission"? Because both psychiatrists A and B have diagnosed the accused as a psychopathic personality, does it follow that they will agree on whether or not the accused "knew that an act or omission was wrong"? Often the psychiatrist's capacity for answering such questions is no better than that of the average layman; for the tools he must use in making the decision are not the tools of his profession, but rather the personalized values and morality he possesses as a private citizen.[148]

IX. Can The Court Call Psychiatric Witnesses?

As early as the fourteenth century, English courts sought the advice of experts on matters of science necessary for them to make an informed determination of the issues being tried.[149] Although these experts were

---

[145] 54 per cent. Depending on how you look at it, this could be considered unanimous agreement "most of the time".

[146] Simon, *The Jury and The Defense of Insanity* (Boston, Little Brown, 1967) at p. 83.

[147] American Psychiatric Assoc. Standard Nomenclature (1952) Washington, D.C.

[148] See Goldstein, "Psychoanalysis and Jurisprudence" (1968), 77 Yale L.J. 1053 at p. 1060; Statement of Dr. Thomas Szasz, "Hearings Before the Subcommittee on Constitutional Rights of the Mentally Ill of the Senate Committee on the Judiciary" (1961) 87 Cong., 1st Sess. pt. 1, 251-72; Waelder, "Psychiatry and the Problem of Criminal Responsibility" (1952), 101 U. Pa. L. Rev. 378. Note also the rather extreme statement by Dr. Gregory Zilboorg, in an address reported in *The Shingle*, April 1949, p. 84, to the effect that a psychiatrist actually *perjures* himself by giving "expert" evidence on an area he knows nothing about.

[149] Simon, at p. 79. See also Law Reform Commission of Canada, *Evidence Project: Opin-*

initially used only as technical assistants to the court, in the seventeenth century, when it had become the duty of juries to find fact, the practice developed of the parties themselves calling these experts as witnesses.[150] The practice of courts appointing experts to be later called flourishes to this day in the United States; statutory provisions in at least 22 states authorize the use of court-appointed psychiatrists to examine the accused and submit reports.[151] Of the American statutes, some take the form of a 30-day remand for mental examination where the accused's capacity to stand trial is at issue, others apply only when responsibility at the time of the offence is questioned, and the rest provide for the appointment of experts in either situation. The Federal Rule, set out in Rule 706 of the 1975 Federal Rules of Evidence[152] provides:

"Rule 706.
"COURT APPOINTED EXPERTS

"(a) Appointment. The court may on its own motion or on the motion of any party enter an order to show cause why expert witnesses should not be appointed, and may request the parties to submit nominations. The court may appoint any expert witnesses agreed upon by the parties, and may appoint witnesses of its own selection. An expert witness shall not be appointed by the court unless he consents to act. A witness so appointed shall be informed of his duties by the judge in writing, a copy of which shall be filed with the clerk, or at a conference in which the parties shall have opportunity to participate. A witness so appointed shall advise the parties of his findings, if any; his deposition may be taken by any party; and he may be called to testify by the court or any party. He shall be subject to cross-examination by each party, including a party calling him as a witness.

"(b) Compensation. Expert witnesses so appointed are entitled to reasonable compensation in whatever sum the court may allow. The compensation thus fixed is payable from funds which may be provided by law in criminal cases and civil actions or proceedings in-

---

ion and Expert Evidence (Study 7) (Ottawa, Information Canada, 1973) at p. 27.

[150] *Ibid.* See also Hand, "Historical and Practical Considerations Regarding Expert Testimony" (1901), 15 Harv. L. Rev. 40; Rosenthal, "The Development of the Use of Expert Testimony" (1935), 2 Law and Contemp. Problems 403.

[151] Weihofen, *Mental Disorder as a Criminal Defense,* at p. 331.

[152] *Federal Rules of Evidence for United States Courts and Magistrates* (St. Paul, West Publishing, 1975) at pp. 84-5. This provision is a slightly altered amendment of what was formerly Rule 28 of the Federal Rules of Criminal Procedure. Along with the amended version (at pp. 85-6) appears this interesting note from the Advisory Committee: "The practice of shopping for experts, the venality of some experts and the reluctance of many reputable experts to involve themselves in litigation, have been matters of deep concern. Though the contention is made that court appointed experts acquire an aura of infallibility to which they are not entitled, ... the trend is increasingly to provide for their use. While experience indicates that actual appointment is a relatively infrequent occurrence, the assumption may be made that the availability of the procedure itself decreases the need for resorting to it. The ever-present possibility that the judge *may* appoint an expert in a given case must inevitably exert a sobering effect on the expert witness of a party and upon the person utilizing his services."

volving just compensation under the Fifth Amendment. In other
civil actions and proceedings the compensation shall be paid by the
parties in such proportion and at such time as the court directs, and
thereafter charged in like manner as other costs.
"(c) Disclosure of appointment. In the exercise of its discretion, the
court may authorize disclosure to the jury of the fact that the court
appointed the expert witness.
"(d) Parties' experts of own selection. Nothing in this rule limits the
parties in calling expert witnesses of their own selection."

Even in the absence of statutory provision, it is clear that the American
courts have the authority at common law to appoint experts to examine
the accused and later call them to testify on his mental condition.[153]

By way of contrast, those provisions in our Criminal Code and provincial mental health acts which allow a court to have accused persons sent
for psychiatric examination fall far short of allowing the judge to call the
examining psychiatrist as a witness. At best, they will place in the possession of the court a written report of the accused's mental condition.
Moreover, such provisions apply only when there is reason to believe
that the accused is mentally ill at the time he appears before the court;
they confer no power to remand for psychiatric examination when it
appears to the judge that the accused may have been insane or in a state
of automatism at the time the offence was allegedly committed.[154] Nevertheless, the writer has been informed that examining psychiatrists will
frequently include in their reports an opinion regarding the accused's
state of mind at the time of the alleged crime. What is the judge to do,
then, if the report, regardless of what it says about the accused person's
fitness to stand trial, suggests that the accused was not responsible at
the time of the offence? Of course, it is open to defence counsel to call
the examining psychiatrist as a witness, but there is the possibility that
for one reason or another he may omit to do so. For example, the
accused might not wish to raise the defence of insanity. Perhaps counsel
is confident in a defence on the merits; or perhaps the accused, who has
since regained his sanity, prefers to be detained in prison rather than in
a mental institution if convicted.[155] In *R. v. Frank*[156] it was held permissible for the Crown to raise, by way of psychiatric testimony, the defence
of insanity before the jury. In *obiter*, Moorhouse J. addressed himself to
the problem of whether it was not also the *duty* of the prosecution to do
so in such circumstances. In that context the learned Justice posed the
following question:

"May I then, with the knowledge I now have, having heard the
evidence of these two psychiatrists yesterday at the inquiry into

---

[153] Weihofen, at p. 332.
[154] Similarly, no authority can be invoked which permits the ordering of a psychiatric
examination for the purpose of confirming a belief that the accused is mentally healthy.
[155] These reasons were suggested by Wright, "Can the prosecutor introduce the defence of
insanity?" (1970), 12 C.R.N.S. 343 at p. 344.
[156] (1971), 12 C.R.N.S. 339 (Ont.).

fitness to stand trial, interfere with Crown counsel's discretion on how he presents his case?"[157]

The question was answered in a rather ambiguous fashion, however. Moorhouse J. said:

"I do not think I *should* do so. In the case of a disease of the mind, such should be made known to the Court. That has been done and, as is the practice, Crown counsel has made available to the defence the psychiatric evidence known to him. The Crown has a discretion as to what evidence he will call."[158]

What Moorhouse J. was saying was that since the Crown had done the correct thing, the court should not have interfered. In other words, he avoided answering his original question; would the court have interferred, had the Crown *not* raised the insanity issue? Although Moorhouse J. said on one hand that Crown counsel has a "discretion", this seems inconsistent with what was said a moment earlier:

"Can it ever be said that a Crown counsel, having knowledge of an accused person, now or heretofore, having a disease of the mind, may keep that information from the Court? I do not think so. It seems to be contrary to my concept of justice that Crown counsel, having such knowledge, should rely on the statutory presumption of sanity."[159]

It was pointed out that according to *Lowther v. The Queen,*[160] it is incumbent upon the trial judge to draw the attention of the jury to any evidence which raises the defence of insanity, regardless of whether counsel pleads it or not. Beyond that, Moorhouse J. suggested that if the trial judge is aware of the possibility of insanity, "he may take steps to have evidence introduced".[161] Although it is unclear whether Moorhouse J. was suggesting that the court could, on its own initiative, call psychiatric evidence, several other enlightening decisions should be referred to in this connection. In *R. v. Chan Ming Luk,*[162] the Supreme Court of Hong Kong, on the basis of an analysis of the English case law, made the following ruling:

"In the present case, there were indications that the accused may have been insane at the time of the alleged crime. At his trial he challenged none of the evidence, gave no evidence and called no witnesses. It is not in the interests of the community or the administration of justice that a man who is insane at the time of an offence should be treated as sane at that time and, whether the present in-

---

[157] *Ibid.,* at p. 341.
[158] *Ibid.* (emphasis added).
[159] *Ibid.*
[160] (1957), 26 C.R. 150 (Que. C.A.).
[161] *Supra,* footnote 156 at p. 340.
[162] [1962] H.K.L.R. 651 (S.C.).

stance be treated as a 'special case' . . . or as an application of a
changing current of thought on this subject, we do not think that
the English decisions, as they stand at the moment, can properly be
taken to preclude the District Judge in the circumstances of the
present case from exercising his discretion so as to call medical evidence on the accused's mental condition at the material time and
from taking account of such evidence, if in his opinion it is desirable
in the interests of justice to do so."[163]

Although no power is expressly given to a judge by the Criminal Code
which enables him to call his own psychiatric witnesses, it may be doubted whether the Code extinguishes the trial judge's traditional right,
referred to in the *Chan Ming Luk* case, to call witnesses of his own
motion in criminal cases when the "interests of justice" demand. Such
right was expressed in the old English cases of *R. v. Chapman*[164] and *R.
v. Holden*[165] and has been re-asserted in later cases such as *R. v. Liddle*[166]
and *R. v. Tregear.*[167] In the latter two cases, however, it was emphasized
that in order for such power not to create an injustice it must only be
used "in a case where a matter arises *ex improviso,* which no human
ingenuity can foresee . . ."[168]. While it is not entirely clear exactly what
limitations are placed on the judge's power, the effect of these words
may well be to undermine the strength of the *Chan Ming Luk* decision.

Perhaps the most interesting item to date is the relatively recent
Nova Scotia County Court case of *R. v. Bouchard.*[169] There, the trial
judge deemed it necessary and proper to call psychiatric evidence of
automatism of his own motion in order to remedy what might have been
a fatal deficiency in the defence's case — a deficiency which the judge
felt he might himself have created. O Hearn Co. Ct. J. explained:

"When I came to consider the matter after the close of the case, I
found it difficult, not from the failure of the defendant to testify, because he did testify, but from a failure of proof of the other material
upon which Dr. Murray based his opinion, in particular his telephone conversation with Dr. Tom Murphy. . . . It seemed clear to
me then that I had probably misled counsel as to the effect of my
ruling with respect to the admissibility of Dr. Murray's evidence of
his telephone conversation with Dr. Murphy. I intended to make
the distinction between admitting the conversation as the basis of
Dr. Murray's opinion on the one hand, and the need to establish the
truthfulness of the material provided by Dr. Murphy. . . . Dr. Murray evidently considered Dr. Murphy's account of the matter of

---

[163] *Per* Hogan C.J. at p. 661.
[164] (1838), 8 C. & P. 558.
[165] (1838), 8 C. & P. 606. But note *R. v. Barnett,* [1956] Crim. L.R. 560 (C.C.A.).
[166] (1928), 21 Cr. App. R. 3.
[167] [1967] 1 All E.R. 989 (C.C.A.). *Dicta* of Avory J. in *R. v. Harris,* [1927] All E.R. Rep.
473 and of Lord Hewart C.J. in *R. v. McMahon* (1933), 24 Cr. App. 97 distinguished by
R. v. Liddle, supra, footnote 166, and this case.
[168] *Supra,* footnote 166 at p. 11.
[169] (1973), 24 C.R.N.S. 31.

considerable confirmatory weight in arriving at his opinion, so that one could say that it was a substantial element upon which he relied in coming to that opinion, and that it should be verified, otherwise the foundation of the opinion would fail.

"Having come to the conclusion that I could well have contributed to a misunderstanding of the legal situation, I determined to take a very unusual step of calling Dr. Murphy to give evidence myself. The situation demanding this seemed to me to have arisen quite ex improviso with the result that the defendant was prejudiced in resting when he did, and I came to this conclusion because it seemed to me that Dr. Murray's opinion provided a basis for the defence of automatism with respect to the first count, sufficient to raise a reasonable doubt, subject to verification of part of the foundation of that opinion by Dr. Murphy."[170]

O Hearn Co. Ct. J. went on to justify his action this way:

"In a criminal trial, the presiding judge has the right to call a witness not called either by the prosecution or the defence and without the consent of either, if, in his opinion, this course is necessary in the interests of justice: All the textbooks, such as Crankshaw, Tremeear, Phipson, and Archbold concur. The power should not be exercised where the defence has closed its case, except where something has arisen on the part of the prisoner ex improviso."[171]

It has been suggested[172] that the decision in this case was a trifle rash inasmuch as the "interests of justice" might have been served in somewhat less drastic a fashion; perhaps simply allowing defence counsel to call the witness would have sufficed. Although this criticism presupposes a willingness on the part of counsel to do so, the facts of this particular case (*i.e.*, both counsel consented to the judge's calling the witness himself) imply such willingness.

X. Conclusions

The frequency with which psychiatric evidence may be used as an adversarial weapon in criminal cases raises some important questions regarding the role of the forensic psychiatrist. Appropriate for discussion at this time is the issue of whether or not Canada should adopt a statutory scheme allowing courts to appoint their own psychiatric experts for the purpose of gathering information and giving sworn testimony.

To many, the most attractive feature of a system whereby the court

---

[170] *Ibid.*, at p. 45.
[171] *Ibid.*, at p. 46.
[172] Stenning, " 'One Blind Man to See Fair Play': The Judge's Right to Call Witnesses" (1974), 24 C.R.N.S. 49 at p. 56.

might call psychiatric evidence is the doctor's resulting stance of inde-
pendence, which would, in theory, eliminate the bias each expert is supposed to have for the party who calls him. It has been pointed out that
"each litigant naturally seeks not the expert who can most objectively
and skillfully assess the problem, but rather, the expert who will be the
best witness for his cause."[173] Presumably, however, under any system of
court-called witnesses, the right of both sides to call their own evidence
would not be dispensed with; any attempt to do so would be "futile",
according to Wigmore, since it would "interfere with the ... traditional
right of the parties to adduce such evidence as they think useful ...".[174]
How, then, would the power of the court to call its own expert evidence
affect in any way the battle of the experts? It has been suggested that
the power of the court to call its own experts would have a "sobering
effect" on the experts called by the parties,[175] but it is difficult to see why
this would be so. Assuming, cynically, that a psychiatrist is willing to
differ disingenuously with the opponent's expert, why would he not be
just as eager to disagree with the court appointee? Both men are col-
leagues of equal status, and a frivolous or insincere opposition to either is
of equal legal and academic consequence. If the doctor is simply ignorant, nothing will change this. Nor will such measure do away with genuine professional difference of opinion.

The chief danger inherent in the use of court-appointed psychiatrists
is that their opinion might be given undue weight,[176] regardless of
whether they are more or less qualified than the experts called by the
parties themselves. Although it has again been argued that the presence
of other psychiatrists in court will affect the testimony of the court
appointee, forcing him to be more cautious than he might otherwise be,
the reasoning here seems to be of dubious merit for the same reasons as
those mentioned earlier. The fact that the opinions of the
"superexperts", as they have been called,[177] will be accorded more weight
than those of the parties' psychiatrists when there is disagreement, can
hardly be doubted. Although the jury is not bound to accept the opinion
of court-appointed experts, where the power resides in Canadian courts
to call their own experts in civil cases[178] the principle has been clearly
stated by the Supreme Court of Canada that:

---

[173] Royal Commission on Capital Punishment, 1949/53, *Report,* England, Cmd. 8932 (London, H.M.S.O., 1953) at p. 36. See also the scathing remarks of Adamson C.J.M. in *R. v.
De Tonnancourt and Paquin* (1956), 115 C.C.C. 155 at pp. 168-9 (Man. C.A.).
[174] *Wigmore On Evidence,·*s. 563, at p. 648. It is interesting to note that in 1928 Louisiana
adopted a statutory provision which purported to do away with the right of the parties
to call their own expert witnesses. The court in *State v. Lange* (1929), 168 La. 958
declared the measure unconstitutional.
[175] *Supra,* footnote 152.
[176] See Goldstein, "The Psychiatrist and The Legal Process" (1963), 33 Am. J. Orthopsy-
chiat. 123.
[177] See Rappeport; "Psychiatrist as an Amicus Curiae" (1972), 18 Medical Trial Technique
Q. 297 at p. 299.
[178] In Ontario, the Supreme Court Rules of Practice and Procedure, R.R.O. 1970, Reg. 545,
Rule 267 provides:
"267(1) The court may obtain the assistance of merchants, engineers, accountants,

"... generally speaking, in favour of the course of adopting the opinion of the judicial experts in preference to that of the experts called as witnesses on behalf of one or the other of the parties, there exists the recognized principle that an independent witness, free of all connection whatever with the parties, should be accorded more weight and consideration than that to which, all conditions being otherwise equal, an interested witness is entitled to."[179]

Even the notion that the independent expert will remain impartial and unbiased in his testimony has been challenged by some critics. One American psychiatrist[180] has commented that the very premise of non-advocacy tends to disarm the psychiatrist, allowing him to fall prey to his prejudices and at the same time delude himself as to the inevitably subjective quality of his testimony.

Perhaps the most compelling argument in favour of court-called psychiatric evidence arises from the situation in which neither side has brought forth evidence of the accused's mental state (nor to they desire to do so), yet the trial judge feels such evidence to be both relevant and necessary. In *Johnson v. U.S.*[181] Frankfurther J. had this to say:

"A trial is not a game of blind man's bluff, and the trial judge — particularly in a case where he himself is the trier of the facts upon which he is to pronounce the law — need not blindfold himself by failing to call an available vital witness simply because the parties, for reason of trial tactics, choose to withold his testimony."

The following provision in the Federal Law Reform Commission's draft Evidence Code[182] would help to guard against the possibility of a trial becoming a game of "blind man's bluff":

"73(1) The judge may, if he considers it desirable, appoint an independent expert who shall, if possible, be a person agreed upon by the parties.

"(2) The judge shall give the independent expert instructions regarding his duties, and these instructions shall, if possible, be agreed upon by all parties.

"(3) The independent expert shall inform the judge and the parties in writing of his opinion, and may thereafter be called to testify by the judge or any party and be subject to examination by each party.

"(4) An independent expert is entitled to reasonable compensa-

---

actuaries, or scientific persons in such way as it thinks fit, the better to enable it to determine any matter of fact in question in any cause or proceeding, and may act on the certificate of such persons.

"(2) The court may fix the remuneration of any such person and may direct payment thereof by any of the parties."

[179] *Per* Rinfret J. in *Citadel Brick Ltd. v. Garneau,* [1937] 3 D.L.R. 169 at pp. 176-7.

[180] Diamond, "The Psychiatrist as Advocate" (1973), 1 Psychiatry and Law 5 at p. 7.

[181] (1948), 366 U.S. 46 at p. 54 (a civil suit).

[182] *Evidence Project: Opinion and Expert Evidence (Study 7)* (Ottawa, Information Canada 1973) at p. 27.

tion in an amount to be determined by the judge, such compensation to be paid in criminal cases, from funds provided by law, and in civil cases, by the parties in such proportion and at such time as the judge directs."[183]

---

[183] Beyond this proposal is the unique suggestion of the Honourable Antoine Rivard (Judge of the Court of Queen's Bench, Quebec) which appears in a chapter entitled "The Functions of Judge, Jury and Counsel — Co-operation in Search for the Truth", *Studies in Canadian Criminal Evidence,* Salhany and Carter, eds (Toronto, Butterworths, 1972) 359 at p. 366:

"Before the trial, at a conference of the judge with counsel, the scientific, artistic, medical or technical question would be fixed in clear and precise terms. For example, in the case of absence of culpability by reason of insanity it would be easy to put the following question: was the accused of sound mind at the moment of committing the crime with which he is charged?

"The Crown thereupon would select an expert from the recognized list of experts which I was discussing above. The defence would do the same, and these two experts would designate a third one. On failure to agree, the third expert would be appointed by the judge. These three men of science would have access to all documents of the case, they would obviously be able to examine the accused or any person susceptible to furnish them with information as well. Together with a detailed report of their work and their inquiry they would submit a unanimous or majority answer to the question referred to them. This answer should be the final statement of the scientific, artistic or technological truth on which the verdict is to be based."

PART III

THE POST-TRIAL STAGE

Chapter 8

Sentencing

I. Introduction

There are no special sentences for mentally disordered offenders to be found in Canada's Criminal Code, aside perhaps from the dangerous offender provision[1] and the section disposing of insane accused persons.[2] Nevertheless, mental illness or disorder, though its presence requires no formal adjudication, is a factor which judges are bound to consider before imposing sentence. But while the law is settled that a failure to take due notice of all relevant psychiatric data will provide grounds for appeal,[3] it is unclear as to what effect must be given to an offender's aberration once it has been adverted to.

As a direct result of this dilemma, Canadian courts have, for the most part, endeavoured to tailor the existing Criminal Code sanctions to fit the mentally disordered offenders' amorphous dimensions. The result, unfortunately, has been a rather patchy and non-uniform design. By weaving provincial mental health legislation into the fabric of Canadian criminal law, the courts have occasionally succeeded in outfitting disordered offenders with a fashionable alternative to prison denims: straightjackets.

The aim of this chapter is to outline the manner in which Canadian courts have attempted to deal with the disposition of mentally abnormal offenders. As will become apparent, the fate of any one such person depends generally on a combination of three factors: (1) the type of offence involved; (2) the nature of the offender's abnormality; and (3) the philosophy of the sentencing judge. In addition to explaining the mechanics of sentencing and enumerating the variety of dispositions

---

[1] Section 688 (enacted 1977 (Can.), c. 53, s. 14).
[2] Subsection 542(2).
[3] *R. v. Roberts,* [1963] 1 O.R. 280 (C.A.); *R. v. D.* (1972), 5 C.C.C. (2d) 366 (Ont. C.A.), discussed *infra* at pp. 241-2; *R. v. Taylor,* [1959] O.W.N. 1 (C.A.).

available to the courts, the discussion will deal with some ethical problems concerning pre-sentence psychiatric information. In the end some conclusions will be drawn and an assessment made regarding possible future alterations — both with regard to judicial sentencing policy and the role of psychiatry in the sentencing process.

II. Remand

When a trial judge wishes to have an offender psychiatrically examined before imposing sentence, he may do so under the authority conferred by s-ss. 543(2) and (2.1) of the Criminal Code. Subsections 608.2(1) and (2) supply an identical procedure for the Court of Appeal. As mentioned earlier,[4] an alternative remand procedure, which is open to both trial and appeal court judges, is that provided by provincial legislation such as Ontario's Mental Health Act.[5]

Although the statutory provisions are silent as to what will constitute sufficient "reason to believe" that an offender fits the pertinent remand requirements, it may be helpful to limit the criteria upon which remand may be ordered. While some might feel psychological screening to be an advisable precaution in the case of all offenders, simple economics would seem to dictate selectivity. For this reason, Walker[6] has given the following categories of offenders priority with respect to remand:

"(i) The mature person who, after years of steady, respectable living, is unexpectedly detected in some 'out of character' offence, such as embezzlement or assault; and, as an extreme case, any first offender over sixty years of age;

"(ii) at the other extreme, the offender with a history of persistent anti-social behaviour which fails to respond to ordinary correctives;

"(iii) the offender whose offences have an irrational quality about them, especially if they follow a stereotyped pattern (for example, the man who picks up and then assaults prostitutes, or steals only women's clothing);

"(iv) the offender who commits serious violence against members of his own family;

"(v) most sexual offenders, apart from those who have simply had intercourse with willing girls just under the age of consent."

In actual practice, judicial use of the psychiatric remand procedures seems to depend upon the personality of the sentencing judge as much as upon that of the offender. Hogarth has noted a direct correlation

---

[4] See Chapter 1 *ante,* pp. 19-22.
[5] R.S.O. 1970, c. 269.
[6] Walker, *Sentencing in a Rational Society* (Pelican, A-1108, 1972) at p. 127.

between the degree to which magistrates perceive mental disorder in offenders and the degree to which they value rehabilitation over the other traditional goals of sentencing.[7] While 44 per cent of those magistrates surveyed considered that none or very few of the offenders appearing before them were mentally ill, 37 per cent felt that a significant minority were, and as many as 14 per cent considered that most offenders were mentally ill.[8] In assessing this data, Hogarth has written:

> "Comparisons were made of the penal philosophy scores of magistrates who differed in the degrees of mental illness they perceived. The positive relationship of belief in reformation to the proportion of offenders seen as mentally ill is very strong. In contrast, the amount of mental illness seen is negatively associated with belief in general deterrence, retribution and incapacitation."[9]

At a later point in his research, he has concluded that "magistrates concerned about the treatment of offenders are more active in their search for information than magistrates concerned to punish crime for deterrent or retributive purposes."[10]

III. Psychiatric Reports

Psychiatrists who are called upon to furnish pre-sentence reports are faced with numerous difficulties. First and foremost is the problem of diagnosis. According to Bartholomew, "it is almost impossible to offer ... a definite psychiatric diagnosis in the majority of criminals...".[11] According to Scott, whom Bartholomew has quoted: "In those cases selected for psychiatric report a classical diagnosis cannot be made in more than 20 per cent. In the other 80 per cent it is impossible to attach a label any more accurate than 'personality disorder' or 'social maladjustment'."[12] While this state of affairs may simply illustrate the understatement that "the science of psychiatry cannot provide absolutely certain answers to many questions",[13] it may also be attributable to the distinct possibility that not all offenders are mentally ill. Unfortunately, however, psychiatrists seem all too often to overlook this contingency. Their reasons for

---

[7] Hogarth, *Sentencing as a Human Process* (Toronto, University of Toronto Press, 1971) at p. 85.

[8] *Ibid.*, at p. 84. The views of this latter group were consistent with the belief of Lord Hale, who declared that "doubtless, most persons that are felons ... are under a degree of partial insanity when they commit these offences."

[9] At p. 85.

[10] At p. 238.

[11] Bartholomew, "The Psychiatric Report for the Court", [1962] Crim. L.R. 19 at p. 21.

[12] Scott, "Psychiatric Reports for Magistrates' Courts" (1953), 4 Brit. J. Delinq. 1, quoted by Bartholomew, at p. 21.

[13] Roberts, "Some Observations on the Problems of the Forensic Psychiatrist" (1965), Wis. L. Rev. 240 at p. 244.

so doing may either be a conscious subscription to Roche's philosophy that "crime is a disturbance of communication, hence a form of mental illness",[14] or else an over-zealous response to the suspicions of the remanding judge. In either case, statistics indicate that persons remanded for psychiatric assessment stand little chance of being found completely normal[15] — despite the examiners' frequent failure to name their illnesses.

Bartholomew has argued that the lack of diagnostic precision on the part of reporting psychiatrists is of no real consequence anyway. The mere affixing of labels such as "psychopathic personality" or "borderline defective" to an offender is of no assistance to the sentencing judge. Rather, it is in supplying a general "dynamic" assessment of the offender's psyche that the examining psychiatrist can be most useful. In essence, a "dynamic" or "multifactorial" diagnosis is one which describes a mental phenomenon in terms of the forces which caused or produced it.[16] The formulation of such a diagnosis naturally requires a great deal of information. In this regard, psychiatrists are oftentimes impeded by the sentencing judges themselves. All too often, Bartholomew has complained, judges fail to supply adequate information concerning their reasons for remanding the accused in the first place:

> "Time and again one reads [on] the form sent from the court to the medical officer under the heading 'Reasons which led the court to request a report on the accused's state of mind' such phrases as 'Demeanour in court'; 'Previous mental history' (without amplification); 'Nature of offence' (this includes all sexual offences without differentiation). Phrases such as 'Not known' and 'For the guidance of the court' demonstrate even more clearly the lack of interest and concern that courts can, and do, display."[17]

In gathering the information he needs, the psychiatrist, in addition to examining the accused and running him through a series of psychological tests, may require previous hospital, prison or police records. He may also consult with the offender's family and friends. Although, needless to say, a great deal of hearsay will have transpired during the course of the doctor's inquiries, *Wilband v. The Queen*[18] seems to have eliminated any and all problems regarding the admissibility of evidence resulting therefrom.

The reporting psychiatrists's troubles are by no means over once he

---

[14] Roche, *The Criminal Mind: A Study of Communication Between Criminal Law and Psychiatry* (New York, Farrar, Strauss and Cudahy, 1958) at p. 241. For criticism of this philosophy, see Szasz, *Law Liberty and Psychiatry: An Inquiry into the Social Uses of Mental Health Practices* (New York, Macmillan, 1963) at pp. 91-108.

[15] In a study made in 1966 in England, it was discovered that only 29 per cent of those persons remanded (143 out of a sample of 494) were considered by the examining doctors to be mentally normal. See Sparks, "The Decision to Remand for Mental Examination" (1966), 6 Brit. J. Criminology 6, table II at p. 10.

[16] Fenichel, *The Psychoanalytic Theory of Neuroses* (St. Paul, Routledge and Kegan, 1946) at p. 11, cited by Bartholomew, at p. 22.

[17] At p. 30.

[18] [1967] S.C.R. 14. Discussed *ante* in Chapter 2 at pp. 37-8.

has arrived at a diagnosis. A court does not, after all, remand an offender simply to learn of his "repressed libidinous fantasies" or "latent homicidal tendencies". What the judge wants to know is (a) whether he is treatable and (b) whether he is dangerous. It is of little comfort to know that the offender's uncontrollable urge to set fire to chickens stems from a neurotic fear of liverwurst.

Although in *R. v. Robinson*[19] the court was told that there was a 66 per cent to 70 per cent chance of the offender's being "cured" by psychotherapy, such predictions are rare indeed. The cautious psychiatrist is more likely to maintain that "one really cannot give prognostic 'odds' as to the efficacy of psychotherapy...";[20] he prefers to state the minimum period of time which would be required to treat the patient effectively. But even this type of estimate should be taken with a grain of salt, for there is no guarantee that the doctor who offers such prediction will be the one who ultimately treats the offender.

Regardless of whether or not a satisfactory answer can be given, it is at least legitimate to question a physician concerning the results one might expect from the therapy he offers. It is doubtful, however, whether an individual's "dangerousness" is a matter which a physician ought properly be called on to assess. Unlike curability, dangerousness is not a subject ostensibly within his field of expertise. It is, for that matter, unlikely that anyone possesses what could be called an expertise in the area of gauging dangerousness. As Halleck has pointed out:

> "Research in the area of dangerous behaviour (other than generalizations from case material) is practically nonexistent. Predictive studies which have examined the probability of recidivism have not focused on the issue of dangerousness. If the psychiatrist or any other behavioural scientist were asked to show proof of his predictive skills, objective data could not be offered."[21]

For this reason, Morris has argued that dangerousness ought to be rejected as a basis for imposing sentences of imprisonment.[22]

Those who adhere to the validity of dangerousness as a workable criminological concept have offered us little in the way of criteria for detecting its presence. Psychiatry's time-honoured epitome of evil incarnate is the ubiquitous psychopath. Also called the sociopath, our elusive stereotype has been credited[23] with the following rather unflattering attributes:

" 1. Superficial charm and good 'intelligence'.

---

[19] (1974), 19 C.C.C. (2d) 193 at p. 196 (Ont. C.A.).
[20] Bartholomew, "Some Problems of the Psychiatrist in Relation to Sentencing" (1972-73), 15 Crim. L.Q. 325 at p. 334.
[21] Halleck, *Psychiatry and the Dilemmas of Crime: A Study of Causes, Punishment and Treatment* (Berkeley, University of California Press, 1971) at p. 314.
[22] Morris, *The Future of Imprisonment* (Chicago, University of Chicago Press, 1974) at p. 62.
[23] Cleckley, *The Mask of Sanity* (St. Louis, Mosby, 1955) at pp. 380-1, cited in Nemeth,

" 2. Absence of delusions and other signs of irrational thinking.
" 3. Absence of 'nervousness' or psycho-neurotic manifestations.
" 4. Unreliability.
" 5. Untruthfulness and insincerity.
" 6. Lack of remorse or shame.
" 7. Inadequately motivated anti-social behaviour.
" 8. Poor judgment and failure to learn by experience.
" 9. Pathological egocentricity and incapacity for love.
"10. General poverty in major affective reactions.
"11. Specific loss of insight.
"12. Unresponsiveness in general inter-personal relations.
"13. Fantastic and uninviting behaviour with drink and sometimes without.
"14. Suicide rarely carried out.
"15. Sex life impersonal, trivial and poorly integrated.
"16. Failure to follow any life plan."

None of us is perfect.

Aware that few really dangerous persons wear "I AM A PSYCHOPATH" buttons, McCaldon[24] has devised his own checklist of ingredients for gauging dangerousness. The characteristics, though they may not add up to stark raving psychopathy, are hardly what one looks for in the ideal baby-sitter:

"(1) A history of violent outbursts, especially if such history involves cruelty to animals.
"(2) Fragmented basic relationships such as broken home, unhappy marriage, etc.
"(3) Exposure to hostile or antisocial environment. . . .
"(4) Violence is seen by the offender as one of the means of his expressing self-esteem.
"(5) A blockage or lack of attainment in normal supportive relationships such as love, sexual relationships, work, friends, etc.
"(6) A rather schizoid or border-line psychotic mental state at the time of examination."

The problem with these criteria, as with those relating to psychopathy, is that their relevance in the prediction of future criminal behaviour is not supported by empirical data.

Perhaps the most serious ethical issue facing a reporting psychiatrist arises after his assessments of the offender's curability and dangerousness have been made. It concerns the inclusion in his report of recommendations pertaining to the actual disposition of the offender. Although some authorities regard it as clearly improper for a psychiatrist to advocate the imposition of one sentence over another,[25] Bartholomew has maintained that:

"Psychopathic Personality — Its Relevance in the Correctional After Care Agency" (1961), 3 Can. J. Corr. at pp. 128-9.
[24] McCaldon, "Reflections on Sentencing" (1974), 16 Can. J. Crimin. and Corr. 291 at pp. 295-6.
[25] See Page, *Sentence of the Court* (London, Faber and Faber, 1948) at p. 170, cited by Bar-

"... a recommendation is implicit in the initial request for a medical and/or psychiatric report. To suppose that the court only requests a diagnostic formulation but does not want any recommendations as to possible 'treatment', or the best method of dealing with the case, is hardly to the credit of the court and would be utterly illogical."[26]

Insofar as an opinion regarding the most effective form of psychotherapy would be difficult to divorce from an endorsement of that treatment, Bartholomew is probably correct in asserting the illogicality of such separation. And it would, of course, be odd for an examining psychiatrist to characterize an individual as treatable without naming the treatment he has in mind. However, the assertion that psychiatrists are logically entitled to advise the court as to the relative values of all forms of sentence is one which must be seriously questioned.

Scott has argued[27] that psychiatrists should never include recommendations for punishment in their reports to the court. The problem with applying this rule, however, lies in the susceptability of the word "punishment" to divergent interpretations. What an offender views as punishment may be seen as treatment by the psychiatrist. When dealing in the area of psychotherapy it is often difficult (if not impossible) to distinguish the two. Indeed, citing the use of aversion therapy, Gunn has observed that "Punishment is of course not entirely alien to psychiatry...".[28] Because many psychiatrists view punishment as therapeutic in some circumstances, they may feel unrestrained in recommending whatever form of disposition they deem appropriate in the interests of rehabilitation. For this reason, Bartholomew has asserted the legitimacy of psychiatric recommendations for imprisonment. "[I]t must be realized," he has written, "that imprisonment is not simply what is left over when all other sanctions have been tried and found to fail or have been rejected in the first place. Imprisonment can be therapeutic and rehabilitative in a number of cases ...".[29] Psychiatrists who view punishment as therapeutic consider one of its uses to be the alleviation of guilt feelings on the part of certain offenders.[30] In illustrating this theory Gunn has reported the following case history:

"... a man, many years ago, remonstrated with his wife's lover, the inevitable fight ensued and the interloper was killed. The man was subsequently convicted of manslaughter. At the time he suffered unbearable guilt and prayed for a stiff punishment. The court took

---

tholomew, *op. cit.* footnote 11, at p. 23.

[26] Bartholomew, *op. cit.* footnote 11, at p. 23. Citing a study made by Radzinowicz, *Sexual Offences* (London, MacMillan, 1957) at p. 74, the author notes that most psychiatric reports do in fact contain recommendations as to the disposal of the prisoner.

[27] Scott, "Psychiatric Reports for Magistrates' Courts" (1953), 4 Brit. J. Delinq. 1, cited by Bartholomew, at p. 24.

[28] Gunn, "Sentencing — As seen by a Psychiatrist" (1971), 11 Med. Sci. and the Law 95 at p. 97.

[29] Bartholomew, *op. cit.* footnote 11, pp. 24-5.

[30] Gunn, at p. 97.

a more lenient view of his behaviour and gave him a conditional discharge. He was amazed and appalled. He felt that he had been deprived of a chance to redeem himself and ran away from home and drowned his sorrows in drink. Since that time he has been a severe and persistent alcoholic and is convinced that if he had a reasonable punishment — say two or three years in prison — he would not have deteriorated."[31]

With all due respect to the chronicler, the credibility of this little melodrama seems a bit thin. One fails to see how staring at a cockroach crawling across the ceiling of his jail cell for three years would have brightened up the offender's outlook on life.

Even if one accepts the legitimacy of therapeutic punishment, a psychiatrist's expertise in matters of psychic rehabilitation will not in itself justify all recommendations he makes with regard to sentence. As the case of *R. v. Doucet*[32] illustrates, a psychiatrist may base his advice on entirely unrelated considerations. In *Doucet* the reporting doctors advocated a sentence of imprisonment for the purposes of general as well as specific deterrence.

A final problem with psychiatric reports concerns their confidentiality. Until the 1968-69 parliamentary session, the general rule in this regard was that set out in *R. v. Benson and Stevenson*,[33] a decision of the British Columbia Court of Appeal. In that case it was held that offenders should be informed of the substance of any detrimental information contained in pre-sentence reports, in order that they might explain or deny it. A crucial exception to this rule was made, however, with regard to psychiatric data, the Court saying:

"In an earlier part of these reasons I referred to an observation by Goddard L.C.J. in *R. v. Dickson* in dealing with the statutory obligation to furnish the prisoner or his counsel with a copy of the representations made to the Court by the Prison Commissioners. He said in part: 'In some cases I think it very undesirable, because it may sometimes give him ideas about his mental condition which he perhaps should not know.' I am in complete agreement with that statement — if I may say so with deference. And for this reason: The fact that a convicted person is suffering from some mental disorder is not a factor which should in ordinary cases influence a Court to impose a higher sentence than would be imposed upon a man of normal mentality. *It is not a fact damaging or detrimental to him in the sense that it would lead to the imposition of a heavy sentence in the ordinary run of cases.*[34] There are cases, involving for instance, sexual crimes, where the Court might well consider the mental instability of the convict renders him a menace to society but it seems to me in that class of case an allegation of that fact con-

---

[31] *Ibid.*
[32] [1971] 1 O.R. 705 at p. 706 (C.A.).
[33] (1951), 100 C.C.C. 247.
[34] See *infra* at pp. 250-1.

tained in a Probation Officer's report is of little value standing alone. A psychiatric examination conducted by a doctor qualified in that field is the method to determine that fact. *The examining doctor would be the best judge as to whether or not the result of his examination should be fully disclosed to the convict.*"[35]

With the enactment of s-s. 662(2) of the Criminal Code the above exception would seem to have been effectively extinguished insofar as it applied to psychiatric information in the hands of the probation officer. Section 662 reads:

> "662(1) Where an accused, other than a corporation, pleads guilty to or is found guilty of an offence, a probation officer shall, if required to do so by a court, prepare and file with the court a report in writing relating to the accused for the purpose of assisting the court in imposing sentence or in determining whether the accused should be discharged pursuant to section 662.1.
>
> "(2) Where a report is filed with the court under subsection (1), the clerk of the court shall forthwith cause a copy of the report to be provided to the accused or his counsel and to the prosecutor."

It is to be noted that this section makes no reference whatsoever to information filed by persons other than the probation officer. With respect to reports filed by the examining psychiatrist personally, the *Benson and Stevenson* exception would therefore appear to have been left intact. Supportive of this view is the wording of s. 17 of Ontario's Mental Health Act. It provides:

> "17. Notwithstanding this or any other Act or any regulation made under any other Act, the senior physician may report *all or any part* of the information compiled by the psychiatric facility to any person *where, in the opinion of the senior physician,* it is in the best interests of the person who is the subject of an order made under section 14 or 15."[36]

IV. Possible Sentences

Nowadays it is commonly assumed in the case of mentally disordered offenders that rehabilitation is the prime consideration for the sentencing judge and that it takes precedence over traditional punitive goals. Thomas has in fact suggested that:

---

[35] *Supra,* footnote 33 at p. 261 (emphasis added).
[36] R.S.O. 1970, c. 269 (emphasis added).

"Where the offender can be shown to be in need of psychiatric treatment, and the necessary treatment is available in an appropriate setting, the Court will normally make an appropriate order *without regard* to considerations of deterrence and retribution . . . . There are some cases in which this approach is not evident, but they are clearly exceptional."[37]

If this is an accurate description of sentencing policy in England, it is doubtful whether it reflects a universally accepted philosophy or practice. Because conviction has historically denoted responsibility, North American jurists have shown reluctance to depart from the logic that those who are mentally blameworthy[38] should be punished. As Halleck has noted, "punishability is equated with the criminal's responsibility for his actions".[39]

More than 20 years ago an American psychoanalyst named Waelder suggested a movement away from the imposition of punative sanctions as an inevitable consequence of conviction. He stated: "It seems advisable, first of all, to reformulate our laws in such a way that they are no longer focused on punishment as the normal consequence of crime, with other dispositions taking place as exceptions from the rule . . .".[40] He went on to recommend[41] the following tables as a guide to sentencing:

Symbol	Diagnostic Characterization	Disposition
1, 1, 1	Dangerous Deterrable Treatable	Punishment and Treatment
1, 1, 2	Dangerous Deterrable Not treatable	Punishment
1, 2, 1	Dangerous Not deterrable Treatable	Preventive Custody and Treatment

---

[37] Thomas, *Principles of Sentencing* (London, Heinemann, 1970) at p. 257 (emphasis added).

[38] *I.e.,* those who, in the case of most offences, have been adjudged to have had *mens rea.*

[39] Halleck, *op. cit.* footnote 21, at p. 207. Even in England, where the rehabilitative ideal is said to flourish, one still finds judicial reasoning like that of Lord Parker C.J. in *R. v. Morris,* [1961] 2 Q.B. 237 at p. 243:

"Of course there may be cases where, although there is a substantial impairment of responsibility, the prisoner is shown on the particular facts of the case nevertheless to have some responsibility for the act he has done, *for which he must be punished* ..." (Emphasis added.)

[40] Waelder, "Psychiatry and the Problem of Criminal Responsibility" (1952), 101 U. of Penn. L. Rev. 378 at p. 389.

[41] *Ibid.,* at p. 390.

1, 2, 2	Dangerous Not deterrable Not treatable	Preventive Custody
2, 1, 1	Not dangerous Deterrable Treatable	Punishment with Probationary Period and Treatment
2, 1, 2	Not dangerous Deterrable Not treatable	Punishment, perhaps with Probationary Period
2, 2, 1	Not dangerous Not deterrable Treatable	Treatment
2, 2, 2	Not dangerous Not deterrable Not treatable	Release

It is submitted that Canadian courts have not yet fully embraced the rehabilitative ideal. Whether or not they articulate their reasons, Canadian judges seem to be operating on a rationale more closely resembling that proposed by Waelder than the one which Thomas has described. Consequently, the sanctions to which mentally abnormal offenders are liable today may entail anything from simple punishment, to elaborate psychiatric treatment, to a combination of the two.

A. FINE

This form of sanction has, on occasion, been employed as a method of dealing with abnormal persons convicted of relatively minor offences. Clearly the purpose behind the imposition of a fine is punative rather than rehabilitative. By punishing the offender, the court seeks only to deter such person from exhibiting the symptoms of his supposed affliction in an unlawful manner; it is not concerned with bringing about a "cure".

The offence of committing an act of gross indecency[42] in public[43] is one for which some judges have considered the levying of a fine suitable. In

---

[42] Criminal Code, s. 157.
[43] Section 158 of the Code provides in part:
     "158(1) Sections 155 and 157 do not apply to any act committed in private between
        (a) a husband and his wife, or
        (b) any two persons, each of whom is twenty-one years or more of age,
     both of whom consent to the commission of the act.
     "(2) For the purposes of subsection (1),
        (a) an act shall be deemed not to have been committed in private if it is committed in a public place, or if more than two persons take part or are present;"

R. v. Five Accused Persons[44] Rice Prov. Ct. J. imposed $100 and $200 fines on several confirmed homosexuals, stating his reasons for so doing as follows:

> "I can see no purpose in suspending sentence. The accused are confirmed homosexualists and have not indicated that they intend to fight off this disease. Even if they did, I doubt whether they could. I do not know how far a successful medical treatment has progressed in this field. . . . I have come to the conclusion that until some other mode of punishment is devised a fine with the alternative of a gaol sentence should be imposed on first offenders — and all the accused are such. There is no need for me to deal with second offenders at this stage. As long as this revolting and sickening offence is a crime, the law can only punish; it is not for courts to prescribe treatment; this is a matter for medical science. It is also not a matter for the courts to say how and where these unfortunates should be incarcerated. There are experts in that field."[45]

Similarly, in *R. v. Boisvert and Lupien*[46] fines of $100 and $750 were imposed by a British Columbia County Court for an offence under what is now s. 157. It is important to note that this section provides for a maximum of five years' imprisonment, thus making fine possible *in lieu of* imprisonment under s-s. 646(1) of the Code.[47] Where the offence is a more serious one and is punishable by more than five years' imprisonment, a fine may be imposed only *in addition* to another authorized punishment.[48] Thus in *R. v. Marple*[49] four defendants convicted of indecent assault on a male person[50] were given a perfunctory prison term of one day and fined in the amount of $500. On appeal by the Crown, the Nova Scotia Supreme Court (Appeal Division) refused to impose a longer term of imprisonment on the grounds that imprisonment would not rehabilitate the offenders and that the fine constituted an adequate deterrent. In the more recent case of *R. v. Dobson*[51] an individual convicted of buggery under s. 155 (which carries a maximum of 14 years)

---

[44] (1961), 4 Crim. L.Q. 124 (Man. Prov. Ct.).

[45] *Ibid.,* at pp. 124-5.

[46] The decision on sentence is reported by Saunders, "Sentencing of Homosexual Offenders" (1967-68), 10 Crim. L.Q. at p. 29. The case of *R. v. Lupien* reached the Supreme Court of Canada on a point of expert evidence and is reported in [1970] S.C.R. 263.

[47] This subsection reads:
   "646(1) an accused who is convicted of an indictable offence punishable with imprisonment for five years or less may be fined in addition to or in lieu of any other punishment that is authorized, but an accused shall not be fined in lieu of imprisonment where the offence of which he is convicted is punishable by a minimum term of imprisonment."

[48] Subsection 646(2) of the Code provides:
   "(2) An accused who is convicted of an indictable offence punishable with imprisonment for more than five years may be fined in addition to, but not in lieu of, any other punishment that is authorized."

[49] (1973), 6 N.S.R. (2d) 389 (C.A.).

[50] Section 156 provides a maximum sentence of ten years for this offence.

[51] (1975), 11 N.S.R. (2d) 81 (C.A.).

was sentenced to one day's imprisonment to be followed by a three-year probation period and was ordered to pay a $600 fine as well. While the trial judge's purpose in handing down this sentence was clearly a punitive one, it is interesting that the Nova Scotia Supreme Court (Appeal Division) saw fit to vary the probation order by making psychiatric treatment a further condition thereof. In doing so, the Court obviously saw nothing contradictory in the aims of punishment and rehabilitation.

B. PROBATION

(i) Following Imprisonment

Judicial recognition that an offender requires psychiatric attention does not necessarily result in the abandonment of such penological considerations as deterrence and retribution. Waelder has pointed out,[52] however, that rehabilitation is generally made more difficult as deterrent or retributive punishment is increased. Capital punishment, for example, tends to make rehabilitation impossible. But short of this ultimate sanction, terms of imprisonment have been considered by judges as not altogether incompatible with the rehabilitative ideal. As Waelder has put it: "Whenever our goals conflict, we have to weigh how much of each of these purposes can be achieved and how much sacrifice in terms of one goal is necessary for the partial realization of another one."[53]

It has been argued with great force that the simultaneous combination of punishment and treatment within a penal institution is counterproductive in terms of rehabilitation.[54] Prison, after all, is hardly the ideal therapeutic environment. It is perhaps for this reason, therefore, that some courts have adopted the "punish now, treat later" approach to sentencing. Utilizing the authority conferred on them by paras. 663(1)(b) and (2)(h),[55] judges have chosen to place suitable offenders on

---

[52] "Psychiatry and the Problem of Criminal Responsibility", at p. 388.
[53] *Ibid.*, at pp. 388-9.
[54] Halleck, *op. cit.* footnote 21, at p. 286 has remarked that:
"The psychiatrist who ventures to offer his services to a prison ... is dismayed to find himself part of a system that is dedicated to the infliction of psychological pain. In fact, the prison environment is almost diabolically conceived to force the offender to experience the pangs of what many psychiatrists would describe as mental illness. A brief look at the prison environment will indicate that it contains the most pernicious factors that are listed as causes of mental illness in our psychiatric textbooks."
[55] Section 663 provides in part:
"663.(1) Where an accused is convicted of an offence the court may, having regard to the age and character of the accused, the nature of the offence and the circumstances surrounding its commission,
...
(b) in addition to fining the accused or sentencing him to imprisonment, whether in default or payment of a fine or otherwise, for a term not exceeding two years, direct that the accused comply with the conditions prescribed in a probation order
...
"(2) The following conditions shall be deemed to be prescribed in a probation

probation, making psychiatric treatment (usually on an out-patient basis) a condition thereof, but only *after* they have served short terms of imprisonment. *R. v. DeCoste*[56] is a case in point. There the defendant pleaded guilty to two charges of indecent assault and was sentenced by the trial court to 18 months' imprisonment. On appeal, the Nova Scotia Supreme Court (Appeal Division) took notice of the fact that he had previously been a psychiatric patient and was diagnosed as schizophrenic. The sentence was varied as follows:

> "In view of all the circumstances of this case, including the fact that the appellant has no previous record, we consider that the protection of the public would best be served here by making every effort *consistent with observance of the principle of deterrence* to ensure that the appellant obtain further psychiatric treatment as soon as possible.
>
> "It is the unanimous opinion of the Court that the sentence be varied to three months in the Halifax County Correction Centre, that the appellant receive psychiatric treatment forthwith, and that he be placed on probation for a period of two years and comply with the conditions of a probation order which shall include those set out in s. 663(2)(a), (d), (f) and (g) of the *Code,* and the further condition, which we regard as of the utmost importance, that he attend and receive such psychiatric treatment as the probation officer shall arrange."[57]

(ii) Following a Conditional Discharge or Suspended Sentence

Subsection 662.1(2) and para. 663(1)(a) provide for the imposition of a probation order in cases where the accused has received a conditional discharge or suspended sentence respectively. Resort to this form of disposition is an obvious sign of judicial adoption of the treatment model. Judges most commonly use this alternative in the case of persons convicted of non-violent sexual offences who are not considered a sufficient danger to the community to require imprisonment. Such sentence has, for example, been employed in cases like *R. v. Holte and Landry;*[58] *R. v. LaChance and Bliss;*[59] *R. v. Desjarlais and Ferguson*[60] and *R. v. Herrmann and Singer*[61] as a method of dealing with homosexuals convicted

---

order, namely, that the accused shall keep the peace and be of good behaviour and shall appear before the court when required to do so by the court, and, in addition, the court may prescribe as conditions in a probation order that the accused shall do any one or more of the following things specified in the order, namely,

...

(h) comply with such other reasonable conditions as the court considers desirable for securing the good conduct of the accused and for preventing a repetition by him of the same offence or the commission of other offences."

[56] (1974), 10 N.S.R. (2d) 94 (C.A.).

[57] *Ibid.,* at pp. 95-6 (emphasis added).

[58] Unreported but cited by Saunders, "Sentencing of Homosexual Offenders" (1967-68), 10 Crim. L.Q. 25 at p. 27.

[59] *Ibid.*

[60] *Ibid.*

[61] *Ibid.*

of acts of gross indecency in public. It has also been used with great frequency in the sentencing of pedophiles. In the case of *R. v. D.*[62] a schoolteacher who had been convicted on two charges of indecently assaulting young girls had been sentenced to a prison term of 12 months definite and six months indeterminate. On appeal the sentence was varied to time served and the accused placed on two years' probation on the condition that he submit to treatment on an out-patient basis at Toronto's Clarke Institute. The court rested its decision upon the following line of reasoning:

> "We have before us material not presented to the trial Judge which disclosed that if the appellant were to continue his treatment with Dr. Tisdall and also take treatment at the Clarke Institute of Psychiatry the chance of being cured is favourable. If such treatment outside the prison is likely to effect such a cure and his imprisonment may not, we think that it is in the general interest of society to have him treated rather than imprisoned."[63]

This statement represents what is perhaps the classic rationale behind the use of probationary psychiatric treatment. It articulates the widely held belief that psychotherapy, if it is to be effective at all, is most properly conducted outside the prison environment.[64] Recognizing that the locking of an individual behind bars may not be the ideal way to effect his healthy readjustment to society, it advances an alternative method of psychic rehabilitation which, though coerced, seems more workable.

The assumption that compulsory psychiatric treatment is either more efficacious or more ethical when the coercive force (in this case, the *threat* of imprisonment) remains hidden, is one which invites examination. With respect to coerced therapy generally, Jonas Rappeport has asserted that "enforced treatment is nonetheless treatment and can, in fact, produce changes which are desirable from the standpoint of the individual and society."[65] Regarding the effectiveness of probationary treatment on an out-patient basis he has made the following observation:

> "The sex offender statistics published by Turner and Mohr from Toronto[66] and by Peters in Philadelphia, and in the initial data that we have developed from almost two years of an enforced group therapy program, have indicated that when close probation supervision forces patients to attend, very satisfactory results can be obtained by outpatient treatment of those with repeated offenses. Those clin-

---

[62] (1971), 5 C.C.C. (2d) 366 (Ont. C.A.).
[63] *Ibid.*, at p. 367.
[64] See *R. v. Hough*, [1965] Crim. L.R. 665 where England's Court of Criminal Appeal utilized probationary psychotherapy in express recognition of the fact that imprisonment would prejudice the chances of therapy being successful.
[65] Rappeport, "Enforced Treatment — Is It Treatment?" (1974), 2 Bulletin of the American Academy of Psychiatry and the Law 148 at p. 148.
[66] The author cites Turner and Mohr, *Pedophilia and Exhibitionism* (Toronto, University of Toronto Press).

ics that have no means of enforcing attendance at treatment sessions have repeatedly reported poor results."[67]

But resort to coerced probationary treatment may involve some rather serious legal and ethical difficulties. Can an offender who has been coerced into treatment ever be said to have given his voluntary informed consent thereto?[68] It may be argued that the probationer's predicament need not negative his capacity to consent at all. He may sincerely wish to be treated.[69] Why should the threat of imprisonment negate freedom of choice? Citizens who are not on probation are also threatened by imprisonment, yet can it be said that whenever persons obey the law they are doing so involuntarily? Hopefully, it is not merely legal constraint which prevents "Citizen Bozo" from attacking his neighbour with a chain saw!

Although there may be legal as well as moral limitations upon the state's right to alter criminal behaviour,[70] the risk of probationary psychotherapy exceeding those limits is no doubt decreased (owing to diminished opportunity) from that which exists in the case of in-patient psychotherapy. Nevertheless, it is significant that some courts have preferred not to make psychiatric treatment a strict condition of probation even where they have felt such treatment advisable. In an apparent attempt to remove the coercive element from the psychiatrist-patient relationship, they have merely offered their recommendation that the probationer undergo psychotherapy. Thus in *R. v. H.*[71] an Ontario County Court sentenced a pedophile who had been convicted on several counts of indecent assault to 12 months' probation with only the usual conditions. The Court further advised the accused, however, to *voluntarily* attend as an out-patient at Toronto's Forensic Clinic. In *R. v. Allen*[72] where the offender had been sentenced on similar charges to two years' imprisonment, the British Columbia Court of Appeal reduced the sentence to time served without imposing probation at all. In stating its reasons the Court noted that the appellant had "recognized the urgency of continuing regular psychiatric treatment ...".[73]

Implicit in the use of out-patient psychotherapy as an alternative to imprisonment is a rejection by the court of general deterrence as a salient consideration in the circumstances. In *R. v. D.* the court felt that: "Deterrence in this case is of small moment because the Court is of the view that the appellant suffers from an illness, as do all pedophiles; they are not deterred by punishment to others."[74] This is not to say, however,

---

[67] At p. 150.

[68] See Chapter 10 *post* at pp. 304-10.

[69] In *R. v. Leech* (1973), 21 C.R.N.S. 1 at p. 12 (Alta.) a psychiatric witness testified: "As a matter of fact [the accused] begged me for psychiatric help. He said that he was frightened if he went to prison that when he would get out he might repeat these acts, and he wanted some form of treatment whereby he would not act in a similar manner".

[70] See Chapter 10 *post* at pp. 304-13.

[71] (1965-66), 8 Crim. L.Q. 11.

[72] (1954), 108 C.C.C. 239.

[73] *Ibid.*, at p. 244.

[74] *Supra,* footnote 62 at p. 368.

that probationary psychiatric treatment may be ordered in the case of all non-deterrable offenders. Before selecting this form of sentence, the court will generally require assurance that the accused's condition is treatable[75] and that his being at large will not unduly endanger the public.[76] Furthermore, the offender must meet the requirement of eligibility contained in the Code's conditional discharge or suspended sentence provisions. The former[77] excludes persons found guilty of offences punishable by a minimum term, 14 years, life, or death; the latter[78] excludes those convicted of crimes for which a minimum punishment is prescribed. This limitation on the use of probation would seem to indicate an unwillingness on the part of Parliament to abandon retribution in the case of more serious offences, regardless of the offender's mental state. Interestingly, the gravity of the crime does not seem to be a relevant consideration in England; probation orders have been imposed for offences such as arson[79] and attempted murder.[80]

Apart from the ethical problems involved in making psychotherapy a condition of probation, there are several practical difficulties inherent in the use of this form of disposition. To begin with, although the Code allows under para. 663(2)(h) for psychiatric treatment to be made a condition of probation, it contains no provision which compels the psychiatric institution to accept the probationer as a patient. This means that unless the reporting psychiatrist is in a position to know for certain that a particular clinic or hospital will accept the offender if released on probation, the individual runs the risk of involuntarily violating his probation.[81] In England such risk is eliminated in part by s. 4 of the Criminal Justice Act 1948[82] which provides that the court must be satisfied that suitable arrangements have been made before including in a probation order a requirement that the offender submit to in-patient treatment.

Another potential problem lies in the fact that the psychiatrist who reports to the sentencing court need not be the one in whose care the offender will be released. Although he might consider the accused suitable for treatment, the facility to whom he is eventually referred may disagree and discharge him from treatment after one session.[83] The result, once again, is that the offender may be placed in violation of his probation. A similar situation may occur even where the reporting psychiatrist is in fact the one who eventually undertakes to treat the accused. Once released, the offender may discover that the doctor's busy schedule allows him to see the accused less frequently than anticipated.[84]

---

[75] See the cases of *Hardy, Silver* and *Wyer,* cited by Thomas, *Principles of Sentencing,* at pp. 259-60, footnote 5.
[76] See *R. v. Greedy,* [1964] Crim. L.R. 669 and *R. v. Cave,* [1965] Crim. L.R. 448.
[77] Subsection 662.1(1).
[78] Paragraph 663(1)(a).
[79] *R. v. Rideout,* cited by Thomas, *op. cit.* footnote 37 at p. 259, footnote 4.
[80] *R. v. Hill,* [1963] Crim. L.R. 525.
[81] Bartholomew, *op. cit.* footnote 20 at p. 333 has raised this problem.
[82] 1948 (U.K.), c. 58 as amended by Sch. 7 to the Mental Health Act, 1959 (U.K.), c. 72.
[83] *Ibid.*
[84] *Ibid.*

C. IMPRISONMENT

(i) With No Special Interest in Treatment

Prison sentences, unaccompanied by any particular recommendation for treatment, are frequently given to offenders whom the courts feel to be mentally ill. Sometimes such dispositions are rationalized on the basis that simple incarceration, if for a long enough period, may itself bring about the prisoner's rehabilitation. In *R. v. Jones,*[85] for instance, the Ontario Court of Appeal sentenced an accused whom psychiatrists had diagnosed as suffering from a personality disorder to 12 years' imprisonment following his conviction on a charge of attempted murder. Arnup J.A. justified the sentence on the grounds *inter alia* that it might "assist in the rehabilitation of the accused, even though the prognosis for the immediate future is very pessimistic indeed."[86] In a similar vein, the Model Sentencing Act prepared by the National Council on Crime and Delinquency (U.S.A.) recommends long sentences for dangerous offenders on the premise that "violent action is a characteristic of the young rather than the old offender."[87] The purpose of a lengthy prison term would be "to continue him until that period of his life when release would be safe and rehabilitation likely."[88] By way of contrast, the Canadian Committee on Corrections was distinctly of the opinion that long-term imprisonment militated strongly against rehabilitation. In the Committee's words, "a person who has received a very long definite sentence, say 20 years, may in fact be more dangerous at the expiration of his sentence and return to freedom than when he was sentenced."[89] This argument would seem to strike also at what is perhaps the chief justification of long-term imprisonment, namely, the protection of the public. Yet judges frequently impose the maximum penalties prescribed for protective purposes. And it is not surprising that mentally abnormal offenders who are considered to be incurable rank as prime candidates for this form of sentencing.[90] As a recent example of such occurence we may take the Ontario Court of Appeal's decision in *R. v. Fisher.*[91] In that case the accused, who was a reformatory inmate, had been convicted of beating up and stabbing a guard while escaping from that institution. He received from the trial court consecutive sentences of one and two years' imprisonment on the escape custody and wounding charges respectively. These were to be added onto the term he was currently serving. On

---

[85] (1971), 3 C.C.C. (2d) 153.

[86] *Ibid.,* at p. 161.

[87] Commentary to s. 5 of the Model Sentencing Act. And see Halleck, who has noted (at p. 285) that "the aging process in itself probably has more to do with reformation than all our correctional endeavours combined."

[88] Commentary to s. 5 of the Act.

[89] Ouimet, *Report of the Canadian Committee on Corrections* (Ottawa, Queen's Printer, 1969) at p. 262.

[90] See *R. v. Aarons,* [1964] Crim. L.R. 484 and *R. v. Saunders,* [1965] Crim. L.R. 250, where the offender's apparent incurability was in each case a factor influencing the court to impose life imprisonment.

[91] (1975), 23 C.C.C. (2d) 449.

appeal by the Crown against sentence, however, a psychiatric report was ordered. It revealed that Fisher was a psychopathic personality who had spent most of his life behind bars — including a 20-year stint at Penetang's centre for the criminally insane. Quite understandably, Fisher was said to be incurable and assessed as unsuitable for further psychiatric treatment. On these facts, the sentence on the wounding charge was raised to the maximum of 14 years. What is interesting is that Houlden J.A. remarked in the course of his judgment that had it not been for the accused's mental disorder, he would only have increased the sentence by three years.

If it is true that imprisonment makes offenders more dangerous than they were before being sentenced, it would seem that total protection of the public can only be achieved by imposing sentences which allow for the unfortunate effects that imprisonment has upon offenders. Psychotherapy not being an option in the case of incurable psychopaths, we are left with the alternative of permanent imprisonment.[92] In the *Fisher* case, this would only have been possible through the subsequent certification of the accused or through his being designated a habitual criminal in accordance with the procedure set forth in former ss. 688 and 690 of the Code. Where the courts have had the option of sentencing an incurable psychopath to life imprisonment, they have seized the opportunity in the name of public protection. In *R. v. Head,* [93] for example, the Saskatchewan Court of Appeal dismissed the appeal of an accused who had been sentenced to a life term for raping a six-year-old girl. Considering the available psychiatric evidence and the fact that he had previously been convicted of indecent assault on a young girl, the Court felt that rehabilitation was beyond question and that the public could only be safeguarded by depriving the accused of his freedom permanently, or at least indefinitely.

Rehabilitation, incurability and dangerousness are not the only criteria upon which the courts have grounded their decisions to imprison mentally abnormal offenders. A very popular alternative consideration is that of general deterrence. This fact is quite surprising, not just in view of the widespread disillusionment which the very concept of general deterrence has encountered in recent years,[94] but because one would have thought it especially difficult to deter irrationally motivated behaviour. Nevertheless, judges commonly invoke the principle, seeing nothing peculiar in the deterrence of symptoms of what they themselves view as an "illness".

Judicial reliance on the principle of general deterrence can be seen in a great many Canadian criminal cases which involve disordered offenders.

---

[92] Conversely, sentences of life imprisonment have on occasion been varied to long fixed terms where the offender has been assessed as treatable on the grounds that the indeterminate nature of the life sentence impeded rehabilitation: see *R. v. Donnelly* (1968), 52 Cr. App. R. 731.

[93] (1970), 1 C.C.C. (2d) 436.

[94] See generally Gardiner, "The Purposes of Criminal Punishment" (1958), 21 Mod.L. Rev. 117 at pp. 121-5; Walker, *op. cit.* footnote 6, at pp. 77-97; Wooton, *Crime and the Criminal Law* (London, Stevens and Sons, 1963) at pp. 97-101.

R. v. Jones[95] involved an accused who was convicted on three charges of
indecently assaulting young girls and was originally fined a total of $450.
Psychiatric evidence showed that he suffered from "sexual repression"
but that there was little likelihood of his committing further such offences. Despite the fact that the reporting psychiatrist had warned that
imprisonment would only worsen the accused's condition, the Ontario
Court of Appeal substituted a prison term of six months definite and
twelve months indeterminate on each count, the sentences to be served
concurrently. The reasoning of the majority[96] was expressed by Pickup
C.J.O. who said:

> "It may be that this particular respondent, after continuation of
> psychiatric treatment, will not repeat the offence and there is a pos-
> sibility of his being cured of his condition by such psychiatric treat-
> ment, but these are matters of grave uncertainty. I think I would
> agree that, so far as the condition of this particular respondent is
> concerned, a prison term may be detrimental to his recovery, but in
> my opinion the offence is too serious for punishment by a fine or by
> suspending sentence and placing the respondent upon probation. It
> is said that the prison term will not have any deterrent effect upon
> other persons who are truly sex perverts. That may be so, but I do
> not think it justifies disregarding the deterrent effect upon those
> persons whom sentence will deter and who might be disposed to
> commit an assault of this character."[97]

With respect, it seems unclear from this reasoning exactly whom the
learned Chief Justice sought to deter. Surely anyone who indecently
assaults young children can be fairly regarded as a "sex pervert".[98] Yet
the Chief Justice admitted that those persons who were *"truly* sex
perverts" would probably not be deterred. Are we to assume that the
sentence was aimed only at deterring *amateur* sex perverts? Or at deterring normal individuals *masquerading* as sex perverts?

Laidlaw J.A. rejected the views of Pickup C.J.O. on the issue of general deterrence. In a dissenting judgment he said:

> "Then, would a term of imprisonment imposed on the respondent
> in the unusual circumstances of this case deter others from commit-
> ting criminal acts of sexual misbehaviour? In my opinion it would
> not. Certainly it would not restrain others who suffer from mental
> maladjustments or illness of a kind that makes them unable to re-
> sist the driving and overpowering sexual impulse to do a wrongful
> act ..."[99]

---

[95] (1956), 115 C.C.C. 273 (Ont. C.A.).
[96] Aylesworth, Chevrier and Schroeder JJ.A. concurring.
[97] *Supra*, footnote 95, at p. 275.
[98] A possible exception may be made in the case of mental defectives: see *R. v. Pascoe*
(1974), 17 Crim. L.Q. 142 (Ont. C.A.), where a mentally defective male was sentenced to
12 months definite and 12 months indefinite for attempting to indecently assault a
seven-year-old boy.
[99] *Supra,* footnote 94 at p. 280.

The Ontario Court of Appeal again adopted the theme of general deterrence in the case of *R. v. Doucet.*[100] That case involved an appellant who was convicted of indecently assaulting a young boy and who had received from the trial court a sentence of imprisonment for two years less a day definite and two years less a day indeterminate. This sentence was affirmed on appeal, the majority of the Court apparently relying (as had the trial judge) upon the opinion of a psychiatrist that a term of imprisonment would deter not only the accused but other pedophiles as well from the practice of their perversion. Brooke J.A. dissented, however, on the grounds (1) that the doctor's evidence had been misconstrued, and (2) that the goal of rehabilitation outweighed that of deterrence. He felt probation with psychiatric treatment was a more suitable sentence in the circumstances.

Once again the goal of general deterrence motivated the Ontario Court of Appeal in *R. v. Murphy.*[101] In that case the accused had been convicted on two charges of rape and one charge of attempted rape. He was sentenced to imprisonment for a total of two years less a day definite and two years less a day indeterminate plus three years' probation. On appeal by the Crown, however, the sentences were raised to a total of seven years' imprisonment. Of interest is the fact that the psychiatric report indicated that the accused had responded well to treatment and was no longer dangerous to others. Furthermore it suggested that a long stay in prison would impede his total recovery. Nevertheless, the Court expressed its view that the original sentences were inadequate in that they failed to sufficiently take into account the aspect of deterrence to others.[102]

(ii) With a Recommendation for Treatment

Where an offender has been assessed as both dangerous to the public and in need of psychiatric treatment, Canadian courts have traditionally given precedence to the need for public protection and treated the accused's mental rehabilitation as a matter of secondary concern. While the priorities here seem faultless, they are, paradoxically, of no help whatsoever in determining the appropriate disposition for disordered offenders who have not committed offences demanding life imprisonment on tariff principles alone. Illustrative of this problem is the case of *R. v. Wallace,*[103] an instance where the Ontario Court of Appeal was

---

[100] [1971] 1 O.R. 705.

[101] (1972), 15 Crim. L.Q. 13.

[102] See also *R. v. Gunnell* (1966), 50 Cr. App. R. 242 at pp. 245-6 where the trial judge refused to issue a hospital order and sentenced the accused to life imprisonment instead saying: "... crimes of this kind ... must ... be dealt with in such a way as to make plain that the law is concerned and ever will be concerned to protect people who suffer as you caused those women to suffer by these quite appalling sexual attacks that you made upon them. Punishment must be an element in this case, and that punishment can only be achieved by imprisonment."

[103] (1973), 11 C.C.C. (2d) 95.

called upon to assess the correctness of a 10-year sentence imposed on a paranoid schizophrenic for the offences of robbery and assault. Acknowledging the fact that the accused's amenability to treatment would decrease with the amount of time spent in prison, Brooke J.A. pondered:

> "If the primary object of the criminal law is the protection of society, how apt is this sentence? Perhaps such a sentence as this one offers immediate protection to society but it clearly does little to protect it for the future."[104]

In these circumstances the accused's mental condition was considered as a factor which could reduce the term of imprisonment from that which might normally have been imposed. Substituting a sentence of four years for the original ten, Brooke J.A. said:

> "It is plain that a sentence the length of that imposed was very much more severe punishment for this man than for a normal person, because of the terror that he experiences, the danger of self-destruction[105] and the loss of amenability to treatment...

> "The best future protection for society lies in imposing a sentence which will make the appellant's rehabilitation probable..."[106]

Surprisingly few Canadian courts have recognized the dilemma articulated by Brooke J.A. In certain cases this fact is no doubt attributable to the nature of mental disorder and type of offence concerned. Where, for example, the accused is considered incurably deranged and has been convicted of an offence punishable by life imprisonment, there is no compunction about imposing the maximum sentence. In *R. v. Hill*[107] Jessup J.A. reasoned that:

> "When an accused has been convicted of a serious crime in itself calling for a substantial sentence and when he suffers from some mental or personality disorder rendering him a danger to the community but not subjecting him to confinement in a mental institution and when it is uncertain when, if ever, the accused will be cured of his affliction, in my opinion the appropriate sentence is one of life. Such a sentence, in such circumstances, amounts to an indefinite sentence under which the parole board can release him to the community when it is satisfied, upon adequate psychiatric examination, it is in the interest of the accused and the community for him to return to society."[108]

---

[104] *Ibid.*, at p. 100.
[105] For an interesting discussion concerning the risk of mentally abnormal offenders committing suicide see Blair, "Life Sentence then Suicide" (1971), 11 Med. Sci. and the Law 162.
[106] *Supra,* footnote 103 at p. 100.
[107] (1974), 15 C.C.C. (2d) 145 (Ont C.A.); affd 23 C.C.C. (2d) 321 (S.C.C.); see also *Hill v. The Queen (No. 2)* (1975), 25 C.C.C. (2d) 6 (S.C.C.).
[108] At pp. 147-8. The rule here was followed in *R. v. Haig* (1974), 26 C.R.N.S. 247 (Ont.

Once a court has imposed a sentence of life imprisonment it has effectively extinguished any dependency of public safety upon the rehabilitation of the offender. If oriented toward reform, however, the court may
choose to deal with the matter by a simple recommendation that the
accused receive whatever pychiatric help may be available to him while
in prison. Thus in *Hill* Jessup J.A. said:

"... I would strongly recommend that the appellant receive psychiatric treatment and I would request the Crown to forward a copy of
this judgment to the Solicitor-General and to the penitentiary
authorities."[109]

Similarly, in *R. v. Leech*[110] the Alberta Supreme Court (Trial Division)
said:

"Whilst under sentence the accused, though not legally insane,
should be considered as a suitable patient for psychiatric care ..."[111]

Because the psychiatric facilities in Canadian prisons are notoriously
inadequate,[112] some judges may feel obligated to recommend that the
offender be transferred under s. 546 of the Criminal Code or s. 19 of the
Penitentiary Act[113] to a provincial mental hospital outside the prison
itself.[114] In *R. v. Robinson*[115] the Ontario Court of Appeal imposed a sentence of eight years' imprisonment "for the express purpose that this
man receive at once such treatment as may be available to him at Penetang or such other hospital for treating persons with mental disorders as
may be available ...".[116] The problem with this recommendation, as with
the others cited, is that it is not in any way binding upon the penitentiary authorities. It therefore offers no assurance that the offender will

---

C.A.). The reasoning is similar to that of the English Court of Criminal Appeal in *R. v.
Hodgson* (1967), 52 Cr. App. R. 113.

[109] *Supra,* footnote 107 at p. 148.

[110] (1973), 21 C.R.N.S. 1.

[111] *Ibid.,* at p. 12.

[112] In 1969 the Ouimet Committee reported, *op. cit.* footnote 89, at p. 237 that "the cross-
Canada picture indicates that most psychiatric services within correctional systems are
minimal and leave much to be desired."

[113] R.S.C. 1970, c. P-6:
"19(1) The Minister may, with the approval of the Governor in Council, enter into
an agreement with the government of any province to provide for the custody, in a
mental hospital or other appropriate institution operated by the province, of persons
who, having been sentenced or committed to a penitentiary, are found to be mentally
ill or mentally defective at any time during confinement in penitentiary."

[114] See Chapter 10 *post* at pp. 290-2.

[115] (1974), 19 C.C.C. (2d) 193.

[116] *Ibid.,* at pp. 198-9. Likewise in *R. v. Bradbury* (1973), 23 C.R.N.S. 293 at p. 298 (Ont.
C.A.) the court said:
"In dismissing the appeal, the members of this Court wish to bring to the attention
of the penitentiary authorities the repeated statements emanating from the Mental
Health Centre at Penetanguishene that Bradbury requires long-term treatment in a
controlled setting such as can be provided by the Mental Health Centre and that the
Mental Health Centre is prepared to accept him for treatment."

receive treatment.[117]

When a disordered offender is convicted of an offence not punishable by life imprisonment his abnormality may modify the court's application of normal tariff principles.[118] In *R. v. Fisher,*[119] for instance, the court considered mental abnormality a factor which could quite properly *increase* a sentence's duration from that which the offence's severity alone would have rated. It should be noted, however, that public safety was the premise upon which this decision rested. Where sentences are geared toward rehabilitation, a popular proposition is that expressed by Norval Morris, namely, *"power over a criminal's life should not be taken in excess of that which would be taken were his reform not considered as one of our purposes."*[120] As Morris has himself pointed out,[121] subscription to this philosophy is by no means universal. Kadish has, for instance, asked: "... why should the rehabilitative purpose be subordinated to the deterrent, vindicatory and incapacitative purposes ...?".[122] Furthermore, if one accepts, as did Brooke J.A. in *Wallace,* that the rehabilitation of dangerous offenders and the protection of society are inseparable goals, one may justify the lengthening of sentences for rehabilitative purposes by applying the reasoning used in *R. v. Fisher.* Indeed, this is what seems to have been done in *R. v. Bradbury.*[123] There the trial judge imposed the maximum sentence of 14 years' imprisonment on a charge of wounding where the accused had been diagnosed as suffering from a "character disorder". Reliance was apparently placed on the opinion of the reporting psychiatrist that a very lengthy period of treatment would be necessary before the accused ceased to be dangerous to others. In dismissing the accused's appeal against sentence, the Ontario Court of Appeal held that in addition to the nature of the offence, the "urgent need for a protracted period of treatment"[124] and "the need for protection of the public"[125] justified the sentence.

In actual practice, therefore, it seems that Morris' proposition has been rather loosely adhered to. In its strictest sense, it suggests that the rehabilitative ideal (though it might give rise to a recommendation for curative therapy) should play *no part whatsoever* in determining the *length* of sentence to be imposed. But as *Bradbury* suggests, the courts

---

[117] See Chapter 10 *post* at p. 291.

[118] Thomas, *Principles of Sentencing,* at p. 272.

[119] (1975), 23 C.C.C. (2d) 449 (Ont. C.A.). See also *R. v. Luknowsky* (1976), 19 Crim. L.Q. 18 (B.C.C.A.).

[120] Morris and Howard, *Studies in Criminal Law* (Oxford, Clarendon, 1964) at p. 175.

[121] Morris, *The Future of Imprisonment* (Chicago, University of Chicago Press, 1974) at p. 18.

[122] Review of Morris and Howard, *Studies in Criminal Law* (1965), 78 Harv. L. Rev. 907 at p. 908. A staunch believer in the primacy of rehabilitation is A. A. Bartholomew. He has complained, *op. cit.* footnote 20 at p. 336, that "... it is almost impossible to undertake psychotherapy with a man on a fixed 'tariff' sentence: apart from the rigidity of a fixed sentence, the tariff invariably is inappropriate to the particular man and his needs. Would anyone expect to be admitted to, say, the surgical ward of a hospital for a fixed period; the period being decided upon in terms of the 'commonest time'?"

[123] (1973), 23 C.R.N.S. 293 (Ont. C.A.).

[124] *Ibid.,* at p. 297.

[125] *Ibid.*

have apparently adopted a more flexible rule. If indeed a governing formula is to be found, perhaps it is that put forward by the English Court of Appeal in *R. v. Moylan*[126] where it said:

">... the court must first determine what are the limits of a proper sentence in respect of the offences charged. Within those limits it may be perfectly proper to increase the sentence in order to enable a cure to be undertaken whilst the prisoner is in prison. But on the authority of *Ford* ... it is clear that it is not correct to increase the sentence above that within the appropriate range for the offence itself merely in order to provide an opportunity for cure."[127]

The Court further stated that it would not consider itself bound by this rule in cases where the protection of the public was involved. Also worth noting is the decision of the same court in *R. v. Turner*[128] where an exception was made to the general rule that the effect of remission must be disregarded when calculating the correct length of sentence. It was reasoned that "when one is considering not punishment but considering reform or mental treatment, something which is in the interests of the prisoner, it would be obviously right for this court to take remission into consideration."[129]

D. HOSPITAL ORDERS?

In determining the length of imprisonment to which a disordered offender should be sentenced, many judges find it virtually impossible to ignore the recommendations made in psychiatric reports. As a result, those judges who are truly reform orientated find a way of scaling their sentences to the length prescribed for treatment purposes, while at the same time paying lip service to Professor Morris' rule. A dramatic example of this tactic in operation may be seen in the recent case of *R. v. Boomhower*.[130] There an offender who had been convicted of discharging a firearm with intent to endanger life was remanded to the Penetanguishene Mental Health Centre for pre-sentence examination. Upon receiving evidence that the offender suffered from a personality disorder which would require up to five years of intensive psychotherapy, the trial judge imposed a sentence of seven years' imprisonment. The offender was thereafter certified under the Ontario Mental Health Act. On appeal against this sentence, Martin J.A. of the Ontario Court of Appeal acknowledged that the learned trial judge had no doubt arranged for the accused's indefinite certification, yet dismissed the appeal on the following grounds:

---

[126] (1969), 53 Cr. App. R. 590.
[127] *Ibid.*, at p. 594.
[128] (1967), 51 Cr. App. R. 72.
[129] *Ibid.*, at p. 73.
[130] (1975), 20 C.C.C. (2d) 89 (Ont. C.A.).

"In our view the learned trial Judge went to great pains to deal with this youthful appellant in a very positive and enlightened manner designed to correct the personality disorder from which he suffers and thereby offer the best long term protection to the public. At the same time the sentence which he imposed upon the appellant does not exceed what is an appropriate sentence in this case, having regard to the very serious nature of the offence committed, apart altogether from the appellant's need for treatment."[131]

The reasoning here demonstrates some pretty fancy footwork on the part of Martin J.A. While the seven-year term (technically the only sentence imposed) may well have been justified by the gravity of the offence alone, it is clear that trial court took power over the offender's life "in excess of that which would [have been] taken were his reform not considered."

Under the English system of hospital orders an express statutory authority is provided whereby courts may accomplish, in a less makeshift fashion, the ends sought in *Boomhower*. Subsection 60(1) of that country's Mental Health Act 1959[132] enables judges to order a mentally disordered offender's admission to and detention in a hospital.[133] This power is exercisable: (1) over persons convicted of offences other than those for which a penalty is fixed by law, or, (2) in the case of magistrates' courts, over persons convicted of summary conviction offences punishable by imprisonment. The authorization of all hospital orders is conditional upon the following criteria being met:

"(a) the court is satisfied, on the written or oral evidence of two medical practitioners ...
   (i)   that the offender is suffering from mental illness, psychopathic disorder, subnormality or severe subnormality, and
   (ii) that the mental disorder is of a nature or degree which warrants the detention of patient in a hospital for medical treatment ... ; and
"(b) the court is of opinion, having regard to all the circumstances including the nature of the offence and the character and the antecedents of the offender, and to the other available methods of dealing with him, that the most suitable method of disposing of the case is by means of an order under this section ..."

Subsection 60(2) of the Act further allows magistrates' courts to make hospital orders *without* first convicting accused persons if satisfied both that they suffer from mental illness or severe abnormality and that they are in fact guilty of the offences with which they have been charged.

A key feature of the English hospital order is that it may not be com-

---

[131] *Ibid.*, at p. 93.
[132] 1959 (U.K.), c. 72.
[133] The fact that this cannot be done in Canada is demonstrated by the case of *R. v. Petrov*, [1973] B.N. 57 (Ont. C.A.).

bined with any other sentence, such as a fixed term of imprisonment. It does not run for any specified period and, although it lapses automatically at the end of 12 months, it may be renewed indefinitely. Furthermore, it may be coupled with a restriction order preventing the patient from being discharged without the permission of the Home Secretary. In proposing what it has called a system of "hospital permits", the Canadian Committee on Corrections has expressly rejected these elements of the English model. As its name suggests, the permit system places the final power over the patient/prisoner in the hands of the hospital rather than the court. In the words of the Committee:

> "It was felt that hospital officials should be able to determine who, based upon appropriate admission criteria, would be admitted to and discharged from psychiatric facilities. . . . Where it is indicated that an offender would benefit from treatment in a psychiatric facility, the court should be empowered to authorize placement of the individual in such a facility. This placement should be conditional upon the circumstances being such that his eligibility otherwise met the terms of the mental health legislation in the particular province involved."[134]

Preferring that the permits be combined with relatively short sentences of imprisonment, the Committee has recommended that the period of hospitalization not exceed the length of sentence *unless* the patient/prisoner is continued as an involuntary patient under provincial mental health legislation.

If adopted, the Committee's permit proposal would do little other than to add a Parliamentary blessing to what may currently be achieved in an unofficial manner. Indeed, the court in *Boomhower* remarked that:

> ". . . the learned trial Judge has utilized existing provincial mental health legislation and facilities, and arrangements made between the provincial mental health authority and the penitentiary services to achieve a result similar to that envisaged by the system of hospital permits recommended by the Report of the Canadian Committee on Corrections . . ."[135]

---

[134] Ouimet, *op. cit.* footnote 89, at pp. 235-6.
[135] *Supra,* footnote 130 at p. 93. The fact that this result can be achieved is apparently not known to all judges, however. In *R. v. Robinson* (1974), 19 C.C.C. (2d) 193 at p. 198 Brooke J.A. of the Ontario Court of Appeal expressed his opinion that the inadequacy of a recommendation that the offender be transferred from prison to a mental hospital "points up the importance of the Committee's recommendation that hospital permits ought to be available". In the case of *R. v. H.,* reported in the Toronto Telegram on September 20, 1962 the judge "bemoaned the fact that there are no laws which would allow him to send the boy to a centre for psychiatric treatment, but said he would recommend that [H] get the treatment he needs." Commenting on this case, Swadron, in his book *Detention of the Mentally Disordered* (Toronto, Butterworths, 1964) at p. 418, has asserted: "The most a sentencing Court can do in Canada under the present law is recommend that the prisoner receive psychiatric treatment."

V. Conclusions

The principle that "like cases should be treated alike" would seem to be nothing more than an empty platitude in the case of mentally disordered offenders.[136] A survey of recent Canadian decisions reveals marked disparities between the sentences imposed on persons who have committed the same crimes and who apparently suffer from the same disorders. As demonstrated by the *Jones*[137] and *Allen*[138] cases, a pedophile convicted of indecent assault may on his first offence receive a suspended sentence with probation or, alternatively, a term of imprisonment — depending on the trial judge he has drawn.[139] A homosexual convicted of gross indency may be fined as in *R. v. Five Accused Persons*[140] and *R. v. Boisvert and Lupien,*[141] may be placed on probation with psychiatric treatment as in *R. v. Holte and Landry;*[142] *R. v. La Chance and Bliss;*[143] *R. v. Desjarlais and Ferguson,*[144] and *R. v. Hermann and Singer,*[145] or may be imprisoned as in *R. v. Marshall;*[146] *R. v. Turpin,*[147] and *R. v. DeSeve.*[148] A psychopath sentenced to life imprisonment may be recommended for transfer to a mental hospital as in *R. v. Robinson*[149] or *R. v. Bradbury,*[150] or he may be considered beyond salvation as in *R. v. Head.*[151]

It is obvious that not all judges rely upon psychiatry as an aid to sentencing. In studying the frequency with which psychiatric reports were used by Ontario magistrates, Hogarth found that such information was requested in only 4.3 per cent of the cases sampled.[152] Though one would have thought this figure to correspond roughly with the number of offenders perceived as mentally abnormal, it was discovered that a great many magistrates refrained as a matter of policy from seeking psychiatric information even where evidence of mental disorder existed.[153] Still, it would appear that most sentencing judges who suspect mental disorder

---

[136] This may indeed be the case with all types of offenders. See the studies cited by Hood and Sparks, *Key Issues in Criminology* (New York, McGraw-Hill, 1970) at pp. 141-70.

[137] (1956), 115 C.C.C. 273 (Ont. C.A.), discussed, *supra.*

[138] (1954), 108 C.C.C. 239 (B.C.C.A.), discussed, *supra.*

[139] The *Jones* and *Allen* cases have been compared by Jaffary, *Sentencing of Adults in Canada* (Toronto, University of Toronto Press, 1963) at pp. 21-2.

[140] (1961), 4 Crim L.Q. 124 (Man. Prov. Ct.), discussed, *supra.*

[141] Unreported, but cited by Saunders, "Sentencing of Homosexual Offenders" (1967-68), 10 Crim. L.Q. 25 and discussed, *supra.*

[142] *Ibid.*

[143] *Ibid.*

[144] *Ibid.*

[145] *Ibid.*

[146] Unreported, but cited by Saunders, "Sentencing of Homosexual Offenders" (1967-68), 10 Crim. L.Q. 25 at p. 27.

[147] *Ibid.*

[148] *Ibid.,* at p. 28.

[149] (1974), 19 C.C.C. (2d) 193 (Ont. C.A.).

[150] (1973), 23 C.R.N.S. 293 (Ont. C.A.), discussed, *supra.*

[151] (1970), 1 C.C.C. (2d) 436 (Sask. C.A.).

[152] Hogarth, *Sentencing as a Human Process,* at p. 240.

[153] *Ibid.,* at p. 238.

do request psychiatric reports.[154] As the cases of *Jones* and *Murphy* [155] indicate, however, the information contained in such reports may not always influence the judge in determining sentence. Even where it is relied upon, the result may be the imposition of sentences which involve no element of psychiatric therapy whatsoever.[156]

In all probability, those judges who do in fact impose psychotherapeutic sentences act on the basis of certain fundamental assumptions about mental disorder and psychiatry. The first is that the accused suffers from a mental "illness" which is capable of being "diagnosed". In this regard it must be stated that the reliability of modern psychiatric diagnoses is a matter of considerable controversy. While sceptics have attacked them for their "gross unreliability",[157] zealots have hailed them as being "as accurate as those in tuberculosis, communicable disease, or other illness."[158] With respect, this latter view seems the less plausible of the two. The fact that psychiatrists frequently disagree in their clinical judgments is one well known to members of that profession and to lawyers and judges as well.[159] However, the reason for this lack of consensus is not entirely clear. Of the several possible explanations which have been offered, one is the existence of the various schools of thought which have developed in the field;[160] divergent clinical judgments may be the result of differing theoretical bases. Another explanation is the susceptibility of each doctor's observations to subjective coloration;[161] individual personalities and experiental backgrounds may account for differences in diagnosis even amongst members of the same school of thought. Perhaps the most compelling explanation is that offered by Thomas Szasz, name-

---

[154] *Ibid.*

[155] *R. v. Jones* (1971), 3 C.C.C. (2d) 153 (Ont. C.A.); *R. v. Murphy* (1972), 15 Crim. L.Q. 13 (Ont. C.A.).

[156] See *R. v. Fisher* (1975), 23 C.C.C. (2d) 449 (Ont. C.A.) and *R. v. Doucet*, [1971] 1 O.R. 705 (C.A.).

[157] Hakeem, "A Critique of the Psychiatric Approach to Crime and Correction" (1958), 23 Law and Contemp. Problems 650 at p. 666.

[158] Bennett, Hargrove and Engle, *The Practice of Psychiatry in General Hospitals* (1956) at p. 91, quoted by Hakeem at p. 662.

[159] See Hakeem, at pp. 660-8; Campbell, "Sentencing: The Use of Psychiatric Information and Presentence Reports" (1972), 60 Ky. L.J. 285 at pp. 313-5; and Beck, "Reliability of Psychiatric Diagnosis: A Study of Consistency of Clinical Judgments and Ratings" (1962), 119 Am. J. Psychiatry 351 where psychiatrists who participated in a study were found to be unanimous in their diagnoses only slightly more than half of the time. But see Overholser, *The Psychiatrist and the Law* (1953) at p. 23, quoted by Hakeem, at p. 662, where it is asserted that "There is general agreement among psychiatrists upon the essential facts and the significance of words and actions, although there are minor differences in theory. The differences and disagreements are much exaggerated by the critics, and constitute one of the alleged reasons for the reluctance of the legal profession to accept any more readily than they do psychiatric concepts and teachings."

[160] Roberts, *op. cit.* footnote 13, at p. 244. But see Watson, "Untying the Knots: The Cross-Examination of the Psychiatric Expert Witness" in Sugarman, *Examining the Medical Expert* (Ann Arbor, Mich., Institute of Continuing Legal Education, 1969) at p. 16, where the author has stated that since today's psychiatric theories are all genetic in concept, the differences between Freudian and Jungian background are really inconsequential.

[161] Diamond and Louisell, "The Psychiatrist as an Expert Witness: Some Ruminations and Speculations" (1965), 63 Mich. L. Rev. 1335 at p. 1341.

ly, that there is in fact no such thing as mental illness to begin with. How can anyone diagnose a disease which does not exist? Szasz's theory is simply that "Strictly speaking . . . disease or illness can affect only the body. Hence, there can be no such thing as mental illness. The term 'mental illness' is a metaphor."[162]

But even the non-existence of mental illness should not in itself remove an offender from the ambit of psychiatric intervention. Although few would disagree as to psychiatry's ability to alter human behaviour, a more important question is whether psychiatry can alter behaviour for the better (*i.e.,* affect a "cure" for the alleged illness). This brings us to our second assumption, namely, that psychiatry can in fact do just that. As Nigel Walker has noted,[163] the effectiveness of present-day psychotherapeutic techniques is a hotly debated issue. Halleck, among others, has observed that "In spite of the enormous effort that has gone into treatment of the mentally ill, there is no scientific proof of the effectiveness of psychotherapy."[164] Ardent anti-psychotherapists such as H.J. Eysenck have cited studies indicating that persons suffering from certain disorders are as likely to recover spontaneously as be cured by psychotherapy.[165] Halleck has questioned the significance of such findings, however, by pointing out that terms such as "cure" and "psychotherapy" are ambiguous and hard to define. He has written:

> "The problem with evaluating psychotherapy in the correctional setting is not only a lack of precision in defining what changes we are looking for but also an unjustified carelessness in deciding what is to be called psychotherapy. There is an unfortunate tendency to label any conversation which takes place between a professional and an offender as psychotherapy. We can hardly expect the offender who receives five to fifty hours of therapy with an untrained psychiatric resident or social worker to respond in the same way as a wealthy neurotic who receives 500 to a thousand hours of therapy from a highly skilled psychoanalyst."[166]

Although he has not cited the evidence being relied upon, Walker has concluded that "there is still more support for the claim that [psychotherapy] is effective . . ."[167] in the treatment of certain mental disorders. In all likelihood, those judges who impose sentences which involve psychotherapy subscribe to this view.

Implicit as well in the psychotherapeutic sentence is another very crucial assumption: that the enforced treatment of mental disorder is

---

[162] Szasz, *The Myth of Mental Illness*, rev. ed. (New York, Harper and Row, 1974) at p. ix. The author asserts at p. 37 that even organic illnesses which are said to affect the mind are not mental illnesses. Rather, they fall into the class of "bodily diseases which, by impairing the functioning of the human body as a machine, create difficulties in social adaptation...".

[163] *Sentencing in a Rational Society,* at p. 111.

[164] *Psychiatry and the Dilemmas of Crime,* at p. 338.

[165] Eysenck, *Crime and Personality* (London, Paladin, 1970) at pp. 151-2.

[166] At p. 339.

[167] At p. 111.

morally and ethically sound. Once again, however, the consensus on this point is far from unanimous. Opinions range from complete endorsement of the coerced cure (with apparent disregard for the nature of the offence involved)[168] to utter rejection of all non-contractual psychiatric treatment.[169]

What then is the proper role for the psychiatrist in the sentencing process? While some commentators subscribe to the view that "it is in recommending disposition where the psychiatrist ... can most helpfully assist the court ...",[170] others have concluded that psychiatric evidence should not be admissible in court.[171] Although the radical nature (and questionable wisdom) of this suggestion makes its implementation unlikely within the near future, it is submitted that for the present psychiatric power must at least be limited in a number of ways. Furthermore, the judge who wishes to impose a psychotherapeutic sentence should be restricted by certain minimum rules of conduct. With these purposes in mind, the following recommendations are offered. They are not intended as a comprehensive guide to the sentencing of mentally disordered offenders, but merely represent a skeleton list of suggestions which come to mind as a direct result of the preceding discussion. Only recommendations 1 and 9 would seem susceptible of legislative implementation. The rest must remain as formulations of suggested policy.

1. Subsections 543(2), 543(2.1) and section 608.2 of the Criminal Code should be repealed. In their place the following remand provision should be substituted:[172]

"(1) A court, judge or magistrate may, when of the opinion, supported by the evidence or, where the prosecutor and the accused consent, by the report in writing, of at least one duly qualified medical practitioner, that there is reason to believe that a person who appears before him charged with or convicted of an offence, suffers from mental disorder, remand the person, by order in writing, to a psychiatric facility for examination for a period not exceeding thirty days.

"(2) The term 'mental disorder', when used in this section, means any organic disease which affects the brain or any mental disability.

"(3) Each of the following, and *only* the following, shall be deemed to constitute sufficient reason to believe that the person being remanded for psychiatric examination 'suffers from mental disorder' within the meaning of subsection (1):

    (a) the person has been charged with or convicted of an offence involving serious violence against a member or members of his own family;

---

[168] Rappeport, *op. cit.* footnote 65, p. 161.

[169] See generally Szasz, *The Manufacture of Madness* (New York, Dell, 1970).

[170] Slovenko, "Psychiatry, Criminal Law, and the Role of the Psychiatrist" (1963), Duke L.J. 395 at p. 407.

[171] Hakeem, *op. cit.* footnote 157, at p. 681.

[172] Because the sections named apply to remands before verdict as well as before sentence,

    (b) the person has been charged with or convicted of an offence under sections 143, 145, 148, 149, 150, 153, 155 or 157;

    (c) the person has been charged with or convicted of an offence the commission of which exhibited a bizarre or irrational quality,

    (d) the person has exhibited a bizarre or irrational manner of behaviour in the courtroom.

"(4) Notwithstanding subsection (3), where a person is remanded under this section the court, judge or magistrate shall, in the order in writing referred to in subsection (1) specify in detail the circumstances which prompted him to remand the person for psychiatric examination.

"(5) Where the person being remanded for psychiatric examination under this section has not been taken into custody or has been released by virtue of any provision contained in Part XIV, the court, judge or magistrate shall stipulate in the order in writing referred to in subsection (2) that the accused be examined as an outpatient and that he not be confined against his will in the psychiatric facility for any period of time in excess of that required for actual examination.

"(6) A court, judge or magistrate shall not make an order under this section until he ascertains from the senior physician of a psychiatric facility that the services of the psychiatric facility are available to the person to be named in the order.

"(7) Where an examination is made under this section, the senior physician of the psychiatric facility shall report in writing to the judge as to the mental condition of the person.

"(8) Where a report is filed with the court under subsection (7), the clerk of the court shall forthwith cause a copy of the report to be provided to the accused or his counsel and to the prosecutor."

It should be noted that many of the safeguards contained in this provision could, of course, be circumvented by using the remand provision contained in provincial mental health legislation. This problem can only be solved by repealing provincial remand provisions.

2. Psychiatric reports should not contain recommendations as to what sentence should be imposed.

Although Bartholomew may have been correct in his assertion[173] that the courts do in fact seek recommendations concerning sentence, such intentions on the part of the judges remain something less than admirable. Szasz has argued that the judges who use psychiatrists in this fashion do so in an attempt to escape responsibility and alleviate their own feelings of guilt.[174] Moreover, the result is to place the psychiatrist in an

---

the wording of the recommended provision allows for the provision's application in identical circumstances.

[173] At pp. 149-50.

[174] Szasz, "Some Observations on the Relationship Between Psychiatry and the Law"

unduly onerous position; in effect, he becomes the sentencing judge.[175] This status may create additional problems, should the reporting psychiatrist ultimately be the one responsible for the offender's treatment; it is not the ideal basis for a therapeutic relationship.

3. Psychiatric reports should confine themselves to diagnoses and assessments of treatability.

Regardless of the dispute concerning reliability of psychiatric diagnoses and effectiveness of psychiatric treatment, these are the only two areas in which psychiatrists claim to have expertise. For this reason, gratuitous opinions on the subjects of non-psychiatric punishment (as opposed to "punitherapy") and general deterrance (see *R. v. Doucet*[176]) are both valueless and prejudicial.

4. "Dangerousness" should be rejected as a basis for imposing sentences of imprisonment.

This recommendation is one made by Norval Morris. The concept of dangerousness, he has argued, "presupposes a capacity to predict future criminal behaviour . . ."[177] far beyond the technical ability which anyone (including psychiatrists) presently possesses. Therefore, he has stated:

> "The distressing moral problem inherent in this situation can be stated as 'whom shall we trust?' For the time being my reply is 'nobody'. I believe that an effective and just system of criminal justice can be constructed without reliance on *increasing* our power over offenders on the grounds of their predicted dangerousness. Within the ambit of power defined by other purposes (most of them retributive), we must frequently relate sentences and parole decisions to our best judgments of the offender's dangerousness; but we should not rely on such inadequate judgments to raise the maxima of punishment."[178]

5. The need for psychiatric treatment should never increase the length of sentence from that which normal tariff principles dictate.

This, again, is Morris' proposition.[179] Strictly speaking, the length of sentence should be determined entirely independently from considerations concerning the length and type of treatment judged appropriate for the offender's disorder. Once this has been done, the offender's mental state should be considered in *mitigation* of sentence only.

6. The effect of remission should never be considered when calculating the correct length of sentence.

(1956), 75 A.M.A. Archives of Neurology and Psychiatry 297, cited by Campbell at p. 311, footnote 150.

[175] Szasz, *The Manufacture of Madness*, at p. 56 has asserted that the mere statement of psychiatric diagnosis is itself a form of sentencing.

[176] [1971] 1 O.R. 705 (C.A.).

[177] *Future of Imprisonment*, at p. 62.

[178] Morris, "Psychiatry and the Dangerous Criminal" (1967-68), 41 So. Cal. L. Rev. 514 at pp. 532-3.

[179] *Supra*, p. 250.

As the case of *R. v. Turner*[180] demonstrates, an exception to the general rule has been made where the offender is considered to be in need of psychiatric treatment. Courts who wish to tailor the length of sentence to correspond to the period prescribed for effective treatment allow for the offender's parole eligibility. The reason offered by the English Court of Appeal for doing this was that psychotherapy was obviously "in the interests of the prisoner."[181] With respect, this is insufficient justification. In the words of Thomas Szasz, it "ignores the possibility that the alleged sufferer ... might prefer to be left alone ...".[182]

7. Where psychiatric treatment is considered appropriate, the type of treatment employed should be no more drastic than the seriousness of the offence merits.

This recommendation is similar to one proposed by Kittrie in his Therapeutic Bill of Rights. In s. 8 he has stated that "Any compulsory treatment must be the least required reasonably to protect society."[183] It is submitted that this section does not go far enough in safeguarding the disordered offender against disproportionate curative treatment. Under Kittrie's proposal, a relatively innocuous fetishist could be subjected to radical behaviour therapy if that was the only way to protect women from having their panties stolen from their clotheslines. It is contended, however, that prolonged treatment with electroshock, emetics, psychotropic drugs or other aversive stimuli would be too severe a penalty for the crime of petty theft.

Because psychiatric treatment is often hard to distinguish from punishment, the above recommendation may be thought of as another expression of the principle of "limited retribution". The principle, in Walker's words, is that *"the unpleasantness of a penal measure must not exceed the limit that is appropriate to the culpability of the offence"*.[184] The recommendation herein stated may perhaps more accurately be referred to as one of "limited reformation"; it seeks to protect the offender from excessive rehabilitation whether that process be unpleasant or enjoyable.

8. Where possible, probationary psychiatric treatment should be voluntary.

Ideally, disordered persons who are placed on probation should be *advised* to undergo therapy (as in the cases of *R. v. H.*[185] and *R. v. Allen*[186]) rather than having treatment made a formal condition.

9. The Criminal Code should be amended to provide for a system of hospital orders.[187]

---

[180] (1969), 53 Cr. App. R. 590, discussed, *supra*.
[181] *Ibid.*
[182] Szasz, *The Manufacture of Madness*, at p. 16.
[183] Kittrie,*The Right to be Different* (Baltimore, Pelican, 1973) at p. 404.
[184] Walker, *op. cit.* footnote 6, at p. 30.
[185] (1965-66), 8 Crim. L.Q. 11.
[186] (1954), 108 C.C.C. 239 (B.C.C.A.).
[187] This was suggested by the Law Reform Commission of Canada, *Working Paper: The*

The provision should look something like this:

"(1) Where a person convicted of an offence is sentenced to imprisonment the court shall, upon application, hear evidence as to whether the offender is suitable for a hospital order.

"(2) Where the following conditions are satisfied, that is to say —

    (a) the court is satisfied, on the written or oral evidence of at least two psychiatrists

        (i) that the offender is suffering from mental disorder, and

        (ii) that the mental disorder is of a nature or degree which warrants the detention of the offender in a hospital for psychiatric treatment;

    (b) the offender has consented in writing to an order under this section;

the court may by order authorize his admission to and detention in such hospital as may be specified in the order.

"(3) An order for the admission of an offender to a hospital (herein referred to as a hospital order) shall not be made under this section unless the court is satisifed that arrangements have been made for the admission of the offender to that hospital in the event of such an order being made by the court, and for his admission thereto within a period of twenty-eight days beginning with the date of the making of such an order.

"(4) A hospital order shall be sufficient authority —

    (a) for a peace officer or any other person directed to do so by the court to convey the patient to the hospital specified in the order within a period of twenty-eight days; and

    (b) for the managers of the hospital to admit him at any time within that period and thereafter to detain him in accordance with the provisions of this section.

"(5) No person detained in a hospital under the authority of a hospital order shall be discharged or transferred therefrom prior to the expiration of his sentence unless parolled or transferred to a correctional institution in accordance with subsections (8) and (9) of this section.

"(6) No person shall be detained in hospital under the authority of a hospital order for a period of time longer than the duration of his sentence.

"(7) Nothing in this Part shall be deemed to affect the offender's eligibility for parole.[188]

"(8) An offender who has been made the subject of a hospital order may at any time request that the balance of his sentence be served in a correctional institution, in which case effect shall forth-

---

Criminal Process and Mental Disorder (Ottawa, Information Canada, 1975) at p. 47.
[188] *Ibid.*

with be given to that request.[189]

"(9) The hospital may, if it considers the offender to be no longer suitable for treatment, request that the balance of the offender's sentence be served in a correctional institution, in which case effect shall forthwith be given to that request.[190]

"(10) An offender serving his sentence under a hospital order is deemed to be serving his sentence in prison for the purposes of escapes and being at large without lawful excuse.[191]

"(11) A court's decision to impose or not to impose a hospital order may be appealed in the same manner as any other sentence of the court."[192]

This provision is basically an embodiment of what can already be achieved informally.[193] As mentioned earlier, many judges are either unaware of the possibility of such procedure, or else wary of its propriety. The purpose behind codification would simply be to alert judges that such an alternative exists. The key element of the provision set out above is the consent of the offender (para. (2)(b)). If an offender himself wishes to be hospitalized rather than imprisoned, and the court is agreeable, there would seem to be no good reason why he should not be. Unfortunately, the enactment of this provision would not preclude an offender from being involuntarily hospitalized by the informal means discussed earlier. Provincial mental health legislation, unless amended, could still be used as a means of circumvention.

One final word. It is by no means suggested that hospital orders, whether consensual or not, are an effective means of dealing with disordered offenders. From the standpoint of repeated hospitalization and recidivism, the English system has been described as "not spectacularly successful".[194]

---

[189] *Ibid.*
[190] *Ibid.*
[191] *Ibid.*
[192] *Ibid.*, at p. 48.
[193] See pp. *supra.*
[194] McCabe, Rollin and Walker, "The Offender and the Mental Health Act" (1964), 4 Med. Sci. and the Law 231 at p. 244.

Chapter 9

Dangerous (Sexual) Offenders

I. Introduction

While it may be true that "no conclusive correlation has been found between mental disorder and dangerous, violent conduct",[1] there is certainly no reason to suppose that disordered offenders are any less dangerous or violent than others who have committed similar offences. This being the case, it seems likely that the mentally ill will continue to contribute their fair share to the class of "dangerous offenders" defined by a recent amendment to the Criminal Code.

Until recently, our law preferred to deal with those offenders it deemed particularly loathsome under two separate headings: habitual offenders and dangerous sexual offenders.[2] Yet a finding that someone fell into either category produced the same result, namely, preventive detention for an indefinite period. With the passage of Bill C-51,[3] Parliament has seen fit to combine the habitual offender and dangerous sexual offender provisions. Being of the point of view that there is in fact no logical reason for separating dangerous sexual offenders from the more general group, it has repealed ss. 687 to 695 of the Criminal Code and replaced them with legislation relating to the sentencing of dangerous offenders generally. The basic provision reads as follows:

"PART XXI
DANGEROUS OFFENDERS
Interpretation

"687. In this Part,
'court' means the court by which an offender in relation to

---

[1] Law Reform Commission of Canada, *Report: The Criminal Process and Mental Disorder (Working Paper 14)* (Information Canada, Ottawa, 1975) at pp. 18-9.
[2] Sections 688 and 689 respectively.
[3] "The Criminal Law Amendment Act, 1977", 1977 (Can.), c. 53, assented to 5 August 1977.

whom an application under this Part is made was convicted, or a superior court of criminal jurisdiction;

'serious personal injury offence' means

(a) an indictable offence (other than high treason, treason, first degree murder or second degree murder) involving

    (i) the use or attempted use of violence against another person, or

    (ii) conduct endangering or likely to endanger the life or safety of another person or inflicting or likely to inflict severe psychological damage upon another person,

and for which the offender may be sentenced to imprisonment for ten years or more, or

(b) an offence mentioned in section 144 (rape) or 145 (attempted rape) or an offence or attempt to commit an offence mentioned in section 146 (sexual intercourse with a female under fourteen or between fourteen and sixteen), 149 (indecent assault on a female), 156 (indecent assault on a male), or 157 (gross indecency).

Dangerous Offenders

"688. Where, upon an application made under this Part following the conviction of a person for an offence but before the offender is sentenced therefor, it is established to the satisfaction of the court

(a) that the offence for which the offender has been convicted is a serious personal injury offence described in paragraph (a) of the definition of that expression in section 687 and the offender constitutes a threat to the life, safety, or physical or mental well-being of other persons on the basis of evidence establishing

    (i) a pattern of repetitive behaviour by the offender, of which the offence for which he has been convicted forms a part, showing a failure to restrain his behaviour and a likelihood of his causing death or injury to other persons, or inflicting severe psychological damage upon other persons, through failure in the future to restrain his behaviour,

    (ii) a pattern of persistent aggressive behaviour by the offender, of which the offence for which he has been convicted forms a part, showing a substantial degree of indifference on the part of the offender as to the reasonably foreseeable consequences to other persons of his behaviour, or

    (iii) any behaviour by the offender, associated with the offence for which he has been convicted, that is of such a brutal nature as to compel the conclusion that his behaviour in the future is unlikely to be inhibited by normal standards of behavioural restraint, or

(b) that the offence for which the offender has been convicted is a serious personal injury offence described in paragraph (b) of the definition of that expression in section 687 and the offender, by his conduct in any sexual matter including that involved in the commission of the offence for which he has been convicted, has shown a failure to control his sexual impulses and a likelihood of his causing injury, pain or other evil to other persons through failure in the future to control his sexual impulses,

the court may find the offender to be a dangerous offender and may thereupon impose a sentence of detention in a penitentiary for an indeterminate period, in lieu of any other sentence that might be imposed for the offence for which the offender has been convicted."

It has been asserted that from a sociological standpoint, there is no reason to suppose that violent sexual offenders owe more to the existence of specifically deviant pathology than to the same "criminogenic factors" of which the non-sexual offender is a product.[4] Moreover, from the standpoint of disposition and treatment there appears to be no sound reason for differentiating between dangerous sexual offenders and dangerous offenders in general, since whatever therapy would ultimately be employed would be substantially the same for both.[5] Nevertheless, the case-law dealing with dangerous sexual offenders has taken a decidedly more psychiatric approach than that dealing with habitual offenders. Principally for this reason, the remainder of this chapter will be devoted to a discussion of the new legislation as it relates to dangerous sexual offenders. As will become apparent, the law has made few real changes in this area, either procedurally or substantively. Despite his change in name, the dangerous sexual offender remains very much a distinct legal entity.

II. The Procedure

The specific sexual offences which may give rise to a dangerous offender application under the new legislation are enumerated in para. 687(b). They include rape, attempted rape, sexual intercourse or attempted sexual intercourse with a female under 14 or between 14 and 16, indecent assault on a female, indecent assault on a male, and gross indecency. Under the former s-s. 689(1) of the Code, the offences of buggery, bestiality, attempted bestiality, attempted indecent assault and attempted gross indecency were included as well. The new provision does not specifically mention these, however, and it would therefore seem that buggery, being punishable by 14 years' imprisonment, is the only offence

---

[4] Spender, "Contribution to the Symposium on Sexual Deviation" (1961), 3 Can. J. Corr. 481 at p. 483.
[5] Guttmacher, "Dangerous Offenders" (1963), Crime and Delinq. 381.

which might be caught by the more general wording in para. (a) of s. 687.

It should be noted that a court has no authority to determine of its own motion whether an individual is a dangerous offender; it is entirely within the discretion of the Crown whether or not an application should be made. With regard to such application, s-s. 689(1) now states:

> "689(1) Where an application under this Part has been made, the Court shall hear and determine the application except that no such application shall be heard unless
> (a) the Attorney General of the province in which the offender was tried has, either before or after the making of the application, consented to the application;[6]
> (b) at least seven days notice has been given to the offender by the prosecutor, following the making of the application, outlining the basis on which it is intended to found the application; and
> (c) a copy of the notice has been filed with the clerk of the court or the magistrate, as the case may be."

Interestingly, this section implies that application can be made only by the prosecutor, and *not* by defence counsel. In *Ponton v. The Queen*,[7] however, it appears that counsel for the accused requested an appeal to have the case remitted for consideration of a term of preventive detention. The accused having been convicted of seduction, indecent assault, gross indecency and distribution of pornagraphic photographs, an appeal against his 12-year sentence was launched on grounds *inter alia* that "'The appellant needs a psychiatrist much more than a gaoler.'"[8] In dismissing the appeal, Galipeault C.J. of the Quebec Queen's Bench (Appeal Side) suggested that the proper course would have been for counsel to have applied to have the accused declared a "criminal sexual psychopath" (under the forerunner of the present provision) at an earlier date. The learned Chief Justice, considering that the accused was not in fact a sexual psychopath, held that there were no grounds for assuming that the trial judge had not received all information necessary for him to pass sentence. Casey J. dissented, saying that a duty rested on the Crown to apply for a finding that the accused was a criminal sexual psychopath where there were strong indications of the fact. Furthermore, he contended that where the Crown failed to make application it was incumbent upon the Court to determine the issue anyway.

It would appear from the Quebec Court of Appeal's recent ruling in *R. v. Bolduc*[9] that, unless objection is raised by defence counsel, a request for a dangerous sexual offender hearing may be made verbally by the Crown attorney at the close of the case for the defence, in which event

---

[6] Under the former provision the consent of the Attorney-General was required only prior to an application for an habitual offender hearing.
[7] (1960), 127 C.C.C. 325 (Que. C.A.).
[8] *Ibid.*, at p. 326.
[9] (1973), 16 C.C.C. (2d) 280.

the requirements of para. 689(1)(b) for service and filing of notice of the application[10] may be dispensed with. In such circumstances, of course, an adjournment would be in order.

When the application is heard, the following provisions are now applicable:

"689(2) An application under this Part shall be heard and determined by the court without a jury.

"(3) For the purposes of an application under this Part, where an offender admits any allegations contained in the notice referred to in paragraph (1)(b), no proof of those allegations is required.

"(4) The production of a document purporting to contain any nomination or consent that may be made or given by the Attorney General under this Part and purporting to be signed by the Attorney General is, in the absence of any evidence to the contrary, proof of that nomination or consent without proof of the signature or the official character of the person appearing to have signed the document.

. . .

"693(1) The offender shall be present at the hearing of the application under this Part and if at the time the application is to be heard

(a) he is confined in a prison, the court may order, in writing, the person having the custody of the accused to bring him before the court; or

(b) he is not confined in a prison, the court shall issue a summons or a warrant to compel the accused to attend before the court and the provisions of Part XIV relating to summons and warrant are applicable *mutatis mutandis.*

"(2) Nowithstanding subsection (1), the court may

(a) cause the offender to be removed and to be kept out of court, where he misconducts himself by interrupting the proceedings so that to continue the proceedings in his presence would not be feasible; or

(b) permit the offender to be out of court during the whole or any part of the hearing on such conditions as the court considers proper."

By s. 691 provision is made for remand of the offender for psychiatric examination.[11]

Upon a finding by the court that the accused is a dangerous offender,

---

[10] For other cases concerning para. 689(1)(b)'s notice requirement see *R. v. Galbraith* (1971), 5 C.C.C. (2d) 37 (B.C.C.A.); leave to appeal to S.C.C. refused 6 C.C.C. (2d) 188n (S.C.C.); *R. v. Bryson*, [1966] 3 C.C.C. 182 (B.C.C.A.); *Re Mark*, [1964] 2 C.C.C. 398 (B.C.); *R. v. Rogers*, [1964] 1 C.C.C. 303 (B.C.); *R. v. Hume, Ex p. Morris*, [1965] 3 C.C.C. 118 (B.C.); revd on other grounds [1965] 3 C.C.C. 349 (C.A.); disapproved in *R. v. Sanders*, [1968] 4 C.C.C. 156 (B.C.C.A.); *Parkes v. The Queen* (1956), 116 C.C.C. 86 (S.C.C.); *R. v. Smith* (1970), 1 C.C.C. (2d) 457 at p. 458 (N.S.C.A.); remitted to trial court for sentence on substantive offence 8 C.C.C. (2d) 279n (S.C.C.).

[11] No such provision formerly existed under the Code.

it must impose a sentence of preventive detention, which is defined in s. 688 as meaning "detention in a penitentiary for an indeterminate period". Such sentence may be imposed as a substitute for any other sentence for which the offender was, by virtue of his offence, liable.[12] Appeal against a sentence of preventive detention is provided for in s. 694.[13]

III. The Substantive Law

Paragraph 688(b) of the new legislation defines the dangerous sexual offender in virtually the same terms as did the former para. 687(b) of the Code. Such person is an offender who has been convicted of a "serious personal injury offence" as defined in para. 687(b), and who

> "... by his conduct in any sexual matter, including that involved in the commission of the offence for which he has been convicted, has shown a failure to control his sexual impulses and a likelihood of his causing injury, pain or other evil to other persons through failure in the future to control his sexual impulses ...".

Prior to 1961 equivalent legislation dealt with the determination of whether or not an accused person was a "criminal sexual psychopath". In para. 659(b) of the 1953-54 Code, such person was defined as follows:

---

[12] Section 688.

[13] Section 694 now provides as follows:

"694(1) A person who is sentenced to detention in a penitentiary for an indeterminate period under this Part may appeal to the court of appeal against that sentence on any ground of law or fact or mixed law and fact.

"(2) The Attorney General may appeal to the court of appeal against the dismissal of an application for an order under this Part on any ground of law.

"(3) On an appeal against a sentence of detention in a pententiary for an indeterminate period the court of appeal may

(a) quash such sentence and impose any sentence that might have been imposed in respect of the offence for which the appellant was convicted, or order a new hearing; or

(b) dismiss the appeal.

"(4) On an appeal against the dismissal of an application for an order under this Part the court of appeal may

(a) allow the appeal, set aside any sentence imposed in respect of the offence for which the respondent was convicted and impose a sentence of detention in a penitentiary for an indeterminate period, or order a new hearing; or

(b) dismiss the appeal.

"(5) A judgment of the court of appeal imposing a sentence pursuant to this section has the same force and effect as if it were a sentence passed by the trial court.

"(6) Notwithstanding subsection 649(1), a sentence imposed on an offender by the court of appeal pursuant to this section shall be deemed to have commenced when the offender was sentenced by the court by which he was convicted.

"(7) The provisions of Part XVIII with respect to procedure on appeals apply, *mutatis mutandis*, to appeals under this section."

"(b)   'criminal sexual psychopath' means a person who, by a course of misconduct in sexual matters, has shown a lack of power to control his sexual impulses and who as a result is likely to attack or otherwise inflict injury, pain or other evil on any person ...".

Both the term "criminal sexual psychopath" and the definition which accompanied it were abandoned for reasons too numerous to examine here.[14] As para. 688(b) now stands, it seems somewhat broader than the pre-1961 section; the change appears to be the result of an effort by Parliament to make the Crown's task easier. As one judge has put it: "A person falling within the old definition could hardly escape falling within the new. The reverse cannot be said."[15]

The present version of para. 688(b) is the result of one further change which occurred in 1968-69. Deleted from the end of the paragraph were the words "or is likely to commit a further sexual offence". The dramatic impact of these words may be seen in the decision of the Supreme Court of Canada in *Klippert v. The Queen*.[16] There it was held that a homosexual who was likely to commit further sexual offences of the same nature (gross indecency) with other consenting males could be found to be a dangerous sexual offender notwithstanding that he had never caused injury, pain or other evil to any other person and was not likely to do so in the future. According to the majority (Fauteux, Judson and Spence JJ.), protection of potential victims was not the sole intent and object of Parliament when it enacted the dangerous sexual offender provisions![17] If this is true, one wonders why the sexual offender, in order to be given a sentence of preventive detention, must first be labelled "dangerous". For this reason, Cartwright and Hall JJ. dissented:

"The intent and object of those sections in the *Criminal Code* which deal with dangerous sexual offenders is to protect persons from becoming the victims of those whose failure to control their sexual impulses renders them a source of danger. To construe the definition as compelling the Court to impose a sentence of preventive detention on a person shown by the evidence led by the Crown not to be a source of danger would be to give it an effect inconsistent with the intent and object of the Part.

"The words 'a further sexual offence' are general words wide enough to embrace every type of offence containing a sexual element and in construing them resort may properly be had to the

---

[14] See McRuer, *Report of the Royal Commission on the Criminal Law Relating to Criminal Sexual Psychopaths* (Ottawa, Queen's Printer, 1958).
[15] *R. v. McAmmond* (1969), 69 W.W.R. 277 (Man. C.A.) *per* Dickson J.A. (as he then was) at p. 286. In this case it was held that a trial judge's improper use of the outdated term in finding that the accused was a "criminal sexual psychopath" instead of a "dangerous sexual offender" did not in itself amount to a miscarriage of justice sufficient to invalidate a sentence of preventive detention.
[16] [1967] S.C.R. 822.
[17] *Per* Fauteux J. (as he then was) at p. 836.

maxim *verba generalia restringunter ad habilitatem rei vel personae* ...

...

"Applying this principle to s. 659(*b*) it is my opinion that the concluding words 'or is likely to commit a further sexual offence' should be given the meaning 'or is likely to commit a further sexual offence involving an element of danger to another person'."[18]

It is probable that the elimination of the words discussed has in itself precluded the possibility of the result in *Klippert* being repeated today. Also significant is the fact that under s. 158,[19] added to the Code as s. 149A during the 1968-69 Parliamentary Session, buggery, bestiality and gross indecency are no longer offences if performed in private between two consenting adults.[20]

A. "FAILURE TO CONTROL HIS SEXUAL IMPULSES"

While evidence of a failure on the part of the accused to control his sexual impulses is a necessary prerequisite to his being adjudged a dangerous offender, it is apparently not required of the Crown to prove that the accused's transgressions resulted *solely* from such failure, to the exclusion of any other motivation. In *R. v. McKenzie*[21] it was held that the adoption of such an interpretation of the statute would involve the unwarranted insertion of limiting words.

It is an interesting question, on the other hand, whether the commission of sex offences necessarily involves the failure of an accused person

---

[18] *Per* Cartwright J. at pp. 830-1.
[19] This section reads:
  "158 (1) Sections 155 and 157 do not apply to any act committed in private between
    (a) a husband and his wife, or
    (b) any two persons, each of whom is twenty-one years or more of age,
  both of whom consent to the commission of the act.
  "(2) For the purposes of subsection (1),
    (a) an act shall be deemed not to have been committed in private if it is committed in a public place, or if more than two persons take part or are present; and
    (b) a person shall be deemed not to consent to the commission of an act
      (i)   if the consent is extorted by force, threats or fear of bodily harm or is obtained by false and fraudulent misrepresentations as to the nature and quality of the act, or
      (ii) if that person is, and the other party to the commission of the act knows or has good reason to believe that that person is feeble-minded, insane, or an idiot or imbecile."
  According to *R. v. Volk* (1973), 12 C.C.C. (2d) 395 (Alta. C.A.) the burden of bringing himself within this exception rests upon the accused.
[20] The question remains open whether a person who commits an act of gross indecency which, though consented to, is not done "in private" within the restricted meaning of para. 158(2)(a) could, upon conviction, be found to be a dangerous sexual offender if he is judged "likely to cause ... *evil* to any person through failure in the future to control his sexual impulses."
[21] [1965] 3 C.C.C. 6 (Alta. C.A.).

to control his sexual impulses. In *R. v. Leshley*,[22] a case decided prior to the 1961 amendment to what was then s. 660, Ferguson J. of the Ontario Supreme Court was of the opinion that it did not. In his judgment he said:

"I have not changed my opinion, expressed in argument that if the acts are deliberate acts, it is illogical to say that the accused had lost the control of his impulses, because if an act is deliberate it surely must be the free manifestation of will. To my mind, it is a manifestation of the exercise of some will power if the act is deliberate. If he has lost his control when he does these acts, then surely that is an indication that the act is not a manifestation of his free will; it is an indication that the acts are not deliberate, an indication of lack of deliberation."

And later:

". . . it is my opinion this man has control of his impulses, that he was deliberate. . . .
"I think his acts are deliberate in the sense that they are not due to loss of the power to control his sexual impulses, and therefore I am going to deal with him as an ordinary man convicted of the offences for which the jury convicted him."

It is significant that in order for the learned Justice to have ruled that the accused was not a criminal sexual psychopath he need only have found that the Crown had not discharged the extremely heavy burden of proving beyond a reasonable doubt[23] that the accused *lacked the power* to control his sexual impulses. Under this test psychiatric witnesses had a difficult time distinguishing between uncontrollable and uncontrolled impulses.[24]

Ferguson J.'s argument that one can commit a sexual offence while in control of his sexual impulses was rejected in the relatively recent case of *R. v. Kelman*.[25] There Verchere J. of the British Columbia Supreme Court held:

"As can be seen I do not think those words are applicable here. I do not think, on the evidence before me, that the acts of the respon-

---

[22] Unreported, but printed in Friedland, *Cases and Materials on Criminal Law and Procedure*, 3rd ed. (Toronto, University of Toronto Press, 1968) at p. 943 and in the McRuer Report, *op. cit.* footnote 14, at p. 45.

[23] This is the standard of proof which Rand J. imposed with regard to the issue of lack of power to control in *R. v. Neil*, [1957] S.C.R. 685 at p. 690.

[24] In the McRuer report at p. 22 it is stated:
"Dr. R. R. Prosser said in evidence before us that one cannot determine lack of power to control. Dr. R. L. Whitman, a lecturer in psychiatry at the University of British Columbia, who is also engaged in private practice in Vancouver, said that he has never tried to distinguish between uncontrolled and uncontrollable impulse. Dr. J. N. Senn, Superintendent of the Ontario Hospital at Hamilton, said that he did not believe in irresistible impulse, he believed impulses were just uncontrolled."

[25] (1971), 4 C.C.C. (2d) 8 (B.C.).

dent in attacking the four young women he has shown to have attacked were *deliberate in the sense that they were not due to the loss of power to control his sexual impulses*. It seems to me that the sexual impulse, being something that is inherent in most, if not all of us, is not controlled when it is gratified. Control, as indicated earlier, means to restrain or to exercise direction upon the free action of, and, it seems to me, then, that if the respondent had controlled his sexual impulses after the opportunity to gratify that sexual impulse had arisen — and I interpolate here that the medical evidence was that because of his personality, disorder gratification of his sexual impulse entailed violence and force — there would not then have been a failure to control.

"I repeat, it seems to me that the gratification of the sexual impulse, especially of one of the type that I have just mentioned, bespeaks loss of control ..."[26]

Notice that Verchere J. held not only that the respondent had failed to control his sexual impulses, but that he in fact *lacked the power* to control them. From this it is clear that the learned Justice was applying the pre-1961 test.[27]

B. "LIKELIHOOD OF HIS CAUSING INJURY, PAIN OR OTHER EVIL THROUGH FAILURE IN THE FUTURE TO CONTROL HIS SEXUAL IMPULSES"

The requirement that a sexual offender must, in order to be sentenced to preventive detention, be proven likely to cause injury, pain or other evil through future failure to control his sexual impulses is basically another way of saying that he must be shown to be dangerous. The significance of the hurdle which this requirement imposes has been succinctly stated in the following observation:

"There may be no more important legal concept linking law and psychiatry than that of dangerousness. Unfortunately, there are few concepts of such importance that are so vaguely conceptualized and poorly measured."[28]

What more nebulous means of gauging dangerousness than in terms of likeliness to cause "other evil"? As was decided in the case of *R. v. Roestad*,[29] the word "evil" is not to be construed *ejusdem generis* with

---

[26] *Ibid.*, at p. 12 (emphasis added).

[27] According to *R. v. McAmmond, supra*, footnote 15, use of the old test does not prejudice the accused. It is probable, however, that a finding that the accused was not a D.S.O. because he did not *lack the power* to control his sexual impulses would have provided the Crown with grounds for appeal.

[28] Steadman, "Some evidence on the inadequacy of the concept and determination of dangerousness in law and psychiatry" (1973), 1 Journal of Psychiatry and Law 409 at p. 409.

[29] (1971), 19 C.R.N.S. 190 (Ont. Co. Ct.); application for leave to appeal to Court of Appeal dismissed 19 C.R.N.S. 235n (C.A.).

the words "injury" and "pain" so as to impart to the word a physical connotation. Accordingly, the word "evil" was held there to be wide enough to encompass moral damage to others. In the words of Graburn Co.Ct.J.:

> "I am convinced, when regard is had to the circumstances and backgrounds of the children to whom Mr. Roestad is attracted, that extensive damage is likely to be caused to the morals of some of those children leading to male prostitution or some other form of exploitative behaviour. This is, in my view, a form of 'evil', the prohibition of which is clearly an aim of Parliament in the section under consideration."[30]

This ruling is particularly interesting in light of Judge Graburn's finding[31] that the young boys, with whom the accused was convicted of committing (with their consent) buggery and indecent assault, had suffered no physical, emotional, moral or psychological harm. Such reasoning was recently upheld by the Alberta Supreme Court (Appellate Division) in *R. v. Dwyer*.[32]

The problem with measuring dangerousness in terms of a propensity for causing evil is that such test, in order to be fair, must assume a uniform standard of morality among judges. Such an assumption is naive, if not bizarre. The well-recognized fact that judges are disparate in their judicial attitudes, and that such inequality is in turn the product of divergent social backgrounds, religions, educational experiences, and individual psychologies and personalities in general, is a problem common to all areas of sentencing.[33] But what differentiates the procedure of sentencing in general from the determination of whether someone is or is not a dangerous sexual offender is this: in the former case it is the likelihood of a certain sentence effecting reform from, deterrence from, or punishment for *crime* which must be subjectively weighed; in the latter it is the likelihood of a concept in itself infinitely more subjective than that of crime which is being subjectively weighed. When one couples this

---

[30] *Ibid.*, at p. 234. The fact that Parliament's intention was indeed to bring those persons who seduce children into commiting acts of gross indecency etc. within the scope of the D.S.O. provisions is clear from the 1961 amendments. In *R. v. Neil, supra*, footnote 23, Cartwright J. was of the opinion that because the pre-1961 test required a likelihood that the accused would "*inflict*...evil", the danger envisioned by Parliament was, in his words (at p. 699), "that of coercive conduct resulting in the active infliction of pain, injury or other evil on the victim, not merely the persuading or seducing of another to participate in sexual misconduct". Although Cartwright J. held the minority opinion on this point, the McRuer Commission recommended in its Report (*supra*, footnote 14, at p. 24) that the word "cause" be substituted for "inflict" for the sake of clarification.

[31] At p. 227.

[32] [1977] 2 W.W.R. 704.

[33] See *The Challenge of Crime in a Free Society — A Report by the President's Commission on Law Enforcement and the Administration of Justice* (Washington, 1967) at p. 145; McGuire and Holtzoff, "The Problems of Sentencing in the Criminal Law" (1940), Boston L. Rev. 413 at pp. 426-33; Gaudet, "The Sentencing Behaviour of the Judge", in Brandom and Katash, *Encyclopedia of Criminology* (New York, 1949) at pp. 449-61; Hogarth, *Sentencing as a Human Process* (Toronto, 1971) at chapters 1, 4-8, 11.

fact with the potential severity of an indeterminate sentence, the dangerousness of the Canadian definition of dangerousness becomes immediately apparent. Oddly enough, from 1961 to 1969, the likelihood of future *criminality* was added to the criteria of dangerousness — despite the fact that the McRuer Commission had concluded in 1958 that "the scientific identification of a potential offender is difficult, if not impossible."[34] Future crime was at least in one sense more susceptible of prediction than future evil; it was after all, codified. On the other hand it could be argued that evil, being a constant, and crime being variable by legislation, it is evil which can more certainly be predicted. The liberal thinker might counter, however, that one's likeliness to commit a future crime of some sort is a safer bet than likeliness to commit a future evil, there being a great many crimes which are not necessarily evil. The moralist might argue the reverse on the premise that there are a great many evils which are not crimes. And so on *ad infinitum*. In any event, the future crime criterion was dropped in 1969, and the vexing question remains why the future evil provision was not eschewed as well.

Even likeliness to cause future injury or pain is a difficult enough thing to predict. We are all likely to cause injury or pain of some sort.[35] Indeed, nearly half of the criteria suggested by Marcus and Conway[36] as a means of measuring dangerousness seem applicable to the majority of the population:

"(1) Brutality sustained in childhood.
(2) Bedwetting, firesetting and cruelty to animals.
(3) Assorted delinquent acts during puberty.
(4) Escalation of the sexual offences.
(5) Inter-related criminality with sexual offences.
(6) Sustained excitement prior to the act and at the time of the offence.
(7) Lack of concern for the victim.
(8) Bizarre fantasies with minor offences.
(9) Explosive outbursts.
(10) Absence of psychosis.
(11) Absence of alcohol consumption.
(12) High I.Q."[37]

---

[34] *Supra*, footnote 14, at p. 60.
[35] See Herman, "Preventive Detention, a Scientific View of Man and State Power" (1973), U. of Ill. L. Forum 637 at pp. 687-8, where the author has written: "In other words the socially determined condition of dangerousness does not consist solely of a determination of real or actually threatened harms; rather it is a resultant of fear, which consists of both rational and irrational factors. The fear of dangerousness in part grows from an awareness of one's own suppressed capacity for violence; under proper circumstances, every person may commit a violent act and inflict harm. Dangerousness, moreover, is not simply an evaluation of the possibility that a person can and may inflict harm, but involves an element of projection onto other individuals of personally felt anxiety, guilt and shame. For instance, many people fear violent sexual assaults. These fears may reflect personally repressed fears and desires."
[36] "Dangerous Sexual Offender Project" (1969), 11 Can. J. Corr. 198.
[37] *Ibid.*, at pp. 204-5

The problem, therefore, becomes a quantitative one. Marcus and Conway have suggested that each factor be scored on a 10 point scale. "A score above ninety", they have concluded, "is indicative of a very high degree of dangerousness."[38] With all due respect to the designers, this system of prediction is remarkably reminiscent of the "sanity meter" a science fiction writer[39] once invented and which Alan Dershowitz has described in a recent article:[40]

> "The meter, installed in all public places, registered from zero to ten. A person scoring up to three was considered normal; one scoring between four and seven, while within the tolerance limit, was advised to undergo therapy; one scoring between eight and ten was required to register with the authorities as highly dangerous and to bring his rating below seven within a specified probation period; anyone failing this probationary requirement, or anyone passing the red line above ten, was required either to undergo immediate surgical alteration or to submit himself to the academy — a mysterious institution from which no one returned."[41]

One problem with the Marcus and Conway scale is that an arbitrary numerical rating designates the threshold limit of dangerousness; there are no research findings to back it up. Furthermore, while the sanity meter was objective and infallible,[42] the Marcus and Conway scale is subject to the notoriously non-uniform[43] judgments of psychiatrists.

In the United States, numerous attempts have been made at devising objective techniques of assessing propensity for violent behaviour. They have, by all reports, failed quite dismally.[44] In actual practice most Canadian psychiatrists do not base their conclusions as to dangerousness upon exhaustive clinical investigation anyway; rather, their opinions are formed on the basis of "one or two interviews, supplemented by the evidence given at trial and an examination of such documentary evidence as may be available. . .".[45] Not surprisingly, the suspicion that predic-

---

[38] *Ibid.*, at p. 205.

[39] Sheckley, *Pilgrimage to Earth* (Bantam, 1957) at pp. 120-40.

[40] Dershowitz, "Preventive Confinement: A Suggested Framework for Constitutional Analysis" (1973), 51 Texas L. Rev. 1277.

[41] *Ibid.*, at p. 1277.

[42] *Ibid.* "Since the machine never erred, everyone in the society knew everyone else's danger rating and acted accordingly. Its widespread use finally succeeded in eliminating crime and other social evils."

[43] See Beck, "Reliability of Psychiatric Diagnosis: A Study of Consistency of Clinical Judgments and Ratings" (1962), 119 American Journal of Psychiatry 351. See also Watson, "Untying the Knots: The Cross-examination of the Psychiatric Expert Witness", in Sugerman, *Examining the Medical Expert* (Ann Arbor, Mich., Institute of Continuing Legal Education, 1969). At p. 16 the author states that differences in diagnosis are usually *quantitative*.

[44] See generally Kozol, "The Diagnosis and Treatment of Dangerousness" (1972), 18 Crime and Delinquency 371; McGee, "Objectivity in Predicting Criminal Behaviour" (1967), 42 F.R.D. 192 and Ginsberg and Klockars, "The Dangerous Offender and Legislative Reform" (1972), 10 Willamette L.J. 167 at pp. 179-82.

[45] Ouimet, *Report of the Canadian Committee on Corrections* (Ottawa, Queen's Printer, 1969) at p. 254.

tions made by psychiatrists tend to be unreliable[46] has been confirmed by investigation. One writer[47] has reported that psychiatric predictions appear to be even less accurate than those of psychologists, social workers, correctional officials and the so-called objective statistical techniques which are an admitted failure. The writer has concluded that "psychiatrists are particularly prone to one type of error — overprediction".[48] The tendency to overpredict is understandable enough. No doubt it stems from the inordinantly onerous position of responsibility in which the psychiatric witness is placed. Despite the supposed fact that the question of whether the accused is a dangerous sexual offender is one for the judge to decide, both as to law and fact,[49] the heavy reliance which the court (and indeed the Criminal Code[50]) places on the psychiatric witness amounts to a near abdication of the court's function in many cases. In *R. v. Sanders*[51] it was discovered that the Magistrate had not bothered to make a specific finding that the accused was a criminal sexual psychopath before imposing a sentence of preventive detention for the following reasons:

> "Both doctors and the Court seem to think that if the doctors concluded or were of the opinion that the applicant was a criminal sexual psychopath because of a course of misconduct in sexual matters and was unable to control his sexual impulses, that the same was sufficient to satisfy statutory requirements."[52]

It is no wonder, therefore, that the psychiatrist, realizing an incorrect decision on his part could mean grief for a sex offender's next victim, chooses to "play it safe" at the expense of someone who, after all, has been convicted of at least one offence. Equally unsurprising, though perhaps more outrageous, is the weight which judges so often accord to psychiatric opinion. Their apparent hesitancy to face the consequences of disregarding uncontradicted "expert evidence" has led them to accept *beyond a reasonable doubt* predictions as to dangerousness which have been statistically shown to have a low probability of accuracy.[53] One

---

[46] *Ibid.* "The Committee has been informed by eminent psychiatrists that it is extremely difficult — if not impossible — to determine on the basis of an interview or two, with any reasonable degree of accuracy, whether an offender is a dangerous sexual offender."

[47] Dershowitz, "Psychiatry and the Legal Process: A Knife that Cuts Both Ways" (1969), 2 Psychology Today 43 at p. 47.

[48] *Ibid.*

[49] *R. v. Binette*, [1965] 3 C.C.C. 216 at pp. 217-8 (B.C.C.A.).

[50] In *R. v. Johnston* (1965), 51 W.W.R. 280 (Man. C.A.), Miller C.J.M. said at p. 287: "I have some doubts that the evidence of the psychiatrists can be brushed aside or disregarded as sec. 661(2) of the *Code* seems to contemplate an important role for the evidence of psychiatrists."

[51] [1966] 2 C.C.C. 345 (B.C.).

[52] *Ibid.*, at p. 354.

[53] Where uncertainty and contradiction in evidence exists, however, the pressure is taken off the judge. In *R. v. Loysen* (1973), 13 C.C.C. (2d) 202 (B.C.), Monroe J. stated at p. 206:

> "I am satisfied beyond a reasonable doubt that the respondent by his conduct in sexual matters has shown a failure to control his sexual impulses but I am not satisfied

cannot help but wonder whether the McRuer Commission's recommendation that the onus of proof be reduced to a mere preponderance of probability[54] was not motivated by a desire to make judicial acceptance of psychiatric predictions seem less ludicrous.

Aside from the practical difficulties inherent in the prediction of dangerousness, there is a fundamental question of philosophy which deserves fuller consideration. Even assuming that infallibility of psychiatric prognosis is capable of achievement in the future,[55] to what extent should the law become involved in the confinement of persons for "evils" which they have not yet committed? Traditionally, the criminal law seems to have been founded on a reactive rather than a preventive theory. Wharton has written that the preventive theory "contradicts one of the fundamental maxims of the English common law, by which not a tendency to crime, but simply crime itself, can be made the subject of a criminal issue".[56] On the other side, Blackstone has argued with great force in his *Commentaries* that "preventive justice is upon every principle of reason, of humanity, and of sound policy preferable in all respects to *punishing* justice ...".[57] Apart from the dangerous offender provisions, it is true that prevention is a basic goal of all sentencing. Indeed Holmes has asserted that prevention comprises the "chief and only universal purpose of punishment."[58]

Preventive detention, as it exists in the Criminal Code, is supposedly mitigated by the fact that the person under detention has in fact already committed a crime. The conclusion that such person is dangerous, therefore, is not drawn solely from psychiatric assessment. As Dershowitz has pointed out:

> "Experience indicates ... that those who have committed sexual assaults in the past, but whose psychological tests appear normal, are more likely to commit rape in the future than those whose psychological tests show a propensity for violence, but who have never committed a sexual assault in the past."[59]

To this it may well be responded that even once past conduct is considered, predictions of dangerousness have not on the whole turned out to be sufficiently accurate to justify long-term imprisonment.

---

beyond a reasonable doubt that it has been proved that he is likely to cause injury, pain or other evil to any person through failure in the future to control his sexual impulses. The evidence and the lack of certainty which I detect in the opinions expressed by the psychiatrists at the hearing and earlier, plus the optimism of the psychologist create in my mind a reasonable doubt — which by law must be resolved in favour of the respondent ...".

[54] McRuer Commission Report, *supra*, footnote 14, at p. 38.

[55] Recent Canadian proposals do in fact indicate a movement toward the "sanity meter" ideal. See the recommendation of the Ouimet Committee, *op. cit.* footnote 45, at p. 264.

[56] Wharton, *Criminal Law*, 12th ed. (1932), s. 2.

[57] Blackstone, *Commentaries on the Laws of England*, Vol. 4 (London, Dawsons of Mall Mall, 1966 Reprint) at p. 248.

[58] Holmes, *The Common Law* (Boston, Little Brown, 1963) at p. 46.

[59] *Supra*, footnote 40, at p. 1313.

IV. Evidence

With regard to the evidence which must be heard upon a dangerous sexual offender application, the former provision of the Criminal Code stated as follows:

> "689(2) On the hearing of an application under subsection (1) the court shall hear any relevant evidence, and shall hear the evidence of at least two psychiatrists, one of whom shall be nominated by the Attorney General."

Bill C-51 has modified and expanded this provision somewhat. Section 690 of the new legislation provides:

> "690(1) On the hearing of an application under this Part, the court shall hear the evidence of at least two psychiatrists and all other evidence that, in its opinion, is relevant, including the evidence of any psychologist or criminologist called as a witness by the prosecution or the offender.
>
> "(2) One of the psychiatrists referred to in subsection (1) shall be nominated by the prosecution and one shall be nominated by the offender.
>
> "(3) If the offender fails or refuses to nominate a psychiatrist pursuant to this section, the court shall nominate a psychiatrist on behalf of the offender.
>
> "(4) Nothing in this section shall be construed to enlarge the number of expert witnesses that may be called without the leave of the court or judge under section 7 of the *Canada Evidence Act.*"

The question of what is meant in s-s. (1) by "all other relevant evidence" may be answered by reference back to the definition of "dangerous sexual offender". Paragraph 688(b) of the new legislation says such person may be judged "by his conduct in any sexual matter". This implies that evidence of previous conduct is admissible even where such conduct did not result in conviction for any offence. This interpretation is confirmed by the new provisions of s. 692:

> "692. Without prejudice to the right of the offender to tender evidence as to his character and repute, evidence of character and repute may, if the court thinks fit, be admitted on the question whether the offender is or is not a dangerous offender."

As stated earlier, the only conviction which must be proved at a dangerous sexual offender hearing is the substantive one.[60] However, where the application is heard after sentence for the substantive offence has been passed and before a magistrate different from the one who tried the case

---

[60] See *R. v. Dawson*, [1970] 3 C.C.C. 212 (B.C.C.A.).

and passed sentence, the transcript of the trial will *not* be considered relevant evidence. Instead, evidence of all sexual misconduct must be given *viva voce* under oath as it was at trial.[61]

Once on the witness stand, it is an interesting question whether expert witnesses will be permitted to express an opinion directly on the issue of whether or not the accused is a dangerous sexual offender. In *R. v. Tousignant*,[62] the Ontario Court of Appeal allowed an appeal on the grounds that, *inter alia*, "certain doctors called to testify as to the mental condition of the accused expressed their opinion on the very question that is left by the statute to the Court for judicial consideration and determination, namely, whether the accused person in question is or is not a criminal sexual psychopath within the meaning of the statute."[63] In the same year, the Supreme Court of Canada solidified the applicability of the ultimate issue rule[64] in sexual psychopath hearings with a finding in *R. v. Neil*[65] similar to that in *Tousignant*. But the distinction in these hearings between what is and what is not an opinion on the ultimate issue may be a fine one — fine to the point being an illusion. In *R. v. McAmmond*[66] the Manitoba Court of Appeal held that a psychiatrist, though not permitted to directly state that he believed the accused to be a dangerous sexual offender, could give his opinion as to whether or not the accused was "likely to cause injury, pain or other evil to any person, through failure in the future to control his sexual impulses." Most recently in *R. v. Bolduc*[67] the Quebec Court of Appeal, relying upon *McAmmond*, had this to say:

"During the examination of the psychiatrists, the following question was asked of both of them: 'Is the accused Bolduc a dangerous sexual offender?'. . .It was a question of fact which was one, of course, to be decided by the Court, but s. 689(1) states that it is upon this question that testimony should be heard, and I do not see how the experts can be prevented from expressing their opinions with regard to the definition that I have cited above, especially in the absence of objection from the defence."[68]

While personal examination may be the best way of obtaining psychiatric information germane to the issue of whether or not an individual is a dangerous sexual offender, it is clear that a psychiatric opinion based on sources of information which are possibly less reliable will nevertheless be admissible. In *Wilband v. The Queen*[69] the Supreme Court of

---

[61] *R. v. Canning*, [1966] 4 C.C.C. 379 (B.C.C.A.).
[62] [1957] O.W.N. 573.
[63] *Ibid.*, at pp. 573-4.
[64] *Halsbury's Laws of England*, 3rd ed., vol. 15 at p. 323 expresses the rule this way: "An expert cannot usually be asked to express an opinion upon any of the issues, whether of law or fact, which the court or jury have to determine...".
[65] [1957] S.C.R. 685.
[66] [1970] 1 C.C.C. 175.
[67] (1973), 16 C.C.C. (2d) 280.
[68] *Ibid.*, at p. 283.
[69] [1967] S.C.R. 14.

Canada ruled admissible the evidence of psychiatrists who had formed their opinions as a result of examining the accused, as well as reading prison reports and listening to the evidence given at trial. In answer to the criticism that the psychiatrists' opinions were no better than the hearsay upon which they were based, Fauteux J. (as he then was) had this to say:

> "The evidence, in this case, indicates that to form an opinion according to recognized normal psychiatric procedures, the psychiatrist must consider all possible sources of information, including second-hand source information, the reliability, accuracy and significance of which are within the recognized scope of his professional activities, skill and training to evaluate. Hence, while ultimately his conclusion may rest, in part, on second-hand source material, it is nonetheless an opinion formed according to recognized normal psychiatric procedures. It is not to be assumed that Parliament contemplated that the opinion, which the psychiatrists would form and give to assist the Court, would be formed by methods other than those recognized in normal psychiatric procedures. *The value of a psychiatrist's opinion may be affected to the extent to which it may rest on second-hand source material; but that goes to the weight and not to the receivability in evidence of the opinion, which opinion is no evidence of the truth of the information but evidence of the opinion formed on the basis of that information.*"[70]

In *R. v. Kanester*[71] the British Columbia Court of Appeal, applying *Wilband*, held that evidence could properly be received from psychiatrists whose views had been formed *entirely* on the basis of medical reports and observation at the accused's trial.

With regard to burden of proof, it is generally accepted that both elements (*i.e.*, failure to control sexual impulses and likelihood of causing future injury, etc.) must be proved beyond a reasonable doubt.[72] Proving beyond a reasonable doubt that someone is *likely* to do something, however, seems somewhat paradoxical; the burden, in effect is probability beyond a reasonable doubt!

---

[70] *Ibid.*, at p. 21 (emphasis added). For a case in which the use of second-hand source material reduced the weight of psychiatric opinion to the point that it was rejected, see *R. v. Knight* (1975), 27 C.C.C. (2d) 343 (Ont.).

[71] [1968] 1 C.C.C. 351.

[72] *R. v. Loysen* (1973), 13 C.C.C. (2d) 202 (B.C.); *R. v. Bolduc* (1973), 16 C.C.C. (2d) 280 (Que. C.A.); *R. v. Roestad* (1971), 19 C.R.N.S. 190 (Ont. Co. Ct.), application for leave to appeal to Court of Appeal dismissed 19 C.R.N.S. 235n (C.A.); *R. v. Dwyer*, [1977] 2 W.W.R. 704 (Alta. C.A.); *R. v. Knight* (1975), 27 C.C.C. (2d) 343 (Ont.).

V. Preventive Detention

As originally conceived, the indeterminate sentence evolved as a means of coping with the problem of habitual offenders.[73] The idea of tailoring the sentence to the prisoner's "rehabilitative progress" was embraced by many penologists as an unquestioned panacea. So fantastic was the concept that proponents of the Treatment Model anticipated with almost manic optimism the prospects for harmonious salvation of criminal souls:

> "The prisoner is given to understand that the date of his release on parole depends entirely upon himself. The authorities desire his release and will help him to earn it; they are not his enemies, but his friends. This disarms him of hostility to them. He is in a favourable state of mind to receive treatment, and is disposed to yield obedience to them, if they keep their promise to him. . . . He is trained and transformed . . ."[74]

More recently, however, evidence has emerged that the transformation which a prisoner is apt to undergo is a total fragmentation of the ego (*i.e.*, psychosis), rendering rehabilitation a near, if not total, impossibility.[75] This reaction has been attributed to the loss of identity implicitly required of a prisoner if he is ever to be released. As one critic has so poignantly expressed the problem:

> "The psychiatrist becomes gentle jailer, polite policeman. His patient is no longer, except marginally, his client. He serves the public order — with such kindness, at best, that constraint permits. . . . His ward . . . to escape, must yield not only outerly but innerly. The wildest tyrants in their wildest fantasies have not required more."[76]

It is not surprising, therefore, that the issue of whether or not preventive detention is "cruel and unusual punishment" has arisen both in Canada and in the United States. In *R. v. Buckler*[77] it was argued that dangerous sexual offender legislation contravened para. 2(b) of the Canadian Bill of Rights.[78] Carson Prov. Ct. J. rejected this submission on

---

[73] Miller, "The Indeterminate Sentence Paradigm: Resocialization or Social Control?", 7 (No. 2) Issues in Criminology 101 at p. 103.

[74] Wines, *Punishment and Reformation* (New York, T.Y. Crowell and Co., 1910) at pp. 36-43, quoted by Miller at p. 107.

[75] See Price, "Mentally Disordered and Dangerous Persons Under the Criminal Law" (1970), 12 Can. J. Corr. 241 at p. 245; Reich, "Therapeutic Implications of the Indeterminate Sentence" (1966), 2 Issues in Criminology 7 at p. 8.

[76] Seely, *The Americanization of the Unconscious* (New York, Jason Aronson Inc, 1967) at p. 43.

[77] [1970] 2 C.C.C. 4 (Ont. Prov. Ct.).

[78] R.S.C. 1970, App. III:

"2. Every law of Canada shall, unless it is expressly declared by an Act of the Parliament of Canada that it shall operate notwithstanding the *Canadian Bill of Rights*,

grounds that (1) the indeterminate nature of the sentence does not in itself amount to cruelty; something in the nature of *physical* pain would have to be inflicted as well, and (2) the infrequent resort to preventive detention does not render it unusual, since persons of unsound mind are being locked away for indeterminate periods all the time.[79]

Paragraph 2(b) was again raised in *R. v. Roestad*,[80] this time in the Ontario County Court. There the Court was of the opinion that indeterminate detention might well be considered cruel without the infliction of physical pain and degradation; it considered that the word "cruelty" was not confined to the physical. However, in determining whether or not a punishment was cruel it was necessary to take into account the *purpose* for which it was being imposed. In the words of Graburn Co.Ct.J.:

> "If the object of indeterminate detention is to punish a person for something he has not yet done I have no doubt that it is cruel. If the man is sentenced to indeterminate detention for the purpose of protecting the public from likely pain, injury or other evil coupled with the safeguards contained in s. 666 I do not consider it would be cruel. Whether punishment is cruel therefore depends upon the object of the punishment as set out in the legislation."[81]

It is submitted, however, that the learned Judge rested his decision on two highly contentious propositions. The first is that detention for public protection is something different from detention as punishment for an act not yet committed. Though it is true that the motives of protection and punishment are theoretically distinguishable, the line separating these two motives becomes infinitely fine in the context of preventive detention. Though Graburn Co.Ct.J. condemned as cruel the practice of punishing a person for something he has not yet done, it is hard to conceive of an example of this practice in operation *except* in cases of preventive detention. Even in the case of conspiracy the punishment imposed by law is for the actual commission of an act of conspiring; surely the learned Judge did not intend to condemn punishment for conspiracy as cruel. Secondly, Graburn Co.Ct.J.'s contention that cruelty is dependant on the motivation of the party alleged to be cruel is one which demands consideration. What the Judge seems to have been

---

be so construed and applied as not to abrogate, abridge or infringe or to authorize the abrogation, abridgment or infringement of any of the rights or freedoms herein recognized and declared, and in particular, no law of Canada shall be construed or applied so as to

       ...

    (b) impose or authorize the imposition of cruel and unusual treatment or punishment"

[79] *Supra*, footnote 77 at p. 12.

[80] (1971), 19 C.R.N.S. 190; application for leave to appeal to C.A. dismissed 19 C.R.N.S. 235n (C.A.).

[81] *Ibid.*, at p. 203. It was also stated that neither lack of a known date of release nor the fact that the prisoner could serve a sentence longer than that actually served by someone sentenced to life imprisonment amounted to cruelty.

saying is that in order for a statutory punishment to be adjudged cruel, some sort of malicious design or *mens rea* must be proved on the part of the legislature. The apparent attempt to transplant the definition of cruelty as it pertains to divorce law[82] into the criminal law is of dubious merit if for no other reason than the legal and practical differences which exist with regard to burden of proof.

In *R. v. Hatchwell*[83] the British Columbia Court of Appeal was called upon to decide whether preventive detention was cruel and unusual *per se*. Robertson J.A. (Bull J.A. concurring) dealt with the issue in one paragraph:

> "Thirdly, it is submitted that a sentence of preventive detention is 'cruel and unusual treatment or punishment' within the meaning of s. 2(*b*) of the Canadian Bill of Rights: cruel because there is no prescribed limit to its length — and I note that the same is true of a term of life imprisonment — and unusual because a precedent of precisely, or almost precisely, the same nature cannot be found elsewhere; counsel did not, as he could not, go so far as to submit that imprisonment in itself is cruel treatment or punishment within the meaning of s. 2(*b*). I feel that I need say no more than that I do not think that this submission can succeed."[84]

One reason for Robertson J.A.'s rather laconic judgment on this point lies perhaps in his awareness at the time of the decision that the cruel and unusual issue was before the Supreme Court of Canada. In a judgment which has not been reported[85] it was held in *Pearson v. LeCorre* that the former s. 688 of the Code[86] was not rendered inoperative by the Canadian Bill of Rights.

Preventive detention has been attacked on other constitutional grounds. In *Ex p. Matticks*[87] it was argued that the enactment of s. 688 was *ultra vires* the Federal Parliament. There the Quebec Court of Appeal easily disposed of the matter by pointing out that despite the fact that preventive detention proceedings are separate proceedings,[88] they nevertheless pertain to the matter of sentencing and as such fall within s-s. 91(27) of the B.N.A. Act, 1867, as an inherent part of "Criminal Law ... and Procedure in Criminal Matters".

In *Re Campbell and The Queen*[89] the argument was raised that the dangerous sexual offender provision, if construed to apply to persons

---

[82] See Bromley, *Family Law*, 5th ed. (London, Butterworths, 1976) at p. 191.
[83] [1974] 1 W.W.R. 307; revd on other grounds [1975] 4 W.W.R. 68 (S.C.C.).
[84] *Ibid.*, at p. 314.
[85] Decided October 3, 1973.
[86] Although this section related to "habitual offenders", in the words of Graburn Co.Ct.J., *supra*, footnote 80 at p. 202 "For the purposes of this branch of the argument no difference would exist between the habitual criminal and dangerous sexual offender provisions of the Criminal Code, a finding of which may result in preventive detention in the former case and must in the latter."
[87] (1972), 10 C.C.C. (2d) 438 (Que. C.A.); affd 15 C.C.C. (2d) 213n (S.C.C.).
[88] See *Wilband v. The Queen*, [1967] S.C.R. 14.
[89] (1974), 16 C.C.C. (2d) 573 (B.C.); affd 22 C.C.C. (2d) 65 (C.A.).

under 18 years of age, would constitute an infringement of the right to equality before the law as guaranteed by para. 1(b) of the Bill of Rights. This contention sprang from the fact that the accused, who was 17 and was tried in British Columbia, could never have been tried in adult court in other provinces. The British Columbia Supreme Court rejected this line of reasoning, referring to the decision of the Supreme Court of Canada in *R. v. Burnshine*[90] where Martland J. said:

> "It is quite clear that, in 1960, when the *Bill of Rights* was enacted, the concept of 'equality before the law' did not and could not include the right of each individual to insist that no statute could be enacted which did not have application to everyone and in all areas of Canada. Such a right would have involved a substantial impairment of the sovereignty of Parliament in the exercise of its legislative powers under s. 91 of the *British North America Act, 1867*, and could only have been created by constitutional amendment, or by statute."[91]

Paragraph 1(b) was invoked in a different context in *R. v. Roestad*.[92] In that case defence counsel, opposing an application by the Crown for preventive detention, took the position that the dangerous sexual offender provision was discriminatory by way of sentence in that it allowed the Crown to treat one group of offenders differently from others. Graburn Co.Ct.J. answered this submission by saying:

> "... in my judgment the concept of equality before the law is not violated here by some groups being treated differently, or more harshly than others, as a result of a decision made by Crown counsel which was authorized by the existing legislation. This concept of equality before the law, in my view, means a fair trial for every person charged in the courts of this country with no deprivation in his right to make a full answer and defence."[93]

The Judge considered himself bound by the decision in *Smythe v. The Queen*,[94] a case involving the Attorney-General's discretion to proceed either summarily or by way of indictment with respect to certain offences. He relied in particular upon the Ontario High Court judgment of Wells C.J.H.C., who said[95] that equality before the law was confined to non-discrimination on the basis of race, national origin, colour, religion or sex.

The inequality before the law argument was again employed in *R. v. Hatchwell*.[96] Once more it was rejected, but this time on slightly differ-

---

[90] (1974), 15 C.C.C. (2d) 505 (S.C.C.).
[91] *Ibid.*, at p. 513
[92] (1971), 19 C.R.N.S. 190 (Ont.Co.Ct.); application for leave to appeal to C.A. dismissed 19 C.R.N.S. 235n (C.A.).
[93] *Ibid.*, at p. 197.
[94] (1971), 13 C.R.N.S. 7 (Ont.); affd 13 C.R.N.S. 33 (C.A.); affd [1971] S.C.R. 680.
[95] (1971), 13 C.R.N.S. 7 at p. 27.
[96] [1974] 1 W.W.R. 307 (B.C.C.A.); revd on other grounds [1975] 4 W.W.R. 68 (S.C.C.).

ent grounds. To defence counsel's contention that indeterminate detention was likely to result in a lengthier sentence than that which would
be served by others who had committed the same offences and was
therefore likely to produce inequality, Robertson J.A. of the British
Columbia Court of Appeal answered:

> "I do not think that this submission is sound; it overlooks that pre-
> ventive detention can only be imposed upon one who has the status
> of an habitual criminal [or dangerous sexual offender], and there is
> no inequality in prescribing for a person who has that status a term
> of imprisonment for a period which is different from that which is
> prescribed for persons who have not that status. Two different
> classes of persons are involved, and all persons coming within each
> class are treated equally with the others in that class."[97]

A final ground on which the provision was argued to contravene the
Bill of Rights in both *Roestad* and *Hatchwell* was that of arbitrariness.
Paragraph 2(a) commands that ". . .no law of Canada shall be construed
or applied so as to (a) authorize or effect the arbitrary detention, imprisonment or exile of any person". Though the submission was rejected
flatly and without discussion by the court in *Hatchwell*,[98] a full page[99] of
discussion was devoted to the matter in *Roestad*. There defence counsel
had alleged three heads under which the former s. 689 of the Code
should be considered arbitrary.

First it was urged that lack of consent to the proceedings by the Attorney-General rendered them arbitrary. To this puzzling line of reasoning,
the court replied simply that with few exceptions prosecutions under the
Criminal Code do not require the Attorney-General's consent.

Next it was urged that the inability of the Crown to predict beforehand who is likely to be a dangerous sexual offender made the proceedings arbitrary. To that the court replied with the obvious: the necessity
for prediction imposed no heavier a burden on the Crown attorney than
a decision as to whether he should prosecute in the case of many offences.

Finally it was urged that since the application cannot be opposed
before it is brought and since selection of the forum is determined by the
Crown and since no guidelines exist with regard to the selection of those
against whom the proceedings might be taken, the unfettered power and
discretion of the Crown tended to make the proceedings arbitrary. This
contention seems somewhat more plausible than the first two in light of
the definition of "arbitrary" quoted by the court. The word "arbitrary",
it said, "is defined in the Concise Oxford Dictionary as meaning 'derived
from mere opinion; capricious; unrestrained; despotic; (Law)
discretionary'."[100] The court responded, however, by pointing out that
by s. 666 of the Code (now s. 695.1) Parliament had directed the

---

[97] *Ibid.*, at p. 313.
[98] *Ibid.*, at p. 314, "I can see nothing 'arbitrary' involved in Code s. 688."
[99] *Supra*, footnote 92 at p. 194.
[100] *Ibid.*

National Parole Board to periodically review the condition, history, and circumstances of a person under preventive detention in order to determine whether he should be granted parole.

Of the constitutional arguments advanced, the ones which strike one as having come closest to the mark are those of "cruel and unusual punishment or treatment" and arbitrariness. As framed, however, these arguments quite obviously lacked appeal as far as the courts were concerned. Another side of the problem which the courts may not have considered is that put forward by a prison inmate from Waugh's satire, "Love Among the Ruins":

> "It's a funny thing but I've settled down here wonderful. Never thought I should. It all seemed a bit too posh at first. Not like the old Scrubs. But it's a real pretty place once you're used to it. Wouldn't mind settling here for a lifer if they'd let me. The trouble is there's no security in crime these days. Time was, you knew just what a job was worth, six months, three years; whatever it was, you knew where you were. Now what with prison commissioners and Preventive Custody and Corrective Treatment they can keep you in or push you out just as it suits them. It's not right."

VI. Conclusions

What are the alternatives to preventive detention of so-called dangerous sexual offenders? One proposal which has been made is the widening of s. 16 of the Criminal Code so as to encompass "irresistable impulse" within the insanity defence.[101] The point here would be to increase the possibility of treatment in a psychiatric facility rather than simple imprisonment. The "sentence" would still be indeterminate, however, regardless of the fact that no conviction would have been imposed, since those persons found not guilty by reason of insanity are detained "in the place and in the manner that the court, judge or magistrate directs, until the pleasure of the lieutenant governor of the province is known."[102] A further point worth making is that the defence of "irresistible impulse" would not, in all liklihood, be available to a large percentage of those persons who would otherwise fall into the category of dangerous sexual offenders. Many sex offenders are diagnosed as psychopaths, as former Criminal Code provisions have indicated. Despite the diversity of opinion regarding the meaning of this term,[103] the current psychiatric con-

---

[101] Bertrand, "Sexual Criminals — Reforms that are Needed in Our Modern Society" (1966), 14 Chitty's L.J. 175 at p. 176.

[102] Criminal Code s-s. 542(2).

[103] One critic of psychiatry has gone so far as to say that "without exception, on every point regarding psychopathic personality, psychiatrists present varying or contradictory views". See Hakeem, "A Critique of the Psychiatric Approach to Crime and Correction" (1958), 23 Law and Contemporary Problems 650 at p. 669.

sensus seems to be that the term connotes, among other things, a combination of defective judgment, explosive behaviour and total lack of conscience or remorse.[104] From the standpoint of the expert witness, therefore, it would follow that the word "irresistible" is a poor one to apply to the impulses of a psychopath, since the psychopath, with his allegedly defective *ego*, makes no real attempt to resist them.

Owing to the numerous difficulties which plague the current dangerous offender provision from start to finish, perhaps the best alternative is the most obvious: elimination of the entire procedure. In the words of the Law Reform Commission of Canada, "Serious offences, including sexual offences, should be dealt with under the ordinary sentencing law."[105]

---

[104] Weihofen, *Mental Disease as a Criminal Defense*, 2nd ed. (Buffalo, Dennis, 1954) at p. 23. See also Cooper, "The Inadequate Psychopath: Some Medico-Legal Problems and a Clinical Profile" (1973), 21 Chitty's L.J. 30.

[105] Law Reform Commission of Canada, *Report: Imprisonment and Release* (Ottawa, Information Canada, 1975).

CHAPTER 10

Psychiatric Treatment

I. Introduction

In the United States, the rapid growth of psychiatric knowledge and power has triggered the emergence of two parallel legal rights: (1) the right of prison inmates and involuntary mental patients to receive such psychiatric treatment as is adequate in light of present knowledge; and (2) the more novel right of such persons *not* to have certain forms of therapy forced upon them. These rights have been litigated in some states, statutorily enacted in others, and have been the subject of widespread commentary and discussion throughout the recent American legal literature. Oddly enough, the right to treatment/right not to be treated dialogue has not caught on in Canada. Despite the near universal advance of institutional psychiatric treatment, related jurisprudence remains virtually non-existent in this country. This state of affairs should particularly disturb the criminal lawyer or criminologist in view of the thorough psychiatrization which Canadian criminal law has undergone in recent years. While the Criminal Code and surrounding case law contain numerous rules pertaining to the trial and responsibility of mentally disordered persons, the law retains an unwholesome ambiguity as to what the disordered accused can expect once he leaves the courtroom. Having been found unfit to stand trial, acquitted on grounds of insanity, sentenced to a prison term, or diverted from the criminal process altogether, what rights and remedies does he possess as far as his psychiatric rehabilitation is concerned?

This chapter will address itself to the foregoing question as well as to the broader philosophical issue of what the law *should* be with regard to the treatment of disordered offenders. It will attempt to examine the problem from the standpoint not only of the offender, but of the institutional psychiatrist as well. As will be seen, there exists no single clear-cut answer which is applicable in the case of all disordered "offenders". While the legal answer may depend on such factors as an individual's criminal law status (*i.e.*, as an unfit accused, federal prisoner, provincial prisoner, etc.), his mental competence, and the province in which he is tried, the ethical solution may hinge upon such additional considerations as the person's supposed dangerousness, the seriousness of the crime involved, the nature of the proposed treatment, and so on.

II. The Right to Treatment

A. UNDER STATUTE

(i) The Insane Accused

Once an accused has been found unfit to stand trial, s-s. 543(6) of the Criminal Code comes into play. It provides:

> "(6) Where the verdict is that the accused is unfit on account of insanity to stand his trial, the court, judge or magistrate shall order that the accused be kept in custody until the pleasure of the lieutenant governor of the province is known ..."

On its face, this section merely provides for custodial care of the accused; it makes no reference whatsoever to treatment. In similar fashion, s-s. 542(2) makes this provision with regard to persons "acquitted" of indictable offences on the ground of insanity:

> "(2) Where the accused is found to have been insane at the time the offence was committed, the court, judge or magistrate before whom the trial is held shall order that he be kept in strict custody in the place and in the manner that the court, judge or magistrate directs, until the pleasure of the lieutenant governor of the province is known."

With regard to "the pleasure of the lieutenant governor", s-s. 545(1) of the Code further states:

> "545(1) Where an accused who is, pursuant to this Part, found to be insane, the lieutenant governor of the province in which he is detained may make an order
> (a) for the safe custody of the accused in a place and manner directed by him ..."

The wording here would seem to indicate two things: first, a lieutenant-governor is under no obligation to make any order at all;[1] and secondly,

---

[1] As indicated by s. 28 of the Interpretation Act, R.S.C. 1970, c.I-23, the word "may" is a permissive term, as opposed to the imperative word "shall".

that a lieutenant-governor possesses an extremely wide discretion as to the place and manner of confinement which may be ordered. This latter impression is supported by the decision of the Nova Scotia Supreme Court in *R. v. Coleman*,[2] where it was held that one of the options open under the forerunner of para. 545(1)(a) was simple incarceration in jail.

(ii) The Federal Prisoner

Prisoners under sentence in federal penitentiaries appear to enjoy the most clearly legislated right to psychiatric treatment. As regards medical treatment generally, Penitentiary Service Regulations,[3] s. 2.06 states:

> "2.06. Every inmate shall be provided, in accordance with directives, with the essential medical and dental care that he requires."

More specific on the matter of psychiatric treatment is s. 3.05.[4] It says:

> "3.05 Where an inmate is found to be suffering from mental disease he shall be segregated immediately from other inmates and shall be provided with psychiatric treatment appropriate for his condition."

One problem with the wording of s. 3.05 is that it does not specify by whom the prisoner must be "found" to be suffering from mental disease. Although a sentencing court may expressly find an offender to be mentally disordered, it is doubtful whether such finding automatically activates the prisoner's rights under s. 3.05. Nevertheless, judges frequently premise sentencing decisions upon the unfounded supposition that their recommendations for psychiatric treatment will be followed. As the Law Reform Commission has pointed out in a recent working paper:

> "Sometimes such recommendations are followed, often they are not. Although it is theoretically possible for prison authorities to transfer mentally disordered offenders to mental hospitals, in practice such transfers are rare. Because of the sparse facilities for psychiatric treatment in prisons generally, many prisoners suffering from serious mental disorders are detained without the prospect of treatment".[5]

Section 3.05 most likely confers upon the penitentiary itself the responsibility of assessing the mental health of its inmates. Unfortunately, however, the lack of diagnostic facilities in Canada's prisons[6]

---

[2] (1927), 47 C.C.C. 148.

[3] SOR/62-90

[4] *Ibid.*

[5] Law Reform Commission of Canada, *Working Paper: The Criminal Process and Mental Disorder* (Ottawa, Information Canada, 1975) at p. 46.

[6] Swadron, *Detention of the Mentally Disordered* (Toronto, Butterworths, 1964) at p. 418, citing the remarks of the Commissioner of Penitentiaries in *Proceedings of the Seminar on the Sentencing of Offenders* (Kingston, Queen's University, 1962) at p. 32.

may preclude a prisoner's right to receive psychiatric treatment from ever arising, since his mental disorder might go undetected.

By using the words "mental disease", s. 3.05 poses another more theoretical problem. Depending upon one's point of view, it may be possible to diagnose an entire prison population as "suffering from mental disease". Philip Q. Roche has asserted that "all felons are mental cases"[7] Szasz, on the other hand, has put forward the diametrically opposing argument that no one is mentally "ill" and that the terms "mental illness" and "mental disease" are mere metaphors.[8]

(iii) The Provincial Prisoner

For those persons who are serving sentences[9] in provincial prisons, s-s. 546(1) of the Code makes the following provision:

> "546(1) The lieutenant governor of a province *may*, upon evidence satisfactory to him that a person who is insane, mentally ill, mentally deficient or feeble-minded is serving a sentence in a prison[10] in that province, order that the person be removed to a place of safekeeping to be named in the order.[11]

This section is analogous to s-s. 19(1) of the Penitentiary Act.[12] As indicated by the permissive word "may",[13] it confers upon the lieutenant-governor of a province a discretion, not a duty, regarding the transfer of mentally disordered prisoners to psychiatric facilities. In a like manner, the mental health or correctional services legislation of some provinces may confer similar discretion upon other provincial officials. Section 21 of Manitoba's Mental Health Act,[14] for instance, empowers the director of psychiatric services to remove mentally disordered prisoners from the common gaol.[15]

---

[7] Roche, *The Criminal Mind: A Study of Communication Between Criminal Law and Psychiatry* (New York, Farrar, Strauss and Cudahy, 1958) at p. 241. For criticism of this philosophy, see Szasz, *Law Liberty and Psychiatry: An Inquiry into the Social Uses of Mental Health Practices* (New York, Macmillan, 1963) at pp. 91-108.

[8] Szasz, *The Myth of Mental Illness*, rev. ed. (New York, Harper and Row, 1974) at p. ix.

[9] Section 70 of the Criminal Law Amendment Act, 1975, 1974-75-76 (Can.), c. 93 has substituted the words "serving a sentence" for the words "in custody" in s-s. 546(1).

[10] Subsection 546(5) states:
"(5) In this section, 'prison' means a prison other than penitentiary, and includes a reformatory school or industrial school."

[11] Emphasis added.

[12] R.S.C. 1970, c. P-6.

[13] Interpretation Act, R.S.C. 1970, c. I-23, s. 28.

[14] R.S.M. 1970, c. M110.

[15] See also Manitoba's Corrections Act, R.S.M. 1970, c. C230, s-s. 35(1), which provides:
"35(1) The minister may direct, in writing, that any inmate of a correctional institution be removed to a hospital for medical, surgical, *or other treatment* as is shown to the minister to be urgently necessary." (Emphasis added.)
While this provision in no way guarantees hospitalization for the disordered prisoner, s. 24 of Quebec's former Mental Patients Institutions Act, R.S.Q. 1964, c. 166, replaced by the Mental Patients Protection Act, 1972 (Que.), c. 44, may be noted by way of contrast. It provided:

(iv) The Hospitalized Offender

Once hospitalized, does the mentally disordered offender enjoy a statutory right to treatment? The answer to this question must, of course, be resolved by reference to the mental health legislation of each province. While the relevant acts and regulations in some provinces provide no clear right to treatment, the provisions in others seem much more favourable. Amongst the more explicit provisions is cl. 11(1)(a) of British Columbia's Mental Health Act.[16] It states:

"11(1) A Director shall ensure that
(a) each patient in a Provincial mental health facility is provided with professional service, care and treatment appropriate to his condition and appropriate to the function of the Provincial mental health facility..."

In other provinces, the right to adequate psychiatric treatment in hospital may be inferred from the statutory enactment of penalties for neglecting mental patients. In Manitoba, for instance, s. 103 of the Mental Health Act warns:

"103. Any superintendent, officer, nurse, attendant, servant or person employed in a hospital or institution, or any person having charge, care, control, or supervision of a mentally disordered person, by reason of any contract or tie of relationship of marriage or otherwise, who ill-treats or wilfully neglects the mentally disordered per-

---

"24. When the sheriff of a district has reason to believe that a person detained in a gaol or other place of correction is suffering from mental illness, he *shall* have him examined by the superintendent of a hospital or by another physician designated by the Minister of Health; if the examination establishes that the prisoner is mentally deranged, the examining physician shall forward forthwith a report to that effect to the Minister of Health.

"The latter *shall* then issue an order for the conveyance of the prisoner to a hospital and such order shall justify the superintendent in keeping the patient there for close treatment; but the latter cannot be admitted to any home contemplated in section 28."

Clearly, the imperative wording here suggested a satutory right to psychiatric hospitalization. And see Reg. 166, R.R.O. 1970 under the Department of Correctional Services Act, R.S.O. 1970, c. 110 (renamed the Ministry of Correctional Services Act by 1972, c. 1, s-s. 59(1)), which contains this rather broad provision:

"17. When an inmate claims to be unable to work *by reason of sickness or other disability*, the medical officer shall examine the inmate and if, in his opinion, the inmate is unfit to work or his employment should be changed, he shall immediately certify the fact in writing to the Superintendent and upon receipt of such certification the inmate shall thereupon be relieved of work duties or have his employment changed or be *admitted to hospital or elsewhere for medical treatment* as directed by the medical officer."

(Emphasis added.) See also s. 3 of Reg. 166, which states, *inter alia*, that the superintendent of a correctional institution is responsible for the "care" and "health" of the institution's inmates. *Quaere* whether this section provides provincial prisoners in Ontario with a right to psychiatric treatment.

[16] 1964 (B.C.), c. 29, as am. by 1973 (2nd Sess.), c. 127, s. 8; 1974, c. 87, s. 28.

son is guilty of an offence."[17]

B. UNDER THE CANADIAN BILL OF RIGHTS

(i) Cruel and Unusual Treatment or Punishment

Insofar as para. 545(1)(a) would appear to authorize the non-treatment of insane accused persons, it is an interesting question whether that provision would be open to challenge on constitutional grounds. Although there exists no Canadian authority on the point, it may be argued that a failure to provide psychiatric treatment for those persons found unfit to stand trial would violate para. 2(b) of the Canadian Bill of Rights,[18] which states:

> "2. Every law of Canada shall, unless it is expressly declared by an Act of the Parliament of Canada that it shall operate notwithstanding the *Canadian Bill of Rights*, be so construed and applied as not to abrogate, abridge or infringe or to authorize the abrogation, abridgement or infringement of any of the rights or freedoms herein recognized and declared, and in particular, no law of Canada shall be construed or applied so as to
>
> . . .
>
> (b) impose or authorize the imposition of cruel and unusual treatment or punishment".

In the United States, detention of an unfit accused without providing treatment would appear to be a clear violation of the Eighth Amendment's prohibition against cruel and unusual punishment. In *Martarella v. Kelley*[19] a United States District Court was of the opinion that "although the State might legally detain non-criminals for compulsory treatment or other legitimate purposes which protect society or the person in custody, detention for mere illness — without a curative program — would be impermissible."[20] From a policy standpoint, there would seem to be no good reason why such reasoning should not be applied in Canada.

It may be questioned, however, whether the same policy considerations could be used to challenge the simple incarceration of someone "acquitted" under s. 16 of the Criminal Code. The case of *Re Kleinys' Habeas Corpus Application*[21] suggests that perhaps they could not. There the accused had been found not guilty by reason of insanity and committed by a magistrate to prison to await the pleasure of the provincial lieutenant-governor. Subsequently, the lieutenant-governor had directed his transfer to a mental hospital; however, at the time of his

---

[17] See also s-s. 29(2) of British Columbia's Mental Health Act, 1964 (B.C.), c. 29.
[18] R.S.C. 1970, App. III.
[19] (1972), 349 F. Supp. 575 (S.D.N.Y.).
[20] *Ibid.*, at p. 599.
[21] (1965), 51 W.W.R. 597 (B.C.).

application for *habeas corpus*, the accused was again being detained in prison. Rejecting the application, the British Columbia Supreme Court apparently saw nothing cruel or unusual about the accused's detention in prison without psychiatric treatment. In the Court's view, the accused was serving a valid indeterminate sentence.[22]

While the decision in *Kleinys* may well have rested upon an assumption that the prisoner no longer required psychiatric treatment (and would, presumably, be released upon application to the lieutenant-governor), the Court's refusal to inquire further into the matter suggests a lack of concern over the possibility that an insane person might continue to be detained without receiving further psychiatric attention. Yet even if the decision implies that non-treatment of an insane accused will not *per se* amount to cruel and unusual punishment, it is submitted that such reasoning is in no way incompatible with that in *Martarella v. Kelley*. It will be remembered that the latter case condemned the imprisonment without treatment of the *non-criminal* insane. But while an unfit accused is clearly non-criminal in status, the same cannot be said of someone "acquitted" on the ground of insanity. This point was made by the Ontario Court of Appeal in *R. v. Trapnell*.[23]

(ii) Due Process

(a) The Diverted Defendant
Owing to the phenomenon of pre-trial diversion, the mentally disordered accused stands a good chance of never being tried. As mentioned earlier,[24] the term "diversion", when used in the context of mentally disordered persons, usually refers to the substitution of civil commitment for criminal trial. In light of the fact that civil commitment entails a "massive curtailment of liberty"[25] which "may in some ways involve a

---

[22] *Ibid.*, at pp. 605-6.

[23] (1910), 22 O.L.R. 219. The case involved the escape from custody of three men found not guilty by reason of insanity. In arriving at its decision, the Court stated at pp. 222-3:

"It is essential to ascertain, in the first place, the character of the custody in which the men who escaped were held. They were confined in that which is called the criminal house of the Provincial Asylum at Hamilton, upon an order of the Lieutenant-Governor of the Province, made under sec. 969 of the Criminal Code; so that their custody must have been as criminals; otherwise the enactment would be *ultra vires*; civil rights, and the establishment, maintenance, and management of asylums, are exclusively provincial matters.

"But it is said that these men had been acquitted, and how, then, could they be detained except as lunatics simply? It is true that they were, in a sense, acquitted by the juries by which they were tried; but the acquittal was a part only of the verdicts; they were special verdicts under sec. 966 of the Criminal Code, the full import of which was that each had committed the crime with which he was charged, but was insane at the time, and on that ground only was acquitted. If they had been found not guilty of the commission of the crime, they would have been entitled to their discharge out of custody; the Criminal Code makes no provision for detention in such a case. It is to be observed, too, that the provisions of the Criminal Code under which these men were tried and imprisoned do not apply to those who are insane at the time of trial, but only to those who are then so sane as to be capable of defending themselves ...".

[24] See Chapter 1 *ante* at p. 7.

[25] *Humphrey v. Cady* (1974), 405 U.S. 504 at p. 509.

more serious abridgement of personal freedom than imprisonment for commission of a crime usually does",[26] the deprivation of criminal law safeguards would seem to demand justification. The rationale traditionally put forward is largely based on the doctrine of *parens patriae*;[27] while the aim of imprisonment is generally punishment, the decision to commit civilly arises either from the subject's supposed need for "observation, care and treatment"[28] or from an assessment that he "require[s] hospitalization in the interests of his own safety or the safety of others".[29] This being the case, it seems only logical that a hospital which commits a patient on such grounds should be bound to actually provide treatment in exchange for the patient's loss of liberty. Unfortunately, however, such reasoning does not necessarily reflect the present law of Canada. As things now stand, the only affirmative "right to treatment" an involuntary mental patient possesses is that which may arise from judicial interpretation of the statute under which he is committed; where no such right is conferred by provincial legislation, the Canadian mental patient may not rely on any higher "constitutional" right to treatment enjoyed by his American counterpart, and may be forced to depend on tort action.

In the United States the courts have invoked the doctrine of substantive due process under the Fourteenth Amendment to demonstrate a constitutional right to psychiatric treatment. As Johnson J. stated in the case of *Wyatt v. Stickney*,[30] "To deprive any citizen of his or her liberty upon the altruistic theory that the confinement is for humane therapeutic reasons and then fail to provide adequate treatment violates the very fundamentals of due process."[31] Similarly, Cutter J. of the Supreme Judicial Court of Massachusetts remarked in *Nason v. Superintendent, Bridgewater Hospital*[32] that, "Confinement of mentally ill persons, not found guilty of crime, without affording them reasonable treatment ... raises serious questions of deprivation of liberty without due process of law."[33]

The first case to clearly articulate the underpinnings of the substantive due process argument was that of *Donaldson v. O'Connor*,[34] a recent decision of the United States Court of Appeals. There Wisdom J. divided the theory into two separate components. The first boils down to three simple propositions, namely: (1) that the "nontrivial governmental abridgement of [any] freedom [which is part of the 'liberty' the Fourteenth Amendment says shall not be denied without due process of law] must be justified in terms of some 'permissible' governmental goal";[35] (2)

---

[26] *Donaldson v. O'Connor* (1974), 493 F. 2d 507 at p. 520.
[27] See Note, "The Nascent Right to Treatment" (1967), 53 Va.L.Rev. 1134 at pp. 1138-9.
[28] See Mental Health Act, R.S.O. 1970, c. 269, s.7.
[29] *Ibid.*, s. 8.
[30] (1971), 325 F. Supp. 781 (M.D. Ala.).
[31] *Ibid.*, at p. 785.
[32] (1968), 233 N.E. 2d 908.
[33] *Ibid.*, at p. 913. See also *Jackson v. Indiana* (1972), U.S. 715 (U.S.S.C.).
[34] (1974), 493 F. 2d 507.
[35] At p. 520, quoting Tribe, "Foreward — Toward a Model of Roles in the Due Process of Life and Law" (1973), 86 Harv. L. Rev. 1 at p. 17.

that "danger to self", "danger to others" and need for "treatment", "care", "custody" or "supervision" are the permissible governmental goals which justify civil commitment;[36] and (3) that "where . . . the rationale for confinement is ... that the patient is *in need of treatment*, the due process clause requires that minimally adequate treatment is in fact provided."[37]

The second part of the due process theory, which applies regardless of whatever rationale is used for commitment, was expressed in these terms:

> "...when the three central limitations on the government's power to detain — that detention be in retribution for specific offence; that it be limited to a fixed term; and that it be permitted after a proceeding where fundamental procedural safeguards are observed — are absent, there must be a *quid pro quo* extended by the government to justify confinement. And the *quid pro quo* most commonly recognized is the provision of rehabilitative treatment ..."[38]

Unfortunately, the due process argument (like the cruel and unusual treatment or punishment argument) cannot be used to provide civilly committed offenders with a right to treatment in Canada. The reason behind this fact is simple: para. 1(a) of the Bill of Rights[39] guarantees that citizens receive due process only where their rights are purportedly affected by federal legislation.[40] While the Criminal Code is a federal statute, mental health acts are not. Even where Criminal Code provisions[41] are used to dispose of mentally disordered defendants, it remains doubtful whether *substantive* due process[42] is a viable safeguard in this country.[43]

Ignoring for the moment the lack of success which substantive due process has had under the Bill of Rights, it is an interesting question whether the failure to provide psychiatric treatment for certain classes of disordered offenders might not compel Canadian adoption of the *Donaldson* rationale in the future. Had the diverted defendant come

---

[36] *Supra*, footnote 34, at p. 520.

[37] *Ibid.*, at p. 521 (emphasis added).

[38] *Ibid.*, at p. 522.

[39] R.S.C. 1970, App. III:

> "1. It is hereby recognized and declared that in Canada there have existed and shall continue to exist without discrimination by reason of race, national origin, colour, religion or sex, the following human rights and fundamental freedoms, namely,
>
>> (a) the right of the individual to life, liberty, security of the person and enjoyment of property, and the right not to be deprived thereof except by due process of law."

[40] Subsection 5(3) provides:

> "(3) The provisions of Part I shall be construed as extending only to matters coming within the legislative authority of the Parliament of Canada."

[41] *I.e.*, s-ss. 543(2) and (2.1), s. 544, s-ss. 738(5) and (6).

[42] As opposed to *procedural* due process.

[43] See the decision of the Supreme Court of Canada in *Curr v. The Queen*, [1972] S.C.R. 889. And see Tarnapolsky, *The Canadian Bill of Rights*, 2nd ed. (Toronto, McClelland and Stewart Ltd., 1975) at pp. 222-35.

within the jurisdiction of the Bill of Rights, he would have been the perfect candidate for application of the *quid pro quo* argument; all three "central limitations on the government's right to detain" are undoubtedly absent from the civil commitment process. In the case of the unfit accused, the dangerous offender or the accused acquitted under s. 16 of the Code, however, the same cannot be said. Although such persons fall within the purview of the Canadian Bill of Rights, their incarceration is limited by the procedural safeguards set out in the Criminal Code. But would not an absence of the other two "central limitations" be sufficient to provide a right to treatment?

(b) The Unfit Accused
It is submitted that the mere provision of procedural safeguards does not alter the *quid pro quo* argument sufficiently to justify the non-treatment of a person found unfit to stand trial. Because in this case the indefinite deprivation of liberty is actuated by purely benevolent design, an obligation must surely rest upon the Crown to endeavour to achieve the purpose for which s. 543 was obviously enacted.

(c) The Dangerous Offender
In theory, the dangerous offender receives his indefinite sentence not as retribution for a specific offence, but simply for his status as such. Nevertheless, it is doubtful that the main purpose of preventive detention is to rehabilitate the offender. Although some American authorities suggest that preventive detainees may enjoy a due process right to treatment,[44] the case for Canadian courts adopting their approach would seem less compelling than that presented by the unfit accused.

(d) The Accused Acquitted Under S. 16
It seems clear that in both England and Canada the main purpose of indefinitely confining someone acquitted by reason of insanity was never the provision of psychiatric treatment. Rather, our jurisprudence indicates that an individual who has received a special verdict under s. 16 but is presently sane (and does *not* necessarily require therapy, therefore) may nevertheless be detained for the public's protection. As the Quebec Superior Court expressed it in *Re Duclos*:[45]

> "The theory of the law... is that the fact of having committed the offence puts him in the class known as dangerous or criminal lunatics. It insists that there should be full subsequent observation and enquiry as to whether his delirium, or his emotional state of mental irresponsibility has run its full course, in other words, whether the lucidity of mind which justified a trial was that of an interval, or permanent."

---

[44] See *Sas v. Maryland* (1964), 334 F. 2d 506 at p. 517 (4th Cir.), cert. dismissed *sub. nom. Murel v. Baltimore City Crim. Ct.* (1972), 407 U.S. 355 (defective delinquent statute); *Davy v. Sullivan* (1973), 354 F. Supp. 1320 (sex offender statute).
[45] (1907), 12 C.C.C. 278 at p. 282.

This being the case, it would seem difficult to support a due process right to treatment for someone who is not necessarily in need of treatment. It is worth noting, however, that such right may accrue to persons found insane in the United States, where statutes committing persons so acquitted to mental institutions have been held to possess a clearly rehabilitative purpose.[46]

C. UNDER TORT LAW

Once a disordered offender has been hospitalized, it is likely that the hospital is under a duty to provide him with proper psychiatric treatment. Nor is such duty necessarily limited to that which may exist under statute. Although there do not appear to be any Canadian cases directly on point, it is submitted that an action for malpractice might lie against any mental institution that neglects to treat its patients. In *Whitree v. State*,[47] an American mental patient brought tort action after receiving 14½ years of mere custodial care in the hospital to which he had been committed pursuant to a finding of incompetence to stand trial. Having ascertained that proper psychiatric treatment would have brought about his release at a much earlier date, the court found the hospital guilty of malpractice and awarded damages for the 12 years of false imprisonment, "moral and mental degradation", and loss of income which resulted therefrom.[48]

---

[46] See *e.g., Ragsdale v. Overholser* (1960), 281 F. 2d 943 at p. 950 (U.S. App. D.C.).

[47] (1968), 290 N.Y.S. 2d 486 (Ct.Cl.).

[48] The court also awarded damages for the pain and suffering which resulted from the following circumstances: "On April 5, 1955, another patient poured hot coffee over him causing first degree burns to his face and chest. On March 4, 1961, he was kicked in the face by another patient causing a fracture to 2 upper incisors, 4 lower incisors to loosen, a fracture of the nose, and a laceration requiring 4 sutures to close. On several occasions, while Whitree was sleeping, he was struck by other patients and his testicles were squeezed. He was struck, kicked, and beaten by attendants. The headaches which Whitree has had through the years since November, 1955, and up to the time of the trial, were causally related to the injuries reflected by his hospitalization on November 2, 1955. On or about September 5, 1950, Whitree sustained a complete fracture of the second metacarpal bone of the left hand which healed with deformity. He sustained a comminuted fracture of the distal end of the right tibia which healed with deformity. He sustained a fracture of the greater tuberosity of the right shoulder which healed with deformity. He sustained fractures of the eighth and ninth ribs posteriorly on the left side. He sustained an injury in the area of the fifth and sixth cervical vertebrae which resulted in a deformity and compression of the bodies of said vertebrae, so that, as a consequence of said injury, he developed an osteoarthritic condition in that area of the cervical spine. As a consequence of the beatings administered to Whitree while a patient during the 12 year period aforesaid, he sustained a permanent and chronic peritonitis of the right shoulder." (p. 504). The hospital provided no treatment for these injuries other than vaseline and rectal suppositories.

III. The Standard of Treatment

Even where the right to psychiatric treatment can be demonstrated, there remains a fundamental question to be answered: To what type and quality of treatment is the disordered offender entitled? The formulation of standards is, of course, essential to the enforcement of any right to treatment. As one commentator has put it:

> "The right to treatment, if it is to become more than mere idealistic rhetoric devoid of practical social consequences, must be measurable by clear standards. The courts, legislatures, treatment personnel, and attorneys must have some precise standard in mind by which they can determine whether the amount of treatment provided or not provided for a patient is an appropriate matter for legal action".[49]

As American jurisprudence indicates, there are basically two approaches which may be taken with regard to the development of treatment standards: (a) the uniform approach; and (b) the individual approach. Advocates of the former argue that unless a treatment programme meets certain objective criteria, the patient is *prima facie* being denied adequate treatment. Among the more commonly propounded indicators is the institution's staff-patient ratio.[50] It has been recommended that the courts choose one ratio as reasonable. Birnbaum has suggested[51] the adoption of the American Psychiatric Association's former *Standards for Hospitals and Clinics*[52] — namely, one physician per 30 patients in admission and intensive care services and one physician per 150 patients in continued treatment services. In *Wyatt v. Stickney*,[53] however, a United States District Court considered a staff-patient ratio of six physicians (two of whom had to be psychiatrists) per 250 patients[54] to be a "medical and constitutional minimum".[55]

Critics of the uniform approach have been quick to point out that adherence to so-called "objective" standards by no means guarantees proper treatment for all patients in mental institutions. As Schwitzgebel has noted, "the minimally adequate staff may be far from sufficient if

---

[49] Schwitzgebel, "Right to Treatment for the Mentally Disabled: The Need for Realistic Standards and Objective Criteria" (1973), 8 Harvard Civil Rights — Civil Liberties, L. Rev. 513 at p. 515.

[50] Others include: the number of hours of individual consultation provided to each patient over a given period of time, the frequency of consultation, etc. See Bazelon, "Implementing the Right to Treatment" (1969), 36 U. Chi. L.Rev. 742 at p. 746.

[51] Birnbaum, "The Right to Treatment" (1960), 46 A.B.A.J. 499 at p. 504, footnote 37.

[52] (1958).

[53] (1972), 344 F. Supp. 373.

[54] *Ibid.*, at p. 383. The Court also held (by way of court order) that for every 250 patients, a mental hospital should employ 12 registered nurses, 6 licensed practical nurses, 4 psychologists, 1 "vocational rehabilitation counselor", 10 "patient activity aides", 10 "mental health technicians", and 10 hospital orderlies.

[55] *Ibid.*, at p. 376.

the institution is attempting to follow particular treatment programs requiring a much higher staff-patient ratio".[56] Furthermore, even a well-staffed hospital may fail to provide patients with whatever forms of treatment suit their particular needs.[57] Conversely, it may be possible for a hospital to administer effective therapy in certain instances despite its lack of compliance with accepted minimum personnel requirements; some patients require less of the hospital's resources than others. For these reasons, the American Psychiatric Association in 1969 eschewed staff-patient ratios from its Standards for Psychiatric Facilities.[58] It was the Association's view that such statistics were "meaningless as a general standard" and that "The type and purpose of the facility, the objectives and methods of treatment, and the physical plant all influence the type and number of personnel required."[59]

The philosophy articulated by Bazelon C.J. in *Rouse v. Cameron*[60] more or less exemplifies the individual approach to the formulation of treatment standards. In that case the learned judge defined the mental patient's right to treatment in terms of a right to receive whatever therapy was "suited to his particular needs",[61] and pointed out that "Treatment that has therapeutic value for some may not have such value for others".[62] This individualized standard seems to have been adopted elsewhere in the United States as well as in Canada. In *Millard v. Cameron*[63] and *Application of D.D.*,[64] for instance, the courts affirmed a right to "suitable" psychiatric treatment. In *People v. Kearse*[65] and *Clatterbuck v. Harris*[66] the courts spoke of "appropriate treatment" and "treatment adequate for his condition" respectively. Similarly, under Penitentiary Service Regulations, s. 3.05 every mentally disordered inmate in Canada's federal penitentiary system is entitled to "psychiatric treatment appropriate for his condition".[67]

But what about those disordered offenders who are not serving time in a federal penitentiary? To what standard of psychiatric care are they entitled? In those provinces where no legislative or judicial authority

---

[56] *Ibid.*, at p. 524.

[57] Halpern, "A Practicing Lawyer Views the Right to Treatment" (1969), 57 Geo. L.J. 782 at p. 792.

[58] (1969), 126 Am. J. Psychiatry 879.

[59] De Marneffe, "The New APA Standards for Psychiatric Facilities" (1969), 126 Am. J. Psychiatry 879.

[60] (1966), 373 F. 2d 451 (D.C. Cir.).

[61] *Ibid.*, at p. 456.

[62] *Ibid.* In an article entitled "Implementing the Right to Treatment" (1969), 36 U.Chi.L.Rev. 742 at p. 746, Judge Bazelon has elaborated as follows: "The mere fact that a hospital can provide some treatment for all patients should not, as some courts have been content to conclude, satisfy the requirement of adequate treatment for the individual patient. The most important facet of the right to treatment is not that the hospital does something for everyone, but that it does the right thing for the right patient. Because individual patients, particularly mental patients, vary so much in their needs, considerable attention must be paid to the patient as an individual."

[63] (1966), 373 F. 2d 468 at p. 472 (D.C. Cir.).

[64] (1971), 118 N.J. Super. 1 at p. 5 (App. Div.).

[65] (1967), 282 N.Y.S. 2d 136 at p. 137 (App. Div.).

[66] (1968), 295 F. Supp. 84 at p. 86 (D.D.C.).

[67] See also cl. 11(1)(a) of British Columbia's Mental Health Act, cited, *supra*, at p. 293.

exists concerning the rights of provincial prisoners to treatment, it may well be that any constitutional protection provided by the Canadian Bill of Rights would be held non-justiciable. In illustration of this dilemma, the case of *Burnham v. Department of Public Health (Georgia)*[68] may be cited. There the plaintiffs, who were patients in a state mental institution, sought to assert their constitutional right to "adequate treatment" by means of a class action for declaratory relief and injunction. Somewhat ironically, the defendants relied upon an argument propounded by Thomas Szasz to defeat the plaintiffs' claim:

> "Levine [M. Levine, Psychotherapy in Medical Practice 17-19 (1942)] lists 40 methods of psychotherapy. Among these, he includes physical treatment, medicinal treatment, reassurance, authoritative firmness, hospitalization, ignoring of certain symptoms and attitudes, satisfaction of neurotic needs and bibliotherapy. In addition, there are physical methods of psychiatric therapy, such as the prescription of sedatives and tranquilizers, the induction of convulsions by drugs and electricity, and brain surgery. Obviously, the term 'psychiatric treatment' covers everything that may be done under medical auspices — and more.
>
> "If mental treatment is all the things Levine and others tell us it is, how are we to determine whether or not patients in mental hospitals receive adequate amounts of it?"[69]

Having quoted this passage, the court declared simply:

> "It is, therefore, the opinion of this Court that the claimed 'duty' (i.e., to 'adequately' or 'constitutionally treat') defies judicial identity and therefore prohibits its breach from being judicially defined."[70]

Even assuming that Canadian courts were to adopt the individualized standard which apparently applies to federal inmates,[71] such decision would not entirely dispose of Szasz's dilemma. Because of the rather wide latitude which the individualized approach allows, it may be possible to bring all sorts of unorthodox forms of psychiatric intervention

---

[68] (1972), 349 F. Supp. 1335 (N.D. Ga.).

[69] Szasz, "The Right to Psychiatric Treatment: Rhetoric and Reality" (1969), 57 Georgetown L.J. 740 at p. 741, quoted in *Burnham* at p. 1342.

[70] *Supra*, footnote 68 at p. 1342.

[71] Canadian courts might prefer the reasoning used in *Donaldson v. O'Connor* (1974), 493 F. 2d 507 at pp. 525-6. There the court expressly disagreed with the decision in *Burnham*, saying: ". . . we doubt whether, even if we were to concede that courts are incapable of formulating standards of adequate treatment in the abstract, we could or should for that reason alone hold that no right to treatment can be recognized or enforced. There will be cases — and the case at bar is one — where it will be possible to make determination whether a given individual has been denied his right to treatment without formulating in the abstract what constitutes 'adequate' treatment". The court went on in fact to formulate an abstract standard, saying (at p. 527) that the patient had a right to "such treatment as will help him to be cured or to improve his mental condition." Such standard follows the individual approach set out in *Rouse v. Cameron*.

under the broad umbrella of "treatment". Indeed, the major difficulty with a *wholly* individualized concept of treatment is that it draws no theoretical distinctions between therapy and non-therapy. This being the case, it would seem possible to justify the simple imprisonment of a disturbed offender should psychiatric evidence indicate such "treatment" appropriate.[72] Moreover, the prisoner for whom "incarceration therapy" was deemed most suitable would have no right to demand a less effective (though perhaps more therapeutic-*looking*) form of therapy involving hospitalization.

In actual fact, the American courts have taken neither a totally uniform nor a totally individual route with regard to the development of treatment standards. Reflecting a more or less hybrid approach, the court in *Wyatt v. Stickney (No. 2)* stated the minimum requirements of adequate treatment to be "(1) a humane psychological and physical environment, (2) qualified staff in numbers sufficient to administer adequate treatment and (3) individualized treatment plans".[73] Similarly, in *Rouse v. Cameron*, Bazelon C.J., though he advocated the individual approach, acknowledged that:

> "The effort should be to provide treatment which is adequate in light of present knowledge. . . .[74] Counsel for the patient and the government can be helpful in presenting pertinent data concerning standards for mental care. . . . Assistance might be obtained from such sources as the American Psychiatric Association, which has published standards . . ."[75]

It is submitted that uniform and individual approaches to treatment standards are quite capable of peaceful co-existence. If for no other reason, uniform minimum standards are useful for establishing the tactical onus of proof where dispute arises as to adequate treatment. Once a plaintiff has established the institution's failure to comply with certain objective treatment criteria, the burden should shift to the institution to demonstrate that it is providing appropriate treatment for the individual despite such failure. Conversely, the adherence to minimum standards should create a presumption of adequate treatment in favour of

---

[72] There is no doubt that some psychiatrists do view imprisonment as a form of therapy in itself. In the case of *Re Maddox* (1957), 88 N.W. 2d 470 four psychiatrists testified that imprisonment was "recognized treatment" for a man with the prisoner's disorder. The Supreme Court of Michigan held, however (at p. 476) that "incarceration in a penitentiary designed and used for the confinement of convicted criminals is not a prescription available upon medical diagnosis . . .". It is to be noted that the prisoner involved in this case had never been convicted of any criminal offence. Where an individual has, in fact, been adjudged criminal, psychiatric support for the theory of "imprisonment as therapy" appears to be quite common. See Bartholomew, "The Psychiatric Report for the Court", [1962] Crim. L.R. 19 at p. 21 and Gunn, "Sentencing — As Seen by a Psychiatrist" (1971), 11 Med. Sci. and the Law 95 at p. 97.

[73] (1971), 334 F. Supp. 1341 at p. 1343 (M.D. Ala.).

[74] See also *Wyatt v. Stickney (No. 1)* (1971), 325 F.Supp. 781 at p. 785; (M.D. Ala.); *Nason v. Superintendent of Bridgewater State Hospital* (1968), 233 N.E. 2d 908; *Cook v. Ciccone* (1970), 312 F. Supp. 822 (W.D. Mo.).

[75] *Supra*, footnote 60 at pp. 456-7.

the institution. But the compliance or lack of compliance with uniform minimums should not in itself decide the issue of adequacy.

IV. The Right Not to be Treated

> " 'Man, what they got going on in there?' McMurphy asks Harding.
> " 'In there? Why, that's right, isn't it? You haven't had the pleasure. Pity. An experience no human should be without?' Harding laces his fingers behind his neck and leans back to look at the door. 'That's the Shock Shop I was telling you about some time back, my friend, the EST, Electro-Shock Therapy. Those fortunate souls in there are being given a free trip to the moon. . . .'
> . . .
> " 'What they do is' — McMurphy listens a moment — 'take some bird in there and shoot *electricity* through his skull?'
> " 'That's a concise way of putting it.'
> " 'What the hell *for*?'
> " 'Why, the patient's good, of course. Everything done here is for the patient's good.' "[76]

As demonstrated by the American experience, the emergence of a legal right to psychiatric treatment may entail some rather far-reaching and perplexing consequences. If the state is obliged as *parens patriae* to provide adequate care and treatment for the institutionalized "mentally ill", the question which naturally arises is this: Can or should the fulfillment of such obligation be frustrated by a patient's wish *not* to be treated?

A. THE DOCTRINE OF VOLUNTARY INFORMED CONSENT

As regards the normal doctor-patient relationship, the legal rules relating to treatment are fairly well established. Generally speaking, it is mandatory for a physican to obtain the consent of his patient before embarking upon any course of treatment. Failure to do so may render the doctor liable in a tort action[77] or subject to possible criminal

---

[76] Kesey, *One Flew Over the Cuckoo's Nest* (New York, Signet Books, 1963) at pp. 162-3.
[77] From basic principles, it is clear that medical treatment in the absence of prior voluntary informed consent will normally constitute a battery: *Younts v. St. Francis Hospital and School of Nursing Inc.* (1970), 205 Kan. 292; *Mohr v. Williams* (1905), 95 Minn. 261; *Pratt v. Davis* (1906), 224 Ill. 300; *Tabor v. Scobel* (1952), 254 S.W. 2d 474 (Ky. C.A.); *Lacey v. Laird* (1956), 166 Ohio St. 12; *Rolater v. Strain* (1914), 39 Okla. 572. Alternatively, such conduct may amount to a negligent omission, either through failure to adequately inform the patient of the procedure involved, or through a failure to warn the patient of the attendant risks: *Kenny v. Lockwood*, [1932] 1 D.L.R. 507 (Ont. C.A.); *Male v. Hopmans*, [1967] 2 O.R. 457 (C.A.). Furthermore, as the decision in *Boase v. Paul*, [1931] 1 D.L.R. 562 (Ont.); affd [1931] 4 D.L.R. 435 (C.A.) suggests, a doctor may be guilty of negligence (in addition to battery) if he exceeds the authority conferred by the patient's instructions.

prosecution.[78] Nor should this situation be any different where the physician involved is a psychiatrist.[79] As one commentator has noted, "no cases have been found that have held that [a privately consulted psychiatrist] is not bound by the same informed consent standards as the regular medical practitioner."[80]

For some peculiar reason, however, American courts seem largely to have abandoned the doctrine of voluntary informed consent when dealing with the incarcerated mental patient. In *Whitree v. State*,[81] for example, the court awarded damages to a patient who had been committed as incompetent to stand trial, but who had not received any treatment for his condition. According to the evidence, the doctors had not treated Whitree with any of the modern tranquilizing drugs available for the simple reason that he had refused them. The court rejected this excuse, however, considering it to be "illogical, unprofessional and not consonant with prevailing medical standards."[82]

The decision in *Whitree* implies that involuntary mental patients possess no right to refuse treatment.[83] This being the case, one might well ask what justifications underlie such a policy. The rationale most frequently put forward is that the mental patient, by definition, is precluded by illness from knowing what is in his own best interest.[84] Paradoxically, however, the courts have chosen to ignore the patient's mental impairment as a possible basis for impugning the validity of his consent when it is purportedly *given*. In *Wilson v. Lehman*,[85] for example, a patient brought action in tort against her psychiatrists, claiming that she had received electroconvulsive therapy without her consent. The Kentucky Court of Appeals rejected her claim, however, relying on the fact that she had voluntarily entered the hospital for the purpose of receiving such treatment. What is significant is the fact that the Court

---

[78] Section 244 of the Criminal Code provides:
"244. A person commits an assault when
   (a) without the consent of another person or with consent, where it is obtained by fraud, he applies force intentionally to the person of another, directly or indirectly".

[79] Sullivan, "The Involuntarily Confined Mental Patient and Informed Consent to Psychiatric Treatment" (1974), 5 Loyola U of Chi. L.J. 478 at p. 596. See also Dawidoff, "The Malpractice of Psychiatrists" (1966), Duke L.J. 696 and Morse, "The Tort Liability of the Psychiatrist" (1967), 19 Bay. L. Rev. 208, both cited by Sullivan.

[80] Sullivan, at p. 596.

[81] (1968), 290 N.Y.S. 2d 486 (Ct.Cl.).

[82] *Ibid.*, at p. 501.

[83] See Rastatter, "The Rights of the Mentally Ill During Incarceration: The Developing Law" (1973), 25 U.Fla. L. Rev. 494 at p. 503.

[84] *Ibid.* And see *Hearings on the Constitutional Rights of the Mentally Ill Before the Subcommittee on Constitutional Rights of the Senate Committee on the Judiciary*, 87th Congress, 1st Sess., part 1 at p. 340 and Ross, "Commitment of the Mentally Ill: Problems of Law and Policy" (1959), 57 Mich. L. Rev. 945 at p. 1004, where the writer explains: "The argument is that mentally ill persons are considered wards of the state. The state as *parens patriae* must provide necessary care and treatment. The care and treatment of mental patients is a governmental function and the basic consideration in the exercise of this function is the patient's welfare, not what the patient or his relatives believe to be in his interests."

[85] (1964), 379 S.W. 2d 478.

did not even consider the possibility that the patient's mental condition could have prevented her from giving a proper consent.[86] A similar result was reached in *Aiken v. Clary*,[87] a case which involved the use of insulin coma therapy on another "voluntary" mental patient. There the court held the patient's apparent agreement to such therapy to be conclusive on the matter of consent, despite the fact that her own physician considered her to be certifiably ill. As a matter of fact, it was the direct threat of involuntary commitment which had been used to coerce the patient's "consent" in the first place.

The disparate results reached in the cases of *Whitree; Wilson* and *Aiken* lead inevitably to the conclusion that American courts tend to determine a patient's ability to consent solely on the basis of whether or not he or she is involuntarily confined in a mental institution, and without considering the nature and effect of a patient's particular mental illness.[88] Commenting on this somewhat arbitrary approach, one critic has written:

> "It seems remarkable that a person suffering from a mental illness could be deemed incapable of giving his informed consent to psychiatric treatment solely because of his status as an involuntary mental patient. There seems to be no logical basis for allowing a private individual the right to give his informed consent to psychiatric treatment while an involuntarily confined mental patient suffering from the same illness can be denied this right."[89]

The use of involuntary confinement as a test of one's ability to give or withhold a valid consent would seem justifiable if it could be shown that only those persons who are incapable of properly consenting are involuntarily confined.[90] With regard to those disordered persons who have lost their liberty as the result of criminal proceedings, such is definitely not the case. In the case of those offenders who have been civilly committed, however, it may more easily be asserted that because involuntary hospitalization implies an inability of the patient to recognize his need for treatment or to act in his own best interests, it also implies that such person lacks the capacity to consent. But while this type of argument holds a certain amount of logic, there is no reason to consider it decisive on the legal issue of consent in Canada. Swadron has asserted that "the statutory authority to detain a person in a mental hospital does not *per se* include the authority to treat him compulsorily".[91] He has further suggested that the question of whether or not an involuntary patient may be treated compulsorily must be resolved solely by means of statutory interpretation.[92] Presumably, the absence of any express

---

[86] See Sullivan, at p. 596.
[87] (1965), 396 S.W. 2d 668 (Mo.).
[88] Sullivan, at p. 597.
[89] *Ibid.*
[90] *Ibid.*
[91] Swadron, *Detention of the Mentally Disordered*, at p. 117.
[92] *Ibid.*

provision removing the patient's right of consent would leave his prerogative intact.[93]

But even if one assumes that imprisonment or involuntary hospitalization need not in itself divest a disordered offender of his right to accept or refuse treatment, the problem of voluntary informed consent is far from solved. For even when a patient/prisoner has apparently "consented" to undergo a form of treatment which has more or less been explained to him, his consent may be rendered ineffective for one of two reasons. First, the individual may in fact be incompetent. If he has been so declared by legal process, a committee of his person may have been appointed,[94] and it may be necessary to secure the committee's consent before administering treatment. If the patient has not been declared incompetent, however, a real dilemma arises. For one thing, the doctors who wish to administer treatment will likely be the ones who determine his competence to consent or refuse.[95] Furthermore, assuming that the staff psychiatrists consider the patient to be incompetent, it is unclear from whom they must then obtain a substitute consent. Generally, if a mental incompetent is not in an emergency state, nor under guardianship, there is no person who can consent for him in the absence of statute.[96] Though the institution's superintendent may actually take the place of a committee,[97] it has been pointed out that provincial mental health legislation seldom gives the director or administrator of a hospital the power of guardianship over the person of his patients.[98] In light of

---

[93] An example of such express provision may be found in cl. 11(1)(a) of British Columbia's Mental Health Act, cited, *supra*, at p. 293. It states:

"11(1) A Director shall ensure that
  (a) each patient in a Provincial mental health facility is provided with professional service, care and treatment appropriate to his condition and appropriate to the function of the Provincial mental health facility, and, *for those purposes, may sign consent to treatment forms for a person admitted under section 23.*"

(Emphasis added.) See also s. 19 of Saskatchewan's Mental Health Act., R.S.S. 1965, c. 345. It provides:

"19(1) Except in case of emergency or where an examination is authorized under section 21, where a patient is detained in an in-patient facility under the authority of section 10, no diagnostic or treatment services or procedures shall be carried out upon the patient except with his consent or that of his nearest relative.

"(2) Where a patient is detained in an in-patient facility under the authority of section 11, 12, 14, 16, 17 or 18, *the medical officer in charge shall have full authority to determine the care and treatment to be provided to the patient and to direct the giving of that care and treatment.*"

(Emphasis added.)

[94] A "committee of the person" is to be distinguished from a "committee of the estate". While some mental health statutes make provision for the appointment of both (see *e.g.*, Manitoba's Mental Health Act, R.S.M. 1970, c. M110, Part III), others make no reference at all to committees of the person as such (see *e.g.*, Ontario's Mental Incompetency Act, R.S.O. 1970, c. 271). Even where provincial legislation provides for both, Swadron has noted that mental incompetency proceedings are "very rarely used to obtain the appointment of a committee of the person". See Swadron, *Mental Retardation — the Law — Guardianship* (Toronto, National Institute on Mental Retardation, 1971) at p. 113.

[95] Swadron, *op. cit.* footnote 6, at p. 115.

[96] Rozovsky, "Consent to Treatment" (1973), 11 Osgoode Hall L.J. 103 at p. 110.

[97] Swadron, *op. cit.* footnote 6, at p. 116.

[98] Rozovsky, at p. 110.

this rather uncertain state of affairs, Gray has offered the following suggestion:

> "In the absence of statutory authority, and where no committee has been appointed, it is recommended that the following procedure be followed. . . . If the patient is mentally incompetent, a consent from his nearest relative should be obtained with an appended statement by one, or preferably two, psychiatrists that the patient is mentally incompetent to consent. If the consent of a near relative cannot be obtained, it is suggested that the consent of a relative be dispensed with, if the treatment is essential to preserve the patient's health."[99]

Whether or not this procedure is legally acceptable remains a moot point.[100] An alternative procedure might be to have the patient declared incompetent under statute so that a committee might be appointed for the patient. It should be noted, however, that even the appointment of a "committee of the person" may not in reality be the panacea it would appear to be. The crucial and unanswered question is what the powers of the committee are. Is such person authorized to consent for a mental incompetent?

Another ground upon which the purported consent of a prisoner or involuntary mental patient may be attacked pertains to the essential element of volition. As the English Court of Appeal explained in the case of *Bowater v. Rowley Regis Corp.*:[101]

> ". . . a man cannot be said to be truly 'willing' unless he is in a position to choose freely, and freedom of choice predicates, not only full knowledge of the circumstances on which the exercise of choice is conditioned, so that he may be able to choose wisely, but the absence from his mind of any feeling of constraint so that nothing shall interfere with the freedom of his will."

It follows from these words that a consent obtained by fraud or given under circumstances of duress is no consent at all.[102] But surely there are "grey areas" as well where, though neither fraud nor duress are present, the consent obtained cannot truly be said to have been given voluntarily. This may be particularly true in the case of institutional and correctional therapy, where release depends in large measure upon co-operation and the use of coercion (whether blatant or implicit) is to some extent inevitable. One writer has recently reported that the practice at Penetanguishene has been to obtain consent to experimental treatment by means of coercive pressure:

---

[99] Gray, *Law and the Practice of Medicine*, 2nd ed. (1955) at pp. 35-6, quoted by Swadron, at p. 119.

[100] See the *Report of the American Bar Foundation on the Rights of the Mentally Ill* at p. 148, quoted by Swadron, *op. cit.* footnote 6, at p. 120, where it is stated: "As to the matter of securing the consent of the inmate's relatives, it is my belief that such is not necessary as a matter of law, but where it is obtained, it is my feeling that such a course is one to be commended."

[101] [1944] K.B. 476 *per* Scott L.J. at p. 479.

[102] *Woods v. Brumlop*, (1962), 71 N.M. 221; *Paulsen v. Gundersen* (1935), 218 Wis. 578.

"A 'management' ward characterized by restricted privileges and movement is reserved for non-volunteers. Patients unwilling to attend ward meeting would, in the words of a staff member 'probably be dragged to the meeting'. In most cases, however, physical coercion is used as a last resort. Most patients are usually convinced by the staff and other patients that 'this is for their own good'. This phrase has a double meaning; in one sense it refers to an attempt at curing the individual's illness; it also refers to the reality of being on an indeterminate sentence, unless you co-operate the psychiatrist is not going to let you go."[103]

Melitta Schmideberg has argued that the use of psychological coercion by prison and hospital authorities is in fact essential to the rehabilitative process:

"Rehabilitation is possible only if the offender wishes to change. To make the very great effort which is necessary the offender needs a strong motivation. This usually stems from a deterrent that has really shaken him. Thus, rehabilitation depends on the (open or implied) threat on the one hand, and on the hope on the other."[104]

But would not such emotional constraint render one's consent to treatment invalid? To use an anology to the confession rule, is not such consent motivated by a "fear of prejudice or hope of advantage [implicitly] held out by a person in authority?"[105] In opposition to this line of reasoning, Seymour Halleck has advanced the following argument:

"It could be argued that in the correctional setting psychotherapy is neither contractual nor voluntary. Many offenders would never seek treatment unless faced with the threat of continued punishment. Some, in fact, are faced with the choice of psychotherapy or prison. Yet in many ways the offender's situation is not different from that of most other people who seek psychiatric help. Few patients are ever eager to see a psychiatrist. A person seeks psychotherapy when he is desperate and unable to ward off the oppressive onslaughts of other people or his own conscience. In the case of the offender, it is sometimes the threat of oppression by society (imprisonment) which drives him to psychotherapy. He chooses treatment in order to avoid or shorten the duration of the psychological pain of imprisonment, just as the neurotic chooses treatment in order to ward off more covert sources of psychological pain. Both

[103] Desroches, "Regional Psychiatric Centres: A Myopic View?" (1973), 15 Can. J. Corr. 200 at p. 212.
[104] Schmideberg, "Re-evaluating the Concepts of Rehabilitation and Punishment" (1968), 12 Internat. J. Offender Therapy, quoted by Rappeport, "Enforced Treatment — Is it Treatment?" (1974), 2 Bulletin of the American Academy of Psychiatry and the Law 148 at p. 150.
[105] *Ibrahim v. The King*, [1914] A.C. 599 *per* Lord Sumner at pp. 609-10 (P.C.); *Walker v. The King*, [1939] S.C.R. 214, *per* Duff C.J.C. at p. 217.

the offender and the neurotic approach therapy with considerable ambivalence."[106]

Perhaps rebuttal of this reasoning may be found, however, in the fairly recent decision of the Wayne County Circuit Court in *Kaimowitz et al v. Department of Mental Health (Mich.).*[107] There it was held that psychosurgery could not be performed on a prison inmate because obtaining voluntary informed consent in the captive environment was an impossibility. The Court said:

> "Although an involuntarily detained mental patient may have a sufficient I.Q. to intellectually comprehend his circumstances ... the very nature of his incarceration diminishes the capacity to consent to psychosurgery. He is particularly vulnerable as a result of his mental condition, the deprivation stemming from involuntary confinement and the effect of the phenomenon of 'institutionalization'."[108]

And later:

> "The Nuremberg standards require that the experimental subjects be so situated as to exercise free power of choice without the intervention of any element of force, fraud, deceit, duress, over-reaching, or other ulterior form of constraint or coercion. It is impossible for an involuntarily detained mental patient to be free of ulterior forms of restraint or coercion when his very release from the institution may depend upon his cooperating with the authorities and giving consent to experimental surgery."[109]

But while the reasoning here seems initially convincing, it is submitted that closer examination will reveal a certain illogicality. In its efforts to safeguard absolute freedom of choice, the Court has itself violated such freedom by refusing to allow the patient to consent.[110] Such usurpation of the mental patient's right to decide what is in his own best interests evinces a paternalistic authoritarianism similar, if not identical, to that which is being condemned.[111]

---

[106] Halleck, *Psychiatry and the Dilemmas of Crime: A Study of Causes, Punishment and Treatment* (Berkeley, University of California Press, 1971) at p. 320.

[107] Unreported, July 10, 1973, Civ. No. 73-19434-AW, Wayne Co. Cir.Ct.; abstracted in (1973), 13 Crim. L. Rept. 2452.

[108] At p. 25 of the original judgment.

[109] At p. 27 of the original judgment.

[110] Cunningham "Aversion Therapy and the Involuntarily Confined: Rehabilitation or Retribution?" (1974), 27 U. Fla. L.Rev. 224 at p. 233; Shapiro, "The Uses of Behaviour Control Technologies" (1972), 7 Issues in Criminology 55 at p. 69.

[111] See Hodson, "Reflections Concerning Violence and the Brain" (1973), 9 Crim. L. Bull. 684 at p. 686, footnote 6.

B. CRUEL AND UNUSUAL TREATMENT OR PUNISHMENT

> " 'But sir', I said, 'how about this new thing they're talking about? How about this new like treatment that gets you out of prison in no time at all and makes sure that you never get back in again?'. . . .
>
> "You could viddy him thinking about that while he puffed away at his cancer, wondering how much to say to me about what he knew about this veshch I'd mentioned. Then he said: 'I take it you're referring to Ludovico's Technique.' He was still very wary.
>
> " 'I don't know what it's called, sir,' I said. All I know is that it gets you out quickly and makes sure that you don't get in again.'
>
> " 'That is so,' he said, his eyebrows like all beetling while he looked down at me. 'That is quite so, 6655321. Of course, it's only in the experimental state at the moment. It's very simple but very drastic.' "[112]

Today, real life psychiatric therapy has become practically indistinguishable from science fiction. The variety of traditional, experimental and *quasi*-experimental techniques which may currently be used to alter criminal behaviour is literally mind-boggling. In addition to the talking and milieu types of treatment, the psychiatric and neurological arsenal includes such somatic therapies as electroshock, insulin coma, psychosurgery, psychotropic drug therapy, operant conditioning, classical conditioning, aversion therapy, hormonal castration, electrical stimulation of the brain, and more. Needless to say, the use of such techniques on prisoners and mental patients raises some rather complex legal and ethical issues. Because of their unpleasantness for the patient,[113] many forms of therapy may be challenged as "cruel and unusual". Nor would such criticism draw its legitimacy solely from the disputed or unproven effectiveness of various techniques;[114] even the certainty of beneficial results need not justify the means by which they are achieved. As Kittrie has pointed out:

> "Mere effectiveness will not justify the imposition of punishment, for certain punishments may be objectionable either because of their method or because of their disproportionate severity. The therapeutic state disclaims penal aims and asserts, therefore, freedom from limitations upon punishment. Moreover, by ignoring or at least bypassing personal culpability and guilt, the therapeutic state finds itself with no measuring stick by which to determine the propriety of its sanctions, other than effectiveness. . . . The time has come to recognize that therapeutic excesses, like penal excesses, need be and can be curbed."[115]

---

[112] Burgess, *A Clockwork Orange* (Penguin Books, 1972), at pp. 66-7.

[113] Commenting on the use of aversion therapy, one psychiatrist has observed that "punishment is of course not entirely alien to psychiatry." See Gunn, "Sentencing — As Seen by a Psychiatrist" (1971), 11 Med. Sci. and the Law 95 at p. 97.

[114] See the studies cited by Schwitzgebel, "The Right to Effective Mental Treatment" (1974), 62 Cal. L. Rev. 936 at pp. 941-8.

[115] Kittrie, *The Right to be Different: Deviance and Enforced Therapy* (Baltimore, Penguin Books, 1973) at pp. 387-8.

Although there are no reported Canadian cases in which para. 2(b) of the Bill of Rights has been used to challenge the legitimacy of certain psychiatric techniques, several American decisions are worth examining. The first is that in *Peek v. Ciccone*,[116] a case which involved the forcible injection of a tranquilizing drug (Thorazine) into a federal prisoner. Refusing the prisoner's application for *habeas corpus*, the United States District Court ruled that he had not been treated cruelly or unusually for two reasons: (1) the medical officers "were not attempting to punish or harm . . ."[117] the prisoner; and (2) the prisoner "was physically restrained by the prison officials only after he refused the oral medication . . .".[118] In saying this, the Court seems to have implied (a) that a particular form of treatment cannot be called cruel or unusual if the prisoner brings it on himself by refusing alternatives, and (b) that such treatment cannot be considered cruel or unusual unless it is intended to be. In other words, the Court viewed the issue of cruel and unusual punishment as one whose resolution depended entirely upon the circumstances. The question of whether or not involuntary tranquilization *per se* "shocks the general conscience of civilized society"[119] seems to have been ignored.

In *Nelson v. Heyne*[120] the involuntary injection of tranquilizing drugs (Thorazine and Sparine) was again challenged by prison inmates asserting their Eighth Amendment rights. This time the cruel and unusual punishment argument succeeded. Noting that the type of drugs used had "potentially serious medical side effects . . .",[121] the court found their forced injection to be "shocking to the conscience and violative of the plaintiffs' 8th and 14th Amendment rights . . .".[122] It should be noted, however, that this decision, like the one in *Peek v. Ciccone*, rested on the particular circumstances of the case. The court expressly distinguished *Peek* on its facts, pointing out that here the prisoner had not been offered the choice between oral and inter-muscular medication.[123]

The Eighth Amendment argument was again raised in the case of *Knecht v. Gillman*,[124] this time with respect to the use of aversive conditioning.[125] There a powerful emetic drug (Apomorphine) had been involuntarily administered to a patient/prisoner as punishment for a breach of prison protocol.[126] The justification given for this procedure

---

[116] (1968), 288 F. Supp. 329 (W.D.Mo.).

[117] *Ibid.*, at p. 337.

[118] *Ibid.*

[119] This is the general standard used by American courts: see *William v. Field* (1969), 416 F. 2d 483 at p. 486 (9th Cir.); *Lee v. Tahash* (1965), 352 F. 2d 970 at p. 972 (8th Cir.).

[120] (1972), 355 F. Supp. 451 (N.D.Ind.); affd 491 F. 2d 352 (U.S.C.A., 7th Cir.).

[121] *Ibid.*, at p. 455.

[122] *Ibid.*

[123] *Ibid.*

[124] (1973), 488 F. 2d 1136 (8th Cir.).

[125] See also *Mackey v. Procunier* (1973), 477 F. 2d 877 (9th Cir.).

[126] *Supra*, footnote 124 at p.1137: "Dr. Leoffelholz testified that the drug could be injected for such pieces of behaviour as not getting up, for giving cigarettes against orders, for talking, for swearing, or for lying. Other inmates or members of the staff would report on these violations of the protocol and the injection would be given by the nurse with-

was that it was "treatment" as opposed to punishment and could not, therefore, be regarded as cruel and unusual punishment. The trial court accepted this. When the case came before the United States Court of Appeals for the Eighth Circuit, however, the procedure was condemned. The Court held: (1) that the mere characterization of a drug's administration as "treatment" did not make it immune from Eighth Amendment scrutiny; and (2) that the use of an emetic drug as an "aversive stimulus" constituted cruel and unusual punishment unless voluntary informed consent was first obtained. While the result in *Knecht* seems desirable, it has been suggested that its rationale remains somewhat anomalous. As one commentator has expressed it: "The court indicated that aversion therapy administered without consent is cruel and unusual punishment. If consent is obtained however, cruel and unusual punishment is miraculously transformed into a legitimate form of treatment."[127] This criticism could be levelled at the *Peek* and *Nelson* decisions as well, since both have likewise failed to stamp any particular form of treatment with the label "cruel and unusual" without taking the surrounding circumstances into account.

Despite their limitations, the three cases discussed clearly demonstrate the viability of the United States' Eighth Amendment as a method of attacking punishment disguised as treatment. Although there would appear to be nothing which prevents para. 2(b) of the Canadian Bill of Rights from being used in a similar fashion, there exists at least one noteworthy feature which distinguishes para. 2(b) from its American counterpart. While the Eighth Amendment's protection extends to all disordered offenders receiving treatment in institutions, the Bill of Rights safeguards are available only to those offenders who receive treatment under the apparent auspices of federal legislation (*i.e.*, the Criminal Code or Penitentiary Act). This means that the diverted defendant, who is committed by civil process rather than prosecuted, may not invoke para. 2(b) as a means of protesting any treatment which he finds unpleasant. Where the section is available, however, its implementation will entail one less difficulty than that of the Eighth Amendment. Because the Canadian provision prohibits "cruel and unusual punishment or treatment", it will not be necessary for the courts to blur the distinction between punishment and treatment in order to find that an individual's rights have been violated.

V. Remedies

By definition, any "right" regarding treatment must carry with it a means of enforcement. Assuming that a disordered offender can establish a legitimate grievance, what legal remedies are available to him?

---

out the nurse or any doctor having personally observed the violation and without specific authorization of the doctor."
[127] Cunningham, *op. cit.* footnote 110, at p. 231.

A. TORT ACTION

As mentioned earlier, the neglect or mistreatment of a patient/prisoner may give rise to an action for damages. Such action may be framed in battery, negligence or malpractice, depending upon the circumstances. Where the offender feels his right to treatment has been violated, a tort suit might avoid difficulties with regard to the formulation of precise treatment standards; "The court need not decide exactly what the right to treatment entails in a given case but merely that this case does not meet the standard."[128] On the other hand, time and expense might render this method of proceeding inconvenient. Furthermore, where the action arises out of a "right not to be treated" situation, the computation of damages might present a problem. In the words of one commentator: "how much damage has an acute catatonic schizophrenic suffered when he has been returned to some form of clinical normalcy by the forcible application of thorazine? Has he actually been benefitted?"[129]

B. HABEAS CORPUS

Although *habeas corpus* has successfully been employed in the United States to end the non-therapeutic confinement of disordered persons,[130] it is doubtful whether such remedy would lie in this country. Under Canadian law, an application for a writ of *habeas corpus* merely empowers the court to consider "whether the prisoner is held in custody by an order of a competent authority pursuant to the provisions of existing legislation."[131] It does not allow the court to look behind a valid warrant or order issued by an authority of competent jurisdiction.[132] Even if this were not the case, the appropriateness of *habeas corpus* might seriously be questioned in many cases. Where the individual concerned is considered dangerous to himself or others, the court might view his outright release as undesirable.[133]

C. MANDAMUS

Mandamus may be used to compel the performance of a legal duty owed to the applicant, and is useful as a means of enforcing a specific legal right for which no other specific remedy exists.[134] It may, therefore, be

---

[128] Schwitzgebel, *op. cit.* footnote 49, at p. 530.
[129] Spece, "Conditioning and other Technologies Used to 'Treat'? 'Rehabilitate'? 'Demolish'? Prisoners and Mental Patients" (1972), 45 So. Cal. L.Rev. 616 at pp. 679-80.
[130] See, *e.g., Rouse v. Cameron* (1966), 373 F. 2d 451 (D.C. Cir.).
[131] Salhany, *Canadian Criminal Procedure*, 2nd ed. (Agincourt, Canada Law Book Ltd., 1972) at p. 290.
[132] *Re Shumiatcher*, [1962] S.C.R. 38; *Re Trepanier* (1885), 12 S.C.R. 111; *Goldhar v. The Queen* (1960), 126 C.C.C. 337 (S.C.C.).
[133] Rastatter, p. 500. And see *Nason v. Superintendent of Bridgewater State Hospital* (1968), 233 N.E. 2d 908.
[134] *Re Bank of Upper Canada v. Baldwin* (1829), Draper 55; *R. ex. rel. Johannesson v. Rural Municipality of Cartier* (1922), 68 D.L.R. 741 (Man.).

used to enforce a statutory right to treatment, provided that the applicant satisfies the court that his demand for treatment has been refused.[135] *Mandamus* may not be used, however, to direct the hospitalization of disordered offenders under para. 545(1)(a) and s-s. 546(1) of the Criminal Code, or under s-s. 19(1) of the Penitentiary Act; the remedy has no power to compel an official to exercise his statutory discretion in any particular manner.[136]

D. INJUNCTION

Injunction may be used as a means of preventing the occurrence or continuance of a legal wrong.[137] In cases where the patient/prisoner wishes to assert his right not to be treated, therefore, this remedy may present an attractive alternative to tort action.

E. OMBUDSMAN

Where no clear-cut right (and therefore no adequate legal remedy) exists, perhaps the most effective means of securing justice is through the provincial ombudsman. Because an express purpose of that office is to receive and act on the complaints of prisoners and mental patients,[138] the ombudsman is in fact frequently resorted to by such persons. Quite often the mere initiation of an investigation (and the concurrent threat of publicity) is sufficient to rectify a given problem.

VI. The Therapist's Dilemma

To treat or not to treat: that is the question. Owing to the dearth of Canadian jurisprudence on the subject, the institutional therapist faces a legal and ethical conundrum of immense peril and complexity. Whether the doctor provides or withholds treatment, he may still end up suffering the slings and arrows of outrageous fortune. (In *Whitree* the outrageous fortune was $300,000 in damages.)

Should prisoners and involuntary mental patients be treated without their consent? It is submitted that the answer to this question may well depend upon the nature of the proposed treatment as well as on the legal status of the patient. Where the treatment contemplated is of an

---

[135] *Re Hamilton Dairies Ltd. and Town of Dundas* (1927), 33 O.W.N. 113 (C.A.); *R. v. Ballard* (1897), 1 C.C.C. 96 (Ont.).
[136] *Re Provincial Board of Health for Ont. and City of Toronto* (1920), 46 O.L.R. 587 (C.A.); *Re Westcott et al. and Corp. of the County of Peterborough* (1873), 33 U.C.Q.B. 280.
[137] Wade, *Administrative Law*, 3rd ed. (Oxford, Clarendon Press, 1971) at p. 111.
[138] See Ontario Ombudsman Act, 1975 (Ont.), c. 42, s-s. 17(2).

experimental nature, reference may be made to the ethical guidelines set forth in the Nuremberg Code. Arising from the historic judgment of the war crimes tribunal in the case of *United States v. Karl Brandt et al.*,[139] the Code provides *inter alia* that "the voluntary consent of the human subject is absolutely essential."[140] A somewhat looser standard is provided, however, by the more recent Helsinki Declaration.[141] Regarding "clinical research combined with professional care", the Declaration has this to say:

> "II.1 In the treatment of the sick person the doctor must be able to use a new therapeutic measure if in his judgment it offers hope of saving life, re-establishing health, or alleviating suffering.
>
> "If at all possible, consistent with patient psychology, the doctor should obtain the patient's freely given consent after the patient has been given a full explanation."[142]

There may in reality be little reason for distinguishing between experimental and non-experimental treatment, especially in the area of social engineering.[143] As Norval Morris has suggested, "A few behavioural modification programs in the community, a few hormonal treatments, a few psychosurgical interventions, and the protection that stems from the 'experimental' label will be removed."[144] This being the case, logic would seem to dictate that the issue of involuntary treatment be resolved by reference to factors other than the transient experimental/ non-experimental distinction. One factor which should be considered is the patient's status vis-à-vis the criminal law. Where the patient is a convicted offender, Rappeport has offered the following justification for coerced therapy:

> "It has generally been accepted and recognized that the criminal convicted of a crime against persons may not have a right to continue such behaviour and remain free. The law, whose very essence

---

[139] *2 Trials of War Criminals Before the Nuremberg Military Tribunals Under Control Council Law No. 10.*

[140] Section 1.

[141] Adopted by the World Medical Assoc. in 1964. See (January 1965) 19 W.H.O. Chronicle at pp. 31-2.

[142] The difficulties inherent in this formulation are many and confusing. The provision states that the doctor may use experimental techniques or measures when "in his judgment" (subjective standard) it "offers hope" (no matter how small in comparison with the risks?) of "saving life, re-establishing health, or alleviating suffering" (of the patient himself or of others to follow?). Moreover, it would appear that the patient might be involuntarily subjected to experimental treatment if the doctor finds that it is not "at all possible, consistent with patient psychology" to obtain consent.

[143] One might well argue that even traditional psychiatric treatment is experimental in nature, since its effectiveness remains at this time a hotly debated issue. See Walker, *Sentencing in a Rational Society* (Pelican, A-1108, 1972) at p. 111, and Halleck, *op. cit.* footnote 106, at p. 338; Schwitzgebel, "The Right to Effective Mental Treatment" (1974), 62 Cal. L.Rev. 936 at pp. 946-7; Eysenck, *Crime and Personality* (London, Paladin, 1970) at pp. 151-2.

[144] Morris, *The Future of Imprisonment* (Chicago, University of Chicago Press, 1974) at p. 25.

is the protection of society, has a right to prevent him from continuing such behaviour by incarcerating him, or at least, placing him under supervision. It would then seem to follow that the law also has the right to force him to enter a treatment program which will change his behaviour so that he no longer harms other persons."[145]

But the difficulty with this statement as a general rationale is that it draws no distinction between the gravity of different offences. It suggests that individuals might forfeit their "right to be different", as Kittrie has called it, upon the commission of any crime — regardless of how trivial it might be.[146]

Where the patient is a minor offender or not technically a criminal at all (*i.e.*, where he has entered the psychiatric facility as the result of pre-trial diversion, or a finding of unfitness to stand trial), it is submitted that other reasons must be found for compulsory treatment besides his commission (or alleged commission) of an offence. One possible justification is the individual's dangerousness to himself or others. By virtue of his position in the community, the institutional psychiatrist may assume moral (if not legal) responsibility for the safety not only of the patient, but of his potential victims as well. As two American commentators have pointed out, "hospitals have not infrequently been held responsible for the death by suicide of the patient himself, as well as for violence perpetrated by him against others."[147] While the relevant case law has generally centred on the hospital's legal duty to provide adequate *custodial* care, one might argue that the hospital's moral duty extends to the provision of compulsory treatment. Support for this position may be found in the judgment of the United States District Court in *Winters v. Miller*,[148] a case which involved the involuntary use of drug therapy. There the Court said:

> "Faced with a patient who had a chronic schizophrenic reaction of a paranoiac type, and who was brought into the hospital by an emergency ambulance, the doctors had to act in accordance with their expertise in treating mental illness. ... For the doctors to have done less would have been a violation of their obligations to the people of New York to seek to cure mentally ill patients so that they will no longer be dangerous or disruptive to themselves, or to the public, and so that they will no longer occupy scarce space in public mental health institutions."[149]

---

[145] Rappeport, "Enforced Treatment — Is It Treatment?" (1974), 2 Bulletin of the American Academy of Psychiatry and the Law 148 at p. 149.
[146] In Rappeport's view, "while the mentally ill may, in Nicholas Kittrie's terms, have a right to be different, this right may be allowed only as long as this difference does not 'interfere' with someone else."
[147] Fleming and Maximov, "The Patient or His Victim: The Therapist's Dilemma" (1974), 62 Cal. L. Rev. 1025 at pp. 1028-9.
[148] (1969), 306 F. Supp. 1158 (E.D.N.Y.).
[149] *Ibid.*, at p. 1168.

The problem with dangerousness as a rationalization for involuntary treatment, however, lies in the extreme difficulty of its assessment. Recent studies tend to indicate that psychiatry simply may not possess sufficient tools to evaluate dangerousness with any high degree of accuracy.[150] A survey of the relevant empirical literature has led Alan Dershowitz to this rather unencouraging conclusion:

"... psychiatrists are rather inaccurate predictors — inaccurate in an absolute sense — and even less accurate when compared with other professionals, such as psychologists, social workers, and correctional officials and when compared to actuarial devices, such as prediction or experience tables. Even more significant for legal purposes, it seems that psychiatrists are particularly prone to one type of error — overprediction. They tend to predict anti-social conduct in many instances where it would not, in fact, occur. Indeed, our research suggests that for every correct psychiatric prediction of violence, there are numerous erroneous predictions. That is, among every group of inmates presently confined on the basis of psychiatric predictions of violence there are only a few who would, and many more who would not, actually engage in such conduct if released."[151]

Likewise, with regard to the assessment of suicidal behaviour, Greenberg has concluded that "a method for distinguishing persons who will suicide from those who will not with a measure of accuracy sufficiently high to permit its use in psychiatric commitments simply does not exist at present."[152] Morover, psychiatrists themselves often disclaim any expertise in the prediction of dangerousness. McCaldon has, for instance, stated:

"As a psychiatrist, I am frequently asked to make an assessment with regard to possible future dangerousness of a patient, and I must confess that I can find no firm psychiatric criteria for so doing. . . . It is unlikely that there are any psychiatrists who can predict dangerousness in a number of individuals with a high level of accuracy."[153]

Similarly, Usdin has asserted that psychiatrists "cannot predict even with reasonable certainty that an individual will be dangerous to himself

---

[150] See generally Kozol, Boucher and Garofolo, "The Diagnosis and Treatment of Dangerousness" (1972), 18 Crime and Delinq. 371; Hunt and Wiley, "Operation Baxtrom after One Year" (1968), 124 Am.J.Psychiat. 974; Steadman and Keveles, "The Community Adjustment and Criminal Activity of the Baxtrom Patients: 1966-70" (1972), 129 Am. J. Psychiat. 304; Wenk, Robinson and Sineth, "Can Violence be Predicted?" (1972), 18 Crime and Delinq. 393.

[151] Dershowitz, "Psychiatry and the Legal Process: A Knife That Cuts Both Ways" (1969), 2 Psychology Today 43 at p. 47.

[152] Greenberg, "Involuntary Psychiatric Commitments to Prevent Suicide" (1974), 49 N.Y.U. L. Rev. 227 at p. 263.

[153] McCaldon, "Reflections on Sentencing" (1974), 16 Can. J. Corr. 291 at p. 295.

or to others."[154] And psychiatrists like Kozol,[155] Rubin,[156] and Halleck[157] have acknowledged the lack of objective proof with regard to the predictive skills of their profession.

This being the case, one finds the institutional psychotherapist in a bit of a bind. Despite his apparent inability to make accurate predictions with regard to dangerousness, he is nevertheless charged with the moral (and perhaps legal)[158] duty of protecting both his patient and his community. Furthermore, economic pressure dictates that he do so not merely by providing custodial care, but by providing the patient with effective treatment. This situation, it is submitted, places the psychiatrist in an unfair predicament as regards the involuntary treatment of those patients he considers dangerous. He may be damned if he does resort to coercive measures, and damned as well if he does not.

Should prisoners and involuntary mental patients be treated if they *do* consent? The answer to this question, once again, is by no means clear-cut. As far as experimental psychosurgery is concerned, Robert Burt has contended that they should not.[159] His point, according to Norval Morris, is that "if there is substantial risk of injury or personality change, the imprisoned and the inmates of a mental hospital should not be permitted to volunteer for experimental treatments not applied to those at liberty."[160] As noted earlier, however, the distinction between experimental and non-experimental treatment is not one which can easily be made. Burt's argument, which is apparently drawn from the *Kaimowitz* case,[161] could therefore be expanded to cover not only psychosurgery but other forms of treatment such as chemotherapy, electroconvulsive therapy or group therapy as well.[162] It is submitted that such an extension would lead to an absurd and paradoxical conflict with any legal right to treatment which prisoners and mental patients might enjoy.[163] Perhaps with these reasons in mind, Morris has expressed the following opinion:

"I adhere to the view that it is possible to protect the inmate's freedom to consent or not; that we must be highly skeptical of consent

[154] Usdin, "Broader Aspects of Dangerousness", in Rappeport ed., *The Clinical Evaluation of the Dangerousness of the Mentally Ill* (Springfield, Ill., Charles C. Thomas, 1967) at p. 43.
[155] Kozol, Boucher and Garofolo, "The Diagnosis and Treatment of Dangerousness".
[156] Rubin, "Prediction of Dangerousness in Mentally Ill Criminals" (1972), 27 Arch. Gen. Psychiat. 397 at pp. 397-8.
[157] Halleck, at p. 314.
[158] See Fleming and Maximov, at pp. 1028-9. At p. 1031 the authors also note: "Hospitals and the medical sciences, like other public institutions and professions, are charged with a public interest. Their image of responsibility in our society makes them prime candidates for converting their moral duties into legal ones."
[159] See Burt, "Biotechnology and Anti-Social Conduct: Controlling the Controllers" (1974), Ohio State Law Forum Lectures, cited by Morris, *op. cit.* footnote 144, at p. 25.
[160] Morris, at p. 25.
[161] Mr. Burt acted as attorney for the mental patient in *Kaimowitz*.
[162] Wexler, "Mental Health Law and the Movement toward Voluntary Treatment" (1974), 62 Cal. L. Rev. 671 at pp. 678-9.
[163] *Ibid.*, at p. 679.

in captivity, particularly to any risky and not well-established procedures; but there seems little value in arbitrarily excluding all prisoners from any treatment, experimental or not. Like free citizens they may consent, under precisely circumscribed conditions (Morris and Mills, 1974) to any medical, psychological, psychiatric, and neurosurgical interventions which are professionally indicated; their protection must be more adequate than that surrounding the free citizen's consent, since they are more vulnerable. It is better directly to confront the potentialities of abuse of power over prisoners than to rely on the temporary exclusion of prisoners from 'experimental' programs."[164]

VII. Conclusions

Canada's laws pertaining to the treatment of mentally disordered offenders are unsatisfactory in a number of respects. While certain federal[165] and provincial[166] statutory provisions and regulations would appear to guarantee a right to psychiatric treatment for some prisoners and mental patients, a survey of the cross-Canada picture reveals some rather serious legislative deficiencies. Although the right to treatment problem may not be susceptible of instant solution, it is submitted that some basic reforms are in order. To begin with, s-ss. 542(3), 543(6), para. 545(1)(a) and s-s. 546(1) of the Criminal Code should be repealed. In their place, a system of hospital orders[167] should be established which makes *mandatory* the psychiatric hospitalization of unfit accused persons and insane offenders upon their request.[168] At the present time, the provincial lieutenant-governor retains too broad a discretion in this regard. By initiating hospital orders, however, Parliament could turn what is now a privilege into a statutory right enforceable by *mandamus.*

Once hospitalized, the disordered offender should be entitled to receive psychiatric treatment which (a) conforms to specific minimum standards and (b) is appropriate for his particular mental condition. The implementation of this right, once again, will require legislative action, though this time on the part of the provincial legislatures. No matter how the provisions are worded, however, it is recognized that certain problems will inevitably arise concerning their interpretation. Will a right to "adequate" or "appropriate" treatment entitle the offender to be *cured* of his affliction? According to Schwitzgebel, "Treatment is not adequate, or appropriate, or proper, or suitable unless it is effective

---

[164] Morris, *op. cit.* footnote 144, at pp. 25-6.

[165] See *supra* pp. 290-2.

[166] See *supra* pp. 292-3.

[167] See s-s. 60(1) of England's Mental Health Act 1959, c. 72; Ouimet, *Report of the Canadian Committee on Corrections* (Ottawa, Queen's Printer, 1969) at p. 235; Law Reform Commission of Canada, *Working Paper: The Criminal Process and Mental Disorder* (Ottawa, Information Canada, 1975) at pp. 46-50.

[168] The hospitalization of disordered prisoners serving sentence should be mandatory as well, *provided* the prisoner does not object. See Chapter 8, *ante* at p. 262.

...".[169] But the problem with legislating a right to effective treatment is that it ignores the fact that certain psychiatric disorders are incurable.[170] For this reason, it is hoped that Canadian courts would adopt the test laid down by Bazelon C.J. in *Rouse v. Cameron,* and decide that "The hospital need not show that the treatment will cure or improve him but only that there is a *bona fide* effort to do so."[171] This is not to say that any sincere attempt to treat the patient, however misguided, will suffice; all treatment ought to conform to accepted professional standards.[172] Nor should lack of staff or facilities provide an excuse for the administration of sub-standard treatment. As the court ruled in *Wyatt v. Aderholt,* "the state may not fail to provide treatment for budgetary reasons alone."[173]

As far as the right not to be treated is concerned, it is further submitted that our laws demand both clarification and alteration. While sufficient ethical justification may exist for the compulsory treatment of some offenders,[174] those mental health statutes which permit the enforced treatment of all involuntary patients[175] ought to be amended. The decision of whether to treat compulsorily or not involves the resolution of some extremely difficult philosophical issues. Because grave social consequences may result from a decision either way, it seems grossly unfair to place this type of responsibility on the shoulders of any one individual. It is therefore proposed that provincial boards be created to decide the question of involuntary therapy on a case-by-case basis. In making their determinations, the boards should take into consideration both the gravity of the offender's crime and the nature of the treatment proposed. As a general rule, it is suggested that the type of treatment employed should be no more drastic than the seriousness of the offence merits. Where the patient has not actually been convicted of a crime or acquitted by reason of insanity (*i.e.,* where he has been found unfit or committed civilly in lieu of trial), especially compelling reasons would be necessary to justify his compulsory treatment.[176]

The creation of psychiatric treatment review boards has recently been

---

[169] Schwitzgebel, *op. cit.* footnote 49, at p. 520. And see *Powell v. Texas* (1968), 392 U.S. 514 at p. 529; *Clatterbuck v. Harris* (1968), 295 F. Supp. 84 at p. 86 (D.D.C.) and *In Re Maddox* (1967), 88 N.W. 2d 470 at p. 472, where the standards of "effective treatment" and "curative treatment" were judicially adopted.

[170] See *Lessard v. Schmidt* (1972), 349 F. Supp. 1078 at p. 1087.

[171] (1963), 373 F. 2d 451 at p. 456.

[172] *Ibid.*

[173] (1974), 503 F. 2d 1305 at p. 1315. See also *Rouse, supra,* footnote 171 at p. 457.

[174] See, *supra,* p. 317.

[175] See, *supra,* footnote 93.

[176] If the individual were, for example, both mentally incompetent and suicidal, there would seem to be little value in adopting the strict civil libertarian which some commentators have taken. As D.A. Treffert has put it: "... in the zeal to impeccably protect the patient's civil liberties and rights, an increasing number of troubled psychotic patients are, what I choose to call. 'dying with their rights on'. ... It seems to me that if there is a right to drown, for example, there must also be a right to be rescued, and somehow there must be a proper balance between these two rights to prevent the several kinds of injustices possible." See Treffert, "Dying With One's Rights On" (1973), 224 J.A.M.A. 1649 at p. 1649.

discussed in the American legal literature. One writer has in fact drafted a detailed model of proposed legislation for the regulation of psychosurgery.[177] A part of that legislation, which might easily be adapted to cover psychiatric treatment generally, is excerpted as follows:

"Section 305. *Special Authorization for Children Seven or Under and Persons Lacking Capacity*
"Notwithstanding any other sections of this Act, when a person is found not capable of giving his informed consent, special authorization for performance of psychosurgery may be granted according to the following requirements:
"(a) The Review Board shall appoint an attorney to represent the person unless he has already retained legal counsel.
"(b) Compelling medical need for the psychosurgery must be found by both the Review Board and the Advisory Board. Such needs include, but are not limited to, the following conditions:
(1) a mental disorder which threatens the life of the patient; or,
(2) severe, intractable pain. . . .
"(e) A hearing shall be held pursuant to section 303 of this Act. A majority of both the Review Board and the Advisory Board must approve of such an operation (for purposes of this subsection, the Advisory Board shall act in both a decision-making and advisory role)."[178]

---

[177] Knowles, "Beyond the Cuckoo's Nest: A Proposal for Federal Regulation of Psychosurgery" (1975), 12 Harv. J. Legis. 610.
[178] *Ibid.*, at p. 663.

Chapter 11

Release

I. Introduction

As the discussion in previous chapters has indicated, the fact that a particular defendant is mentally disordered may affect his relationship to the criminal justice system in a number of ways. It may be relevant to the issues of fitness to stand trial, responsibility, disposition, or to the basic question of whether the criminal law should be applied in the first place.[1] Another way in which the presence of mental disorder may entail special consequences for an accused concerns the matter of release from custody. One unfortunate consequence is that "it generally leads to longer periods of incarceration than would result if offenders were treated by the system on grounds other than therapeutic ones ... ".[2]

This chapter will outline the various release procedures which apply to disordered individuals and offer some suggestions for their improvement.

II. Release From A Warrant Of The Lieutenant-Governor

The length of time for which an individual may be detained on a warrant of the lieutenant-governor seems to be a matter entirely within the discretion of that official. As to the options which are open to him regarding the release of persons detained pursuant to an order under s-s. 546(1) of the Code, s. 546 further provides:

---

[1] See Law Reform Commission of Canada, *Report: Mental Disorder in the Criminal Process* (Ottawa, Information Canada, 1976) at p. 3.

[2] Cragg, "Psychiatry, the Inmate and the Law" (1976), 3 Dalhousie L.J. 510 at p. 517.

"(3) Where the lieutenant governor is satisfied that a person to whom subsection (2) applies has recovered, he may order that the person

    (a) be returned to the prison from which he was removed pursuant to subsection (1), if he is liable to further custody in prison, or

    (b) be discharged, if he is not liable to further custody in prison.

"(4) Where the lieutenant governor is satisfied that a person to whom subsection (2) applies has partially recovered, he may, where the person is not liable to further custody in prison, order that the person shall be subject to the direction of the minister of health for the province, or such other person as the lieutenant governor may designate, and the minister of health or other person designated may make an order or direction in respect of the custody and care of the person that he considers proper."

Another option implicit in the wording of both para. 545(1)(a) and s-s. 546(2) is that of "loosening" the original warrant to allow for gradual release of the patient/prisoner. In practice, the loosened warrant is employed in a manner analogous to probation, out-patient psychiatric care being the standard condition thereof.

Subsection (4) of s. 546 is vague and rather curious in its wording. It confers upon entirely unspecified individuals ("the minister of health for the province, *or such other person as the lieutenant governor may designate*") the broad discretionary power of making "any order or direction in respect of the custody and care" of partially recovered persons that they consider proper. Though it has been suggested[3] that the provision allows for a form of conditional release which renders the accused responsible to the person designated in the order, certain questions remain unanswered. As one commentator has pondered:

"Supposing the Minister or 'other person' decides that in the social interest the released person should be re-hospitalized, or deprived of his human rights in other respects? Should the determination of such conditions be a unilateral decision by the executive? No doubt the officials concerned can be relied upon to act in good faith and only after taking advantage of the best of medical advice, but, as a democratic principle, should not the individual concerned be entitled to a hearing? We grant him as much when the state expropriates his property; should the argument not be equally as strong where his personal liberty is at stake?"[4]

It is unclear, moreover, whether a person who is re-hospitalized pursuant to an exercise of administrative discretion under s-s. 546(4) is entitled to review of his detention. By s-s. 547(1), the board is technically

---

[3] Jobson, "Commitment and Release of the Mentally Ill under Criminal Law" (1969), 11 Crim. L.Q. 186 at pp. 194-5.

[4] *Ibid.*, at p. 195.

entitled to review the case only of those persons being held pursuant to orders under s. 545, s-ss. 546(1) or (2).

Although the Code provides for the appointment by the lieutenant-governor of a board of review,[5] it is important to note that such appointment is by no means mandatory.[6] As s-s. 547(1) states:

> "547(1) The lieutenant governor of a province *may* appoint a board to review the case of every person in custody in a place in that province by virtue of an order made pursuant to section 545 or subsection 546(1) or (2)."[7]

If appointed, a board of review must consist of between three and five members,[8] at least two of whom must be duly qualified psychiatrists entitled to practice medicine in the province for which the board is appointed.[9] At least one member must be a member of the bar of the province.[10] To constitute a quorum of the board, at least three members must be present; amongst them must be one psychiatrist and one lawyer.[11] With regard to the board's functions, s-s. (5) of s. 547 further provides:

> "(5) The board shall review the case of every person referred to in subsection (1)
>
> (a) not later than six months after the making of the order referred to in that subsection relating to that person, and
> (b) at least once in every twelve month period following the review required pursuant to paragraph (a) so long as the person remains in custody under the order,
>
> and forthwith after each review the board shall report to the lieutenant governor setting out fully the results of such review and stating
>
> (c) where the person in custody was found unfit on account of insanity to stand his trial, whether, in the opinion of the board, that person has recovered sufficiently to stand his trial,
> (d) where the person in custody was found not guilty on account of insanity, whether, in the opinion of the board, that person has recovered and, if so, whether in its opinion it is in the interest of the public and of that person for the lieutenant governor to order that he be discharged absolutely or subject to such conditions as the lieutenant governor may prescribe,
> (e) where the person in custody was removed from prison pur-

---

[5] See also s. 31 of the Ontario Mental Health Act.
[6] Note the use in s-s. 547(1) of the word "may" which, according to s. 28 of the Interpretation Act, R.S.C. 1970, c. I-23, is a permissive term (as opposed to the imperative "shall").
[7] Emphasis added.
[8] Subsection 547(2).
[9] Subsection 547(3).
[10] *Ibid.*
[11] Subsection 547(4).

suant to subsection 546(1), whether, in the opinion of the
board, that person has recovered or partially recovered, or

(f) any recommendations that it considers desirable in the interests of recovery of the person to whom such review relates and that are not contrary to the public interest."

In addition to making any review which may be required under s-s. (5),
the board may be requested by the lieutenant-governor to review any
other case he chooses, in which case the board must again report to him
in accordance with s-s. (5).

While the decision of a board of review may be reviewed by the Federal Court,[12] it is important to note that the mere detention under a lieutenant-governor's order is not in itself reviewable by the courts. Unless
the board has acted or the lieutenant-governor has refused direct application from the prisoner, no remedy will lie by means of *habeas corpus*.
As the British Columbia Supreme Court said in *Re Kleiny's Habeas Corpus Application*,[13] "once it is established that the accused may be law-
fully detained by valid warrant until the lieutenant-governor exercises
his discretion to direct his release, then no writ of *habeas corpus* may
issue until that discretion has been exercised." Once an application for
release has been rejected by the lieutenant-governor it is still not
entirely clear upon what ground a writ of *habeas corpus* might issue.
The only judicial opinion to be found on point is that expressed in *obiter*
by the Alberta Supreme Court in *Re Brooks' Detention*,[14] *per* Milvain J.:

"I am ... firmly of the view that the lieutenant-governor cannot
exercise his discretionary powers in any arbitrary fashion ... If an
arbitrary decision were made, I feel that the matter could then be
reviewed by way of *habeas corpus* under the common-law right of
the court to intervene where the liberty of the subject is involved."

The learned Justice further pointed out[15] that both arbitrary detention
and deprivation of the remedy of *habeas corpus* were prohibited by
paras. 2(a) and (c)(iii) of the Canadian Bill of Rights and suggested as
well that the onus lay on the lieutenant-governor to justify his continued detention of a prisoner.

---

[12] See *Lingley v. Hickman*, [1972] F.C. 171 and *Lingley v. New Brunswick Board of
Review*, [1973] F.C. 861.
[13] (1965), 51 W.W.R. 597, *per* Ruttan J. at p. 603.
[14] (1962), 38 W.W.R. 51 at p. 53.
[15] *Ibid.*, at pp. 53-4.

III. The Civilly Committed Defendant

Once an accused has been involuntarily hospitalized, there are basically two methods by which he may seek to secure his release: (1) application for review under the provisions of the province's Mental Health Act; and (2) application by way of *habeas corpus*. In Ontario, the former procedure is set out in s. 28 of the Mental Health Act. Subsection (1) states:

> "28(1) An involuntary patient, or any person on his behalf, may apply in the prescribed form to the chairman of the review board having jurisdiction to inquire into whether the patient suffers from mental disorder of a nature or degree so as to require hospitalization in the interests of his own safety or the safety of others."

Such application may be made immediately upon becoming an involuntary patient[16] and whenever a certificate of renewal[17] comes into force.[18] Where no application is made, the patient does not enjoy an automatic review of his case and is eligible for discharge only once he is "no longer in need of ... observation, care and treatment ... ".[19]

The review board envisioned by s. 27 of the Mental Health Act is similar in nature to that described in s. 547 of the Criminal Code. Although a review board has in fact been appointed in Ontario, its creation, once again, appears to have been entirely within the discretion of the provincial lieutenant-governor; s-s. 27(1) of the Act merely states that the lieutenant-governor in council "may appoint a review board for any one or more psychiatric facilities."[20] This situation seems rather odd in light of the imperative instructions which are given regarding the board's composition. By s-s. (2) of s. 27 the board *shall* consist of three or five members; one (and not more than two) must be a lawyer, one (and not more than two) must be a psychiatrist, and one must be a lay person. By s-s. (5) persons with a financial interest in the psychiatric facility where an applicant is being detained *shall not* sit as members of that applicant's review board. While these provisions reflect an obvious concern for impartiality and administrative fairness, it is indeed peculiar that their purpose might have been utterly defeated by the lieutenant-governor's failure to appoint a review board in the first place.

Once a patient's application has been received by the review board's chairman, an inquiry into that person's case becomes mandatory.[21] The inquiry need not necessarily take the form of a hearing, however, since

---

[16] Mental Health Act, R.S.O. 1970, c. 269, cl. 28(2)(b).
[17] Section 13.
[18] Clause 28(2)(a).
[19] Subsection 26(1).
[20] The permissive wording of this section puzzled the McRuer Civil Rights Commission, who wondered why the usual phraseology in such matters was not followed: see McRuer, *Royal Commission Inquiry Into Civil Rights* Report No. 1, Vol. 3 (Ottawa, Queen's Printer, 1963) at p. 1235.
[21] Subsection 29(1).

only such investigations as the board "considers necessary to reach a decision" are required.[22] Where a hearing is in fact held the applicant enjoys no absolute right to be present,[23] though it appears he does retain the right to be represented.[24] With regard to the calling and cross-examination of witnesses, s-s. 29(3) provides:

> "(3) Where a hearing is held, the patient or his representative may call witnesses and make submissions and, with the permission of the chairman, may cross-examine witnesses."

This provision met with criticism from the McRuer Civil Rights Commission on the grounds that it unduly limited the right to cross-examine witnesses. As the Commission put it:

> "We realize that in cases that may come before the board of review, an unlimited right to cross-examine witnesses would frustrate the purposes of the Act, but there would appear to be no reason why counsel appearing for a patient should not have the same right to cross-examine witnesses as at any other hearing."[25]

While the unsatisfactory aspects of review procedure may be avoided by resorting to *habeas corpus* application, it should be remembered that the usefulness of this remedy depends entirely upon the laws of the particular jurisdiction in which it is sought.[26] The *habeas corpus* provisions in some provinces, for instance, render it effective only in cases where a defect is discovered in the original proceedings for commitment. Where no such irregularity can be found, the court may not inquire into the applicant's state of mind to determine whether he is properly detained at the time the writ is returned.[27] In Ontario, however, this is fortunately not the case. Section 7 of the Habeas Corpus Act[28] provides:

> "7. Although the return to a writ of *habeas corpus* is good and sufficient in law, the court or judge before whom the writ is returnable may examine into the truth of the facts set forth in the return, by affidavit or other evidence, and may order and determine touching the discharging, bailing or remanding the person."

Under this provision the court may, if it chooses, have the applicant examined by an independent physician in order to ascertain his present state of mind. This was done in the cases of *Re Carnochan;*[29] *Re Dack,*[30] *and Re O'Donnell.*[31] In *Re Minehan*[32] the section was interpreted as

---

[22] *Ibid.*
[23] Subsection 29(2).
[24] *Ibid.*
[25] *Supra,* footnote 20 at p. 1235.
[26] Swadron, *Detention of the Mentally Disordered* (Toronto, Butterworths, 1964) at p. 198.
[27] See *Re Reid* (1953), 10 W.W.R.(N.S.) 383 (B.C.).
[28] R.S.O. 1970, c. 197.
[29] [1941] S.C.R. 470.
[30] (1914), 5 O.W.N. 774.
[31] (1915), 7 O.W.N. 605.
[32] (1925), 28 O.W.N. 263.

allowing for a full-scale inquiry into the applicant's sanity (*i.e.*, a trial of the issue).[33] Having apparently adopted this latter procedure, the court in *Re Davidson*[34] found that the applicant was not in fact insane and ordered that he be discharged from custody.

In Ontario, as elsewhere in Canada, irregularities in the original commitment procedure will provide *prima facie* grounds for an applicant's release.[35] As demonstrated by the case of *Re Gibson*,[36] however, such defects are not conclusive on the matter. Where there is evidence that an applicant's release might endanger the public's safety, the court may direct that the issues of his sanity and potential dangerousness[37] be tried. In *Re Bowyer*,[38] Middleton J.A. remarked that "It would obviously be against the public interest to set free an insane person merely because there has been some slip in the preparation of the committal papers."[39] The learned Justice further suggested that once the applicant's discharge was contested, it became incumbent upon the applicant to satisfy the court as to his sanity.[40] This latter statement remains somewhat questionable, however, in light of earlier decisions such as *Re Shuttleworth*[41] and *Re King*.[42] In *King*, the court's discretion to refuse discharge was held to be conditional upon its being satisfied both as to the applicant's insanity and dangerousness.[43]

IV. The Preventive Detainee

Prior to the passage of Bill C-51,[44] the National Parole Board was commanded to review the case of each person under preventive detention at least once a year.[45] By s. 695.1 of the new legislation, however, this has been changed. That provision states in part:

---

[33] At such trial, the onus rests on the plaintiff to establish his sanity on a balance of probabilities. See *Fawcett v. A.-G. Ont.* (1963), 40 D.L.R. (2d) 942 (Ont.), *per* Spence J. (as he then was) at p. 945; affd 45 D.L.R. (2d) at p. 579 (C.A.); affd [1964] S.C.R. 625.

[34] (1915), 8 O.W.N. 481.

[35] *Re Gibson* (1907), 15 O.L.R. 245 (C.A.), *per* Osler J.A. at pp. 247-8.

[36] *Supra*, footnote 35.

[37] In *Re Greenwood* (1855), 24 L.J.Q.B. 148 an applicant was discharged from an asylum because, though possibly insane, he was not considered dangerous.

[38] (1930), 66 O.L.R. 378.

[39] *Ibid.*, at p. 380.

[40] *Ibid.*

[41] (1846), 9 Q.B.D. 651.

[42] [1917] 1 W.W.R. 132 (Man.).

[43] *Ibid.*, at p. 133.

[44] "Criminal Law Amendment Act, 1977", 1977 (Can.), c. 53, assented to 5 August, 1977.

[45] The former provision, s. 694, provided:

> "694. Where a person is in custody under a sentence of preventive detention, the National Parole Board shall, at least once in every year, review the condition, history and circumstances of that person for the purpose of determining whether he should be granted parole under the *Parole Act*, and if so, on what conditions."

"695.1 (1) Subject to subsection (2), where a person is in custody under a sentence of detention in a penitentiary for an indeterminate period, the National Parole Board shall, forthwith after the expiration of three years from the day on which that person was taken into custody and not later than every two years thereafter, review the condition, history and circumstances of that person for the purpose of determining whether he should be granted parole under the *Parole Act* and, if so, on what conditions."[46]

Although this amendment would appear simply to have increased the severity of preventive detention as a sanction, there are those who would argue that the measure has beneficial effects for the prisoner in terms of his rehabilitation. Commenting on the disruptive effect of frequent parole hearings, one criminologist has written:

"The meaning of the impending hearing to the inmate cannot be over-stressed, nor does the staff overlook the opportunity to use this reminder as a manipulative device, much as a concerned yet stern parent might admonish an unremorseful child. This periodic stress and uncertainty appear to damage psyches unmercifully, and to mitigate against any therapeutic progress."[47]

The Parole Board's review is accomplished primarily by means of an interview conducted by members visiting the institution, plus the evaluation of a report submitted by three psychiatrists.[48] The difficulties which arise here are twofold and mutually contradictory. First, the complaint has arisen that change in the prisoner's personality cannot accurately be measured against the backdrop of unreality which is the prison environment. As one prison psychiatric panel has put it:

"These men are now in an institutional setting with its own atmosphere and structured routine. The difference between this and the outside world is vast. Co-operativeness, no trouble, and a routine existence with adaptation to the setting judged normally by correctional staff and with the offender naturally trying to cast himself in a favourable light, are no indication of future outside performance."[49]

---

[46] The section continues:

"(2) Where a person is in custody under a sentence of detention in a penitentiary for an indeterminate period that was imposed before the *Criminal Law Amendment Act, 1977* came into force, the National Parole Board shall, at least once in every year, review the condition, history and circumstances of that person for the purpose of determining whether he should be granted parole under the *Parole Act* and, if so, on what conditions."

[47] Miller, "The Indeterminite Sentence Paradigm: Resocialization or Social Control?" (1972), 7 (No. 2) Issues in Crimin. 101 at p. 113.

[48] Marcus, "A Multi-Disciplinary Two Part Study of Those Individuals Designated Dangerous Sexual Offenders Held in Federal Custody in British Columbia, Canada" (1968), 8 Can J. Corr. 90 at p. 99.

[49] *Ibid.*, at p. 100.

Diametrically opposed to this complaint is the criticism that rather than appear falsely rehabilitated, a prisoner is likely to exhibit an uncharacteristically poor image of himself in response to the immense pressure which is placed on him by the Board's review. Miller has suggested[50] that he may, in effect, "flunk" the psychological tests as a result:

"The MMPI[51] is given during this 'stressful' stripping-of-identity period and is used as a means of classification and prediction throughout his inmate and parole career. It is possible that the MMPI administered at another time, or as a later follow-up might not correlate highly with earlier results and diagnoses."[52]

V. The Psychiatrist as Jailer

As the foregoing discussion has hopefully made clear, retribution and deterrence are not the only justifications offered for involuntary confinement in Canada. The acceptance of mental disorder and supposed dangerousness as grounds for the protracted confinement of certain individuals has had the inevitable effect of casting the institutional psychiatrist in the role of jailer. Even where the Criminal Code has nominated the provincial lieutenant-governor or National Parole Board as official arbiter, it is apparent that these authorities, in reaching their decisions, must rely heavily (if not exclusively) upon the advice of psychiatrists. The patient/inmate, moreover, is not unaware of this fact. Commenting on the effect which the psychiatrist's dual role as therapist/jailer may produce, one critic[53] has written:

"This decision-making role [of the psychiatrist] has a decided impact upon the social control effectiveness of the program, for the inmate eventually realizes that outward compliance is the key to doing easy time and obtaining early release. The system sponsors 'a systematic confusion between obedience to others and one's own personal adjustment.'[54] Poor adjustment in the institution is equated with the likelihood of failure outside, rather than seen as dissatisfaction with the regime. Each act against the institution is met with a more punitive reaction, and is taken as a further indication of the problems of the individual, not of the institution.

"The individual soon learns that the easiest way out is to sell out. He learns what to make of his treators so that he can be on the make with them. Of course, it is possible that such a system might

---

[50] *Supra*, footnote 47, p. 113.
[51] Minnesota Multiphasic Personality Inventory — a psychological test.
[52] *Supra*, footnote 47, p. 113.
[53] Ericson, "Penal Psychiatry in Canada: The Method of Our Madness" (1976), 26 U.T.L.J. 17 at p. 26.
[54] Quoting Goffman, *Asylums* (New York, Anchor, 1961) at p. 385.

eventually inure rather than cure him. Thus, it should not be surprising to find in some cases that although this system of social control is effective while the person is in custody, it may have quite the opposite effect when the individual returns to the society on whose behalf this system operates."

VI. Conclusions

If warrants of the lieutenant-governor are retained, it is submitted that some basic changes ought to be made in the current Criminal Code provisions. To begin with, s-s. 547(1) should be amended to make the appointment of a board of review mandatory. Furthermore, s-s. 546(4), which provides for the continued treatment (and possible incarceration) of partially-recovered inmates who are "not liable to further custody in prison" at the discretion of the lieutenant-governor should be repealed. Once an offender has served his term in prison, he should not be subjected to the possibility of further incarceration without a hearing.

Review of the cases of involuntarily detained patients (*i.e.*, persons "committed" by civil process) should not depend upon application as it presently does. It should be automatic, as should the holding of a hearing.[55] At the review hearing, the patient should enjoy rights similar to those to which a defendant in a criminal trial is entitled. These would include the right to cross-examine witnesses and the presumption of sanity.

With regard to the case of preventive detainees, very little need be said. As stated in an earlier chapter,[56] preventive detention should be abolished. Although it would not entirely eliminate the problem, it is submitted that such a measure would assist penal psychiatrists in making the difficult transition from jailers to therapists.

---

[55] See Chapter 1, *ante*, under the heading "Conclusions".
[56] See Chapter 8, *ante*, under the heading "Conclusions".

Table of Statutes

Bill of Rights, R.S.C. 1970, App. III
s. 1(a) 297
   2(b) 281, 282, 294
   (e) 68
   5(3) 297
British North America Act, 1867 (Imp.), c. 3
s. 91(27) 22
   92(7) 23
   (13) 23
Canada Evidence Act, R.S.C. 1970, c. E-10
s. 7 196
Corrections Act, R.S.M. 1970, c. C230
s. 35(1) 292
Criminal Code, R.S.C. 1970, c. C-34
s. 2 127
   16 .... 13, 72, 89, 126, 133, 298
   (1) 121, 122
   (2) 121, 122, 132
   (3) 109, 121, 136
   (4) 121
   157 .... 237, 238
   158 .... 237, 270
   205(4) 178
   214(2) 166
   215 .... 169, 187
   (1) 170, 176
   (2) 170, 176
   (3) 175
   216 .... 178, 179
   220 178
   223 96
   457 52
   457.1 52
   465(1) 19, 20
   (2) 19
   542(1) 122
   (2) 116, 124, 227, 290
   543 78
   (1) 58, 62, 63, 65
   (2) 19, 20, 52, 53, 54, 55, 228

Criminal Code – *continued*

543(2.1) 19, 20, 52, 54, 228
(4) 58, 59, 60
(6) 77, 290
(7) 58, 59
(8) 78
544 .... 19, 20, 53
545 .... 77, 78
(1) 124, 125, 290
546 249
(1) 125, 292, 332
(2) 125
(3) 126, 324
(4) 324
547(1) 325, 332
(2) 325
(3) 325
(4) 325
(5) 325, 326
577(3) 51, 68, 69, 114
589(3) 178
603(1) 123
(2) 62, 123
608.2 228
613 123
(1) 214
618(2) 124
620 123
646 238
661(2) 38
662 235
662.1(2) 240
663(1) 239, 240
(2) 243
687 .... 263, 264
688 .... 227, 264, 265, 268, 269
689(1) 266
(2) 267
690 278
691 267
692 278
693 267
694 329
695.1(1) 329, 330
(2) 330
737(1) 122
771(2) 123

Habeas Corpus Act, R.S.O. 1970, c. 197
s. 7 328
Health and Public Welfare Act, R.S.N. 1970, c. 151
s. 108 12

Interpretation Act, R.S.C. 1970, c. I-23
s. 28 .... 62, 292

Interpretation Act, R.S.O. 1970, c. 225
  s. 30 28

Mental Health Act, 1972 (Alta.), c. 118
  s. 34 12
Mental Health Act, 1964 (B.C.), c. 29
  s. 11(1) 293, 307
    27 12
    28 .... 17, 18
Mental Health Act, R.S.M. 1970, c. M110
  s. 21 292
    103 293
Mental Health Act, R.S.N.B. 1973, c. M-10
  s. 10 12
Mental Health Act, R.S.O. 1970, c. 269
  s. 1 11
    8 11
    8(1) 25
    9(1) 10
    10 .... 10, 11, 13, 14, 15
    11 11
    14 54
      (1) 19, 21, 22, 23, 52, 54
      (2) 55
      (3) 19, 24, 54
    15(1) 21, 22, 23, 52, 54
      (2) 55
    17 235
    26(1) 327
    27 327
      (1) 28
    28(1) 327
      (2) 327
    29(1) 28, 327
    29(3) 328
      (12) 328
Mental Health Act, R.S.P.E.I. 1974, c. M-9
  s. 12 12
Mental Health Act, R.S.S. 1965, c. 345
  s. 16(1) 17
    20 12
Mental Hospitals Act, R.S.O. 1937, c. 294
  s. 35 24
Mental Hospitals Act, R.S.O. 1950, c. 229
  s. 35 23
Mental Hospitals Act, R.S.O. 1960, c. 236
  s. 38 24
Mental Patients Institutions Act, R.S.Q. 1964, c. 166
  s. 24 18
    25 18
Mental Patients Protection Act, 1972 (Que.), c. 44
  s. 64 18

Penitentiary Act, R.S.C. 1970, c. P-6
    s. 19(1) 249, 292
Police Act, R.S.O. 1970, c. 351
    s. 46(1) 9, 10

Index

A

Actus reus
  automatism as denial, 83, 84
Amnesia
  automatism, relationship, 88, 89
  fitness to stand trial, 67-69
Appeal
  insanity acquittals, 123, 124
Arteriosclerosis
  automatism, exclusion, 93, 94
Automatism
  amnesia, 88, 89
  causes
    head injury, 99, 100
    hypnosis, 111, 112
    hypoglycemia, 100, 101
    psychological
      blow, 101-107
    sleep, 107-110
  definition, 83, 84
  delusions, relationship, 109, 110
  denial of *actus reus*, 83, 84
  exclusion of defence
    disease of the mind
      brain tumour, 94
      cerebral arterio-
        sclerosis, 93, 94
      epilepsy, 90-93
      generally, 89, 90
    drugs, 96-99
    drunkenness, 95
  judicial attitude, 83
  knowledge, 87, 88
  proof
    evidential burden, 112-114
    foundation, 114, 115

  rebuttal, 115-118
  reform proposals, 118, 119
  unconsciousness
    degrees of, 87
    meaning, 85-87
  volition, 84

B

Bill of Rights
  cruel and unusual
    punishment
      preventive deten-
        tion, 281-283
      psychiatric treatment
        right to obtain, 294, 295
        right to refuse, 311-313
  due process
    psychiatric treat-
      ment, 295-299
Brain tumour
  automatism, exclusion, 94

C

Character
  psychiatric evidence as
    to, 195, 196
Civil commitment
  release, 327-329
Competence
  psychiatric evidence as
    to, 190
Conditional discharge
  probation after, 240-244
Confession
  statements to
    psychiatrist, 37-40

337

Counsel
  instructing
    liability, 67
Court
  diversion by. *See* Diversion
  witnesses called by, 216-221
Credibility
  psychiatric evidence as
    to, 191-194

D

Dangerous offender
  Crown discretion, 266
  effect of finding, 267
  evidence
    convictions, 278, 279
    opinions, 279, 280
    psychiatric, 278
  history of provisions, 263
  offences included, 265
  preventive detention
    aims of, 281
    constitutionality, 283-286
    cruel and unusual
      punishment, 281, 283
    disadvantages, 281
    release, 329-331
    review, 329-331
  procedure, 265-268
  reform proposals, 286, 287
  sentencing, 267, 268
  sexual
    definition, 268-270
    failure to control im-
      pulses, 270-272
    likelihood of future
      injury, 272-277
    private acts, 270
  statutory provisions, 263-265
Defences
  automatism. *See* Automatism
  diminished
    responsibility, 183-185
  incapacity to form intent.
    See Intent
  infanticide. *See* Infanticide
  insanity. *See* Insanity
  provocation. *See* Provocation
  reduced responsibility
    generally, 153
    reform proposals, 186-188
Delusions
  automatism,
    relationship, 109, 110

insanity defence, 136-138
Diminished responsibility
  English defence, 183-185
Disease of the mind
  meaning
    insanity defence, 127-130
Diversion
  changes suggested, 28, 29
  court, by
    constitutional
      questions, 22-25
    remand as patient, 21, 22
    remand for examina-
      tion, 19-21
  effects of, 26, 27
  importance of, 7
  Lieutenant-Governor
    order, 18
  meaning, 7
  police screening
    common law powers, 9, 10
    dangerousness, 13-15
    discretion in charging, 9
    disorderly conduct, 13
    Mental Health Act func-
      tions, 10-12
    Police Act functions, 9, 10
    problems in, 14-16
  policy basis, 25
  problems in, 25, 26
  process, 8, 9
  prosecutor, by, 16, 17
  provincial authorities,
    by, 17, 18
  purpose, 7, 8
Drugs
  incapacity to form in-
    tent, 160-163

E

Epilepsy
  automatism, exclusion, 90-93
Evidence
  psychiatric. *See* Psychiatric
    evidence

F

Fine
  sentence of, use of, 237-239
Fitness to stand trial
  determination
    criteria, 56

out-patient examina-
    tion,   54, 55
problems,   57, 58
remand for examination
    practice,   52-55
reports,   55, 56
tests,   52, 53
issue, trial of
appeal, on, 61, 62.
expert evidence,   76, 77
judicial discretion,   62-65
onus of proof,   73-76
results,   77, 78
test
    amnesia,   67-69
    insanity,   69, 70
    instructing counsel,   67
    psychosis, 71-73
    understanding
        proceedings,   65-67
timing,   58-62
origin of rule,   51
problems in,   78, 79

H

Habeas corpus
ending confinement by,   314
release from civil commit-
    ment,   328, 329
Habitual offender. *See*
Dangerous offender
Head injury
automatism after,   99, 100
Hospital order
use of,   251-253
Hypnosis
automatism,   111, 112
Hypoglycemia
automatism after,   100, 101

I

Imbecility
natural,   126, 127
Imprisonment
probation after,   239, 240
treatment not recom-
    mended,   244-247
treatment recom-
    mended,   247-251
Infanticide
definition,   178
effect of giving birth,   180-182
effect of lactation,   182, 183

onus of proof,   178-180
Injunction
restraining treatment,   315
Insanity
acquittal
    appeal,   123, 124
    summary conviction of-
        fence,   124
defence
    reform proposals,   145-152
    rules, evaluation,   144, 145
detention warrant,   124, 125
evidence
    burden of proof,   143, 144
    inferences,   143
    jury direction,   122, 123
    right to adduce,   141-143
    sufficiency of,   122
fitness to stand trial. *See*
    Fitness to stand trial
meaning
    appreciating nature and
        quality of act,   130, 131
    delusions,   136-138
    disease of the
        mind,   127-130
    irresistible im-
        pulse,   138-141
    knowing act
        wrong,   132-136
    natural imbecility,   126, 127
removal from prison,   125, 126
statutory defence,   121
Intent
incapacity to form
    drug impairment,   160-163
    intoxication
        generally,   153, 154
        proof,   157, 158
        specific intent,   154-156
        types of,   158-160
    mental disorder
        evidence,   169
        lack of knowledge,   165
        lack of planning,   166-169
        lack of specific in-
            tent,   163-165
Intoxication
incapacity to form intent. *See*
    Intent
Irresistible impulse
insanity defence,   138-141

L

Lieutenant-Governor
detention order,
making, 18
release. *See* Release

M

Mandamus
enforcing right to
treatment, 314, 315
Mental disorder
incapacity to form intent. *See*
Intent
Mentally disordered person
pre-trial diversion. *See*
Diversion

N

National Parole Board
review of preventive
detention, 329-331

O

Ombudsman
protection of prisoner's
rights, 315

P

Pre-trial diversion. *See* Diversion
Preventive detention. *See*
Dangerous offender
Police
diversion by. *See* Diversion
screening by. *See* Diversion
Privilege
psychiatric evidence. *See*
Psychiatric evidence
self-incrimination. *See*
Self-incrimination
Probation
sentence of, use of, 240-244
Prosecutor
diversion by, 16, 17
Provincial authority
diversion by, 17, 18
Provocation
definition, 170
nature of defence, 170
tests
objective, 171-176

subjective, 176, 177
Psychiatric evidence
admissibility
character, 195, 196
competence, 190
credibility, 191-194
generally, 189
court calling, powers, 216-221
dangerous offenders, 278
disagreement, reasons
for, 215, 216
fitness to stand trial, 76, 77
hypothetical
questions, 202-208
necessity for, 31
opinion, basis of, 201, 202
privilege
extension, 34-36
need for, 46-50
restriction, 32
qualifications of witness, 196-
201
reform proposals, 221-224
self-incrimination. *See*
Self-incrimination
ultimate issue rule, 208-210
weight, 211-215
Psychiatric examination
compulsory
privilege
need for, 42
procedure
interview, 43-45
mental tests, 45, 46
physical tests, 45
provisions for, 36
Psychiatric treatment
consent problems, 315, 316,
319, 320
experimental, 316
justification, 316, 317
prisoner's rights
enforcement
generally, 313
habeas corpus, 314
injunction, 315
mandamus, 314, 315
Ombudsman, 315
tort action, 314
obtaining
Bill of Rights, 294-299
federal prisoner, 291, 292
generally, 289, 290
hospitalized offen-
der, 293

insane accused, 290, 291
provincial prisoner, 292
tort law, 299
refusing
cruel and unusual
punishment, 311-313
generally, 289, 290
voluntary informed
consent, 304-310
standard, 300-304
problems in, 315-320
reform proposals, 320-322
Psychiatrist
pre-trial consultation
exclusion of evidence, 32,
33
privilege
extension, 34-36
restriction, 32
problems, 31, 32
Psychiatry
function
after trial, 3
defences at trial, 2
generally, 1, 2
pre-trial, 2
Psychosis
fitness to stand trial, 71-73

R

Reduced responsibility
defences involving, 153
reform proposals, 186-188
Release
civil commitment
board of review, 327, 328
habeas corpus, 328, 329
preventive detention, 329-331
psychiatrist role, 331, 332
reform proposals, 332
warrant of Lieutenant-
Governor
board of review, 325, 326
discretion, 323
gradual release from, 324
Remand
sentencing, before, 228-229
Report
fitness to stand trial,
before, 52-58
remand and diversion. *See*
Diversion
sentencing, before, 229-235

S

Self-incrimination
pre-trial statements
confessions rule, 37-40
constructive waiver, 41
onus of proof, 41, 42
person in authority, 36, 37
problems, 36
real evidence fiction, 40, 41
Sentencing
general principles, 227, 228
possibilities
fine, 237-239
generally, 235-237
hospital orders, 251-253
imprisonment
treatment not
recommended, 244-247
treatment recom-
mended, 247-251
probation
after conditional
discharge, 240-244
after imprisonment, 239,
240
after suspended sen-
tence, 240-244
practical application, 255
problems in, 255-257
reform proposals, 257-262
remand before, 228, 229
reports before, 229-235
variations in, 254, 255
Sexual offender
dangerous. *See* Dangerous
offender
Somnambulism
defence, 107-110
Suspended sentence
probation after, 240-244

T

Tort action
protection of rights, 314
Treatment, psychiatric. *See*
Psychiatric treatment
Trial
evidence at. *See* Evidence
fitness to stand. *See* Fitness to
stand trial
sentencing. *See* Sentencing
Truth drugs
use of, pre-trial, 43, 44

W

Witness
    court, power to call,   216-221
    qualifications, psychiatric
        evidence,   196-201